THE FORUM, CAPITOL AND PALATINE.

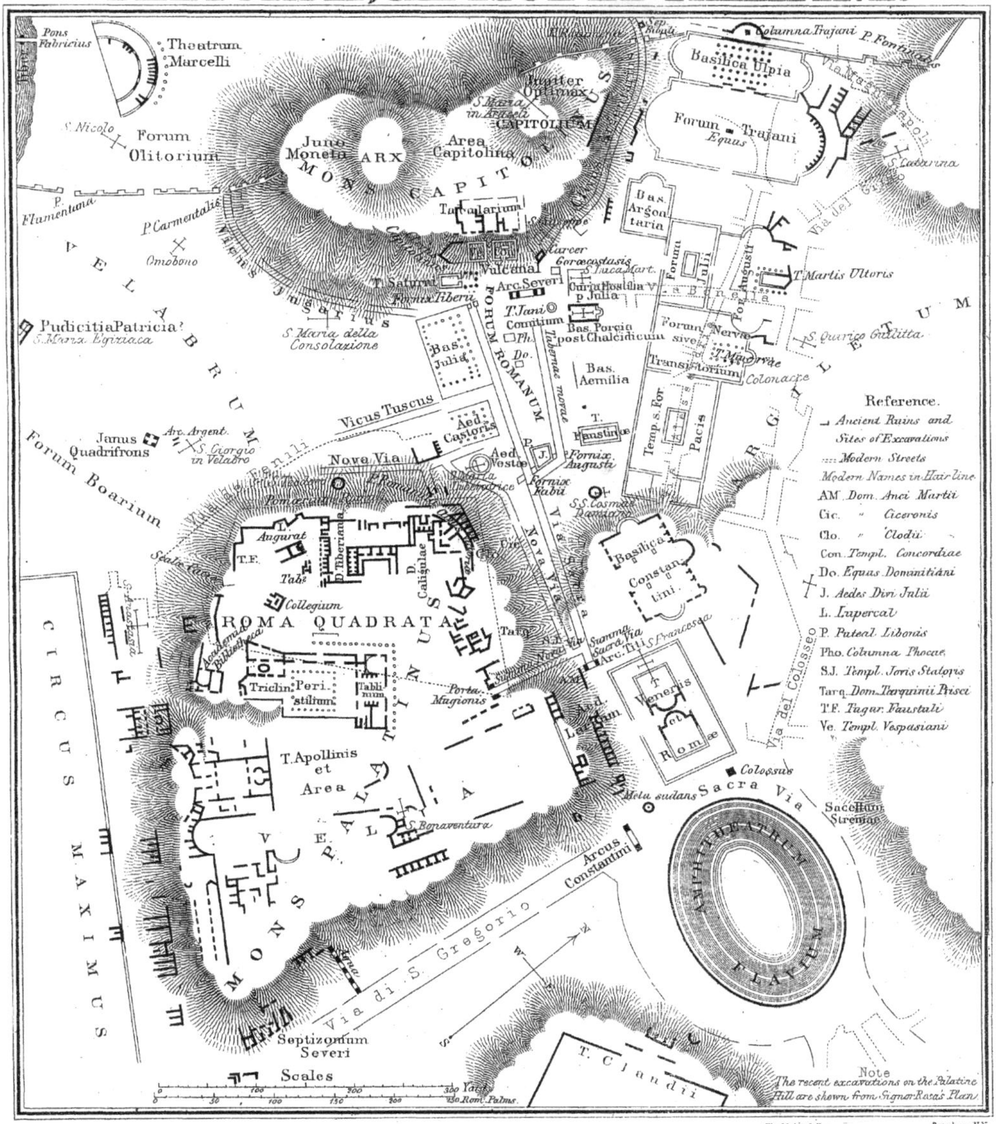

Reference.

- Ancient Ruins and Sites of Excavations
- Modern Streets
- Modern Names in Hair line.
- AM. Dom. Anci Martii
- Cic. " Ciceronis
- Clo. " Clodii
- Con. Templ. Concordiae
- Do. Equus Domnitiani
- J. Aedes Divi Julii
- L. Lupercal
- P. Pateal Libonis
- Pho. Columna Phocae
- S.J. Templ. Jovis Statoris
- Tarq. Dom. Tarquinii Prisci
- T.F. Tagur. Faustali
- Ve. Templ. Vespasiani

Note
The recent excavations on the Palatine Hill are shown from Signor Rosa's Plan

Scales
0 100 200 300 Yards
0 50 100 150 200 250 Rom. Palms

Broadway N.Y.

THE

OLD ROMAN WORLD

THE

GRANDEUR AND FAILURE OF ITS CIVILIZATION

BY

JOHN LORD, LL. D.

NEW YORK
CHARLES SCRIBNER AND COMPANY
1867

RIVERSIDE, CAMBRIDGE:
STEREOTYPED AND PRINTED BY
H. O. HOUGHTON AND COMPANY

CONTENTS.

CHAPTER I.

THE CONQUESTS OF THE ROMANS.

PAGE

Early History of Rome — Wars under the Kings — Their Results — Gradual Subjection of Italy — Great Heroes of the Republic — Their Virtues and Victories — Military Aggrandizement — The Carthaginian, Macedonian, and Asiatic Wars — Their Consequences — Civil Wars of Marius and Sulla, of Pompey and Cæsar — The Conquests of the Barbarians — Extension of Roman Dominion in the East — Conquests of the Emperors — The Military Forces of the Empire — Military Science — The Roman Legion — The Military Genius of the Romans,........ 19

CHAPTER II.

THE MATERIAL GRANDEUR AND GLORY OF THE ROMAN EMPIRE.

The vast Extent of the Empire — Boundaries — Rivers and Mountains — The Mediterranean and its Islands — The Provinces — Principal Cities — Great Architectural Monuments — Roads — Commerce — Agriculture — Manufactures — Wealth — Population — Unity of the Empire,..................... 71

CHAPTER III.

THE WONDERS OF ANCIENT ROME.

Original Settlement — The Seven Hills — Progress of the City — Principal Architectural Monuments — A Description of the Temples, Bridges, Aqueducts, Forums, Basilicas, Palaces, Amphitheatres, Theatres, Circuses, Columns, Arches, Baths, Obe-

PAGE

lisks, Tombs — Miscellaneous Antiquities — Streets — Gardens — Private Houses — Populous Quarters — Famous Statues and Pictures — General Magnificence — Population, ... 100

CHAPTER IV.

ART IN THE ROMAN EMPIRE.

The great Wonders of Ancient Architecture, Sculpture, and Painting — Famous Artists of Antiquity — How far the Romans copied the Greeks — How far they extended Art — Its Principles — Its Perfection — Causes of its Decline — Permanence of its grand Creations, ... 139

CHAPTER V.

THE ROMAN CONSTITUTION.

The Original Citizens — Comitia Calata — Comitia Curiata — Comitia Centuriata — Comitia Tributa — The Plebs — Great Patrician Families — The Aristocratic Structure of ancient Roman Society — The Dignity and Power of the Senate — The Knights — The Growth of the Democracy — Contests between Patricians and Plebeians — Rise of Tribunes — Popular Leaders — Their Laws — The Great Officers of State — Provincial Governors — Usurpations of fortunate Generals — The Revolution under Julius Cæsar and Augustus — Imperial Despotism — Preservation of the Forms of the Republic, and utter Prostration of its Spirit, ... 189

CHAPTER VI.

ROMAN JURISPRUDENCE.

Genius of the Romans for Government and Laws — Development of Jurisprudence — Legislative Sources — Judicial Power — Courts of Law — The Profession of Law — Great Lawyers and Jurists — Ancient Codes — Imperial Codes — The Law of Persons — Rights of Citizens, of Foreigners, of Slaves — Laws of Marriage, of Divorce, of Adoption — Paternal Power — Guardianship — Laws relating to Real Rights — Law of Obligations — Laws of Succession — Testaments and Legacies — Actions and Procedure in Civil Suits — Criminal Law, ... 223

CHAPTER VII.

ROMAN LITERATURE.

PAGE

The Grecian Models — How far they contributed to Roman Creations — The Development of the Latin Language — The Orators, Poets, Dramatists, Satirists, Historians, and their chief Works — How far Literature was cultivated — Schools — Libraries — Literary Legacies of the Romans,................ 262

CHAPTER VIII.

GRECIAN PHILOSOPHY.

Its gradual Development from Thales to Aristotle — How far the Romans adopted the Greek Philosophy — What Additions they made to it — How far it modified Roman Thought and Life — Influence of Philosophy on Christianity — Influence on modern Civilization, ... 306

CHAPTER IX.

SCIENTIFIC KNOWLEDGE AMONG THE ROMANS.

The Mathematical Genius of the Old Astronomers — Their Labors and Discoveries — Extent of Astronomical Knowledge — The Alexandrian School — The Science of Geometry and how far carried — Great Names — Medicine — Geography — Other Physical Sciences and their limited Triumphs, ... 353

CHAPTER X.

INTERNAL CONDITION OF THE ROMAN EMPIRE.

The Vices and Miseries of Roman Society — Social Inequalities — Disproportionate Fortunes — The Wealth and Corruption of Nobles — Degradation of the People — Vast Extent of Slavery — The Condition of Women — Demoralizing Games and Spectacles — Excessive Luxury and squalid Misery — Money-making — Imperial Misrule — Universal Egotism and Insensibility to grand Sentiments — Hopelessness of Reform — Preparation for Ruin,.................................... 387

CHAPTER XI.

THE FALL OF THE EMPIRE.

PAGE

False Security of the Roman People — Their stupendous Delusions — The Invasion of Barbarians — Their Characteristics — Their alternate Victory and Defeat — Desolation of the Provinces — The Degeneracy of the Legions — General Imbecility and Cowardice — Great public Misfortunes — General Union of the Germanic Nations — Their Leaders — Noble but vain Efforts of a Succession of warlike Emperors — The rising Tide of Barbarians — Their irresistible Advance — The Siege and Sack of Rome — The Fall of Cities — Miseries of all Classes — Universal Despair and Ruin — The Greatness of the Catastrophe — Reflections on the Fall of Rome, ... 436

CHAPTER XII.

THE REASONS WHY THE CONSERVATIVE INFLUENCES OF PAGAN CIVILIZATION DID NOT ARREST THE RUIN OF THE ROMAN WORLD.

Necessary Corruption of all Institutions under Paganism — Glory succeeded by Shame — The Army a worn-out Mechanism — The low Aims of Government — Difficulties of the Emperors — Laws perverted or unenforced — The Degeneracy of Art — The Frivolity of Literature — The imperfect Triumph of Philosophy — Nothing Conservative in human Creations — Necessity of Aid from foreign and Divine Sources, ... 493

CHAPTER XIII.

WHY CHRISTIANITY DID NOT ARREST THE RUIN OF THE ROMAN EMPIRE.

The Victories of Christianity came too late — Small Number of Converts when Christianity was a renovating Power — Their comparative Unimportance in a political and social View for three Centuries — The Church constructs a Polity for Itself rather than seeks to change established Institutions — Rapid Corruption of Christianity when established, and Adoption of Pagan Ideas and Influences — No Renovation of worn-out Races — No Material on which Christianity could work — Not

PAGE
the Mission of the Church to save Empires, but the Race — A diseased Body must die, ... 537

CHAPTER XIV.

THE LEGACY OF THE EARLY CHURCH TO FUTURE GENERATIONS.

The great Ideas which the Fathers propounded — The Principle of Self-sacrifice, seen especially in early Martyrdoms — The Idea of Benevolence in connection with public and private Charities — Importance of public Preaching — Pulpit Oratory — The Elaboration of Christian Doctrine — Its Connection with Philosophy — Church Psalmody — The Principle of Christian Equality — Its Effects on Slavery and the Elevation of the People — The Social Equality of the Sexes — Superiority in the condition of the modern over the ancient Woman — The Idea of Popular Education — The Unity of the Church, ... 576

INTRODUCTION.

I PROPOSE to describe the Greatness and the Misery of the old Roman world; nor is there any thing in history more suggestive and instructive.

A little city, founded by robbers on the banks of the Tiber, rises gradually into importance, although the great cities of the East are scarcely conscious of its existence. Its early struggles simply arrest the attention, and excite the jealousy, of the neighboring nations. The citizens of this little state are warriors, and, either for defense or glory, they subdue one after another the cities of Latium and Etruria, then the whole of Italy, and finally the old monarchies and empires of the world. In two hundred and fifty years the citizens have become nobles, and a great aristocracy is founded, which lasts eight hundred years. Their aggressive policy and unbounded ambition involve the whole world in war, which does not cease until all the nations known to the Greeks acknowledge their sway. Everywhere Roman laws, language, and institutions spread. A vast empire arises, larger than the Assyrian and the Macedonian combined, — a universal empire, — a great wonder and mystery, having all the grandeur of a providential event. It becomes too great to be governed by an oligarchy of nobles. Civil wars create an imperator, who, uniting in himself all the great offices of state, and sustained by the conquering legions, rules from East to West and from North to South, with absolute and undivided sovereignty. The Cæsars reach the summit of human greatness and power, and the city of Romulus becomes the haughty mistress of the world. The emperor is worshiped as a deity, and the proud metropolis calls herself eternal. An empire is established by force of arms and by a uniform policy, such as this world has not seen before or since.

Early Roman history is chiefly the detail of successful wars, aggressive and uncompromising, in which we see a fierce and selfish patriotism, an indomitable will, a hard unpitying temper, great practical sagacity, patience, and perseverance, superiority to adverse fortune, faith in national destinies, heroic sentiments, and grand ambition. We see a nation of citizen soldiers, an iron race of conquerors, bent on conquest, on glory, on self-exaltation, attaching but little value to the individual man, but exalting the integrity and unity of the state. We see no fitful policy, no abandonment to the enjoyment of the fruits of victory, no rest, no repose, no love of art or literature, but an unbounded passion for domination. The Romans toiled, and suffered, and died, — never wearied, never discouraged, never satisfied, until their mission was accomplished and the world lay bleeding and prostrate at their feet.

In the latter days of the Republic, the Roman citizen, originally contented with a few acres in the plains and valleys through which the Tiber flowed, becomes a great landed proprietor, owning extensive estates in the conquered territories, an aristocrat, a knight, a senator, a noble, while his dependents disdained to labor and were fed at the public expense. The state could afford to give them corn, oil, and wine, for it was the owner of Egypt, of Greece, of Asia Minor, of Syria, of Spain, of Gaul, of Africa, — a belt of territory around the Mediterranean Sea one thousand miles in breadth, embracing the whole temperate zone, from the Atlantic Ocean to the wilds of Scythia. The Romans revel in the spoils of the nations they have conquered, adorn their capital with the wonders of Grecian art, and abandon themselves to pleasure and money-making. The Roman grandees divide among themselves the lands and riches of the world, and this dwelling-place of princes looms up the proud centre of mundane glory and power.

In the great success of the Romans, we notice not only their own heroic qualities, but the hopeless degeneracy of the older nations and the reckless turbulence of the western barbarians, both of whom needed masters.

The conquered world must be governed. The Romans had a genius for administration as well as for war. While war was reduced to a science, government became an art. Seven hundred years of war and administration gave experience and skill, and the wisdom thus learned became a legacy to future civilizations.

It was well, both for enervated orientals and wild barbarians, to be ruled by such iron masters. The nations at last enjoyed peace and prosperity, and Christianity was born and spread. A new power silently arose, which was destined to change government, and science, and all the relations of social life, and lay a foundation for a new and more glorious structure of society than what Paganism could possibly create. We see the hand of Providence in all these mighty changes, and it is equally august in overruling the glories and the shame of a vast empire for the ultimate good of the human race.

If we more minutely examine the history of either Republican or Imperial Rome, we read lessons of great significance. In the Republic we see a constant war of classes and interests, — plebeians arrayed against patricians; the poor opposed to the rich; the struggle between capital and labor, between an aristocracy and democracy. Although the favored classes on the whole retained ascendancy, yet the people constantly gained privileges, and at last were enabled, by throwing their influence into the hands of demagogues, to overturn the constitution. Julius Cæsar, the greatest name in ancient history, himself a patrician, by courting the people triumphed over the aristocratical oligarchy and introduced a new régime. His dictatorship was the consummation of the victories of the people over nobles as signally as the submission of all classes to fortunate and unscrupulous generals.

We err, however, in supposing that the Republic was ever a democracy, as we understand the term, or as it was understood in Athens. Power was always in the hands of senators, nobles, and rich men, as it still is in England, and was in Venice. Popular liberty was a name, and democratic institutions were feeble and shackled. The citizen-noble was free, not the proletarian. The latter had the redress of laws, but only such as the former gave. How exclusive must have been an aristocracy when the Claudian family boasted that, for five hundred years, it had never received any one into it by adoption, and when the Emperor Nero was the first who received its privileges! It is with the senatorial families, who contrived to retain all the great offices of the state, that everything interesting in the history of Republican Rome is identified, — whether political quarrels, or private feuds, or legislation, or the control of armies, or the improvements of the city, or the government of provinces. It was they, as senators, governors, consuls, generals, quæstors, who gave the people baths, theatres, and temples. They headed factions as well as armies. They were the state.

The main object to which the reigning classes gave their attention was war, — the extension of the empire. "*Ubi castra, ibi respublica.*" Republican Rome was a camp, controlled by aristocratic generals. Dominion and conquest were their great ideas, their aim, their ambition. To these were sacrificed pleasure, gain, ease, luxury, learning, and art. And when they had conquered they sought to rule, and they knew how to rule. Aside from conquest and government there is nothing peculiarly impressive in Roman history, except the struggles of political leaders and the war of classes.

But in these there is wonderful fascination. The mythic period under kings; the contests with Latins, Etruscans, Volscians, Samnites, and Gauls; the legends of Porsenna, of Cincinnatus, of Coriolanus, of Virginia; the heroism of Camillus, of Fabius, of Decius, of Scipio; the great struggle with Pyrrhus and Hannibal; the wars with Carthage, Macedonia, and Asia Minor; the rivalries between patrician and plebeian families; the rise of tribunes; the Mænian, Hortensian, and Agrarian laws; the noble efforts of the Gracchi; the censorship of Cato; the civil wars of Marius and Sulla, and their exploits, followed by the still greater conquests of Pompey and Julius; these, and other feats of heroism and strength, are full of interest which can never be exhausted. We ponder on them in youth; we return to them in old age.

And yet the real grandeur of Rome is associated with the emperors. With their accession there is a change in the policy of the state from war to peace. There is a greater desire to preserve than extend the limits of the empire. The passion for war is succeeded by a passion for government and laws. Labor and toil give place to leisure and enjoyment. Great works of art appear, and these become historical, — the Pantheon, the Forum Augusti, the Flavian Amphitheatre, the Column of Trajan, the Baths of Caracalla, the Aqua Claudia, the golden house of Nero, the Mausoleum of Hadrian, the Temple of Venus and Rome, the Arch of Septimus Severus. The city is changed from brick to marble, and palaces and theatres and temples become colossal. Painting and sculpture ornament every part of the city. There are more marble busts than living men. Life becomes more complicated and factitious. Enormous fortunes are accumulated. A liberal patronage is extended to artists. Literature declines, but great masterpieces of genius are still produced.

Medicine, law, and science flourish. A beautiful suburban life is seen on all the hills, while gardens and villas are the object of perpetual panegyric. From all corners of the earth strangers flock to see the wonders of the mighty metropolis, more crowded than London, more magnificent than Paris, more luxurious than New York. Fêtes, shows, processions, gladiatorial combats, chariot races, form the amusement of the vast populace. A majestic centralized power controls all kingdoms, and races, and peoples. The highest state of prosperity is reached that the ancient world knew, and all bow down to Cæsar and behold in him the representative of divine providence, from whose will there is no appeal, and from whose arm it is impossible to fly.

But *mene, mene, tekel, upharsin*, is written on the walls of the banqueting chambers of the palace of the Cæsars. The dream of omnipotence is disturbed by the invasion of Germanic barbarians. They press toward the old seats of power and riches to improve their condition. They are warlike, fierce, implacable. They fear not death, and are urged onward by the lust of rapine and military zeal. The old legions, which penetrated the Macedonian phalanx and withstood the Gauls, cannot resist the shock of their undisciplined armies; for martial glory has fled, and the people prefer their pleasures to the empire. Great emperors are raised up, but they are unequal to the task of preserving the crumbling empire. The people, enervated and egotistical, are scattered like sheep or are made slaves. The proud capitals of the world fall before the ruthless invaders. Desolation is everywhere. The barbarians trample beneath their heavy feet the proud trophies of ancient art and power. The glimmering life-sparks of the old civilization disappear. The world is abandoned to fear, misery, and despair, and there is no help, for retributive justice marches on with impressive solemnity. Imperial despotism, disproportionate fortunes, unequal divisions of society, the degradation of woman, slavery, Epicurean pleasures, practical atheism, bring forth their wretched fruits. The vices and miseries of society cannot be arrested. Glory is succeeded by shame; all strength is in mechanism, and that wears out; vitality passes away; the empire is weak from internal decay, and falls easily into the hands of the new races. "Violence was only a secondary cause of the ruin; the vices of self-interest were the primary causes. A world, as fair and glorious as our own, crumbles away." Our admiration is changed to sadness and awe. The majesty of man is rebuked by the majesty of God.

Such a history is suggestive. Why was such an empire permitted to rise over the bleeding surface of the world, and what was its influence on the general destiny of the race? How far has its civilization perished, and how far has it entered into new combinations? Was its strength material, or moral, or intellectual? How far did literature, art, science, laws, philosophy, prove conservative forces? Why did Christianity fail to arrest so total an eclipse of the glory of man? Why did a magnificent civilization prove so feeble a barrier against corruption and decay? Why was the world to be involved in such universal gloom and wretchedness as followed the great catastrophe? Could nothing arrest the stupendous downfall?

And when we pass from the great facts of Roman history to the questions which it suggests to a contemplative mind in reference to the state of society among ourselves, on which history ought to shed light, what enigmas remain to be solved. Does moral worth necessarily keep pace with æsthetic culture, or intellectual triumphs, or material strength? Do the boasted triumphs of civilization create those holy certitudes on which happiness is based? Can vitality in states be preserved by mechanical inventions? Does society expand from inherent laws of development, or from influences altogether foreign to man? Is it the settled destiny of nations to rise to a certain height in wisdom and power, and then pass away in ignominy and gloom? Is there permanence in any human institutions? Will society move round in perpetual circles, incapable of progression and incapable of rest, or will it indefinitely improve? May there not be the highest triumphs of art, literature, and science, where the mainsprings of society are sensuality and egotism? Is the tendency of society to democratic, or aristocratic, or despotic governments? Does Christianity, in this dispensation, merely furnish witnesses of truth, or will it achieve successive conquests over human degeneracy till the race is emancipated and saved? Can it arrest the downward tendency of society, when it is undermined by vices which blunt the conscience of mankind, and which are sustained by all that is proud in rank, brilliant in fashion, and powerful in wealth?

These are inquiries on which Roman history sheds light. If history is a guide or oracle, they are full of impressive significance. Can we afford to reject all the examples of the past in our sanguine hopes for the future? Human nature is the same in any age, and human experiences point to some great elemental truths, which the Bible confirms. *We* may be unmoved by them, but they remain in solemn dignity for all generations; "and foremost of them," as Charles Kingsley has so well said, "stands a law which man has been trying in all ages, as now, to deny, or at least to ignore, and that is, — that as the fruit of righteousness is wealth and peace, strength and honor, the fruit of unrighteousness is poverty and anarchy, weakness and shame; for not upon *mind*, but upon *morals*, is human welfare founded. Science is indeed great; but she is not the greatest. She is an instrument, and not a power. But her lawful mistress, the only one under whom she can truly grow, and prosper, and prove her divine descent, is Virtue, the likeness of Almighty God, — an ancient doctrine, yet one ever young, and which no discoveries in science will ever abrogate."

Hence the great aim of history should be a dispassionate inquiry into the genius of past civilizations, especially in a moral point of view. Wherein were they weak or strong, vital or mechanical, permanent or transient? We wish to know that we may compare them with our own, and learn lessons of wisdom. The rise and fall of the Roman Empire is especially rich in the facts which bear on our own development. Nor can modern history be comprehended without a survey of the civilization which has entered into our own, and forms the basis of many of our own institutions. Rome perished, but not wholly her civilization. So far as it was founded on the immutable principles of justice, or beauty, or love, it will never die, but will remain a precious legacy to all generations. So far as it was founded on pride, injustice, and selfishness, it ignobly disappeared. *Men* die, and their trophies of pride are buried in the dust, but their truths live. All truth is indestructible, and survives both names and marbles.

Roman history, so grand and so mournful, on the whole suggests cheering views for humanity, since out of the ruins, amid the storms, aloft above the conflagration, there came certain indestructible forces, which, when united with Christianity, developed a new and more glorious condition of humanity. Creation succeeded destruction. All that was valuable in art, in science, in literature, in philosophy, in laws, has been preserved. The useless alone has perished with the worn-out races themselves. The light which scholars, and artists, and poets, and philosophers, and lawgivers kindled, illuminated the path of the future guides of mankind. And especially the great ideas which the persecuted Christians unfolded, projected themselves into the shadows of mediæval Europe, and gave a new direction to human thought and life. New sentiments arose, more poetic and majestic than ever existed in the ancient world, giving radiance to homes, peace to families, elevation to woman, liberty to the slave, compassion for the miserable, self-respect to the man of toil, exultation to the martyr, patience to the poor, and glorious hopes to all; so that in rudeness, in poverty, in discomfort, in slavery, in isolation, in obloquy, peace and happiness were born, and a new race, with noble elements of character, arose in the majesty of renovated strength to achieve still grander victories, and confer higher blessings on mankind.

Thus the Roman Empire, whose fall was so inglorious, and whose chastisement was so severe, was made by Providence to favor the ultimate progress of society, since its civilization entered into new combinations, and still remains one of the proudest monuments of human genius.

It is this civilization, in its varied aspects, both good and evil, lofty and degraded, which in the following chapters I seek to show. This is the real point of interest in Roman history. Let us see what the Romans really accomplished — the results of their great enterprises; the systems they matured with so much thought; the institutions they bequeathed to our times; yea, even those vices and follies which they originally despised, and which, if allowed to become dominant, *must*, according to all those laws of which we have cognizance, ultimately overwhelm *any* land in misery, shame, and ruin.

In presenting this civilization, I aim to generalize the most important facts, leaving the reader to examine at his leisure recondite authorities, in which, too often, the argument is obscured by minute details, and art is buried in learning.

THE OLD ROMAN WORLD.

CHAPTER I.

THE CONQUESTS OF THE ROMANS.

One of the features of Roman greatness, which preëminently arrests attention, is military genius and strength. The Romans surpassed all the nations of antiquity in the brilliancy and solidity of their conquests. They conquered the world, and held it in subjection. For many centuries they stamped their iron heel on the necks of prostrate and suppliant kings, from the Atlantic Ocean to the Caspian Sea. Nothing could impede, except for a time, their irresistible progress from conquering to conquer. They were warriors from the earliest period of their history, and all their energies were concentrated upon conquest. Their aggressive policy never changed so long as there was a field for its development. They commenced as a band of robbers; they ended by becoming masters of all the countries and kingdoms which tempted their cupidity or aroused their ambition. Their empire was universal, — the only universal empire which ever existed on this earth, — and it was won with the sword. It was not a rapid conquest, but it was systematic and irresistible, evincing great genius, perseverance, and fortitude.

The successive and fortunate conquests of the Romans were the admiration, the envy, and the fear of all nations — so marvelous and successful that they

The Romans fight from a fixed purpose

have the majesty of a providential event. They cannot be called a mystery, since we see the persistent adaptation of means to an end. But no other nation ever evinced this uniform military policy, except for a limited period, or under the stimulus of a temporary enthusiasm, such as characterized the Saracens and the Germanic barbarians. The Romans fought when there was no apparent need of fighting, when their empire already embraced most of the countries known to the ancients. The Egyptians, the Assyrians, the Persians, and the Greeks made magnificent conquests, but their empire was partial and limited, and soon passed away. The Greeks evinced great military genius, and the enterprises of Alexander have been regarded as a wonder. But the Greeks did not fight, as the Romans did, from a fixed purpose to bring all nations under their sway, and they yielded, in turn, to the Romans. The Romans were never subdued, but all nations were subdued by them — even superior races. They erected a universal monarchy, which fell to pieces by its own weight, when the vices of self-interest had accomplished their work. They became the prey of barbarians in a very different sense from that which reduced the ancient empires. They did not yield to any powerful, warlike neighbor, as the Persians yielded to the Greeks, but to successive waves of unknown warriors who came in quest of settlement, and then only when all Roman vigor had fled, and the whole policy of the empire was changed — when it was the aim of emperors to conserve old conquests, not make new ones.

War a passion with the Romans.

With the Romans, for a thousand years, war was a passion; and, while it lasted, it consumed all other passions. It animated statesmen, rulers, generals, and citizens alike, ever burning, never at rest, — a passion unscrupulous, resistless, all-pervading, all-absorbing, all-conquering. Success in war gave consideration, dignity, honor beyond all other successes. It always has called out popular admiration, and its glory has ever been highly prized, and it always will be so, but it has not monopolized all offices and dignities as among the Romans. The Greeks thought of art, of literature, and of philosophy as well as of war, and gave their crowns of glory for civic and artistic excellence as well as for military success. The Greeks fought to preserve or extend their civilization; the Romans, in order to rule. They had very little respect for any thing beyond military genius. The successful warrior alone was the founder of a great family. The Roman aristocracy, so proud, so rich, so powerful, was based on the glory of battle-fields. Every citizen was trained to arms, and senators and statesmen commanded armies. The whole fabric of the State was built up on war, and for many centuries it was the leading occupation of the people. How insignificant was a poet, or a painter, or a philosopher by the side of a warrior! Rome was a city of generals, and they preoccupied the public mind.

Value placed by the Romans on military art.

To a Roman, military art was the highest of all. It was constantly being improved, until it reached absolute perfection, with the old weapons and implements of war. To its perfection the whole genius of the people was consecrated; it was to them what the fine arts were to the Greeks, what priestly domination was to the Middle Ages, and what material inventions to abridge human labor are to us. The Romans despised literature, art, philosophy, commerce, agriculture, and even luxury, when they were making their grand conquests; they only respected their fortunate generals. Hence there was no great encouragement to genius or ambition in any other field; but in this field, the horizon perpetually expanded. Every new conquest prepared the way for successive conquests; ambition here was untrammeled, energy was unbounded, visions of glory were most dazzling, warlike schemes were most fertile, until the whole world lay bleeding and prostrate.

Military genius, however, does not present man in the

highest state of wisdom or beauty. It is very attractive, but "there is a greater than the warrior's excellence," at least to a contemplative or religious eye. When men save nations, in fearful crises, by their military genius, as Napoleon did France when surrounded with hostile armies, or Gustavus Adolphus did Germany when it was struggling for religious rights, then they render the greatest possible services, and receive no unmerited honors. The heart of the world cherishes the fame of Miltiades, of Charlemagne, of Henry IV., of Washington; for they were identified with great causes. War is one of the occasional necessities of our world. No nation can live, or is worthy to live, without military virtues. They rescue nations on the verge of ruin, and establish great rights, without which life is nothing. War, however much to be lamented as an evil, is the last appeal and resource of nations, and settles what cannot be settled without it; and it will probably continue so long as there are blindness, ambition, and avarice among men. Nor, under certain circumstances, of which nations can only be the proper judges, is it inconsistent with the law of love. Hence, as it is a great necessity, it will ever be valued as a great science. Civilization accepts it and claims it. It calls into exercise great qualities, and these intoxicate the people, who bow down to them as godlike.

Lawfulness of war.

Still, military genius, however lauded and honored, is too often allied with ambition and selfishness to secure the highest favor of philosophers or Christians. It does not reveal the soul in its loftiest aspirations. Men of a coarser type are often most successful, — men insensible to pity and to reproach, whose greatest merit is in will, nerve, energy, and power of making rapid combinations. We revere the intellect of the Greeks more than that of the Romans, though they were inferior to the latter in military success. We have more respect for those qualities which add to the domain of truth

Those who are most successful in war.

than those which secure power. A wise man elevates the Bacons, the Newtons, and the Shakespeares above all the Marlboroughs and Wellingtons. Plato is surrounded with a brighter halo than Themistocles, and Cicero than Marius.

The general evils of war.

War as a trade is unscrupulous, hard, rapacious, destructive. It foments all the evil passions; it is allied with all the vices; it is antagonistic to human welfare. It glories merely in strength; it worships only success. It raises wicked men to power; it prostrates and hides the good. It extinguishes what is most lovely, and spurns what is most exalted. It makes a pandemonium of earth, and drags to its triumphal car the venerated relics of ages. It is an awful crime, making slaves of the helpless, and spreading consternation, misery, and death wherever it goes — marking its progress with a trail of blood, and filling the earth with imprecations and curses. It is the greatest scourge which God uses to chastise enervated nations, and cannot be contemplated with any satisfaction except as the wrath which is made to praise the Sovereign Ruler who employs what means He chooses to punish or exalt.

Spirit of the Romans in their wars.

Now the Romans, in a general sense, pursued war as a trade, to gratify a thirst for power, to raise themselves on the ruins of ancient monarchies, to enrich themselves with the spoils of the world, and to govern it for selfish purposes. There were many Roman wars which were exceptions, when an exalted patriotism was the animating principle; but aggressive war was the policy and shame of Rome. Her citizens did not generally fight to preserve liberties or rights or national existence, but for self-aggrandizement. Incessant campaigns for a thousand years brought out military science, courage, energy, and a grasping and selfish patriotism. They gave power, skill to rule, executive talents; and these qualities, eminently adapted to worldly greatness, made the Romans universal masters, even if they do not make them interesting. They developed great strength, resource, will, and even made them wise in administration, possibly great civilizers, since centralized power is better than anarchies; yet these traits do not make us love them, or revere them. Providence doubtless ordered the universal monarchy, which only universal war could establish, for the good of the world at that time, for the advancement of civilization itself. Universal dominion must be succeeded by universal peace, and in such a peace the higher qualities and virtues and talents can only be manifested, so that the Roman rule was not a calamity, but a very desirable despotism. Yet despotism it was, — cold, remorseless, self-seeking. War made the Romans practical, calculating, overbearing, proud, scornful, imperious.

Success of the Romans in war.

But war made them a great people, and made them eminent in certain great qualities. Their success in war is tantamount to saying that in one great field of genius, which civilization honors, they not merely distinguished themselves, and gained a proud fame which will never die out of the memory of man, but that they have had no equals in any age. War enabled them to build up a vast empire, which empire gave a great impulse to ancient civilization.

There is something very singular and mysterious in the results of wars which are caused and carried on by unprincipled and unscrupulous men. They are made to end in substantial benefits to the human race. The wrath of man, in other words, is made to praise God, showing that He is the Sovereign ruler on this earth, and uses what instruments He pleases to carry out his great and benevolent designs. However atrocious the causes of wars, and execrable the spirit in which they are carried out, they are ever made to subserve the benefit of future ages, and the great cause of civilization in its vast connections. Men may be guilty, and may be punished for their wickedness, and execrated through all time by enlightened nations; still they are but tools of the higher power. I do not say that God is the author of wars any more than He is of sin; but wars are yet sent as a punishment to those whom they directly and immediately affect, while they unbind the cords of slavery, and relax the hold of tyrants. They are like storms in the natural world: they create a healthier moral life, after the disasters are past. Those ambitious men, who seek to add province to province and kingdom to kingdom, and for whom no maledictions are too severe, since they shed innocent blood, rarely succeed unless they quarrel with doomed nations incapable of renovation. Thus Babylon fell before Cyrus when her day had come, and she could do no more for civilization. Thus Persia, in her turn, yielded to the Grecian heroes when she became enervated with the luxuries of the conquered kingdoms. Thus Greece again succumbed to Rome when she had degenerated into a land where every vice was rampant. The passions which inflamed Cyrus, and Alexander, and Pompey were alike imperious, and their policy was alike unscrupulous. They simply were bent on conquest, and on establishing powerful empires, which conquests doubtless resulted in the improvement of the condition of mankind. There is also something hard and forbidding in the policy of successful statesmen. We are shocked at their injustice, cruelty, and rapaciousness; but they are often used by Providence to raise nations to preëminence, when their ascendency is, on the whole, a benefit to the world. There is nothing amiable or benign in the characters of such men as Oxenstiern, Richelieu, or Bismarck, but who can doubt the wisdom of their administration? It is seldom that any nation is allowed to have a great ascendency over other nations unless the general influence of the dominant State is favorable to civilization; and when this influence is perverted the ascendency passes away. This is remarkably seen in the history of the Persian, the Greek, and the Roman Em-

Providence seen in the ascendency of great nations.

pires, and still more forcibly in the empire of the popes in the Middle Ages, and of the vast influence of France and England during the last hundred years. This is both a mystery and a fact. It is mysterious that bad men should be allowed to succeed so often, but it is one of the sternest facts of life, only to be explained on the principle that they are instruments in the hands of the Great Moral Governor whose designs we are not able to fathom, yet the wisdom of which is subsequently, though imperfectly, made known. It was wicked in the sons of Jacob to sell Joseph to the Ishmaelites; their craft and lies were successful: they deceived their father and accomplished their purposes; yet his bondage was the means of their preservation from the evils of famine. The rise and fall of empires are to be explained on the same principles as the rise and fall of families. A coarse, unscrupulous but enterprising man gets rich, but his wealth is made to subserve interests far greater than that of his children. Hospitals, colleges, and libraries are endowed as monasteries were in the Middle Ages. If vice, selfishness, and pride were not overruled, what would become of our world? The whole history of civilization is the good which is made to spring out of evil. Men are nothing in comparison with Omnipotence. What are human plans? Yet enterprise and virtue and talent are rewarded. In the affairs of life we see that goodness does not lose its recompense, and that vice is punished; but beyond, what more impressively do we behold than this, that the instruments of punishment are often the wicked themselves.

The results of the Crusades.

Among the worst wars in history — uncalled for, unscrupulous, fanatical — were the Crusades. And when were wars more unfortunate, more unsuccessful? Five millions of Crusaders perished miserably in those mad expeditions stimulated by hatred of Mohammedanism. No trophies consoled Europe for its enormous losses, extended over two hundred years. But those wars developed the resources of Europe; they broke the power of feudal barons; they promoted commerce and the arts of life; they led to greater liberality of mind; they opened the horizon of knowledge; they introduced learned men into rising universities; they centralized the power of kings; they weakened the temporal jurisdiction of the popes; they improved architecture, sculpture, and painting; they built free cities; they gave a new stimulus to all the energies of the European nations. Their benefits to civilization were not the legitimate result of destructive passions. The natural penalty of folly and crime was paid in hardship, sorrow, disease, captivity, disappointment, poverty, and death. But out of the ashes a new creation arose, not what any of the leaders of those movements ever contemplated — infinitely removed from the thoughts of Bernard, Urban, Philip, and Richard, great men as they were, far-sighted statesmen, who expected other results. The hand which guided that warfare between Europe and Asia was the hand that led the Israelites out of Egypt across the Red Sea. Moreover, *quem deus vult perdere prius dementat.* What uprising more foolish, insane, disastrous, than the great Southern rebellion! Its result was never dreamed of for a moment by those Southern leaders. They hoped to see the establishment of a great empire based on slavery; they saw the utter destruction of slavery itself. The course by which they anticipated dominion and riches ended in their temporal ruin. They were made the destroyers of their own pet system, when it could not have been destroyed in any other way. It was only by a great war that the fetters of the slave could be removed, and God sent war so soon as it pleased Him to bring the wicked bondage to an end. If any thing shows the hand of God it is the wars of the nations. They are sent like the famine and the pestilence. All human wisdom and power sink into insignificance when they are put forth to stop these scourges of the Almighty.

Their immediate consequences are disastrous; their ultimate, beneficial.

It is against all reason that they ever come; yet they do come, and then crimes are avenged; evil punishes evil, and succeeding generations are made to see that the progress of the race is through sorrow and suffering. No great empire is built up but with the will of God. No empire falls without deserving the chastisement and the ruin. But God has promised to save and to redeem, and the world moves on in accordance with natural laws, and each successive century witnesses somehow or other a great advance in the general condition of mankind. It is not the great rulers who plan this improvement. It comes from Heaven. It comes in spite of human degeneracy, which, if left to itself, would doubtless soon produce a state of society like that which is attributed to the nations "before the flood came and destroyed them all."

Wars overruled for the good of nations.

With this view of war — always aggressive with one party, always a calamity to both; the greatest calamity known to the nations, exhausting, bloody, cruel, sweeping every thing before it; a moral conflagration, bringing every kind of suffering and sorrow in its train, yet made to result as a retribution to worn-out and degenerate races, and a means of vast development of resources among those peoples which have life and energy, — we see the providence of God in the Roman Conquests. The gradual growth of Rome as a warlike state is a most impressive example of the agency of a great Moral Governor in breaking up states that deserved to perish, and in building up a power such as the world needed in order to facilitate both a magnificent civilization and the peaceful spread of a new religion. The Greeks created art and literature; the Romans, laws and government, by which society everywhere was made more secure and tranquil, until the good which arose from the evil was itself perverted.

Growth of Rome under the kings.

Under the kingly rule Rome becomes the most important and powerful of the cities of Latium, and a foundation is laid of social, religious, and political institutions which are destined to achieve a magnificent triumph. The kings of Rome are all great men — wise and statesmanlike, patrons of civilization among a rude and primitive people. No state for more than two hundred years was ever ruled by more enlightened princes, ambitious indeed, sometimes unscrupulous, but fortunate and successful. The benefits derived from the conquests and ascendency of the city of Romulus were seen in the union of several petty states, and the fusion of their customs and manners. Before the foundation of the city, Italy was of no account with the older empires. In less than two hundred and fifty years a great Italian power grows up on the banks of the Tiber, imbued to some extent with the civilization of Greece, which it receives through Etruria and the Tarquins.

Effect of the expulsion of the Tarquins.

But the growth of Rome under the kings was too rapid for its moral health. A series of disasters produced by the expulsion of the Tarquins, during which the Roman state dwindles into a small territory on the left bank of the Tiber, develops strength and martial virtue. It takes Rome one hundred and fifty years to recover what it had lost. Moreover its great prosperity has provoked envy, and all the small neighboring nations are leagued against it. These must be subdued, or Italy will remain divided and subdivided, with no central power.

The heroic period of Roman history begins really with the expulsion of the kings; also the growth of aristocratical power. It is not under kings nor democratic influences and institutions that Rome reaches preëminence, but under an aristocracy. All that is most glorious in Roman annals took place under the rule of the Patricians.

Rome struggles for existence for 150 years.

During the one hundred and fifty years — when the future mistress of the world struggled for its existence with the cities and inhabitants of Latium, Samnium, and Etruria, whose united territories scarcely extended fifty miles from Rome, were developed the virtues of a martial aristocracy. Our minds kindle with the contemplation of their courage, fortitude, patience, hope, perseverance, energy, self-devotion, patriotism, and religious faith. They deserved success. The long and bitter struggle of one hundred and fifty years had more of the nature of self-preservation than military ambition. The history of those petty wars is interesting, because it is romantic. Beautiful legends of early patriotism and heroism have been reproduced in all the histories from Livy to our times, like those of the knights of king Arthur and the paladins of Charlemagne in the popular literature of Europe. Poets have made them the themes of their inspiration. Painters have chosen them as favorite subjects of art. We love to ponder on the bitter exile of Coriolanus, his treasonable revenge, and the noble patriotism of his weeping and indignant mother, who saved her country but lost her son; on Cincinnatus, taken from the plow and sent as general and dictator against the Acquians; on the Fabian gens, defending Rome a whole year from the attacks of the Veientines until they were all cut off, like the Spartan band at Thermopylæ; on Siccius Dentatus, the veteran captain of one hundred and twenty battles, who was only slain by rolling a stone from a high rock upon his head; on Cossos, slaying the king of Veii with his own hand; on the siege of Veii, itself, a city as large as Rome, lasting ten years, and only finally taken by draining the Alban lake; on the pride and avarice of the banished Camillus, and his subsequent rescue of Rome from the Gauls; on the sacred geese of the capitol, and Manlius who slew its assailants; on the siege of the capitol for seven months by these Celtic invaders, and the burning and sack of the city, and its deliverance by the great Camillus. These legends are not legitimate history, but they show the self-devotion and bravery, the simplicity and virtue of those primitive ages, when luxury was unknown and crime was

Beautiful legends of the heroic period.

They indicate the existence of great virtues.

severely punished. It was in those days of danger and hardship that the foundation of the future military strength of the empire was laid. We do not read of military science, of war as an art or trade, or even of great military ambition, for the sphere of military operations was narrow and obscure, but of preparation for victories, under men of genius, in the time to come. That part of Roman history bears the same relation to the age of Marius and Sulla, that the conquests of the Puritans over the Indians, and the difficulties with which they contended, do to the gigantic warfare of the North and South in the late rebellion. The Puritans laid the foundation of the military virtues of the Americans, in their colonial state, as the Patricians of Rome did for one hundred and fifty years after the expulsion of the kings. Those petty wars with Volscians and Acquians brought out the Roman character, and are the germ of subsequent greatness. They took place in the infancy of the republic, under the rule of Patricians, who were not then great nobles, but brave and poor citizens, animated with patriotic zeal and characterized, like the Puritans, for stern and lofty virtues and religious faith, — superstitious and unenlightened, yet elevated and grand, — qualities on which the strength of man is based. It is not puerile to dwell with delight on the legends of that heroic age, for the philosopher sees in those little struggles the germs of imperial power. They were small and insignificant, like the battles of the American Revolution, when measured with the marshaling of vast armies on the plains of Pharsalia or Waterloo, but they were great in their inherent heroism and in their future results. Who shall say which is greater to the eye of the Infinite — the battle of Leipsic, or the fight on Bunker Hill? It is the cause, the principles involved, the spirit of a contest, which give dignity and importance to the battle-field. Hence all nations and ages have felt great interest in the early struggles of Rome. They are full of poetry and philosophical importance.

Petty wars with neighboring states develop patriotism.

The Roman historians themselves dwelt upon them with peculiar enthusiasm; and the record of them lives in the school-books of all generations, and has not been deemed unworthy of the critical genius of Niebuhr, of Arnold, or of Mommsen.

The result of this protracted warfare with petty cities and states for one hundred and fifty years was the complete independence of the City of the Seven Hills, the regaining of the conquests lost by the expulsion of Tarquin, the conquest of Latium, the dissolution of the Latin League, the possession of the Pontine district, and the extension of Roman power to the valleys of the Apennines. The war with the Gauls was not a systematic contest. It was a raid of these Celts across the Apennines, and the temporary humiliation of the Roman capital. The Gauls burned and sacked the city, but soon retreated, and Rome was never again invaded by a foreign foe until the hordes of Alaric appeared. The disaster was soon recovered, and the Romans made more united by the lesson.

The complete independence of Rome.

The Gaulish invasion.

With the retreat of the Gauls, B. C. 350, and the recovery of Latium, B. C. 341 and four hundred and sixteen years from the foundation of the city, the aggressive period of Roman warfare begins. By this time the Plebeians made their power felt, and had obtained one of the two consulships; but for a long time after, the Patricians, though shorn of undivided sovereignty, still monopolized most of the great offices of state — indeed were the controlling power, socially and politically. At no period was Rome a democratic state; never had Plebeians the ascendency. But now the plebeian influence begins to modify the old constitution. All classes, after incessant warfare for a century and a half, and exposed to innumerable feuds, united in enterprises of conquest. Rome begins to appear on the stage of political history.

The aggressive nature of Roman warfare commenced with Samnium. The Samnites were a warlike and pastoral people who inhabited the rugged mountain district between the valleys of the Vulturnus and the Calor, but they were nevertheless barbarians, and the contest between them and the Romans was for the sovereignty of Italy. I need not mention the alleged causes, or the details of a sanguinary war. The alleged causes were not the true ones, and the details are complicated and obscure. We deal with results. The war began B. C. 326, and lasted, with short intervals of peace, thirty-six years. The Roman heroes were M. Valerius Corvus, L. Papirius Cursor, Q. Fabius Maximus, and P. Decius the younger. All of these were great generals, and were consuls or dictators. As in all great contests, lasting a whole generation, there was alternate victory and defeat, disgraced by treachery and bad faith. The Romans fought, assisted by Latins, Campanians, and Apulians. The Samnites defended themselves in their mountain fastnesses with inflexible obstinacy, and obtained no assistance from allies until nearly worn out, when Umbrians, Etrurians, and Senonian Gauls came to the rescue. About sixty thousand men fought on each side. The battle of Sentinum determined the fate of Samnium and Italy, gained by Fabius and Decius, and the Samnites laid down their arms and yielded to their rivals. Their brave general, Pontius, was beheaded in the prison under the capitol, — an act of inhumanity which sullied the laurels of Fabius. The Roman power is now established over central and lower Italy, and with the exception of a few Greek cities on the coast, Latium, Campania, Apulia, and Samnium are added to the territories of the republic.

War with the Samnites.

Decisive battle of Sentinum.

In the mean time the political inequality between Patricians and Plebeians had been removed, and a plebeian nobility had grown up, created by success in war and domestic factions. The great man in civil history, during this war, was Appius Claudius the Censor, a proud and inflexible Patrician. His great

Works of Appius Claudius.

3

works were the Appian road and aqueduct. The road led to Capua through the Pontine marshes one hundred and twenty miles, and was paved with blocks of basalt; the aqueduct passed under ground, and was the first of those vast works which supplied the city with water.

About ten years elapsed between the conquest of the Samnites and the landing of Pyrrhus in Italy, B. C. 280, during which the Romans were brought in contact with Magna Grecia and Syracuse.

The chief of the Greek-Italian cities was Tarentum, a very ancient Lacedæmonian colony. It was admirably situated for commerce on the gulf which bears its name, was very rich, and abounded in fearless sailors. But like most commercial cities, it intrusted its defense to mercenaries. It viewed with alarm the growing power of Rome, and unable to meet her face to face, called in the aid of Pyrrhus, king of Epirus, the greatest general of the age, which was followed by a general rising of the Italian states, to shake off the Roman yoke.

Tarentum invokes the aid of Pyrrhus.

Pyrrhus was a soldier of fortune, and practiced war as an art, and delighted in it like Alexander or Charles XII. He readily responded to the overture of the Tarentine Ambassador, and sent over a general with three thousand men to secure a footing, and soon followed with twenty thousand foot, five thousand horse, and a number of elephants. Among his troops were five thousand Macedonian soldiers, a phalanx such as the Romans had never encountered. The Macedonians fought in masses; the Romans in lines. The first encounter was disastrous to the Romans, whose cavalry was frightened by the elephants. But Pyrrhus, contented with victory, did not pursue his advantages, and advanced with easy marches towards Rome with seventy thousand men. The battle of Heraclea, however, had greatly weakened his forces; his allies proved treacherous; and he was glad to offer terms of peace, which were promptly rejected by the

Expedition of Pyrrhus into Italy.

Senate. After spending nearly three years in Italy he retired to Syracuse, but again tried his fortune against the Romans, and was signally routed at the battle of Beneventum by Curius Dentatus. He hastily left Italy to her fate, and the fall of Tarentum speedily followed, which made the Romans masters of the whole peninsula. The Macedonian phalanx, which had conquered Asia, yielded to the Roman legion, and a new lesson was learned in the art of war.

He is defeated at the battle of Beneventum.

The Romans, by the fall of Tarentum, were now the undisputed masters of Italy, and had made the first great step towards the conquest of the world. The city of Romulus was now four hundred and eighty years old, and the national domain extended from the Ciminian wood in Etruria to the middle of the Campania. It was called the Ager Romanus, in which was a population of two hundred and ninety-three thousand men capable of bearing arms; and the citizens of the various conquered cities, who had served certain magistracies in them, were enrolled among Roman citizens, with all the rights to which the citizens of the capital were entitled, — absolute authority over wife, children, and slaves, security from capital punishment except by a vote of the people, or under military authority in the camp, access to all the honors and employments of the state, the right of suffrage, and the possession of Quirinal property. They felt themselves to be allies of Rome, and henceforward lent efficient aid in war. To all practical intents, they were Romans as completely as the inhabitants of Marseilles are French. Tarentum, Neapolis, Tibur, Præneste, and other large cities, enjoyed peculiar privileges; but armed garrisons were maintained in them, under the form of colonies. The administration of them was organized after the model of Rome. Military roads were constructed between all places of importance.

Results of the fall of Tarentum.

The Romans complete masters of Italy.

The same sterling virtues which characterized the absolute rule of the Patricians still continued, and patriotism partook of the nature of religious sentiment. Three Decii surrendered their lives for the Roman army, and Manlius immolated his son to the genius of discipline; Rufinus is degraded from the Senate for possessing ten pounds of silver plate, although twice consul and once dictator; Regulus, twice consul, possessed no more than one little field in the barren district of Papinice. Curius like Fabricius prepared his simple meal with his own hand, and refused the gold of the Samnites, as Fabricius refused that of Pyrrhus. The new masters of Italy deserved their empire. There was union because there was now political equality. The "new men, like Fabricius and Curius Dentatus, were not less numerous in the Senate than the old Curial families. The aristocracy of blood was blended with the aristocracy of merit. The consulship gave unity of command, the Senate wisdom and the proper strength, preserving a happy equilibrium of forces, — the combination of royalty, aristocracy, and democracy, which, with military virtues and austere manners, made an irresistible force."[1] This period, the fifth century of the existence of the Roman state, was its heroic age.

The virtues of eminent Patricians.

But now military aggrandizement became the master-passion of the people, and the uniform policy of the government. Military virtues still remained, but the morals of state began to decline. Aggressive wars, for conquest and power, henceforth, mark the progress of the Romans; and not merely aggressive wars, but unjust and foreign wars. The step of the Roman is now proud and defiant. Visions of unlimited conquest rise up before his eye. He is cold, practical, imperious. The eagles of the legions are the real objects of pride and reverence. Mars is the presiding deity. Success is the only road to honor.

Rome prepares for aggressive and unjust war.

[1] Durny, *Hist. des Romains.*

While Rome was completing the reduction of Italy, Carthage, a Tyrian colony on the opposite coast of Africa, was extending her conquests in the Islands of the Mediterranean. The Greek colonies of Sicily had fallen under her sway. She was a rival whose power was formidable, enriched by the commerce of the world, and proud in the number of her allies. The city contained seven hundred thousand inhabitants, and the walls measured twenty miles in circumference.

Rivalry between Carthage and Rome.

Between such ambitious and unscrupulous rivals, peace could not long be maintained. To the eye of the philosopher the ascendency of Carthage or of Rome over the countries which border on the Mediterranean was clearly seen. Which were better? Shall the world be governed by a martial, law-making, law-loving, heroic commonwealth, not yet seduced and corrupted by luxury and wealth, or by a commercial, luxurious, selfish nation of merchants, whose only desire is self-indulgence and folly. Providence sides with Rome — although Rome cannot be commended, and is ruled by ambitious and unscrupulous chieftains whose delight is power. If there is to be one great empire more, before Christianity is proclaimed, which shall absorb all other empires, now degenerate and corrupt, let that be given to a people who know how to civilize after they have conquered. Let the sword rather than gold rule the world — enlightened statesmen rather than self-indulgent merchants. So Carthage falls, after three memorable struggles, extending over more than a century, during which she produced the greatest general of antiquity, next to Cæsar and Alexander. But not even Hannibal could restore the fortunes of his country, after having inflicted a bitter humiliation on his enemies. That city of merchants, like Tyre and Sidon, must drink of the cup of divine chastisement. Another type of civilization than that furnished by a "mistress of the sea," was needed for Europe, and an-

Shall Rome or Carthage have the preeminence.

Carthage falls after a long and memorable struggle.

other rule for Asia and Africa. The Carthaginians taught the Romans, in their contest, how to build ships of war and fight naval battles. As many as three hundred thousand men were engaged in that memorable sea-fight of Ecnomus which opened to Regulus the way to Africa. Three times did the Romans lose their fleets by tempests, and yet they persevered in building new ones. The fortitude of the Romans, in view of the brilliant successes of Hannibal, can never be sufficiently admired. The defeat at Cannæ was a catastrophe, but the troops of Fabius, to whom was left the defense of the city, were not discouraged, and with Scipio — religious, self-reliant, and lofty — the tide of victory turned. By the first Punic war, which lasted twenty-two years, Rome gained Sicily; by the second, which opened twenty-three years after the first, and lasted seventeen years, she gained Sardinia, a foothold in Spain and Gaul, and a preponderance throughout the western regions of Europe and Africa; by the third, which occurred fifty years after the second, and continued but four years, she gained all the provinces of Africa ruled by Carthage, and a great part of Spain. Nothing was allowed to remain of the African capital. The departing troops left behind complete desolation. The captives were sold as slaves, or put to death, and enough of spoil rewarded the victors to adorn a triumph only surpassed by that of Paulus on his return from the conquest of Greece.

Territories acquired by the fall of Carthage.

In the mean time, in the interval between the second and third Punic wars, occurred the Macedonian wars, which prepared the way for conquests in the East. The great Macedonian empire was split up into several monarchies among the generals of Alexander and their successors. The Ptolemies reigned in Egypt; the successors of Seleucus in Babylonia; those of Antigonus in Syria and Asia Minor; those of Lysimachus in Thrace; and of Cassander in Macedonia. It was the mission of

Condition of the Macedonian empire.

Rome to subdue these monarchies, or rather her good fortune, for she was destined to conquer the world. The principles which animated these wars cannot be defended on high moral grounds, any more than the conquest of India by England, or of Algeria by France. They were based entirely upon ambition — upon the passion for political aggrandizement. I confess I have no sympathy with them. Roman liberties were not jeopardized, nor were these monarchies dangerous rivals like Carthage. The subjugation of Italy was in accordance with what we now call the Monroe doctrine — to obtain the ascendency on her own soil; and even the conquest of Sicily was no worse than the conquest of Ireland, or what would be the future absorption of Cuba and Jamaica within the limits of the United States. The Emperor Napoleon would probably justify both the humiliation of Carthage and the conquest of Greece and Asia and Egypt, and others would echo his voice in defense of aggressive domination, on some plea of pretended schemes of colonization, and the progress of civilization. But I do not believe in overturning the immutable laws of moral obligation for any questionable policy of expediency. I look upon the great civil wars of the Romans, which followed these conquests, in which so much blood was shed, and in which Marius and Sulla and Cæsar and Pompey exhausted the resources of the state, and made an imperial *régime* necessary, only as the visitation of God in rebuke of such wicked ambition.

Principles and passions which led to the conquest of Greece.

The conquest over the Macedonians, however, by the Romans, was not an unmixed calamity, and was a righteous judgment on the Greeks. Nothing could be more unscrupulous than the career of Alexander and his generals. Again, the principle which had animated the Oriental kings before him was indefensible. We could go back still further, and show from the whole history of Asiatic conquests that their object was to aggrandize ambitious conquerors. The Persians, at first,

Greece reaps the penalty of the unscrupulous wars of Alexander.

were a brave and religious people, hardy and severe, and their conquest of older monarchies resulted in a certain good. But they became corrupt by prosperity and power, and fell a prey to the Greeks. The Greeks, at that period, were the noblest race of the ancient world — immortal for genius and art. But power dazzled them, and little remained of that glorious spirit which was seen at Thermopylæ and Marathon. The Greek ascendency in Asia and Egypt was followed by the same luxury and extravagance and effeminacy that resulted from the rule of Persia. The Greeks had done great things, and contributed to the march of civilization, but they had done their work, and their turn of humiliation must come. Their vast empire fell into the hands of the Romans, and the change was beneficial to humanity. They who had abused their trust were punished, and those were exalted above them who were as yet uncorrupted by those vices which are most fatal to nations. The great fruit of these wars were the treasures of Greece, especially precious marbles, and other works of art. The victory at Pydna, B. C. 168, which gave the final superiority to the Roman legion over the Macedonian phalanx, was followed by the triumph of Paulus himself — the grandest display ever seen at Rome. First passed the spoils of Greece — statues and pictures — in two hundred and fifty wagons; then the arms and accoutrements of the Macedonian soldiers; then three thousand men, each carrying a vase of silver coin; then victims for sacrifice, with youths and maidens with garlands; then men bearing vases of gold and precious stones; then the royal chariot of the conquered king laden with armor and trophies; then his wife and children, and the fallen monarch on foot; then the triumphal car of the victorious general, preceded by men bearing four hundred crowns of gold — the gift of the Grecian cities — and followed by his two sons on horseback, and

Degeneracy of the Greeks.

Spoils of Greece fall into the hands of the Romans.

The triumph of Paulus.

the whole army in order. The sack of Corinth by Mummius was the finale of Grecian humiliation, soon followed by the total subjection of Macedonia, Greece, and Illyria, forming three provinces. Nine provinces now composed the territories of Rome, while the kings of Asia Minor, Syria, and Egypt were vassals rather than allies, B. C. 133.

Grecian provinces added to the empire.

The manners and habits of the imperial capital had undergone a gradual change since the close of the second Punic War. During these fifty years, the sack of so many Grecian cities, the fall of Carthage, and the prestige of so many victories, had filled Rome with pride and luxury. In vain did M. Portius Cato, the most remarkable man who adorned this degenerate age, lift up his voice against increasing corruption. In vain were his stringent measures as censor. In vain did he strike senators from the list, and make an onslaught on the abuses of his day. In vain were his eloquence, his simple manners, his rustic garb, and his patriotic warnings. That hard, narrow, self-sufficient, arbitrary, worldly-wise old statesman, whose many virtues redeemed his defects, and whose splendid abilities were the glory of his countrymen, could not restore the simplicities of former times. An age of "progress" had set in, of Grecian arts and culture, of material wealth, of sumptuous banquets, of splendid palaces, of rich temples, of theatrical shows, of circus games, of female gallantries, of effeminated manners — all the usual accompaniments of civilization, when it is most proud of its triumphs; and there was no resisting its march — to the eye of many a great improvement; to the eye of honest old Cato, the *descensus averni*. Wealth had become a great power; senatorial families grew immensely rich; the divisions of society widened; slavery was enormously increased, while the rural population lost independence and influence.

Change of manners and morals at Rome.

Reforms of Cato the Censor.

Great degeneracy produced by the Grecian wars.

Then took place the memorable struggles of Rome, not merely with foreign enemies, but against herself. Factions and parties convulsed the city; civil war wasted the national resources.

It was in that period of civic strife, when factions and parties struggled for ascendency — when the Gracchi were both reformers and demagogues, patriots and disorganizers, heroes and martyrs — when fortunate generals aimed at supreme power, and sought to overturn the liberties of their country, that Rome was seriously threatened by the barbarians. Both Celts and Teutones, from Gaul and Germany, formed a general union for the invasion of Italy. They had successively defeated five consular armies, in which one hundred and twenty thousand men were slain. They rolled on like a devastating storm — some three hundred thousand warriors from unconquered countries beyond the Alps. They were met by Marius the hero of the African war, who had added Numidia, to the empire — now old, fierce, and cruel, a plebeian who had arisen by force of military genius — and the Gaulish hordes were annihilated on the Rhone and the Po. The Romans at first viewed those half-naked warriors — so full of strength and courage, so confident of victory, so reckless of life, so impetuous and savage — with terror and awe. But their time had not yet come. Numbers were of no avail against science, when science was itself directed by genius and sustained by enthusiasm. The result of the decisive battles of Aquæ Sextiæ and Vercellæ was to roll back the tide of northern immigration for three hundred years, and to prepare the way for the conquests of Cæsar in Gaul.

Wars with the Cimbri and Teutones.

Success of Marius, who rolls back the tide of northern emigration.

Then followed that great insurrection of the old states of Italy against their imperious mistress — their last struggle for independence, called the Social War, in which three hundred thousand of the young men of Italy fell, and in which Sulla so much distinguished himself

The Social War.

as to be regarded as the rival of Marius, who had ruled Rome since the slaughter of the Cimbrians and Teutones. Sulla, who had served under Marius in Africa, dissolute like Antony, but cultivated like Cæsar — a man full of ambition and genius, and belonging to one of the oldest and proudest patrician families, the Cornelian gens — was no mean rival of the old tyrant and demagogue, and he was sent against Mithridates, the most powerful of all the Oriental kings.

Rise of Sulla.

This Asiatic potentate had encouraged the insurgents in Italy, and was also at war with the Romans. Marius viewed with envy and hatred the preference shown to Sulla in the conduct of the Mithridatic War, and succeeded, by his intrigues and influence with the people, in causing Sulla to be superseded, and himself to be appointed in his place.

Hence that dreadful civil contest between these two generals, in which Rome was alternately at the mercy of both, and in which the most horrible butcheries took place that had ever befallen the city — a reign of terror, a burst of savage passion, especially on the part of Marius, who had lately abandoned himself to wine and riotous living. He died B. C. 86, victor in the contest, in his seventh consulate, worn out by labor and dissolute habits, nearly seventy years of age.

Civil wars between Marius and Sulla.

His opportune death relieved Rome of a tyrannical rule, and opened the way for the splendid achievements of Sulla in the East. A great warrior had arisen in a quarter least expected. In the mountainous region along the north side of the Euxine, the kingdom of Pontus had grown from a principality to a kingdom, and Mithridates, ruling over Cappadocia, Paphlagonia, and Phrygia, aspired for the sovereignty of the East. He was an accomplished and enlightened prince, and could speak twenty-five languages, hardy, adventurous, and bold, like an ancient Persian. By conquests and

Death of Marius.

alliances he had made himself the most powerful sovereign in Asia.

Mithridates.

Availing himself of the disturbance growing out of the Social War, he fomented a rebellion of the provinces of Asia Minor, seized Bithynia, and encouraged Athens to shake off the Roman yoke. Most of the Greek communities joined the Athenian insurrection, and Asia rallied around the man who hoped to cope successfully with Rome herself.

Conquests of Sulla in Greece.

At this juncture, Sulla was sent into Greece with fifty thousand men. Athens fell before his conquering legions, B. C. 88, and the lieutenants of Mithridates retreated before the Romans with one hundred thousand foot and ten thousand horse, and one hundred armed chariots. On the plains of Chæronea, where Grecian liberties had been overthrown by Philip of Macedon, two hundred and fifty years before, a desperate conflict took place, and the Pontic army was signally defeated. Shortly after, Sulla gained another great victory over the generals of the King of Pontus, and compelled him to accept peace, the terms of which he himself dictated, after exacting heavy contributions from the cities of Greece and Asia Minor.

Death of Sulla.

The civil war between Sulla and the chiefs of the popular faction that had been created by Marius, which ended in his complete ascendency in Italy, stopped for a while the Roman conquests in the East. Sulla, having undone the popular measures of the last half century, and reigned supreme over all factions as dictator, died B. C. 78, after a most successful career, and left his mantle to the most enterprising of his lieutenants, Cnæus Pompey, who was destined to complete the Mithridatic war.

Character of Sulla.

If Sulla had not been so inordinately fond of pleasure and luxurious self-indulgence, he might have seized the sceptre of universal dominion, and have made himself undisputed master of the empire. He was a man of extraordinary genius, fond of literature, and a great diplomatist. But he was not preëminently ambitious like Cæsar, and was diverted by the fascinations of elegant leisure; nor was he naturally cruel, though his passions, when aroused, were fierce and vindictive. He lived in an age of exceeding corruption, when it was evident to contemplative minds that Roman liberties could not be much longer preserved. He had, for a time, restored the ascendency of the senatorial families, but faction was at work among the unprincipled chiefs of the republic.

Lucullus marches against Mithridates.

On the death of the great dictator, Mithridates broke the peace he had concluded, and marched into Bithynia, which had been left by will to the Roman people by Nicomedes, with the hope of its reconquest. He had an army of one hundred and twenty thousand foot and fifteen thousand horse. Lucullus, with thirty thousand foot and one thousand horse, advanced against him, and the vast forces of Mithridates were defeated, and the king was driven into Armenia, and sought the aid of Tigranes, his son-in-law, king of that powerful country. He, too, was subdued by the Roman legions, and all the nations from the Halys to the Euphrates acknowledged the dominion of Rome.

Rising greatness of Pompey.

Still, Mithridates was not subdued, and Pompey, who had annihilated the Mediterranean pirates, was deemed the only person fit to finish the Mithridatic war. His successes had been more brilliant than even those of Sulla, or Lucullus, or Metellus. He was made Dictator of the East, with greater powers than had ever before been intrusted to a Roman general. He had success equal to his fame; drove Mithridates across the Caucasus; reduced Pontus, and took possession of Syria, which had been subject to Tigranes. The defeated King of Pontus, who had sought to unite all the barbarous tribes of Eastern Europe against Rome, destroyed himself. Pompey, after seven years' continued successes, returned to Italy to claim his triumph, having subdued the East, and added the old monarchy of the Seleucidæ to the dominion of Rome, B. C. 61.

The early career of Julius Cæsar.

But while Pompey was pursuing his victories over the effeminate people of Asia, a still more brilliant career in the West marked the rising fortunes of Julius Cæsar. I need not dwell on the steps by which he arose to become the formidable rival of the conqueror of the East. He bears the most august name of antiquity. A patrician by birth, a demagogue in his principles, popular in his manners, unscrupulous in his means, he successively passed through the various great offices of state, which he discharged with prodigious talent. As leader of the old popular party of Marius, he sought the humiliation of the Senate, while his ambition led him to favor every enterprise which promised to advance his own interests. Leaving the province of Spain, after his prætorship, before Pompey's return to Italy, his great career of conquest commenced. He first availed himself of some disturbances in Lusitania to declare war against its gallant people, overran their country, and then turned his arms against the Gallicians. In two years he had obtained spoils more than sufficient to pay his enormous debts, the result of his prodigality, by which, however, he won the hearts of the thoughtless citizens, and paved the way for honor. Conqueror of Spain, and idol of the people, he returned to Rome, B. C. 60, when Pompey was quarreling with the Senate, formed an alliance with him and Crassus, and by their aid was elected consul. His measures in that high office all tended to secure his popularity with the people, and supported by Pompey and Crassus, he triumphed over the Senate. He then secured the government of Cisalpine Gaul and Illyricum, with two legions, for the extraordinary term of five years. The Senate added the province of Transalpine Gaul, then

His victories in Spain.

Cæsar sent into Gaul.

threatened by the Allobrogians, Suevi, Helvetians, and other barbaric tribes, with the intention of confining him to a dangerous and uncertain field of warfare.

That field, however, established his military fame, and paved the way for his subsequent usurpations. The conquests of Cæsar in Western Europe are unique in the history of war, and furnish no parallel. Other conquests may have been equally brilliant and more imposing, but none were ever more difficult and arduous, requiring greater perseverance, energy, promptness, and fertility of resources. The splendid successes of Lucullus and Pompey in Asia resembled those of Alexander. We see military discipline and bravery triumphing over the force of multitudes, and a few thousand men routing vast armies of enervated or undisciplined mercenaries. Such were the conquests of the English in India. They make a great impression, but the fortunes of an empire are decided by a single battle. It was not so with the conflicts of Cæsar in Gaul. He had to fight with successive waves of barbarians, inured to danger, adventurous and hardy, holding life in little estimation, willing to die in battle, intrepid in soul, and bent on ultimate victory. He had to fight in hostile territories, unacquainted with the face of the country, at a great distance from the base of his supplies, exposed to perpetual perils, and surrounded with unknown difficulties. And these were appreciated by his warlike countrymen, who gave him the credit he deserved. The ten years he spent in Gaul were the years of his truest glory, and the most momentous in their consequences on the future civilization of the world, since it was not worn-out monarchies he added to the empire, but a new territory, inhabited by brave and simple races, who were to learn the arts and laws and literature of Rome, and supply the government with powerful aid in the decline of its strength. It was the conquered barbarians who, henceforth, were to furnish Rome with

His great military genius.

His difficulties in the conquest of Gaul.

Results of the Gaulish wars.

soldiers, and even scholars and statesmen and generals. Among them the old civilization was to take root, among them new states were to arise on which the Romans could impress their own remarkable characteristics. It was the western provinces of the empire that alone were vital with energy and strength, and which were destined to perpetuate the spirit of Roman institutions. The eastern provinces never lost the impress of the Greek mind and manners. They remained Greek even when subdued by the imperial legions. Syria, Asia Minor, Egypt, were filled with Grecian cities, and Asiatic customs were modified by Grecian civilization. The West was purely Roman, and the Latin language, laws, and arts were continued, in a modified form, through the whole period of the Middle Ages. Even Christianity had a different influence in the West from what it had in the East. In other words, the West was completely Latinized, while the East remained Grecian. Though the East was governed by Roman proconsuls, they could not change the Græco-Asiatic character of its institutions and manners; but the barbarians were willing to learn new lessons from their Roman masters.

Gaul becomes Latinized.

It would require a volume to describe the various campaigns of Cæsar in Gaul, in which a million of people were destroyed. But I only aim to show results. Most people are familiar with the marvelous generalship and enterprises of the Roman conqueror — the conquest and reconquest of the brave barbarians, most of whom were Celts; the uprising of Germanic tribes as well, and their fearful slaughter near Coblentz; the bloody battles, the fearful massacres, the unscrupulous cruelties which he directed; the formidable insurrection organized by Vercingetorix; the spirit he infused into his army; the incessant hardships of the soldiers, crossing rivers, mountains, and valleys, marching with their heavy burdens — fighting amid every disadvantage, until all the

Greatness of Cæsar.

countries north of the Alps and west of the Rhine acknowledged his sway — all these things are narrated by Cæsar himself with matchless force and simplicity of language.

Cæsar now probably aspired to the sovereignty of the empire, as Napoleon did after the conquest of Italy. But he had a great rival in Pompey, who had remained chiefly at Rome, during his Gaulish campaigns, virtually dictator, certainly the strongest citizen. And Pompey had also his ambitious schemes. One was the conqueror of the East; the other of the West. One leaned to the aristocratic party, the other to the popular. Pompey was proud, pompous, and self-sufficient. Cæsar was politic, patient, and intriguing. Both had an inordinate ambition, and both were unscrupulous. Pompey had more prestige, Cæsar more genius. Pompey was a greater tactician, Cæsar a greater strategist. The Senate rallied around the former, the people around the latter. Cicero distrusted both, and flattered each by turns, but inclined to the side of Pompey, as belonging to the aristocratic party.

Rivalry between Cæsar and Pompey.

Between such ambitious rivals coalition for any length of time could not continue. Dissensions arose between them, and then war. The contest was decided at Pharsalia. On the 6th of June, B. C. 48, "Greek met Greek," yet with forces by no means great on either side. Pompey had only forty thousand, and Cæsar less, but they were veterans, and the victory was complete. Pompey fled to Egypt, without evincing his former greatness, paralyzed, broken, and without hope. There he miserably died, by the assassin's dagger, at the age of sixty, and the way was now prepared for the absolute rule of Cæsar.

Battle of Pharsalia.

Death of Pompey.

But the party of Pompey rallied, connected with which were some of the noblest names of Rome. The battle of Thapsus proved as disastrous to Cato as Pharsalia did to

Pompey. Cæsar was uniformly victorious, not merely over the party which had sustained Pompey, but in Asia, Africa, and Spain, which were in revolt. His presence was everywhere required, and wherever he appeared his presence was enough. He was now dictator for ten years. He had overturned the constitution of his country. He was virtually the supreme ruler of the world. In the brief period which passed from his last triumphs to his death, he was occupied in legislative labors, in settling military colonies, in restoring the wasted population of Italy, in improving the city, in reforming the calendar, and other internal improvements, evincing an enlarged and liberal mind.

Dictatorship of Cæsar.

But the nobles hated him, and had cause, in spite of his abilities, his affability, magnanimity, and forbearance. He had usurped unlimited authority, and was too strong to be removed except by assassination. I need not dwell on the conspiracy under the leadership of Brutus, and his tragic end in the senate-house, where he fell, pierced by twenty-two wounds, at the base of Pompey's statue, the greatest man in Roman history — great as an orator, a writer, a general, and a statesman; a man without vanity, devoted to business, unseduced by pleasure, unscrupulous of means to effect an end; profligate, but not more so than his times; ambitious of power, but to rule, when power was once secured, for the benefit of his country, like many other despots immortal on a bloody catalogue. After his passage of the Rubicon his career can only be compared with that of Napoleon.

Death of Cæsar. His character.

But Roman territories were not much enlarged by Cæsar after the conquest of Celtic Europe. His later wars were either against rivals or to settle distracted provinces. Nor were they increased in the civil wars which succeeded his death, between the various aspirants for the imperial power and those who made one more stand for the old constitution. At the fatal battle of

Character of his later wars.

Philippi, when the hopes of Roman patriots vanished forever, double the number of soldiers were engaged on both sides than at Pharsalia, but fortune had left the senatorial party, of which Brutus was the avenger and the victim.

Civil wars after the death of Cæsar.

Civil war was carried on most vigorously after the death of Julius. But it was now plainly a matter between rival generals and statesmen for supreme command. The chief contest was between Octavian and Antony, the former young, artful, self-controlled, and with transcendent abilities as a statesman ; the latter bold, impetuous, luxurious, and the ablest of all Cæsar's lieutenants as a general. Had he not yielded to the fascinations of Cleopatra, he would probably have been the master of the world. But the sea-fight of Actium, one of the great decisive battles of history, gave the empire of the world to Octavian B. C. 31, and two years after the victor celebrated three magnificent triumphs, after the example of his uncle, for Dalmatia, Actium, and Egypt. The kingdom of the Ptolemies passed under the rule of Cæsar. The Temple of Janus was shut, for the first time for more than two hundred years ; and the imperial power was peaceably established over the civilized world.

Ascendency of Octavian.

The friends of liberty may justly mourn over the fall of republican Rome, and the centralization of all power in the hands of Augustus. But it was a calamity which could not be averted, and was a revolution which was in accordance with the necessities of the times. Fifty years' civil war taught the Romans the hopelessness of the struggle to maintain their old institutions so long as the people were corrupt, and fortunate generals would sacrifice the public welfare to their ambition. Order was better than anarchy, even though a despot reigned supreme. When men are worse than governments, they must submit to the despotism of tyrants. It is idle to dream of liberty with a substratum of folly and vice. The

Necessity for the empire.

strongest man will rule, but whether he rule wisely or unwisely, there is no remedy. Providence gave the world to the Romans, after continual and protracted wars for seven hundred years; and when the people who had conquered the world by their energy, prudence, and perseverance, were no longer capable of governing themselves, then the state fell into the possession of a single man.

Change in the imperial policy.

Under the emperors, the whole policy of the government was changed. They no longer thought of further aggrandizement, but of retaining the conquests which were already made. And if they occasionally embarked in new wars, those wars were of necessity rather than of ambition, were defensive rather than aggressive. New provinces were from time to time added, but in consequence of wars which were waged in defense of the empire. The conquest of Britain and Judea was completed, and various conflicts took place with the Germanic nations, who, in the reign of Antoninus, formed a general union for the invasion of the Roman world. These barbarians were the future aggressors on the peace of the empire, until it fell into their hands. The empire of Augustus may be said to have reached the utmost limits it ever permanently retained, extending from the Rhine and the Danube to the Euphrates and Mount Atlas, embracing a population variously estimated from one hundred to one hundred and thirty millions.

Perfection of military art.

When Augustus became the sovereign ruler of this vast empire, military art had reached the highest perfection it ever attained among any of the nations of antiquity. It required centuries to perfect this science, if science it may be called, and the Romans doubtless borrowed from the people whom they subdued. They learned to resist the impetuous assaults of semi-barbarous warriors, the elephants of the East, and the phalanx of the Greeks. Military discipline was carried to the severest extent by Marius, Pompey, and Cæsar.

The Roman soldier was trained to march twenty miles a day, under a burden of eighty pounds; yea, to swim rivers, to climb mountains, to penetrate forests, and to encounter every kind of danger. He was taught that his destiny was to die in battle. He expected death. He was ready to die. Death was his duty, and his glory. He enlisted in the armies with little hope of revisiting his home. He crossed seas and deserts and forests with the idea of spending his life in the service of his country. His pay was only a denarius daily, equal to about sixteen cents of our money. Marriage was discouraged or forbidden. He belonged to the state, and the state was exacting and hard. He was reduced to abject obedience, yet he held in his hand the destinies of the empire. And however insignificant was the legionary as a man, he gained importance from the great body with which he was identified. He was the servant and the master of the state. He had an intense *esprit de corps.* He was bound up in the glory of his legion. Both religion and honor bound him to his standards. The golden eagle which glittered in his front was the object of his fondest devotion. Nor was it possible to escape the penalty of cowardice or treachery, or disobedience. He could be chastised with blows by his centurion; his general could doom him to death. Never was the severity of military discipline relaxed. Military exercises were incessant, in winter as in summer. In the midst of peace the Roman troops were familiarized with the practice of war.

The spirit of the Roman soldier.

It was the spirit which animated the Roman legions, and the discipline to which they were inured, which gave them their irresistible strength. When we remember that they had not our fire-arms, we are surprised at their efficiency, especially in taking strongly fortified cities. Jerusalem was defended by a triple wall, and the most elaborate fortifications, and twenty-four thousand soldiers, beside the aid received from the citizens; and yet

Military genius of the Romans.

it fell in little more than four months before an army of eighty thousand under Titus. How great the science to reduce a place of such strength, in so short a time, without the aid of other artillery than the ancient catapult and battering-ram! Whether the military science of the Romans was superior or inferior to our own, no one can question that it was carried to utmost perfection before the invention of gunpowder. We are only superior in the application of this great invention, especially in artillery. There can be no doubt that a Roman army was superior to a feudal army in the brightest days of chivalry. The world has produced no generals superior to Cæsar, Pompey, Sulla, and Marius. No armies ever won greater victories over superior numbers than the Roman, and no armies of their size, ever retained in submission so great an empire, and for so long a time. At no period in the history of the empire were the armies so large as those sustained by France in time of peace. Two hundred thousand legionaries, and as many more auxiliaries, controlled diverse nations and powerful monarchies. The single province of Syria once boasted of a military force equal in the number of soldiers to that wielded by Tiberius. Twenty-five legions made the conquest of the world, and retained that conquest for five hundred years. The self-sustained energy of Cæsar in Gaul puts to the blush the efforts of all modern generals, except Frederic II., Marlborough, Napoleon, Wellington, Grant, Sherman, and a few other great geniuses which a warlike age developed; nor is there a better text-book on the art of war than that furnished by Cæsar himself in his Commentaries. And the great victories of the Romans over barbarians, over Gauls, over Carthaginians, over Greeks, over Syrians, over Persians, were not the result of a short-lived enthusiasm, like those of Attila and Tamerlane, but extended over a thousand years. The Romans were essentially military in all their tastes and habits.

The perfection of military art.

Luxurious senators and nobles showed the greatest courage and skill in the most difficult campaigns. Antony, Cæsar, Pompey, and Lucullus were, at home, enervated and luxurious, but, at the head of the legions, were capable of any privation and fatigue. The Roman legion was a most perfect organization, a great mechanical force, and could sustain furious attacks after vigor, patriotism, and public spirit had fled. For three hundred years a vast empire was sustained by mechanism alone.

The Roman Legion.

The legion is coeval with the foundation of Rome, but the number of the troops of which it was composed varied at different periods. It rarely exceeded six thousand men. Gibbon estimates the number at six thousand eight hundred and twenty-six men. For many centuries it was composed exclusively of Roman citizens. Up to the year B. C. 107, no one was permitted to serve among the regular troops except those who were regarded as possessing a strong personal interest in the stability of the republic. Marius admitted all orders of citizens; and after the close of the Social War, B. C. 87, the whole free population of Italy was allowed to serve in the regular army. Claudius incorporated with the legion the vanquished Goths, and after him the barbarians filled up the ranks, on account of the degeneracy of the times. But during the period when the Romans were conquering the world every citizen was trained to arms, and was liable to be called upon to serve in the armies. In the early age of the republic, the legion was disbanded as soon as the special service was performed, and was in all essential respects a militia. For three centuries, we have no record of a Roman army wintering in the field; but when Southern Italy became the seat of war, and especially when Rome was menaced by foreign enemies, and still more when a protracted foreign service became inevitable, the same soldiers remained in activity for several years. Gradually the distinction between the

Its composition.

soldier and the civilian was entirely obliterated. The distant wars of the republic, like the prolonged operations of Cæsar in Gaul, and the civil contests, made a standing army a necessity. During the civil wars between Cæsar and Pompey, the legions were forty in number; under Augustus but twenty-five. Alexander Severus increased them to thirty-two. This was the standing force of the empire, from one hundred and fifty to two hundred and forty thousand men, and this was stationed in the various provinces. The main dependence of the legion was on the infantry, which wore heavy armor consisting of helmet, breastplate, greaves on the legs, and buckler on the left arm four feet in length and two and a half in width. The helmet was originally made of leather or skin, strengthened and adorned by bronze or gold, and surmounted by a crest which was often of horse-hair, and so made as to give an imposing look. The crest not only served for ornament but to distinguish the different centurions. The breastplate or cuirass was generally made of metal, and sometimes was highly ornamented. Chain-mail was also used. The greaves were of bronze or brass, with a lining of leather or felt, and reached above the knees. The shield, worn by the heavy-armed infantry, was not round, like that of the Greeks, but oval or oblong, adapted to the shape of the body, and was made of wood or wicker-work. The weapons were a light spear, a pilum or javelin six feet long, terminated by a steel point, and a sword with a double edge, adapted to striking or pushing. The legion was drawn up eight deep, and three feet intervened between rank and file, which disposition gave great activity, and made it superior to the Macedonian phalanx, the strength of which depended on sixteen ranks of long pikes wedged together. The cavalry attached to each legion were three hundred men, and they originally were selected from the leading men in the

The infantry the strength of the legion.

Its armor.

Its weapons.

The cavalry.

state. They were mounted at the expense of the state, and formed a distinct order. The cavalry was divided into ten squadrons; and to each legion was attached a train of ten military engines of the largest size, and fifty-five of the smaller, — all of which discharged stones and darts with great effect. This train corresponded with our artillery. Besides the armor and weapons of the legionaries, they usually carried on their marches provisions for two weeks, and three or four stakes used in forming the palisade of the camp, beside various tools, — altogether a burden of sixty or eighty pounds per man. The general period of service for the infantry was twenty years, after which the soldier received a discharge together with a bounty in money or land.

Term of military service.

The Roman legion, whether it was composed of four thousand men, as in the early ages of the republic, or six thousand, as in the time of Augustus, was divided into ten cohorts, and each cohort was composed of Hastati, Principes, Triarii, and Velites. The soldiers of the first line, called Hastati, consisted of youths in the bloom of manhood, and were distributed into fifteen companies or maniples. Each company contained sixty privates, two centurions, and a standard-bearer. Two thirds were heavily armed, and bore the long shield, the remainder carried only a spear and light javelins. The second line, the Principes, was composed of men in the full vigor of life, divided also into fifteen companies, all heavily armed, and distinguished by the splendor of their equipments. The third body, the Triarii, was also composed of tried veterans, in fifteen companies, the least trustworthy of which were placed in the rear. These formed three lines. The Velites were light-armed troops, employed on out-post duty, and mingled with the horsemen. The Hastati were so called because they were armed with the hasta; the Principes, for being placed so near to the front; the

Organization of the legion.

The Hastati.

The Principes and Velites.

Triarii, from having been arrayed behind the first two lines as a body of reserve, armed with the pilum, thicker and stronger than the Grecian lance,— four and a half feet long, of wood, with a barbed head of iron,—so that the whole length of the weapon was six feet nine inches. It was used either to throw or thrust with, and when it pierced the enemy's shield,[1] the iron head was bent, and the spear, owing to the twist in the iron, still held to the shield.[2] Each soldier carried two of these weapons.[3] The Principes were in the front ranks of the phalanx, clad in complete defensive armor, —men in the vigor of strength. The Pilarii were in the rear, who threw the heavy pilum over the heads of their comrades, in order to break the enemy's line. In the time of the empire, when the legion was modified, the infantry wore cuirasses and helmets, and two swords; namely, a long one and a dagger. The select infantry carried a long spear and a shield, the rest a pilum. Each man carried a saw, a basket, a mattock, a hatchet, a leather strap, a hook, a chain, and provisions for three days. The Equites wore helmets and cuirasses, like the infantry, with a broad sword at the right side, and in their hand a long pole. A buckler swung at the horse's flank. They were also furnished with a quiver containing three or four javelins.

The Triarii.

The Pilarii.

The Equites.

The artillery were used both for hurling missiles in battle, and for the attack of fortresses. The *tormentum*, which was an elastic instrument, discharged stones and darts, and was continued until the discovery of gunpowder. In besieging a city, the ram was employed for destroying the lower part of a wall, and the balista, which discharged stones, was used to overthrow the battlements. The balista would project a stone weighing from fifty to three hundred pounds. The *aries*, or battering-ram, consisted of a large beam made of the

The artillery.

1 Liv. viii. 8. 2 Plut. Mar. 25. 3 Polyb. vi. 23.

trunk of a tree, frequently one hundred feet in length, to one end of which was fastened a mace of iron or bronze, which resembled in form the head of a ram, and was often suspended by ropes from a beam fixed transversely over it, so that the soldiers were relieved from supporting its weight, and were able to give it a rapid and forcible motion backward and forward. And when this machine was further aided by placing a frame in which it was suspended upon wheels, and constructing over it a roof, so as to form a *testudo*, which protected the besieging party from the assaults of the besieged, there was no tower so strong, no wall so thick, as to resist a long-continued attack. Its great length enabled the soldiers to work across the ditch, and as many as one hundred men were often employed upon it. The Romans learned from the Greeks the art of building this formidable engine, which was used with great effect by Alexander, but with still greater by Vespasian in the siege of Jerusalem. It was first used by the Romans in the siege of Syracuse. The *vinea* was a sort of roof under which the soldiers protected themselves when they undermined walls. The *helepolis*, also used in the attack of cities, was a square tower furnished with all the means of assault. This also was a Greek invention, and that used by Demetrius at the siege of Rhodes, B. C. 306, was one hundred and thirty-five feet high and sixty-eight wide, divided into nine stories. Towers of this description were used at the siege of Jerusalem,[1] and were manned by two hundred men employed upon the catapults and rams. The *turris*, a tower of the same class, was used both by Greeks and Romans, and even by Asiatics. Mithridates used one at the siege of Cyzicus one hundred and fifty feet in height. This most formidable engine was generally made of beams of wood covered on three sides with iron and sometimes with raw hides. They were

The Testudo.

The Helepolis.

The Turris.

1 Josephus, *B. J.*, ii. 19.

higher than the walls and all the other fortifications of a besieged place, divided into stories pierced with windows. In and upon them were stationed archers and slingers, and in the lower story was a battering-ram. They also carried scaling-ladders, so that when the wall was cleared, these were placed against the walls. They were placed upon wheels, and brought as near the walls as possible. It was impossible to resist these powerful engines, unless they were burned, or the ground undermined upon which they stood, except by overturning them with stones or iron-shod beams hung from a mast on the wall, or by increasing the height of the wall, or the erection of temporary towers on the wall beside them.

Scaling-ladders.

Thus there was no ancient fortification capable of withstanding a long siege when the besieged city was short of defenders or provisions. With equal forces an attack was generally a failure, for the defenders had always a great advantage. But when the number of defenders was reduced, or when famine pressed, the skill and courage of the assailants would ultimately triumph. Some ancient cities made a most obstinate resistance, like Tarentum; Carthage, which stood a siege of four years; Numantia in Spain, and Jerusalem. When cities were of immense size, population, and resources, like Rome when besieged by Alaric, it was easier to take them by cutting off all ingress and egress, so as to produce famine. Tyre was only taken by Alexander by cutting off the harbor. Babylon could not have been taken by Cyrus by assault, since the walls were three hundred and thirty-seven feet high, according to Herodotus, and the ditch too wide for the use of battering-rams. He resorted to an expedient of which the blinded inhabitants of that doomed city never dreamed, which rendered their impregnable fortifications useless. Nor would the Romans have probably prevailed against Jerusalem had not famine decimated and weakened the people. Fortified cities, though scarcely ever

The advantages of defenders.

Ordinary way of capture.

impregnable, were yet more in use in ancient than modern times, and greatly delayed the operations of advancing armies. And it was probably the fortified camp of the Romans, which protected an army against surprises and other misfortunes, which gave such efficacy to the legions.

Strength and advantage of fortresses.

The chief officers of the legion were the tribunes, and originally there was one in each legion from the three tribes — the Ramnes, Luceres, and Tities. In the time of Polybius the number in each legion was six. Their authority extended equally over the whole legion; but, to prevent confusion, it was the custom for these military tribunes to divide themselves into three sections of two, and each pair undertook the routine duties for two months out of six. They nominated the centurions, and assigned to each the company to which he belonged. These tribunes, at first, were chosen by the commander-in-chief, — by the kings and consuls; but during the palmy days of the republic, when the patrician power was preëminent, they were elected by the people, that is, the citizens. Later they were named half by the Senate and half by the consuls. No one was eligible to this great office who had not served ten years in the infantry or five in the cavalry. They were distinguished by their dress from the common soldier. Next in rank to the tribunes, who corresponded to the rank of brigadiers and colonels in our times, were the centurions, of whom there were sixty in each legion, — men who were more remarkable for calmness and sagacity than for courage and daring valor; men who would keep their posts at all hazards. It was their duty to drill the soldiers, to inspect arms, clothing, and food, to visit the sentinels, and regulate the conduct of the men. They had the power of inflicting corporal punishment. They were chosen for merit solely, until the later ages of the empire, when their posts were bought, as in the English army. These centu-

The Tribunes.

The Centurions.

rions were of unequal rank, — those of the Triarii before those of the Principes, and those of the Principes before those of the Hastati. The first centurion of the first maniple of the Triarii stood next in rank to the tribunes, and had a seat in the military councils, and his office was very lucrative. To his charge was intrusted the eagle of the legion.[1] As the centurion could rise from the ranks, and rose by regular gradation through the different maniples of the Hastati, Principes, and Triarii, there was great inducement held out to the soldiers. In the Roman legion it would seem that there was a regular gradation of rank, although there were but few distinct offices. But the gradation was not determined by length of service, but for merit alone, of which the tribunes were the sole judges. Hence the tribune of a Roman legion had more power than that of a modern colonel. As the tribunes named the centurions, so the centurions appointed their lieutenants, who were called sub-centurions.

Gradation of ranks.

There was a change in the constitution and disposition of the legion after the time of Marius, until the fall of the republic. The legions were thrown open to men of all grades; they were all armed and equipped alike; the lines were reduced to two, with a space between each cohort, of which there were five in each line; the young soldiers were placed in the rear, and not the van; the distinction between Hastati, Principes, and Triarii ceased; the Velites disappeared, their work being done by the foreign mercenaries; the cavalry ceased to be part of the legion, and became a distinct body; and the military was completely severed from the rest of the state. Formerly no one could aspire to office who had not completed ten years of military service, but in the time of Cicero a man could pass through all the great dignities of the state with a very limited experience of military life. Cicero himself served but one campaign.

Change in the organization of legions.

[1] Liv. xxv. 5; Cæs. *B. C.*, vi. 6.

Under the emperors, there were still other changes. The regular army consisted of legions and supplementa, — the latter being subdivided into the imperial guards and the auxiliary troops.

Changes under the emperors.

The auxiliaries (Socii) consisted of troops from the states in alliance with Rome, or those compelled to furnish subsidies. The infantry of the allies was generally more numerous than that of the Romans, while the cavalry was three times as numerous. All the auxiliaries were paid by the state; the infantry received the same pay as the Roman infantry, but the cavalry only two thirds of what was paid to the Roman cavalry. The common foot-soldier received in the time of Polybius three and a half asses a day, equal to about six farthings sterling money; the horseman three times as much. The prætorian cohorts received twice as much as the legionaries. Julius Cæsar allowed about six asses a day as the pay of the legionary, and under Augustus the daily pay was raised to ten asses — little more than four pence per day. Domitian raised the stipend still higher. The soldier, however, was fed and clothed by the government.

Pay of soldiers.

The prætorian cohort was a select body of troops instituted by Augustus to protect his person, and consisted of ten cohorts, each of one thousand men, chosen from Italy. This number was increased by Vitellius to sixteen thousand, and they were assembled by Tiberius in a permanent camp, which was strongly fortified. They had peculiar privileges, and when they had served sixteen years, received twenty thousand sesterces, or more than one hundred pounds sterling. Each prætorian had the rank of a centurion in the regular army. Like the body-guard of Louis XIV., they were all gentlemen, and formed gradually a great power, like the janissaries at Constantinople, and frequently disposed of the purple itself. It would thus appear that the centurion only received twice the pay of the ordinary legionary.

The Prætorian cohort.

There was not therefore so much difference in rank between a private and a captain as in our day. There were no aristocratic distinctions in the ancient world so marked as in the modern.

Our notice of the Roman legion would be incomplete without allusion to the camp in which the soldier virtually lived. A Roman army never halted for a single night without forming a regular intrenchment capable of holding all the fighting men, the beasts of burden, and the baggage. When the army could not retire, during the winter months, into some city, it was compelled to live in the camp. It was arranged and fortified according to a uniform plan, so that every company and individual had a place assigned. We cannot tell when this practice of intrenchment began; it was matured gradually, like all other things pertaining to the art of war. The system was probably brought to perfection during the wars with Hannibal. Skill in the choice of ground, giving facilities for attack and defense, and for procuring water and other necessities, was of great account with the generals. An area of about five thousand square feet was allowed for a company of infantry, and ten thousand feet for a troop of thirty dragoons. The form of a camp was an exact square, the length of each side being two thousand and seventeen feet. There was a space between the ramparts and the tents of two hundred feet to facilitate the marching in and out of soldiers, and to guard the cattle and booty. The principal street was one hundred feet wide, and was called Principia. The defenses of the camp consisted of a ditch, the earth from which was thrown inwards, and strong palisades of wooden stakes upon the top of the earthwork so formed. The ditch was sometimes fifteen feet deep, and the vallum or rampart ten feet in height. When the army encamped for the first time the tribunes administered an oath to each individual, including slaves, to the effect that they would

The Roman camp.

steal nothing out of the camp. Every morning at day-break, the centurions and the equites presented themselves before the tents of the tribunes, and the tribunes in like manner presented themselves to the prætorian, to learn the orders of the consuls, which through the centurions were communicated to the soldiers. Four companies took charge of the principal street, to see that it was properly cleaned and watered. One company took charge of the tent of the tribune, a strong guard attended to the horses, and another of fifty men stood beside the tent of the general that he might be protected from open danger and secret treachery. The velites mounted guard the whole night and day along the whole extent of the vallum, and each gate was guarded by ten men. The equites were intrusted with the duty of acting as sentinels during the night, and most ingenious measures were adopted to secure their watchfulness and fidelity. The watchword for the night was given by the commander-in-chief. "On the first signal being given by the trumpet, the tents were all struck and the baggage packed. At the second signal, the baggage was placed upon the beasts of burden; and at the third the whole army began to move. Then the herald, standing at the right hand of the general, demands thrice if they are ready for war, to which they all respond with loud and repeated cheers that they are ready, and for the most part, being filled with martial ardor, anticipate the question, 'and raise their right hands on high with a shout.'"[1]

The guardianship of the camp.

The breaking up of the camp.

Josephus gives an account of the line of march in which the army of Vespasian entered Galilee. "1. The light-armed auxiliaries and bowmen, advancing to reconnoiter. 2. A detachment of Roman heavy-armed troops, horse and foot. 3. Ten men out of every century or company, carrying their own equipments and the measures of the camp. 4. The baggage of Vespasian

Line of March.

[1] Smith, *Dict. of Ant.*, art. *Castra.*

and his legati guarded by a strong body of horse. 5. Vespasian himself, attended by his horse-guard and a body of spearmen. 6. The peculiar cavalry of the legion. 7. The artillery dragged by mules. 8. The legati, tribunes, and præfects of cohorts, guarded by a body of picked soldiers. 9. The standards, surrounding the eagle. 10. The trumpeters. 11. The main body of the infantry, six abreast, accompanied by a centurion, whose duty it was to see that the men kept their ranks. 12. The whole body of slaves attached to each legion, driving the mules and beasts of burden loaded with the baggage. 13. Behind all the legions followed the mercenaries. 14. The rear was brought up by a strong body of cavalry and infantry." [1]

Excitements of military life.

From what has come down to us of Roman military life, it appears to have been full of excitement, toil, danger, and hardship. The pecuniary rewards of the soldier were small. He was paid in glory. No profession brought so much honor as the military. And from the undivided attention of a great people to this profession, it was carried to all the perfection which could be attained until the great invention of gunpowder changed the art of war. It was not the number of men employed in the armies which particularly arrests attention, but the spirit and genius which animated them. The Romans loved war, but so reduced it to a science that it required comparatively small armies to conquer the world. Sulla defeated Mithridates with only thirty thousand men, while his adversary marshaled against him over one hundred thousand; and Cæsar had only ten legions to effect the conquest of Gaul, and none of these were of Italian origin. At the great decisive battle of Pharsalia, when most of the available forces of the empire were employed, on one side or the other, Pompey commanded a legionary army of forty-five thousand men; and the cavalry amounted to seven thousand more, but among

Smallness of the Roman armies.

[1] Josephus, *B. J.*, iii. 6, § 2.

them were included the flower of the Roman nobility. The auxiliary force has not been computed, although it was probably numerous. Cæsar had under him only twenty-two thousand of legionaries and one thousand cavalry. But every man in both armies was prepared to conquer or die. The forces were posted on the open plain, and the battle was really a hand-to-hand encounter, in which the soldiers, after hurling their lances, fought with their swords chiefly. And when the cavalry of Pompey rushed upon the legionaries of Cæsar, no blows were wasted on the mailed panoply of the mounted Romans, but were aimed at the face alone, as that alone was unprotected. The battle was decided by the coolness, bravery, and discipline of veterans, inspired by the genius of the greatest general of antiquity. Less than one hundred thousand men, in all probability, were engaged in one of the most memorable conflicts which the world has seen.

How battles were decided.

Thus it was, by unparalleled heroism in war, and a uniform policy in government, that Rome became the mistress of the world. The Roman conquests have never been surpassed, for they were retained until the empire fell. I wish that I could have dwelt on these conquests more in detail, and presented more fully the brilliant achievements of individuals. It took nearly two hundred years, after the expulsion of the kings, to regain supremacy over the neighboring people, and another century to conquer Italy. The Romans did not contend with regular armies until they were brought in conflict with the king of Epirus and the phalanx of the Greeks, "which improved their military tactics, and introduced between the combatants those mutual regards of civilized nations which teach men to honor their adversaries, to spare the vanquished, and to lay aside wrath when the struggle is ended." In the fifth century of her existence, the republic appears in peculiar splendor. Military

Gradual organization of military power.

chieftains do not transcend their trusts; the aristocracy are equally distinguished for exploits and virtues; the magistrates maintain simplicity of manners and protect the rights of the citizens; the citizens are self-sacrificing and ever ready to obey the call to arms, laying aside great commands and retiring poor to private stations. Marcus Valerius Corvus, after filling twenty-one curule offices, returns to agricultural life; Marcus Curius Dentatus retains no part of the rich spoils of the Sabines; Fabricius rejects the gold of the Samnites and the presents of Pyrrhus. The most trustworthy are elevated to places of dignity and power. Senators mingle in the ranks of the legions, and eighty of them die on the field of Cannæ. Discipline is enforced to cruelty, and Manlius Torquatus punishes with death a disobedient son. Soldiers who desert the field are decimated or branded with dishonor. Faith is kept even with enemies, and Regulus returns a voluntary prisoner to his deadly enemies.

Magnanimity of the early generals.

After the consolidation of Roman power in Italy, it took one hundred and fifty years more only to complete the conquest of the world — of Northern Africa, Spain, Gaul, Illyria, Epirus, Greece, Macedonia, Asia Minor, Pontus, Syria, Egypt, Bithynia, Cappadocia, Pergamus, and the islands of the Mediterranean. The conquest of Carthage left Rome without a rival in the Mediterranean, and promoted intercourse with the Greeks. The Illyrian wars opened to the Romans the road to Greece and Asia, and destroyed the pirates of the Adriatic. The invasion of Cisalpine Gaul, now that part of Italy which is north of the Apennines, protected Italy from the invasion of barbarians. The Macedonian War against Philip put Greece under the protection of Rome, and that against Antiochus laid Syria at her mercy; and when these kingdoms were reduced to provinces, the way was opened to further conquests in the East, and the Mediterranean became a Roman lake.

Results of different wars.

But these conquests introduce luxury, wealth, pride, and avarice, with arts, refinements, and literature. These degrade while they elevate. Civilization becomes the alternate triumph of good and evil influences, and a doubtful boon. Successful war creates great generals, and founds great families, increases slavery, and promotes inequalities. Demagogues arise who seduce and deceive the people, and they enroll themselves under the standards of their idols. Rome is governed by an oligarchy of military chieftains, and has become more aristocratic and more democratic at the same time. The people gain rights, only to yield to the supremacy of demagogues. The Senate is humbled, but remains the ascendant power, for generals compose it, and those who have held great offices. Meanwhile the great generals struggle for supremacy. Civil wars follow in the train of foreign conquests. Marius, Sulla, Pompey, Julius, Antony, Augustus, sacrifice the state to their ambition. Good men lament, and protest, and hide themselves. Cato, Cicero, Brutus, speak in vain. Degenerate morals keep pace with civil contests. Rome revels in the spoils of all kingdoms and countries, is intoxicated with power, becomes cruel and tyrannical, and, after yielding up the lives of citizens to fortunate generals, yields at last her liberties, and imperial despotism begins its reign, — hard, immovable, resolute, — under which genius is crushed, and life becomes epicurean, but under which property and order are preserved. The regime is bad; but it is a change for the better. War has produced its fruits. It has added empire, but undermined prosperity; it has created a great military monarchy, but destroyed liberty; it has brought wealth, but introduced inequalities; it has filled the city with spoils, but sown the vices of self-interest. The machinery is perfect, but life has fled. It is henceforth the labor of emperors to keep together their vast possessions with this machinery, which at

Effect of Roman conquests on society.

Degeneracy of morals undermines military power.

last wears out, since there is neither genius to repair it nor patriotism to work it. It lasts three hundred years, but is broken to pieces by the Goths and Vandals.

The highest authority in relation to the construction of an army is Polybius, who was contemporary with Scipio, at a period when Roman discipline was most perfect. A fragment from his sixth book gives considerable information. A chapter of Livy — the eighth — is also very much prized. Salmasius and Lepsius have also written learned treatises. Smith's Dictionary, which is full of details in every thing pertaining to the weapons, the armor, the military engines, the rewards and punishments of the soldiers, refers to Folard's *Commentaire*, to *Mémoires Militaires sur les Grecs et les Romains*, by Guischard, and to the *Histoire des Campagnes d'Hannibal en Italie*, by Vaudencourt. Tacitus, Sallust, Livy, Dion Cassius, Pliny, and Cæsar reveal incidentally much that we wish to know. Gibbon gives some important facts in his first chapter. The subject of ancient machines is treated by Folard's Commentary attached to his translation of Polybius. Cæsar's Commentaries give us, after all, the liveliest idea of the military habits and tactics of the Romans. Josephus describes with great vividness the siege of Jerusalem. The article on *Exercitus*, by Prof. Ramsay, in Smith's Dictionary, is the fullest I have read pertaining to the structure of a Roman army.

For the narrative of wars, the reader is referred to ordinary Roman histories — to Livy and Cæsar especially; to Niebuhr, Mommsen, Arnold, and Liddell. See also Durny, *Hist. des Romains;* Michelet, *Hist. de Rom.* Napoleon's History of Cæsar should be read, admirable in style, and interesting in matter, although a sophistical defense of usurpation.

CHAPTER II.

THE MATERIAL GRANDEUR AND GLORY OF THE ROMAN EMPIRE.

To the eye of an ancient traveler there must have been something very grand and impressive in the external aspects of wealth and power which the Roman Empire, in the period of its greatest glory, presented in every city and province. It will therefore be my aim in this chapter to present those objects of pride and strength which appealed to the senses of an ordinary observer, and such as would first arrest his attention were he to describe the wonders he beheld to those who were imperfectly acquainted with them.

Culmination of Roman greatness.

It is generally admitted that Roman greatness culminated during the reigns of the Antonines, about the middle of the second century of the Christian era. At that period we perceive the highest triumphs of material civilization and the proudest spirit of panygeric and self-confidence. To the eye of contemporaries it seemed that Rome was destined to be the mistress of the world forever.

We naturally glance, in the first place, to the extent of that vast empire which has had no parallel in ancient or modern times, and which was erected on the ruins of all the powerful states of antiquity. It was a most wonderful centralization of power, spreading its arms of hopeless despotism from the Pillars of Hercules to the Caspian Sea; from the Rhine and the Danube to the Euphrates and Tigris; from the forests of Sarmatia to the deserts of Africa. The empire extended three thousand miles from east to west, and two thousand from north to south. It stretched over thirty-five degrees of latitude, and sixty-five of longitude, and embraced within its limits nearly all the seas, lakes, and gulfs which commerce explored. It contained 1,600,000 square miles, for the most part cultivated, and populated by peoples in various stages of civilization, some of whom were famous for arts and wealth, and could boast of heroes and cities, — of a past history brilliant and impressive. In nearly the centre of this great empire was the Mediterranean Sea, which was only, as it were, an inland lake, upon whose shores the great cities of antiquity had flourished, and towards which the tide of Assyrian and Persian conquests had rolled and then retreated forever. The great rivers — the Nile, the Po, and the Danube — flowed into this basin and its connecting seas, wafting the produce of distant provinces to the great central city on the Tiber. The boundaries of the empire were great oceans, deserts, and mountains, beyond which it was difficult to extend or to retain conquests. On the west was the Atlantic Ocean, unknown and unexplored — that mysterious expanse of waters which filled navigators with awe and dread, and which was not destined to be crossed until the stars should cease to be the only guide. On the northwest was the undefined region of Scandinavia, into which the Roman arms never penetrated, peopled by those barbarians who were to be the future conquerors of Rome, and the creators of a new and more glorious civilization, — those Germanic tribes which, under different names, had substantially the same manners, customs, and language, — a race more unconquerable and heroic than the Romans themselves, the future lords of mediæval Europe, the ancestors of the English, the French, the Spaniards, and the Germans. On the northwest were the Sarmatians

Extent of the empire. **Square miles.** **Seas and rivers.** **Boundaries.** **Scandinavia.**

and Scythians — Sclavonic tribes, able to conquer, but not to reconstruct; savages repulsive and hideous even to the Goths themselves. On the east lay the Parthian empire, separated from Roman territories by the Euphrates, the Tigris, and the Armenian mountains. The Caucasian range between the Euxine and the Caspian seas presented an insuperable barrier, as did the deserts of Arabia to the Roman legions. The Atlas, the African desert, and the cataracts of the Nile formed the southern boundaries. The vulnerable part of the empire lay between the Danube and Rhine, from which issued, in successive waves, the Germanic foes of Rome. To protect the empire against their incursions, the Emperor Probus constructed a wall, which, however, proved but a feeble defense.

Sarmatia.

Mountains.

This immense empire was divided into thirty-six provinces, exclusive of Italy, each of which was governed by a proconsul. The most important of these were Spain, Gaul, Sicily, Achaia, Asia Minor, Syria, and Egypt. Gaul was more extensive than modern France. Achaia included Greece and the Ionian Islands. The empire embraced the modern states of England, France, Spain, Holland, Belgium, Switzerland, Bavaria, Austria, Styria, the Tyrol, Hungary, Egypt, Morocco, Algiers, and the empire of Turkey both in Europe and Asia. It took the Romans nearly five hundred years to subdue the various states of Italy, the complete subjugation of which took place with the fall of Tarentum, a Grecian city, which introduced Grecian arts and literature. Sicily, the granary of Rome, was the next conquest, the fruit of the first Punic War. The second Punic War added to the empire Sardinia, Corsica, and the two Spanish provinces of Bætica and Tarraconensis — about two thirds of the peninsula — fertile in the productions of the earth, and enriched by mines of silver and gold, and peopled by Iberians and Celts. The

Provinces.

Results of successive conquests.

rich province of Illyricum was added to the empire about one hundred and eighty years before Christ. Before the battle of Actium, the empire extended over Achaia, Asia Minor, Macedonia, Narbonensic Gaul, Cyrenaica, Crete, Cilicia, Cyprus, Bithynia, Syria, Aquitania, Belgic and Celtic Gaul. Augustus added Egypt, Lusitania, Numidia, Galatia, the Maritime Alps, Noricum, Vindelicia, Rhætia, Pannonia, and Mœsia. Tiberius increased the empire by the addition of Cappadocia. Claudius incorporated the two Mauritanias, Lycia, Judæa, Thrace, and Britain. Nero added Pontus. These various and extensive countries had every variety of climate and productions, and boasted of celebrated cities. They composed most of the provinces known to the ancients west of the Euphrates, and together formed an empire in comparison with which the Assyrian and Egyptian monarchies, and even the Grecian conquests, were vastly inferior. The Saracenic conquests in the Middle Ages were not to be compared with these, and the great empires of Charlemagne and Napoleon could be included in less than half the limits. What a proud position it was to be a Roman emperor, whose will was the law over the whole civilized world! Well may the Roman empire be called universal, since it controlled all the nations of the earth known to the Greeks. It was the vastest centralization of power which this world has seen, or probably will ever see, extending nearly over the whole of Europe, and the finest parts of Asia and Africa. We are amazed that a single city of Italy could thus occupy with her armies and reign supremely over so many diverse countries and nations, speaking different languages, and having different religions and customs. And when we contemplate this great fact, we cannot but feel that it was a providential event, designed for some grand benefit to the human race. That benefit was the preparation for the reception of a new and universal religion. No system

Vastness of the political power.

Empire universal.

of "balance of power," no political or military combinations, no hostilities could prevent the absorption of the civilized world in the empire of the Cæsars.

If we more particularly examine this great empire, we observe that it was substantially composed of the various countries and kingdoms which bordered on the Mediterranean, and those other seas with which it was connected. Roman power was scarcely felt on the shores of the Baltic, or the eastern coasts of the Euxine, or on the Arabian and Persian gulfs. The central part of the empire was Italy, the province which was first conquered, and most densely populated. It was the richest in art, in cities, in commerce, and in agriculture.

The Mediterranean the centre of the empire.

Italy itself was no inconsiderable state — a beautiful peninsula, extending six hundred and sixty geographical miles from the foot of the Alps to the promontory of Leucopetra. Its greatest breadth is about one hundred and thirty miles. It was always renowned for beauty and fertility. Its climate on the south was that of Greece, and on the north that of the south of France. The lofty range of the Apennines extended through its entire length, while the waters of the Mediterranean and the Adriatic tempered and varied its climate. Its natural advantages were unequaled, with a soil favorable to agriculture, to the culture of fruits, and the rearing of flocks. Its magnificent forests furnished timber for ships; its rich pastures fed innumerable sheep, goats, cattle, and horses; its olive groves were nowhere surpassed; its mountains contained nearly every kind of metals; its coasts furnished a great variety of fish; while its mineral springs supplied luxurious baths. There were no extremes of heat and cold; the sky was clear and serene; the face of the country was a garden. It was a paradise to the eye of Virgil and Varro, the most favored of all the countries of antiquity in those productions which sus-

Italy.

Natural productions.

tain the life of man or beast. The plains of Lombardy furnished maize and rice; oranges grew to great perfection on the Ligurian coast; aloes and cactuses clothed the rocks of the southern provinces; while the olive and the grape abounded in every section. The mineral wealth of Italy was extolled by the ancient writers, and the fisheries were as remarkable as agricultural products. The population numbered over four millions who were free, and could furnish seven hundred thousand foot and seventy thousand horse for the armies of the republic, if they were all called into requisition. The whole country was dotted with beautiful villas and farms, as well as villages and cities. It contained twelve hundred cities or large towns which had municipal privileges. Mediolanum, now Milan, the chief city in Cisalpine Gaul, in the time of Ambrose, was adorned with palaces and temples and baths. It was so populous that it lost it is said at one time three hundred thousand male citizens in the inroads of the Goths. It was surrounded with a double range of walls, and the houses were elegantly built. It was also celebrated as the seat of learning and culture. Verona had an amphitheatre of marble, whose remains are among the most striking monuments of antiquity, capable of seating twenty-two thousand people. Ravenna, near the mouth of the Padus (Po), built on piles, was a great naval depot, and had an artificial harbor capable of containing two hundred and fifty ships of war, and was the seat of government after the fall of the empire. Padua counted among its inhabitants five hundred Roman knights, and was able to send twenty thousand men into the field. Aquileia was a great emporium of the trade in wine, oil, and salted provisions. Pola had a magnificent amphitheatre. Luna, now Spezzia, was famous for white marbles, and for cheeses which often weighed a thousand pounds. Arutium, now Avezzo, an Etrurian city, was celebrated for its potteries, many beau-

Population.

Cities.

Italian cities.

itful specimens of which now ornament the galleries of Florence. Cortona had walls of massive thickness, which can be traced to the Pelasgians. Clusium, the capital of Porsenna, had a splendid mausoleum. Volsinii boasted of two thousand statues. Veii had been the rival of Rome. In Umbria, we may mention Sarsina, the birthplace of Plautus; Mevania, the birthplace of Propertius; and Sentinum, famous for the self-devotion of Decius. In Picenum were Ancona, celebrated for its purple dye; and Picenum, surrounded by walls and inaccessible heights, memorable for a siege against Pompey. Of the Sabine cities were Antemnæ, more ancient than Rome; Nomentum, famous for wine; Regillum, the birthplace of Appius Claudius, the founder of the great Claudian family; Reate, famous for asses, which sometimes brought the enormous price of 60,000 sesterces, about $2320; Cutiliæ, celebrated for its mineral waters; and Alba, in which captives of rank were secluded. In Latium were Ostia, the seaport of Rome; Laurentum, the capital of Latinus; Lavinium, fabled to have been founded by Æneas; Lanuvium, the birthplace of Roscius and the Antonines; Alba Longa, founded four hundred years before Rome; Tusculum, where Cicero had his villa; Tibur, whose temple was famous through Italy; Præneste, now Palestrio, remarkable for its citadel and its temple of Fortune; Antium, to which Coriolanus retired after his banishment, a favorite residence of Augustus, and the birthplace of Nero, celebrated also for a magnificent temple, amid whose ruins was found the Apollo Belvidere; Forum Appii, mentioned by St. Paul, from which travelers on the Appian Way embarked on a canal; Arpinum, the birthplace of Cicero; Aquium, where Juvenal and Thomas Aquinas were born, famous for a purple dye; Formiæ, a favorite residence of Cicero. In Campania were Cumæ, the abode of the Sibyl; Misenum, a great naval station; Baiæ, celebrated for its spas and villas; Puteoli, famous for sulphur

Memorable cities.

springs; Neapolis, the abode of literary idlers; Herculaneum and Pompeii, destroyed by an eruption of Vesuvius; Capua, the capital of Campania, and inferior to Rome alone; and Salernum, a great military stronghold. In Samnium were Bovianum, a very opulent city; Beneventum, and Sepinum. In Apulia were Sarinum; Venusia, the birthplace of Horace; Cannæ, memorable for the great victory of Hannibal; Brundusium, a city of great antiquity on the Adriatic, and one of the great naval stations of the Romans; and Tarentum, the rival of Brundusium, a great military stronghold. In Lucania were Metapontum, at one time the residence of Pythagoras; Heraclea, the seat of a general council; Sybaris, which once was the mistress of twenty-five dependent cities, fifty stadia in circumference, and capable of sending an army of three hundred thousand [1] men into the field, — a city so prosperous and luxurious that the very name of Sybarite was synonymous with voluptuousness.

Such were among the principal cities of Italy. More than two hundred and fifty towns or cities are historical, and were famous for the residence of great men, or for wines, wool, dyes, and various articles of luxury. The ruins of Pompeii prove it to have been a city of great luxury and elegance. The excavations, which have brought to light the wonders of this buried city, attest a very high material civilization; yet it was only a second-rate provincial town, of which not much is commemorated in history. It was simply a resort for Roman nobles who had villas in its neighborhood. It was surrounded with a wall, and was built with great regularity. Its streets were paved, and it had its forum, its amphitheatre, its theatre, its temples, its basilicas, its baths, its arches, and its monuments. The basilica was two hundred and twenty feet in length by eighty feet in width, the roof of which was supported by twenty-eight Ionic col-

Pompeii.

[1] Anthon, *Geog. Dict.*

umns. The temple of Venus was profusely ornamented with paintings. One of the theatres was built of marble, and was capable of seating five thousand spectators, and the amphitheatre would seat ten thousand.

But Italy, so grand in cities, so varied in architectural wonders, so fertile in soil, so salubrious in climate, so rich in minerals, so prolific in fruits and vegetables and canals, was only a small part of the empire of the Cæsars. The Punic wars, undertaken soon after the expulsion of Pyrrhus, resulted in the acquisition of Sicily, Sardinia, and Africa, from which the Romans were supplied with inexhaustible quantities of grain, and in the creation of a great naval power. Sicily, the largest island of the Mediterranean, was not inferior to Italy in any kind of produce. It was, it was supposed, the native country of wheat. Its honey, its saffron, its sheep, its horses, were all equally celebrated. The island, intersected by numerous streamy and beautiful valleys, was admirably adapted for the growth of the vine and olive. Its colonies, founded by Phœnicians and Greeks, cultivated all the arts of civilization. Long before the Roman conquest, its cities were famous for learning and art. Syracuse, a Corinthian colony, as old as Rome, had a fortress a mile in length and half a mile in breadth; a temple of Diana whose doors were celebrated throughout the Grecian world, and a theatre which could accommodate twenty-four thousand people. No city in Greece, except Athens, can produce structures which vie with those of which the remains are still visible at Agrigentum, Selinus, and Segesta.

Sicily and Sardinia.

Richness of Sicily.

Syracuse.

Africa was one of the great provinces of the empire. It virtually embraced the Carthaginian empire, and was settled chiefly by the Phœnicians. Its capital, Carthage, so long the rival of Rome, was probably the greatest maritime mart of antiquity, next to Alexandria. Though it had been completely destroyed,

Carthage.

yet it became under the emperors no inconsiderable city, and was the capital of a belt of territory extending one hundred and sixty miles, from the Pillars of Hercules to the bottom of the great Syrtis, unrivaled for fertility. Its population once numbered seven hundred thousand inhabitants, and ruled over three hundred dependent cities, and could boast of a navy carrying one hundred and fifty thousand men.

Greece, included under the province called Achaia, was the next great conquest of the Romans, the fruit of the Macedonian wars. Though small in territory, it was the richest of all the Roman acquisitions in its results on civilization. The great peninsula to which Hellas belonged extended from the Euxine to the Adriatic; but Hellas proper was not more than two hundred and fifty miles in length and one hundred and eighty in breadth. Attica contained but seven hundred and twenty square miles, yet how great in associations, deeds, and heroes! When added to the empire, it was rich in every element of civilization, in cities, in arts, in literature, in commerce, in manufactures, in domestic animals, in fruits, in cereals. It was a mountainous country, but had an extensive sea-coast, and a flourishing trade with all the countries of the world. Almost all the Grecian states had easy access to the sea, and each of the great cities were isolated from the rest by lofty mountains difficult to surmount. But the Roman arms and the Roman laws penetrated to the most inaccessible retreats.

The richness of Greece.

In her political degradation, Greece still was the most interesting country on the globe. Every city had a history; every monument betokened a triumph of human genius. On her classic soil the great miracles of civilization had been wrought — the immortal teacher of all the nations in art, in literature, in philosophy, in war itself. Every cultivated Roman traveled in Greece; every great noble sent his sons to be educated in her schools;

Her monuments and arts and schools.

every great general sent to the banks of the Tiber some memento of her former greatness, some wonder of artistic skill. The wonders of Rome herself were but spoliations of this glorious land.

First in interest and glory was Athens, which was never more splendid than in the time of the Antonines. The great works of the age of Pericles still retained their original beauty and freshness; and the city of Minerva still remained the centre of all that was elegant or learned of the ancient civilization, and was held everywhere in the profoundest veneration. There still flourished the various schools of philosophy, to which young men from all parts of the empire resorted to be educated — the Oxford and the Edinburgh, the Berlin and Paris of the ancient world. In spite of successive conquests, there still towered upon the Acropolis the temple of Minerva, that famous Parthenon whose architectural wonders have never been even equaled, built of Pentelic marble, and adorned with the finest sculptures of Pheidias — a Doric temple, whose severe simplicity and matchless beauty have been the wonder of all ages — often imitated, never equaled, majestic even in its ruins. Side by side, on that lofty fortification in the centre of the city, on its western slope, was the Propylæa, one of the masterpieces of ancient art, also of Pentelic marble, costing 2000 talents, or $23,000,000,[1] when gold was worth more than twenty times what it is now. Then there was the Erechtheum, the temple of Athena Polias, the most revered of all the sanctuaries of Athens, with its three Ionic porticos, and its frieze of black marble, with its olive statue of the goddess, and its sacred inclosures. The great temple of Zeus Olympius, commenced by Peisistratus and completed by Hadrian, the largest ever dedicated to the deity among the Greeks, was four stadia in circumference. It

The glory of Athens.

Temples.

[1] Smith, *Geog. Dict.*

6

was surrounded by a peristyle which had ten columns in front and twenty on its sides. The peristyle being double on the sides, and having a triple range at either end, besides three columns between the antæ at each end of the cella, consisted altogether of one hundred and twenty columns. These were sixty feet high and six and a half feet in diameter, the largest which now remain of ancient architecture in marble, or which still exist in Europe. This vast temple was three hundred and fifty-four feet in length and one hundred and seventy-one in breadth, and was full of statues. The ruins of this temple, of which sixteen columns are still standing, are among the most imposing in the world, and indicate a grandeur and majesty in the city of which we can scarcely conceive. The theatre of Bacchus, the most beautiful in the ancient world, would seat thirty thousand spectators. I need not mention the various architectural monuments of this classic city, each of which was a study — the Temple of Theseus, the Agora, the Odeum, the Areopagus, the Gymnasium of Hadrian, the Lyceum, and other buildings of singular beauty, built mostly of marble, and adorned with paintings and statues. What work of genius in the whole world more interesting than the ivory and gold statue of Athena in the Parthenon, the masterpiece of Pheidias, forty feet high, the gold of which weighed forty talents, — a model for all succeeding sculptors, and to see which travelers came from all parts of Greece? Athens, a city of five hundred thousand inhabitants, was filled with wonders of art, which time has not yet fully destroyed.

Corinth.

Corinth was another grand centre of Grecian civilization, richer and more luxurious than Athens. When taken by the Romans she possessed the most valuable pictures in Greece. Among them was one of Dionysus by Aristides for which Attalus offered 600,000 sesterces. Rich commercial cities have ever been patrons of the fine arts. These they can appreciate better than poetry or philosophy. The Corinthians invented the most elaborate style of architecture known to antiquity, and which was generally adopted at Rome. They were also patrons of statuary, especially of works in bronze, for which the city was celebrated. The Corinthian vessels of terra cotta were the finest in Greece. All articles of elegant luxury were manufactured here, especially elaborate tables, chests, and sideboards. If there had been a great exhibition in Rome, the works of the Corinthians would have been the most admired, and would have suited the taste of the luxurious senators, among whom literature and the higher developments of art were unappreciated. There was no literature in Corinth after Periander, and among the illustrious writers of Greece not a single Corinthian appeared. Nor did it ever produce an orator. What could be expected of a city whose patron goddess was Aphrodite! But Lais was honored in the city, and rich merchants frequented her house. The city was most famous for courtesans, and female slaves, and extravagant luxury. It was like Antioch and Tyre and Carthage. Corinth was probably the richest city in Greece, and one of the largest. It had, it is said, four hundred and sixty thousand slaves. Its streets, three miles in length, were adorned with costly edifices. Its fortress was one thousand eight hundred and eighty-six feet above the sea and very strong.

The wonders of Corinth.

Its luxury.

Sparta, of historic fame, was not magnificent except in public buildings. It had a famous portico, the columns of which, of white marble, represented the illustrious persons among the vanquished Medes.

Sparta.

Olympia, the holy city, was celebrated for its temple and its consecrated garden, where stood some of the great masterpieces of ancient art, among them the famous statue of Jupiter, the work of Pheidias, — an impersonation of majesty and power, — a work which furnished models from which Michael Angelo drew his inspiration.

Olympia.

Delphi, another consecrated city, was enriched with the contributions of all Greece, and was the seat of the Dorian religion. So rich were the shrines of its oracle that Nero carried away from it five hundred statues of bronze at one time.

Delphi.

Such was Greece, every city of which was famous for art, or literature, or commerce, or manufacture, or for deeds which live in history It had established a great empire in the East, but fell, like all other conquering nations, from the luxury which conquest engendered. It was no longer able to protect itself. Its phalanx, which resisted the shock of the Persian hosts, yielded to the all-conquering legion. When Æmilius Paulus marched up the Via Sacra with the spoils of the Macedonian kingdom in his grand and brilliant triumph, he was preceded by two hundred and fifty wagons containing pictures and statues, and three thousand men, each carrying a vase of silver coin, and four hundred more bearing crowns of gold. Yet this was but the commencement of the plunder of Greece.

Greece enriches Rome.

And not merely Greece herself, but the islands which she had colonized formed no slight addition to the glories of the empire. Rhodes was the seat of a famous school for sculpture and painting, from which issued the Laocoön and the Farnese Bull. It contained three thousand statues and one hundred and six colossi, among them the famous statue of the sun, one hundred and five feet high, one of the seven wonders of the world, containing 3000 talents — more than $3,000,000. Its school of rhetoric was so celebrated that Cicero resorted to it to perfect himself in oratory.

Islands colonized by Greeks.

If we pass from Greece to Asia Minor and Syria, with their dependent provinces, all of which were added to the empire by the victories of Sulla and Pompey, we are still more impressed with the extent of the Roman rule. Asia Minor, a vast peninsula between the

Asia Minor.

Mediterranean, Ægean, and Euxine seas, included several of the old monarchies of the world. It extended from Ilium on the west to the banks of the Euphrates, from the northern parts of Bithynia and Pontus to Syria and Cilicia, nine hundred miles from east to west, and nearly three hundred from north to south. It was the scene of some of the grandest conquests of the oriental world, Babylonian, Persian, and Grecian. Syria embraced all countries from the eastern coasts of the Mediterranean to the Arabian deserts. No conquests of the Romans were attended with more eclat than the subjection of these wealthy and populous sections of the oriental world; and they introduced a boundless wealth and luxury into Italy. But in spite of the sack of cities and the devastations of armies, the old monarchy of the Seleucidæ remained rich and grand. Both Syria and Asia Minor could boast of large and flourishing cities, as well as every kind of luxury and art. Antioch was the third city in the empire, the capital of the Greek kings of Syria, and like Alexandria a monument of the Macedonian age. It was built on a regular and magnificent plan, and abounded in temples and monuments. Its most striking feature was a street four miles in length, perfectly level, with double colonnades through its whole length, built by Antiochus Epiphanes. In magnitude the city was not much inferior to Paris at the present day, and covered more land than Rome. It had its baths, its theatres and amphitheatres, its fora, its museums, its aqueducts, its temples, and its palaces. It was the most luxurious of all the cities of the East, and had a population of three hundred thousand who were free. In the latter days of the empire it was famous as the scene of the labors of Chrysostom.

Its extent.

Cities.

Antioch.

Ephesus, one of the twelve of the Ionian cities in Asia, was the glory of Lydia, — a sacred city of which the temple of Diana was the greatest ornament. This famous temple was four times as large as the Parthe-

Ephesus.

non, and covered as much ground as Cologne Cathedral, and was two hundred and twenty years in building. It had one hundred and twenty-eight columns sixty feet high, of which thirty-six were carved, each contributed by a king — the largest of all the Grecian temples, and probably the most splendid. It was a city of great trade and wealth. Its theatre was the largest in the world, six hundred and sixty feet in diameter,[1] and capable of holding sixty thousand spectators. Ephesus gave birth to Apelles the painter, and was the metropolis of five hundred cities.

Jerusalem.

Jerusalem, so dear to Christians as the most sacred spot on earth, inclosed by lofty walls and towers, not so beautiful or populous as in the days of Solomon and David, was, before its destruction by Titus, one of the finest cities of the East. Its royal palace, surrounded by a wall thirty cubits high, with decorated towers at equal intervals, contained enormous banqueting halls and chambers most profusely ornamented; and this palace, magnificent beyond description, was connected with porticos and gardens filled with statues and reservoirs of water. It occupied a larger space than the present fortress, from the western edge of Mount Zion to the present garden of the Armenian Convent.

The Temple.

The Temple, so famous, was small compared with the great wonders of Grecian architecture, being only about one hundred and fifty feet by seventy; but its front was covered with plates of gold, and some of the stones of which it was composed were more than sixty feet in length and nine in width. Its magnificence consisted in its decorations and the vast quantity of gold and precious woods used in its varied ornaments, and vessels of gold, so as to make it one of the most costly edifices ever erected to the worship of God.

The Acropolis.

The Acropolis, which was the fortress of the Temple, combined the strength of a castle with the magnificence of a palace, and

[1] Müller, *Anc. Art.*

was like a city in extent, towering seventy cubits above the elevated rock upon which it was built. So strongly fortified was Jerusalem, even in its latter days, that it took Titus five months, with an army of one hundred thousand men, to subdue it; one of the most memorable sieges on record. It probably would have held out against the whole power of Rome, had not famine done more than battering rams.

Many other interesting cities might be mentioned both in Syria and Asia Minor, which were centres of trade, or seats of philosophy, or homes of art. Tarsus in Cilicia was a great mercantile city, to which strangers from all parts resorted. Damascus, the oldest city in the world, and the old capital of Syria, was both beautiful and rich. Laodicea was famous for tapestries, Hierapolis for its iron wares, Cybara for its dyes, Sardis for its wines, Smyrna for its beautiful monuments, Delos for its slave-trade, Cyrene for its horses, Paphos for its temple of Venus, in which were a hundred altars. Seleucia, on the Tigris, had a population of four hundred thousand. Cæsarea, founded by Herod the Great, and the principal seat of government to the Roman prefects, had a harbor equal in size to the renowned Piræus, and was secured against the southwest winds by a mole of such massive construction that the blocks of stone, sunk under the water, were fifty feet in length and eighteen in width, and nine in thickness.[1] The city itself was constructed of polished stone, with an agora, a theatre, a circus, a prætorium, and a temple to Cæsar. Tyre, which had resisted for seven months the armies of Alexander, remained to the fall of the empire a great emporium of trade. It monopolized the manufacture of imperial purple. Sidon was equally celebrated for its glass and embroidered robes. The Sidonians cast glass mirrors, and imitated precious stones. But the glory of both Tyre and Sidon was in ships, which visited all the coasts of the Mediterranean, and even penetrated to Britain and India.

Damascus and other cities.

[1] Josephus, *Ant.*, xv.

But greater than Tyre, or Antioch, or any eastern city, was Alexandria, the capital of Egypt, which was one of the last provinces added to the empire. Egypt alone was a mighty monarchy — the oldest which history commemorates, august in records and memories. What pride, what pomp, what glory are associated with the land of the Pharaohs, with its mighty river reaching to the centre of a great continent, flowing thousands of miles to the sea, irrigating and enriching the most fertile valley of the world! What noble and populous cities arose upon its banks three thousand years before Roman power was felt! What enduring monuments remain of a very ancient yet extinct civilization! What successive races of conquerors have triumphed in the granite palaces of Thebes and Memphis! Old, sacred, rich, populous, and learned, Egypt becomes a province of the Roman empire. The sceptre of three hundred kings passes from Cleopatra, the last of the Ptolemies, to Augustus Cæsar, the conqueror at Actium; and six millions of different races, once the most civilized on the earth, are amalgamated with the other races and peoples which compose the universal monarchy. At one time the military force of Egypt is said to have amounted to seven hundred thousand men, in the period of its greatest prosperity. The annual revenues of this state under the Ptolemies amounted to about $17,000,000 in gold and silver, beside the produce of the earth. A single feast cost Philadelphus more than half a million of pounds sterling, and he had accumulated treasures to the amount of 740,000 talents, or about $860,000,000.[1] What European monarch ever possessed such a sum? The kings of Egypt were richer in the gold and silver they could command than Louis XIV., in the proudest hour of his life. What monarchs ever reigned with more absolute power than the kings of this ancient seat of learning and art! The

Egypt.

Its ancient grandeur.

Glories of Egypt.

Thebes.

[1] Napoleon, *Life of Cæsar.*

foundation of Thebes goes back to the mythical period of Egyptian history, and it covered as much ground as Rome or Paris, equally the centre of religion, of trade, of manufactures, and of government, — the sacerdotal capital of all who worshiped Ammon from Pelusium to Axume, from the Red Sea to the Oases of Libya. The palaces of Thebes, though ruins two thousand years ago as they are ruins now, were the largest and probably the most magnificent ever erected by the hand of man. What must be thought of a palace whose central hall was eighty feet in height, three hundred and twenty-five feet in length, and one hundred and seventy-nine in breadth ; the roof of which was supported by one hundred and thirty-four columns, eleven feet in diameter and seventy-six feet in height, with their pedestals ; and where the cornices of the finest marble were inlaid with ivory moldings or sheathed with beaten gold ! But I do not now refer to the glories of Egypt under Sesostris or Rameses, but to what they were when Alexandria was the capital of the country, — what it was under the Roman domination.

The ground-plan of this great city was traced by Alexander himself, but it was not completed until the reign of Ptolemy Philadelphus. It continued to receive embellishments from nearly every monarch of the Lagian line. Its circumference was about fifteen miles ; the streets were regular, and crossed one another at right angles, and were wide enough to admit both carriages and foot passengers. The harbor was large enough to admit the largest fleet ever constructed ; its walls and gates were constructed with all the skill and strength known to antiquity ; its population numbered six hundred thousand, and all nations were represented in its crowded streets. The wealth of the city may be inferred from the fact that in one year 6250 talents, or more than $6,000,000, were paid to the public treasury for port dues. The library was the largest in the world, and num-

Extent and population of Alexandria.

Library.

bered over seven hundred thousand volumes, and this was connected with a museum, a menagerie, a botanical garden, and various halls for lectures, altogether forming the most famous university in the empire. The inhabitants were chiefly Greek, and had all their cultivated tastes and mercantile thrift. In a commercial point of view it was the most important in the empire, and its ships whitened every sea. Alexandria was of remarkable beauty, and was called by Ammianus *Vertex omnium civitatum.* Its dry atmosphere preserved for centuries the sharp outlines and gay colors of its buildings, some of which were remarkably imposing. The Mausoleum of the Ptolemies, the High Court of Justice, the Stadium, the Gymnasium, the Palæstra, the Amphitheatre, and the Temple of the Cæsars, all called out the admiration of travelers. The Emporium far surpassed the quays of the Tiber. But the most imposing structure was the Exchange, to which, for eight hundred years, all the nations sent their representatives. It was commerce which made Alexandria so rich and beautiful, for which it was more distinguished than both Tyre and Carthage. Unlike most commercial cities, it was intellectual, and its schools of poetry, mathematics, medicine, philosophy, and theology were more renowned than even those of Athens during the third and fourth centuries. For wealth, population, intelligence, and art, it was the second city of the world. It would be a great capital in these times.

Public buildings.

Commerce.

Such were Egypt, Syria, Asia Minor, Greece, and Africa, all of which had been great empires, but all of which were incorporated with the Roman in less than two hundred years after Italy succumbed to the fortunate city on the Tiber. But these old and venerated monarchies, with their dependent states and provinces, though imposing and majestic, did not compose the vital part of the empire of the Cæsars. It was those new provinces which were rescued from the barba-

Power of the empire seated in the western provinces.

rians, chiefly Celts, where the life of the empire centred. It was Spain, Gaul, Britain, and Illyricum, countries which now compose the most powerful European monarchies, which the more truly show the strength of the Roman world. And these countries were added last, and were not fully incorporated with the empire until imperial power had culminated in the Antonines. From a comparative wilderness, Spain and Gaul especially became populous and flourishing states, dotted with cities, and instructed in all the departments of Roman art and science. From these provinces the armies were recruited, the schools were filled, and even the great generals and emperors were furnished. These provinces embraced nearly the whole of modern Europe.

Spain had been added to the empire after the destruction of Carthage, but only after a bitter and protracted warfare. It was completed by the reduction of Numantia, a city of the Celtiberians in the valley of the Douro, and its siege is more famous than that of Carthage, having defied for a long time the whole power of the empire, as Tyre did Alexander, and Jerusalem the armies of Titus. It yielded to the genius of Scipio, the conqueror of Africa, as La Rochelle, in later times, fell before Richelieu, but not until famine had done its work. The civilization of Spain was rapid after the fall of Numantia, and in the time of the Antonines was one of the richest and most prized of the Roman provinces. It embraced the whole peninsula, from the Pillars of Hercules to the Pyrenees; and the warlike nations who composed it became completely Latinized. It was divided into three provinces — Bætica, Lusitania, and Tarraconensis — all governed by prætors, the last of whom had consular power, and resided in Carthago Nova, on the Mediterranean. Under Constantine, Spain, with its islands, was divided into seven provinces, and stood out from the rest of the em-

Spain.

Its provinces.

pire like a round bastion tower from the walls of an old fortified town. This magnificent possession, extending four hundred and sixty miles from north to south, and five hundred and seventy from east to west, including, with the Balearic Isles, 171,300 square miles, with a rich and fertile soil and inexhaustible mineral resources, was worth more to the Romans than all the conquests of Pompey and Sulla, since it furnished men for the armies, and materials for a new civilization. It furnished corn, oil, wine, fruits, pasturage, metals of all kinds, and precious stones. Bætica was famed for its harvests, Lusitania for its flocks, Tarraconensis for its timber, and the fields around Carthago Nova for materials of which cordage was made. But the great value of the peninsula to the eyes of the Romans was in its rich mines of gold, silver, and other metals. The bulk of the population was Iberian. The Celtic element was the next most prominent. There were six hundred and ninety-three towns and cities in which justice was administered. New Carthage, on the Mediterranean, had a magnificent harbor, was strongly fortified, and was twenty stadia in circumference, was a great emporium of trade, and was in the near vicinity of the richest silver mines of Spain, which employed forty thousand men. Gades (New Cadiz), a Phœnician colony, on the Atlantic Ocean, was another commercial centre, and numbered five hundred Equites among the population, and was immensely rich. Corduba, on the Bætis (Guadalquivir), the capital of Bætica, was a populous city before the Roman conquest, and was second only to Gades as a commercial mart. It was the birthplace of Seneca and Lucan.

Productions.

Its towns and cities.

Its commercial centres.

Gaul, which was the first of Cæsar's most brilliant conquests, and which took him ten years to accomplish, was a still more extensive province. It was inhabited chiefly by Celtic tribes, who, uniting with Germanic nations, made a most obstinate defense. When incorporated with the empire, Gaul became rapidly civilized. It was a splendid country, extending from the Pyrenees to the Rhine, with a sea-coast of more than six hundred miles, and separated from Italy by the Alps, having 200,-000 square miles. Great rivers, as in Spain, favored an extensive commerce with the interior, and on their banks were populous and beautiful cities. Its large coast on both the Mediterranean and the Atlantic gave it a communication with all the world. It produced corn, oil, and wine, those great staples, in great abundance. It had a beautiful climate, and a healthy and hardy population, warlike, courageous, and generous. Gaul was a populous country even in Cæsar's time, and possessed twelve hundred towns and cities, some of which were of great importance. Burdigala, now Bordeaux, the chief city of Aquitania, on the Garonne, was famous for its schools of rhetoric and grammar. Massolia (Marseilles), before the Punic wars was a strong fortified city, and was largely engaged in commerce. Vienne, a city of the Allobroges, was inclosed with lofty walls, and had an amphitheatre whose long diameter was five hundred feet, and the aqueducts supplied the city with water. Lugdunum (Lyons) on the Rhone, was a place of great trade, and was filled with temples, theatres, palaces, and aqueducts. Nemausus (Nîmes) had subject to it twenty-four villages, and from the monuments which remain, must have been a city of considerable importance. Its amphitheatre would seat seventeen thousand people; and its aqueduct constructed of three successive tiers of arches, one hundred and fifty-five feet high, eight hundred and seventy feet long, and fifty feet wide, is still one of the finest monuments of antiquity, built of stone without cement. It is still solid and strong, and gives us a vivid conception of the magnificence of Roman masonry. Narbo (Narbonne) was another commercial centre, adorned with public buildings which called

Richness of Gaul.

Population and cities.

Splendor of Gaulish cities.

forth the admiration of ancient travelers. The modern cities of Treves, Boulogne, Rheims, Chalons, Cologne, Metz, Dijon, Sens, Orleans, Poictiers, Clermont, Rouen, Paris, Basil, Geneva, were all considerable places under the Roman rule, and some were of great antiquity.

Illyricum.

Illyricum is not famous in Roman history, but was a very considerable province, equal to the whole Austrian empire in our times, and was as completely reclaimed from barbarism as Gaul or Spain. Both Jerome and Diocletian were born in a little Dalmatian town

Cultivated face of nature.

Nothing could surpass the countries which bordered on the Mediterranean in all those things which give material prosperity. They were salubrious in climate, fertile in soil, cultivated like a garden, abounding in nearly all the fruits, vegetables, and grains now known to civilization. The beautiful face of nature was the subject of universal panegyric to the fall of the empire. There were no destructive wars. All the various provinces were controlled by the central power which emanated from Rome. There was scope for commerce, and all kinds of manufacturing skill. Italy, Sicily, and Egypt were especially fertile. The latter country furnished corn in countless quantities for the Roman market. Italy could boast of fifty kinds of wine, and was covered with luxurious villas in which were fish-ponds, preserves for game, wide olive groves and vineyards, to say nothing of the farms which produced milk, cheese, honey, and poultry. Syria was so prosperous that its inhabitants divided their time between the field, the banquet, and the gymnasium, and indulged in continual festivals. It was so rich that Antiochus III. was able to furnish at one time a tribute of 15,000 talents, beside 540,000 measures of wheat. The luxury of Nineveh and Babylon was revived in the Phœnician cities.

Agricultural wealth.

Spain produced horses, mules, wool, oil, figs, wine, corn, honey, beer, flax, linen, beside mines of copper, silver, gold, quicksilver, tin, lead, and steel. Gaul was so cultivated that there was little waste land, and produced the same fruits and vegetables as at the present day. Its hams and sausages were much prized. Sicily was famous for wheat, Sardinia for wool, Epirus for horses, Macedonia for goats, Thessaly for oil, Bœotia for flax, Scythia for furs, and Greece for honey. Almost all the flowers, herbs, and fruits that grow in European gardens were known to the Romans — the apricot, the peach, the pomegranate, the citron, the orange, the quince, the apple, the pear, the plum, the cherry, the fig, the date, the olive. Martial speaks of pepper, beans, pulp, lentils, barley, beets, lettuce, radishes, cabbage sprouts, leeks, turnips, asparagus, mushrooms, truffles, as well as all sorts of game and birds.[1] In no age of the world was agriculture more honored than before the fall of the empire.

Natural productions of the various provinces.

And all these provinces were connected with each other and with the capital by magnificent roads, perfectly straight, and paved with large blocks of stone. They were originally constructed for military purposes, but were used by travelers, and on them posts were regularly established. They crossed valleys upon arches, and penetrated mountains. In Italy, especially, they were great works of art, and connected all the provinces. Among the great roads which conveyed to Rome as a centre were the Clodian and Cassian roads which passed through Etruria ; the Amerina and Flavinia through Umbria ; the Via Valeria, which had its terminus at Alternum on the Adriatic ; the Via Latina, which, passing through Latium and Campania, extended to the southern extremity of Italy ; the Via Appia also passed through Latium, Campania, Lucania, Iapygia to Brundusium, on the Adriatic. Again, from the central terminus at Milan, several lines passed through the gorges of the Alps, and connected Italy with

Roads.

[1] Martial, B. 13.

Lyons and Mayence on the one side, and with the Tyrol and Danubian provinces on the other. Spain and southern Gaul were connected by a grand road from Cadiz to Narbonne and Arles. Lyons was another centre from which branched out military roads to Saintes, Marseilles, Boulogne, and Mayence. In fact, the Roman legion could traverse every province in the empire over these grandly built public roads, as great and important in the second century as railroads are at the present time. There was an uninterrupted communication from the Wall of Antonius through York, London, Sandwich, Boulogne, Rheims, Lyons, Milan, Rome, Brundusium, Dyrrachium, Byzantium, Ancyra, Tarsus, Antioch, Tyre, Jerusalem — a distance of 3740 miles. And these roads were divided by mile-stones, and houses for travelers erected every five or six miles.

Commerce.

Commerce under the emperors was not what it now is, but still was very considerable, and thus united the various provinces together. The most remote countries were ransacked to furnish luxuries for Rome. Every year a fleet of one hundred and twenty vessels sailed from the Red Sea for the islands of the Indian Ocean. But the Mediterranean, with the rivers which flowed into it, was the great highway of the ancient navigator. Navigation by the ancients was even more rapid than in modern times before the invention of steam, since oars were employed as well as sails. In summer one hundred and sixty-two Roman miles were sailed over in twenty-four hours. This was the average speed, or about seven knots. From the mouth of the Tiber, vessels could usually reach Africa in two days, Massilia in three, Tarraco in four, and the Pillars of Hercules in seven. From Puteoli the passage to Alexandria had been effected, with moderate winds, in nine days. But these facts apply only to the summer, and to favorable winds. The Romans did not navigate in the inclement seasons. But in summer the

Objects of ancient commerce.

great inland sea was white with sails. Great fleets brought corn from Gaul, Spain, Sardinia, Africa, Sicily, and Egypt. This was the most important trade. But a considerable commerce was carried on in ivory, tortoise-shell, cotton and silk fabrics, pearls and precious stones, gums, spices, wines, wool, oil. Greek and Asiatic wines, especially the Chian and Lesbian, were in great demand at Rome. The transport of earthenware, made generally in the Grecian cities; of wild animals for the amphitheatre; of marble, of the spoils of eastern cities, of military engines, and stores, and horses, required very large fleets and thousands of mariners, which probably belonged, chiefly, to great maritime cities like Alexandria, Corinth, Carthage, Rhodes, Cyrene, Massalia, Neapolis, Tarentum, and Syracuse. These great cities with their dependencies, required even more vessels for communication with each other than for Rome herself — the great central object of enterprise and cupidity.

The metropolis of the empire.

In this survey of the provinces and cities which composed the empire of the Cæsars, I have not yet spoken of the great central city — the City of the Seven Hills, to which all the world was tributary. Rome was so grand, so vast, so important in every sense, political and social; she was such a concentration of riches and wonders, that it demands a separate and fuller notice than what I have been able to give of those proud capitals which finally yielded to her majestic domination. All other cities not merely yielded precedence, but contributed to her greatness. Whatever was costly, or rare, or beautiful in Greece, or Asia, or Egypt, was appropriated by her citizen kings, since citizens were provincial governors. All the great roads, from the Atlantic to the Tigris, converged to Rome. All the ships of Alexandria and Carthage and Tarentum, and other commercial capitals, were employed in furnishing her with luxuries or necessities. Never was there so proud a city as this "Epitome of the Universe."

7

London, Paris, Vienna, Constantinople, St. Petersburg, Berlin, are great centres of fashion and power; but they are rivals, and excel only in some great department of human enterprise and genius, as in letters, or fashions, or commerce, or manufactures — centres of influence and power in the countries of which they are capitals, yet they do not monopolize the wealth and energies of the world. London may contain more people than ancient Rome, and may possess more commercial wealth; but London represents only the British monarchy, not a universal empire. Rome, however, monopolized every thing, and controlled all nations and peoples. She could shut up the schools of Athens, or disperse the ships of Alexandria, or regulate the shops of Antioch. What Lyons or Bordeaux is to Paris, Corinth or Babylon was to Rome — secondary cities, dependent cities. Paul condemned at Jerusalem, stretched out his arms to Rome, and Rome protects him. The philosophers of Greece are the tutors of Roman nobility. The kings of the East resort to the palaces of Mount Palatine for favors or safety. The governors of Syria and Egypt, reigning in the palaces of ancient kings, return to Rome to squander the riches they have accumulated. Senators and nobles take their turn as sovereign rulers of all the known countries of the world. The halls in which Darius, and Alexander, and Pericles, and Crœsus, and Solomon, and Cleopatra have feasted, if unspared by the conflagrations of war, witness the banquets of Roman proconsuls. Babylon and Thebes and Athens were only what Delhi and Calcutta are to the English of our day — cities to be ruled by the delegates of the Roman Senate. Rome was the only "home" of the proud governors who reigned on the banks of the Thames, of the Seine, of the Rhine, of the Nile, of the Tigris. After they had enriched themselves with the spoils of the ancient monarchies they returned to their estates in Italy, or to their palaces on the Aventine, for the earth had but *one* capital

The centre and the pride of the world.

— one great centre of attraction. To an Egyptian even, Alexandria was only provincial. He must travel to the banks of the Tiber to see something greater than his own capital. It was the seat of government for one hundred and twenty millions of people. It was the arbiter of taste and fashion. It was the home of generals and senators and statesmen, of artists and scholars and merchants, who were renowned throughout the empire. It was enriched by the contributions of conquered nations for eight hundred years. It contained more marble statues than living inhabitants. Every spot was consecrated by associations; every temple had a history; every palace had been the scene of festivities which made it famous; every monument pointed to the deeds of the illustrious dead, and swelled the pride of the most powerful families which aristocratic ages had created.

Its varied objects of interest.

For the ancient authorities, see Strabo, Pliny, Polybius, Diodorus Siculus, Titus Livius, Pausanias, and Herodotus. There is an able chapter on Mediterranean prosperity in Napoleon's *History of Cæsar.* Smith, *Dictionary of Ancient Geography*, is exhaustive. See, also, Müller, article on *Atticus*, in Ersch, and Gruber's *Encyclopedia*, translated by Lockhart; Stuart and Revett, *Antiquities of Atticus;* Dodwell, *Tour through Greece;* Wilkinson, *Hand-book for Travelers in Egypt;* Becker, *Hand-book of Rome.* Anthon has compiled a useful work on ancient geography, but the most accessible and valuable book on the material aspects of the old Roman world is the great dictionary of Smith, from which this chapter is chiefly compiled.

CHAPTER III.

THE WONDERS OF ANCIENT ROME.

THE great capital of the ancient world had a very humble beginning, and that is involved in myth and mystery. Even the Latin stock, inhabiting the country from the Tiber to the Volscian mountains, which furnished the first inhabitants of the city, cannot be clearly traced, since we have no traditions of the first migration of the human race into Italy. It is supposed by Mommsen that the peoples which inhabited Latium belong to the Indo-Germanic family. Among these were probably the independent cantons of the Ramnians, Tities, and Luceres, which united to form a single commonwealth, and occupied the hills which arose about fourteen miles from the mouth of the Tiber. Around these hills was a rural population which tilled the fields. From these settlements a fortified fort arose on the Palatine Hill, fitted to be a place of trade from its situation on the Tiber, and also a fortress to protect the urban villages. Though unhealthy in its site, it was admirably adapted for these purposes, and thus early became an important place.

Early inhabitants of Italy.

The legends attribute a different foundation of the "Eternal City." But these also assign the Palatine as the nucleus of ancient Rome. It was on this hill that Romulus and Remus grew up to manhood, and it was this hill which Romulus selected as the site of the city he was so desirous to build. But modern critics suppose that he did not occupy the whole hill, but only the western part of it. Varro, whose authority is generally received, assigns the year 753 before Christ as the date for the foundation of the city. The first memorable incident in the history of this little city of robbers was the care of Romulus to increase its population by opening an asylum for fugitive slaves on the Capitoline Hill. But this supplied only males who had no wives. And when the proposal of the founder to solicit intermarriage with the neighboring nations was rejected, he resorted to stratagem and force. He invites the Sabines and the people of other Latin towns to witness games. A crowd of men and women are assembled, and while all are intent on the games, the unmarried women are seized by the Roman youth. Then ensues, of course, a war with the Sabines, the result of which is that the Sabines are united with the Romans and settle on the Quirinal. The Saturnian Hill is left in possession of the Sabines, while Romulus assumes the Sabine name of Quirinus, from which we infer that the Sabines had the best of the conflict. Callius, who, it is said, assisted Romulus, receives as a compensation the hill known as the Cælian. At the death of Romulus, who reigned thirty-seven years, Rome comprised the Palatine, the Quirinal, the Cælian, and the Capitoline hills.[1] The Sabines thus occupy two of the seven hills, and furnish not only people for the infant city, but laws, customs, and manners, especially religious observances.

Foundation of Rome.

Settlement under Romulus.

Extent of the city at the death of Romulus.

The reign of Numa was devoted to the consolidation of the power which Romulus had acquired, to the civilization of his subjects, and the improvement of the city. He fixed his residence between the Roman and the Sabine city, and erected adjoining to the Regia a temple to Vesta, which was probably only an *ædes sacra.* It was probably along with these buildings that the Sacra Via came into existence. The Regia became in after times the residence of the Pontifex Maximus. Numa estab-

The public works of Numa.

[1] M. Ampère, *Hist. Rom.*, tom. i. ch. xii.

lished on the Palatine the Curia Saliorum, and built on the Quirinal a temple of Romulus, afterwards rebuilt by Augustus. He also erected on the Quirinal a citadel connected with a temple of Jupiter, with cells of Juno and Minerva. He converted the gate which formed the entrance of the Sabine city into a temple of Janus, and laid the foundation upon the Capitoline of a large temple to Fides Publica, the public faith.

The reign of Tullus Hostilius. Under the reign of Tullus Hostilius was the capture of Alba Longa, the old capital of Latium, where Numa had reigned, and the transfer of its inhabitants to Rome, which thus became the chief city of the Latin league. They were located on the Cælian, which also became the residence of the king. He built the Curia Hostilia, a senate chamber, to accommodate the noble Alban families, in which the Roman Senate assembled, at the northwest corner of the Forum, to the latest times of the republic. It was a templum, but not dedicated for divine services, adjoining the eastern side of the Vulcanal.

Improvement of the city made by Tullus. Out of the spoils of Alba Longa, Tullus improved the Comitium, a space at the northwest end of the Forum, fronting the Curia, the common meeting place of the Romans and Sabines. On the Quirinal Hill he erected a Curia Saliorum in imitation of that of Numa on the Palatine, devoted to the worship of Quirinus.

Growth of Rome during the reign of Ancus Martius. Ancus Martius, a grandson of Numa, succeeded Tullus after a reign of thirty-two years. Under him the city was greatly augmented by the inhabitants of various Latin cities which he subdued. These settled on the Aventine, and in the valley which separated it from the Palatine, supposed by Niebuhr to be the origin of the Roman Plebs, though it is maintained by Lewis that the Plebeian order was coëval with the foundation of the city. Ancus fortified Mons Janiculus, the hill on the western bank of the Tiber, for the protection of the city. He connected it with Rome by the Pons Sublicius, the earliest of the Roman bridges, built on piles. The Janiculum was not much occupied by residences until the time of Augustus. Ancus founded Ostia, at the mouth of the Tiber, which became the port of Rome. It was this king who built the famous Mamertine Prison, near the Forum, below the northern height of the Capitoline.

A new dynasty succeeded this king, who reigned twenty-four years; that of the Tarquins, an Etrurian family of Greek extraction, which came from Corinth, the cradle of Grecian art, celebrated as the birth-place of painting and for its works of pottery and bronze. Tarquinius Priscus constructed the Cloaca Maxima, that vast sewer which drained the Forum and Velabrum, and which is regarded by Niebuhr as one of the most stupendous monuments of antiquity. It was composed of three semicircular arches inclosing one another, the innermost of which had a diameter of twelve feet, large enough to be traversed by a Roman hay-cart.[1] It was built without cement, and still remains a magnificent specimen of the perfection of the old Tuscan masonry. Along the southern side of the Forum this enlightened monarch constructed a row of shops occupied by butchers and other tradesmen. At the head of the Forum and under the Capitoline he founded the Temple of Saturn, the ruins of which attest considerable splendor. But his greatest work was the foundation of the Capitoline Temple of Jupiter, completed by Tarquinius Superbus, the consecrated citadel in which was deposited whatever was most valued by the Romans.

Tarquinius Priscus.

The Cloaca Maxima.

Temple of the Capitoline Jupiter.

During the reign of Servius Tullius, who succeeded Tarquin B. C. 578, the various elements of the population were amalgamated, and the seven hills, namely, the Palatine, the Capitoline, the Quirinal, the Cælian, the Viminal, the Esquiline, and the Aventine, were covered with houses, and inclosed by a wall about six

Accession of Servius Tullius.

[1] Arnold, *Hist. of Rom.*, vol. i. p. 52.

miles in circuit. A temple of Diana was erected on the Aventine, besides two temples to Fortune, one to Juno, and one to Luna. Servius also dedicated the Campus Martius, and enlarged the Mamertine Prison by adding a subterranean dungeon of impenetrable strength.

Tarquinius Superbus. On the assassination of Servius Tullius, B. C. 535, his son-in-law, Tarquinius Superbus, usurped the power, and did much for the adornment of the city. The Capitoline Temple was completed on an artificial platform, having a triple row of columns in front, and a double row at the sides. It was two hundred feet wide, having three cells adjoining one another, the centre appropriated to Jupiter, with Juno and Minerva on either hand. The temple had a single roof, and lasted nearly five hundred years before it was burned down, and rebuilt with greater splendor.

Rome under the early consuls. Such were the chief improvements of the city during the kingly rule. Under the consuls the growth was constant, but was not marked by grand edifices. Portunus, the conqueror of the Tarquins at Lake Regillus, erected a temple to Ceres, Liber, and Libera, at the western extremity of the Circus Maximus. Camillus founded a celebrated temple to Juno on the Aventine. But these, and a few other temples, were destroyed when the Gauls held possession of the city. The city was rebuilt hastily and without much regard to regularity. There was nothing memorable in its architectural monuments till the time of Appius Claudius, who constructed the Via Appia, the first Roman aqueduct. In fact the constant wars of the Romans prevented much improvement in the city till the fall of Tarentum, although the ambassadors of Pyrrhus were struck with its grandeur. M. Curius Dentatus commenced the aqueduct called Anio Vetus B. C. 273, the greater part of which was under ground. Its total length was forty-three miles. Q. Flaminius, B. C. 220, between the first and second Punic wars, constructed the great highway, called after him the Via Flaminia — the great northern road of Italy, as the Via Appia was the southern. These roads were very elaborately built. In constructing them, the earth was excavated till a solid foundation was obtained; over this a layer of loose stones was laid, then another layer nine inches thick of rubble-work of broken stones cemented with lime, then another layer of broken pottery cemented in like manner, over which was a pavement of large polygonal blocks of hard stone nicely fitted together. Roads thus constructed were exceedingly durable, so that portions of them, constructed two thousand years ago, are still in a high state of preservation.

Roman roads.

The improvements of Rome were rapid after the conquest of Greece, although destructive fires frequently laid large parts of the city in ruins. The deities of the conquered nations were introduced into the Roman worship, and temples erected to them. In the beginning of the second century before Christ we notice the erection of basilicas, used as courts of law and a sort of exchange, the first of which was built by M. Portius Cato, B. C. 184, on the north side of the Forum. It was of an oblong form, open to the air, surrounded with columns, at one end of which was the tribunal of the judge. The Basilica Portia was soon followed by the Basilica Fulvia behind the Argentariæ Novæ, which had replaced the butchers' shops. Fulvius Nobilia further adorned the city with a temple of Hercules on the Campus Martius, and brought from Ambrasia, once the residence of Pyrrhus, two hundred and thirty marble and two hundred and eighty-five bronze statues, beside pictures. L. Æmilius Paulus founded an emporium on the banks of the Tiber as a place of landing and sale for goods transported by sea, and built a bridge over the Tiber. Sempronius Gracchus, the father of the two demagogue patriots, erected a third Basilica B. C. 169, on the south side of the Forum

Ancient basilicas.

Temple of Hercules.

on the site of the house of Scipio Africanus. The triumph of Æmilius Paulus introduced into the city pictures and statues enough to load two hundred and fifty chariots, and a vast quantity of gold and silver. Cornelius Octavius, B. C. 167, built a grand palace on the Palatine, one of the first examples of elegant domestic architecture, and erected a magnificent double portico with capitals of Corinthian bronze. With the growing taste for architectural display, various Asiatic luxuries were introduced — bronze beds, massive sideboards, tables of costly woods, cooks, pantomimists, female dancers, and luxurious banquets. Metellus erected the first marble temple seen in Rome, before which he placed the twenty-five bronze statues which Lysippus had executed for Alexander the Great.

Asiatic luxuries.

The same year that witnessed the triumph of Metellus, B. C. 146, also saw the fall of Carthage and the sack of Corinth by Mummius, so that many of the choicest specimens of Grecian art were brought to the banks of the Tiber. Among these was the celebrated picture of Bacchus by Aristides, which was placed in the Temple of Bacchus, Ceres, and Proserpine. The Forum now contained many gems of Grecian art, among which were the statues of Alcibiades and Pythagoras which stood near the comitium, the Three Sibyls placed before the rostra, and a picture by Serapion, which covered the balconies of the tabernæ on the south side of the Forum.

Sack of Corinth.

Adornment of the Forum.

In the year 144 B. C., Q. Marcius Rex constructed the Aqua Marcia, one of the noblest of the Roman monuments, sixty-two miles in length, seven of which were on arches, sufficiently lofty to supply the Capitoline with pure and cold water. Seventeen years after, the Aqua Tepula was added to the aqueducts of Rome.

Aqua Marcia.

The first triumphal arch erected to commemorate victories was in the year B. C. 196, by L. Sertinius. Scipio Africanus erected another on the Capi-

Triumphal arches.

toline, and Q. Fabius, B. C. 121, raised another in honor of his victories over the Allobroges. This spanned the Via Sacra where it entered the Forum, and at that time was a conspicuous monument, though vastly inferior to the arches of the imperial regime.

When tranquillity was restored to Rome after the riots connected with the murder of the Gracchi, the Senate ordered a Temple of Concord to be built, B. C. 121, in commemoration of the event. This temple was on the elevated part of the Vulcanal, and was of considerable magnitude. It was used for the occasional meetings of the Senate, and contained many valuable works of art. Adjoining this temple, Opimius, the consul, erected the Basilica Opimia, which was used by the silversmiths, who were the bankers and pawnbrokers of Rome. The whole quarter on the north side of the Forum, where this basilica stood, was the Roman exchange — the focus for all monetary transactions.

Temple of Concord.

Basilica Opimia.

The increasing wealth and luxury of Rome, especially caused by the conquest of Asia, led to the erection on the Palatine of those magnificent private residences, which became one of the most striking features of the capital. The first of these historical houses was built by M. Livius Drusus, and overlooked the city. It afterwards passed into the hands of Crassus, Cicero, and Censorinus. Pompey had a house on the Palatine, but afterwards transferred his residence to the Casinæ, another aristocratic quarter. M. Æmilius Lepidus also lived in a magnificent palace; the house of Crassus was still more splendid, adorned with columns of marble from Mount Hymettus. The house of Catullus excelled even that of Crassus. This again was excelled by that of Aquillius on the Viminal, which for some time was the most splendid in Rome, until Lucullus occupied nearly the whole of the Pincian Hill with his gardens and galleries of art, which contained some of the *chefs d'œuvre* of antiquity. The

Private palaces.

gardens of Servilius, which lay on the declivity of the Aventine, were adorned with Greek statues, exceeded in beauty by those of Sallust between the Pincian and the Quirinal hills, built with the spoils of Numidia, and ultimately the property of the emperors. The house of Clodius on the Palatine, near to that of Cicero, was one of the finest in Rome, occupied before him by Scaurus, who gave for it nearly fifteen million sesterces, about $650,000. It was adorned with Greek paintings and sculptures. The house of Cicero, which he bought of Crassus, cost him $150,000. Its atrium was adorned with Greek marble columns thirty-eight feet high. Hortensius lived in a house on the Palatine, afterwards occupied by Augustus. The residence of his friend Atticus, on the Quirinal, was more modest, whose chief ornament was a grove. Pompey surrounded his house with gardens and porticos.

Houses of the nobles.

The year 83 B. C. was marked by the destruction by fire of the old Capitoline Temple, which had withstood the ravages of the Gauls. Sulla aspired to rebuild it, and caused to be transported to Rome for that purpose the column of the Olympian Zeus at Athens. It was completed by Cæsar, and its roof was gilded at an expense of $15,000,000. The pediment was adorned with statuary, and near it was a colossal statue of Jupiter.

Destruction and rebuilding of the Capitol.

In the early ages of the republic there were no theatres at Rome, theatrical representations being regarded as demoralizing. The regular drama was the last development even of Grecian genius. The Roman aristocracy set their faces against dramatic entertainments till after the conquest of Greece. These plays were introduced and performed on temporary stages in the open air, or in wooden buildings. There was no grand theatre till Pompey erected one of stone, B. C. 55, in the Campus Martius, which was capable of holding eighty thousand

Theatre of Pompey.

spectators, and it had between its numerous pillars three thousand bronze statues.[1] He also erected, behind his theatre, a grand portico of one hundred pillars, which became one of the most fashionable lounging-places of Rome, and which was adorned with statues and images. Pompey also built various temples.

His great rival however surpassed him in labors to ornament the capital. Cæsar enlarged the Forum, or rather added a new one, the ground of which cost $2,500,000. It was called the Forum Julian, and was three hundred and forty feet long by two hundred wide, containing a temple of Venus. He did not live, however, to carry out his magnificent plans. He contemplated building an edifice, for the assembly of the Comitia Tributa, of marble, with a portico inclosing a space of a mile square, and also the erection of a temple to Mars of unparalleled size and magnificence. He commenced the Basilica Julia and the Curia Julia — vast buildings, which were completed under the emperors.

Forum Julian.

Basilica Julia.

Such were the principal edifices of Rome until the imperial sway. Augustus boasted that he found the city of brick and left it of marble. It was not until the emperors embellished the city with amphitheatres, theatres, baths, and vast architectural monuments that it was really worthy to be regarded as the metropolis of the world. The great improvements of Rome in the republican period were of a private nature, such as the palaces of senatorial families. There were no temples equal to those in the Grecian cities either for size, ornament, or beauty. Indeed, Rome was never famous for temples, but for edifices of material utility rather than for the worship of the gods; yet the Romans, under the rule of the aristocracy, were more religious than the Corinthians or Athenians.

Rome under the Emperors.

On the destruction of the senatorial or constitutional party that had ruled since the expulsion of the kings, and

[1] *Plin. H. N.*, xxxvi. 24.

probably before, and the peaceful accession of Augustus, B. C. 31, a great impulse was given to the embellishments of the city. His long reign, his severe taste, and his immense resources, — undisputed master of one hundred and fifty millions of subjects, — enabled him to carry out the designs of Julius, and to restore an immense number of monuments falling to decay. But Rome was even then deficient in those things which most attract attention in our modern capitals — the streets and squares. The longest street of Rome was scarcely three fourths of a mile in length; but the houses upon it were of great altitude. Moreover the streets were narrow and dark — scarcely more than fifteen feet in width. But they were not encumbered with carriages. Private equipages, which form one of the most imposing features of a modern city, were unknown. There was nothing attractive in a Roman street, dark, narrow, and dirty, with but few vehicles, and with dingy shops, like those of Paris in the Middle Ages. The sun scarcely ever penetrated to them. They were damp and cold. The greater part of the city belonged to wealthy and selfish capitalists, like Crassus, who thought more of their gains than the health or beauty of the city. The Subura, the Sub Velia, and the Velabrum, built in the valleys, were choked up with tall houses, frequently more, and seldom less, than seventy feet in height. The hills alone were covered with aristocratic residences, temples, and public monuments. The only open space, where the poor people could get fresh air and extensive prospect, was the Circus Maximus and the Forum Romanum. The former was three fourths of a mile in length and one eighth in breadth, surrounded with a double row of benches, the lower of stone and the upper of wood, and would seat two hundred and eighty-five thousand spectators. The Forum was the centre of architectural splendor, as well as of life and business. Its original site

Works of Augustus.

The Subura.

Forum Romanum.

extended from the eastern part of the Capitoline to the spot where the Velia begins to ascend, and was bounded on the south by the Via Sacra, which extended to the arx or citadel. It was that consecrated street by which the augurs descended when they inaugurated the great festivals of the republic, and in which lived the Pontifex Maximus. Although the Forum Romanum was only seven hundred feet by four hundred and seventy, yet it was surrounded by and connected with basilicas, halls, porticoes, temples, and shops. It was a place of great public resort for all classes of people — a scene of life and splendor rarely if ever equaled, and having some resemblance to the crowded square of Venice on which St. Mark's stands. Originally it was a market-place, busy and lively, a great resort where might be seen "good men walking quietly by themselves,"[1] "flash men strutting about without a denarius in their purses," "gourmands clubbing for a dinner," "scandal-mongers living in glass houses," "perjured witnesses, liars, braggarts, rich and erring husbands, worn-out harlots," and all the various classes which now appear in the crowded places of London or Paris. In this open space the people were assembled on great public occasions, and here they were addressed by orators and tribunes. Immediately surrounding the Forum Romanum, or in close proximity to it, were the most important public buildings of the city in which business was transacted — the courts of law, the administrative bureaus, the senate chamber and the principal temples, as well as monuments and shops. On the north side was the Comitium, an open space for holding the Comitia Curiata and heavy lawsuits, and making speeches to the assembled people. During the kingly government the temples of Janus and Vesta and Saturn were erected, also the Curia Hostilia, a senate-house, the Senaculum, the Mamertine Prison, and the Tabernæ or

Its magnificence

Surrounding buildings.

[1] *Plautus Cuve*, iv. 1.

porticoes and shops inclosing the Forum. During the republic the temple of Castor and Pollux, which served for the assembly of the Senate and judicial business, was erected, not of the largest size, but very rich and beautiful. The Basilica Portia, where the tribunes of the people held their assemblies, was founded by Cato the Censor, and this was followed by the Basilica Fulvia, with columns of Phrygian marble, admired by Pliny for its magnificence, the Basilica Sempronia, the Temple of Concord, and the Triumphal Arch of Fabius, to commemorate his victories over the Allobroges. Under the empire, the magnificent Basilica Julia was erected for the sittings of the law courts, and its immense size may be inferred from the fact that one hundred and eighty judges, divided into four courts, with four separate tribunals, with seats for advocates and spectators, were accustomed to assemble. Tiberius erected a triumphal arch near the Temple of Saturn. Domitian built the Temple of Vespasian and Titus, and erected to himself a colossal equestrian statue. Near it rose the temples of Divus-Julius and of Antoninus and Faustina. Beside these were the Triumphal Arch of Septimius Severus, still standing; the Columns of Phocas and Trajan, the latter of which is the finest monument of its kind in the world, one hundred and twenty-seven feet high, with a spiral band of admirable reliefs containing two thousand five hundred human figures. Beside these, new fora of immense size were constructed by various emperors, not for political business so much as courts of justice. The Forum Julium, which connected with the old Forum Romanum, was virtually a temple of great magnificence. In front of it was the celebrated bronze horse of Lysippus, and the temple was enriched with precious offerings and adorned with pictures from the best Greek artists. It was devoted to legal business. The Forum Augusti

Temple of Castor and Pollux.

Basilica Julia.

Arch of Septimius Severus, and columns of Trajan.

Forum Julium.

Forum Augusti.

was still larger, and also inclosed a temple, in which the Senate assembled to consult about wars and triumphs, and was surrounded with porticoes in which the statues of the most eminent Roman generals were placed, while on each side were the triumphal arches of Germanicus and Drusus. More extensive and magnificent than either of the old fora was the one which Trajan erected, in the centre of which was the celebrated column of the emperor, so universally admired, while the sides were ornamented with a double colonnade of gray Egyptian marble, the columns of which were fifty-five feet in height. This was one of the most gigantic structures in Rome, covering more ground than the Flavian Amphitheatre, and built by the celebrated Apollodorus of Damascus. It filled the whole space between the Capitoline and Quirinal. The Basilica Ulpia was only one division of this vast edifice, divided internally by four rows of columns of gray granite, and paved with slabs of marble.

Forum of Trajan.

Basilica Ulpia.

Nothing in Rome, or perhaps any modern city, exceeded the glory and beauty of the Forum, with the adjoining basilica, and other public buildings, filled with statues and pictures, and crowded with people. The more aristocratic loungers sought the retired promenade afforded by the porticoes near the Circus Flaminius, where the noise and clamor of the crowded streets, the cries of venders, the sports of boys, and the curses of wagoners, could not reach them. The Forum was the peculiar glory of the republican period, where the Gracchi enlightened the people on their political rights, where Cato calmed the passions of the mob, where Cicero and Hortensius delivered their magnificent harangues.

Beauty of the Roman Forum.

The glory of the Augustan age was more seen in the magnificent buildings which arose upon the hills, although he gave attention to the completion of many works of utility or beauty in other parts of the city. He restored the Capitoline temple and the theatre of Pom-

Works of Augustus.

pey; repaired aqueducts; finished the Forum and Basilica Julia; and entirely built the Curia Julia. He founded, on the Palatine, the Imperial Palace, afterwards enlarged by his successors until it entirely covered the original city of Romulus. Among the most beautiful of his works was

Temple of Apollo. the Temple of Apollo, the columns of which were of African marble, between which were the statues of the fifty Danaids. In the temple was a magnificent statue of Apollo, and around the altar were the images of four oxen — the work of Miron, so beautifully sculptured that they seemed alive. The temple was of the finest marble; its gates were of ivory, finely sculptured. Attached to this temple was a library, where the poets, orators, and philosophers assembled, and recited their productions. The Forum Augusti was another of the noblest monuments of this emperor, in order to provide accommodation for the crowds which overflowed the Forum Ro-

Theatre of Marcellus. manum. He also built the theatre of Marcellus, capable of holding twenty thousand spectators.

Nor was Augustus alone the patron of the arts. His son-in-law, and prime minister, Agrippa, adorned the city

Pantheon. with many noble structures, of which the Pantheon remains to attest his munificence. This temple, the best preserved of all the monuments of ancient splendor, stood in the centre of the Campus Martius, and contained only the images of the deities immediately connected with the Julian race and the early history of Rome. Agrippa was the first to establish those famous baths, which became the most splendid monuments of imperial

Thermæ Agrippæ. munificence. The Thermæ Agrippæ stood at the back of the Pantheon. It was fed by the Aqua Virgo, an aqueduct which Agrippa purposely constructed to furnish water for his baths. Many other architectural monuments marked the public spirit of this en-

Campus Martius. lightened and liberal minister, especially in the quarter of the Circus Flaminius and the Campus

Martius. This quarter was like a separate town, more magnificent than any part of the ancient city. It was adorned with temples, porticoes, and theatres, and other buildings devoted to amusement and recreation. It had not many private houses, but these were of remarkable splendor. Other courtiers of Augustus followed his example for the embellishment of the city. Statilius Taurus built the first permanent amphitheatre of stone in the Campus Martius. L. Cornelius Balbur built at his own expense a stone theatre. L. Marcius Philippus rebuilt the temple of Hercules Musarum, and surrounded it with a portico. L. Cornificius built a temple of Diana. Asininius Pollio an Atrium Libertatis; and Munatius Plaucus a temple of Saturn. Mæcenas, who lived upon the Esquiline, converted the Campus Esquilinus, near the Subura, a pauper burial-ground offensive to both sight and health, into beautiful gardens, called the Horti Mæcenatis.

Works of the Nobles.

> Nunc licet esquiliis habitare salubribus atque,
> Aggere in Aprico Spatiari, quo modo tristes,
> Albis informem spectabant ossibus agrum.[1]

Near these gardens Virgil lived, also Propertius, and probably Horace. The Esquiline, once a plebeian quarter, seems to have been selected by the literary men, who sought the favor of Mæcenas, for their abode. Ovid lived near the capitol, at the southern extremity of the Quirinal.

Among the other buildings which Augustus erected, should not be omitted the magnificent Mausoleum, or the tomb of the imperial family at the northern part of the Campus Martius, near which lay the remains of Sulla and of Cæsar, and which remained the burial-place of his family down to the time of Hadrian.[2]

Mausoleum of Augustus.

[1] Horace, *Sat.* i. 8.

[2] "This enduring structure, which survived the conflagrations, the wars, and the anarchies of fifteen hundred years, consisted of a large tumulus of earth, raised on a lofty basement of white marble, and covered on the summit with evergreens in the manner of a hang-

Mausoleum of Augustus.

He also brought from Egypt the obelisk which now stands on Mount Citorio, and which was placed in that receptacle for monuments — the Campus Martius.

Tiberius did but little for the improvement of his capital beyond erecting a triumphal arch, in commemoration of the exploits of Germanicus, on the Via Sacra, and establishing the Prætorian Camp near the Servian Agger.

Imperial palace. Caligula extended the imperial palace, and began the Circus Neronis in the gardens of Agrippa, near where St. Peter's now stands.

Claudius constructed the two noble aqueducts, the Aqua Claudia and Arno Novis, — the longest of all these magnificent Roman monuments, — the latter of which was fifty-nine miles in length, and some of its arches were one hundred and nine feet in height.

Claudian aqueduct.

Nero still further extended the precincts of the imperial palace, and included the Esquiline. The great fire which occurred in his reign, A. D. 65, and which lasted six days and seven nights, destroyed some of the most ancient of the Roman structures surrounding the Palatine, and very much damaged the Forum, to say nothing of the statues and treasures which perished. But the city soon arose from her ashes more beautiful than before. The streets were laid out on a more regular plan and made wider,

ing garden. On the summit was a bronze statue of Augustus himself, and beneath the tumulus was a large central hall, round which ran a range of fourteen sepulchral chambers, opening into this common vestibule. At the entrance were two Egyptian obelisks, fifty feet in height, and all around was an extensive grove divided into walks and terraces. The young Marcellus, whose fate was bewailed by Virgil, was its first occupant. Here was placed Octavia, the neglected wife of Antony, and Agrippa, the builder of the Parthenon, and Livia, the beloved wife of Augustus, and beside them the first imperator himself. Here were the poisoned ashes of the noble Germanicus, borne from Syria; here the young Drusus, the pride of the Claudian family, and at his side the second Drusus, the son of Tiberius. Here reposed the dust of Agrippina, after years of exile, by the side of her husband, Germanicus; here Nero and his mother, Agrippina, and his victim, Britannicus; here Tiberius, Caligula, Claudius, and all the other Cæsars to Nerva. Then the marble door was closed, for the sepulchral cells were full." — Story's *Roba di Roma*.

Those who were buried in it.

the houses were built lower, and brick was substituted for wood.

The great work of Nero was the construction of the Imperial Palace on the site of the buildings which had been destroyed by the fire. He gave to it the name of Aurea Domus, and, if we may credit Suetonius,[1] its richness and splendor surpassed any other similar edifice in ancient times. It fronted the Forum and Capitol, and in its vestibule stood a colossal statue of the emperor, one hundred and twenty feet high. The palace was surrounded by three porticoes, each one thousand feet in length. The back front of the palace looked upon the artificial lake, afterwards occupied by the Flavian Amphitheatre. Within the area were gardens and vineyards. It was entirely overlaid with gold, and adorned with jewels and mother-of-pearl. The supper rooms were vaulted, and the compartments of the ceiling, inlaid with ivory, were made to revolve and scatter flowers upon the banqueters below. The chief banqueting-room was circular, and perpetually revolved in imitation of the motion of the celestial bodies. There are scarcely no remains of this extensive palace, which engrossed so large a part of the city, and which covered the site of so many famous temples and palaces, and which exhausted even the imperial revenues, great as they were, even as Versailles taxed the magnificent resources of Louis XIV., and St. Peter's obliged the Popes to appeal to the contributions of Christendom.

The Imperial Palace.

The next great edifice which added to the architectural wonders of the city, was the temple built by Vespasian after the destruction of Jerusalem, which he called the Temple of Peace. It was adorned with the richest sculptures and paintings of Greece, taken from Nero's palace, which Vespasian demolished as a monument of insane extravagance. In this temple were

Temple of Peace.

1 Suet. *Ner.*, 31.

deposited also the Jewish spoils, except the laws and veil of the temple.

Flavian Amphitheatre. But the great work of this emperor, and the greatest architectural wonder of the world, was the amphitheatre which he built on the ground covered by Nero's lake, in the middle of the city, between the Velia and the Esquiline. For magnitude it can only be compared with the pyramids of Egypt, and its remains are the most striking monument we have of the material greatness of the Romans. The Colosseum. Though not the first of the amphitheatres which were erected, its enormous size rendered the erection of subsequent ones unnecessary. It was here that emperors, senators, generals, knights, and people, met together to witness the most exciting and sanguinary amusements ever seen in the world. It was built in the middle of the city, with a perfect recklessness of expense, and could accommodate eighty-seven thousand spectators, round an arena large enough for the combats of several hundred animals at a time. It was a building of an elliptical form, founded on eighty arches, and rising to the height of one hundred and forty feet, with four successive orders of architecture, six hundred and twenty feet by five hundred and thirteen, inclosing six acres. It was built of travertine, faced with marble, and decorated with statues. The eighty arches of the lower story formed entrances for the spectators. The seats were of marble covered with cushions. The spectators were protected from the sun and rain by ample canopies, while the air was refreshed by scented fountains. The nets designed as a protection from the wild beasts were made of golden wire. The porticoes were gilded; the circle which divided the several ranks of spectators was studded with a precious mosaic of beautiful stones. The arena was strewed with the finest sand, and assumed, at different times, the most different forms. Subterranean pipes conveyed water into the arena. The furniture of the amphitheatre consisted of gold, silver, and amber. The passages of ingress and egress were so numerous that the spectators could go in and out without confusion. Only a third part of this wonderful structure remains, and whole palaces have been built of its spoils.[1]

Another great fire which took place A. D. 80, — the same in which Titus dedicated the Colosseum, — and which raged three days and nights, destroyed the region of the Circus Flaminius, including some of the finest temples of the city, and especially on the Capitoline, and created the necessity for new improvements. These were made by Domitian, who rebuilt the Capitol itself with greater splendor on its old site, and erected several new edifices. Martial speaks with peculiar admiration of the Temple of the Gens Flavia.[2] He also erected that beautiful arch to his brother Titus which still remains one of the finest monuments of the imperial city. The Odeum, a roofed theatre, was erected by him, capable of holding twelve thousand people. He also made many additions to his palace on the Palatine — so lofty, that Martial, his flatterer, described it as towering above the clouds, and Statius compared the ceiling to the cope of heaven.

Rebuilding of the Capitol.

Arch of Titus.

No great improvements were made in the city until Trajan commenced his beneficent and splendid reign. His greatest work was the Forum which bears his name, to which allusion has been made, eleven hundred feet long, in the centre of which was that beautiful pillar, one hundred and twenty-eight feet high, which is still standing. The Forum, the Basilica Ulpia, and the temple dedicated by Hadrian to Trajan, were all parts of this magnificent structure, one of the most imposing ever built, filled with colossal statues and surrounded with colonnades.

Forum Trajanum.

Basilica Ulpia.

1 Dyer, *Hist. of the City of Rome*, p. 245. Gibbon, chap. 12. Montaigne, *Essays*, iii. 6. Lipsius, *de Amphitheatro*.

2 Martial, *L.*, ix. Ep. 4, 35.

None of the Roman emperors had so great a passion for building as Hadrian, who succeeded Trajan A. D. 117. He erected a vast number of edifices, and in his reign Rome attained its greatest height of architectural splendor. The most remarkable among the edifices which he built was the Temple of Venus and Rome, facing on one side the Colosseum, and the other the Forum, on the site of the Atrium, or the golden house of Nero. This seems to have been one of the largest of the Roman temples, erected on an artificial terrace five hundred feet long and three hundred broad. It was surrounded with a portico four hundred feet by two hundred, and another portico of four hundred columns inclosed the terrace on which the temple was built, the columns of which were forty feet in height. The roof was covered with bronze tiles. Ammianus Marcellinus classes this magnificent temple with the Capitoline Temple, the Flavian Amphitheatre, and the Pantheon. The next greatest work of Hadrian was the Mausoleum, which is now converted into the Castle of St. Angelo, built on a platform of which each side was two hundred and fifty-three feet in length. From the magnificent colonnade which supported the platform on which it was built, and the successive stories supported by arches and pillars, between which were celebrated statues, this circular edifice, one hundred and eighty-eight feet in diameter, must have been one of the most imposing edifices in the city. After eighteen centuries, it still remains a monument of architectural strength, and it served for one of the strongest fortresses in Italy during the Middle Ages. I pass by, without notice, the villa this emperor erected at Tivoli, the ruins of which are among the most interesting which remain of that great age.

Temple of Venus and Rome.

Mausoleum of Hadrian.

Hadrian's Villa.

Under Hadrian Rome attained its greatest splendor, and after him, there was a progressive decline in the arts, since the public taste was corrupted. Still successive emperors continued to adorn the city. Marcus Aurelius, the wisest and best of all the emperors, erected a column similar to that of Trajan, to represent his wars with the Germanic tribes, and this still remains; he also built a triumphal arch. Septimius Severus erected the most beautiful of the triumphal arches, of which the Arc de Triumph in Paris is an imitation; and Caracalla built one of the greatest of the Roman baths, which, with the porticoes which surrounded it, formed a square of eleven hundred feet on each side — so enormous were these structures of luxury and utility, designed not only for the people as a sanitary measure, but for places of gymnastic exercises, popular lectures, and the disputations of philosophers. The Pantheon was merely an entrance to the baths of Agrippa. The baths of Trajan covered an area nearly as great. But those of Caracalla surpassed them all in magnificence. Nothing was more striking to a traveler than the painted corridors, the arched ceilings, the variegated columns, the elaborate mosaic pavements, the immortal statues, and the exquisite paintings which ornamented these places of luxury and pleasure. From amid their ruins have been dug out the most priceless of the statues which ornament the museums of Italy — the Farnese Hercules, the colossal Floræ, the Torso Farnese, the Torso Belvidere, the Atreus and Thyestes, the Laocoön, beside granite and basaltic vases beautifully polished, cameos, bronzes, medals, and other valuable relics of ancient art. To supply these baths new aqueducts were built, and the treasures of the empire expended. Those subsequently erected by Diocletian contained three thousand two hundred marble seats, and the main hall now forms one of the most splendid of the Roman churches.

Column of Marcus Aurelius.

Arch of Septimius Severus.

Baths of Caracalla.

Such is a brief view of the progress of those architectural wonders which made Rome the most magnificent city of antiquity, and perhaps the grandest, in its public monuments, of any city in ancient or modern times. What a concentration of works of art on the hills, and around the Forum, and in the Campus Martius, and other celebrated quarters! There were temples rivaling those of Athens and Ephesus; baths covering more ground than the Pyramids, surrounded with Corinthian columns and filled with the choicest treasures, ransacked from the cities of Greece and Asia; palaces in comparison with which the Tuileries and Versailles are small; theatres which seated more people than any present public buildings in Europe; amphitheatres more extensive and costly than Cologne, Milan, and York Minster cathedrals combined, and seating eight times as many people as could be crowded into St. Peter's Church; circuses where, it is said, three hundred and eighty-five thousand spectators could witness the games and chariot-races at a time; bridges, still standing, which have furnished models for the most beautiful at Paris and London; aqueducts carried over arches one hundred feet in height, through which flowed the surplus water of distant lakes; drains of solid masonry in which large boats could float; pillars more than one hundred feet in height, coated with precious marbles or plates of brass, and covered with bass-reliefs; obelisks brought from Egypt; fora and basilicæ connected together, and extending more than three thousand feet in length, every part of which was filled with "animated busts" of conquerors, kings, and statesmen, poets, publicists, and philosophers; mausoleums greater and more splendid than that Artemisia erected to the memory of her husband; triumphal arches under which marched in stately procession the victorious armies of the Eternal City, preceded by the spoils and trophies of conquered empires, — such was the proud capital — a city of palaces, a residence of nobles who were virtually kings, enriched with the accumulated treasurés of ancient civilization. Great were the capitals

Temples and Palaces.

General aspect of the city.

of Greece and Asia, but how preëminent was Rome, since all were subordinate to her. How bewildering and bewitching to a traveler must have been the varied wonders of the city! Go where he would, his eye rested on something which was both a study and a marvel. Let him drive or walk about the suburbs, there were villas, tombs, aqueducts looking like railroads on arches, sculptured monuments, and gardens of surpassing beauty and luxury. Let him approach the walls — they were great fortifications extending twenty-one miles in circuit, according to the measurement of Ammon as adopted by Gibbon, and forty-five miles according to other authorities. Let him enter any of the various gates which opened into the city from the roads which radiated to all parts of Italy — they were of monumental brass covered with bass-reliefs, on which the victories of generals for a thousand years were commemorated. Let him pass up the Via Appia, or the Via Flaminia, or the Via Cabra — they were lined with temples and shops and palaces. Let him pass through any of the crowded thoroughfares, he saw houses towering scarcely ever less than seventy feet — as tall as those of Edinburgh in its oldest sections. Let him pass through the varied quarters of the city, or wards as we should now call them, he finds some fourteen regions, as constituted by Augustus, all marked by architectural monuments, and containing, according to Lipsius, a population larger than London or Paris, guarded and watched by a police of ten thousand armed men. Most of the houses in which this vast population lived, according to Strabo, possessed pipes which gave a never-failing supply of water from the rivers which flowed into the city through the aqueducts and out again through the sewers into the Tiber. Let him walk up the Via Sacra — that short street, scarcely half a mile in length — and he passes the Flavian Amphitheatre, the Temple of Venus and Rome, the Arch of Titus, the temples of Peace, of

What a traveler would see in a walk.

The Via Sacra.

Vesta, and of Castor, the Forum Romanum, the Basilica Julia, the Arch of Severus, and the Temple of Saturn, and stands before the majestic ascent to the Capitoline Jupiter, with its magnificent portico and ornamented pediment, surpassing the façade of any modern church. On his left, as he emerges from beneath the sculptured Arch of Titus, is the Palatine Mount, nearly covered by the palace of the Cæsars, the magnificent residences of the higher nobility, and various temples, of which that of Apollo was the most magnificent, built by Augustus of solid white marble from Luna. Here were the palaces of Vaccus, of Flaccus, of Cicero, of Catiline, of Scaurus, of Antonius, of Clodius, of Agrippa, and of Hortensius. Still on his left, in the valley between the Palatine and the Capitoline, though he cannot see it, concealed from view by the great temples of Vesta and of Castor, and the still greater edifice known as the Basilica Julia, is the quarter called the Velabrum, extending to the river, where the Pons Æmilius crosses it — a low quarter of narrow streets and tall houses where the rabble lived and died. On his right, concealed from view by the Ædes Divi Julii and the Forum Romanum, is that magnificent series of edifices extending from the Temple of Peace to the Temple of Trajan, including the Basilica Pauli, the Forum Julii, the Forum Augusti, the Forum Trajani, the Basilica Ulpia, more than three thousand feet in length and six hundred in breadth, almost entirely surrounded by porticoes and colonnades, and filled with statues and pictures — on the whole the grandest series of public buildings clustered together probably ever erected, especially if we take in the Forum Romanum and the various temples and basilicas which connected the whole together — a forest of marble pillars and statues. He ascends the steps which lead from the Temple of Concord to the Temple of Juno Moneta upon the Arx or Tarpeian Rock, on the southwestern sum-

The Velabrum.

The Fora.

mit of the hill, itself one of the most beautiful temples in Rome, erected by Camillus on the spot where the house of M. Manlius Capitolinus had stood. Here is established the Roman mint. Near this is the temple erected by Augustus to Jupiter Tonans and that built by Domitian to Jupiter Custos. But all the sacred edifices which crown the Capitoline are subordinate to the Templum Jovis Capitolini, standing on a platform of eight thousand square feet, and built of the richest materials. The portico which faces the Via Sacra consists of three rows of Doric columns, the pediment is profusely ornamented with the choicest sculptures, the apex of the roof is surmounted by the bronze horses of Lysippus, and the roof itself is covered with gilded tiles. The temple has three separate cells, though covered with one roof; in front of each stand colossal statues of the three deities to whom it is consecrated. Here are preserved what was most sacred in the eyes of Romans, and it is itself the richest of all the temples of the city. What a beautiful panorama is presented to the view from the summit of this consecrated hill, only mounted by a steep ascent of one hundred steps. To the south is the Via Sacra extending to the Colosseum, and beyond it is the Appia Via, lined with monuments as far as the eye can reach. Little beyond the fora to the east is the Carinæ, a fashionable quarter of beautiful shops and houses, and still further off are the Baths of Titus, extending from the Carinæ to the Esquiline Mount. This hill, once a burial-ground, is now covered with the house and gardens of Mæcenas, and of the poets whom he patronized. It is not rich in temples, but its gardens and groves are beautiful. To the northeast are the Viminal and Quirinal hills, after the Palatine the most ancient part of the city — the seat of the Sabine population. Abounding in fanes and temples, the most splendid of which is the Temple of Quirinus, erected originally to Romulus by Numa, but

View from the summit of the Capitoline Hill.

rebuilt by Augustus, with a double row of columns on each of its sides, seventy-six in number. Near by was the house of Atticus, and the gardens of Sallust in the valley between the Quirinal and Pincian, afterwards the property of the emperor. Far back on the Quirinal, near the wall of Servius, were the Baths of Diocletian, and still further to the east the Pretorian Camp established by Tiberius, and included within the wall of Aurelian. To the northeast the eye lights on the Pincian Hill covered by the gardens of Lucullus, to possess which Messalina caused the death of Valerius Asiaticus, into whose possession they had fallen. In the valley which lay between the fora and the Quirinal was the celebrated Subura, — the quarter of shops, markets, and artificers, — a busy, noisy, vulgar section, not beautiful, but full of life and enterprise and wickedness. The eye now turns to the north, and the whole length of the Via Flaminia is exposed to view, extending from the Capitoline to the Flaminian gate, perfectly straight, the finest street in Rome, and parallel to the modern Corso. It is the great highway to the north of Italy. Monuments and temples and palaces line this celebrated street. It is spanned by the triumphal arches of Claudius and Marcus Aurelius. To the west of it is the Campus Martius, with its innumerable objects of interest, — the Baths of Agrippa, the Pantheon, the Thermæ Alexandrinæ, the Column of Marcus Aurelius, and the Mausoleum of Augustus. Beneath the Capitoline on the west, toward the river, is the Circus Flaminius, the Portico of Octavius, the Theatre of Balbus, and the Theatre of Pompey, where forty thousand spectators were accommodated. Stretching beyond the Thermæ Alexandrinæ, near the Pantheon, is the magnificent bridge which crosses the Tiber, built by Hadrian when he founded his Mausoleum, to which it leads, still standing under the name of the Ponte S. Angelo. The eye takes in eight or nine bridges

Gardens of Lucullus.

The Subura.

over the Tiber, some of wood, but generally of stone, of beautiful masonry, and crowned with statues. At the foot of the Capitoline, toward the southwest, are the Portico of Octavius and the Theatre of Marcellus, near the Pons Cestius. Still further southwest, between the Capitoline and the Aventine, in a low valley, are the Velabrum and the Forum Boarium, once a marsh, but now rich in temples and monuments, among which are those of Hercules Fortuna and Mater Matuta. There are no less than four temples consecrated to Hercules in the Forum Boarium, one of the most celebrated places in Rome, devoted to trade and commerce. Beyond still, in the valley between the Palatine and the Aventine, is the great Circus Maximus, founded by the early Tarquin. It is the largest open space inclosed by walls and porticoes in the city. It seats three hundred and eighty-five thousand people. How vast a city, which can spare nearly four hundred thousand of its population to see the chariot-races! Beyond is the Aventine itself. This also is rich in legendary monuments and in the palaces of the great, though originally a plebeian quarter. Here dwelt Trajan, before he was emperor, and Ennius the poet, and Paula, the friend of St. Jerome. Beneath the Aventine, and a little south of the Circus Maximus, west of the Appian Way, are the great baths of Caracalla, the ruins of which, next to those of the Colosseum, made on my mind the strongest impression of any thing that pertains to antiquity, though these were not so large as those of Diocletian. The view south takes in the Cælian Hill, the ancient residence of Tullus Hostilius. The beautiful Temple of Divus Claudius, the Arch of Dolabella, the Macellum Magnum, — a market founded by Nero, — the Castra Peregrina, the Temple of Isis, the Campus Martialis, are among the most conspicuous objects of interest. This hill is the residence of many distinguished Romans. It is covered with palaces. Among them is the

Circus Maximus.

View of Rome from the Capitol.

house of Claudius Centumalus — so high, that the augurs command him to lower it. It towers ten or twelve stories into the air. Scarcely inferior in size is the house of Mamura, whose splendor is described by Pliny. Here also is the house of Annius Verus, the father of Marcus Aurelius, surrounded with gardens. But grander than any of these palaces is that of Plautius Lateranus, the *egregiæ Lateranorum ædes*, which became imperial property in the time of Nero, and on whose site stands the basilica of St. John Lateran, — the gift of Constantine to the bishop of Rome, — one of the most ancient of the Christian churches, in which, for fifteen hundred years, daily services have been performed.

Such are the objects of interest and grandeur which strike the eye as it is turned toward the various quarters of the city. But these are only the more important. The seven hills, appearing considerably higher than at the present day, as the valleys are raised fifteen or twenty feet above their ancient level, are covered with temples, palaces, and gardens; the valleys are densely crowded with shops, houses, baths, and theatres. The houses rise frequently to the tenth platform or story. The suburban population, beyond the walls, is probably greater than that within. The city, virtually, contains between three and four millions of people. Lipsius estimates four millions as the population, including slaves, women, children, and strangers. Though this estimate is regarded as too large by Merivale and others, yet how enormous must have been the number of the people when there were nine thousand and twenty-five baths, and when those of Diocletian could accommodate three thousand two hundred people at a time. The wooden theatre of Scaurus contained eighty thousand seats; that of Marcellus would seat twenty thousand; the Colosseum would seat eighty-seven thousand, and give standing space for twenty-two thousand more. The Circus Maximus would hold three

Population.

hundred and eighty-five thousand spectators. If only one person out of four of the free population witnessed the games and spectacles at a time, we thus must have four millions of people altogether in the city. The Aurelian walls are now only thirteen miles in circumference, but Lipsius estimates the circumference at forty-five miles, and Vopiscus nearly fifty. The diameter of the city must have been eleven miles, since Strabo tells us that the actual limit of Rome was at a place between the fifth and sixth milestone from the column of Trajan in the Forum — the central and most conspicuous object in the city except the capitol.[1] Even in the sixth century, after Rome had been sacked and plundered by Goths and Vandals, Zacharia, a traveler, asserts that there were three hundred and eighty-four spacious streets, eighty golden statues of the gods; sixty-six large ivory statues of the gods; forty-six thousand six hundred and three houses; seventeen thousand and ninety-seven palaces; thirteen thousand and fifty-two fountains; three thousand seven hundred and eighty-five bronze statues of emperors and generals; twenty-two great horses in bronze; two colossi; two spiral columns; thirty-one theatres; eleven amphitheatres; nine thousand and twenty-six baths; two thousand three hundred shops of perfumers; two thousand and ninety-one prisons.[2] This seems to be incredible. "But," says Story, "Augustus divided the city into eighteen regions: each region contained twenty-two vici; each vicus contained about two hundred and thirty dwelling-houses, so that there must have been seventy-five thousand houses; of these houses, seventeen thousand were palaces, or domus. If each contained two hundred persons, (and four hundred slaves were maintained in a single palace,) reckoning family, freedmen, and slaves, we have three millions four hundred thousand people, and supposing the remaining fifty-eight thousand houses to have contained twenty-five

Number of houses.

[1] Strabo, lib. v. ch. 3.

[2] St. Ampère, *Hist. Romaine à Rome.*

persons each, we have in them one million four hundred and fifty thousand, which would give an entire population of four millions eight hundred and fifty thousand." If Mr. Merivale's estimate of seven hundred thousand is correct, then the Colosseum would hold nearly one in six of the whole population, which is incredible. Indeed, it is probable that even four millions was under than above the true estimate, which would make Rome the most populous city ever seen upon our globe. Nor is it extravagant to suppose this. The city numbered, according to the census, eighty thousand people in the year 197; and in 683 it had risen to four hundred and fifty thousand. Is it strange it should have numbered four millions in the time of Augustus, or even six millions in the time of Aurelian, when we bear in mind that it was the political and social centre of a vast empire, and that empire the world? If London contains three millions at the present day, and Paris two millions, why should not a capital which had no rival, and which controlled at least one hundred and twenty millions of people? So that Pliny was not probably wrong when he said, "*Si quis altitudinem tectorum addat, dignam profecto æstimationem concipiat, fateatur qui nullius urbis magnitudinem potuisse ei comparare.*" "If any one considers the height of the roofs, so as to form a just estimate, he will confess that no city could be compared with it for magnitude."

Modern writers, taking London and Paris for their measure of material civilization, seem unwilling to admit that Rome could have reached such a pitch of glory and wealth and power. To him who stands within the narrow limits of the Forum, as it now appears, it seems incredible that it could have been the centre of a much larger city than Europe can now boast of. Grave historians are loth to compromise their dignity and character for truth, by admitting statements which seem, to men of limited views, to be fabulous, and which transcend modern experience.

But we should remember that most of the monuments of ancient Rome have entirely disappeared. Nothing remains of the Palace of the Cæsars, which nearly covered the Palatine Hill; little of the fora which, connected together, covered a space twice as large as that inclosed by the palaces of the Louvre and Tuileries with all their galleries and courts; almost nothing of the glories of the Capitoline Hill; and little comparatively of those Thermæ which were a mile in circuit. But what does remain attests an unparalleled grandeur — the broken pillars of the Forum; the lofty columns of Trajan and Marcus Aurelius; the Pantheon, lifting its spacious dome two hundred feet into the air; the mere vestibule of the Baths of Agrippa; the triumphal arches of Titus and Trajan and Constantine; the bridges which span the Tiber; the aqueducts which cross the Campagna; the Cloaca Maxima, which drained the marshes and lakes of the infant city; but above all, the Colosseum. What glory and shame are associated with that single edifice! That alone, if nothing else remained of Pagan antiquity, would indicate a grandeur and a folly such as cannot now be seen on earth. It reveals a wonderful skill in masonry, and great architectural strength; it shows the wealth and resources of rulers who must have had the treasures of the world at their command; it indicates an enormous population, since it would seat all the male adults of the city of New York; it shows the restless passions of the people for excitement, and the necessity on the part of government of yielding to this taste. What leisure and indolence marked a city which could afford to give up so much time to the demoralizing sports! What facilities for transportation were afforded, when so many wild beasts could be brought to the capital from the central parts of Africa without calling out unusual comment! How imperious a populace that compels the government to provide such expensive pleasures! The games of Titus, on

The monuments which survive.

Games of Titus.

its dedication, last one hundred days, and five thousand wild beasts are slaughtered in the arena. The number of the gladiators who fought surpasses belief. At the triumph of Trajan over the Dacians, ten thousand gladiators were exhibited, and the emperor himself presides under a gilded canopy, surrounded by thousands of his lords. Underneath the arena, strewed with yellow sand and sawdust, is a solid pavement so closely cemented that it can be turned into an artificial lake on which naval battles are fought. But it is the conflict of gladiators which most deeply stimulates the passions of the people. The benches are crowded with eager spectators, and the voices of one hundred thousand are raised in triumph or rage as the miserable victims sink exhausted in the bloody sport.

But it is not the gladiatorial sports of the amphitheatre which most strikingly attest the greatness and splendor of the city; nor the palaces, in which as many as four hundred slaves are sometimes maintained as domestic servants, twelve hundred in number according to the lowest estimate, but probably five times as numerous, since every senator, every knight, and every rich man was proud to possess a residence which would attract attention; nor the temples, which numbered four hundred and twenty-four, most of which were of marble, filled with statues, the contributions of ages, and surrounded with groves; nor the fora and basilicæ, with their porticoes, statues, and pictures, covering more space than any cluster of public buildings in Europe, a mile and a half in circuit; nor the baths, nearly as large, still more completely filled with works of art; nor the Circus Maximus, where more people witnessed the chariot races at a time than are nightly assembled in all the places of public amusement in Paris, London, and New York combined — more than could be seated in all the cathedrals of England and France; it is not these which most impressively make us feel that Rome was the mistress of the world and the centre of all civilization. The triumphal processions of the conquering generals were still more exciting to behold, for these appeal more directly to the imagination, and excite those passions which urged the Romans to a career of conquest from generation to generation. No military review of modern times equaled those gorgeous triumphs, even as no scenic performance compares with the gladiatorial shows. The sun has never shone upon any human assemblage so magnificent and so grand, so imposing and yet so guilty. And we recall the picture of it with solemn awe as it moves along the Via Sacra and ascends the Capitoline Hill, or passes through the theatres of Pompey and Marcellus, that all the people might witness the brilliant spectacle. Not only were displayed the spoils of conquered kingdoms, and the triumphal cars of generals, but the whole military strength of the capital. An army of one hundred thousand men, flushed with victory, follows the gorgeous procession of nobles and princes. The triumph of Aurelian, on his return from the East, gives us some idea of the grandeur of that ovation to conquerors. "The pomp was opened by twenty elephants, four royal tigers, and two hundred of the most curious animals from every climate, north, south, east, and west. These were followed by one thousand six hundred gladiators, devoted to the cruel amusement of the amphitheatre. Then were displayed the arms and ensigns of conquered nations, the plate and wardrobe of the Syrian queen. Then ambassadors from all parts of the earth — all remarkable in their rich dresses, with their crowns and offerings. Then the captives taken in the various wars, Goths, Vandals, Samaritans, Alemanni, Franks, Gauls, Syrians, and Egyptians, each marked by their national costume. Then the Queen of the East, the beautiful Zenobia, confined by fetters of gold, and fainting under the weight of jewels, preceding the beautiful chariot in which she had hoped to enter the gates of Rome. Then the chariot of the Persian king. Then the triumphal

Roman triumphs

car of Aurelian himself, drawn by elephants. Finally the most illustrious of the Senate, the people, and the army closed the solemn procession, amid the acclamations of the people, and the sound of musical instruments. It took from dawn of day until the ninth hour for the procession to pass to the capitol, and the festival was protracted by theatrical representations, the games of the circus, the hunting of wild beasts, combats of gladiators, and naval engagements. Liberal donations were presented to the army, and a portion of the spoils dedicated to the gods. All the temples glittered with the offerings of ostentatious piety, and the Temple of the Sun received fifteen thousand pounds of gold. The soldiers and the citizens were then surfeited with meat and wine. The disbanded soldiery thronged the amphitheatre, and yelled their fiendish applause at the infernal games, — "the gorged robbers of the world, drunk in a festival of hell,"[1] — a representation of war as terrible as war itself, compensating to the Roman people the massacres which they could not see.

If any thing more were wanted to give us an idea of Roman magnificence, we would turn our eyes from public monuments, demoralizing games, and grand processions; we would forget the statues in brass and marble, which outnumbered the living inhabitants, so numerous that one hundred thousand have been recovered and still embellish Italy, and would descend into the lower sphere of material life — to those things which attest luxury and taste — to ornaments, dresses, sumptuous living, and rich furniture. The art of working metals and cutting precious stones surpassed any thing known at the present day. In the decoration of houses, in social entertainments, in cookery, the Romans were remarkable. The mosaics, signet rings, cameos, bracelets, bronzes, chains, vases, couches, banqueting tables, lamps, chariots, colored glass, gildings, mirrors, mattresses, cosmetics, perfumes, hair dyes, silk robes, potteries,

[1] Henry Giles.

all attest great elegance and beauty. The tables of thuga root and Delian bronze were as expensive as the sideboards of Spanish walnut, so much admired in the great exhibition at London. Wood and ivory were carved as exquisitely as in Japan and China. Mirrors were made of polished silver. Glass-cutters could imitate the colors of precious stones so well, that the Portland vase, from the tomb of Alexander Severus, was long considered as a genuine sardonix. Brass could be hardened so as to cut stone. The palace of Nero glittered with gold and jewels. Perfumes and flowers were showered from ivory ceilings. The halls of Heliogabulus were hung with cloth of gold, enriched with jewels. His beds were silver, and his tables of gold. Tiberius gave a million of sesterces for a picture for his bed-room. A banquet dish of Drusillus weighed five hundred pounds of silver. The cups of Drusus were of gold. Tunics were embroidered with the figures of various animals. Sandals were garnished with precious stones. Paulina wore jewels, when she paid visits, valued at $800,000. Drinking-cups were engraved with scenes from the poets. Libraries were adorned with busts, and presses of rare woods. Sofas were inlaid with tortoise-shell, and covered with gorgeous purple. The Roman grandees rode in gilded chariots, bathed in marble baths, dined from golden plate, drank from crystal cups, slept on beds of down, reclined on luxurious couches, wore embroidered robes, and were adorned with precious stones. They ransacked the earth and the seas for rare dishes for their banquets, and ornamented their houses with carpets from Babylon, onyx cups from Bythinia, marbles from Numidia, bronzes from Corinth, statues from Athens — whatever, in short, was precious or rare or curious in the most distant countries. The luxuries of the bath almost exceed belief, and on the walls were magnificent frescoes and paintings, exhibiting an inexhaustible productiveness in landscape and mythological scenes, executed in lively colors. From the praises of Cicero, Seneca, and Pliny, and other great critics, we have a right to infer that painting was as much prized as statuary, and equaled it in artistic excellence, although so little remains of antiquity from which we can form an enlightened judgment. We certainly infer from designs on vases great skill in drawing, and from the excavations of Pompeii, the most beautiful colors. The walls of the great hall of the baths of Titus represent flowers, birds, and animals, drawn with wonderful accuracy. In the long corridor of these baths the ceiling is painted with colors which are still fresh, and Raphael is said to have studied the frescoes with admiration, even as Michael Angelo found in the Pantheon a model for the dome of St. Peter's, and in the statues which were dug up from the ruins of the baths, studies for his own immortal masterpieces.

Thus every thing which gilds the material wonders of our day with glory and splendor, also marked the old capitol of the world. That which is most prized by us, distinguished to an eminent degree the Roman grandees. In an architectural point of view no modern city approaches Rome. It contained more statues than all the Museums of Europe. It had every thing which we have except machinery. It surpassed every modern capitol in population. It was richer than any modern city, since the people were not obliged to toil for their daily bread. The poor were fed by the government, and had time and leisure for the luxuries of the bath and the excitements of the amphitheatre. The citizen nobles owned whole provinces. Even Paula could call a whole city her own. Rich senators, in some cases, were the proprietors of twenty thousand slaves. Their incomes were known to be £1000 sterling a day, when gold and silver were worth four times as much as at the present day. Rome was made up of these citizen kings and their dependants, for most of the senators had been, at some time, governors of provinces, which they rifled and robbed. In Rome were accumulated the choicest treasures of the world. Her hills were covered with the palaces of the proudest nobles that ever walked the earth. Rome was the centre, and the glory, and the pride of all the nations of antiquity. It seemed impossible that such a city could ever be taken by enemies, or fall into decay. "*Quando cadet Roma cadet et mundus*," said the admiring Saxons three hundred years after the injuries inflicted by Goths and Vandals. Nor has Rome died. Never has she entirely passed into the hands of her enemies. A hundred times on the verge of annihilation, she was never annihilated. She never accepted the stranger's yoke — she never was permanently subjected to the barbarian. She continued to be Roman after the imperial presence had departed. She was Roman when fires, and inundations, and pestilence, and famine, and barbaric soldiers desolated the city. She was Roman when the Pope held Christendom in a base subserviency. She was Roman when Rienzi attempted to revive the virtues of the heroic ages, and when Michael Angelo restored the wonders of Apollodorus. And Roman that city will remain, whether as the home of princes, or the future capitol of the kings of Italy, or the resort of travelers, or the school of artists, or the seat of a spiritual despotism which gains strength as political and temporal power passes away before the ideas of the new races and the new civilization.

The most valuable book of reference for this chapter is the late work of Dr. Dyer, author of the article "Roma" in Smith's Dictionary. In fact this chapter is a mere compilation of that elaborate work, ("History of the City of Rome,") which may be said to be exhaustive. Mabillon and Montfauçon — two French Benedictines — rendered great service in the seventeenth century to Roman topography. Edward Burton and Richard Burgess wrote descriptions of Roman antiquities, now superseded by the writings of those great German scholars, who made a new epoch of Roman topography — Niebuhr,

Bunsen, Platner, Gerhard, and Röstell, who, however, have succeeded in throwing doubt on many things supposed to be established. One of the most learned treatises on ancient Rome is the celebrated *Handbuch* of Becker. Stephano Piale and Luigi Canina are the most approved of the modern Italian antiquarians.

CHAPTER IV.

ART IN THE ROMAN EMPIRE.

In my enumeration of the external glories of the Roman world, I only attempted to glance at those wonders which were calculated to strike a traveler with admiration. Among these were the great developments of Art, displayed in architecture, in statuary, and in painting. But I only enumerated the more remarkable objects of attraction; I did not attempt to show the genius displayed in them. But ancient art, as a proud creation of the genius of man, demands additional notice. We wish to know to what heights the Romans soared in that great realm of beauty and grace and majesty.

The æsthetic glories of art are among the grandest triumphs of civilization, and attest as well as demand no ordinary force of genius. Art claims to be creative, and to be based on eternal principles of beauty, and artists in all ages have claimed a proud niche in the temple of fame. They rank with poets and musicians, and even philosophers and historians, in the world's regard. They are favored sons of inspiration, urged to their work by ideal conceptions of the beautiful and the true. Their productions are material, but the spirit which led to their creation is of the soul and mind. Imagination is tasked to the uttermost to portray sentiments and passions. The bust is "animated," and the temple, though built of marble, and by man, is called "religious." Art appeals to every cultivated mind, and excites poetic feelings. It is impressive even to every order, class, and condition of men, not, perhaps, in its severest forms, since the taste must be cultivated to appreciate its higher beauties, but to a certain extent. The pyramids and the granite image temples of Egypt must have filled even the rude people with a certain awe and wonder, even as the majestic cathedrals of mediæval Europe, with their imposing pomps, stimulated the poetic conceptions of the Gothic nations. Art is popular. The rude savage admires a gaudy picture even as the cultivated Leo X. or Cardinal Mazarini bent in admiration before the great creations of Raphael or Domenichino. Art appeals to the senses as well as to the intellect and the heart, and is capable of inspiring the passions as well as the loftiest emotions and sentiments. The Grecian mind was trained to the contemplation of æsthetic beauty in temples, in statues, and in pictures; and the great artist was rewarded with honors and material gains. The love of art is easier kindled than the love of literary excellence, and is more generally diffused. It is coeval with songs and epic poetry. Before Socrates or Plato speculated on the great certitudes of philosophy, temples and statues were the pride and boast of their countrymen. And as the taste for art precedes the taste for letters, so it survives, when the literature has lost its life and freshness. The luxurious citizens of Rome ornamented their baths and palaces with exquisite pictures and statues long after genius ceased to soar to the heights of philosophy and poetry. The proudest triumphs of genius are in a realm which art can never approach, yet the wonders of art are still among the great triumphs of civilization. Zeuxis or Praxiteles may not have equaled Homer or Plato in profundity of genius, but it was only a great age which could have produced a Zeuxis or Praxiteles. I cannot place Raphael on so exalted a pinnacle as Luther, or Bacon, or Newton, and yet his fame will last as long as civilization shall exist. The creations of the chisel will ever be held in reverence by

Origin and principles of art.

Fascinations of art.

mankind, and probably in proportion as wealth, elegance, and material prosperity shall flourish. In an important sense, Corinth was as wonderful as Athens, although to Athens will be assigned the highest place in the ancient world. It was art rather than literature or philosophy which was the glory of Rome in the period of her decline. As great capitals become centres of luxury and display, artists will be rewarded and honored. The pride of a commercial metropolis is in those material wonders which appeal to the senses, and which wealth can purchase. A rich merchant can give employment to the architect, when he would be disinclined to reward the critic or the historian. Even where liberty and lofty aspirations for truth and moral excellence have left a state, the arts suffer but little decline. The grandest monuments of Rome date to the imperial regime, not to the republican sway. When the voice of a Cicero was mute, the Flavian amphitheatre arose in its sublime proportions. Imperial despotism is favorable to the adornment of Paris and St. Petersburg, even as wealth and luxury will beautify New York. When the early lights of the Church were unheeded in the old capitals of the world, new temples and palaces were the glory of the state. Art was the first to be revived of the trophies of the old civilization, and it will be the last to be relinquished by those whom civilization has enriched. Art excites no dangerous passions or sentiments in a decaying monarchy, and it is a fresh and perpetual pleasure, not merely to the people, but to the arbiters of taste and fashion. The Popes rewarded artists when they crushed reformers, and persecuted inquiring genius. The developments of art appeal to material life and interests rather than to the spiritual and eternal. St. Paul scarcely alludes to the material wonders of the cities he visited, even as Luther was insensible to the ornaments of Italy in his absorbing desire for the spiritual and moral welfare of society. Art is purely the creation of man. It

Development of art.

receives no inspiration from Heaven ; and yet the principles on which it is based are eternal and unchangeable, and when it is made to be the handmaid of virtue, it is capable of exciting the loftiest sentiments. So pure, so exalted, and so wrapt are the feelings which arise from the contemplation of a great picture or statue, that we sometimes ascribe a religious force to the art itself, while all that is divine springs from the conception of the artist, and all that is divine in his conception arises from sentiments independent of his art, as he is stimulated by emotions of religion, or patriotism, or public virtue, and which he could never have embodied had he not been a good man, rather than a great artist, or, at least, affected by sentiments which he learned from other sources. There can be no doubt that, through the vehicle of art, the grandest and noblest sentiments may be expressed. Hence artists may be great benefactors; yet sometimes their works are demoralizing, as they appeal to perverted taste and passions. This was especially true in the later days of Rome, when artists sought to please their corrupt but wealthy patrons. The great artists of Greece, however, had in view a lofty ideal of beauty and grace which they sought to realize without reference to profit, or worldly advantage, or utilitarian necessities. Art, when true and exalted, as it sometimes is, and always should be, has its end in itself. Like virtue, it is its own reward. Michael Angelo worked, preoccupied and wrapt, without the stimulus of even praise, even as Dante lived in the visions to which his imagination gave form and reality. Art is therefore self-sustained, unselfish, lofty. It is the soul going forth triumphant over external circumstances, jubilant and melodious even in poverty and neglect, rising above the evils of life in its absorbing contemplation of ideal loveliness. The fortunate accidents of earth are nothing to the true artist, striving to reach his ideal of excellence, — no more than carpets and chairs are

Glory of art.

to a great woman pining for sympathy or love. And it is only when there is this soul-longing to reach the excellence it has conceived for itself alone that great works have been produced. The sweetest strains of music sometimes come from women where no one listens to their melodies. Nor does a great artist seek or need commiseration, if ever so unfortunate in worldly circumstances. He may be sad and sorrowful, but only in the profound seriousness of superior knowledge, in that isolation to which all genius is doomed.

Great artists labor from inspiration.

We have reason to believe that the great artists of antiquity lived, as did the Ionic philosophers, in their own glorious realms of thought and feeling, which the world could neither understand nor share. Their ideas of grace and beauty were realized to the highest degree ever known on earth. They were expressed in their temples, their statues, and their pictures. They did not live for utilities. When art became a utility, it degenerated. It became more pretentious, artificial, complicated, elaborate, ornamental even, but it lacked genius, the simplicity of power, the glory of originality. The horses of the sun cannot be made to go round in a mill. The spiritual must keep within its own seclusion, in its inner temple of mystery and meditation.

Grecian art consecrated to Paganism.

Grecian art was consecrated to Paganism, and could not therefore soar beyond what Paganism revealed. It did not typify those exalted sentiments which even a Gothic cathedral portrayed — sacrifice; the man on the cross; the man in the tomb; the man ascending to heaven. Nor did it paint, like Raphael, etherial beauty, such as was expressed in the mother of our Lord, her whom all generations shall bless, *regina angelorum, mater divinæ gratiæ.* But whatever has been reached by the unaided powers of man, it reproduced and consecrated, and it realized the highest conceptions of beauty and grace that have ever been represented. All that the mind and

Greatness and beauty of Grecian art.

the soul could, by their inherent force, reach, it has attained. Modern civilization has no prouder triumphs than those achieved by the artists of Pagan antiquity in those things which pertain to beauty and grace. Grecian artists have been the schoolmasters of all nations and all ages in architecture, sculpture, and painting. How far they themselves were original we cannot decide, although they were probably somewhat indebted to the Assyrians and Egyptians. But they struck out so new a style, and so different from the older monuments of Asia and Egypt, that we consider them the great creators of art. But whether original or not, they have never been surpassed. In some respects their immortal productions remain objects of hopeless imitation. In the realization of ideas of beauty which are eternal, like those on which Plato built his system of philosophy, they reached absolute perfection. And hence we infer that art can flourish under Pagan as well as Christian influences. We can go no higher than those ancient Pagans in one of the proudest fields of civilization ; for art has as sincere and warm admirers as it had in Grecian and Roman times, but the limit of excellence has been reached. It is the mission of our age to apply creative genius to enterprises and works which have not been tried, if any thing new is to be found under the sun. Nor was it the number and extent of the works of art among the Greeks and Romans, nor their perfection, which made art so distinguishing an element of the old civilization. It was the spirit of the age, the absorption of the public mind, the great prominence which art had in the eyes of the people. Art was to the Greeks what tournaments and churches were to the men of the Middle Ages, what the Reformation was to Germany and England in the sixteenth century, what theories of political rights were to the era of the French Revolution, what mechanical inventions to abridge human labor are to us. The creation of a great statue was an era, an object of popular interest — the subject of universal comment. It kindled popular inspirations. It was the great form of progress in which that age rejoiced. Public benefactors erected temples, and lavished upon them the superfluous wealth of the State. And public benefactors, in turn, had statues erected to their memory by their grateful admirers. The genius of the age expressed itself in marble histories. And these histories stand in the mystery of absolute perfection — the glory and the characteristic of a great and peculiar people.

Grecian admiration of art.

Much has been written on those principles upon which art is founded, and great ingenuity displayed. But treatises on taste, on beauty, on grace, and other perceptions of intellectual pleasure, are not very satisfactory, and must be necessarily indefinite. In what does beauty consist? Do we arrive at any clearer conceptions of it by definitions? Whether beauty, the chief glory of the fine arts, consists in certain arrangements and proportions of the parts to a whole, or in the fitness of means to an end, or is dependent on associations which excite pleasure, or is a revelation of truth, or is an appeal to sensibilities, or is an imitation of Nature, or the realization of ideal excellence, it is difficult to settle and almost useless to inquire. "Metaphysics, mathematics, music, and philosophy have been called in to analyze, define, demonstrate, and generalize."[1] Great writers have written ingenious treatises, like Burke, Alison, and Stewart. Beauty, according to Plato, is the contemplation of mind; Leibnitz maintained it consists in perfection; Diderot referred beauty to the idea of relation; Blondel asserted it was harmonic proportions; Peter Leigh speaks of it as the music of the eye. Yet everybody understands what beauty is, and that it is derived from Nature, agreeable to the purest models which Nature presents. Such was the ideal of Phidias. Such was it to the minds of the Greeks, who united every ad-

Principles of art.

[1] Cleghorn, *Ancient and Modern Art*, vol. i. p. 67.

vantage, physical and mental, for the perfection of art. Nor could art have been so wonderfully developed had it not been for the influence which the great poets, orators, dramatists, historians, and philosophers exercised on the inspiration of the artists. Phidias, being asked how he conceived the idea of his Olympian Jupiter, answered by repeating a passage of Homer. We can scarcely conceive of the enthusiasm which the Greeks exhibited in the cultivation of art. Hence it has obtained an ascendency over that of all other nations. Roman art was the continuation of the Grecian. The Romans appreciated and rewarded Grecian artists. They adopted their architecture, their sculpture, and their paintings; and, though art never attained the estimation and dignity in Rome that it did in Greece, it still can boast of a great development. But, inasmuch as all the great models were Grecian, and appropriated and copied by the Romans, — inasmuch as the great wonders of the "Eternal City" were made by Greeks, —we cannot treat of Roman art in distinction from Grecian. And as I wish to show simply the triumph of Pagan genius in the realm of art, and most of the immortal creations of the great artists were transported to Rome, and adorned Rome, it is within my province to go where they were originally found.

Devotion of the Greeks for art.

> "Tu, regere imperio populos, Romane, memento!
> Hae tibi erunt artes."

The first development of art was in architecture, not merely among the Greeks, but among the older nations. Although it refers, in a certain sense, to all buildings, yet it is ordinarily restricted to those edifices in which we recognize the principle of beauty, such as symmetrical arrangement, and attractive ornaments, like pillars, cornices, and sculptured leaves.

Art first impressive in architecture.

The earliest buildings were houses to protect men from the inclemencies of the weather, and built without much regard to beauty; but it is in temples for the worship of

God, that architecture lays claim to dignity. It was the result of devotional feelings ; nor is there a single instance of supreme excellence in art being reached, which was not sacred, and connected with reverential tendencies. In the erection and decoration of sacred buildings there was a profound sentiment that they were to be the sanctuaries of God, and genius was stimulated by pious emotions. In India, in Egypt, in Greece, in Italy, the various temples all originated in blended superstition and devotion. Nor did the edifice, erected for religious worship, reach its culminating height of beauty and grandeur until that earnest and profoundly religious epoch which felt as injuries the insults offered to the tomb which covered the remains of the Saviour of the world. Then arose those hoary and Gothic vaults of Cologne and Westminster, the only modern structures which would probably have called out the admiration of an ancient Greek.

Egyptian architecture.

But architecture is conventional, and demands a knowledge of its system and a mind informed as to the principles on which it depends for beauty. Hence, in the oldest temples of India and Egypt, there was probably vastness, without elegance or even embellishment. But no nation ever left structures that, in extent and grandeur, can compare with those of ancient Egypt ; and these were chiefly temples. Nothing remains of the ancient monuments of Thebes but the ruins of edifices consecrated to the deity — neither bridges, nor quays, nor baths, nor theatres. It was when the Israelites were oppressed by Pharaoh that the great city of Heliopolis, which the Greeks called Thebes, arose, with its hundred gates, and stately public buildings, and magnificent temples. The ruins of these attest grandeur and vastness. They were built of stone, in huge blocks, and we are still at a loss to comprehend how such heavy stones could have been transported and erected. All the monuments of the Pharaohs are wonders of science and art, especially such as appear in the ruins of Carnack — a temple formerly designated as that of Jupiter Ammon. It was in the time of Sesostris, or Rameses the Great, the first of the Pharaohs of the nineteenth dynasty, that architecture in Egypt reached its greatest development. Then we find the rectangular cut blocks of stone in parallel courses, and the heavy piers, and the cylindrical column, with its bell-shaped capital, and the bold and massive rectangular architraves extending from pier to pier and column to column, surmounted by a deep covered coping or cornice. But the imposing architecture of Egypt was chiefly owing to the vast proportions of the public buildings. It was not produced by beauty of proportion, or graceful embellishments. It was designed to awe the people, and kindle sentiments of wonder and astonishment. So far as this end was contemplated, it was nobly reached. Even to this day the traveller stands in admiring amazement before those monuments which were old three thousand years ago. No structures have been so enduring as the Pyramids. No ruins are more extensive and majestic than those of Thebes. The temple of Carnack and the palace of Rameses the Great, were probably the most imposing ever built by man. This temple was built of blocks of stone seventy feet in length, on a platform one thousand feet long and three hundred wide, with pillars sixty feet in height. But this and other structures did not possess that unity of design, which marked the Grecian temples. Alleys of colossal sphinxes form the approach. At Carnack the alley was six thousand feet long, and before the main body of the edifice stand two obelisks commemorative of the dedication. The principal structures do not follow the straight line, but begin with pyramidical towers which flank the gateways. Then follows, usually, a court surrounded with colonnades, subordinate temples, and houses for the priests. A second pylon, or pyramidical tower, now leads to the interior and most con-

Monuments of Egypt.

Temple of Carnack.

siderable part of the temple, a portico inclosed with walls, which only receives light through the entablature or openings in the roof. Adjoining to this is the cella of the temple, without columns, inclosed by several walls, often divided into various small chambers, with monolith receptacles for idols or mummies or animals. The columns stand within the walls. The Egyptians had no perpetual temples. The colonnade is not, as among the Greeks, an expansion of the temple ; it is merely the wall with apertures. The walls, composed of square blocks, are perpendicular only on the inside, and beveled externally, so that the thickness at the bottom sometimes amounts to twenty-four feet, and thus the whole building assumes a pyramidical form, the fundamental principle of Egyptian architecture. The columns are more slender than the early Doric, are placed close together, and have bases of circular plinths ; the shaft diminishes, and is ornamented with perpendicular or oblique furrows, but not fluted like Grecian columns. The capitals are of the bell form, ornamented with all kinds of foliage, and have a narrow but high abacus, or bulge out below, and are contracted above, with low, but projecting abacus. They abound with sculptured decorations, borrowed from the vegetation of the country. The highest of the columns of the temple of Luxor is five and a quarter times the greatest diameter.[1]

Features of Egyptian art.

But no monuments have ever excited so much curiosity and wonder as the Pyramids, not in consequence of any particular beauty or ingenuity, as from their immense size and unknown age. None but sacerdotal monarchs would ever have erected them — none but a fanatical people would ever have toiled upon them. They do not indicate civilization, but despotism. We do not know for what purpose they were raised, except as sepulchres for kings. They do not even indicate as high a culture as the temples of Thebes, although they were built

The Pyramids.

[1] Müller.

at a considerable period subsequently, even several generations after Sesostris reigned in splendor. The pyramid of Cheops, at Memphis, covers a square whose side is seven hundred and sixty-eight feet, and rises into the air four hundred and fifty-two, and is a solid mass of stone, which has suffered less from time than the mountains near it. And it is probable that it stands over an immense substructure, in which may yet be found the lore of ancient Egypt, and which may even prove to be the famous labyrinth of which Herodotus speaks, built by the twelve kings of Egypt. According to this author, one hundred thousand men worked on this monument for forty years. What a waste of labor!

The palaces of the kings are mere imitations of the temples, and the only difference of architecture is this, that the rooms are larger and in greater numbers. Some think that the labyrinth was a collective palace of many rulers.

Such was the massive grandeur of Egyptian antiquities: at the best curiosities, but of slight avail for moral or æsthetic culture, they yet indicate a considerable civilization at a very remote period—proving not merely by architectural monuments, but by their system of writing, an original and intellectual people.[1]

Babylonian architecture.

Of Babylonian architecture we know but little, beyond what the Scriptures and ancient authors allude to in scattered notices. But, though nothing survives of ancient magnificence, we feel that a city whose walls, according to Herodotus, were eighty-seven feet in thickness, three hundred and thirty-seven in height, and sixty miles in circumference, and in which were one hundred gates of brass, must have had considerable architectural splendor. The Tower of Belus, the Palace of Nebuchadnezzar, and the Obelisk of Semiramis, were probably wonderful structures, certainly in size, which is one of the conditions of architectural effect.

[1] Müller, *Ancient Art;* Wilkinson, *Topog. of Thebes;* Champollion, *Lettres Écrites d'Egypt; Journal des Sav.* 1836; *Encyclopedia Britannica;* Strabo.

The Tyrians must have carried architecture to considerable perfection, since the Temple of Solomon, one of the most magnificent in the ancient world, was probably built by Phœnician artists. It was not remarkable for size; it was, indeed, very small; but it had great splendor of decoration. It was of quadrangular outline, erected upon a solid platform of stone, and having a striking resemblance to the oldest Greek temples, like those of Ægina and Pæstum. The portico of the temple, in the time of Herod, was one hundred and eighty feet high, and the temple itself was entered by nine gates thickly coated with silver and gold. The inner sanctuary was covered on all sides with plates of gold, and was dazzling to the eye. The various courts and porticoes and palaces with which it was surrounded, gave to it a very imposing effect.

Tyrian monuments.

Architecture, however, as the expression of genius and high civilization, was perfected only by the Greeks. Egyptian monuments were curiosities to the Greek and Roman mind, as they are to us objects of awe and wonder. And as we propose to treat of the arts in their culminating excellence chiefly, — to show what the Pagan intellect of man could accomplish, unaided by light from heaven, we turn to the great teacher of the last two thousand years. It was among the ancient Dorians, who descended from the mountains of Northern Greece eighty years after the fall of Troy, that art first appeared. The Pelasgi, supposed to be Phœnicians, erected cyclopean structures fifteen hundred years before Christ, as seen in the giant walls of the Acropolis,[1] constructed of huge blocks of hewn stone, and the palaces of the princes of heroic times,[2] like the Mycenæan treasury, the lintel of the doorway of which is one stone twenty-seven feet long and sixteen broad.[3] But these edifices, which aimed at splen-

Early Doric monuments.

1 *Dodwell's Classical Tour*, Müller.
2 Homer's description of the palace of Odysseus.
3 Mure, *Tour in Greece.*

dor and richness merely, were deficient in that simplicity and harmony which have given immortality to the temples of the Dorians. In this style of architecture every thing was suitable to its object, and was grand and noble. The great thickness of the columns, the beautiful entablature, the ample proportion of the capital; the great horizontal lines of the architrave and cornice, predominating over the vertical lines of the columns; the severity of geometrical forms, produced for the most part by straight lines, gave an imposing simplicity to the Doric temple. How far the Greek architects were indebted to the Egyptian we cannot tell, for though columns are found amid the ruins of the Egyptian temples, they are of different shape from any made by the Greeks. In the structures of Thebes we find both the tumescent and the cylindrical columns, from which amalgamation might have been produced the Doric column. The Greeks seized on beauty wherever they found it, and improved upon it. The Doric column was not, probably, an entirely new creation, but shaped after the models furnished by the most original of all the ancient nations, even the Egyptians. The Doric style was used exclusively until after the Macedonian conquest, and was chiefly applied to temples. The Doric temples are uniform in plan. The columns were fluted, and were generally about six diameters in height. They diminished gradually from the base, with a slight convexed swelling downward. They were superimposed by capitals proportionate, and coming within their height. The entablature which the column supported is also of so many diameters in height. So regular and perfect was the plan of the temple, that, "if the dimensions of a single column, and the proportion the entablature should bear to it, were given to two individuals acquainted with the style, with directions to compose a temple, they would produce designs exactly similar in size, arrangement, and general proportions." Then the Doric order possessed a peculiar har-

The principles of Doric achitecture.

mony, but taste and skill were nevertheless necessary in order to determine the number of diameters a column should have, and, accordingly, the height of the entablature. The Doric was the favorite order of European Greece for one thousand years, and also of her colonies in Sicily and Magna Græcia. The massive temples of Pæstum, the colossal magnificence of the Sicilian ruins, and the more elegant proportions of the Athenian structures, like the Parthenon and Temple of Theseus, show the perfection of the Doric architecture. Although the general style of all the Doric temples is so uniform, yet hardly two temples were alike. The earlier Doric was more massive; the latter were more elegant, and were rich in sculptured decorations. Nothing could surpass the beauty of a Doric temple in the time of Pericles. The stylobate or pedestal, from two thirds to a whole diameter of a column in height, was built in three equal courses, which gradually receded from the one below, and formed steps, as it were, of a grand platform on which the pillars rested. The column was from four to six diameters in height, with twenty flutes, with a capital of half a diameter supporting the entablature. This again, two diameters in height, was divided into architrave, frieze, and cornice. But the great beauty of the temple was the portico in front, a forest of columns, supporting the pediment, about a diameter and a half to the apex, making an angle at the base of about 14°. From the pediment projects the cornice, while, at the apex and at the base of it, are sculptured ornaments, generally, the figures of men or animals. The whole outline of columns supporting the entablature is graceful, while the variety of light and shade arising from the arrangement of mouldings and capitals produce a grand effect. The Parthenon, the most beautiful specimen of the Doric, has never been equaled, and it still stands august in its ruins — the glory of the old Acropolis, and the pride of Athens. It was built of Pentelic marble,

The features of the Doric order.

The Parthenon.

and rested on a basement of limestone. It was two hundred and twenty-seven feet in length, and one hundred and one in breadth, and sixty-five in height, surrounded with forty-eight fluted columns, six feet and two inches at the base, and thirty-four feet in height, while within the peristyle, at either end, was an interior range of columns, standing before the end of the cella. The frieze and the pediment were elaborately ornamented with reliefs and statues, while the cella, within and without, was adorned with the choicest sculptures of Phidias. The grandest was the colossal statue of Minerva, in the eastern apartment of the cella, forty feet in height, composed of gold and ivory; while the inner walls were decorated with paintings, and the temple itself was a repository of countless treasure. But the Parthenon, so regular, with its vertical and horizontal lines, was curved in every line, with the exception of the gable, — pillars, architrave, entablature, frieze, and cornice, together with the basement—all arched upwards, though so slightly as not to be perceptible, and these curved lines gave to it a peculiar grace which cannot be imitated, as well as solidity.

Nearly coeval with the Doric was the Ionic order, invented by the Asiatic Greeks, still more graceful, though not so imposing. The Acropolis is a perfect example of this order. The column is nine diameters in height, with a base, while the capital is more ornamented. The shaft is fluted with twenty-four flutes and alternate fillets, and the fillet is about a quarter the width of the flute. The pediment is flatter than of the Doric order, and more elaborate. The great distinction of the Ionic column is a base, and a capital formed with volutes, with a more slender shaft. Vitruvius, the greatest authority among the ancients in architecture, says that, "the Greeks, in inventing these two kinds of columns, imitated in the one the naked simplicity and dignity of a man, and in the other, the delicacy and ornaments of a

The Acropolis.

woman; the base of the Ionic was the imitation of sandals, and the volutes of ringlets."

The Corinthian order exhibits a still greater refinement and elegance than the other two, and was introduced toward the end of the Peloponnesian war. Its peculiarity is columns with foliated capitals, and still greater height, about ten diameters, with a more ornamented entablature. Of this order, the most famous temple in Greece was that of Minerva at Tegea, built by Scopas of Paros, but destroyed by fire four hundred years before Christ.

Temple of Minerva.

Nothing more distinguished Greek architecture than the variety, the grace, and the beauty of the mouldings, generally in eccentric curves. The general outline of the moulding is a gracefully flowing cyma, or wave, concave at one end, and convex at the other, like an Italic *f*, the concavity and convexity being exactly in the same curve, according to the line of beauty which Hogarth describes.

The most beautiful application of Grecian architecture was in the temples, which were very numerous, and of extraordinary grandeur, long before the Persian war. Their entrance was always to the west or the east. They were built either in an oblong or round form, and were mostly adorned with columns. Those of an oblong form had columns either in the front alone, in the fore and back fronts, or on all the four sides. They generally had porticoes attached to them. They had no windows, receiving their light from the door or from above. The friezes were adorned with various sculptures, as were sometimes the pediments, and no expense was spared upon them. The most important part of the temple was the cella, where the statue of the deity was kept, and was generally surrounded with a balustrade. Beside the cella was the vestibule, and a chamber in the rear or back front in which the treasures of the temple were kept. Names were applied to the

Architecture among the Greeks seen in greatest perfection in temples.

temples, as well as the porticoes, according to the number of columns in the portico at either end of the temple, such as the tetrastyle with four columns in front, or hexastyle when there were six. There were never more than ten columns in front. The Parthenon had eight, but six was the usual number. It was the rule to have twice as many columns along the sides as in front, and one more. Some of the temples had double rows of columns on all sides, like that of Diana at Ephesus, and of Quirinus at Rome. The distance between the columns varied from a diameter and half of a column to four diameters. About five eighths of a Doric temple were occupied by the cella, and three eighths by the portico.

Simplicity of Grecian temples.

That which gives so much simplicity and harmony in the Greek temples, which are the great elements of beauty in architecture, is the simple outline, in parallelogrammic and pyramidal forms, in which the lines are straight and uninterrupted through their entire length. This simplicity and harmony are more apparent in the Doric than in any of the other orders, and pertain to all the temples of which we have knowledge. Nor can any improvement be made upon them, or any alteration which does not conflict with established principles. The Ionic and Corinthian, or the Voluted and Foliated orders, do not possess that harmony which pervades the Doric, but the more beautiful compositions are so consummate that they will ever be taken as models of study.

It is not the magnitude of the Grecian temples and other works of art which most impresses us. It is not for this that they are important models. It is not for this that they are copied and reproduced in all the modern nations of Europe. They were generally small compared with the temples of Egypt, or the vast dimensions of Roman amphitheatres. Only three or four would compare in size with a Gothic cathedral, like the Parthenon, the Temple of Zeus at Olympia, and the Temple of Diana at Ephesus. Even the Pantheon at Rome is small, compared with the later monuments of the Cæsars. The traveler is always disappointed in contemplating their remains, so far as size is concerned. But it is their matchless proportions, their severe symmetry, the grandeur of effect, the undying beauty, the graceful form which impress us, and make us feel that they are perfect. By the side of the Colosseum they are insignificant in magnitude. They do not cover acres like the baths of Caracalla. Yet who has copied the Flavian amphitheatre? Who erects an edifice after the style of the Thermæ? But all artists copy the Parthenon. That, and not the colossal monuments of the Cæsars, reappears in the capitals of Europe, and stimulates the genius of a Michael Angelo or a Christopher Wren.

Matchless proportions of the Grecian temples.

The flourishing period of Greek architecture was during the period from Pericles to Alexander — one hundred and thirteen years. The Macedonian conquest introduced more magnificence and less simplicity. The Roman conquest accelerated the decline in severe taste, when different orders were used indiscriminately.

In this state the art passed into the hands of the masters of the world, and they inaugurated a new era in architecture. The art was still essentially Greek, although the Romans derived their first knowledge from the Etruscans. The Cloaca Maxima was built during the reign of the second Tarquin — the grandest monument of the reign of the kings. It is not probable that temples and other public buildings were either beautiful or magnificent until the conquest of Greece, when Grecian architects were employed. The Romans adopted the Corinthian style, which they made even more ornamental, and by the successful combination of the Etruscan arch with the Grecian column, laid the foundation of a new and original style, susceptible of great variety and magnificence. They entered into architecture with the enthusi-

Beginning of Roman art.

asm of their teachers, but, in their passion for novelty, lost sight of the simplicity which is the great fascination of a Doric Temple. "And they deemed that lightness and grace were to be attained not so much by proportion between the vertical and the horizontal, as by the comparative slenderness of the former. Hence we see a poverty in Roman architecture in the midst of profuse ornament. The great error was a constant aim to lessen the diameter, while they increased the elevation, of the columns. Hence the massive simplicity and severe grandeur of the ancient Doric disappear in the Roman, the characteristics of the order being frittered down into a multiplicity of minute details."[1] And when they used the Doric at all, they used the base, which was never done at Athens. They also altered the Doric capital, which cannot be improved. Again, most of the Grecian Doric temples were peripteral, that is, were surrounded with pillars on all the sides. But the Romans did not build with porticoes even on each front, but only on one, which had a greater projection than the Grecian. They generally are projected three columns. Many of the Roman temples are circular, like the Pantheon, which has a portico of eight columns projected to the depth of three. Nor did the Romans construct hypæthral temples, or uncovered, with internal columns, like the Greeks. The Pantheon is an exception, since the dome has an open eye; and one great ornament of this beautiful structure is in the arrangement of internal columns placed in the front of niches, composed with antæ, or pier-formed ends of walls, to carry an entablature round under an attic on which the cupola rests. They also adopted coupled columns, broken and recessed entablatures, and pedestals, which are considered blemishes. They again paid more attention to the interior than to the exterior decoration of their palaces and baths, as we may infer from the ruins of Adrian's villa at Tivoli, and the excavations of Pompeii.

Romans copied the Greeks.

[1] Memes, *Sculpture and Architecture.*

The Roman Corinthian, like the Greek orders, consisted of three parts, stylobate, column, and entablature, but the stylobate was much loftier, and was not graduated, except in the access before a portico. The column varied from nine and a half to ten diameters, and was always fluted with twenty-four flutes and fillets. The height of the capital is a diameter and one eighth; the entablature varies from one diameter and seven eighths to two diameters and a half. The portico of the Pantheon is one of the best specimens of the Corinthian order. The entablature of the temple of Jupiter Stator, like that of the Pantheon, is two diameters and one half. The pediments are steeper than those made by the Greeks, varying in inclination from eighteen to twenty-five degrees. The mouldings used in Roman architectural works are the same as the Grecian in general form, although they differ from them in contour. They are less delicate and graceful, but were used in great profusion. Roman architecture is overdone with ornament, every moulding carved, and every straight surface sculptured with foliage or historical subjects in relief. The ornaments of the frieze consist of foliage and animals, with a variety of other things. The great exuberance of ornament is considered a defect, although when applied to some structures it is exceedingly beautiful. In the time of the first Cæsars architecture had a character of grandeur and magnificence. Columns and arches appeared in all the leading public buildings, columns generally forming the external, and arches the internal construction. Fabric after fabric arose on the ruins of others. The Flavii supplanted the edifices of Nero, which ministered to debauchery, by structures of public utility.

The Romans invented no new principle in architecture, except the arch, which was not known to the Greeks, and carried out by them to greater perfection than by the Romans; but this, for simplicity, harmony, and beauty, has never been surpassed in any age, or by any nation.

The Romans were a practical and utilitarian people, and needed for their various structures greater economy of material than large blocks of stone, especially for such as were carried to great altitudes. The arch supplied this want, and is perhaps the greatest invention ever made in architecture. No instance of its adoption occurs in the construction of Greek edifices, before Greece became a part of the Roman Empire. Its application dates back to the Cloaca Maxima, and may have been of Etrurian invention. It was not known to Egyptians, or Persians, or Indians, or Greeks. Some maintain that Archimedes of Sicily was the inventor, but to whomsoever the glory of the invention is due, it is certain that the Romans were the first to make a practical application of its wonderful qualities. It enabled them to rear vast edifices into the air with the humblest materials, to build bridges, aqueducts, sewers, amphitheatres, and triumphal arches, as well as temples and palaces; its merits have never been lost sight of by succeeding generations, and it is at the foundation of the magnificent Gothic cathedrals of the Middle Ages. Its application extends to domes and cupolas, to arched floors and corridors and roofs, and to various other parts of buildings where economy of material and labor is desired. It was applied extensively to doorways and windows, and is an ornament as well as a utility. The most imposing forms of Roman architecture may be traced to a knowledge of the properties of the arch, and as brick was more extensively used than any other material, the arch was invaluable. The imperial palace on Mount Palatine, the Pantheon, except its portico and internal columns, the temples of Peace, of Venus and Rome, and of Minerva Medica, were of brick. So were the great baths of Titus, Caracalla, and Diocletian, the villa of Adrian, the city walls, the villa of Mecænas at Tivoli, and most of the palaces of the nobility; although, like many of the temples, they were faced with stone. The Colosseum

Changes made by the Romans.

Invention of the arch.

was of travertine faced with marble. It was the custom to stucco the surface of the walls, as favorable to decorations. In consequence of this invention, the Romans erected a greater variety of fine structures than either the Greeks or Egyptians, whose public edifices were chiefly confined to temples. The arch entered into almost every structure, public or private, and superseded the use of long stone beams, which were necessary in the Grecian temples, as also of wooden timbers, in the use of which the Romans were not skilled, and which do not really pertain to the art of architecture. An imposing building must always be constructed of stone or brick. The arch also enabled the Romans to economize in the use of costly marbles, of which they were very fond, as well as of other stones. Some of the finest columns were made of Egyptian granite, very highly polished.

Uses of the arch.

The extensive application of the arch doubtless led to the deterioration of the Grecian architecture, since it blended columns with arcades, and thus impaired the harmony which so peculiarly marked the temples of Athens and Corinth. And as taste became vitiated with the decline of the Empire, monstrous combinations took place, which were a great fall from the simplicity of the Parthenon, and the interior of the Pantheon.

But whatever defects marked the age of Diocletian and Constantine, it can never be questioned that the Romans carried architecture to a perfection rarely attained in our times. They may not have equaled the severe simplicity of their teachers, the Greeks, but they surpassed them in the richness of their decorations, and in all buildings designed for utility, especially in private houses and baths and theatres.

Magnificence of Roman architecture.

The Romans do not seem to have used other than semicircular arches. The Gothic, or Pointed, or Christian architecture, as it has been variously called, was the creation of the Middle Ages, and arose nearly simultaneously in Europe after the first Crusade, so that it would seem to be of Eastern origin. But it was a graft on the old Roman arch, — in the shape of an ellipse rather than a circle. Aside from this invention, to which we are indebted for the most beautiful ecclesiastical structures ever erected, we owe every thing in architecture to the Greeks and Romans. We have found out no new principles which were not equally known to Vitruvius. No one man was the inventor or creator of the wonderful structures which ornamented the cities of the ancient world. We have the names of great architects, who reared various and faultless models, but they all worked upon the same principles. And these can never be subverted. So that in architecture the ancients are our schoolmasters, whose genius we revere the more we are acquainted with their works. What more beautiful than one of those grand temples which the heathen but cultivated Greeks erected to the worship of their unknown gods: the graduated and receding stylobate as a base for the fluted columns, rising at regular distances, in all their severe proportion and matchless harmony, with their richly carved capitals, supporting an entablature of heavy stones, most elaborately moulded and ornamented with the figures of plants and animals, and rising above this, on the ends of the temple, or over a portico several columns deep, the pediment, covered by chiseled cornices, with still richer ornaments rising from the apices and at the feet; all carved in white marble, and then spread over an area larger than any modern churches, making a forest of columns to bear aloft those ponderous beams of stone, without any thing tending to break the continuity of horizontal lines, by which the harmony and simplicity of the whole are seen. So accurately squared and nicely adjusted were the stones and pillars of which these temples were built, that there was scarcely need of even cement. Without noise or confusion or sound of hammers did those temples

The effect of columns in architecture.

rise, since all their parts were cut and carved in the distant quarries, and with mathematical precision. And within the cella, nearly concealed by the surrounding columns, were the statues of the gods, and the altars on which incense was offered, or sacrifices made. In every part, interior and exterior, do we see a matchless proportion and beauty, whether in the shaft, or the capital, or the frieze, or the pilaster, or the pediment, or the cornices, or even the mouldings — everywhere grace and harmony, which grow upon the mind the more they are contemplated. The greatest evidence of the matchless creative genius displayed in those architectural wonders is that, after two thousand years, and with all the inventions of Roman and modern artists, no improvement can be made, and those edifices which are the admiration of our own times are deemed beautiful as they approximate the ancient models which will forever remain objects of imitation. No science can make two and two other than four. No art can make a Doric temple different from the Parthenon without departing from the settled principles of beauty and proportion which all ages have endorsed. Such were the Greeks and Romans in an art which is one of the greatest indices of material civilization, and which by them was derived from geometrical forms, or the imitation of Nature.

The genius displayed by the ancients in sculpture, is even more remarkable than in architecture. It was carried to perfection, however, only by the Greeks. But they did not originate the art, since we read of sculptured images from the remotest antiquity. The earliest names of sculptors are furnished by the Old Testament. Assyria and Egypt are full of relics to show how early this art was cultivated. It was not carried to perfection as early, probably, as architecture; but rude images of gods, carved in wood, are as old as the history of idolatry. The history of sculpture is in fact identified with that of idols. It was from Phœnicia that Solomon obtained the workmen for the decoration of his Temple. But the Egyptians were probably the first who made considerable advances in the execution of statues. They are rude, simple, uniform, without beauty or grace, but colossal and grand. Nearly two thousand years before Christ, the walls of Thebes were ornamented with sculptured figures, even as the gates of Babylon were of sculptured bronze. The dimensions of Egyptian colossal figures surpass those of any other nation. The sitting figures of Memnon at Thebes are fifty feet in height, and the Sphinx is twenty-five, and these are of granite. The number of colossal statues was almost incredible. The sculptures found among the ruins of Carnac must have been made nearly four thousand years ago.[1] They exhibit great simplicity of design, but without much variety of expression. They are generally carved from the hardest stones, and finished so nicely that we infer that the Egyptians were acquainted with the art of hardening metals to a degree not known in our times. But we see no ideal grandeur among any of the remains of Egyptian sculpture. However symmetrical or colossal, there is no expression, no trace of emotion, no intellectual force. Every thing is calm, impassive, imperturbable. It was not until sculpture came into the hands of the Greeks that any remarkable excellence was reached. But the progress of development was slow. The earliest carvings were rude wooden images of the gods, and more than a thousand years elapsed before the great masters were produced which marked the age of Pericles.

Perfection of Grecian sculpture.

It is not my object to give a history of the development of the plastic art, but to show the great excellence it attained in the hands of immortal sculptors.

The Greeks had an intuitive perception of the beautiful,

[1] Wilkinson's *Ancient Egyptians.*

and to this great national trait we ascribe the wonderful progress which sculpture made. Nature was most carefully studied, and that which was most beautiful in Nature became the object of imitation. They ever attained to an ideal excellence, since they combined in a single statue what could not be found in a single individual, as Zeuxis is said to have studied the beautiful forms of seven virgins of Crotona in order to paint his famous picture of Venus. Great as was the beauty of Thryne, or Aspasia, or Lais, yet no one of them could have served for a perfect model. And it required a great sensibility to beauty in order to select and idealize what was most perfect in the human figure. Beauty was adored in Greece, and every means were used to perfect it, especially beauty of form, which is the characteristic excellence of Grecian statuary. The gymnasia were universally frequented, and the great prizes of the games, bestowed for feats of strength and agility, were regarded as the highest honors which men could receive — the subject of the poet's ode and the people's admiration. Statues of the victors perpetuated their fame and improved the sculptor's art. From the study of these statues were produced those great creations which all subsequent ages have admired. And from the application of the principles seen in these forms we owe the perpetuation of the ideas of grandeur and beauty such as no other people have ever discovered and scarcely appreciated. The sculpture of the human figure became a noble object of ambition, and was most munificently rewarded. Great artists arose, whose works adorned the temples of Greece, so long as she preserved her indepenence; and when it was lost, their priceless productions were scattered over Asia and Europe. The Romans especially seized what was most prized, whether or not they could tell what was most perfect. Greece lived in her marble statues more than in her government or laws. And when we remember the es-

Admiration for sculpture among the Greeks.

High estimation of sculpture among the Greeks.

timation in which sculpture was held, the great prices paid for masterpieces, the care and attention with which they were guarded and preserved, and the innumerable works which were produced, filling all the public buildings, especially consecrated places, and even open spaces, and the houses of the rich and great, — calling from all classes admiration and praise, — it is improbable that so great perfection will ever be reached again in those figures which are designed to represent beauty of form. Even the comparatively few statues which have survived the wars and violence of two thousand years, convince us that the moderns can only imitate. They can produce no creations which were not surpassed by Athenian artists. "No mechanical copying of Greek statues, however skillful the copyist, can ever secure for modern sculpture the same noble and effective character it possessed among the Greeks, for the simple reason that the imitation, close as may be the resemblance, is but the result of the eye and hand, while the original is the expression of a true and deeply felt sentiment. Art was not sustained by the patronage of a few who affect to have what is called *taste.* In Greece, the artist, having a common feeling for the beautiful with his countrymen, produced his works for the public, which were erected in places of honor and dedicated in temples of the gods." [1]

But it was not until the Persian wars awakened in Greece the slumbering consciousness of national power, and Athens became the central point of Grecian civilization, that sculpture, like architecture and painting, reached its culminating point of excellence, under Phidias and his contemporaries. Great artists, however, had previously made themselves famous, like Miron, Polycletus, and Ageladas; but the great riches which flowed into Athens at this time gave a peculiar stimulus to art, especially under the encouragement of such a ruler as

Phidias and his contemporaries.

[1] *Encyclopedia Britannica*, "Sculpture," R. W. T.

Pericles, whose age was the golden era of Grecian history. Pheidias or Phidias was to sculpture what Æschylus was to tragic poetry, sublime and grand. He was born four hundred and eighty-four years before Christ, and was the pupil of Ageladas. He stands at the head of the ancient sculptors, not from what *we* know of him, for his masterpieces have perished, but from the estimation in which he was held by the greatest critics of antiquity. It was to him that Pericles intrusted the adornment of the Parthenon, and the numerous and beautiful sculptures of the frieze and the pediment were the work of artists whom he directed. *His* great work in that wonderful edifice was the statue of the goddess Minerva herself, made of gold and ivory, forty feet in height, standing victorious with a spear in her left hand and an image of victory in her right; girded with the ægis, with helmet on her head, and her shield resting by her side. The cost of this statue may be estimated when the gold alone of which it was composed was valued at forty-four talents.[1] Another of his famous works was a colossal bronze statue of Athena Promachus, sixty feet in height, on the Acropolis, between the Propylæa and the Parthenon. But both of these yielded to the colossal statue of Zeus in his great temple at Olympia, represented in a sitting posture, forty feet high, on a pedestal of twenty. In this, his greatest work, the artist sought to embody the idea of majesty and repose, — of a supreme deity no longer engaged in war with Titans and Giants, but enthroned as a conqueror, ruling with a nod the subject world, and giving his blessing to those victories which gave glory to the Greeks.[2] So famous was this

The statue of Zeus by Phidias.

[1] This sum was equal to $500,000 of our money, an immense sum in that age. Some critics suppose that this statue was overloaded with ornament, but all antiquity was unanimous in its admiration. The exactness and finish of detail were as remarkable as the grandeur of the proportions.

[2] The god was seated on a throne. Ebony, gold, ivory, and precious stones formed, with a multitude of sculptured and painted figures, the wonderful composition of this throne.

statue, which was regarded as the masterpiece of Grecian art, that it was considered a calamity to die without seeing it; and this served for a model for all subsequent representations of majesty and power in repose among the ancients. It was removed to Constantinople by Theodosius I., and was destroyed by fire in the year 475. Phidias executed various other famous works, which have perished; but even those that were executed under his superintendence, that have come down to our times, like the statues which ornamented the pediment of the Parthenon, are among the finest specimens of art which exist, and exhibit the most graceful and appropriate forms which could have been selected, uniting grandeur with simplicity, and beauty with accuracy of anatomical structure. His distinguishing excellence was ideal beauty, and that of the sublimest order.[1]

Colossal statues of ivory and gold.

Of all the wonders and mysteries of ancient art, the colossal statues of ivory and gold were perhaps the most remarkable, and the difficulty of executing them has been set forth by the ablest of modern critics, like Winkelmann, Heyne, and De Quincy. "The grandeur of their dimensions, the perfection of their workmanship, the richness of their materials; their majesty, beauty, and ideal truth; the splendor of the architecture and pictorial decoration with which they were associated, all conspired to impress the beholder with wonder and awe, and induce a belief of the actual presence of the god."

The school of Praxiteles.

After the Peloponnesian War, a new school of art arose in Athens, which appealed more to the passions. Of this school was Praxiteles, who aimed to please, without seeking to elevate or instruct. No one has probably ever surpassed him in execution. He wrought in bronze and marble, and was one of the artists who adorned the Mausoleum of Artemisia. Without attempt-

[1] Müller, *De Phidiæ Vita.*

ing the sublime impersonation of the deity, in which Phidias excelled, he was unsurpassed in the softer graces and beauties of the human form, especially in female figures. His most famous work was an undraped statue of Venus, for his native town of Cnidus, which was so remarkable that people flocked from all parts of Greece to see it. He did not aim at ideal majesty so much as ideal gracefulness, and his works were imitated from the most beautiful living models, and hence expressed only the ideal of sensual charms. It is probable that the Venus de Medici of Cleomenes was a mere copy of the Aphrodite of Praxiteles, which was so highly extolled by the ancient authors. It was of Parian marble, and modeled from the celebrated Phryne. His statues of Dionysus also expressed the most consummate physical beauty, representing the god as a beautiful youth, crowned with ivy, engirt with a nebris, and expressing tender and dreamy emotions. Praxiteles sculptured several figures of Eros, or the god of love, of which that at Thespiæ attracted visitors to the city in the time of Cicero. It was subsequently carried to Rome, and perished by a conflagration in the time of Titus. One of the most celebrated statues of this artist was an Apollo, many copies of which still exist. His works were very numerous, but chiefly from the circle of Dionysus, Aphrodite, and Eros, in which adoration for corporeal attractions is the most marked peculiarity, and for which the artist was fitted by his life with the hetæræ.

Scopas.

Scopas was his contemporary, and was the author of the celebrated group of Niobe, which is one of the chief ornaments of the gallery of sculpture at Florence. He flourished about three hundred and fifty years before Christ, and wrought chiefly in marble. He was employed in decorating the Mausoleum which Artemisia erected to her husband, one of the wonders of the world. His masterpiece is said to have been a group representing Achilles conducted to the island of Leuce by the divinities of the sea, which ornamented the shrine of Domitius in the Flaminian Circus. In this, tender grace, heroic grandeur, daring power, and luxurious fullness of life were combined with wonderful harmony.[1] Like the other great artists of this school, there was the grandeur and sublimity for which Phidias was celebrated, but a greater refinement and luxury, and skill in the use of drapery.

Lysippus.

Sculpture in Greece culminated, as an art, in Lysippus, who worked chiefly in bronze. He is said to have executed fifteen hundred statues, and was much esteemed by Alexander the Great, by whom he was extensively patronized. He represented men, not as they were, but as they appeared to be ; and, if he exaggerated, he displayed great energy of action. He aimed to idealize merely human beauty, and his imitation of Nature was carried out in the minutest details. None of his works are extant ; but as he alone was permitted to make the statue of Alexander, we infer that he had no equals. The Emperor Tiberius transferred one of his statues, that of an athlete, from the baths of Agrippa to his own chamber, which so incensed the people that he was obliged to restore it. His favorite subject was Hercules, and a colossal statue of this god was carried to Rome by Fabius Maximus, when he took Tarentum, and afterwards was transferred to Constantinople. The Farnese Hercules and the Belvidere Torso are probably copies of this work. He left many eminent scholars, among whom were Chares, who executed the famous Colossus of Rhodes, Agesander, Polydorus, and Athenodorus, who sculptured the group of the "Laocoon." The Rhodian School was the immediate offshoot from the school of Lysippus at Sicyon, and from this small island of Rhodes the Romans, when they conquered it, carried away three thousand statues. The Colossus was one of the wonders of the world, seventy

The works of Lysippus.

[1] Muller, 125.

cubits in height, and the Laocoon is a perfect miracle of art, in which group pathos is exhibited in the highest degree ever attained in sculpture. It was discovered in 1506 near the baths of Titus, and is one of the choicest remains of ancient plastic art.

The great artists of antiquity did not confine themselves to the representation of man; but they also carved animals with exceeding accuracy and beauty. Nicias was famous for his dogs, Myron for his cows, and Lysippus for his horses. Praxiteles composed his celebrated lion after a living animal. "The horses of the frieze of the Elgin Marbles appear to live and move; to roll their eyes, to gallop, prance, and curvet; the veins of their faces and legs seem distended with circulation. The beholder is charmed with the deer-like lightness and elegance of their make; and although the relief is not above an inch from the back-ground, and they are so much smaller than nature, we can scarcely suffer reason to persuade us they are not alive." [1]

The Greeks also carved gems, cameos, medals, and vases, with unapproachable excellence. Very few specimens have come down to our times, but those which we possess show great beauty both in design and execution.

Cameos and medals.

Grecian statuary commenced with ideal representations of deities, and was carried to the greatest perfection by Phidias in his statues of Jupiter and Minerva. Then succeeded the school of Praxiteles, in which the figures of gods and goddesses were still represented, but in mortal forms. The school of Lysippus was famous for the statues of celebrated men, especially in cities where Macedonian rulers resided. Artists were expected henceforth to glorify kings and powerful nobles and rulers by portrait statues. The plastic art then degenerated. Nor were works of original genius produced, but rather copies or varieties from the three great

[1] Flaxman, *Lectures on Sculpture.*

schools to which allusion has been made. Sculpture may have multiplied, but not new creations; although some imitations of great merit were produced, like the "Hermaphrodite," the "Torso," the Farnese "Hercules," and the "Fighting Gladiator." When Corinth was sacked by Mummius, some of the finest statues of Greece were carried to Rome, and after the civil war between Cæsar and Pompey the Greek artists emigrated to Italy. The fall of Syracuse introduced many works of priceless value into Rome; but it was from Athens, Delphi, Corinth, Elis, and other great centres of art, that the richest treasures were brought. Greece was despoiled to ornament Italy. The Romans did not create a school of sculpture. They borrowed wholly from the Greeks, yet made, especially in the time of Hadrian, many beautiful statues. They were fond of this art, and all eminent men had statues erected to their memory. The busts of emperors were found in every great city, and Rome was filled with statues. The monuments of the Romans were even more numerous than those of the Greeks, and among them some admirable portraits are found. These sculptures did not express that consummation of beauty and grace, of refinement and sentiment, which marked the Greeks; but the imitations were good. Art had reached its perfection under Lysippus; there was nothing more to learn. Genius in that department could soar no higher. It will never rise to loftier heights.

Sack of the Grecian cities.

It is noteworthy that the purest forms of Grecian art arose in its earlier stages. In a moral point of view, sculpture declined from the time of Phidias. It was prostituted at Rome under the emperors. The specimens which have often been found among the ruins of ancient baths make us blush for human nature. The skill of execution did not decline for several centuries; but the lofty ideal was lost sight of, and gross appeals to human passions were made by those who sought to

Degeneracy of art among the Romans.

please corrupt leaders of society in an effeminate age. The turgidity and luxuriance of art gradually passed into tameness and poverty. The reliefs on the Arch of Constantine are rude and clumsy compared with those on the Column of Marcus Aurelius.

But I do not wish to describe the decline of art, or enumerate the names of the celebrated masters who exalted sculpture in the palmy days of Pericles, or even Alexander. I simply allude to sculpture as an art which reached a great perfection among the Greeks and Romans, as we have a right to infer from the specimens which have been preserved. How many more must have perished, we may infer from the criticisms of the ancient authors! The finest productions of our own age are in a measure reproductions. They cannot be called creations, like the statue of the Olympian Jove. Even the Moses of Michael Angelo is a Grecian god, and the Greek Slave a copy of an ancient Venus. The very tints which have been admired in some of the works of modern sculptors are borrowed from Praxiteles, who succeeded in giving an appearance of living flesh. The Museum of the Vatican alone contains several thousand specimens of ancient sculpture which have been found among the debris of former magnificence, many of which are the productions of Grecian artists transported to Rome. Among them are antique copies of the Cupid and the Faun of Praxiteles, the statue of Demosthenes, the Minerva Medica, the Athlete of Lysippus, the Torso Belvidere, sculptured by Apollonius, the Belvidere Antinous, of faultless anatomy and a study for Domenichino, the Laocoon, so panegyrized by Pliny, the Apollo Belvidere the work of Agasias of Ephesus, the Sleepy Ariadne, with numerous other statues of gods and goddesses, emperors, philosophers, poets, and statesmen of antiquity. The Dying Gladiator, which ornaments the capitol, alone is a magnificent proof of the perfection to which sculpture was brought centuries

Imitation of ancient art.

after the art had culminated at Athens. And these are only a few which stand out among the twenty thousand recovered statues which now embellish Italy, to say nothing of those which are scattered over Europe. We have the names of hundreds of artists who were famous in their day. Not merely the figures of men are chiseled, but animals and plants. Nature, in all her forms, was imitated; and not merely Nature, but the dresses of the ancients are perpetuated in marble. No modern sculptor has equaled, in delicacy of finish, the draperies even of those ancient statues, as they appear to us after the exposure and accidents of two thousand years. No one, after a careful study of the museums of Europe, can question that, of all the nations who have claimed to be civilized, the ancient Greek and Roman deserve a proud preëminence in an art which is still regarded as among the highest triumphs of human genius. All these matchless productions of antiquity, it should be remembered, are the result of native genius alone, without the aid of Christian ideas. Nor, with the aid of Christianity, are we sure that any nation will ever soar to loftier heights than did the Greeks in that proud realm which was consecrated to Paganism.

We are not so certain in regard to the excellence of the ancients in the art of painting as we are in reference to sculpture and architecture, since so few specimens have been preserved. We have only the testimony of the ancients themselves; and as they had so severe a taste and so great susceptibility to beauty in all its forms, we cannot suppose that their notions were crude in this great art which the moderns have carried to so great perfection. In this art the moderns may be superior, especially in perspective and drawing, and light and shade. No age, we fancy, can surpass Italy in the fifteenth and sixteenth centuries, when the genius of Raphael, Correggio, and Domenichino blazed with such wonderful brilliancy.

Nevertheless, we read of celebrated schools among the ancients, all of which recognized *form* as the great prin ciple and basis of the art, even like the moderns. The schools of Sicyon, Corinth, Athens, and Rhodes were indebted for their renown, like those of Bologna, Florence, and Rome, to their strict observance of this fundamental law.

Painting, in some form, is very ancient, though not so ancient as the temples of the gods and the statues which were erected to their worship. It arose with the susceptibility to beauty of form and color, and with the view of conveying thoughts and emotions of the soul by imitation. The walls of Babylon were painted after Nature with different species of animals and combats. Semiramis was represented on horseback, striking a leopard with a dart, and her husband Ninus wounding a lion. Ezekiel (viii. 10) represents various idols and beasts portrayed upon the walls, and even princes, painted in vermilion, with girdles around their loins (xxiii. 14, 15). In ages almost fabulous there were some rude attempts in this art, which probably arose from the coloring of statues and reliefs. The wooden chests of Egyptian mummies are painted and written with religious subjects, but the colors were laid without regard to light and shade. The Egyptians did not seek to represent the passions and emotions which agitate the soul, but rather to authenticate events and actions; and hence their paintings, like hieroglyphics, are inscriptions. It was their great festivals and religious rites which they sought to perpetuate, not ideas of beauty or grace. Hence their paintings abound with dismembered animals, plants, and flowers, censers, entrails, — whatever was used in their religious worship. In Greece, also, the original painting consisted in coloring statues and reliefs of wood and clay. At Corinth, painting was early united with the fabrication of vases, on which were rudely painted figures of men and animals.

Antiquity of painting.

Painting among the Egyptians.

Among the Etruscans, before Rome was founded, it is said there were beautiful paintings, and it is probable they were advanced in art before the Greeks. There were paintings in some of the old Etruscan cities which the Roman emperors wished to remove, so much admired were they even in the days of the greatest splendor. The ancient Etruscan vases are famous for designs which have never been exceeded in purity of form, but it is probable that these were copied from the Greeks.

But whether the Greeks or the Etruscans were the first to paint, the art was certainly carried to the greatest perfection among the former. The development of it was, like all arts, very gradual. It probably commenced by drawing the outline of a shadow, without intermediate markings; the next step was the complete outline with the inner markings, such as are represented on the ancient vases, or like the designs of Flaxman. They were originally practiced on a white ground. Then light and shade were introduced, and then the application of colors in accordance with Nature. We read of a great painting by Bularchus, of the battle of Magnete, purchased by a king of Lydia seven hundred and eighteen years before Christ. And as the subject was a battle, it must have represented the movement of figures, although we know nothing of the coloring, or of the real excellence of the work, except that the artist was paid munificently. Cimon of Cleona is the first great name connected with the art in Greece, and is praised by Pliny, to whom we owe the history of ancient painting more than to any other author. He was contemporary with Dionysius in the eightieth Olympiad. He was not satisfied with drawing simply the outlines of his figures, such as we see in the oldest painted vases, but he also represented limbs, and folds of garments. He invented the art of foreshortening, or the various positions of figures, as they appear when looking upward or downward and sideways, and hence is the first painter of

Cimon of Cleona.

perspective. He first made muscular articulations, indicated the veins, and gave natural folds to drapery.[1]

A much greater painter than he was Polygnotus of Thasos, the contemporary of Phidias, who came to Athens about the year 463 B. C., one of the greatest geniuses of any age, and one of the most magnanimous; and had the good fortune to live in an age of exceeding intellectual activity. He was employed on the public buildings of Athens, and on the great temple of Delphi, the hall of which he painted gratuitously. He also decorated the Propylæa, which was erected under the superintendence of Phidias. His greatness lay in statuesque painting, which he brought nearly to perfection by the ideal expression, the accurate drawing, and improved coloring. He used but few colors, and softened the rigidity of his predecessors by making the mouth of beauty smile. He was the first who painted woman with brilliant drapery and variegated head-dresses. He gave great expression to the face and figure, and his pictures were models of excellence for the beauty of the eyebrows, the blush upon the cheeks, and the gracefulness of the draperies. He was a great epic painter, as Phidias was a sculptor, and Homer a poet, since he expressed not passion and emotion only, but ideal character. He imitated the personages and the subjects of the old mythology, and treated them in an epic spirit. He strove, like Phidias, to express character in repose. His subjects were almost invariably taken from Homer and the Epic cycle. His pictures had nothing of that elaborate grouping, aided by the powers of perspective, so much admired in modern art. His figures were grouped in regular lines, as in the bas-reliefs upon a frieze. He painted on panels which were afterward let into the walls. He used the pencil, instead of painting in encaustic with the cestrum.

Greatness of Polygnotus and his school.

Among the works of Polygnotus, as mentioned by

[1] Pliny, xxxv. 34.

Pliny,[1] are his paintings in the Temple at Delphi, in the Portico called Poecile at Athens, in the Propylæa of the Acropolis, in the Temple of Theseus, and in the Temple of the Dioscuri at Athens. He took his subjects from the whole range of Epic poetry, but we know nothing of them except from the praises of his contemporaries.[2] His great merit is said to have consisted in accurate drawing, and in giving grace and charm to his female figures. He painted in a truly religious spirit, and upon symmetrical principles, with great grandeur and freedom, resembling Michael Angelo more than any other modern artist. Like the Greeks, he painted with wax, resins, and in water colors, to which the proper consistency was given with gum and glue. The use of oil was unknown. The artists painted upon wood, clay, plaster, stone, parchment, but not upon canvas, which was not used till the time of Nero. They painted upon tablets or panels, and not upon the walls. These panels were framed and encased in the walls. The style or cestrum used in drawing, and for spreading the wax colors, was pointed on one end and flat on the other, and generally made of metal. Wax was prepared by purifying and bleaching, and then mixed with colors. When painting was practiced in water colors, glue was used with the white of an egg or with gums, but wax and resins were also worked with water, with certain preparations. This latter was called encaustic, and was, according to Plutarch, the most durable of all methods. It was not generally adopted till the time of Alexander the Great. Wax was a most essential ingredient, since it prevented the colors from cracking. Encaustic painting was practiced both with the cestrum and the pencil, and the colors were also burnt in. Fresco was used for coloring walls, which were divided into compartments or panels. The composition of the stucco, and the method of preparing the walls for painting, is described by

Peculiarities of Polygnotus.

Fresco painting.

[1] H. N. xxx. 9, s. 35. [2] Pausanias, x. 25–31.

the ancient writers: "They first covered the walls with a layer of ordinary plaster, over which, when dry, were successively added three other layers of a finer quality, mixed with sand. Above these were placed three layers of a composition of chalk and marble-dust, the upper one being laid on before the under one was dry, by which process the different layers were so bound together that the whole mass formed one beautiful and solid slab, resembling marble, and was capable of being detached from the wall and transported in a wooden frame to any distance. The colors were applied when the composition was still wet. The fresco wall, when painted, was covered with an encaustic varnish, both to heighten the color and preserve it from the effects of the sun or the weather. But this process required so much care, and was attended with so much expense, that it was used only in the better houses and palaces." The later discoveries at Pompeii show the same correctness of design in painting as in sculpture, and also considerable perfection in coloring. The great artists of Greece were both sculptors and painters, like Michael Angelo. Phidias and Euphranor, Zeuxis and Protogenes, Polygnotus and Lysippus, were both. And the ancient writers praise the paintings of these great artists as much as their sculpture. The Aldobrandini Marriage, found on the Esquiline Mount, during the pontificate of Clement VIII., and placed in the Vatican by Pius VII., is admired both for drawing and color. Polygnotus was praised by Aristotle for his designs and by Lucian for his color.[1]

Contemporaries of Polygnotus.

Dionysius and Micon were the great contemporaries of Polygnotus, the former of whom was celebrated for his portraits. His pictures were deficient in the ideal, but were remarkable for expression and elegant drawing.[2] Micon was particularly skilled in painting horses, and was the first who used for a color the

1 *Poetica of Aristotle*, c. 286. *Imagines of Lucian*, c. 7.
2 Plutarch, *Timol.* 36.

light Attic ochre, and the black made from burnt vine twigs. He painted three of the walls of the Temple of Theseus, and also the walls of the Temple of the Dioscuri.

The school of Apollodorus.

With Apollodorus, of Athens, a new development was made in the art of painting. Through his labors, about 408 B. C., dramatic effect was added to the style of Polygnotus, without departing from his pictures as models. "The acuteness of his taste," says Fuseli, "led him to discover that, as all men were connected by one general form, so they were separated each by some predominant power, which fixed character and bound them to a class. Thence he drew his line of imitation and personified the central form of the class to which his object belonged, and to which the rest of its qualities administered, without being absorbed; agility was not suffered to destroy firmness, solidity, or weight; nor strength and weight agility; elegance did not degenerate to effeminacy, nor grandeur swell to hugeness."[1] His aim was to deceive the eye of the spectator by the semblance of reality. He painted men and things as they really appeared. He also made a great advance in coloring. He invented chiaro-oscuro. Other painters had given attention to the proper gradation of light and shade; he heightened this effect by the gradation of tints, and thus obtained what the moderns call *tone*. He was the first who conferred due honor on the pencil — "primusque gloriam penicillo jure contulit."[2]

Peculiarities of Zeuxis as a painter.

This great painter prepared the way for Zeuxis,[3] who belonged to his school, but who surpassed him in the power to give ideal form to rich effects. He began his great career four hundred and twenty-four years before Christ, and was most remarkable for his female figures. His "Helen," painted from five of the most beautiful women of Croton, was one of the most renowned productions of antiquity, to see which the painter demanded

[1] Fuseli, Lect. I. [2] Pliny, H. N. xxxv. 11. [3] Born 455 B. C.

money. He gave away his pictures, because, with an artist's pride, he maintained that their price could not be estimated. There is a tradition that Zeuxis laughed himself to death over an old woman painted by him. He arrived at illusion of the senses, regarded as a high attainment in art, as in the instance recorded of his grapes. He belonged to the Asiatic school, whose head-quarters were at Ephesus, the peculiarities of which were accuracy of imitation, the exhibition of sensual charms, and the gratification of sensual tastes. He went to Athens about the time that the sculpture of Phidias was completed, which modified his style. His marvelous powers were displayed in the contrast of light and shade which he learned from Apollodorus. He gave ideal beauty to his figures, but it was in form rather than in expression. He taught the true method of grouping, by making each figure the perfect representation of the class to which it belonged. His works were deficient in those qualities which elevate the feelings and the character. He was the Euripides rather than the Homer of his art. He exactly imitated natural objects, which are incapable of ideal representation. His works were not so numerous as they were perfect in their way, in some of which, as in the Infant Hercules strangling the Serpent, he displayed great dramatic power.[1] Lucian highly praises his Female Centaur as one of the most remarkable paintings of the world, in which he showed great ingenuity in his contrasts. His Jupiter Enthroned is also extolled by Pliny, as one of his finest works. He acquired a great fortune, and lived ostentatiously.

Parrhasius of Ephesus

Contemporaneous with him, and equal in fame, was Parrhasius, a native of Ephesus, whose skill lay in accuracy of drawing, and power of expression. He gave to painting true proportion, and attended to minute details of the countenance and the hair. In his gods and heroes, he did for painting what Phidias did in sculpt-

[1] Lucian *on Zeuxis.*

ure. His outlines were so perfect as to indicate those parts of the figure which they did not express. He established a rule of proportion which was followed by all succeeding artists. While many of his pieces were of a lofty character, some were demoralizing. Zeuxis yielded the palm to him, since he painted a curtain which deceived his rival, whereas Zeuxis painted grapes which deceived only birds. He was exceedingly arrogant and luxurious, and boasted of having reached the utmost limits of his art. He combined the magic tone of Apollodorus with the exquisite design of Zeuxis, and the classic expression of Polygnotus.

Contemporaries of Zeuxis.

Many were the eminent painters that adorned the fifth century before Christ, not only in Athens, but the Ionian cities of Asia. Timanthes of Sicyon was distinguished for invention, and Eupompus of the same city founded a school. His advice to Lysippus is memorable — " Let Nature, not an artist, be your model." Protogenes was celebrated for his high finish. His Talissus took him seven years to complete. Pamphilus was celebrated for composition, Antiphilus for facility, Theon of Samos for prolific fancy, Apelles for grace, Pausias for his chiaro-oscuro, Nicomachus for his bold and rapid pencil, Aristides for depth of expression.

Art culminates in Apelles.

The art probably culminated in Apelles, the Titian of his age, who united the rich coloring and sensual charms of the Ionian with the scientific severity of the Sicyonian school. He was contemporaneous with Alexander, and was alone allowed to paint the picture of the great conqueror. He was a native of Ephesus, studied under Pamphilus of Amphipolis, and when he had gained reputation he went to Sicyon and took lessons from Melanthius. He spent the best part of his life at the court of Philip and Alexander, and painted many portraits of these great men and of their generals. He excelled in portraits, and labored so assiduously to perfect himself in drawing that he never spent a day without practicing.[1] He made great improvement in the mechanical part of his art, and also was the first who covered his picture with a thin varnish, both to preserve it and bring out the colors. He invented ivory black. His distinguishing excellence was grace, "that artless balance of motion and repose, springing from character, founded on propriety, which neither falls short of the demands nor overleaps the modesty of Nature."[2] His great contemporaries may have equaled him in perspective, accuracy, and finish; but he added a grace of conception and refinement of taste which placed him, by the general consent of ancient authors, at the head of all the painters of the world. His greatest work was his Venus Anadyomene, or Venus rising out of the sea, in which female grace was personified. The falling drops of water from her hair form a transparent silver veil over her form. It cost one hundred talents,[3] and was painted for the Temple of Æsculapius at Cos, and afterwards placed by Augustus in the temple which he dedicated to Julius Cæsar. The lower part of it becoming injured, no one could be found to repair it. Nor was there an artist who could complete an unfinished picture which he left. He was a man who courted criticism, and who was unenvious of the fame of rivals. He was a great admirer and friend of Protogenes of Rhodes, who was his equal in finish, but who never knew, as Apelles did, when to cease correcting.[4]

The Venus of Apelles.

After Apelles, the art of painting declined, although great painters occasionally appeared, especially from the school of Sicyon, which was renowned for nearly two hundred years. The destruction of Corinth by Mummius, B. C. 146, gave a severe blow to Grecian art. He carried

1 Pliny, xxxv. 12.

2 Fuseli, Lect. I.

3 £243×100=£24300×5=$121,500.

4 Cicero, *Brut.* 18; *De Orat.* iii. 7. Martial, xxx. 9. Ovid, *Art. Anc.* iii. 403. Pliny, xxxv. 37.

to Rome more works, or destroyed them, than all his predecessors combined. Sylla, when he spoiled Athens, inflicted a still greater injury, and, from that time, artists resorted to Rome and Alexandria and other flourishing cities for patronage and remuneration. The masterpieces of famous artists brought enormous prices, and Greece and Asia were ransacked for old pictures. The paintings which Æmilius Paulus brought from Greece required two hundred and fifty wagons to carry them in the triumphal procession. With the spoliation of Greece, the migration of artists commenced, and this spoliation of Greece and Asia and Sicily continued for two centuries; and such was the wealth of Rhodes in works of art that three thousand statues were found for the conquerors. Nor could there have been less at Athens, Olympia, or Delphi. Scaurus had all the public pictures of Sicyon transported to Rome. Verres plundered every temple and public building in Sicily.

Introduction of pictures into Rome.

Thus Rome was possessed of the finest paintings of the world, without the slightest claim to the advancement of the art. And if the opinion of Sir Joshua Reynolds is correct, art could soar no higher in the realm of painting, as well as of statuary. Yet the Romans learned to place as high value on the works of Grecian genius as the English do on the paintings of the old masters of Italy and Flanders. And if they did not add to the art, they gave such encouragement that, under the emperors, it may be said to have been flourishing. Varro had a gallery of seven hundred portraits of eminent men.[1] The portraits as well as the statues of the great were placed in the temples, libraries, and public buildings. The baths especially were filled with paintings.

High value placed by them on painting.

The great masterpieces of the Greeks were either historical or mythological. Paintings of gods and heroes, groups of men and women, in which

Subjects among the Greeks.

[1] Pliny, H. N. xxx. 2.

character and passion could be delineated, were the most highly prized. It was in the expression given to the human figure — in beauty of form and countenance, in which all the emotions of the soul as well as the graces of the body were portrayed — that the Greek artists sought to reach the ideal, and to gain immortality. And they painted for people who naturally had taste and sensibility.

Among the Romans, portrait, decorative, and scene painting engrossed the art, much to the regret of such critics as Pliny and Vitruvius. Nothing could be in more execrable taste than a colossal painting of Nero, one hundred and twenty feet high. From the time of Augustus, landscape decorations were common, and were carried out with every species of license. Among the Greeks we do not read of landscape painting. This has been reserved for our age, and is much admired, as it was at Rome in its latter days. Mosaic gradually superseded painting in Rome. It was first used for floors, but finally walls and ceilings were ornamented with it, like St. Peter's at Rome. Many ancient mosaics have been preserved which attest beauty of design of the highest character, like the Battle of Issus, lately discovered at Pompeii.

Landscape painting.

In fact, neither statuary nor painting was advanced by the Romans. They had no sensibility, or conception of ideal beauty. The divine spark of genius animated the Greeks alone. Still the wonders of Grecian art were possessed by the Romans, and were made to adorn those grand architectural monuments for which they had a taste. Greek productions were not merely matters of property, they were copied and reproduced in all the cities of the Mediterranean; and though no artist of original genius arose from Augustus to Constantine, galleries of art existed everywhere in which the masterpieces of Polygnotus, Pausias, Aristides, Timanthes, Zeuxis, Parrhasius, Pamphilus, Euphranor, Protogenes, Apelles, Timomachus, and of other illustrious men, were objects of as much praise as the galleries of Dresden and Florence.

"The glorious art of these masters, as far as regards tone, light, and local color," says Müller, "is lost to us, and we know nothing of it except from obscure notices and later imitations; on the contrary, the pictures on vases give us the most exalted idea of the progress and achievements of the arts of design."[1] It is surprising that, with four colors, the Greeks should have achieved such miracles of beauty and finish as are represented by the greatest cities of antiquity. The great wonders of the schools of Ephesus, Athens, and Sicyon have perished, and we cannot judge of their merits as we can of the statues which have fortunately been preserved. Whether Polygnotus was equal to Michael Angelo, Zeuxis to Raphael, and Apelles to Titian, we have no means of settling. But it is scarcely to be questioned that critics like the Greeks, whose opinions respecting architecture and sculpture coincide with our own, could have erred in their verdicts respecting those great paintings which extorted the admiration of the world, and were held, even in the decline of art, in such high value, not merely in the cities where they were painted, but in those to which they were transferred. What *has* descended to our times, like the mural decorations of Pompeii and the designs on vases, go to prove the perfection which was attained in painting, as well as sculpture and architecture.

Probable perfection of the ancients in painting.

And thus, in all those arts of which modern civilization is proudest, and in which the genius of man has soared to the loftiest heights, the ancients were not merely our equals: they were our superiors. It is greater to originate than to copy. In architecture, in sculpture, and in painting the Greeks attained absolute perfection. Any architect of our time, who should build an edifice in different proportions than those which were recognized

Perfection of art among the ancients.

[1] Müller, *Ancient Art*, 143.

in the great cities of antiquity, would make a mistake. Who can improve upon the Doric columns of the Parthenon, or the Corinthian capitals of the Temple of Jupiter? Indeed, it is in proportion as we accurately copy the faultless models of the age of Pericles that excellence with us is attained. When we differ from them we furnish grounds of just criticism. So, in sculpture, the Greek Slave is a reproduction of an ancient Venus, and the Moses of Michael Angelo is a Jupiter in repose. It is only when the artist seeks to bring out the purest and loftiest sentiments of the soul, and such as only Christianity can inspire, that he may hope to surpass the sculpture of antiquity in one department of the art alone — in expression, rather than beauty of form, on which no improvement can be made. And if we possessed the Venus of Apelles, as we can boast of having the sculptured Venus of Cleomenes, we should probably discover greater richness of coloring, as well as grace of figure, than in that famous Titian which is one of the proudest ornaments of the galleries of Florence, and one of the greatest marvels of Italian art.

REFERENCES. — Winckelmann's History of Ancient Art; Müller's Remains of Ancient Art; A. J. Guattani, Antiq. de la Grande Grèce; Mazois, Antiq. de Pomp.; Sir W. Gill, Pompeiana; Donaldson's Antiquities of Athens; Vitruvius, Stuart, Chandler, Clarke, Dodwell, Cleghorn, De Quincey. These are some of the innumerable authorities on Architecture among the ancients.

In Sculpture, Pliny and Cicero are the most noted critics. There is a fine article in the Encyclopedia Britannica on this subject. In Smith's Dictionary are the lives and works of the most noted masters. Müller's Ancient Art alludes to the leading masterpieces. Montfauçon's Antiquité expliquée en Figures; Specimens of Ancient Sculpture, by the Society of Diettanti, London, 1809; Ancient Marbles of the British Museum, by Taylor Combe; Millin, Introduction à l'Étude des Monumens Antiques; Monumens Inédits d'Antiquité figurée, recuellis et publiés par Raoul-Rochette; Gerhard's Archäol. Zeit.; David's Essai sur le Classement Chronol. des Sculpteurs Grecs les plus célèbres.

In Painting, see Caylus, Mémoires de l'ac des Inscr. Levesque, sur les Progrès successifs de la Peinture chez les Grecs; I. I. Grund, Mahlerei der Griechen; Meyer's Kunstgischichte; Müller, Hist. of Ancient Art; Article on Painting, Ency. Brit., Article "Pictura," Smith's Dict.; Fuseli's Lectures; Sir Joshua Reynolds' Lectures. Lanzi's History of Painting refers to the revival of the art. Vitruvius speaks at some length on ancient wall paintings. The finest specimens of ancient painting are found in catacombs, the baths, and the ruins of Pompeii. On this subject, Winckelmann is the great authority.

CHAPTER V.

THE ROMAN CONSTITUTION.

It is not from a survey of the material grandeur, or the arts, or the military prowess of Rome that we get the highest idea of her civilization. These indicate strength and even genius; but the checks and balances which were gradually introduced into the government of the city and empire, by which society was kept together, and a great prosperity secured for centuries, also show great foresight and practical wisdom. A State which favored individual development while it promoted law and order; which secured liberty, while it made the government stable and respectable; which guaranteed rights to the poorer citizens, while it placed power in the hands of those who were most capable of wielding it for the general good, is well worth our contemplation. The idea of aggrandizement was, it must be confessed, the most powerful which entered into the Roman mind; but the principles of national unity, the welfare of citizens, the reign of law, the security of property, the network of trades and professions, also received attention there. The aspirations for liberty and national prosperity never left the Roman mind. The Romans were great creators of civilization, though in a different sense from the Greeks. What the principles of art were to the Greeks, those of government were to the Romans. If the Greeks made statues, the Romans made laws. If the former speculated on the beautiful, or the good, or the true, the latter realized the boast of Diogenes — the power to govern men. The passion for government was the most powerful which a Roman citizen

The Roman creators of civilization.

The Romans sought to govern

felt, next to the passion for war. For five hundred years after the expulsion of the kings, there was the most perfect system of checks and balances in the government of the state known in the ancient world, and which is scarcely rivaled in the modern. Power was so wisely distributed that not even a successful general was able to gain a dangerous preëminence. Every citizen was a politician, and every Senator a statesman. For five hundred years there was neither anarchy nor military despotism. If every citizen knew how to fight, every citizen also knew how to govern, to submit. No consul dared to exceed his trust; no general, till Cæsar, ventured to cross the Rubicon. The Roman Senate never lost its dignity — a supreme body which controlled all public interests. The Romans were sufficiently wise to bend to circumstances. Though proud, the patricians made concessions to plebeians whenever it was necessary. The right of citizenship was gradually extended throughout the Empire. Paul lived in a remote city of Asia Minor, but, by virtue of his citizenship, could appeal to a higher court than that of the governor. The Romans succeeded, by their wisdom, in extending their institutions over the countries they had conquered; and every part of the Empire was well governed even when military despotism had overturned the ancient constitution. There were, of course, cases of extortion and injustice, and most governors made large fortunes; yet the provinces were better administered, and the rule was more in accordance with justice than under the native princes. Throughout the vast limits of the Empire, life and property were safe, and the roads were free of robbers; nor were there riots in the cities, except on very rare occasions, in which they were put down with merciless severity. Yet a few hundred men were enough to preserve order in the largest cities, and a few thousand in the most extensive provinces.

The Romans sought to govern through laws.

Even under the most tyrannical emperors, justice and order were enforced. The government was never better administered than by Tiberius, and further, was never better administered than when he was abandoned to pleasure in his guarded villa at Capri. There was the passion to govern the world, but in accordance with laws. The rule of the Romans was not that of brute force, even when the army was at the control of the Emperors. The citizens, to the last, enjoyed great social and political rights. They had great immunities, in reference to marriage, and the making of wills, and the possession of property. Their persons were secured from the disgrace of corporal punishment; they could appeal from the decision of magistrates; they were eligible to public offices; they were exempted from many oppressive taxes which still grind down the people in the most civilized states of Europe. The government of Octavius was the mildest despotism ever known to the ancient world. That Ulysses of state craft exercised the most extensive powers under the ancient forms, and all the early emperors disguised rather than paraded their powers. Contented with real power, the Roman was careless of its display. He had the tact to rule without seeming to rule; but rule he must, though not until he had first learned to obey — obedience to laws and domination were inseparably connected. This made the Roman yoke endurable, because it was not offensive or unjust. The Romans were masters of the world by conquest, yet ruled the world they had subdued by arms in accordance with laws based on the principles of equity. This sense of justice, in the enjoyment of unbounded domination, undoubtedly gave permanence to their government. The centurion was ever present to enforce a decree, but the decree was in accordance with justice. This was the idea, the recognized principle of government, although often abused. Paul appealed to Cæsar. He might have been released by the governor, had he not appealed. Here was justice to Paul in allowing the appeal; and still greater justice in keeping him in bonds until acquitted by Cæsar himself.

Roman sense of justice.

It must, however, be confessed that, after the Cæsars were fairly established on their throne, a great indifference to public affairs ensued. Every office was then, directly or indirectly, in the hands of the emperor. Cicero expressed the popular sentiment of his day when he said, "that was the most perfect government which was a combination of popular and aristocratic authority;"—but in the eighth century of the city, the system of checks and balances would have fallen to pieces in the hands of a degenerate people. A constitutional monarchy even was no longer possible. The vices of the oligarchy, and the fierce reactions of the democracy, had destroyed all the dreams of the earlier patriots. The mass of the people had long been passive under the sway of factions and political intriguers, and they resigned themselves to the despotism of the emperor without a struggle. But even in this degradation the power of government remained among the leading classes. The governors of provinces, taken generally from the Senate and the nobles, were skillful in their administration of public affairs. They were enlightened in all political duties. The traditional ideas of government survived for several generations, even as the mechanism of the army made it powerful after all real spirit had fled. The Roman still regarded himself as the favorite of the gods, destined to achieve a vast mission, even the reduction of the world to political unity. Augustus made every effort, while he reigned, in the ruin of political institutions, to revive the forms and traditions of other days. The patricians were favored and honored, and the Senate still was made to appear august, with a prostrate world at its feet, to which it was bound to dictate laws and institutions. Political unity was the grand idea of the Romans, and this idea has survived to our own times. It was one of the great elements of Roman civilization. Universal empire was based, in the better days of the Republic, on public morality,

Degeueracy under emperors.

Skill of the Romans for government.

On what the prosperity was based.

in the iron discipline of families, in a marvelously well-trained soldiery, in a military system which made the civil society an army almost ready for the field, in a recognition of public rights and duties, in a wise system of colonization, in conciliatory conduct to the conquered races, and in a central power as the dispenser of all honor and emoluments. The civil wars broke up, in a measure, this wise and considerate policy; still citizenship extended to all parts of the empire, even when it was manifest it must soon fall into the hands of barbarians. And as for the administration of justice, it was probably better conducted under the emperors than under the supreme rule of the Senate. Even bad emperors knew how to govern. To the Roman mind every thing was subordinate to the art of government. And every characteristic fitted the Romans to govern — energy of will, practical good sense, the conception of justice, an unyielding pride, fortitude, courage, and lust of power. And the spirit of domination was carried out into every thing. It was made a science, an art. Whatever would contribute to the ascendency of the state was remorselessly adopted; whatever would interfere with it was abandoned or swept away. Fierce and tolerant by turns, and as circumstances prompted — such was the Roman. With submission life was easy, and the government was mild. And the supreme government rarely entrusted power except to faithful, capable, and patriotic rulers. The wisest and best were selected for important offices. The governors of provinces were men of great experience; they were generals and senators who had passed their term of active service. They easily made great mistakes. They carried out the policy of the State. They were acquainted with laws, and the customs of the people whom they ruled. They were versed in the literature of their day. They were men of dignity and fortune. They were moderate, conciliatory, and firm. They were models for rulers for

Government the great art and science of the Romans.

all subsequent ages. There were, of course, exceptions, but the small number of riots and rebellions shows the contentment of the people, for they were not ground down by oppressive laws and exactions, until their spirit was broken. How munificent were the emperors to such cities as Athens and Alexandria! Athens was the seat of learning and culture, to the very end of the empire. Arts and literature and science were fostered in all the cities. They were adopted as parts of the empire, not treated like conquered territories. After the destruction of Carthage, the Romans had no jealousy of cities that once were equals. Their arts were made to subserve Roman greatness, indeed, but they were left free to develop their resources. The development of resources was a vital principle of the Roman government. Spain, Syria, and Egypt, were never more prosperous than under the imperial rule. All the provinces were more thriving under the emperors than they had been under their ancient kings, until the era of barbaric invasions. If war had been the mission of the republic, peace was the pride of the empire. There were no wars of importance for three hundred years, except those of necessity. The end of the emperors was to govern, to preserve peace, and secure obedience to the laws.

Prosperity of the government.

But we must bear in mind that, whatever were the popular rights enjoyed in the republican era, and however vast were the powers wielded by the emperors after liberty had fled, yet the constitution of Roman society was essentially aristocratic. All the great conquests were made under the rule of patricians, and all the leading men under the emperors were nobles. The government was virtually, from first to last, in the hands of the aristocracy. Still there was an important popular element, especially in the latter days of the republic, to which revolutionary leaders appealed, like the Gracchi, Marius, Catiline, and Cæsar. One of the most

The aristocracy the real rulers of the state.

humiliating lessons which we learn of antiquity, we are forced to own, was the signal incapacity of the people to govern themselves, when they had obtained a greater share of power than the old constitution had allowed. The republic did not long survive when successful generals and eloquent demagogues were sustained by the people. Had Rome been a democracy, as some suppose, the empire never could have been established. We comfort ourselves, however, by the reflection, that when the people surrendered themselves to factions and demagogues and tyrants, they were both ignorant and depraved. Self-government has never yet succeeded, because there have never been virtue and intelligence among the masses. So long as we can boast of virtue and intelligence among the people, we need not despair with the government in their hands. An enlightened self-interest will suggest the wisest policy. We only despair of the government of the people when they are ignorant, brutal, and wicked. As there was no period in the ancient world when they were not unenlightened, we are reconciled to the fact that a wise and vigorous administration of public affairs was always conducted by kings or nobles who had intelligence and patriotism, if they were proud and imperious. Whatever faith we may justly cherish in reference to popular sovereignty, grounded on the principles of natural justice, and the hopes which are held out as the fruit of Christian ideas, still, as a fact, there is but little in the history of the Roman commonwealth which reflects much glory on the people, except when controlled and marshalled by the aristocracy. Just so far as the popular element prevailed, the state was hurried on to ruin. The aristocratical element had the ascendency when Rome was most prosperous and most respected. Yet, while the Roman constitution was essentially aristocratic for five hundred years, it had a strong popular element mingled with it. The

Defects of Democratic ascendency.

The people unfit to govern when unenlightened.

Popular element in the Roman State.

patricians had the chief power, but they were not lords and masters in so absolute a sense as to trample on the people with impunity, nor were they able to deprive them of their rights, or of all share in the government. They were not feudal nobles, nor a Venetian oligarchy. And yet it were a mistake to suppose that the distinction between the classes implied that the aristocratic power was lodged with the patricians alone. The patricians were not necessarily aristocrats, nor the plebeians a rabble. The political distinctions passed away without destroying social inequalities. There were great families among the plebeians which really belonged to the aristocratic class, at least in the time of Cicero. Aristocracy may have been based on birth, as in England, but it was sustained by wealth, as in that country. A very rich man gained, ultimately, admission to the noble class, as Rothschild has in London. Without wealth to uphold distinctions, any aristocracy soon becomes contemptible. That organization of society is most aristocratic which confers great political and social privileges on a few men, and retains these privileges from generation to generation, as in France during the reign of Louis XV. The state of society at Rome under the republic, favored the monopoly of offices among powerful families. It was considered very remarkable for even Cicero to rise to the highest honors of the state with his magnificent genius, character, attainments, and services; but he shared the consulship with a man of very ordinary capacity. The great offices were all in the hands of the aristocracy, from the expulsion of the kings to the times of Julius Cæsar. Even the tribunes of the people ultimately were selected from powerful families.

Rich Plebeians had a great influence in the government.

The Roman people — *Romanus populus* — under the kings, the original citizens, were the warriors who built Rome, and conquered the surrounding cities and districts. They were called *patres*, which is sy-

The Patricians.

nonymous with Patricians.[1] They were united among themselves by kindred and by political and religious ties. They supported themselves by agriculture, although engaged continually in war. They consisted originally of three tribes, which gradually were united into the sovereign people. The first tribe was a Latin colony, and settled on the Palatine Hill; the second were Sabine settlers on the Quirinal; the third were Etruscans, who occupied the Cælian. They were distinct, at first, and were not united fully till the time of Tarquinius Priscus, himself an Etruscan.[2] As there were no other Roman citizens but these patricians, they had no exclusive rights under the kings, and hence there was then no aristocracy of birth. Each of these three tribes of citizens consisted of ten curiæ, and each curia of ten decuries, or gentes. The three tribes, therefore, contained three hundred gentes. A gens was a family, and the gentes were aggregates of kindred families.[3] The name of a gens was generally characterized by the termination *eia* or *ia*, as Julia, Cornelia, and it is to be presumed that each gens had a common ancestor. But with the growth of the city it came to pass that a gens often included a great number of families; we read of three hundred Fabii forming the gens Fabia in the year 275. These families composed, ultimately, the aristocracy. They were the people who filled all offices, and alone had the right of voting in the assemblies. As the gentes were subdivisions of the three ancient tribes, the *populus* alone had *gentes*, so that to be a patrician and to have a gens were synonymous. With the growth of Rome new gentes or families were added which did not claim descent from the ancient tribes. The powerful gens of the Claudia came to Rome with Atta Claudius, their head, after the expulsion of the kings. Tullus Hostilius incorporated the Julii, Servilii and other gentes with the patri-

The Roman *Gens.*

1 Cicero, *De Repub.*, ii. 12. Liv., i. 8.
2 Dionys., ii. 62.
3 Nieb., Lect. V.

cians. This ruling class, the descendants of the conquerors, became a powerful aristocracy, and ultimately learned to value pride of blood. There are very few names in Roman history, until the time of Marius, which did not belong to this noble class. What proud families were the Servilii, the Claudii, the Julii, the Cornelii, the Fabii, the Valerii, the Sempronii, the Octavii, the Sergii, and others.[1]

The *Equites* were originally elected from the patricians, and were cavalry soldiers, and did not form a distinct class till the time of the Gracchi. They were composed of rich citizens, whose wealth enabled them to become judices. They had the privilege of wearing a gold ring, and had seats reserved for them, like the Senate, at the theatre and circus. They increased in number with the increase of wealth, and formed an honorable corps from which the highest officers of the army and the civil magistrates were chosen. Admission to this body was an introduction to public life, and was a test of social position. It was composed of rich plebeians as well as patricians, and was based wholly on wealth. Pliny says, "It became the third order in the state, and to the title of *Senatus Populusque Romanus*, there began to be added, *et Equestris ordo*."

Beside this *Romanus populus*, which constituted the ruling class under kings, was another body, made up of conquered people. In early times their number was small, nor did they appear as a distinct class until the reign of Tullus Hostilius. After the subjection of Alba, the head of the Latin Confederacy, great numbers were transferred to Rome, and received settlements on the Cælian Hill, and were kept under submission to the patricians. As the Roman conquests extended, their numbers increased, until they formed the larger part of the population. They were called *plebs*, or commonalty, and had no political privileges whatever. They had not even the right of suffrage; but they were enrolled in

The Roman plebs.

[1] Liv., i. 33. Dionys., iii. 31.

the army,[1] and made to bear the expenses of the state. At first they were not allowed to intermarry with the patricians. Their oppression provoked resistance. The struggle which ensued is one of the most memorable in Roman history. The haughty oligarchy were obliged gradually to concede rights. These rights the *plebs* retained. First they gained a law which prevented patricians from taking usurious interest. They secured the appointment of tribunes for their protection. Soon after they had the right of summoning before their own *Comitia tributa* any one who violated their rights. In 449 they had influence sufficient to establish the Connubium, by which they could intermarry with patricians. In 421 the plebeians were admitted to the quæstorship. Then, after a fierce contest, they were made decemvirs. Their next right was the dignity of the consulship, and this led to the dictatorship. In 351 they secured the censorship, and in 336 the prætorship. Political distinctions now vanished. The possession of a share of the great offices created powerful families, and these were incorporated with the aristocracy. The great privilege of securing tribunes was the first step to political power, and the most important in the constitutional history of the state. And it was the tribunes who gradually usurped the greatest powers. They assumed the right, in 456, of convoking even the Senate. They also had the right to be present in the deliberations of the Senate; as their persons were inviolable, they interceded against any action which a magistrate might undertake during his term of office, and even a command issued by a prætor. They could compel the Senate to submit a question to a fresh consultation, and ultimately compelled the consuls to appoint a dictator. Their power grew to such a height that they acquired the right of proposing to the *Comitia tributa*, or the Senate, measures on nearly all

The tribunes.

Gradual increase of their power.

Their usurpations.

[1] Liv., i. 33. Dionys., iii. 31.

the important affairs of the state, and finally were elected from among the Senators themselves.

Advancement of the Plebeians.

Through the institution of tribunes, and other circumstances, especially the increase of wealth, the plebeians, originally so unimportant and insignificant that they could not obtain admission into the Senate, nor the high offices of state, nor the occupancy of the public lands, ultimately obtained all the rights of the patricians, so that gradually the political distinctions between patricians and plebeians vanished altogether, 286 B. C., and the term *populus* was applied to them as well as to the patricians.[1]

Gradual increase of their power.

These rights were only secured by bitter and fierce contests. The plebeians, during their long struggle, did not seek power to gratify their ambition, but to protect themselves from oppression. Nor was the power which they obtained abused until near the close of the Republic.

But while they ultimately were blended, politically, with the patricians, still the latter monopolized most of the great offices of the state until the time of Cicero, and socially, always were preëminent. Yet there were many noble plebeian families who were blended with the aristocratic class. Aristocracy survived, after the political distinctions between the two classes were abrogated. Rome was never a democracy. Great families, whether patrician or plebeian, controlled the State, either by their wealth or social connections. The Roman nobility was really composed of all the families rendered illustrious by the offices they had filled. And as the great officers were taken generally from the Senate, that body was particularly august.

The Senate.

Until the usurpation of Cæsar, the Senate was the great controlling power of the republic. It not only had peculiar privileges and powers, but a monop-

[1] Liv., iv. 44; v. 11, 12. Cicero *de Repub.*, ii. 37.

oly of offices. It always remained powerful, in spite of the victories of the plebeians. The laws proclaimed equality, but for fifty-nine years after the plebeians had the right of appointment as military tribunes, only eighteen were plebeians,[1] while two hundred and forty-six were patricians; and while the right of admission to the Senate was acknowledged on principle, yet no one could enter it without having obtained a decree of the censor, or exercised a curule magistracy, — favors almost always reserved for the aristocracy. The Senate was a judicial and legislative body, and numbered for several centuries but three hundred men, selected from the patricians. At first they were appointed by the kings, afterwards by the consuls, and subsequently by the censors. But as all those who had been appointed by the *populus* to the great offices had admission into this body, the people, that is, the patricians, virtually nominated the candidates for the Senate. But all magistrates were not necessarily members of the Senate, only those whom the censors selected from among them, and the curule magistrates during their office. It was from these curule magistrates that vacancies were filled up. The office of senator was for life. When the plebeians obtained the great offices, the Senate of course represented the whole people, as it formerly had represented the *populus*. But it was never a democratic assembly, for all its members belonged to the nobles. It required, under Augustus, 1,200,000 sesterces to support the senatorial dignity. Only a rich man could be, therefore, a senator. Nor could he carry on any mercantile business. The Senate was ever composed of men who had rendered great public services, or who were distinguished for wealth and talents. It was probably the most dignified and the proudest body of men ever assembled. The powers of the Senate were enormous. It had the general superintendence of matters of religion and foreign rela-

Character and defects of senators.

[1] *Hist. Julius Cæsar*, by Napoleon; chap. ii. 5.

tions; it commanded the levies of troops; it regulated duties and taxes; it gave audience to ambassadors; it proposed, for a long time, the candidates for office to the *Comitia;* it determined upon the way that war should be conducted; it decreed to what provinces the consuls and prætors should be sent; it appointed governors of provinces; it sent out embassies to foreign states; it carried on the negotiations with foreign ambassadors; it declared martial law in the appointment of dictators, and it decreed triumphs to fortunate generals. In short it was the supreme power in the state, and was the medium through which all the affairs of government passed. It was neither an hereditary, nor a popular body, yet represented the state — at first the patrician order, and finally the whole people, retaining to the end its aristocratic character. The senators wore on their tunics a broad purple stripe, — a badge of distinction, like a modern decoration, — and they had the exclusive rights of the orchestra at theatres and amphitheatres.[1] Under the emperors, the Senate was degraded, and was made entirely subservient to their will, and a mouth-piece; still it survived all the changes of the constitution, and was always a dignified and privileged body. It combined, in its glory, more functions than the English Parliament; it was convoked by the curule magistrates, and finally by the tribunes. The most ancient place of assembly was the Curia Hostilia, though subsequently many temples were used. The majority of votes decided a question, and the order in which senators spoke and voted was determined by their rank, in the following order: president of the Senate, consuls, censors, prætors, ædiles, tribunes, quæstors. Their decisions, called *Senatus Consulta*, were laws — *leges* — and were entrusted to the care of ædiles and tribunes.[2]

The prerogative of Senators.

Such was the Roman Senate — an assembly of nobles,

[1] See article in Smith's *Dict. of Ant.*, by Dr. Schmitz.

[2] Nieb. *Roman Hist.*, viii. p. 264.

whether patrician or plebeian. The descendants of all who had filled curule magistracies were *nobiles*, and had the privilege of placing in the atrium of the house the images and titles of their ancestors — an heraldic distinction in substance. And as the patricians carried back their pedigree to the remotest historical period, there was great pride of blood. Few plebeians could boast of a remote and illustrious ancestry, and every plebeian who obtained a curule office, was the founder of his family's nobility, like Cicero — a *novus homo*. This nobility contrived to keep possession of all the great offices, and it was difficult for a new man to get access to their ranks. The distinction of Patrician and Plebeian was secondary, after the *Gracchi*, to that of *Nobilitas*, yet it was rare to find a patrician gens the families of which had not enjoyed the highest honors many times over. Thus the aristocracy was composed of the families of those who had held the highest offices of the state; but as these offices were controlled by the Senate and enjoyed by the patricians chiefly, it was difficult to determine whether nobility was the result of patrician blood, or the possession of great offices. A man could scarcely be a patrician who had not held a great office; nor could he often hold a great office unless he were a patrician. The great offices were held in succession by the members of the Senate. The two consuls, the ten tribunes, the eight prætors in the time of Sulla — the twenty quæstors, together with the governors of provinces, and the generals who were selected from the Senate, or belonged to it, would necessarily compose a large part of the nobility, when their term of office lasted but a limited time, so that a senator with any ability was sure, in the course of his life, of the highest honors of the state.

The Senate composed of patricians and plebeians.

The Senate hold the great offices of state.

The great executive officers, therefore, belonged to the noble class, not of necessity, but as a general thing. Cicero was a *novus homo*, and yet rose by his talents to the highest dignities. It was rare, however, to confer the highest offices on those who had not distinguished themselves in war. Military fame, after all, gave the greatest prestige to the Roman name. Consuls commanded armies, but they would not have been chosen consuls except for military, as well as political, talent.

But only those who had distinguished themselves.

The consul was, after the abolition of the monarchy, the highest officer of the state. It was not till the year 366 B. C. that a plebeian obtained this dignity. The powers of consuls were virtually those of the old kings, with the exception of priestly authority. They convened the Senate, introduced ambassadors, called together the people, conducted elections, commanded the armies and never appeared in public without lictors. Nor were they shorn of their powers till Julius Cæsar assumed the dictatorship. The whole internal machinery of the state was under their control. But their term of office lasted only a single year. Their election took place in the *Comitia Centuriata.*

The consuls.

The censors were next in dignity, and like the consuls, there were two, and elected in the same manner under the presidency of a consul; only men of consular rank were chosen to this high office, and hence it was really higher than the consulship. The censors were chosen for a longer term than the consuls, and had the oversight of the public morals, the care of the census, and the administration of the finances. They could brand with ignominy the highest persons of the state, and could elect to the Senate, and exclude from it unworthy men. They had, with the ædiles, the control of the public buildings and all public works. They could take away from a knight his horse, and punish extravagance in living, or the improper dissolution of the marriage rite. They were held in the greatest reverence, and when they died were honored with magnificent funerals.

The censors.

Next in rank were the prætors, at first two in number, and ultimately sixteen. They exercised the judicial power, both in civil and criminal cases. The prætors.

The ædiles were also curule magistrates, and to them was entrusted the care of the public buildings, and the superintendence of public festivals. They were the keepers of the decrees of the Senate, and of the plebiscita. They superintended the distribution of water, the care of the streets, the drainage of the city, and the distribution of corn to the people. It was their business to see that no new deities were introduced, and they had the general superintendence of the police, and the inspection of baths. Their office entailed large expenses, and they were forced into great extravagance to gain popularity, as in the case of Julius Cæsar and Æmilius Scaurus; but the ædiles exercised extensive powers, which, however, were essentially diminished under the emperors. The ædiles.

Allusion has already been made to the tribunes in connection with the development of the plebeian power. At first they were only two, then increased to five, and finally to ten. It was their business to protect the plebs from the oppression of nobles, but their authority was so much increased in the time of Julius Cæsar that they could veto an ordinance of the Senate.[1] They not only could stop a magistrate in his proceedings, but command their viatores to seize a consul or a censor, to imprison him, or throw him from the Tarpeian rock.[2] The college of tribunes had the power of making edicts. After the passage of the Hortensian law, there was no power equal to theirs, and they could dictate even to the Senate itself. In the latter days of the republic, the tribunes were generally elected from among the senators. It was the vast influence which the people had obtained through the tribunes which led to the usurpation of Cæsar; for he, as The tribunes.

[1] Cæsar, *De Bell. Civ.*, 1, 2. [2] Liv. ii. 56, iv. 26; Cicero, *De Legibus*, iii. 9.

well as Marius, rose into power by courting them against the interests of the aristocracy.

The quæstors. The last of the great magistrates whose office entitled them to a seat in the Senate were the quæstors, who had charge of the public money. Originally only two in number, they were raised by Sulla to twenty, and by Cæsar to forty, for political influence. As the Senate had the supreme direction of the finances they were merely its agents or paymasters. The proconsul or prætor, who had the administration of a province, was attended with a quæstor to regulate the collection of the revenues. The quæstors also were the paymasters of the army.

Such were the great executive officers of the state, having a seat in the Senate, and belonging to the noble class by their official position as well as by birth. No one could be consul until he had passed through all these offices successively, except the censorship.

Pontifex Maximus. There was, however, another great Roman dignitary who held his office for life, which was one of transcendent importance. He was at the head of the college of priests, which had the superintendence of all matters of religion. The college of pontiffs, of which, under Julius Cæsar, there were sixteen, were not priests, but stood above all priests, and regulated the worship of the gods, and punished offenses against religion. The chief pontiff lived in a public palace in the Via Sacra, and might also hold other offices. It is a great proof of the talents of Cæsar and of the estimation in which he was held, that, at the age of thirty-seven, he was chosen to this high dignity, against the powerful opposition of Catulus, prince of the Senate, and when he had only reached the ædileship.

Assemblies of the people. In regard to the assemblies of the people, where they voted for the great officers of state, it must be borne in mind that they were not made up of the rabble, but of the populus or the patricians till nearly the close of the republic. Each of the thirty curia had its building for the discussion of political and legal questions. They had also collectively an assembly, called *Comitia Curiata*, where the people voted on the measures proposed by the magistrates. The votes were given by the curiæ, each curia having one collective vote. The assembly originated nothing, but decided upon the life of Roman citizens, upon peace and war, and the election of magistrates. This was the primitive form under the kings. But Servius Tullius instituted the *Comitia Centuriata*, and hence divided the populus into six property classes, and one hundred and ninety-three centuriæ. The first class was composed of ninety-eight centuriæ, with a property qualification of one hundred thousand asses; the second of twenty-two centuriæ with seventy-five thousand asses; the third of twenty, with fifty thousand asses; the fourth of twenty-two, with twenty-five thousand asses; the fifth of thirty, with eleven thousand asses; and the sixth of any one of those below twelve and a half minæ. Yet this class was the most numerous. The wealthier classes voted first, and when a majority of the centuries was obtained the voting stopped. Hence the power was virtually in the hands of the rich; for, united, they made a majority before the poorer classes were called upon to vote. The *Comitia Centuriata* elected the magistrates and made laws, and formed the highest court of appeal, but all its decisions had to be sanctioned by the curiæ, although in course of time the curia was a formality. The centuries met in the Campus Martius, and were presided over by the consuls, who read the names of the candidates. In the assemblies by centuries, the vote of the first class prevailed over all the others; in the *comitia* by curiæ the patricians were supreme.

The Comitia Centuriata.

The *Comitia Tributa* represented the thirty Roman tribes according to the Servian constitution, to whom was originally given the right to elect in-

The Comitia Tributa.

ferior magistrates. This was a plebian assembly, and had very insignificant powers, chiefly relating to the local affairs of the tribes. But when these tribes began to be real representatives of the people, with the increase of the plebeian classes, matters affecting the whole state were brought before them by the tribunes. This gave to the assembly the initiative of measures, which was sanctioned by a law of L. Valerius Publicola, B. C. 449. This law gave to the decrees passed by the tribes the power of a real *lex*, binding upon the whole people, provided it had the sanction of the Senate and the populus in the *Comitia Centuriata*. In 287 B. C. the Hortensian law made the plebiscita independent of the sanction of the Senate. When the plebeians began to be recognized as an essential element in the state, it was found inconvenient to have the first class, which included the equites, so greatly preponderant in the comitia of the centuries; and it was designed to blend the *Comitia Centuriata* and *the Tributa* in such a manner as to make only one assembly. This took place after the completion of the thirty-five tribes, B. C. 241. The citizens of each tribe were divided into five property classes, and each tribe into ten centuries, making three hundred and fifty centuries. This comitia was far more democratic than the comitia of the centuries, and was guided by the tribunes. When all the Italians were incorporated with the thirty-five tribes, violence and bribery became the order of the day. Sulla took away the jurisdiction of the people, and Julius Cæsar encroached still more on popular rights when he decided upon peace and war in connection with the Senate—which great question was formerly settled by the comitia alone. The people retained nothing under him but the election of magistrates, which amounted to little, since Cæsar had the right to appoint half the magistrates himself, with the exception of the consuls. After the death of Cæsar, the comitia continued to be held, but was always controlled by the rulers, whose unlimited

Decline of power of the comitia.

powers were ultimately complied with without resistance. Finally the comitia became a mere farce, and all legislation passed away forever, and was completely in the hands of the emperor and Senate.

Thus it would appear that the Roman constitution was essentially aristocratic, especially for three hundred years after the expulsion of kings. The *Senate* and the *populus* had the whole power. Gradually, as wealth increased, the *equites* became an influential order, not less aristocratical than the patricians. The *plebs* were not of much consideration till the time of the Gracchi, and always obtained office with difficulty. It was two hundred years after the expulsion of kings before the plebeians could even obtain a share of the public lands. So long as the aristocracy preserved their virtue and patriotism, the state was most ably administered, and continually increased in wealth and power. The conquest of Italy was entirely under the regime of nobles, and even when wealthy plebeian families mingled with the ancient patricians there was still great difficulty in reaching preferment, without the advantages of birth.[1] In fourteen years, from 399 to 412, the patricians allowed only six plebeians to reach the consulship. The lives of the citizens were protected by the laws, but public opinion remained powerless at the assassination of those who incurred the hatred of the Senate. The comitia were free, but the Senate had at its disposal either the veto of the tribunes or the religious scruples of the people, for a consul could prevent the meeting of the assemblies, and the augurs could cut short their deliberations. Even the dictatorship was often a means of oppressing the plebs, and was a lever in the hands of the aristocracy, since the dictator was appointed by the consuls under the direction of the Senate.[2] He was a patrician as a matter of course, until the political distinctions between patrician and plebeian were

The nobles retain the chief ascendency.

The dictator

[1] Mommsen, *Roman Hist.*, i. p. 241.

[2] Liv., viii. 23.

removed, and had absolute authority for six months. He was not held responsible for his acts while in office,[1] nor was there any appeal from his decisions. He was preceded by twenty-four lictors, and was virtually supreme. Between 390 and 416 there were eighteen dictators. The Senate thus remained all-powerful, in spite of the victories of the plebeians, and such were its patriotism and intelligence that it preserved its preponderance. It was during the conquest of Italy that aristocratic power shone in all its splendor, and the most able men were entrusted with public affairs. Every thing was sacrificed to patriotism, and discipline was enforced with cruelty. The most powerful patricians readily exposed their lives in battle, and a town became a people which ultimately embraced the world. When the plebeians had grown to be a power the decline of the republic commenced, and a new organization was necessary. Great chieftains became dictators for life, and the imperial sceptre was seized by an unscrupulous but enlightened general. The Roman *populus* in an important sense carried out the great idea of self-government, but, strictly speaking, self-government, as applied to the people generally, never existed in the Roman Commonwealth. But the idea was advanced which gave birth to future republics. Nor did the fall of the old patrician oligarchy divest the Roman commonwealth of its aristocratic character, for a new aristocracy arose. When the plebeian families obtained the consulate and other high offices of state, they were put on a level with the old patrician families, and were allowed the privilege of placing the wax images of their illustrious ancestors in the family hall, and to have these images carried in the funeral procession. As curule magistrates, they had a seat in the Senate, and wore the insignia of rank — the gold finger-ring and the purple border on the toga. "The result of the Licinian

The idea of popular government.

[1] Becker, *Handbuch der Romanisch Alterthümer*, vii. p. 2; Nieb. *History of Rome*, vol. i. p. 563.

laws," says Mommsen, "in reality, only amounted to what we now call the creation of a new batch of officers."[1] As all the descendants of those who had enjoyed the curule magistracy were entitled to the privilege of these distinctions, the nobility became hereditary. And as the great officers of state were generally selected from this class, since they controlled the comitia, the nobility was not merely hereditary, but it was a *governing* nobility. The nobility had the possession of the Senate itself. It monopolized the great offices of state. The stability of the Roman aristocracy is seen in the fact, that, from the year 388 to 581, when the consulate was held by one patrician and one plebeian, one hundred and forty of the consuls, out of the three hundred and eighty-six, belonged to sixteen great houses. The Cornelii furnished thirty consuls in one hundred and ninety-three years, the Valerii eighteen, the Claudii twelve, the Æmilii fifteen, the Fabii twelve, the Manlii ten, the Postumii eight, the Servilii seven, the Sulpicii eight, the Papirii four, to say nothing of other curule offices. Thus the nobility was not composed exclusively of patrician families, although these were the most numerous, but of old plebeian families also, in the same way that the English House of Lords is composed of families which trace their origin to Saxons as well as Normans, although the Normans, for several centuries, were the governing class. And as the House of Lords has accessions occasionally from the ranks of the people, in consequence of great wealth, or political interest, or eminent genius, or signal success in war, so the Roman nobility was increased, as old families died out, by the successful generals who gained the great offices of state. Marius arose from the people, but his exploits in the field of battle insured his entrance among the nobility in consequence of the offices he held, even as the Lord Chancellors of England, who have been eminent lawyers merely, are made herditary peers in consequence of their judicial position.

The Senate retains all real power.

[1] Mommsen, B. III. c. xi.

The Roman burgesses again were any thing but a rabble. They were composed of men of standing and wealth. If they did not compose the motive-power, they constituted a firm foundation of the state. They had a clear conception of the common good, and a sagacity in the election of rulers, and a spirit of sacrifice for the general interests. They had a lofty patriotism that nothing could seduce. The rabble of Rome were of no account until the enormous wealth of the senatorial houses raised up clients and parasites. And when this rabble, who were merely the dependents of the rich, obtained the privilege of voting, then the decline of liberties was rapid and fearful, since they were merely the tools of powerful demagogues.

Roman citizens.

Thus among the Romans, until the prostration of their liberties, the powers of government were not in the hands of kings, as among the Orientals, nor in those of the aristocracy, exclusively, nor in those of the people; but in all combined, one class acting as a check against another class. They were shared between the Senate, the magistrates, and the people in their assemblies. Theoretically, the *populus* was the real sovereign by whom power was delegated; but, for several centuries, the *populus* meant the patricians, who alone could take part in the assemblies. The preponderating influence was exercised by the Senate. The judicial, the legislative, and the executive authority were as clearly defined as in our times. The magistrates were all elected by the Senate or the people, and sometimes proposed by the one and confirmed by the other. No case, involving the life of a Roman citizen, could be decided except by the *Comitia Centuriata.* The election of a magistrate, or the passing of a law, though made on the ground of a *senatus consultum,* yet required the sanction of the curiæ. In legislative measures, a *senatus consultum* was brought before the people by the consul, or the senator who originated the measure, after it had

Balance of power.

previously been exhibited in public for seventeen days. The inferior magistrates, whose office it was to superintend affairs of local interest, were elected by the *Comitia Tributa.* All the magistrates, however great their power, could, at the expiration of their office, be punished for transcending their trust. No person was above the authority of the laws. No one class could subvert the liberties and prerogatives of another. The Senate had the most power, but it could not ride over the Constitution. The consuls were not the creatures of the Senate; they were elected by the centuries, and presided over the Senate, as well as the assembly of the people. The abuse of power by a consul was prevented by his colleague, and by the certainty of being called to account on the expiration of his office. His power was also limited by the Senate, since he was dependent upon it. There was no absolute power exercised at Rome, except by the dictators, but they were appointed only in a national crisis, and then only for six months. Unless their power were perpetuated, not even they could overturn the constitution. The senators again, the most powerful body in the state, were not entirely independent. They could not elect members of their own body, nor keep them in office. The censors had the right of electing the senators from among the ex-magistrates and the equites, and of excluding such as they deemed unworthy. And as the Senate was thus composed wholly of men who had held the highest offices or had great wealth, it was a body of great experience and wisdom. Yet even this august assembly was obliged to submit to the introduction of any subject of discussion by the tribune. What a counterpoise to the authority of this powerful body were the tribunes! From their right of appearing in the Senate, and of taking part in its discussions, and from their being the representatives of the whole people, in whom power was supposed primarily to be lodged, they gradually obtained the right of intercession against any action which a magistrate might undertake during the time of his office, and without giving a reason. They could not only prevent a consul from convening the Senate, but could veto an ordinance of the Senate itself. They could even seize a consul and a censor and imprison him. Thus was power marvelously distributed, even while it remained in the hands of the higher classes. The people were not powerless when their assemblies could make laws and appoint magistrates, and when their tribunes could veto the most important measures. The consuls could not remain in office long enough to be dangerous, and the senators could be ejected from their high position when flagrantly unworthy. "The *nobiles* had no legal privileges like a feudal aristocracy, but they were bound together by a common distinction derived from a legal title, and by a common interest; and their common interest was to endeavor to confine the election to all the high magistracies to the members of their own body." The term *nobilitas* implied that some one of a man's ancestors had filled a curule magistracy, and it also implied the possession of wealth. Theoretically it would seem that the *nobiles* were very numerous, since so many people can ordinarily boast of an illustrious ancestor; but practically the class was not so large as we might expect. A noble might be poor, but still, like Sulla, he remained noble. The distinction of patrician was, long before the reforms of the Gracchi, of secondary importance; that of *nobilitas* remained to the close of the republic. The nobility kept themselves exclusive and powerful from the possession of the great offices of state from generation to generation; they prevented their own extinction by admitting into their ranks those who distinguished themselves to an eminent degree.

The reign of demagogues.

But this state of things applied only to the republic in its palmy days. When democratical influences favored the ascendency of demagogues, — thus far in the history of our world, the inevitable consequence of a greater extension of popular liberties than what the people are prepared for, — then wholesome restraints were removed, and the people were the most enslaved, when they thought themselves most free. There is no more melancholy slavery than the slavery of the passions. Ignorant self-indulgent people are led by their passions; they are rarely influenced by reason or by enlightened self-interest. Those who most skillfully and unscrupulously appeal to popular passions, when the people have power, have necessarily the ascendency in the community. The people, deceived, flattered, headstrong, follow them willingly. In times of war, and especially among a martial people, military chieftains, by inflaming the warlike passions, by holding out exaggerated notions of glory, by appealing to vanity and patriotism mingled, have ever had a most extraordinary influence in republics. They have also great influence in monarchies, when the monarch is crazed by the passion of military success. Monarchs, with the passions of the people, are led by men who flatter them even as the people are led. Hence the reign of favorites with kings. The ascendency of favorites, with sovereigns like Louis XIII., or even like Louis XIV., is maintained by the same policy as that which animated Marius and Cæsar, or animates the popular favorites of our times. And this ascendency may be for the better or the worse, according to the character of the demagogue rulers, or royal favorites. When a Richelieu or a Cavour holds the reins, a country may be indirectly benefited by the wisdom of their public acts. When a Buckingham or a Catiline prevails, a nation suffers a calamity. In either case, the power which is conceded to be legitimate becomes a mockery. With Cæsar, the popular power is a mere name, even, as with Richelieu, the kingly is a shadow. In the better days of the Roman republic, the executive power was kept in a healthy state by the great authority of the Senate, and the senatorial influence was prevented from undue encroachment by the watchfulness of the tribunes. And when the aristocratical ascendency was most marked, the aristocratical body had too much virtue and ability to be enslaved by ambitious and able men of their own number. Had the Roman Senate, in the height of its power, been composed of ignorant, inexperienced, selfish, unpatriotic members, then it would have been easy for a great intellect among them, whether accompanied by virtue or not, by appealing perpetually to their pride, to their rank, to their privileges, to their peculiar passions, to have led them, as Pitt led the House of Commons. The real rulers of our world are few, in any community, or under any form of government. They are always dangerous, when there is a low degree of virtue or intelligence among those whom they represent. Certain it is, that their power is nearly absolute when they are sustained by passion or prejudice. The representative of a fanatical constituency has no continued power, unless he perpetually flatters those whom, in his heart, he knows to be lost to the control of reason. And his influence is greater or less, according to the strength of the popular passions which he inflames, or in which, as is often the case, he shares. The honest representative of fanatics is himself a fanatic. Thus Cromwell had so great an ascendency with his party, because he felt more strongly than they in matters where they sympathized. But the liberties of Rome were not overturned by fanatical rulers, but by those who availed themselves of the passions which they themselves did not feel, in order to compass their selfish ends. And that is the greater danger in republics — that bad men rise by the suffrage of foolish people whom they deceive, by affecting to fall in with their wishes, like Napoleon and Cæsar, rather than that honest men climb to power by the very excess of their enthusiasm, like Cromwell, or Peter the Hermit. Hence a Mirabeau is more dangerous than a Robespierre. The former would have betrayed the people he led; the latter would have urged them on to consistent courses, even if the way was lined with death. Had Mirabeau lived, and retained his power, he would have compromised the Revolution, of which Napoleon was the product, and the work would have had to be done over. But Robespierre pushed his principles to their utmost logical sequence, and the nation was satisfied with their folly, in a practical point of view. Napoleon arose to rebuke anarchy as well as feudal kings, and though maddened and intoxicated by war, so that his name is a Moloch, he never dreamed of restoring the unequal privileges which the Revolution swept away.

Greatness of the constitution.

The Roman constitution, as gradually developed by the necessities and crises which arose, is a wonderful monument of human wisdom. The people were not ground down. They had rights which they never relinquished; and they constantly gained new privileges, as they were prepared to appreciate them, or as they were in danger of subjection by the governing classes. They never had the ascendency, but they enjoyed renewed and increasing power, until they were strong enough to tempt aristocratic demagogues and successful generals. When Cæsar condescended to flatter the people, they had become a power, but a power incapable of holding its own, or using it for the welfare of the state. Then it was subverted, as Napoleon rode into absolute dominion over the bridge which the Revolution had built. And the Roman constitution was remarkable, not only because it prevented a degrading subjection of the masses, even while it refused them the rights of government, but because it maintained a balance among the governing classes themselves, and restricted the usurpations of powerful families, as well as military heroes. For nearly five hundred years, not a man arose whom the Romans feared, or whom they could not control — whom they could not at any time have hurled from the Tarpeian rock had he contemplated the subversion, I will not say of the liberties of the people, but of the constitution which made the aristocracy supreme. There were ambitious and unscrupulous men, doubtless, among those fortunate generals whom the Senate snubbed, and whom the people adored. But, great as they were in war, and powerful from family interest and vast wealth, no one of them ever dared to make himself supreme until Cæsar passed the Rubicon — not Scipio, crowned with the laurels which he had taken from the head of Hannibal; not Marius, fresh from his great victories over the barbaric hosts of northern Europe; not even Sulla, after his magnificent conquests in the east, and his triumph over all the parties and factions which democracy raised against him. Pompey may have contemplated what it was the fortune of Cæsar to secure. But that pompous magnate could have succeeded only by using the watchwords and practicing the acts to which none but a demagogue could have stooped. Before his time, at least for fifty years, there were too many men in the Senate who had the spirit of Cato, of Cicero, and of Brutus.

The Revolution.

But, *tempora mutantur.* When the Senate was made up of men whom great generals selected, whether aristocratic sycophants or rich plebeians; when the tribunes played into the hands of the very men whom they were created to oppose; when the high priest of a people, originally religious, was chosen without regard to either moral or religious considerations, but purely political; when the high offices of the state were filled by senators who had never seen military life except for some brief campaign; when factions and parties set old customs aside; when the most aristocratic nobles sought entrance into plebeian ranks in order, like Mirabeau, to steal the few offices which the people controlled, and when the people, mad and fierce from demoralizing spectacles, raised mobs and subverted law, then the constitution, under which the Romans had advanced to the conquest of the world, became subverted. Under the emperors, there was no constitution. They controlled the Senate, the army, the tribunals of the law, the distant provinces, the city itself, and regulated taxes and imposed burdens, and appointed to high offices whomever they wished. The Senate lost its independence, the courts their justice, the army its spirit, and the people their hopes. Yet the old form remained. The Senate met as in the days of the Gracchi. There were consuls and prætors still. But it was merely equites or rich men who filled the senatorial benches — tools of the emperor, as were all the officers of the state. The government of nobles was succeeded by the government of emperors who, in their turn, were too often the tools of favorites, or of prætorian guards, until the assassin's dagger cut short their days.

Effects of imperial rule.

This is not the place to speculate on the good or evil which resulted from this change in the Roman government. Most historians and philosophers agree that the change was inevitable, and proved, on the whole, benignant. It was simply the question whether the Romans should have civil wars and anarchies and factions, which decimated the people, and kept society in a state of fear and insecurity, and prevented the triumph of law, or whether they should submit to an absolute ruler, who had unbounded means of doing good, and whom interest and duty alike prompted to secure the public welfare. The people wanted, above all things, safety, and the means of prosecuting their various interests. Under the emperors they obtained the greatest boons possible, when the condition of society was hollow and rotten to the core. The people were governed, sometimes wisely, sometimes recklessly, but there were order and law for three hundred years. It little mattered to the vast population of the empire who was supreme master, provided they were not oppressed. The proud *Imperator*, the title

The rule of emperors a necessity.

and prænomen of all the Roman monarchs, and which had been invented for Octavian, remained the fountain of law, the arbiter of all interests, the undisputed ruler of the world. The old offices nominally remained, but, by virtue of the censorship, the emperor had the power of excluding persons from the Senate, and of calling others into it. Thus the august body which was, under the republic, the counterpoise to executive authority, was rendered dependent on the imperial will. There was no Senate, but in name, when it could be controlled by the government. It became a mere form, or an instrument in the hands of the administration, to facilitate business. By obtaining the proconsular power over the whole of the Roman Empire, Octavian made the provincial governors his vicegerents. The *tribunicia potestas* which he also enjoyed, enabled him to annul any decree of the Senate, and of interfering in all the acts of the magistrates. An appeal was open to him, as tribune, from all the courts of justice; he had a right to convoke the Senate, and to put any subject under consideration to the vote of senators. Augustus even seized the pontificate, which office, that of Pontifex Maximus, put into his hands all the ecclesiastical courts. As tribune and censor, he also controlled the treasury, so that all the powers of the state were concentrated in him alone — that of consul, tribune, censor, prætor, and high priest. What a power to be exercised by one man in so great an empire! The Roman constitution was subverted when one man usurped the offices which were formerly shared by many. No sovereign was ever so absolute as the Roman Imperator, since he combined all the judicial, the executive, and the legislative branches of the government; that is, he controlled them all.

The old forms of government preserved.

Yet the old machinery was kept up, the old forms, the old offices in name, otherwise even Augustus might not have been secure on his throne. The Comitia still elected magistrates, but only such as were proposed by the government. The Senate assembled as usual, but it was composed of rich men, merely to register the decrees of the Imperator. The consuls were elected as before, but they were mere shadows in authority. The only respectable part of the magistracy was that which interpreted the laws. The only final authority was the edict of the emperor, who not only controlled all the great offices of state, but was possessed of enormous and almost unlimited private property. They owned whole principalities. Augustus changed the whole registration of property in Gaul on his own responsibility, without consulting any one.[1] His power was so unlimited that soldiers took the oath of allegiance to him, as they once did to the *imperium populi Romani.* His armies, his fleets, and his officers were everywhere, and no one dreamed of resisting a power which absorbed every thing into itself.

It is altogether another question whether the prosperity of the state was greater or less after the subversion of the constitution. For three hundred years the state was probably kept together by the ancient mechanism controlled by one central will. The change from civil war and party faction to imperial centralized power, considering the demoralized condition of society, was doubtless beneficial. The emperor could rule; he could not, however, conserve the empire. Doubtless, in most cases, he ruled well, since he ruled by the aid of great experience and ability. It is peculiarly the interest of despots to have able men as ministers. They never select those whom they deem to be weak and corrupt; they are simply deceived in their estimate of ability and fidelity. For several generations, the provinces had experienced governors, the armies had able generals, the courts of law learned judges. The provinces were not so inexorably robbed as in the time of Cicero. The people had their pleasures and spectacles and baths. Property

The imperial power unable to save the state.

[1] Niebuhr, Lecture 105.

was secure, unless enormous fortunes tempted the cupidity of the emperors. Justice was well administered. Cities were rebuilt and adorned. Rome owed its greatest monuments of art to the emperors. There was a cold and remorseless despotism; but the unnoticed millions toiled in peace. Literature did not thrive, since that can only live with freedom, but art received great encouragement, and genius, in the useful professions, did not go unrewarded. The empire did not fall till luxury and prosperity enervated the people and rendered them unable to cope with the barbarian hosts. Rome was never so rich as when she fell into the hands of Goths and Vandals. But the empire, under the old constitution, might have protected itself against external enemies. The mortal wound to Roman power and glory was inflicted by traitors.

AUTHORITIES. — Niebuhr, Lectures on the History of Rome; Mommsen, History of Rome; Arnold, History of Rome; Merivale, History of the Romans; Gibbon, Decline and Fall; Smith's Dictionary of Greek and Roman Antiquities gives the details, and points out the old classical authorities, as does Napoleon's Life of Cæsar. Dionysius, Polybius, Livy, Plutarch, Cicero, Sallust, all shed light on important points. See also Göttling, *Gesch der Rom. Staat.* A large catalogue of writers could be mentioned, but allusion is only made to those most accessible to American readers.

CHAPTER VI.

ROMAN JURISPRUDENCE.

If the Romans showed great practical sagacity in distributing political power among different classes and persons, their laws evince still greater wisdom. Jurisprudence is generally considered to be their indigenous science. It is for this they were most distinguished, and by this they have given the greatest impulse to civilization. Their laws were most admirably adapted for the government of mankind, but they had a still higher merit; they were framed, to a considerable degree, upon the principles of equity or natural justice, and hence are adapted for all ages and nations, and have indeed been reproduced by modern lawgivers, and so extensively, as to have formed the basis of many modern codes. Hence it is by their laws that the Romans have had the greatest influence on modern times, and these constitute a wonderful monument of human genius. If the Romans had bequeathed nothing but laws to posterity, they would not have lived in vain. These have more powerfully affected the interests of civilization than the arts of Greece. They are as permanent in their effects as any thing can be in this world — more so than palaces and marbles. The latter crumble away, but the legacy of Gaius, of Ulpian, of Paulus, of Tribonian, will be prized to the remotest ages, not only as a wonderful work of genius, but for its practical utility. The enduring influence of Moses is chiefly seen in his legislation, for this has entered into the Christian codes, and is also founded on the principles of justice. It is for this chiefly that he ranks with the greatest intellects of earth, whether he was divinely instructed or not.

Object for which the laws were made.

Roman laws were first made in reference to the political exigencies and changes of the state, and afterwards to the relations of the state with individuals, or of individuals with individuals. The former pertain more properly to constitutional history; the latter belong to what is called the science of jurisprudence, and only fall in with the scope of this chapter. The laws enacted by the Roman people in their centuries, or by the Senate, pertaining to political rights and privileges — those by which power passed from the hands of patricians to plebeians, or from the *populus* to great executive officers — are highly important and interesting in an historical or political sense. But the genius of the Romans was most strikingly seen in the government of mankind; and it is therefore the relations between the governing and the governed, the laws created for the general good, pertaining to property and crime and individual rights, which, in this chapter, it is my chief object to show.

Greeks inferior to the Romans in jurisprudence.

The Greeks, with all their genius, their great creations in literature, philosophy, and art, did very little for civilization, which we can trace, in the science of jurisprudence. They were too speculative for such a practical science. Nevertheless their speculative wisdom was made use of by Roman jurists. It was only so far as philosophy modified laws, that the influence of Greece was of much account.

Jurisprudence culminates with emperors.

Nor did Roman jurisprudence culminate in its serene majesty till the time of the emperors. It was not perfectly developed, until Justinian consolidated it in the Code, the Pandects, and the Institutes. The classical jurists may have laid the foundation; the superstructure was raised under the auspices of those whom we regard as despots.

Ingenious writers, like Vico and Niebuhr, have extended

their researches to the government of the kings, and advanced many plausible speculations; but the earliest legislation worthy of notice, was the celebrated code called the Twelve Tables, framed from the reports of the commissioners whom the Romans sent to Athens and other Greek states, to collect what was most useful in their legal systems. But scarcely any part of the civil law contained in the Twelve Tables has come down to us. All we know with certainty, is that it was the intention of the decemviral legislation to bring the estates into closer connection, and to equalize the laws for both. Nor do the provisions of the decemviral code, with which we are acquainted, show that enlightened regard to natural justice which characterized jurisprudence in its subsequent development. It allowed insolvent debtors to be treated with great cruelty; they could be imprisoned for sixty days, loaded with chains, and then might be sold into foreign slavery. It sanctioned a barbarous retaliation — an eye for an eye, and a tooth for a tooth. But it gave a redress for lampoons or libels, allowed an appeal from the magistrate to the people, and forbid capital punishment except by a decision of the centuries.[1] Niebuhr maintains,[2] in his lectures on the History of Rome, that the Twelve Tables conceded the right to every *pater familias* of making a will, by which regulation the child of a plebeian, by a patrician mother, could succeed to his father's property, which was of great importance, and a great step in natural justice. It is supposed that the most important part of the decemviral legislation was the *jus publicum*,[3] or that which refers to the Roman constitution. The Twelve Tables obtained among the Romans a peculiar reverence; they were committed to memory by the young; they were transcribed with the greatest care, and were considered as the fountain of right. They were approved by the *comitia centuriata*, which was

Early legislation.

The Twelve Tables.

1 Lord Mackenzie, part 6. 2 Lecture 25. 3 Cicero, *De Legibus*.

15

the supreme authority, and in the time of Appius Claudius was composed of patricians alone. If Niebuhr is right in his statement that the power of making wills was given to plebeians, it shows a greater liberality on the part of patricians than what they generally have had credit for, and is hardly to be reconciled with the statement of Lord Mackenzie, that all marriages between patricians and plebeians were prohibited by the new code.

The Twelve Tables the basis of Roman law.

The laws of the Twelve Tables were the basis of all the laws, civil and religious. But the edicts of the prætors, who were the great equity judges, as well as the common-law magistrates,[1] proclaimed certain changes which custom and the practice of the courts had introduced, and these, added to the *leges populi* or laws proposed by the consul and passed by the centuries, the *plebiscita* or laws proposed by the tribunes and passed by the tribes, and the *senatus consulta*, gradually swelled the laws to a great number. Three thousand plates of brass, containing these various laws, were deposited in the capitol.[2] Subtleties and fictions were introduced by the lawyers to defeat the written statutes, and jurisprudence became complicated, even in the time of Cicero. The opinions of eminent lawyers were even adopted by the legal profession, and were recognized by the courts. The evils of a complicated jurisprudence were so evident in the seventh century of the city, that Q. Mucius Scævola, a great lawyer, when consul, published a scientific elaboration of the civil law. Cicero studied law under him, and his contemporaries, Alfenus Varus and Ælius Gallus, wrote learned treatises, from which extracts appear in the Digest. Cæsar contemplated a complete revision of the laws, but did not live long enough to carry out his intentions. His legislation, so far as he directed his mind to it, was very just. Among other laws was one which ordained that creditors should accept lands as payment for their outstand-

1 Maine's *Ancient Law*, p. 67.

2 Suetonius, *In Vespa.*

ing debts, according to the value determined by commissioners. In his time, the relative value of money had changed, and was greatly diminished. The most important law of Augustus, was the *lex ælia sentia*, deserving of all praise, which rélated to the manumission of slaves. But he did not interfere with the social relations of the people after he had deprived them of political liberty. He once attempted, by his *Lex Julia et Papia Poppæa*, to counteract the custom which then prevailed, of abstaining from legal marriage and substituting concubinage instead, by which the free population declined; but this attempt to improve the morals of the people met with such opposition from the tribes or centuries, that the next emperor abolished popular assemblies altogether, which Augustus feared to do. The Senate, in the time of the emperors, composed chiefly of lawyers and magistrates, and entirely dependent upon them, became the great fountain of law. By the original constitution, the people were the source of power, and the Senate merely gave or refused its approbation to the laws proposed, but under the emperors the comitia disappeared, and the Senate passed decrees, which have the force of laws, subject to the veto of the emperor. It was not until the time of Septimus Severus and Caracalla, that the legislative action of the Senate ceased, and the edicts and rescripts of emperors took the place of all legislation.

Progress of Roman law.

The golden age of Roman jurisprudence was from the birth of Cicero to the reign of Alexander Severus. Before this period it was an occult science, confined to prætors, pontiffs, and patrician lawyers. There were no books nor schools to teach its principles. But in the latter days of the republic law became the fashionable study of Roman youth, and eminent masters arose. The first great lawyer who left behind him important works, was the teacher of Cicero, Q. Mucius Scævola, who wrote a treatise in eighteen books on the civil law.

Q. Mucius Scævola.

"He was,"[1] says Cicero, "the most eloquent of jurists, and the most learned of orators." This work, George Long thinks, had a great influence on contemporaries and on subsequent jurists, who followed it as a model. It is the oldest work from which there are any excerpts in the Digest.

Servius Sulpicius, the friend of Cicero, and fellow-student of oratory, surpassed his teachers Balbus and Gallus, and was the equal in reputation of the great Mucius Scævola, the Pontifex Maximus, who said it was disgraceful for a patrician and a noble to be ignorant of the law with which he had to do. Cicero ascribes his great superiority as a lawyer to the study of philosophy, which disciplined and developed his mind, and enabled him to deduce his conclusions from his premises with logical precision. He left behind him one hundred and eighty treatises, and had numerous pupils, among whom A. Ofilius and Alfenus Varus, Cato, Cæsar, Antony, and Cicero, were great lawyers. Labeo, in the time of Augustus, wrote four hundred books on jurisprudence, spending six months in the year in giving instruction to his pupils, and in answering legal questions, and the other six months in the country in writing books. Like all the great Roman jurists, he was versed in literature and philosophy, and so devoted to his profession that he refused political office. His rival, Capito, was equally learned in all departments of the law, and left behind him as many treatises as Labeo. These two jurists were the founders of celebrated schools, like the ancient philosophers, and each had distinguished followers. Masurius Sabinus Gaius and Pomponius, were of the school of Capito. M. Cocceius Nerva, Sempronius Proculus, and Juventius Celsus, were of the school of Labeo. Gaius, who flourished in the time of the Antonines, was a great legal authority; and the recent discovery of his Institutes has revealed

Servius Sulpicius.

Labeo.

Gaius.

[1] Cicero, *De Or.* i. 39.

the least mutilated fragment of Roman jurisprudence which exists, and one of the most valuable, and sheds great light on ancient Roman law. It was found in the library of Verona. No Roman jurist had a higher reputation than Papinian, who was *præfectus prætorio* under Septimius Severus, an office which made him only secondary to the emperor — a sort of grand vizier — whose power extended over all departments of the state. He was beheaded by Caracalla. The great commentator Cujacius, declares that he was the first of all lawyers who have been, or who are to be; that no one ever surpassed him in legal knowledge, and no one will ever equal him. Paulus was his contemporary, and held the same office as Papinian. He was the most fertile of Roman law-writers, and there is more taken from him in the Digest than from any other jurist, except Ulpian. There are two thousand and eighty-three excerpts from this writer, one sixth of the whole Digest. No legal writer, ancient or modern, has handled so many subjects. In perspicuity, he is said to be inferior to Ulpian, one of the most famous of jurists, who was his contemporary. He has exercised a great influence on modern jurisprudence from the copious extracts of his writings in Justinian's Digest. He was the chief adviser of Alexander Severus, and like Paulus was *præfectus prætorio*. The number of excerpts in the Digest from him, is said to be two thousand four hundred and sixty-two, and they form a third part of it. Some fragments of his writings remain. The last of the great civilians associated with Gaius, Papinian, Paulus, and Ulpian, as oracles of jurisprudence, was Modestinus, who was a pupil of Ulpian. He wrote both in Greek and Latin. There are three hundred and forty-five excerpts in the Digest from his writings, the titles of which show the extent and variety of his labors.[1]

Papinian.

Paulus.

These great lawyers shed great glory on the Roman

[1] These facts are drawn from the different articles of George Long, in *Smith's Dictionary*.

civilization. In the earliest times men sought distinction on the fields of battle, but in the latter days of the republic honor was conferred for forensic ability. The first pleaders of Rome were not jurisconsults, but aristocratic patrons who looked after their clients. But when law became complicated, a class of men arose to interpret it, and these men were held in great honor, and reached, by their services, the highest offices — like Cicero and Hortensius. No remuneration was given originally for forensic pleading, beyond the services which the client gave to a patron, but gradually the practice of the law became lucrative. Hortensius, as well as Cicero, gained an immense fortune. He had several villas, a gallery of paintings, a large stock of wines, parks, fish-ponds, and aviaries. Cicero had villas in all parts of Italy ; a house on the Palatine with columns of Numidian marble, and a fortune of twenty millions of sesterces, equal to $800,000. Most of the great statesmen of Rome, in the time of Cicero, were either lawyers or generals. Crassus, Pompey, P. Sextus, M. Marcellus, P. Clodius, Calidius, Messala Niger, Asinius Pollio, C. Cicero, M. Antonius, Cæsar, Calvus, Cælius, Brutus, Catulus, Messala Cervirus, were all celebrated for their forensic efforts. Candidates for the bar studied four years under a distinguished jurist, and were required to pass a rigorous examination. The judges were chosen from members of the bar, as well as, in later times, the senators. The great lawyers were not only learned in the law, but possessed great accomplishments. Varro was a lawyer, and was the most learned man that Rome produced. But, under the emperors, the lawyers were chiefly distinguished for their legal attainments, like Paulus and Ulpian.

The profession of law.

During this golden age of Roman jurisprudence, many commentaries were written on the Twelve Tables, the Perpetual Edict, the Laws of the People, and the Decrees of the Senate, as well as a vast mass of treatises on every department of the law, most of which have perished. The Institutes of Gaius, which have reached us nearly in their original form, are the most valuable which remain, and have thrown great light on some important branches previously involved in obscurity. Their use in explaining the Institutes of Justinian, is spoken of very highly by Mackenzie, since the latter are mainly founded on the long lost work of Gaius. A treatise of Ulpian, preserved in the Vatican, entitled "*Tituli ex corpore Ulpiani*," also contains valuable information, as well as the "*Receptæ Sententiæ*" of Julius Paulus, his great contemporary, both of which works, as well as others of inferior importance, were lately published at Rome by Dr. Gneist, called "*Corpus Juris Romani Antejustinianii.*"[1] The great lawyers who flourished from Trajan to Alexander Severus, like Gaius, Ulpian, Paulus, Papinian, and Modestinus, had no successors who can be compared with them, and their works became standard authorities in the courts of law.

Roman jurists.

After the death of Alexander Severus no great accession was made to Roman law, until Theodosius II. caused the constitutions, from Constantine to his own time, to be collected and arranged in sixteen books. This was called the Theodosian Code, which in the West was held in high esteem, although superseded shortly after in the East by the Justinian Code.

Justinian labors.

To Justinian belongs the immortal glory of reforming the jurisprudence of the Romans. "In the space of ten centuries," says Gibbon, "the infinite variety of laws and legal opinions had filled many thousand volumes, which no fortune could purchase, and no capacity could digest. Books could not easily be found and the judges, poor in the midst of riches, were reduced to the exercise of their illiterate discretion."[2] Justinian determined to unite in one body all the rules of law, whatever may have been their origin, and in the year

[1] Mackenzie, p. 16.

[2] Gibbon, ch. 44.

528, appointed ten jurisconsults, among whom was the celebrated Tribonian, to select and arrange the imperial constitutions, leaving out what was obsolete or useless or contradictory, and to make such alterations as the circumstances required. This was called the *Code*, divided into twelve books, and comprising the constitutions from Hadrian to Justinian. This was published in fourteen months after it was undertaken.

Tribomian.

Justinian authorized Tribonian, then quaestor, "*vir magnificus magisteria dignitate inter agentes decoratus*," for great titles were now given to the officers of the crown, to prepare, with the assistance of seventeen associates, a collection of extracts from the writings of the most eminent jurists, so as to form a body of law for the government of the empire, with power to select and omit and alter; and this immense work was done in three years, and published under the title of Digest or Pandects. "All the judicial learning of former times," says Lord Mackenzie, "was laid under contribution by Tribonian and his colleagues. Selections from the works of thirty-nine of the ablest lawyers, scattered over two thousand separate treatises, were collected in one volume; and care was taken to inform posterity that three millions of lines were abridged and reduced, in these extracts, to the modest number of one hundred and fifty thousand. Among the selected jurists, only three names belonged to the age of the republic; the civilians who flourished under the first emperors are seldom appealed to; so that most of the writers, whose works have contributed to the Pandects, lived within a period of one hundred years. More than a

The code of Pandects.

third of the whole Pandects is from Ulpian, and next to him, the principal writers are Paulus, Papinian, Salvius Julianus, Pomponius, Q. Cervidius Scævola, and Gaius. Though the variety of subjects is immense, the Digest has no claims to scientific arrangement. It is a vast cyclopedia of heterogeneous law badly arranged; every thing is there, but every thing is not in its proper place."[1]

But neither the Digest nor the Code was adapted to elementary instruction. It was necessary to prepare a treatise on the principles of Roman law. This was entrusted to Tribonian, and two professors, Theophilus and Dorotheus. It is probable that Tribonian merely superintended the work, which was founded chiefly on the Institutes of Gaius, and was divided into four books, and has been universally admired for its method and elegant precision. It was intended merely as an introduction to the Pandects and the Code.

The Institutes.

The *Novels of Justinian* were subsequently published, being the new ordinances of the emperor, and the changes he thought proper to make, and are therefore a high authority.

The Novels of Justinian.

The Code, Pandects, Institutes, and Novels of Justinian, comprise the Roman law, as received in Europe, in the form given by the school of Bologna, and is called the "*Corpus Juris Civilis.*" "It was in that form," says Savigny, "that the Roman law became the common law of Europe; and when, four centuries later, other sources came to be added to it, the *Corpus Juris* of the school of Bologna had been so universally received, and so long established as a basis of practice, that the new discoveries remained in the domain of science, and served only for the theory of the law. For the same reason, the Anti-Justinian law is excluded from practice."[2] After Justinian, the old texts were left to moulder as useless though venerable, and they have nearly all disappeared. The Code, the Pandects, and the Institutes, were declared to be the only legitimate authority and alone were admitted to the tribunals or taught in the schools. The rescripts of the early emperors recognized too many popular rights to suit the despotic character of Justinian, and the older jurists, like the Scævolas, Sul-

[1] Mackenzie, p. 25.

[2] Savigny, *Droit Romani*, vol. i. p. 68.

picius, and Labeo, were distasteful from their sympathy with free institutions. Different opinions have been expressed by the jurisconsults as to the merits of the Justinian collection. By some it is regarded as a vast mass of legal lumber; by others, as a beautiful monument of human labor. After the lapse of so many centuries, it is certain that a large portion of it is of no practical utility, since it is not applicable to modern wants. But again, no one doubts that it has exercised a great and good influence on moral and political science, and introduced many enlightened views concerning the administration of justice, as well as the nature of civil government, and thus has modified the codes of the Teutonic nations, which sprang up on the ruins of the old Roman world. It was used in the Greek empire until the fall of Constantinople. It never entirely lost authority in Italy, although it remained buried till the discovery of the Florentine copy of the Pandects at the siege of Amalfi in 1135. Peter Valence, in the eleventh century, made use of it in a law-book which he published. With the rise of the Italian cities, the study of Roman law revived, and Bologna became the seat from which it spread over Europe. In the sixteenth century, the science of theoretical law passed from Italy to France, under the auspices of Francis I., when Cujas or Cujacius became the great ornament of the school of Bourges, and the greatest commentator on Roman law until Dumoulin appeared. Grotius, in Holland, excited the same interest in civil law that Dumoulin did in France, followed by eminent professors in Leyden and the German universities. It was reserved for Pothier, in the middle of the eighteenth century, to reduce the Roman law to systematic order — one of the most gigantic tasks which ever taxed the industry of man. The recent discoveries, especially that made by Niebuhr, of the long lost work of Gaius have given a great impulse to the study of Roman law in Germany, and to this impulse no one has contributed so greatly as Savigny of Berlin.

The great importance of the subject demands a more minute notice of the principles of the Roman law, than what the limits of this work should properly allow. I shall therefore endeavor to abridge what has been written by the more eminent authorities, taking as a basis the late work of Lord Mackenzie and the learned and interesting essay of Professor Maine.

Law of persons.

The Institutes of Justinian commenced with the law of persons, recognizing the distinction of ranks. All persons are capable of enjoying civil rights, but not all in the same degree. Greater privileges are allowed to men than to women, to freemen than to slaves, to fathers than to children.

Equality of citizens.

In the eye of the law all Roman citizens were equal, wherever they lived, whether in the capital or the provinces. Citizenship embraced both political and civil rights. The political rights had reference to the right of voting in the comitia, but this was not considered the essence of citizenship, which was the enjoyment of the *connubium* and *commercium*. By the former the citizen could contract a valid marriage, and acquire the rights resulting from it, particularly the paternal power; by the latter he could acquire and dispose of property. Citizenship was acquired by birth and by manumission; it was lost when a Roman became a prisoner of war, or had been exiled for crime, or became a citizen of another state. An unsullied reputation was necessary for a citizen to exercise his rights to their full extent.

Slaves.

The Roman jurists acknowledged all persons originally free by natural law; and, while they recognized slavery, ascribed the power of masters entirely to the law and custom of nations. Persons taken in war were considered at the absolute control of their captors, and were therefore, *de facto*, slaves; and the children of a female slave followed the condition of their mother, and belonged to her master. But masters could manumit their slaves, who thus became Roman citizens, with some restrictions. Until the time of Justinian, they were not allowed to wear the gold ring, the distinguishing symbol of a man born free. This emperor removed all restrictions between freedmen and citizens. Previously, after the emancipation of a slave, he was bound to render certain services to his former master as patron, and if the freedman died intestate his property reverted to his patron.

Marriage.

Marriage was contracted by the simple consent of the parties, though in early times, equality of condition was required. The *lex Canuleia*, A. U. C. 309, authorized connubium between patricians and plebeians, and the *lex Julia*, A. U. C. 757, allowed it between freedmen and freeborn. By the *conventio in manum*, a wife passed out of her family into that of her husband, who acquired all her property; without it, the woman remained in the power of her father, and retained the free disposition of her property. Poligamy was not permitted; and relationship within certain degrees rendered the parties incapable of contracting marriage, and these rules as to forbidden degrees have been substantially adopted in England. Celibacy was discouraged. The law of Augustus *Julia et Papia Poppœa* contained some seven regulations against it, which were abolished by Constantine. Concubinage was allowed, if a man had not a wife, and provided the concubine was not the wife of another man. This heathenish custom was abrogated by Justinian.[1] The wife was entitled to protection and support from her husband, and she retained her property independent of her husband, when the *conventio* was abandoned, as it was ultimately. The father gave his daughter, on her marriage, a dowry in proportion to his means, the management of which, with its fruits during marriage, belonged to the husband; but he could not alienate real estate without the wife's consent, and on the dissolution of marriage the *dos* reverted to the

[1] D. 25. 7. C. 5, 26.

wife. Divorce existed in all ages at Rome, and was very common at the commencement of the empire. To check its prevalence, laws were passed inflicting severe penalties on those whose bad conduct led to it. Every man, whether married or not, could adopt children, under certain restrictions, and they passed entirely under paternal power. But the marriage relation among the Romans did not accord after all with those principles of justice which we see in other parts of their legislative code. The Roman husband, like the father, was a tyrant. The facility of divorce destroyed mutual confidence, and inflamed every trifling dispute, for a word, or a message, or a letter, or the mandate of a freedman, was quite sufficient to secure a separation. It was not until Christianity became the religion of the empire, that divorce could not be easily effected without a just cause.

Nothing is more remarkable in the Roman laws than the extent of paternal power. It was unjust, and bears the image of a barbarous age. Moreover, it seems to have been coeval with the foundation of the city. A father could chastise his children by stripes, by imprisonment, by exile, by sending them to the country with chains on their feet. He was even armed with the power of life and death. "Neither age nor rank, nor the consular office, could exempt the most illustrious citizen from the bonds of filial subjection. Without fear, though not without danger of abuse, the Roman legislators had reposed unbounded confidence in the sentiments of paternal love, and the oppression was tempered by the assurance that each generation must succeed in its turn to the awful dignity of parent and master."[1] By an express law of the Twelve Tables a father could sell his children as slaves. But the abuse of paternal power was checked in the republic by the censors, and afterwards by emperors. Alexander Severus limited the right of the father to simple

Paternal power.

[1] Gibbon, c. xliv.

correction, and Constantine declared the father who should kill his son to be guilty of murder.[1] The rigor of parents in reference to the disposition of the property of children, was also gradually relaxed. Under Augustus, the son could keep absolute possession of what he had acquired in war. Under Constantine, he could retain any property acquired in the civil service, and all property inherited from the mother could also be retained. In later times, a father could not give his son or daughter to another by adoption without their consent. Thus this *patria potestas* was gradually relaxed as civilization advanced, though it remained a peculiarity of Roman law to the latest times, and severer than is ever seen in the modern world.[2] No one but a Roman citizen could exercise this awful paternal power, nor did it cease until the father died, or the daughter had entered into marriage with the *conventio in manum*. Illegitimate children were treated as if they had no father, and the mother was bound to support them until Justinian gave to natural children a right to demand aliment from their father.[3] Fathers were bound to maintain their children when they had no separate means to supply their wants, and children were also bound to maintain their parents in want. These reciprocal duties, creditable to the Roman law-givers, are recognized in the French Code, but not in the English, which also recognizes the right of a father to bequeath his whole estate to strangers, which the Roman fathers had not power to do.[4] The age when children attain majority among the Romans, was twenty-five years. Women were condemned to the perpetual tutelage of parents, husbands, or guardians, as it was supposed they never could attain to the age of reason and experience. The relation of guardian and ward was strictly observed by the Romans. They made a distinction between the right to govern a person, and the right to man-

[1] Ch. iv. 17.
[2] Maine, *Ancient Law*, p. 143.
[3] N. 89, ch. xii.
[4] Lord Mackenzie, p. 142.

age his estate, although the tutor could do both. If the pupil was an infant, the tutor could act without the intervention of the pupil; if the pupil was above seven years of age, he was considered to have an imperfect will. The tutor managed the estate of the pupil, but was liable for loss occasioned by bad management. He could sell movable property when expedient, but not real estate, without judicial authority. The tutor named by the father was preferred to all others.

Real rights.

The Institutes of Justinian pass from persons to things, or the law relating to real rights; in other words, that which pertains to property. Some things, common to all, like air, light, the ocean, and things sacred, like temples and churches, are not classed as property. Originally, the Romans divided things into *res mancipi*, and *res nec mancipi.* The former comprehended houses, lands, slaves, and beasts of burden, and could only be acquired by certain solemn forms, which, if not observed, the property was not legally transferred. The latter included all other things, and admitted of being transferred by simple tradition.

Occupancy.

Occupancy, one of the original modes of acquiring property, was applied to goods and persons taken in war; to things lost by negligence, or chance, or thrown away by necessity; to pearls, shells, and precious stones found on the sea-shore; to wild animals, to fish, to hidden treasure.

Acquisition, by accession, pertained to the natural and industrial fruits of the land, the rents of houses, interest on money, the increase of animals, lands gained from the sea, and movables.

Transfer of property.

Two things were required for the transfer of property, for it is the essence of property that the owner of a thing should have the right to transfer it, — first, the consent of the former owner to transfer the thing upon some just ground; and secondly, the actual delivery of the thing to the person who is to acquire it. Movables were presumed to be the property of the possessors, until positive evidence was produced to the contrary. A prescriptive title to movables was acquired by possession for one year, and to immovables by possession for two years. Undisturbed possession for thirty years constituted in general a valid title. When a Roman died, his heirs succeeded to all his property, by hereditary right. If he left no will, his estate devolved upon his relations in a certain order prescribed by law. The power of making a testament only belonged to citizens above puberty. Children under the paternal power could not make a will. Males above fourteen, and females above twelve, when not under power, could make wills without the authority of their guardian ; but pupils, lunatics, prisoners of war, criminals, and various other persons, were incapable of making a testament. The testator could divide his property among his heirs in such proportions as he saw fit; but if there was no distribution, all the heirs participated equally. A man could disinherit either of his children by declaring his intentions in his will, but only for grave reasons, such as grievously injuring his person or character or feelings, or attempting his life. No will was effectual unless one or more persons were appointed heirs to represent the deceased. Wills were required to be signed by the testator, or some person for him, in the presence of seven witnesses who were Roman citizens. If a will was made by a parent for distributing his property solely among his children, no witnesses were required, and the ordinary formalities were dispensed with among soldiers in actual service, and during the prevalence of pestilence. The testament was opened in the presence of the witnesses, or a majority of them; and after they had acknowledged their seals, a copy was made, and the original was deposited in the public archives. According to the Twelve Tables, the powers of a testator in disposing of his property were unlim-

Testaments and legacies.

ited, but in process of time laws were enacted to restrain immoderate or unnatural bequests. By the Falcidian law, in the time of Augustus, no one could leave in legacies more than three fourths of his estate, so that the heirs could inherit at least one fourth. Again a law was passed, by which the descendants were entitled to one third of the succession, and to one half if there were more than four. In France if a man die leaving one lawful child, he can only dispose of half of his estate by will; if he leaves two children, the third; if he leaves three or more, the fourth.[1] In England a man can cut off both his wife and children.[2] The Romans recognized bequests in trust, besides testaments, by which property descended directly to the heir. The person charged with a trust was bound to restore the subject at the time appointed by the testator. The trustee could not alienate an estate without the consent of all the parties interested, except for the payment of debts. All persons capable of making a will could leave legacies, real or personal, but these were not due if the testator died insolvent. When a man died intestate, the succession devolved on the descendants of the deceased; but, these failing, the nearest ascendants were called; if there were brothers and sisters, they were entitled to succeed together along with the ascendants in the same class. Children succeeded to property, if their father died intestate, in equal portions, without distinction of sex, and if there was only one child he took the whole estate. A descendant of either sex, or any degree, was preferred to all ascendants and collaterals. The descendants of a son or daughter, who had predeceased, took the same share of the succession that their parent would have done had he been alive. In England, if all the children are dead, and only grandchildren exist, they all take, not by families, but *per capita*, equal shares in their own right as next of kin, and Mackenzie thinks this arrangement is more equitable

Laws of succession.

1 *Code Civil*, Art. 913.

2 Williams, *Exec.*, p. 3.

than the Roman.[1] If there were no descendants, the Roman father and mother, and other ascendants, excluded all collaterals from the succession except brothers and sisters of the whole blood, and the children of deceased brothers and sisters. When ascendants stood alone, the father and mother succeeded in equal portions, and if only one survived, he or she succeeded to the whole, so that grandparents were excluded. If there were brothers and sisters of the whole blood, the estate was divided among them *in capita*, according to the number of persons, including the father and mother. The children of a deceased brother were not admitted to the succession along with ascendants and surviving brothers and sisters.[2] If a person died leaving neither ascendants nor descendants, his brothers and sisters succeeded to his estate in equal shares. And if the intestate left also nephews and nieces by a deceased brother or sister, these succeeded, along with their uncles and aunts, to the share their parent would have taken. On the failure of brothers and sisters by the whole blood, the brother and sisters by the half blood succeeded, and if any of these brothers and sisters have died leaving children, the right of representation was extended to them also, just as in the case of children of brothers-german. When husband or wife died, without leaving relations, the survivor was called to the succession. A widow who was poor and unprovided for had a right to share in the succession of her deceased husband. When he left more than three descendants, she was entitled to participate with them equally. If there were only three or fewer, she was entitled to one fourth of the estate. If she had children by the deceased, she had only the usufruct of her portion during her life, and was bound to preserve it for them. If a man had no legitimate children, he could leave his whole inheritance to his natural children, or to their mother; but if he had lawful children, he could

The laws in inheritance.

1 Mackenzie, p. 288.

2 *Ibid.* 290.

leave only one twelfth to the natural children and their mother. If the father died intestate, without leaving a lawful wife or issue, his natural children and their mother were entitled to one sixth of the succession, and the rest was divided among the lawful heirs.

Contracts.

In the matter of contracts, the Roman law was especially comprehensive, and the laws of France and Scotland are substantially based upon the Roman system. The Institutes of Gaius and Justinian distinguish four sorts of obligation, — aut *re*, aut *verbis*, aut *literis*, aut *consenser*. Gibbon, in his learned chapter, prefers to consider the specific obligations of men to each other under promises, benefits, and injuries. Lord Mackenzie treats the subject in the order of the Institutes.

"Obligations contracted *re* — by the intervention of things — are called by the moderns real contracts, because they are not perfected till something has passed from one party to another. Of this description are the contracts of loan, deposit, and pledge. Till the subject is actually lent, deposited, or pledged, it does not form the special contract of loan, deposit, or pledge." [1]

Loans.

In regard to loans, the borrower was obliged to take care of it as if it were his own. *In rebus commodatis talis diligentia præstanda est, qualem quisque diligentissimus paterfamilias suis rebus adhibet.*[2] He could only use a thing for the purpose for which it was lent; he could not keep it beyond the time agreed upon, nor detain it as a set-off against any debt. He was bound to restore the article in the same condition as received, subject only to the deterioration arising from reasonable use, whether a horse, a house, or a carriage. And he was required to make good all injuries caused by his own fault or negligence. If the article perished, without any blame or neglect, the loss fell on the owner. If the loan was for consumption, which was called *mutuum*, like corn, or oil,

[1] Mackenzie.

[2] D. 13, 6, 1 pr.

or wine, the borrower was required to return as much of the same kind and quality, whether the price of the commodity had risen or fallen. In a loan of money, under *mutuum*, the borrower was not required to pay interest. Interest was only due *ex lege*, or by agreement. The rate varied at different times ; generally, it was eight and one third per cent., and even more than this in the latter years of the republic. Justinian introduced a scale which varied with different classes of society. Persons of illustrious rank could lend money at four per cent., ordinary people at six, and for maritime risks twelve ; but it was unlawful to charge interest upon interest.[1] Property would double, at eight and one third, in twelve years, not so rapidly as by our system of compound interest, especially at the rate of seven per cent. In England the usury laws of different monarchs limited interest from ten per cent. to five ; but these were repealed in 1854. Only five per cent. can now be recovered upon any contract.

Deposits.

A deposit differed from a loan in this, — that the depositary was not entitled to any use of a thing deposited, and was bound to preserve it with reasonable care, and restore it on demand. As he derived no advantage, he was entitled to be reimbursed for all necessary charges. Ship-masters, innkeepers, and stablers, were responsible for the luggage and effects of travellers intrusted to their care, which policy is now adopted in both Europe and America, on the ground that if they were not held strictly to their charge, being not a very reputable class of men in ancient times, they might be in league with thieves. An innkeeper was therefore held responsible for loss, or damage, or theft, to secure the protection of travellers, whose patronage was a compensation. In case of robbery, when goods were taken by superior force, he was not responsible, nor was he for loss occasioned by inevitable accident.

At Rome, pledges were customary, as a security for

[1] C. 4, 32, 26, § 1.

money due, on condition of their restoration after the payment of a debt. Real property, like houses and lands, as well as movables, were the subject of pledge.[1] The creditor was bound to bestow ordinary care and diligence in the preservation of the subject, but he could not use it, or take the profits of it, without a special contract. By the *pactum antichresis*, the creditor was allowed to take the profits in lieu of the interest on his debt; by the *lex commissoria*, the thing pledged became the absolute property of the creditor if the debt was not paid at the time agreed on. But as this condition was found to be a source of oppression, it was prohibited by a law of Constantine.[2] When the debt, interest, and all necessary expenses were paid, the debtor was entitled to have his pledge restored to him. After the time of payment was passed, the creditor had a right to sell the pledge, and retain his debt out of the produce of the sale; if there was a deficiency, the balance could be recovered by an action; if there was a surplus, the debtor was entitled to it. The Roman pledge was of the nature of the modern business of pawnbroking and of a mortgage.

Pledges and securities.

Next to the perfection of contracts by the intervention of things *re*, were obligations contracted by *verbis* — solemn words — and by *literis* or writing. The *verborum obligatio* was contracted by uttering certain formal words of style, an interrogation being put by one party and an answer given by the other. These stipulations were binding. In England all guarantees must be in writing.

Verbal contracts.

The *obligatio literis* was a written acknowledgment of debt chiefly employed when money was borrowed, but the creditor could not sue upon the note within two years from its date, without being called upon also to prove that the money was in fact paid to the debtor.

Written obligations.

Contracts perfected by consent — *consenses* — had refer-

[1] D. 20, 1.

[2] C. 7, 35.

ence to sale, hiring, partnership, and mandate. All contracts of sale were good without writing. When an article was sold and delivered, the market price, as fixed by custom, determined the price, if nothing had been said about it. The seller was bound to warrant that the thing sold was free from defects, and when the subject did not answer this implied warranty, the sale might be set aside. But the seller could stipulate that he should not be held to warrant against defects. Property was not transferred without actual delivery. When the sale was completed, all the risks of the thing sold passed to the purchaser. In the case of commodities sold by weight, number, or measure, the contract was not completed until the goods were weighed, counted, or measured, which sometimes caused considerable difficulty. After delivery, the seller was bound to warrant the title to the buyer, and to indemnify him for any loss.[1]

Sales.

In regard to hiring, all sorts of things, which were the subject of commerce, may be let for hire. Leases of land and houses come under this head. They were generally given for five years, and unless there was an express stipulation, the lessee might sublet to another. The lessor was required to deliver the subject in a good state of repair, and maintain it in that condition, and to guarantee its peaceable enjoyment; the lessee was bound to use the subject well, to put it to no use except that for which it was let, to preserve it in good condition, and restore it at the end of the term. He was bound also to pay the rent at the stipulated period, and when two years' rent were in arrear, the tenant could be ejected. The tenant of a farm was entitled to a remission of his rent if his crop was destroyed by an unforeseen accident or calamity. A contractor who agreed to undertake a piece of work was required to finish it in a proper manner, and if from negligence or ignorance the work was defective, he was liable to

Leases.

[1] D. 22, 2. C. 8, 45.

damages. In a partnership, if there were no express agreement, the shares of profit and loss were divided equally. Each partner was bound to exercise the same care for the joint concern as if it were his own. The acts of one partner were not binding on another, if he acted beyond the scope of the partnership. If one of the partners advanced money on account of the partnership, each of the partners were bound to contribute to the indemnity in proportion to his share of the concern; and if any of them became insolvent, the solvent shareholders were obliged to make up the deficiency.[1] An agent could be employed to transact business for another, but was required to act strictly according to his orders, and the mandant, who gave the orders, was bound to ratify what was done by the mandatary, and to reimburse him for all advances and expenses incurred in executing the commission. By the Roman law agents were not remunerated. Donations could not be made beyond a certain maximum. Justinian ordered that when gifts exceeded five hundred solidi, a formal act stating the particulars of the donation should be inscribed in a public register.

Agents and Partners.

When a person spontaneously assumed the management of the affairs of another in his absence, and without any mandate, this was called *negotiorum gestio*, and the person was bound to perform any act which he had begun, as if he held a proper mandate, and strictly account for his management, while the principal was bound to indemnify him for all advances and expenses.

When money was paid through error it could be recovered, under certain circumstances. But this point is a matter concerning which the jurists differ.

Acts which caused damage to another obliged the wrongdoer to make reparation, and this responsibility extended to damages arising not only from positive acts, but from negligence or imprudence. In an action of libel or slan-

[1] D. 17, 2, 67.

der, the truth of the allegation might be pleaded in justification.[1] In all cases it was necessary to show that an injury had been committed maliciously. But if damage arose in the exercise of a right, as killing a slave in self-defense, no claim for reparation could be maintained. If any one exercised a profession or trade for which he was not qualified, he was liable to all the damage his want of skill or knowledge might occasion. When any damage was done by a slave or an animal, the owner of the same was liable for the loss, though the mischief was done without his knowledge and against his will. If any thing was thrown from a window of a house near the public thoroughfare, so as to injure any one by the fall, the occupier was bound to repair the damage, though done by a stranger. Claims arising under obligations might be transferred to a third person, by sale, exchange, or donation ; but to prevent speculators from purchasing debts at low prices, it was ordered that the assignee should not be entitled to exact from the debtor more than he himself had paid to acquire the debt with interest, — a wise and just regulation which it would be well for us to copy. In regard to the extinction of obligations the creditor is not bound to accept of payments by instalments, or any thing short of proper payment at the time and place agreed upon. When several debts were due, the debtor, in making payment, could appropriate it to any one he pleased.[2] When performance became impossible, without any fault of the debtor, such as when the specific subject had perished by unavoidable accident, the obligation was extinguished ; but if the impossibility was caused by the fault of the debtor, he was still liable. This was a great modification of the severity of the ancient code, when a debtor could be sold into slavery for his debt. As certain contracts are formed by consent alone, so they could be extinguished by the mutual consent of the contracting par-

Libels.

Damages.

[1] D. 47, 10, 18.

[2] D. 46, 3, 1.

ties, without performance on either side. In some cases the mere lapse of time extinguished an obligation, as in accordance with the modern system of outlawry.

The next great department of Roman jurisprudence pertained to actions and procedure. The state conferred on a magistrate or judge jurisdiction to determine questions according to law. Civil jurisdiction pertains to questions of private right; criminal jurisdiction takes cognizance of crimes. When jurisdiction was conferred on a Roman magistrate, he acquired all the powers necessary to exercise it. The *imperium merum* gave the power to inflict punishment; the *imperium mixtum* was the power to carry civil decrees into execution. A *real action* was directed against a person in the territory where the subject in dispute was located.

Law of actions.

By the ancient constitution, the king had the prerogative of determining civil causes. The right then devolved on the consuls, afterwards on the prætor, and in certain cases on the curule and plebeian ediles, who were charged with the internal police of the city.

The prætor, a magistrate next in dignity to the consuls, acted as supreme judge of the civil courts, assisted by a council of jurisconsults to determine questions in law. At first one prætor was sufficient, but as the limits of the city and empire extended, he was joined by a colleague. After the conquest of Sicily, Sardinia, and the two Spains, new prætors were appointed to administer justice in the provinces. The prætor held his court in the comitium, wore a robe bordered with purple, sat in a curule chair, and was attended by lictors.

The Prætors.

The prætor delegated his power to judges, called Judex, Arbiter, and Recuperatores. When parties were at issue about facts, it was the custom for the prætor to fix the question of law upon which the action turned, and then to remit to a delegate to inquire into the facts and pronounce judgment according to them. In the time

Other judges.

of Augustus there were four thousand judices, who were merely private citizens, generally senators or men of consideration. The judex was invested by the magistrate with a judicial commission for a single case only. After being sworn to duty, he received from the prætor a formula containing a summary of all the points under litigation, from which he was not allowed to depart. He was required not merely to investigate facts, but to give sentence. And as law questions were more or less mixed up with the case, he was allowed to consult one or more jurisconsults. If the case was beyond his power to decide, he could decline to give judgment. The arbiter, like the judex, received a formula from the prætor, and seemed to have more extensive power. The recuperatores heard and determined cases, but the number appointed for each case was usually three or five.

The centumvirs.

The centumvirs constituted a permanent tribunal composed of members annually elected, in equal numbers, from each tribe, and this tribunal was presided over by the prætor, and divided into four chambers, which, under the republic, was placed under the ancient quæstors. The centumvirs decided questions of property, embracing a wide range of subjects.[1] The Romans had no class of men like the judges of modern times. The superior magistrates were changed annually, and political duties were mixed with judicial. The evil was partially remedied by the institution of legal assessors, selected from the most learned jurisconsults. Under the empire, the prætors were greatly increased. Under Tiberius, there were sixteen who administered justice, beside the consuls, six ediles, and ten tribunes of the people. The emperor himself became the supreme judge, and he was assisted in the discharge of his judicial duties by a council composed of the consuls, a magistrate of each grade, and fifteen senators. The prætorian prefects, although, at first, their duties were purely

[1] *Cicero de Orat.*, i. 38.

military, finally discharged important judicial functions. The prefect of the city, in the time of the emperors, was a great judicial personage, who heard appeals from the prætors themselves.

In all cases brought before the courts, the burden of proof was with the party asserting an affirmative fact. Proof by writing was generally considered most certain, but proof by witnesses was also admitted. Pupils, lunatics, infamous persons, interested parties, near relations, and slaves, could not bear evidence, or any person who had a strong enmity against the party. The witnesses were required to give their testimony on oath. Two witnesses were enough to prove a fact, in most instances. When witnesses gave conflicting testimony, the judge regarded those who were worthy of credit rather than numbers. In the English courts, the custom used to be as with the Romans, of refusing testimony from those who were interested, but this has been removed. On the failure of regular proof, the Roman law allowed a party to refer the facts in a civil action to the oath of his adversary.

Witnesses.

Under the empire every judgment was reduced to writing and signed by the judge, and then entered upon a register.[1] After the sentence, the debtor was allowed thirty days for the payment of his debt, after which he was assigned over to the creditor and kept in chains for sixty days, during which he was publicly exposed for three market days, and if no one released him by paying the debt, he could be sold as a slave. Justinian extended the period to four months for the payment of a judgment debt, after which, if the debt was not paid, the debtor could be imprisoned, but not, as formerly, in the creditor's house. At first the goods of the debtor were sold in favor of any one who offered to pay the largest dividend, but in process of time, the goods of the debtor were

Condition of debtors.

[1] C. vii. 45, 12.

sold in detail, and all creditors were paid a ratable dividend. In no respect are modern codes superior to the Roman, so much as in reference to imprisonment for debt. In the United States it has practically ceased, and in England no one can be imprisoned for a debt under £20, and in France under £8.

Appeal.

Under the Roman republic, there was no appeal in civil suits, but under the emperors a regular system was established. Under Augustus, there was an appeal from all the magistrates to the prefect of the city, and from him to the prætorian prefect or emperor. In the provinces there was an appeal from the municipal magistrates to the governors, and from them to the emperor. Under Justinian, no appeal was allowed from a suit which did not involve at least twenty pounds in gold.

Criminal courts.

In regard to criminal courts, among the Romans, during the republic, the only body which had absolute power of life and death was the *comitia centuriata*. The Senate had no jurisdiction in criminal cases, so far as Roman citizens were concerned. It was only in extraordinary emergencies that the Senate, with the consuls, assumed the responsibility of inflicting summary punishment. Under the emperors, the Senate was armed with the power of criminal jurisdiction. And as the Senate was the tool of the imperator, he could crush whomsoever he pleased.

As it was inconvenient, when Rome had become a very great city, to convene the comitia for the trial of offenders, the expedient was adopted of delegating the jurisdiction of the people to persons invested with temporary authority, called *quæsitores*. These were established at length into regular and permanent courts, called *quæstiones perpetuæ*. Every case submitted to these courts was tried by a judge and jury. It was the duty of the judge to preside and regulate proceedings according to law; and it was the duty of the jury, after hearing the evidence and pleadings, to decide upon the guilt or innocence of the accused. As many as fifty persons frequently composed the jury, whose names were drawn out of an urn. Each party had a right to challenge a certain number, and the verdict was decided by a majority of votes. At first the judices were chosen from the Senate, and afterwards from the Equestrians, and then again from both orders. But in process of time the *quæstiones perpetuæ* gave place to imperial magistrates. The accused defended himself in person or by counsel.

The Romans divided *crimes* into public and private. Private crimes could only be prosecuted by the party injured, and were generally punished by pecuniary fines, as among the old Germanic nations.

Crimes.

Of public crimes, the *crimen læsæ majestatis*, or treason, was regarded as the greatest, and this was punished with death, and with confiscation of goods,[1] while the memory of the offender was declared infamous. Greater severity could scarcely be visited on a culprit. Treason comprehended conspiracy against the government, assisting the enemies of Rome, and misconduct in the command of armies. Thus Manlius, in spite of his magnificent services, was hurled from the Tarpeian Rock, because he was convicted of an intention to seize upon the government. Under the empire, not only any attempt on the life of the emperor was treason, but disrespectful words or acts. The criminal was even tried after death,[2] that his memory might become infamous, and this barbarous practice existed even in France and Scotland, as late as the beginning of the seventeenth century. In England, men have been executed for treasonable words. Beside treason there were other crimes against the state, such as a breach of the peace, extortion on the part of provincial governors, embezzlement of public property, stealing sacred things, bribery, most of which offenses were punished by pecuniary penalties.

Treason.

[1] I. 4, 18, 3.

[2] C. 9, 8, 6.

But there were also crimes against individuals which were punished with the death penalty. Willful murder, poisoning, parricide, were capitally punished. Adultery was punished by banishment, beside a forfeiture of considerable property.[1] Constantine made it a capital offense. The Romans made adultery to consist in sexual intercourse with another man's wife, but not with a woman who was not married, even if he were married. Rape was punished with death[2] and confiscation of goods, as in England till a late period, when transportation for life became the penalty. The punishments inflicted for forgery, coining base money, and perjury, were arbitrary. Robbery, theft, patrimonial damage, and injury to person and property, were private trespasses, and not punished by the state. After a lapse of twenty years, without accusation, crimes were supposed to be extinguished. The Cornelian, Pompeian, and Julian laws formed the foundation of criminal jurisprudence, which never attained the perfection that was seen in the Civil Code. It was in this that the full maturity of wisdom was seen. The emperors greatly increased the severity of punishments, as probably necessary in a corrupt state of society. After the decemviral laws fell into disuse, the Romans, in the days of the republic, passed from extreme rigor to great lenity, as is observable in the transition from the Puritan regime to our times in the United States. Capital punishment for several centuries was exceedingly rare, and this was prevented by voluntary exile. Under the empire, public executions were frequent and revolting.

Capital punishments.

Criminal law gradually ameliorated.

Fines were a common mode of punishment with the Romans, as with the early Germans. Imprisonment in a public jail was also rare, the custom of bail being in general use. Although retaliation was authorized by the Twelve Tables for bodily injuries, it was seldom exacted, since pecuniary compensation was taken in lieu.

Fines.

[1] D. 48, 5. [2] C. 9, 13.

Corporal punishments were inflicted upon slaves, but rarely upon citizens, except for military crimes. But Roman citizens could be sold into slavery for various offenses, chiefly military, and criminals were often condemned to labor in the mines or upon public works. Banishment was common — *aquæ et ignis interdictio* — and this was equivalent to the deprivation of the necessities of life, and incapacitating a person from exercising the rights of citizenship. Under the emperors, persons were confined often on the rocky islands off the coast, or a compulsory residence in a particular place assigned. Thus Chrysostom was sent to a dreary place on the banks of the Euxine. Ovid was banished to Tomi. Death, when inflicted, was by hanging, scourging, and beheading, also by strangling in prison. Slaves were often crucified, and were compelled to carry their cross to the place of execution. This was the most ignominious and lingering of all deaths. It was abolished by Constantine from reverence to the sacred symbol. Under the emperors, execution took place also by burning alive and exposure to wild beasts. It was thus the early Christians were tormented, since their offense was associated with treason. Persons of distinction were treated with more favor than the lower classes, and the punishment was less cruel and ignominious. Thus Seneca, condemned for privity to treason, was allowed to choose his mode of death. The criminal laws of modern European states followed too often the barbarous custom of the emperors until a recent date. Since the French Revolution, the severity of the penal codes has been much modified.

Exile.

The penal statutes of Rome, as Gibbon emphatically remarks, "formed a very small portion of the Code and the Pandects; and in all judicial proceedings, the life or death of the citizen was determined with less caution and delay than the most ordinary question of covenant or inheritance." This was owing to the complicated relations of society, by which obligations are created or annulled, while duties to the state are explicit and well known, being inscribed not only on tables of brass, but on the conscience itself. It was natural, with the growth and development of commerce and dominion, that questions would arise which could not be ordinarily settled by ancient customs, and the practice of lawyers and the decisions of judges continually raised new difficulties, to be met only by new edicts. It is a pleasing fact to record that jurisprudence became more just and enlightened as it became more intricate. The principles of equity were more regarded under the emperors than in the time of Cato. It is in the application of these principles that the laws of the Romans have obtained so high consideration. Their abuse consisted in the expense of litigation, and the advantages which the rich thus obtained over the poor. But if delays and forms led to an expensive and vexatious administration of justice, these were more than compensated by the checks which a complicated jurisprudence gave to hasty or partial decisions. It was in the minuteness and precision of the forms of law, and in the foresight with which questions were anticipated in the various transactions of business, that prove that the Romans, in their civil and social relations, were very much on a level with modern times. And it would be difficult to find, in the most enlightened of modern codes, greater wisdom and foresight than what appear in the legacy of Justinian, as to all questions pertaining to the nature, the acquisition, the possession, the use, and the transfer of property. Civil obligations are most admirably defined, and all contracts are determined by the wisest application of the natural principles of justice. What can be more enlightened than the laws which relate to leases, to sales, to partnerships, to damages, to pledges, to hiring of work, and to quasi contracts! How clear the laws pertaining to the succession to property, to the duties of guardians, to the rights of wards, to legacies, to bequests in trust, and to

Excellence of laws pertaining to property.

the general limitation of testamentary powers! How wise the regulations in reference to intestate succession, and to the division of property among males and females. We find no laws of entail, no unequal rights, no absurd distinctions between brothers, no peculiar privileges given to males over females, or to older sons. In the Institutes of Justinian, we see on every page a regard to the principles of natural justice. We discover that the property of the wife cannot be alienated nor mortgaged by a prodigal husband; that wards are to be protected from the cupidity of guardians; that property could be bequeathed by will, and that wills are sacred; that all promises are to be fulfilled; that he who is intrusted with the property of another is bound to restitution by the most imperative obligations; that usury should be restrained; that all injuries should be repaired; that cattle and slaves should be protected from malice and negligence; that atrocious cruelties in punishment should not be inflicted; that malicious witnesses should be punished; that corrupt judges should be visited with severe penalties; that libels and satires should subject their authors to severe chastisement; that every culprit should be considered innocent until his guilt was proved. In short, every thing pertaining to property and contracts and wills is guarded with the most zealous care. A man was sure of possessing his own, and of transmitting it to his children. No infringement on personal rights could be tolerated. A citizen was free to go where he pleased, to do whatsoever he would, if he did not trespass on the rights of another; to seek his pleasure unobstructed, and pursue his business without vexatious incumbrances. If he was injured or cheated, he was sure of redress. Nor could he be easily defrauded with the sanction of the laws. A rigorous police guarded his person, his house, and his property. He was supreme and uncontrolled within his family. And this security to property and life and personal rights was guaranteed by the

Rights of citizens.

greatest tyrants. The fullest personal liberty was enjoyed under the emperors, and it was under their sanction that jurisprudence, in some of the most important departments of life, reached perfection. If injustice was suffered, it was not on account of the laws, but the depravity of men, the venality of the rich, and the tricks of lawyers. But the laws were wise and equal. The civil jurisprudence could be copied with safety by the most enlightened of European states. And, indeed, it is the foundation of their civil codes, especially in France and Germany.

That there were some features in the Roman laws which we, in these Christian times, cannot indorse, and which we reprehend, cannot be denied. Under the republic, there was not sufficient limit to paternal power, and the *paterfamilias* was necessarily a tyrant. It was unjust that the father should control the property of his son, and cruel that he was allowed such absolute control, not only over his children, but his wife. But the limits of paternal power were more and more curtailed, so that under the latter emperors, fathers were not allowed to have more authority than was perhaps expedient.

Abuse of paternal power.

The recognition of slavery as a domestic institution was another blot, and slaves could be treated with the grossest cruelty and injustice without redress. But here the Romans were not sinners beyond all other nations, and our modern times have witnessed a parallel.

Evils of slavery.

It was not the existence of slavery which was the greatest evil, but the facility by which slaves could be made. The laws pertaining to debt were severe, and it was most disgraceful to doom a debtor to the absolute power of a creditor. To subject men of the same blood to slavery for trifling debts, which they could not discharge, was the great defect of the Roman laws. But even these cruel regulations were modified, so that in the corrupt times of the empire, there was no greater practical severity than what was common in England one hundred years ago. The temptations to fraud were enormous in a wicked state of society, and demanded a severe remedy. It is possible that future ages may see too great leniency shown to debtors, who are not merely unfortunate but dishonest, in these our times; and the problem is not yet solved, whether men should be severely handled who are guilty of reckless and unprincipled speculations and unscrupulous dealings, or whether they should be allowed immunity to prosecute their dangerous and disgraceful courses.

Evils of divorce.

The facility of divorce was another stigma on the Roman laws, and the degradation of woman was the principal consequence. But woman never was honored in any pagan land. Her condition at Rome was better than it was at Athens. She always was regarded as a possession rather than as a free person. Her virtue was mistrusted, and her aspirations were scorned. She was hampered and guarded more like a slave than the equal companion of man. But the whole progress of legislation was in her favor, and she continued to gain new privileges to the fall of the empire.

Severity of penal law.

Moreover, the penal code of the Romans, in reference to breaches of trust, or carelessness, or ignorance, by which property was lost or squandered, may have been too severe, as is the case in England in reference to hunting game on another's grounds. It was hard to doom a man to death who drove away his neighbor's cattle, or entered in the night his neighbor's house. But severe penalties alone will keep men from crimes where there is a low state of virtue and religion, and society becomes impossible when there is no efficient protection to property. If sheep can be killed by dogs, if orchards can be stripped of their fruit, and jewelry be appropriated by servants with impunity, a great stimulus to honest industry is taken away, and men will be forced to seek more distant homes where they can reap the fruits of toil, or will give up in despair. Society was never more secure and happy in England than when vagabonds could be arrested, and when petty larcenies were visited with certain retribution. Every traveler in France and England feels that in regard to the punishment of crime, those old countries, restricted as are political privileges, are vastly superior to our own. The Romans lost, under the emperors, their political rights ; but they gained protection and safety in their relations with society. And where quiet and industrious citizens feel safe in their homes, and are protected in their dealings from scoundrels, and have ample scope for industrial enterprise, and are free to choose their private pleasures, they resign themselves to the loss of electing their rulers without great unhappiness. There are greater evils in the world than the deprivation of the elective franchise, great and glorious as is this privilege. The arbitrary rule of the emperors was fatal to political aspirations and rights, but the evils of political slavery were qualified and set off by the excellence of the civil code, and the privileges of social freedom.

Certainty of punishment.

The great practical evil connected with Roman jurisprudence was the intricacy and perplexity and uncertainty of the laws, together with the expense involved in litigation. The class of lawyers was large, and their gains were extortionate. Justice was not always to be found on the side of right. The law was uncertain as well as costly. The most learned counsel could only be employed by the rich, and even judges were venal. So that the poor did not easily find adequate redress, and the good became an evil. But all this is the necessary attendant on a factitious state of society. Material civilization will lead to an undue estimate of money. And when money purchases all that artificial people desire, then all classes will prostitute themselves for its possession, and justice, dignity, and elevation of sentiment are forced to retreat, as hermits sought a solitude, when society had

Intricacy and uncertainty of the law.

reached its lowest degradation, out of pure despair of its renovation.

The authorities for this chapter are very numerous. Since the Institutes of Gaius have been recovered, very many eminent writers on Roman law have appeared, especially in Germany and France. Among those who could be cited, are Beaufort, Histoire de la Republique Romaine; Colquhoun, Summary of the Roman Civil Law; De Fresquet, Traité Elementaire de Droit Romain; Ducaurroy (A. M. Professor of Roman Law at Paris), Les Institutes de Justinien nouvellement expliquées; Gneist (Dr. Reed), Institutionum et Regularum Juris Romani; Halifax (Dr. Samuel), Analysis of the Roman Civil Law; Heineccius (Jo. Gott.), Elementa Juris Civilis Secundum Ordinem Institutionum; Laboulaye, Essai sur les Lois Criminelles des Romains; Long's Articles on Roman Law in Dr. Smith's Dictionary; Maine's Ancient Law; Gaius, Institutionum Commentarii Quatuor; Marezole (Theodore, Professor at Leipsic), Lebruch der Institutionem des Römischen Rechts; Maynz (Charles, Professor of Law at Brussels), Elements du Droit Romain; Ortolan (M., Professor at Paris), Explication Historique des Institutes de l'Empereur Justinien; Phillimore, Introduction to the Study and History of Roman Law; Pothier, Pandectæ Justinianæ in Novum Ordinem Digestæ; Savigny, Geschichte des Röm. Rechts; Walter, Histoire de la Procédure Civile Chez Romains.

I have found the late work of Lord Mackenzie, on Roman Law, together with the articles of George Long, in Smith's Dictionary, the most useful in compiling this notice of Roman jurisprudence. Mr. Maine's Treatise on Roman Law is exceedingly interesting and valuable. Gibbon's famous chapter should also be read by every student. There is a fine translation of the Institutes of Justinian, which is quite accessible, by Dr. Harris of Oxford. The Code, Pandects, Institutes, and Novels, are, of course, the original authority, with the long-lost Institutes of Gaius.

In connection with the study of the Roman law, it would be well to read Sir George Bowyer's Commentaries on the Modern Civil Law; Irving, Introduction to the Study of the Civil Law; Lindley, Introduction to the Study of Jurisprudence; and Wheaton's Elements of International Law; Vattel, Le Droit des Gens.

CHAPTER VII.

ROMAN LITERATURE.

If the ancient civilization rivaled the modern in the realm of *art*, it was equally remarkable in the field of letters. It is not my object to show that it was equal, or superior, or inferior to modern literature, either in original genius or artistic excellence. That point would be difficult to settle, and unprofitable to discuss. There is no doubt as to the superior advantage which the modern world derives in consequence of the invention of printing, and the consequent diffusion of knowledge. But the question is in reference to the height which was attained by the ancient pagan intellect, unaided by Christianity. I simply wish to show that the ancients were distinguished in all departments of literature, and that some of the masterpieces of genius were created by them.

Nor is it my object to write a summary of the literature of antiquity. It would be as dull as a catalogue, or a dictionary, or a compendium of universal history for the use of schools in a single volume. And it would be as profitless. My aim is simply to show that the old civilization can boast of its glories in literature, as well as in art, and that the mind of man never more nobly asserted its power than in Greece and Rome. Our present civilization delights in those philosophers, poets, and historians, who caught their inspiration from the great pagan models which have survived the wreck of material greatness. The human intellect achieved some of its greatest feats before Christianity was born. The inborn dignity of the mind and soul was never more nobly asserted than by Plato and

Aristotle, by Thucydides and Tacitus, by Homer and Virgil, by Demosthenes and Cicero. In attestation, therefore, of the glory of the ancient civilization, in the realm of literature, it is quite sufficient for our purpose to point out some of those great lights which, after the lapse of two thousand years or more, still continue to shine, and which are objects of hopeless imitation, even as they are of universal admiration. If we can show that the great heights were reached, even by a few, we prove the extent of civilization. If genius can soar, under Pagan, as well as under Christian influences, it would appear that civilization, in an intellectual point of view, may be the work of man, unaided by inspiration. It is the triumph of the native intellect of man which I wish to show.

Romans borrow from the Greeks.

Although it is my chief aim to present the magnificent civilization of the Roman empire under the emperors, I must cite the examples of Grecian as well as Roman genius, since Greece became a part of that grand empire, and since Grecian and Roman culture is mixed up and blended together. Roman youth were trained in the Grecian schools. Young men were sent to Athens and Rhodes after they had finished their education in the capital. Athens continued to be, for several hundred years after her political glory had passed away, the great university city of the world. Educated Romans were as familiar with the Greek classics as they were with those of their own country, and could talk Greek as modern Germans can talk French. The poems which kindled the enthusiasm of Roman youth are as worthy of notice as the statues which the conquerors brought from the Ionian cities, to ornament their palaces and baths. They equally attest the richness of the old civilization. And as it is the triumph of the pagan intellect which I wish to show, it matters but little whether we draw our illustrations from Greece or Rome. Without the aid of Greece, Rome could never have reached the height she attained.

Now how rich in poetry was classical antiquity, whether sung in the Greek or Latin languages. In all those qualities which give immortality, it has never been surpassed, whether in simplicity, in passion, in fervor, in fidelity to nature, in wit, or in imagination. It existed from the early ages, and continued to within a brief period of the fall of the empire. With the rich accumulation of ages, the Romans were familiar. They knew nothing indeed of the solitary grandeur of the Jewish muse, or the mythological myths of the Ante-Homeric songsters; but they possessed the Iliad and the Odyssey, with their wonderful truthfulness, and clear portraiture of character, their absence of all affectation, their serenity and cheerfulness, their good sense and healthful sentiments, yet so original that the germ of almost every character which has since figured in epic poetry can be found in them. We see in Homer[1] a poet of the first class, holding the same place in literature that Plato does in philosophy, or Newton in science, and exercising a mighty influence on all the ages which have succeeded him. For nearly three thousand years his immortal creations have been the delight and the inspiration of men of genius, and they are as marvelous to us as they were to the Athenians, since they are exponents of the learning, as well as of the consecrated sentiments of the heroic ages. We see no pomp of words, no far-fetched thoughts, no theatrical turgidity, no ambitious speculations, no indefinite longings; but we read the manners and customs of the primitive nations, and lessons of moral wisdom and human nature as it is, and the sights and wonders of the external world, all narrated with singular simplicity, yet marvelous artistic skill. We find accuracy, delicacy, naturalness, yet grandeur, sentiment, and beauty, such as Pheidias represented in his statues of

Richness of Greek poetry.

The Homeric poems.

1 Born probably at Smyrna, an Ionian city, about one hundred and fifty years after the Trojan War.

Jupiter. No poems have ever been more popular, and none have extorted greater admiration from critics. Like Shakespeare, Homer is a kind of Bible to both the learned and unlearned among all people and ages — one of the prodigies of this world. His poems form the basis of Greek literature, and are the best understood and the most widely popular of all Grecian composition. The unconscious simplicity of the Homeric narrative, its vivid pictures, its graphic details and religious spirit, create an enthusiasm such as few works of genius can claim. Moreover, it presents a painting of society, with its simplicity and ferocity, its good and evil passions, its compassion and its fierceness, such as no other poem affords.[1] Nor is it necessary to speak of any other Grecian epic, when the Iliad and the Odyssey attest the perfection which was attained one hundred and twenty years before Hesiod was born. Grote thinks that the Iliad and the Odyssey were produced at some period between 850 B. C., and 776 B. C.

Pindar.

In lyrical poetry the Greeks were no less remarkable, and indeed they attained to absolute perfection, owing to the intimate connection between poetry and music. Who has surpassed Pindar in artistic skill? His *triumphal odes* are pæans, in which piety breaks out in expressions of the deepest awe, and the most elevated sentiments of moral wisdom. They alone of all his writings have descended to us, but all possess fragments of odes, songs, dirges, and panegyrics, which show the great excellence to which he attained. He was so celebrated that he was employed by the different states and princes of Greece to compose choral songs for special occasions, especially the public games. Although a Theban, he was

[1] The Homeric poems have been translated into nearly all the European languages, and several times into English. The last translation is by the Earl of Derby — a most remarkable work. Guizot, *Cours d'Hist. Mod.*, Lecon 7me; Grote, vol. ii. p. 277; *Studies in Homer*, by Hon. W. E. Gladstone; Mure, *Critical Hist. of Lang. and Lit. of Greece;* Müller, *Hist. of the Lit. of Ancient Greece*, translated by Donaldson.

held in the highest estimation by the Athenians, and was courted by kings and princes.[1] We possess, also, fragments of Sappho, Simonides, Anacreon, and others, enough to show that, could the lyrical poetry of Greece be recovered, we should probably possess the richest collection that the world has produced.

Greek dramatic poetry.

But dramatic poetry was still more varied and remarkable. Even the great masterpieces of Sophocles and Euripides, were regarded by contemporaries as inferior to many tragedies utterly unknown to us. The great creator of the Greek drama was Æschylus, born at Eleusis, 525 B. C. It was not till the age of forty-one that he gained his first prize. Sixteen years afterwards, defeated by Sophocles, he quitted Athens in disgust, and went to the court of Hiero, king of Syracuse. But he was always held, even at Athens, in the highest honor, and his pieces were frequently reproduced upon the stage. It was not so much his object to amuse an audience, as to instruct and elevate it. He combined religious feeling with lofty moral sentiment. And he had unrivaled power over the realm of astonishment and terror. "At his summons," says Sir Walter Scott, "the mysterious and tremendous volume of destiny, in which is inscribed the doom of gods and men, seemed to display its leaves of iron before the appalled spectators; the more than mortal voices of Deities, Titans, and departed heroes, were heard in awful conference; heaven bowed, and its divinities descended; earth yawned and gave up the pale spectres of the dead, and yet more undefined and ghastly forms of those infernal deities who struck horror into the gods themselves." His imagination dwells in the loftiest regions of the old mythology of Greece; his tone is always pure and moral, though stern and harsh. He appeals to the most violent passions, and he is full of the boldest

Æschylus.

[1] Born in Thebes 522 B. C., and died probably in his eightieth year, and was contemporary with Æschylus and the battle of Marathon.

metaphors. In sublimity he has never been surpassed. He was in poetry, what Pheidias and Michael Angelo were in art. The critics say that his sublimity of diction is sometimes carried to an extreme, so that his language becomes inflated. His characters are sublime, like his sentiments; they were gods and heroes of colossal magnitude. His religious views were Homeric, and he sought to animate his countrymen to deeds of glory, as it became one of the generals who fought at Marathon to do. He was an unconscious genius, and worked, like Homer, without a knowledge of artistical laws. He was proud and impatient, and his poetry was religious rather than moral. He wrote seventy plays, of which only seven are extant; but these are immortal, among the greatest creations of human genius, like the dramas of Shakespeare. He died in Sicily in the sixty-ninth year of his age. The principal English translation of his plays are by Potter, Harford, and Medwin.[1]

Sophocles.

The fame of Sophocles is scarcely less than that of Æschylus. He was twenty-seven years of age when he appeared as a rival. He was born in Colonus, in the suburbs of Athens, 495 B. C., and was the contemporary of Herodotus, of Pericles, of Pindar, of Pheidias, of Socrates, of Cimon, of Euripides — the era of great men; the period of the Peloponnesian War, when every thing that was elegant and intellectual culminated at Athens. Sophocles had every element of character and person which fascinated the Greeks: beauty of person, symmetry of form, skill in gymnastics, calmness and dignity of manner, a cheerful and amiable temper, a ready wit, a meditative piety, a spontaneity of genius, an affectionate admiration for talent, and patriotic devotion to his country. His tragedies, by the universal consent of the best critics, are the perfection of the Grecian drama, and they, moreover, maintain that he has no rival, Shakespeare

[1] See Müller and Bode, histories of Greek Literature.

alone excepted, in the whole realm of dramatic poetry, unless it be Æschylus himself, to whom he bears the same relation in poetry that Raphael does to Michael Angelo in the world of art. It was his peculiarity to excite emotions of sorrow and compassion. He loved to paint forlorn heroes. He was human in all his sympathies, not so religious as his great rival, but as severely ethical; not so sublime, but more perfect in art. His sufferers are not the victims of an inexorable destiny, but of their own follies. Nor does he even excite emotion apart from a moral end. He lived to be ninety years old, and produced the most beautiful of his tragedies in his eightieth year, the "Œdipus at Colonus." He wrote the astonishing number of one hundred and thirty plays, and carried off the first prize twenty-four times. His "Antigone" was written when he was forty-five, and when Euripides had already gained a prize. Only seven of his tragedies have survived, but these are priceless treasures. The fertility of his genius was only equaled by his artistic skill.[1]

Euripides.

Euripides, the last of the great triumvirate of the Greek tragic poets, was born at Athens, B. C. 485. He had not the sublimity of Æschylus, nor the touching pathos of Sophocles, but, in seductive beauty and successful appeal to passion, was superior to both. Nor had he their stern simplicity. In his tragedies the passion of love predominates, nor does it breathe the purity of sentiment. It approaches rather to the tone of the modern drama. He paints the weakness and corruptions of society, and brings his subjects to the level of common life. He was the pet of the Sophists, and was pantheistic in his views. He does not paint ideal excellence, and his characters are not as men ought to be, but as they are, especially in corrupt states of society. He wrote ninety-five plays, of which eighteen are extant. Whatever objection may be

[1] Schlegel, *Lectures on Dramatic Art;* Müller, *Hist. Lit.*; Donaldson's *Antigone;* Lessing, *Leben des Sophokles;* Philip Smith, article in Smith's *Dict.*

urged in reference to his dramas on the score of morality, nobody can question their transcendent art, or his great originality. With the exception of Shakespeare, all succeeding dramatists have copied these three great poets, especially Racine, who took Sophocles for his model.[1]

The Greeks were no less distinguished for comedy. Both tragedy and comedy sprung from feasts in honor of Bacchus; and as the jests and frolics were found misplaced when introduced into grave scenes, a separate province of the drama was formed, and comedy arose. At first it did not derogate from the religious purposes which were at the foundation of the Greek drama. It turned upon parodies, in which the adventures of the gods are introduced by way of sport, like the appetite of Hercules, or the cowardice of Bacchus. Then the comic authors entertained spectators by fantastic and gross displays; by the exhibition of buffoons and pantomimes. But the taste of the Athenians was too severe to relish such entertainments, and comedy passed into ridicule of public men and measures, and of the fashions of the day. The people loved to see their great men brought down to their own level. Nor did comedy flourish until the morals of society were degenerated, and ridicule had become the most effective weapon to assail prevailing follies. Comedy reached its culminating point when society was both the most corrupt and the most intellectual, as in France, when Molière pointed his envenomed shafts against popular vices. It pertained to the age of Socrates and the Sophists, when there was great bitterness in political parties, and an irrepressible desire for novelties. In Cratinus, comedy first made herself felt as a great power, who espoused the side of Cimon against Pericles, with great bitterness and vehemence. Many were the comic writers of that age of wickedness and genius, but all yielded precedence to

Greek comedy.

1 Müller, Schlegel. Sir Walter Scott on the Drama; Grote, vol. viii. p. 442, Thorne, *Mag. Vita. Eurip.* Potter has made a translation of all his plays.

Aristophanes, whose plays only have reached us. Never were libels on persons of authority and influence uttered with such terrible license. He attacked the gods, the politicians, the philosophers, and the poets of Athens; even private citizens did not escape from his shafts, and women were subjects of his irony. Socrates was made the butt of his ridicule, when most revered, and Cleon in the height of his power, and Euripides when he had gained the highest prizes. He has furnished jests for Rabelais, and hints to Swift, and humor for Molière. In satire, in derision, in invective, and bitter scorn, he has never been surpassed. No modern capital would tolerate such unbounded license. Yet no plays were ever more popular, or more fully exposed follies which could not otherwise be reached. He is called the Father of Comedy, and his comedies are of great historical importance, although his descriptions are doubtless caricatures. He was patriotic in his intentions, and set up for a reformer. His peculiar genius shines out in his "Clouds," the greatest of his pieces, in which he attacks the Sophists. He wrote fifty-four plays. He was born B. C. 444, and died B. C. 380. His best comedies are translated by Mitchell.

Aristophanes.

Thus it would appear that in the three great departments of poetry, — the epic, the lyric, and the dramatic, — the old Greeks were great masters, and have been the teachers of all subsequent nations and ages.

The Romans, in these departments, were not their equals, but they were very successful copyists, and will bear competition with modern nations. If the Romans did not produce a Homer, they can boast of a Virgil; if they had no Pindar, they furnished a Horace, while in satire they transcended the Greeks.

The Romans, however, produced no poetry worthy of notice until the Greek language and literature were introduced. It was not till the fall of Tarentum that we read of a Roman poet. Livius Andronicus, a Greek slave,

B. C. 240, rudely translated the Odyssey into Latin, and was the author of various plays, all of which have perished, and none of which, according to Cicero, were worth a second perusal. Still he was the first to substitute the Greek drama for the old lyrical stage poetry. One year after the first Punic War, he exhibited the first Roman play. As the creator of the drama, he deserves historical notice, though he has no claim to originality, and like a schoolmaster as he was, pedantically labored to imitate the culture of the Greeks. And his plays formed the commencement of Roman translation-literature, and naturalized the Greek metres in Latium, even though they were curiosities rather than works of art.[1] Nævius, B. C. 235, produced a play at Rome, and wrote both epic and dramatic poetry, but so little has survived, that no judgment can be formed of his merits. He was banished for his invectives against the aristocracy, who did not relish severity of comedy.[2] Mommsen regards Nævius as the first among the Romans who deserves to be ranked among the poets. He flourished about the year 550, and closely adhered to Andronicus in metres. His language is free from stiffness and affectation, and his verses have a graceful flow. Plautus was perhaps the first great poet whom the Romans produced, and his comedies are still admired by critics, as both original and fresh. He was born in Umbria, B. C. 257, and was contemporaneous with Publius and Cneius Scipio. He died B. C. 184.

Nævius.

The first development of Roman genius in the field of poetry, seems to have been the dramatic, in which the Greek authors were copied. Plautus might be mistaken for a Greek, were it not for the painting of Roman manners. His garb is essentially Greek. He wrote one hundred and thirty plays, not always for the stage, but for the reading public. He lived about the time of the second Punic War, before the theatre was fairly

Plautus.

[1] Mommsen, vol. ii. b. iii. ch. xiv.

[2] Horace, *Ep.* ii. 1, 53.

established at Rome. His characters, although founded on Greek models, act, speak, and joke like Romans. He enjoyed great popularity down to the latest times of the empire, while the purity of his language, as well as the felicity of his wit, was celebrated by the ancient critics.[1] Cicero places his wit on a par with the old Attic comedy,[2] while Jerome spent much time in reading his comedies, even though they afterward cost him tears of bitter regret. Modern dramatists owe much to him. Molière has imitated him in his "*Avare*," and Shakespeare in his "Comedy of Errors." Lessing pronounces the "*Captivi*" to be the finest comedy ever brought upon the stage.[3] He has translated this play into German. It has also been admirably translated into English. The great excellence of Plautus was the masterly handling of the language, and the adjusting the parts for dramatic effect. His humor, broad and fresh, produced irresistible comic effects. No one ever surpassed him in his vocabulary of nicknames, and his happy jokes. Hence he maintained his popularity in spite of his vulgarity.[4]

Terence.

Terence shares with Plautus the throne of Roman comedy. He was a Carthaginian slave, and was born B. C. 160, but was educated by a wealthy Roman, into whose hands he fell, and ever after associated with the best society, and traveled extensively into Greece. He was greatly inferior to Plautus in originality, nor has he exerted a lasting influence like him ; but he wrote comedies characterized by great purity of diction, and which have been translated into all modern languages.[5] Anterior to the Augustan age, no tragic production has reached us, although Quintilian speaks highly of Accius,[6] especially of the vigor of his style. But he merely imitated the Greeks. Terence closely copied Menander, whom Mommsen re-

1 Quint., x. i. § 99.
2 Cicero, *De Off.*, i. 29.
3 Smith, *Dict. of Ant.* art. *Plaut.*
4 Mommsen, vol. ii. b. iii. ch. xiv.
5 Coleman's *Terence ;* Dryden, *On Dram. Poet. ;* Mommsen, vol. iii. b. v. ch. xiii.
6 Quint., x. l. § 97.

gards as the most polished, elegant, and chaste of all the poets of the newer comedy. Unlike Plautus, he draws his characters from good society, and his comedies, if not moral, were decent. Plautus wrote for the multitude; Terence for the few. Plautus delighted in a noisy dialogue and slang expressions; Terence confines himself to quiet conversation and elegant expressions, for which he was admired by Cicero and Quintilian, and other great critics. He aspired to the approval of the good, rather than the applause of the vulgar; and it is a remarkable fact that his comedies supplanted the more original productions of Plautus in the latter years of the republic, showing that the literature of the aristocracy was more prized than that of the people, even in a degenerate age. The "*Thyestes*"[1] of Varius, was regarded in its day as equal to Greek tragedies. Ennius composed tragedies in a vigorous style, and was regarded by the Romans as the parent of their literature, although most of his works have perished.[2] Virgil borrowed many of his thoughts, and he was regarded as the prince of Roman song in the time of Cicero. The Latin language is greatly indebted to him. Pacuvius imitated Æschylus in the loftiness of his style.[3] The only tragedy of the Romans which has reached us was written by Seneca the philosopher.

The Æneid.

In epic poetry the Romans accomplished more, though still inferior to the Greeks. The "Æneid" has certainly survived the material glories of Rome. It may not have come up to the exalted ideal of its author; it may be defaced by political flatteries; it may not have the force and originality of the "Iliad," but it is superior in art, and delineates the passion of love with more delicacy than can be found in any Greek author. In soundness of judgment, in tenderness of feeling, in chastened fancy, in picturesque description, in delineation of character, in matchless beauty of diction, and in splendor of versification, it has never been surpassed by any poem in any lan-

1 Hor., *Sat.* i. 9; Martial, viii. 18. 2 Born B. C. 239. 3 Born B. C. 170.

18

guage, and proudly takes its place among the imperishable works of genius. "Availing himself of the pride and superstition of the Roman people, the poet traces the origin and establishment of the 'Eternal City,' to those heroes and actions which had enough in them of what was human and ordinary to excite the sympathies of his countrymen, intermingled with persons and circumstances of an extraordinary and superhuman character to awaken their admiration and awe. No subject could have been more happily chosen. It has been admired also for its perfect unity of action; for while the episodes command the richest variety of description, they are always subordinate to the main object of the poem, which is to impress the divine authority under which Æneas first settled in Italy. The wrath of Juno, upon which the whole fate of Æneas seems to turn, is at once that of a woman and a goddess; the passion of Dido, and her general character, bring us nearer to the present world; but the poet is continually introducing higher and more effectual influences, until, by the intervention of gods and men, the Trojan name is to be continued in the Roman, and thus heaven and earth are appeased."[1] No one work of man has probably had such a wide and profound influence as this poem of Virgil, — a text-book in all schools since the revival of learning, the model of the Carlovingian poets, the guide of Dante, the oracle of Tasso.[2]

Virgil.

In lyrical poetry, the Romans can boast of one of the greatest masters of any age or nation. The Odes of Horace have never been transcended, and will probably remain through all the ages, the delight of scholars. They may not have the deep religious sentiment, and

Horace.

1 Thompson, *Hist. Rom. Lit.*, p. 92.

2 Virgil was born seventy years before Christ, and was seven years older than Augustus. His parentage was humble, but his facilities of education were great. He was a most fortunate man, enjoying the friendship of Augustus and Mæcenas, fame in his own lifetime, leisure to prosecute his studies, and ample rewards for his labors. He died at Brundusium at the age of fifty.

the unity of imagination and passion which belong to the Greek lyrical poets, but as works of art, of exquisite felicity of expression, of agreeable images, they are unrivaled. Even in the time of Juvenal, his poems were the common school books of Roman youth. Horace, like Virgil, was a favored man, enjoying the friendship of the great with ease, fame, and fortune. But his longings for retirement, and his disgust at the frivolities around him, are a sad commentary on satisfied desires.[1] His odes compose but a small part of his writings. His epistles are the most perfect of his productions, and rank with the Georgics of Virgil and the satires of Juvenal, as the most perfect form of Roman verse. His satires are also admirable, but without the fierce vehemence and lofty indignation that characterized Juvenal. It is the folly rather than the wickedness of vice which he describes with such playful skill and such keenness of observation. He was the first to mould the Latin tongue to the Greek lyric measures. Quintilian's criticism is indorsed by all scholars. "*Lyricorum Horatius fere solus legi dignus, in verbis felicissime audax.*" No poetry was ever more severely elaborated than that of Horace, and the melody of the language imparts to it a peculiar fascination. If inferior to Pindar in passion and loftiness, it glows with a more genial humanity, and with purer wit. It cannot be enjoyed fully, except by those versed in the experiences of life. Such perceive a calm wisdom, a penetrating sagacity, a sober enthusiasm, and a refined taste, which are unusual even among the masters of human thought. It is the fashion to depreciate the original merits of this poet, as well as those of Virgil and Plautus and Terence, because they derived so much assistance from the Greeks. But the Greeks borrowed from each other. Pure originality is impossible. It is the mission of art to add to its stores, without hoping to monopolize the whole realm.

[1] Born B. C. 65. The best translation of his works is by Francis; but Horace is untranslatable.

Even Shakespeare, the most original of modern poets, was vastly indebted to those who went before him, and even he has not escaped the hypercriticism of minute observers.

Catullus.

In this allusion to lyrical poetry, I have not spoken of Catullus, unrivaled in tender lyric, and the greatest poet before the Augustan era. He was born B. C. 87, and enjoyed the friendship of the most celebrated characters. One hundred and sixteen of his poems have come down to us, most of which are short, and many of them defiled by great coarseness and sensuality. Critics say, however, that whatever he touched he adorned; that his vigorous simplicity, pungent wit, startling invective, and felicity of expression, make him one of the great poets of the Latin language.

Lucretius.

In didactic poetry, Lucretius was preëminent, and is regarded by Schlegel as the first of Roman poets in native genius.[1] He lived before the Augustan era, and died at the age of forty-two by his own hand. His great poem "De Rerum Natura," is a delineation of the epicurean philosophy, and treats of all the great subjects of thought with which his age is conversant. It somewhat resembles Pope's "Essay on Man," in style and subject, but immeasurably superior in poetical genius. It is a lengthened disquisition, in seven thousand four hundred lines, of the great phenomena of the outward world. As a painter and worshiper of nature, he was superior to all the poets of antiquity. His skill in presenting abstruse speculations is marvelous, and his outbursts of poetic genius are matchless in power and beauty. Into all subjects he casts a fearless eye, and writes with sustained enthusiasm. But he was not fully appreciated by his countrymen, although no other poet has so fully brought out the power of the Latin language. Professor Ramsay,[2] while alluding to the

[1] Born B. C. 95, died B. C. 52. Smith's *Dict.*

[2] The translation of Lucretius into English was made by I. M. Goode, Evelyn, and Drummond.

melancholy tenderness of Tibullus, the exquisite ingenuity of Ovid, the inimitable felicity and taste of Horace, the gentleness and splendor of Virgil, and the vehement declamation of Juvenal, thinks that, had the verses of Lucretius perished, we should never have known that it could give utterance to the grandest conceptions with all that self-sustained majesty and harmonious swell, in which the Grecian muse rolls forth her loftiest outpourings. The eulogium of Ovid is —

> "Carmina sublimis tunc sunt peritura Lucreti,
> Exitio terras quum dabit una dies."

Ovid.

Elegiac poetry has an honorable place in Roman literature. To this school belongs Ovid,[1] whose "Metamorphoses" will always retain their interest. He, with that self-conscious genius common to poets, declares that his poem would be proof against sword, fire, thunder, and time, — a prediction, says Bayle,[2] which has not yet proved false. Niebuhr[3] thinks that, next to Catullus, he was the most poetical of his countrymen. Milton thinks he could have surpassed Virgil had he attempted epic poetry. He was nearest to the romantic school of all the classical authors, and Chaucer, Ariosto, and Spenser owe to him great obligations. Like Pope, his verses flowed spontaneously. His "Tristia" were more admired by the Romans than his "Amores" or "Metamorphoses,"— probably from the doleful description of his exile,— a fact which shows that contemporaries are not always the best judges of real merit. His poems, great as was their genius, are deficient in the severe taste which marked the Greeks, and are immoral in their tendency. He had great advantages, but was banished by Augustus for his description of licentious love, "Carmina per libidinosa." Nor did he support exile with dignity. He died of a broken heart, and languished, like Cicero, when doomed to a similar fate. But few intel-

1 Born B. C. 43. Died A. D. 18.
2 Bayle, *Dict.*
3 *Lect.*, vol. ii. p. 166.

lectual men have ever been able to live at a distance from the scene of their glories, and without the stimulus of high society. Chrysostom is one of the few exceptions. Ovid, as an immoral man, was justly punished.

Tibullus. Tibullus was also a famous elegiac poet, and was born the same year as Ovid, and was the friend of Horace. He lived in retirement, and was both gentle and amiable. At his beautiful country seat he soothed his soul with the charms of literature and the simple pleasures of the country. Niebuhr pronounces his elegies doleful,[1] but Merivale[2] thinks that "the tone of tender melancholy in which he sung his unprosperous loves had a deeper and purer source than the caprices of three inconstant paramours." "His spirit is eminently religious, though it bids him fold his hands in resignation rather than open them in hope. He alone of all the great poets of his day remained undazzled by the glitter of the Cæsarian usurpation, and pined away in unavailing despondency, in beholding the subjugation of his country."

Propertius. His contemporary, Propertius,[3] was, on the contrary, the most eager of all the flatterers of Augustus, — a man of wit and pleasure, whose object of idolatry was Cynthia, a poetess and a courtesan. He was an imitator of the Greeks, but had a great contemporary fame,[4] and shows great warmth of passion, but he never soared into the sublime heights of poetry, like his rival. Such were among the great elegiac poets of Rome, generally devoted to the delineation of the passion of love. The older English poets resembled them in this respect, but none of them have soared to such lofty heights as the later ones, like Wordsworth and Tennyson. It is in lyric poetry that the moderns have chiefly excelled the ancients, in variety, in elevation of sentiment, and in imagination.

1 *Lect.*, vol. iii. p. 143.
2 *Hist.*, vol. iv. p. 602.
3 Born B. C. 51.
4 Quint., x. l. § 93.

The grandeur and originality of the ancients were displayed rather in epic and dramatic poetry.

In *satire* the Romans transcended both the Greeks and the moderns. There is nothing in any language which equals the fire, the intensity, and the bitterness of Juvenal, — not even Swift and Pope. But he flourished in the decline of literature, and has neither the taste nor elegance of the Augustan writers. He was the son of a freedman, and was born A. D. 38, and was the contemporary of Martial. He was banished by Domitian on account of a lampoon against a favorite dancer, but under the reign of Nerva he returned to Rome, and the imperial tyranny was the subject of his bitterest denunciation, next to the degradation of public morals. His great rival in satire was Horace, who laughed at follies; but he, more austere, exaggerated and denounced them. His sarcasms on women have never been equaled in severity, and we cannot but hope that they were unjust. In an historical point of view, as a delineation of the manners of his age, his satires are priceless, even like the epigrams of Martial. Satire arose with Lucilius,[1] in the time of Marius, an age when freedom of speech was tolerated. Horace was the first to gain immortality in this department. Persius comes next, born A. D. 34, the friend of Lucan and Seneca in the time of Nero; and he painted the vices of his age when it was passing to that degradation which marked the reign of Domitian when Juvenal appeared, who, disdaining fear, boldly set forth the abominations of the times, and struck without distinction all who departed from duty and conscience. This uncompromising poet, not pliant and easy like Horace, animadverted, like an incorruptible censor, on the vices which were undermining the moral health and preparing the way for violence; on the hypocrisy of philosophers and the cruelty of tyrants; on the weakness of women and the de-

Juvenal.

Persius.

[1] Born B. C. 148.

bauchery of men. He discourses on the vanity of human wishes with the moral wisdom of Dr. Johnson, and urges self-improvement like Socrates and Epictetus.[1]

I might speak of other celebrated poets, — of Lucan, of Martial, of Petronius; but I only wish to show that the great poets of antiquity, both Greek and Roman, have never been surpassed in genius, in taste, and in art, and few were ever more honored in their lifetime by appreciating admirers showing the advanced state of civilization which was reached in every thing pertaining to the realm of thought.

But the genius of the ancients was displayed in prose composition as well as in poetry, although perfection was not so soon attained. The poets were the great creators of the languages of antiquity. It was not until they had produced their immortal works that the languages were sufficiently softened and refined to admit of great beauty in prose. But prose requires art as well as poetry. There is an artistic rhythm in the writings of the classical authors, like those of Cicero and Herodotus and Thucydides, as marked as in the beautiful measure of Homer and Virgil. Burke and Macaulay are as great artists in style as Tennyson himself. Plato did not write poetry, but his prose is as "musical as Apollo's lyre." And it is seldom that men, either in ancient or modern times, have been distinguished for both kinds of composition, although Voltaire, Schiller, Milton, Swift, and Scott are among the exceptions. Cicero, the greatest prose writer of antiquity, produced only an inferior poem, laughed at by his contemporaries. Bacon could not write poetry, with all his affluence of thought and vigor of imagination and command of language, any easier than Pope could write prose.

All sorts of prose compositions were carried to perfection by both Greeks and Romans, in history, in criticism, in philosophy, in oratory, in epistles.

1 The best translations of Juvenal are those of Dryden, Gifford, and Badham.

Herodotus.

The earliest great prose writer among the Greeks was Herodotus,[1] from which we may infer that *History* was the first form of prose composition which attained development. But Herodotus was not born until Æschylus had gained a prize for tragedy, more than two hundred years after Simonides, the lyric poet, flourished, and probably six hundred years after Homer sung his immortal epics. After more than two thousand years the style of this great "Father of History" is admired by every critic; while his history, as a work of art, is still a study and a marvel. It is difficult to understand why no anterior work in prose is worthy of note, since the Greeks had attained a high civilization two hundred years before he appeared, and the language had reached a high point of development under Homer for more than five hundred years. The history of Herodotus was probably written in the decline of life, when his mind was enriched with great attainments in all the varied learning of his age, and when he had conversed with most of the celebrated men of the various countries which he visited. It pertains chiefly to the wars of the Greeks with the Persians; but, in his frequent episodes, which do not impair the unity of the work, he is led to speak of the manners and customs of the oriental nations. It was once the fashion to speak of Herodotus as a credulous man, who embodied the most improbable, though interesting stories. But now it is believed that no historian was ever more profound, conscientious, and careful; and all modern investigations confirm his sagacity and impartiality. He was one of the most accomplished men of antiquity, or of any age, — an enlightened and curious traveler, a profound thinker, a man of universal knowledge, familiar with the whole range of literature, art, and science in his day, acquainted with all the great men of Greece and at the courts of Asiatic princes, the friend of Sophocles, of Pericles, of Thucydides, of Aspasia, of Socrates, of Damon, of Zeno, of Pheidias, of

[1] Born B. C. 484.

Protagoras, of Euripides, of Polygnotus, of Anaxagoras, of Xenophon, of Alcibiades, of Lysias, of Aristophanes, — the most brilliant constellation of men of genius who were ever found together within the walls of a Grecian city, respected and admired by these great lights, all of whom he transcended in knowledge. Thus was he fitted for his task by travel, by study, and by intercourse with the great, to say nothing of his original genius, and the greatest prose work which had yet appeared in Greece was produced, — a prose epic, severe in taste, perfect in unity, rich in moral wisdom, charming in style, religious in spirit, grand in subject, without a coarse passage ; simple, unaffected, and beautiful, like the narratives of the Bible ; amusing, yet instructive, easy to understand, yet extending to the utmost boundaries of human research — a model for all subsequent historians. So highly was it valued by the Athenians, when their city was at the height of its splendor, that they decreed to its author ten talents, about twelve thousand dollars, for reciting it. He even went from city to city, a sort of prose rhapsodist, or like a modern lecturer, reciting his history — an honored and extraordinary man, a sort of Humboldt, having mastered every thing. And he wrote, not for fame, but to communicate the results of his inquiries, from the pure love of truth which he learned by personal investigation at Dodona, at Delphi, at Samos, at Athens, at Corinth, at Thebes, at Tyre ; yea, he traveled into Egypt, Scythia, Asia Minor, Palestine, Babylonia, Italy, and the islands of the sea. His episode in Egypt is worth more, in an historical point of view, than every thing combined which has descended to us from antiquity. Herodotus was the first to give dignity to history ; nor, in truthfulness, candor, and impartiality, has he ever been surpassed. His very simplicity of style is a proof of his transcendent art, even as it is the evidence of his severity of taste.[1]

[1] Dahlman has written an admirable life of Herodotus; but Rawlinson's translation, with his notes, is invaluable.

To Thucydides, as an historian, the modern world also assigns a proud preëminence. He treated only of a short period, during the Peloponnesian War; but the various facts connected with that great event could only be known by the most minute and careful inquiries. He devoted twenty-seven years to the composition of his narration, and he weighed his testimony with the most scrupulous care. His style has not the fascination of Herodotus, but it is more concise. In a single volume he relates what could scarcely be compressed into eight volumes of a modern history. As a work of art, of its kind, it is unrivaled. In his description of the plague of Athens he is minute as he is simple. He abounds with rich moral reflections, and has a keen perception of human character. His pictures are striking and tragic. He is vigorous and intense, and every word he uses has a meaning. But some of his sentences are not always easily understood. One of the greatest tributes which can be paid to him is, that, according to the estimate of an able critic,[1] we have a more exact history of a long and eventful period by Thucydides than we have of any period in modern history, equally long and eventful; and all this is compressed into a volume.[2]

Thucydides.

Xenophon is the last of the trio of the Greek historians, whose writings are classical and inimitable.[3] He is characterized by great simplicity and absence of affectation. His "Anabasis," in which he describes the expedition of the younger Cyrus and the retreat of the ten thousand Greeks, is his most famous book. But his "Cyropædia," in which the history of Cyrus is the subject, although still used as a classic in colleges for the beauty of the style, has no value as a history, since the author merely adopted the current stories of his hero without

Xenophon.

1 George Long, Oxford.

2 Born 471 B. C.; lived twenty years in exile on account of a military failure.

3 Born probably about 444 B. C.

sufficient investigation. Xenophon wrote a variety of treatises and dialogues, but his "Memorabilia" of Socrates is the most valuable. All antiquity and all modern writers unite in giving to Xenophon great merit as a writer, and great moral elevation as a man.

If we pass from the Greek to the Latin historians, — to those who were as famous as the Greek, and whose merit has scarcely been transcended in our modern times, if, indeed, it has been equaled, — the great names of Sallust, of Cæsar, of Livy, of Tacitus, rise up before us, together with a host of other names we have not room or disposition to present, since we only aim to show that the ancients were at least our equals in this great department of prose composition. The first great masters of the Greek language in prose were the historians, so far as their writings have descended, although it is probable that the orators may have shaped the language before them, and given it flexibility and refinement. The first great prose writers of Rome were the orators. Nor was the Latin language fully developed and polished until Cicero appeared. But we do not write a history of the language: we speak only of those who wrote immortal works in the various departments of learning.

As Herodotus did not arise until the Greek language had been already formed by the poets, so no great prose writer appeared among the Romans for a considerable time after Plautus, Terence, Ennius, and Lucretius flourished.

Sallust.

The first great historian was Sallust, the contemporary of Cicero, born B. C. 86, the year that Marius died. Q. Fabius Pictor, M. Portius Cato, L. Cal. Piso had already written works which are mentioned with respect by the Latin authors, but they were mere annalists or antiquarians, like the chroniclers of the Middle Ages, and had no claim as artists. Sallust made Thucydides his model, but fell below him in genius and elevated sentiment. He was born a plebeian, and rose to distinction by his talents, but was ejected from the Senate for his profligacy. Afterwards he made a great fortune as prætor and governor of Numidia, and lived in magnificence on the Quirinal — one of the most profligate of the literary men of antiquity. We possess but a small portion of his works, but the fragments which have come down to us show peculiar merit. He sought to penetrate the human heart, and reveal the secret motives which actuate the conduct of men. His style is brilliant, but his art is always apparent. He is clear and lively, but rhetorical. Like Voltaire, who inaugurated modern history, he thought more of style than of accuracy of facts. He was a party man, and never soared beyond his party. He aped the moralist, but erected egotism and love of pleasure into proper springs of action, and honored talent disconnected with virtue. Like Carlyle, he exalted *strong* men, and *because* they were strong. He was not comprehensive like Cicero, or philosophical like Thucydides, although he affected philosophy as he did morality. He was the first who deviated from the strict narratives of events, and also introduced much rhetorical declamation, which he puts into the mouths of his heroes.[1] He wrote for éclat.

Cæsar.

Cæsar, as an historian, ranks higher, and no Roman ever wrote purer Latin than he. But his historical works, however great their merit, but feebly represent his transcendent genius — the most august name of antiquity. He was mathematician, architect, poet, philologist, orator, jurist, general, statesman — imperator. In eloquence he was only second to Cicero. The great value of his history is in the sketches of the productions, the manners, the customs, and the political state of Gaul, Britain, and Germany. His observations on military science, on the operation of sieges, and construction of bridges and military engines, are valuable. But the description of

1 The best translations of this author are those by Stewart, 1806, and Murphy, 1807.

his military operations is only a studied apology for his crimes, even as the bulletins of Napoleon were set forth to show his victories in the most favorable light. His fame rests on his victories and successes as a statesman rather than on his merits as an historian, even as Louis Napoleon will live in history for his deeds rather than as the apologist of Cæsar.[1] The "Commentaries" resemble the history of Herodotus more than any other Latin production, at least in style; they are simple and unaffected, precise and elegant, plain and without pretension.

Cæsar was born B. C. 100, and while I admire his genius and his generosity, I hold in detestation the ambition which led him to overturn the constitution of his country on the plea of revolutionary necessity. It is true that there was the strife of parties and factions, greedy of revenge, and still more of spoils. It was a period of "*great offenses*," but it was also the brightest period in Roman history, so far as pertains to the development of genius. It was more favorable to literature than the lauded "Augustan era." It was an age of free opinions, in which liberty gave her last sigh, and when heroic efforts were made to bring back the ancient virtue, and to save the state from despotism. The lives of Piso, of Milo, of Cinna, of Lepidus, of Cotta, of Dolabella, of Crassus, of Quintus Maximus, of Aquila, of Pompey, of Brutus, of Cassius, of Antony, show what extraordinary men of action were then upon the stage, both good and evil, while Varro, Cicero, Catullus, Lucretius, and Sallust gave glory to the world of letters. It may have resulted favorably to the peace of society that the imperial rule supplanted the aristocratic regime, but it was a change fatal to liberty of speech and all independent action — a change, the good of which was on the outside, and in favor of material interests, but the evil of which was internal, and consumed secretly, but surely, the real greatness of the empire.

[1] See *History of Cæsar*, by Napoleon, a work more learned than popular, however greatly he may be indebted to the labors of others.

The Augustan age, though it produced a constellation of poets who shed glory upon the throne before which they prostrated themselves in abject homage, like the courtiers of Louis XIV., still was unfavorable to prose composition, — to history as well as eloquence. Of the historians, Livy is the only one whose writings are known to us, and only fragments of his history.[1] He was a man of distinction at court, and had a great literary reputation — so great that a Spaniard traveled from Cadiz on purpose to see him. Most of the great historians of the world have occupied places of honor and rank, which were given to them not as prizes for literary successes, but for the experience, knowledge, and culture which high social position and ample means secured. Herodotus lived in courts; Thucydides was a great general, also Xenophon; Cæsar wrote his own exploits; Sallust was prætor and governor; Livy was tutor to Claudius; Tacitus was prætor and consul suffectus; Eusebius was bishop and favorite of Constantine; Ammianus was the friend of the Emperor Julian; Gregory of Tours was one of the leading prelates of the West; Froissart attended in person, as a man of rank, the military expeditions of his day; Clarendon was Lord Chancellor; Burnet was a bishop and favorite of William III.; Thiers and Guizot both were prime ministers; while Gibbon, Hume, Robertson, Macaulay, Grote, Milman, Neander, Niebuhr, Müller, Dahlman, Buckle, Prescott, Irving, Bancroft, Motley, have all been men of wealth or position. Nor do I remember a single illustrious historian who has been poor and neglected.

Prose composition.

High social position of historians.

The ancients regarded Livy as the greatest of historians, — an opinion not indorsed by modern critics, on account of his inaccuracies. But his narrative is always interesting, and his language pure. He did not sift evidence like Grote, nor generalize like Gibbon; but

Livy.

[1] Born B. C. 59.

he was, like Voltaire and Macaulay, an artist in style, and possessed undoubted genius. His annals are comprised in one hundred and forty-two books, extending from the foundation of the city to the death of Drusus, B. C. 9, of which only thirty-five have come down to us — an impressive commentary on the vandalism of the Middle Ages, and the ignorance of the monks who could not preserve so great a treasure. "His story flows in a calm, clear, sparkling current, with every charm which simplicity and ease can give." He delineates character with great clearness and power; his speeches are noble rhetorical compositions; his sentences are rhythmical cadences. He was not a critical historian, like Herodotus, for he took his materials secondhand, and he was ignorant of geography; nor did he write with the exalted ideal of Thucydides, but as a painter of beautiful forms, which only a rich imagination could conjure, he is unrivaled in the history of literature. Moreover, he was honest and sound in heart, and was just and impartial in reference to those facts with which he was conversant.

Tacitus.

In the estimation of modern critics, the highest rank, as an historian, is assigned to Tacitus, and it would be difficult to find his rival in any age or country. He was born A. D. 57, about forty-three years after the death of Augustus. He belonged to the equestrian rank, and was a man of consular dignity. He had every facility for literary labors that leisure, wealth, friends, and social position could give, and he lived under a reign when truth could be told.

The extant works of this great writer are the "Life of Agricola," his father-in-law; his "Annales," which commence with the death of Augustus, A. D. 14, and close with the death of Nero, A. D. 68; the "Historiæ," which comprise the period from the second consulate of Galba, A. D. 68, to the death of Domitian; and a treatise on the Germans.

His histories describe Rome in the fullness of imperial glory, when the will of one man was the supreme law of the empire. He also wrote of events when liberty had fled, and the yoke of despotism was nearly insupportable. He describes a period of great moral degradation, nor does he hesitate to lift the veil of hypocrisy in which his generation had wrapped itself. He fearlessly exposes the cruelties and iniquities of the early emperors, and writes with judicial impartiality respecting all the great characters he describes. No ancient writer shows greater moral dignity and integrity of purpose than Tacitus. In point of artistic unity he is superior to Livy and equal to Thucydides, whom he resembles in conciseness of style. His distinguishing excellence as an historian is his sagacity and impartiality. Nothing escapes his penetrating eye; and he inflicts merited chastisement on the tyrants who reveled in the prostrated liberties of his country, while he immortalizes those few who were faithful to duty and conscience in a degenerate age. But his writings were not so popular as those of Livy. Neither princes nor people relished his intellectual independence and moral elevation. He does not satisfy Dr. Arnold, who thinks he ought to have been better versed in the history of the Jews, and who dislikes his speeches because they were fictitious.

Histories of Tacitus.

Neither the Latin nor Greek historians are admired by those dry critics, who seek to give to rare antiquarian matter a disproportionate importance, and to make this matter as fixed and certain as the truths of natural science. History can never be other than an approximation to the truth, even when it relates to the events and characters of our own age. History does not give positive knowledge which cannot be disputed except in general terms. We *know* that Cæsar was ambitious, but we do not know whether he was more or less so than Pompey, nor do we know how far he was justified in his usurpation. A great history must have other merits

Qualities which give immortality to historians.

than mere accuracy, or antiquarian research, or display of authorities and notes. It must be a work of art, and art has reference to style and language, to grouping of details and richness of illustration, to eloquence and poetry and beauty. A dry history, if ever so learned, will never be read; it will only be consulted, like a law-book, or Mosheim's "Commentaries." We wish *life* in history, and it is for the life that the writings of Livy and Tacitus will be perpetuated. Voltaire and Schiller have no great merit as historians, in a technical sense, but the "Life of Charles XII." and the "Thirty Years' War" are still classics. Neander has written one of the most searching and recondite histories of modern times, but it is too dry, too deficient in art, to be cherished, and may pass away, like the voluminous writings of Varro, the most learned of the Romans. It is the *art* which is immortal in a book, not the knowledge, or even the thoughts. What keeps alive the "Provincial Letters"? It is the style, the irony, the elegance. It is the exquisite delineation of character, the moral wisdom, the purity and force of language, the artistic arrangement, and the lively and interesting narratives, appealing to all minds, like the "Arabian Nights," or Froissart's "Chronicles," which give immortality to the classic authors of antiquity. We will not let them perish, because they amuse us, and inspire us. Livy doubtless was too ambitious in aspiring to write accurately the whole history of his country. He would have been wiser had he confined himself to a particular epoch, of which he was conversant, like Tacitus and Thucydides. But it is taking a narrow view of history to make all writers after the same pattern, even as it would be bigoted to make all Christians belong to the same sect. Some will be remarkable for style, others for learning, and others again for moral and philosophical wisdom. Some will be minute, and others generalizing. Some dig out a multiplicity of facts without apparent object, and others induce from those facts. Some will make essays, and others chronicles. We have need of all styles and all kinds of excellence. A great and original thinker may not have the time or opportunity or taste for a minute and searching criticism of original authorities; but he may be able to generalize previously established facts, so as to draw most valuable moral instruction. History is a boundless field of inquiry. No man can master it, in all its departments and periods. What he gains in minute details, he is apt to lose in generalization. If he attempts to embody too much learning, he may be deficient in originality; if he would say every thing, he is apt to be dry; if he elaborates too much, he loses life. Society, too, requires different kinds and styles of history, — history for students, history for ladies, histories for old men, histories for young men, histories to amuse, and histories to instruct. If all men were to write history according to Dr. Arnold's views, then we should have histories of interest only to classical scholars. A fellow of Christ Church may demand authorities, even if he never consults one of them, but a member of Congress may wish to see learning embodied in the text, and animated by genius, after the fashion of the ancient historians, who never quoted their sources of knowledge, and who were valued for the richness of thoughts and artistic beauty of style. The ages in which they flourished, attached no value to pedantic displays of labor, or evidences of learning paraded in foot-notes.

Greatness of the ancient historians.

Thus the great historians whom I have alluded to, both Greek and Latin, have few equals and no superiors, in our own times, in those things which are most to be admired. They were not pedants, but men of immense genius and learning, who blended the profoundest principles of moral wisdom with the most fascinating narratives, men universally popular among learned and unlearned, and men who were great artists in style, and masters of the language in which they wrote. We claim a superiority to them, because we are more recondite and critical; but the decline of Roman literature can be dated to times when commentaries became the fashion. We improve on commentaries. They are chiefly confined to biblical questions. *We* write dictionaries and encyclopedias. In this respect we are superior to the ancients. Our latest fashion of histories makes them very long, and very uncertain, containing much irrelevant matter, and more remarkable for learning than for genius, or elegance of diction. Yet Macaulay, Prescott, and Motley have few equals among the ancients in interest or artistic beauty.

Suetonius. Rome can boast of no great historian after Tacitus, who should have belonged to the Ciceronian epoch. Suetonius, born about the year A. D. 70, shortly after Nero's death, was rather a biographer than historian. Nor as a biographer does he take a high rank. His "Lives of the Cæsars," like Diogenes Laertius' "Lives of the Philosophers," are rather anecdotical than historical. L. A. Florus, who flourished during the reign of Trajan, has left a series of sketches of the different wars from the days of Romulus to those of Augustus. Frontinus epitomized **Marcellinus.** the large histories of Pompeius. Marcellinus wrote a history from Nerva to Valens, and is often quoted by Gibbon. But none wrote who should be adduced as examples of the triumph of genius, except Sallust, Cæsar, Livy, and Tacitus.

Ancient orators. There is another field of prose compositions in which the Greeks and Romans gained great distinction, and proved themselves equal to any nation of modern times, and this was that of eloquence. It is true we have not a rich collection of ancient speeches. But we have every reason to believe that both Greeks and Romans were most severely trained in the art of public speaking, and that forensic eloquence was highly prized and munificently rewarded. It commenced with democratic institutions, and flourished as long as the people were a great power in the state. It declined whenever and as soon as tyrants bore rule. Eloquence and liberty flourished together; nor can there be eloquence when there is not freedom of debate. In the fifth century before Christ — the first century of democracy — great orators arose, for without the power and the opportunity of defending himself against accusation, no man could hold an ascendent position. Socrates insisted upon the gift of oratory to a general in the army,[1] as well as to a leader in political life. In Athens the courts of justice were numerous, and those who could not defend themselves were obliged to secure the services of those who were trained in the use of public speaking. Thus the lawyers arose, among whom eloquence has been more in demand, and more richly paid than in any other class, certainly of ancient times. Rhetoric became connected with dialectics, and in Greece, Sicily, and Italy, both were most extensively cultivated. Empedocles was distinguished as much for rhetoric as for philosophy. It was not, however, in the courts of law that eloquence displayed the greatest fire and passion, but in political assemblies. These could only coexist with liberty; and a democracy was more favorable than an aristocracy to a large concourse of citizens. In the Grecian republics, eloquence as an art, may be said to have been born. It was nursed and fed by political agitations; by the strife of parties. It arose from appeals to the people as a source of power; and, when the people were not cultivated, it appealed chiefly to popular passions and prejudices. When they were enlightened, it appealed to interests.

Ancient eloquence.

It was in Athens, where there existed the purest form of democratic institutions, that eloquence rose to the loftiest heights in the ancient world, so far as eloquence appeals to popular passions. Pericles, the greatest statesman of Greece, was celebrated for his eloquence,

Pericles.

[1] Xen. *Mem.*, iii. 3, 11.

although no specimens remain to us. It was conceded by the ancient authors, that his oratory was of the highest kind, and the epithet of Olympian was given him as carrying the weapons of Zeus upon his tongue.[1] His voice was sweet, and his utterance distinct and rapid. Pisistratus was also famous for his eloquence, although he was a usurper and a tyrant. Isocrates [2] was a professed rhetorician, and endeavored to base it upon sound moral principles, and rescue it from the influence of the Sophists. He was the great teacher of the most eminent statesmen of his day. Twenty-one of his orations have come down to us, and they are excessively polished and elaborated; but they were written to be read; they were not extemporary. His language is the purest and most refined Attic dialect. Lysias [3] was a fertile writer of orations also, and he is reputed to have produced as many as four hundred and twenty-five. Of these only thirty-five are extant. They are characterized by peculiar gracefulness and elegance, which did not interfere with strength. So able were these orations, that only two were unsuccessful. They were so pure that they were regarded as the best canon of the Attic idiom.[4]

Demosthenes.

But all the orators of Greece — and Greece was the land of orators — gave way to Demosthenes, born B. C. 385. He received a good education, and is said to have been instructed in philosophy by Plato, and in eloquence by Isocrates. But it is more probable that he privately prepared himself for his brilliant career. As soon as he attained his majority, he brought suits against the men whom his father had appointed his guardians for their waste of property, and was, after two years, successful, conducting the prosecution himself. It was not until the age of thirty that he appeared as a speaker in the public assembly on political matters, and he enjoyed universal respect, and

1 Plutarch; Cic. *De Orat.*, iii. 34; Quin., x. i. § 82; Plat. *Phed.*, p. 262.
2 Born 436 B C.
3 Born B. C. 458.
4 Dion. *Lys.*, ii. 3.

became one of the leading statesmen of Athens, and henceforth he took an active part in every question that concerned the state. He especially distinguished himself in his speeches against Macedonian aggrandizements, and his Philippics are, perhaps, the most brilliant of his orations. But the cause which he advocated was unfortunate. The battle of Cheronea, B. C. 338, put an end to the independence of Greece, and Philip of Macedon was all-powerful. For this catastrophe Demosthenes was somewhat responsible, but his motives were pure and his patriotism lofty, and he retained the confidence of his countrymen. Accused by Æschines, he delivered his famous Oration on the Crown. Afterwards, during the supremacy of Alexander, he was again accused, and suffered exile. Recalled from exile, on the death of Alexander, he roused himself for the deliverance of Greece, without success, and, hunted by his enemies, he took poison in the sixty-third year of his age, having vainly contended for the freedom of his country, — one of the noblest spirits of antiquity, spotless in his public career, and lofty in his private life. As an orator, he has not probably been equaled by any man of any country. By his contemporaries he was regarded as faultless as a public speaker, and when it is remembered that he struggled against physical difficulties which, in the early part of his career, would have utterly discouraged any ordinary man, we feel that he deserves the highest commendation. He never spoke without preparation, and most of his orations were severely elaborated. He never trusted to the impulse of the occasion. And all his orations exhibit him as a pure and noble patriot, and are full of the loftiest sentiments. He was a great artist, and his oratorical successes were greatly owing to the arrangement of his speeches and the application of the strongest arguments in their proper places. Added to this moral and intellectual superiority was the "magic power of his language, majestic and simple at the same time, rich yet not bombastic, strange and yet familiar, solemn without being ornamented, grave and yet pleasing, concise and yet fluent, sweet and yet impressive, which altogether carried away the minds of his hearers."[1] His orations were most highly prized by the ancients, who wrote innumerable commentaries on them, but most of these criticisms are lost. Sixty, however, of these great productions of genius have come down to us, and are contained in the various collections of the Attic orators by Aldus, Stephens, Taylor, Reiske, Dukas, Bekker, Dobson, and Sauppe. Demosthenes, like other orators, first became known as the composer of speeches for litigants; but his great fame was based on the orations he pronounced in great political emergencies. His rival was Æschines, but he was vastly inferior to Demosthenes, although bold, vigorous, and brilliant. Indeed, the opinions of mankind, for two thousand years, have been unanimous in ascribing to Demosthenes the highest position as an orator of all the men of ancient and modern times. David Hume says of him, "that, could his manner be copied, its success would be infallible over a modern audience." "It is rapid harmony exactly adjusted to the sense. It is vehement reasoning, without any appearance of art. It is disdain, anger, boldness, freedom involved in a continual stream of argument; so that, of all human productions, his orations present to us the models which approach the nearest to perfection."[2]

Roman orators.

It is probable that the Romans were behind the Athenians in all the arts of rhetoric; and yet in the days of the republic celebrated orators arose, called out by the practice of the law and political meetings. It was, in fact, in forensic eloquence that Latin prose first appears as a cultivated language; for the forum was to the Romans what libraries are to us. And the art of public speaking was very early developed. Cato, Lælius, Carbo, and the Gracchi are said to have been majestic and har-

[1] Leonhard Schmitz.

[2] *Dissertation of Lord Brougham on the Eloquence of the Ancients.*

monious in speech. Their merits were eclipsed by Antonius, Crassus, Cotta, Sulpitius, and Hortensius. The last had a very brilliant career as an orator, although his orations were too florid to be read. Cæsar was also distinguished for his eloquence, the characteristics of which were force and purity. Cælius was noted for lofty sentiment; Brutus for philosophical wisdom; Callidus for a delicate and harmonious style, and Calvus for sententious force.

Cicero.

But all the Roman orators yielded to Cicero, as the Greeks did to Demosthenes. These two men are always coupled together when allusion is made to eloquence. They were preëminent in the ancient world, and have never been equaled in the modern.

Cicero was not probably equal to his great Grecian rival in vehemence, in force, in fiery argument, which swept every thing away before him; and he was not probably equal to him in original genius; but he was his superior in learning, in culture, and in breadth.[1] He distinguished himself very early as an advocate; but his first great public effort was in the prosecution of Verres for corruption. Although defended by Hortensius, and the whole influence of the Metelli and other powerful families, Cicero gained his cause, — more fortunate than Burke in his prosecution of Warren Hastings, who was also sustained by powerful interests and families. Burke also resembled Cicero in his peculiarities and in his fortunes more than any modern orator. His speech on the Manilian law, when he appeared as a political orator, greatly contributed to his popularity. I need not describe his memorable career; his successive election to all the highest offices of state, his detection of Catiline's conspiracy, his opposition to turbulent and ambitious partisans, his alienations and friendships, his brilliant career as a statesman, his misfortunes and sorrows, his exile and recall, his splendid services to the state, his greatness and his defects, his virtues and weak-

[1] Born B. C. 106.

nesses, his triumphs and martyrdom. These are foreign to my purpose. No man of heathen antiquity is better known to us, and no man, by pure genius, ever won more glorious laurels. His life and labors are immortal. His virtues and services are embalmed in the heart of the world. Few men ever performed greater literary labors, and in most of its departments. Next to Aristotle, he was the most learned man of antiquity, but performed more varied labors than he, since he was not only great as a writer and speaker, but as a statesman, and was the most conspicuous man in Rome after Pompey and Cæsar. He may not have had the moral greatness of Socrates, nor the philosophical genius of Plato, nor the overpowering eloquence of Demosthenes, but he was a master of all the wisdom of antiquity. Even civil law, the great science of the Romans, became interesting in his hands, and is divested of its dryness and technicality. He popularized history, and paid honor to all art, even to the stage. He made the Romans conversant with the philosophy of Greece, and systematized the various speculations. He may not have added to the science, but no Roman, after him, understood so well the practical bearing of all the various systems. His glory is purely intellectual, and it was by pure genius that he rose to his exalted position and influence.

But it was in forensic eloquence that he was preëminent, and in which he had but one equal in ancient times. Roman eloquence culminated in him. He composed about eighty orations, of which fifty-nine are preserved. Some were delivered from the rostrum to the people, and some in the Senate. Some were mere philippics, as savage in denunciation as those of Demosthenes. Some were laudatory; some were judicial; but all were severely logical, full of historical allusion, profound in philosophical wisdom, and pervaded with the spirit of patriotism. "He goes round and round his object, surveys it in every light, examines it in all its parts, retires and then advances, compares and contrasts it, illustrates, confirms, and enforces it, till the hearer feels ashamed of doubting a position which seems built on a foundation so strictly argumentative. And having established his case, he opens upon his opponent a discharge of raillery so delicate and good natured that it is impossible for the latter to maintain his ground against it; or, when the subject is too grave, he colors his exaggerations with all the bitterness of irony and vehemence of passion. But the appeal to the gentler emotions is reserved for the close of the oration, as in the defense of Cluentius, Cælius, Milo, and Flaccus; the most striking instances of which are the poetical bursts of feeling with which he addresses his client, Plaucius, and his picture of the desolate condition of the vestal Fonteia, should her brother be condemned. At other times his peroration contains more heroic and elevated sentiments, as in the invocation of the Alban Altars, and in his defense of Sextius, and that on liberty at the close of the third Philippic."[1]

Critics have uniformly admired his style as peculiarly suited to the Latin language, which, being scanty and unmusical, requires more redundancy than the Greek. The simplicity of the Attic writers would make Latin composition bold and tame. To be perspicuous, the Latin must be full. Thus Arnold thinks that what Tacitus gained in energy he lost in elegance and perspicuity. But Cicero, dealing with a barren and unphilosophical language, enriched it with circumlocutions and metaphors, while he formed it of harsh and uncouth expressions, and thus became the greatest master of composition the world has seen. He was a great artist, making use of his scanty materials to the best effect; and since he could not attain the elegance of the Greeks, he sought to excel them in vigor. He had absolute control over the resources of his vernacular tongue, and not only unrivaled skill in composition, but tact and judgment. Thus he was gener-

[1] Newman, *Hist. Rom. Lit.*, p. 305.

ally successful, in spite of the venality and corruption of the times. The courts of justice were the scene of his earliest triumphs; nor did he speak from the rostra until he was prætor on mere political questions, as in reference to the Manilian and Agrarian laws. It is in his political discourses that he rises to the highest ranks. In his speeches against Verres, Catiline, and Antony, he kindles in his countrymen lofty feelings for the honor of his country, and abhorrence of tyranny and corruption. Indeed, he hated bloodshed, injustice, and strife, and beheld the downfall of liberty with indescribable sorrow.

Cicero held a very exalted position as a philosophical writer and critic; but we defer what we have to say on this point until we speak of the philosophy of the ancients. Upon eloquence his main efforts were, however, directed, and eloquence was the most perfect fruit of his talents. Nor can we here speak of Cicero as a man. He has his admirers and detractors. He had great faults and weaknesses as well as virtues. He was egotistical, vain, and vacillating. But he was industrious, amiable, witty, and public spirited. In his official position he was incorruptible. He was no soldier, but he had a greater than a warrior's excellence. In spite of his faults, his name is one of the brightest of the ancients. His integrity was never impeached, even in an age of unparalleled corruption, and he was pure in morals. He was free from rancor and jealousy, was true in his friendships, and indulgent to his dependents.[1]

Thus in oratory, as in history, the ancients can boast of most illustrious examples, never even equaled. Still, we cannot tell the comparative merits of the great classical

[1] Professor Ramsay, of Glasgow, has written a most admirable article on Cicero in Smith's *Dictionary*. It is very full and impartial. Cicero's own writings are the best commentary on his life. Plutarch has afforded much anecdote. Forsythe is the last work of erudition. The critics sneer at Middleton's *Life of Cicero;* but it has lasted one hundred years. It is, perhaps, too eulogistic. Drumann is said to have most completely exhausted his subject in his *Geschichte Roms.*

orators of antiquity, with the more distinguished of our times. Only Mirabeau, Pitt, Fox, Burke, Brougham, Webster, and Clay, can even be compared with them. In power of moving the people, some of our modern reformers and agitators may be mentioned favorably; but their harangues are comparatively tame when read.

In philosophy, the Greeks and Romans distinguished themselves more than even in poetry, or history, or eloquence. Their speculations pertained to the loftiest subjects which ever tasked the intellect of man. But this great department deserves a separate chapter. There were respectable writers, too, in various other departments of literature, but no very great names whose writings have descended to us. Contemporaries had an exalted opinion of Varro, who was considered the most learned of the Romans, as well as their most voluminous author. He was born ten years before Cicero, and he is highly commended by Augustine.[1] He was entirely devoted to literature, took no interest in passing events, and lived to a good old age. St. Augustine says of him, "that he wrote so much that one wonders how he had time to read; and that he read so much, we are astonished how he found time to write." He composed four hundred and ninety books. Of these only one has descended to us entire — "De Re Rustica"— written at the age of eighty; but it is the best treatise which has come down from antiquity on ancient agriculture. We have parts of his other books, and we know of books which have entirely perished which, for their information, would be invaluable; especially his "Divine Antiquities," in sixteen books — his great work, from which St. Augustine drew his materials for his "City of God." He wrote treatises on language, on the poets, on philosophy, on geography, and various other subjects. He wrote satire and criticism. But although his writings were learned, his style was so bad that

Varro.

[1] Born B. C. 116; *Civ. Dei.*, vi. 2.

the ages have failed to preserve him. It is singular that the truly immortal books are most valued for their artistic excellences. No man, however great his genius, can afford to be dull. Style is to written composition, what delivery is to a public speaker. John Foster, one of the finest intellects of the last generation, preached to a "handful" of hearers, while "Satan" Montgomery drew ecstatic crowds. Nobody goes to hear the man of thoughts, every body to hear the man of words, being repelled or attracted by *manner*.

Seneca.

Seneca was another great writer among the Romans, but he belongs to the domain of philosophy, although it is his ethical works which have given him immortality, as may be truly said of Socrates and Epictetus, although they are usually classed among the philosophers. He was a Spaniard, and was born a few years before the Christian era, was a lawyer and a rhetorician, a teacher and minister of Nero. It was his misfortune to know one of the most detestable princes that ever scandalized humanity, and it is not to his credit to have accumulated, in four years, one of the largest fortunes in Rome, while serving such a master. But since he lived to experience his ingratitude, he is more commonly regarded as a martyr. Had he lived in the republican period, he would have been a great orator. He wrote voluminously on many subjects, and was devoted to a literary life. He rejected the superstitions of his country, and looked upon the ritualism of religion as a mere fashion; but his religion was a mere deism, and he dishonored his own virtues by a compliance with the vices of others. He saw much of life, and died at fifty-three. What is remarkable in his writings, which are clear but labored, is, that under pagan influences and imperial tyranny, he should have presented such lofty moral truth; and it is a mark of almost transcendent talent that he should, unaided by Christianity, have soared so high in the realm of ethical inquiry. Nor is it easy to find any modern author who has treated great questions in so attractive a way.

Quintilian is a Latin classic, and belonged to the class of rhetoricians, and should have been mentioned among the orators, like Lysias the Greek, a teacher, however, of eloquence, rather than an orator. He was born A. D. 40, and taught the younger Pliny, also two nephews of Domitian, receiving a regular salary from the imperial treasury. His great work is a complete system of rhetoric. "*Institutiones Oratoriæ*" is one of the clearest and fullest of all rhetorical manuals ever written in any language, although, as a literary production, inferior to the "*De Oratore*" of Cicero. It is very practical and sensible, and a complete compendium of every topic likely to be useful in the education of an aspirant for the honors of eloquence. In systematic arrangement, it falls short of a similar work by Aristotle; but it is celebrated for its sound judgment and keen discrimination, showing great reading and reflection. He should be viewed as a critic rather than as a rhetorician, since he entered into the merits and defects of the great masters of Greek and Roman literature. In his peculiar province he has had no superior. Like Cicero, or Demosthenes, or Plato, or Thucydides, or Tacitus, he would be a great man if he lived in our times, and could proudly challenge the modern world to produce a better teacher than he in the art of public speaking.

Quintilian.

There are other writers of immense fame, who do not represent any particular class in the field of literature, which can be compared with the modern. But I can only draw attention to Lucian, a witty and voluminous Greek author, who lived in the reign of Commodus, wrote rhetorical, critical, and biographical works, and even romances which have given hints to modern authors. But his fame rests on his "Dialogues," intended to ridicule the heathen philosophy and religion, and which show him to have been one of the great masters of ancient satire and mockery. His style of dialogue — a combina-

Lucian.

tion of Plato and Aristophanes — is not much used by modern writers, and his peculiar kind of ridicule is reserved now for the stage. Yet he cannot be called a writer of comedy, like Molière. He resembles Rabelais and Swift more than any other modern writers, and has their indignant wit, indecent jokes, and pungent sarcasms. He paints, like Juvenal, the vices and follies of his time, and exposes the hypocrisy that reigns in the high places of fashion and power. His dialogues have been imitated by Fontanelle and Lord Lyttleton, but they do not possess his humor or pungency. Lucian does not grapple with great truths, but contents himself in ridiculing those who have proclaimed them; and, in his cold cynicism, depreciates human knowledge, and all the great moral teachers of mankind. He is even shallow and flippant upon Socrates. But he was well read in human nature, and superficially acquainted with all the learning of antiquity. In wit and sarcasm, he may be compared with Voltaire, and his end was the same, to demolish and pull down, without substituting any thing in its stead. His skepticism was universal, and extended to religion, to philosophy, and to every thing venerated and ancient. His purity of style was admired by Erasmus, and he has been translated into most European languages. The best English version is rendered by Dr. Franklin, London, 2 vols. 4to. In strong contrast to the "Dialogues" is the "City of God," by Saint Augustine, in which he demolishes with keener ridicule all the gods of antiquity, but substitutes instead the knowledge of the true God.

Thus the Romans, as well as Greeks, produced works in all departments of literature which will bear comparison with the masterpieces of modern times. And where would have been the literature of the early Church, or of modern nations, had not the great original writers of Athens and Rome been our schoolmasters? And when we further remember that their glorious literature was created by native genius, without the aid of Christianity, we are filled with amazement, and may almost be excused if we deify the reason of man. At least we are assured that literature as well as art may flourish under pagan influences, and that Christianity has a higher mission than the culture of the mind. Religious skepticism cannot be disarmed if we appeal to Christianity as the test of intellectual culture. The realm of reason has no fairer fields than those which are adorned by pagan art. Nor have greater triumphs of intellect been witnessed in these, our Christian times, than among that class which is the least influenced by Christian ideas. Some of the proudest trophies of genius have been won by infidels, or by men stigmatized as such. Witness Voltaire, Rousseau, Diderot, Hegel, Fichte, Gibbon, Hume, Buckle. And then how many great works are written without the inspiration of the spirit of a living Christianity! How little Bulwer, or Byron, or Dumas, or Goethe owe, apparently, to Christian teachings! Is Emerson superior to Epictetus, in an ethical point of view? Was Franklin a great philosopher, or Jefferson a great statesman, because they were surrounded by Christian examples? May there not be the greatest practical infidelity, with the most artistic beauty and native reach of thought? Milton justly ascribes the most sublime intelligence to Satan and his angels on the point of rebellion against the majesty of Heaven. A great genius may be kindled by the fires of discontent and ambition, which will quicken the intellectual faculties, even while they consume the soul, and spread their devastating influence on the homes and hopes of man.

REFERENCES. — There are no better authorities than the classical authors themselves, and their works must be studied in order to comprehend the spirit of ancient literature. Modern historians of Roman literature are merely critics, like Drumann, Schlegel, Niebuhr, Müller, Mommsen, Mure, Arnold, Dunlap, and Thompson. Nor do I know of an exhaustive history of Roman literature in the English language. Yet nearly every great writer has occasional criticisms, entitled to respect. The Germans, in this department, have no equals. As critics and commentators they are unrivaled.

CHAPTER VIII.

GRECIAN PHILOSOPHY.

WHATEVER may be said of the inferiority of the ancients to the moderns in natural and mechanical science, which no one is disposed to question, or even in the realm of literature, which can be questioned, there was one department which they carried to absolute perfection, and to which we have added nothing of consequence. In the realm of art they were our equals, and probably our superiors; in philosophy they carried logical deductions to their utmost limit. They created the science. They advanced, from a few crude speculations on material phenomena, to an analysis of all the powers of the mind, and finally to the establishment of ethical principles which even Christianity did not overturn. The progress of the science, from Thales to Plato, is the most stupendous triumph of the human understanding. The reason of man soared to the loftiest flights that it has ever attained. It cast its searching eye into the most abstruse inquiries which ever tasked the famous intellects of the world. It exhausted all the subjects which dialectical subtlety ever raised. It originated and it carried out the boldest speculations respecting the nature of the soul and its future existence. It established most important psychological truths. It created a method for the solution of the most abstruse questions. It went on, from point to point, until all the faculties of the mind were severely analyzed, and all its operations were subjected to a rigid method. The Romans never added a single principle to the philosophy which the Greeks elabc rated; the ingenious scholastics of the Middle Ages merely reproduced their ideas; and even the profound and patient Germans have gone round in the same circles that Plato and Aristotle marked out more than two thousand years ago. It was Greek philosophy in which noble Roman youth were educated, and hence, as it was expounded by a Cicero, a Marcus Aurelius, and an Epictetus, it was as much the inheritance of the Romans as it was of the Greeks themselves, after their political liberties were swept away, and the Grecian cities formed a part of the Roman empire. The Romans learned, or might have learned, what the Greeks created and taught, and philosophy became, as well as art, identified with the civilization which extended from the Rhine and the Po to the Nile and the Tigris. Grecian philosophy was one of the distinctive features of ancient civilization long after the Greeks had ceased to speculate on the laws of mind, or the nature of the soul, or the existence of God, or future rewards and punishments. Although it was purely Grecian in its origin and development, it cannot be left out of the survey of the triumphs of the human mind when the Romans were masters of the world, and monopolized the fruits of all the arts and sciences. It became one of the grand ornaments of the Roman schools, one of the priceless possessions of the Roman conquerors. The Romans did not originate medicine, but Galen was one of its greatest lights; they did not invent the hexameter verse, but Virgil sung to its measure; they did not create Ionic capitals, but their cities were ornamented with marble temples on the same principles as those which called out the admiration of Pericles. So, if they did not originate philosophy, and generally had but little taste for it, still its truths were systematized and explained by Cicero, and formed no small accession to the treasures with which cultivated intellects sought everywhere to be enriched. It formed an essential part of the intellectual wealth of the civilized world, when civilization could not prevent the world from falling into decay and ruin. And as it was the noblest triumph which the human mind, under pagan influences, ever achieved, so it was followed by the most degrading imbecility into which man, in civilized countries, was ever allowed to fall. Philosophy, like art, like literature, like science, arose, shined, grew dim, and passed away, and left the world in night. Why was so bright a glory followed by so dismal a shame? What a comment is this on the greatness and littleness of man!

Commencement of Grecian speculations.

The development of Greek philosophy is doubtless one of the most interesting and instructive subjects in the whole history of mind. In all probability it originated with the Ionian Sophoi, though many suppose it was derived from the East. It is questionable whether the oriental nations had any philosophy distinct from religion. The Germans are fond of tracing resemblances in the early speculations of the Greeks to the systems which prevailed in Asia from a very remote antiquity. Gladish sees in the Pythagorean system an adoption of Chinese doctrines; in the Heraclitic system, the influence of Persia; in the Empedoclean, Egyptian speculations; and in the Anaxagorean, the Jewish creeds.[1] But the Orientals had theogonies, not philosophies. The Indian speculations aim to an exposition of ancient revelation. They profess to liberate the soul from the evils of mortal life — to arrive at eternal beatitudes. But the state of perfectibility could only be reached by religious ceremonial observances and devout contemplation. The Indian systems do not disdain logical discussions, or a search after the principles of which the universe is composed; and hence we find great refinements in sophistry, and a wonderful subtlety of logical discussion; but these are directed to unattainable ends, — to the connection of good with evil, and the union of the supreme with nature. Nothing came out of these speculations but an

[1] Lewes, *Biog. Hist. of Philos.*, Introd.

occasional elevation of mind among the learned, and a profound conviction of the misery of man and the obstacles to his perfection.[1] The Greeks, starting from physical phenomena, went on in successive series of inquiries, until they elevated themselves above matter, above experience, even to the loftiest abstractions, and until they classified the laws of thought. It is curious how speculation led to demonstration, and how inquiries into the world of matter prepared the way for the solution of intellectual phenomena. Philosophy kept pace with geometry, and those who observed nature also gloried in abstruse calculations. Philosophy and mathematics seem to have been allied with the worship of art among the same men, and it is difficult to say which more distinguished them, æsthetic culture or power of abstruse reasoning.

We do not read of any remarkable philosophical inquirer until Thales arose, the first of the Ionian school. He was born at Miletus, a Greek colony in Asia Minor, about the year B. C. 636, when Ancus Martius was king of Rome, and Josiah reigned at Jerusalem. He has left no writings behind him, but he was numbered as one of the seven wise men of Greece. He was numbered with the wise men on account of his political sagacity and wisdom in public affairs.[2]

Thales.

> "And he, 't is said, did first compute the stars
> Which beam in Charles' wain, and guide the bark
> Of the Phœnician sailor o'er the sea."

He was the first who attempted a logical solution of material phenomena, without resorting to mythical representations. Thales felt that there was a grand question to be answered relative to the *beginning of things*. "Philosophy," it has been well said, "may be a history of *errors*, but not of *follies*." It was not a folly, in a rude age, to speculate on the first or fundamental principle of things.

[1] See Archer Butler's fine lecture on the *Indian Philosophies*.
[2] Müller, *Hist. of Grec. Lit.*, ch. xvii.

He looked around him upon Nature, upon the sea and earth and sky, and concluded that water or moisture was the vital principle. He felt it in the air, he saw it in the clouds above, and in the ground beneath his feet. He saw that plants were sustained by rain and by the dew, that neither animal nor man could live without water, and that to fishes it was the native element. What more important or vital than water? It was the *prima materia*, the ἀρχή, the beginning of all things — the origin of the world.[1] I do not here speak of his astronomical and geometrical labors — as the first to have divided the year into three hundred and sixty-five days. He is celebrated also for practical wisdom. "Know thyself," is one of his remarkable sayings. But the foundation principle of his philosophy was that water is the first cause of all things — the explanation of the origin of the universe. How so crude a speculation could have been maintained by so wise a man it is difficult to conjecture. It is not, however, the *reason* which he assigns for the beginning of things which is noteworthy, so much as the *fact* that his mind was directed to the solution of questions pertaining to the origin of the universe. It was these questions which marked the Ionian philosophers. It was these which showed the inquiring nature of their minds. What is the great first cause of all things? Thales saw it in one of the four elements of nature, as the ancients divided them. And it is the earliest recorded theory among the Greeks of the origin of the world. It is an induction from the phenomena of animated nature — the nutrition and production of a seed.[2] He regarded the entire world in the light of a living being gradually maturing and forming itself from an imperfect seed state, which was of a moist nature. This moisture endues the universe with vitality. The world, he thought, was full of gods, but they had their origin in water.

Water the vital principle of Nature.

[1] Aristotle, *Metaph.*, l. c. 3; Diog. Laertius, *Thales.*
[2] Ritter, b. iii. c. 3; Lewes, ch. 1.

He had no conception of God as *Intelligence*, or as a *creative* power. He had a great and inquiring mind, but he was a pagan, with no knowledge of a spiritual and controlling and personal deity.

Anaximenes. Air the *animus mundi.*

Anaximenes, his disciple, pursued his inquiries, and adopted his method. He also was born in Miletus, but at what time is unknown, probably B. C. 529. Like Thales, he held to the eternity of matter. Like him, he disbelieved in the existence of any thing immaterial, for even a human soul is formed out of matter. He, too, speculated on the origin of the universe, but thought that *air*, not water, was the primal cause.[1] This seemed to be universal. We breathe it; all things are sustained by it. It is Life — that is pregnant with vital energy, and capable of infinite transmutations. All things are produced by it; all is again resolved into it; it supports all things; it surrounds the world; it has infinitude; it has eternal motion. Thus did this philosopher reason, comparing the world with our own living existence, — which he took to be air, — an imperishable principle of life. He thus advanced a step on Thales, since he regarded the world not after the analogy of an imperfect seed-state, but that of the highest condition of life, — the human soul.[2] And he attempted to refer to one general law all the transformations of the first simple substance into its successive states, for the cause of change is the eternal motion of the air.

Diogenes. — Air and soul identical.

Diogenes of Apollonia, in Crete, one of his disciples, born B. C. 460, also believed that air was the principle of the universe, but he imputed to it an intellectual energy, yet without recognizing any distinction between mind and matter.[3] He made air and the soul identical. "For," says he, "man and all other animals breathe and live by means of the air, and therein consists

1 Cicero, *De Nat. D.*, i. 10.

2 Ritter, b. iii. c. 3.

3 Diog. Laert., ii. 3; Bayle, *Dict. Hist. et Crit.*

their soul."[1] And as it is the primary being from which all is derived, it is necessarily an eternal and imperishable body; but, as *soul*, it is also endued with consciousness. Diogenes thus refers the origin of the world to an intelligent being — to a soul which knows and vivifies. Anaximenes regarded air as having Life. Diogenes saw in it also Intelligence. Thus philosophy advanced step by step, though still groping in the dark; for the origin of all things, according to Diogenes, must exist in *Intelligence.*

Heraclitus. — Fire the principle of life.

Heraclitus of Ephesus, classed by Ritter among the Ionian philosophers, was born B. C. 503. Like others of his school, he sought a physical ground for all phenomena. The elemental principle he regarded as *fire*, since all things are convertible into it. In one of its modifications, this fire, or fluid, self-kindled, permeating every thing as the soul or principle of life, is endowed with intelligence and powers of ceaseless activity. "If Anaximenes discovered that he had within him a power and principle which ruled over all the acts and functions of his bodily frame, Heraclitus found that there was life within him which he could not call his own, and yet it was, in the very highest sense, *himself*, so that without it he would have been a poor, helpless, isolated creature; a universal life which connected him with his fellow-men, — with the absolute source and original fountain of life."[2] "He proclaimed the absolute vitality of nature, the endless change of matter, the mutability and perishability of all individual things in contrast with the eternal Being — the supreme harmony which rules over all."[3] To trace the divine energy of life in all things was the general problem of his philosophy, and this spirit was akin to the pantheism of the East. But he was one of the greatest speculative intellects that preceded Plato, and of all the physical theorists arrived nearest to spiritual truth. He taught the germs

1 Ritter, b. iii. c. 3.
2 Maurice, *Moral and Metaph. Phil.*
3 Lewes, *Biog. Hist. of Phil.*

of what was afterwards more completely developed. "From his theory of perpetual fluxion Plato derived the necessity of seeking a stable basis for the universal system in his world of ideas."[1]

Anaxagoras, the most famous of the Ionian philosophers, was born B. C. 500, and belonged to a rich and noble family. Regarding philosophy as the noblest pursuit of earth, he abandoned his inheritance for the study of nature. He went to Athens in the most brilliant period of her history, and had Pericles, Euripides, and Socrates for pupils. He taught that the great moving force of nature was intellect (νοῦς). Intelligence was the cause of the world and of order, and mind was the principle of motion; yet this intelligence was not a moral intelligence, but simply the *primum mobile* — the all-knowing motive force by which the order of nature is effected. He thus laid the foundation of a new system which, under the Attic philosophers, sought to explain nature, not by regarding matter in its different forms, as the cause of all things, but rather mind, thought, intelligence, which both knows and acts — a grand conception unrivaled in ancient speculation. This explanation of material phenomena by intellectual causes was his peculiar merit, and places him in a very high rank among the thinkers of the world. Moreover, he recognized the reason as the only faculty by which we become cognizant of truth, the senses being too weak to discover the real component particles of things. Like all the great inquirers, he was impressed with the limited degree of positive knowledge, compared with what there is to be learned. "Nothing," says he, "can be known; nothing is certain; sense is limited, intellect is weak, life is short"[2] — the complaint, not of a skeptic, but of a man overwhelmed with the sense of his incapacity to solve the problems which arose before his active mind.[3] Anax-

[1] Archer Butler, series i. lect. v.; Hegel, *Gesch. D. Phil.*, i. p. 334.
[2] Cicero, *Qu. Ac.*, i. 12.
[3] Lucret., lib. i. 834–875.

agoras thought that this spirit (Νοῦς) gave to all those material atoms, which, in the beginning of the world, lay in disorder, the impulse by which they took the forms of individual things, and that this impulse was given in a circular direction. Hence that the sun, moon, and stars, and even the air, are constantly moving in a circle.[1]

Anaximander thought that the Infinite is the origin of things.

In the mean time another sect of philosophers arose, who, like the Ionians, sought to explain nature, but by a different method. Anaximander, born B. C. 610, was one of the original mathematicians of Greece, yet, like Pythagoras and Thales, speculated on the beginning of things. His principle was that the *Infinite* is the origin of all things. He used the word ἀρχή to denote the material out of which all things were formed, as the everlasting and divine.[2] The idea of elevating an abstraction into a great first cause is certainly puerile, nor is it easy to understand his meaning, other than that the abstract has a higher significance than the concrete. The speculations of Thales tended toward discovering the material constitution of the universe, upon an *induction* from observed facts, and thus made water to be the origin of all things. Anaximander, accustomed to view things in the abstract, could not accept so concrete a thing as water; his speculations tended toward mathematics, to the science of pure *deduction*. The primary being is a unity, one in all, comprising within itself the multiplicity of elements from which all mundane things are composed. It is only in infinity that the perpetual changes of things can take place.[3] This original but obscure thinker prepared the way for Pythagoras.

Pythagoras. — Number the essence of things.

This philosopher and mathematician, born about the year B. C. 570, is one of the great names of antiquity; but his life is shrouded in dim magnificence. The old historians paint him as "clothed in robes

[1] Müller, *Hist. Lit. of Greece*, chap. xvii. [2] Arist., *Phy.*, iii. 4.
[3] Diog. Laert., i. 119; Cicero, *Tus. Qu.*, i. 16; Tennemann, p. 1, ch. i. § 86.

of white, his head covered with gold, his aspect grave and majestic, wrapt in the contemplation of the mysteries of existence, listening to the music of Homer and Hesiod, or to the harmony of the spheres."[1] To him is ascribed the use of the word *philosopher* rather than *sophos*, a lover of wisdom, not wise man. He taught his doctrines to a select few, the members of which society lived in common, and venerated him as an oracle. His great doctrine is, that *number* is the essence of things, by which is understood the *form* and not the *matter* of the sensible. The elements of numbers are the *odd* and *even*, the former being regarded as limited, the latter unlimited. Diogenes Laertius thus sums up his doctrines, which were that "the *monad* is the beginning of every thing. From the monad proceeds an indefinite *duad*. From the monad and the duad proceed *numbers*, and from numbers *signs*, and from these *lines*, of which plain figures consist. And from plain figures are derived solid bodies, and from these sensible bodies, of which there are four elements, fire, water, earth, and air. The world results from a combination of these elements."[2] All this is unintelligible or indefinite. We cannot comprehend how the number theory will account for the production of corporeal magnitude any easier than we can identify monads with mathematical points. But underlying this mysticism is the thought that there prevails in the phenomena of nature a rational *order*, *harmony*, and conformity to *law*, and that these laws can be represented by numbers. Number or harmony is the principle of the universe, and order holds together the world. Like Anaximander, he passes from the region of physics to metaphysics, and thus opens a new world of speculation. His method was purely deductive, and his science mathematical. "The *Infinite* of Anaximander became the *One* of Pythagoras." Assuming that number is the essence of the

Order and harmony in nature.

[1] Lewes, *Biog. Hist. Phil.*

[2] Diog. Laert., *Lives of Phil.*

world, he deduced that the world is regulated by numerical proportions, in other words, by a system of laws, and these laws, regular and harmonious in their operation, *may* have suggested to the great mind of Pythagoras, so religious and lofty, the necessity for an intelligent creator of the universe. It was in moral truth that he delighted as well as metaphysical, and his life and the lives of his disciples were disciplined to a severe virtue, as if he recognized in numbers or order the necessity of a conformity to all law, and saw in obedience to it both harmony and beauty. But we have no *direct* and positive evidence of the kind or amount of knowledge which this great intellect acquired. All that can be affirmed is, that he was a man of extensive attainments; that he was a great mathematician, that he was very religious, that he devoted himself to doing good, that he placed happiness in the virtues of the soul or the perfect science of numbers, and made a likeness to the Deity the object of all endeavors. He believed that the soul was incorporeal,[1] and is put into the body by the means of number and harmonical relation, and thus subject to a divine regulation. Every thing was regarded by him in a moral light. The order of the universe is only a harmonical development of the first principle of all things to virtue and wisdom.[2] He attached great value to music, as a subject of precise mathematical calculation, and an art which has a great effect on the affections. Hence morals and mathematics were linked together in his mind. As the heavens were ordered in consonance with number, they must move in eternal order. "The spheres" revolved in harmonious order around the great centre of light and heat — the sun — "the throne of the elemental world." Hence the doctrine of "the music of the spheres." *Pythagoras ad harmoniam canere mundum existimat.*[3] The

[1] Ritter, b. iv. chap. i.

[2] Our knowledge of Pythagoras is chiefly derived from Aristotle. Both Ritter and Brandis have presented his views elaborately, but with more clearness than was to be expected.

[3] Cicero, *De Nat. D.*, iii. ii. 27.

tendency of his speculations, obscure as they are to us, was to raise the soul to a contemplation of order and beauty and law, in the material universe, and hence to the contemplation of a supreme intelligence reigning in justice and truth. Justice and truth became therefore paramount virtues, to be practiced, to be sought as the great end of life, allied with the order of the universe, and with mathematical essences — the attributes of the deity, the sublime unity which he adored.

The Ionic philosophers, and the Pythagoreans, sought to find the nature or first principle of all things in the *elements*, or in *numbers*. But the Eleatics went beyond the realm of physics to pure metaphysical inquiries. This is the second stage in the history of philosophy — an idealistic pantheism, which disregarded the sensible and maintained that the source of all truth is independent of sense.

Xenophanes. — God the first great cause.

The founder of this school was Xenophanes, born in Colophon, an Ionian city of Asia Minor, from which, being expelled, he wandered over Sicily as a rhapsodist or minstrel, reciting his elegiac poetry on the loftiest truths; and at last came to Elea, about the year 536, where he settled. The great subject of his inquiries was God himself — the first great cause — the supreme intelligence of the universe. "From the principle *ex nihilo nihil fit*, he concluded that nothing could pass from non-existence to existence. All things that exist are eternal and immutable. God, as the most perfect essence, is eternally *One*, unalterable, neither finite nor infinite, neither movable nor immovable, and not to be represented under any human semblance."[1] What a great stride was this! Whence did he derive his opinions? He starts with the proposition that God is an all-powerful being, and denies all beginning of being, and hence infers that God must be from eternity. From this truth he ad-

[1] Tennemann, *Hist. of Phil.*, p. 1, § 98.

vances to deny all multiplicity. A plurality of gods is impossible. With these sublime views — the unity and eternity and omnipotence of God — he boldly attacked the popular errors of his day. He denounced the transference to the deity of the human form; he inveighed against Homer and Hesiod; he ridiculed the doctrine of migration of souls. Thus he sings, —

> "Such things of the gods are related by Homer and Hesiod,
> As would be shame and abiding disgrace to mankind, —
> Promises broken, and thefts, and the one deceiving the other." [1]

And, again, respecting anthropomorphic representations of the Deity, —

> "But men foolishly think that gods are born like as men are,
> And have, too, a dress like their own, and their voice and their figure;
> But there 's but one God alone, the greatest of gods and of mortals,
> Neither in body, to mankind resembling, neither in ideas."

Such were his sublime meditations. He believed in the *One*, which is God; but this all-pervading, unmoved, undivided being was not a personal God, nor a moral governor, but the deity pervading all space. He could not separate God from the world, nor could he admit the existence of world which is not God. He was a monotheist, but his monotheism was pantheism. He saw God in all the manifestations of nature. This did not satisfy him, nor resolve his doubts, and he therefore confessed that reason could not compass the exalted aims of philosophy. But there was no cynicism in his doubt. It was the soul-sickening consciousness that Reason was incapable of solving the mighty questions that he burned to know. There was no way to arrive at the truth, "for," as he said, "error is spread over all things." It was not disdain of knowledge, it was the combat of contradictory opinions that oppressed him. He could not solve the questions pertaining to God. What uninstructed reason can? "Canst thou by searching find out God, canst thou know

God seen in all the manifestations of nature.

[1] See Ritter, on Xenophanes. See note 20, in Archer Butler, series i. lect vi.

the Almighty unto perfection." What was impossible to Job, was not possible to him. But he had attained a recognition of the unity and perfections of God, and this conviction he would spread abroad, and tear down the superstitions which hid the face of truth. I have great admiration of this philosopher, so sad, so earnest, so enthusiastic, wandering from city to city, indifferent to money, comfort, friends, fame, that he might kindle the knowledge of God. This was a lofty aim indeed for philosophy in that age. It was a higher mission than that of Homer,[1] great as his was, but not so successful.

He sought to create a knowledge of God.

Parmenides of Elea, born about the year B. C. 536, followed out the system of Xenophanes, the central idea of which was the existence of God. With him the central idea was the notion of *being*. Being is uncreated and unchangeable; the fullness of all being is *thought;* the *All* is thought and intelligence. He maintained the uncertainty of knowledge; but meant the knowledge derived through the senses. He did not deny the certainty of reason. He was the first who drew a distinction between knowledge obtained by the senses, and that obtained through the reason; and thus he anticipated the doctrine of innate ideas. From the uncertainty of knowledge derived through the senses, he deduced the twofold system of true and apparent knowledge.[2]

Zeno of Elea, the friend and pupil of Parmenides, born B. C. 500, brought nothing new to the system, but invented *Dialectics*, that logic which afterwards became so powerful in the hands of Plato and Aristotle, and so generally admired among the schoolmen. It seeks to establish truth by refuting error by the *reductio ad absurdum.* While Parmenides sought to establish the doc-

Zeno introduces a new method.

[1] Lewes has some shallow remarks on this point, although spirited and readable. Ritter is more earnest.

[2] Prof. Brandis's article in Smith's *Dictionary.*

trine of the *One*, Zeno proved the non-existence of the *Many*. He denied that appearances were real existences, but did not deny existences. It was the mission of Zeno to establish the doctrines of his master. But, in order to convince his listeners, he was obliged to use a new method of argument. So he carried on his argumentation by question and answer, and was, therefore, the first who used dialogue as a medium of philosophical communication.[1]

Empedocles. — Love the moving cause of all things.

Empedocles, born B. C. 444, like others of the Eleatics, complained of the imperfection of the senses, and looked for truth only in reason. He regarded truth as a perfect unity, ruled by love, — the only true force, the one moving cause of all things, — the first creative power by whom the world was formed. Thus "God is love," a sublime doctrine which philosophy revealed to the Greeks.

The loftiness of the Eleatic philosophers.

Thus did the Eleatic philosophers speculate almost contemporaneously with the Ionians, on the beginning of things and the origin of knowledge, taking different grounds, and attempting to correct the representations of sense by the notions of reason. But both schools, although they did not establish many truths, raised an inquisitive spirit and awakened freedom of thought and inquiry. They raised up workmen for more enlightened times, even as scholastic inquirers in the Middle Ages prepared the way for the revival of philosophy on sounder principles. They were all men of remarkable elevation of character as well as genius. They hated superstitions and attacked the Anthropomorphism of their day. They handled gods and goddesses with allegorizing boldness, and hence were often persecuted by the people. They did not establish moral truths by scientific processes, but they set examples of lofty disdain of wealth and factitious advantages, and devoted themselves with holy enthu-

[1] Cousin, *Nouveaux Fragments Philosophiques.*

siasm to the solution of the great questions which pertain to God and nature. Thales won the respect of his countrymen by devotion to studies. Pythagoras spent twenty-two years in Egypt to learn its science. Xenophanes wandered over Sicily as a rhapsodist of truth. Parmenides, born to wealth and splendor, forsook the feverish pursuit of sensual enjoyments to contemplate "the quiet and still air of delightful studies." Zeno declined all worldly honors to diffuse the doctrines of his master. Heraclitus refused the chief magistracy of Ephesus that he might have leisure to explore the depths of his own nature. Anaxagoras allowed his patrimony to run to waste in order to solve problems. "To philosophy," said he, "I owe my worldly ruin and my soul's prosperity." They were, without exception, the greatest and best men of their times. They laid the foundation of the beautiful temple which was constructed after they were dead, in which both physics and psychology reached the dignity of science.[1]

Nevertheless, these great men, lofty as were their inquiries, and blameless their lives, had not established any system, nor any theories which were incontrovertible. They had simply speculated, and the world ridiculed their speculations. They were one-sided; and, when pushed out to their extreme logical sequence, were antagonistic to each other, which had a tendency to produce doubt and skepticism. Men denied the existence of the gods, and the grounds of certainty fell away from the human mind.

Circumstances which favored the Sophists.

This spirit of skepticism was favored by the tide of worldliness and prosperity which followed the Persian War. Athens became a great centre of art, of taste, of elegance, and of wealth. Politics absorbed the minds of the people. Glory and splendor were followed by corruption of morals and the pursuit of material

[1] Archer Butler in his lecture on the Eleatic school follows closely, and expounds clearly, the views of Ritter.

pleasures. Philosophy went out of fashion, since it brought no outward and tangible good. More scientific studies were pursued — those which could be applied to purposes of utility and material gains ; even, as in our day, geology, chemistry, mechanics, engineering, having reference to the practical wants of men, command talent, and lead to certain reward. In Athens, rhetoric, mathematics, and natural history supplanted rhapsodies and speculations on God and Providence. Renown and wealth could only be secured by readiness and felicity of speech, and that was most valued which brought immediate reward, like eloquence. Men began to practice eloquence as an *art*, and to employ it in furthering their interests. They made special pleadings, since it was their object to gain their point, at any expense of law and justice. Hence they taught that nothing was immutably right, but only so by convention. They undermined all confidence in truth and religion by teaching its uncertainty. They denied to men even the capability of arriving at truth. They practically affirmed the cold and cynical doctrine that there is nothing better for a man than that he should eat and drink. *Qui bono*, the cry of the Epicureans, of the latter Romans, and of most men in a period of great outward prosperity, was the popular inquiry, — who shall show us any good ? — how can we become rich, strong, honorable ? — this was the spirit of that class of public teachers who arose in Athens when art and eloquence and wealth and splendor were at their height in the fifth century before Christ, and when the elegant Pericles was the leader of fashion and of political power.

Character of the Sophists.

These men were the Sophists — rhetorical men who taught the children of the rich ; worldly men who sought honor and power ; frivolous men, trifling with philosophical ideas ; skeptical men, denying all certainty to truths ; men who, as teachers, added nothing to the realm of science, but who yet established certain dia-

Power and popularity of the Sophists.

lectical rules useful to later philosophers. They were a wealthy, powerful, honored class, not much esteemed by men of thought, but sought out as very successful teachers of rhetoric. They were full of logical tricks, and contrived to throw ridicule upon profound inquiries. They taught also mathematics, astronomy, philology, and natural history with success. They were polished men of society, not profound nor religious, but very brilliant as talkers, and very ready in wit and sophistry. And some of them were men of great learning and talent, like Democritus, Leucippus, and Gorgias. They were not pretenders and quacks; they were skeptics who denied subjective truths, and labored for outward advantage. They were men of general information, skilled in subtleties, of powerful social and political connections, and were generally selected as ambassadors on difficult missions. They taught the art of disputation, and sought systematic methods of proof. They thus prepared the way for a more perfect philosophy than that taught by the Ionians, the Pythagoreans, or the Eleatæ, since they showed the vagueness of their inquiries, conjectural rather than scientific. They had no doctrines in common. They were the barristers of their age, *paid* to make the "worse appear the better reason," yet not teachers of immorality any more than the lawyers of our day, — men of talents, the intellectual leaders of society. If they did not advance positive truths, they were useful in the method they created. They taught the art of disputation. They doubtless quibbled when they had a bad cause to present. They brought out the truth more forcibly when they defended a good cause. They had no hostility to truth; they only doubted whether it could be reached in the realm of psychological inquiries, and sought to apply it to their own purposes, or rather to distort it in order to gain a case. They are not a class of men whom I admire, as I do the old sages they ridiculed, but they were not without their

Influence of the Sophists.

use in the development of philosophy.[1] The Sophists also rendered a service to literature by giving definiteness to language, and creating style in prose writing. Protagoras investigated the principles of accurate composition; Prodicus busied himself with inquiries into the significance of words; Gorgias proposed a captivating style. He gave symmetry to the structure of sentences.

Socrates.

The ridicule and skepticism of the Sophists brought out the great powers of Socrates, to whom philosophy is probably more indebted than to any man who ever lived, not so much for a perfect system, but for the impulse he gave to philosophical inquiries, and his successful exposure of error. He inaugurated a new era. Born in Athens in the year 470 B. C., the son of a poor sculptor, he devoted his life to the search for truth, for its own sake, and sought to base it on immutable foundations. He was the mortal enemy of the Sophists, whom he encountered, as Pascal did the Jesuits, with wit, irony, puzzling questions, and remorseless logic. Like the earlier philosophers, he disdained wealth, ease, and comfort, but with greater devotion than they, since he lived in a more corrupt age, when poverty was a disgrace and misfortune a crime, when success was the standard of merit, and every man was supposed to be the arbiter of his own fortune, ignoring that Providence who so often refuses the race to the swift and the battle to the strong. He was what in our time would be called eccentric. He walked barefooted, meanly clad, and withal not over cleanly, seeking public places, disputing with every body willing to talk with him, making every body ridiculous, especially if one assumed airs of wisdom or knowledge, — an exasperating opponent, since he wove a web around a man from which he could not be extricated, and then exposed him to ridicule, in the wittiest city of the world. He attacked every body, and yet was generally respected, since it was *errors* and

The method of Socrates.

[1] Grote has a fine chapter on the Sophists (part ii. ch. 67).

not the person, *opinions* rather than vices; and this he did with bewitching eloquence and irresistible fascination; so that, though he was poor and barefooted, a Silenus in appearance, with thick lips, upturned nose, projecting eyes, unwieldy belly, he was sought by Alcibiades and admired by Aspasia. Even Xantippe, a beautiful young woman, very much younger than he, a woman fond of the comforts and pleasures of life, was willing to be his wife, even if she did afterwards torment him, when the *res angusta domi* disenchanted her from the music of his voice and the divinity of his nature. "I have heard Pericles," said the most dissipated and voluptuous man in Athens, "and other excellent orators, but was not moved by them; while this Marsyas — this Satyr — so affects me that the life I lead is hardly worth living, and I stop my ears, as from the Syrens, and flee as fast as possible, that I may not sit down and grow old in listening to his talk." He learned his philosophy from no one, and struck out an entirely new path. He declared his own ignorance, and sought to convince other people of theirs. He did not seek to reveal truth so much as to expose error. And yet it was his object to attain correct ideas as to moral obligations. He was the first who recognized natural right, and held that virtue and vice are inseparably united. He proclaimed the sovereignty of virtue, and the immutability of justice. He sought to delineate and enforce the practical duties of life. His great object was the elucidation of morals, and he was the first to teach ethics sytematically, and from the immutable principles of moral obligation. Moral certitude was the lofty platform from which he surveyed the world, and upon which, as a rock, he rested in the storms of life. Thus he was a reformer and a moralist. It was his ethical doctrines which were most antagonistic to the age, and the least appreciated. He was a profoundly religious man, recognized Providence, and believed in the immortality of the soul. From the

Ethical inquiries of Socrates.

abyss of doubt, which succeeded the speculations of the first philosophers, he would plant grounds of certitude — a ladder on which he would mount to the sublime regions of absolute truth. He did not presume to inquire into the Divine essence, yet he believed that the gods were omniscient and omnipresent, that they ruled by the law of goodness, and that, in spite of their multiplicity, there was unity — a supreme intelligence that governed the world. Hence he was hated by the Sophists, who denied the certainty of arriving at the knowledge of God. From the comparative worthlessness of the body he deduced the immortality of the soul. With him, the end of life was reason and intelligence. He proved the existence of God by the order and harmony of nature, which belief was certain. He endeavored to connect the moral with the religious consciousness, and then he proclaimed his convictions for the practical welfare of society. In this light Socrates stands out the grandest personage of pagan antiquity, — as a moralist, as a teacher of ethics, as a man who recognized the Divine.

The mission of Socrates.

So far as he was concerned in the development of Grecian philosophy proper, he was probably inferior to some of his disciples. Yet he gave a turning-point to a new period, when he awakened the *idea* of knowledge, and was the founder of the theory of scientific knowledge, since he separated the legitimate bounds of inquiry, and was thus the precursor of Bacon and Pascal. He did not attempt to make physics explain metaphysics, nor metaphysics the phenomena of the natural world. And he only reasoned from what was assumed to be true and invariable. He was a great pioneer of philosophy, since he resorted to inductive methods of proof, and gave general definiteness to ideas.[1] He gave a new method, and used great precision of language. Although he employed induction, it was his aim to withdraw the mind from the contemplation of nature, and to fix it on its own phenomena,

[1] Arist., *Metaph.*, xiii. 4.

— to look inward rather than outward, as carried out so admirably by Plato. The previous philosophers had given their attention to external nature; he gave up speculations about material phenomena, and directed his inquiries solely to the nature of knowledge. And, as he considered knowledge to be identical with virtue, he speculated on ethical questions mainly, and the method which he taught was that by which alone man could become better and wiser. To know one's self, in other words, "that the proper study of mankind is man," he was the first to proclaim. He did not disdain the subjects which chiefly interested the Sophists, — astronomy, rhetoric, physics; but he discussed moral questions, such as, what is piety? what is the just and the unjust? what is temperance? what is courage? what is the character fit for a citizen? — and such like ethical points. And he discussed them in a peculiar manner, in a method peculiarly his own. "Professing ignorance, he put perhaps this question — What is law? It was familiar and was answered off-hand. Socrates, having got the answer, then put fresh questions applicable to specific cases, to which the respondent was compelled to give an answer inconsistent with the first, thus showing that the *definition* was too narrow or too wide, or defective in some essential condition.[1] The respondent then amended his answer; but this was a prelude to other questions, which could only be answered in ways inconsistent with the amendment; and the respondent, after many attempts to disentangle himself, was obliged to plead guilty to his inconsistencies, with an admission that he could make no satisfactory answer to the original inquiry which had at first appeared so easy." Thus, by this system of cross-examination, he showed the intimate connection between the dialectic method, and the logical distribution of particulars into species and genera. The discussion first turns upon the meaning of some generic term; the queries bring the answers into collision with

[1] Grote, part ii. ch. 68.

various particulars which it ought not to comprehend, or which it ought to comprehend, but does not. He broke up the one into many by his analytical string of questions, which was a novel mode of argument. This was the method which he invented, and by which he separated *real* knowledge from the *conceit* of knowledge, and led to precision in the use of definitions. It was thus that he exposed the false, without aiming even to teach the true; for he generally professed ignorance, and put himself in the attitude of a learner, while he made by his cross-examinations the man from whom he apparently sought knowledge to be as ignorant as himself, or, still worse, absolutely ridiculous. Thus he pulled away all the foundations on which a false science had been erected, and indicated the way by which alone the true could be established. Here he was not unlike Bacon, who pointed out the way that science could be advanced, without founding any school or advocating any system; but he was unlike Bacon in the object of his inquiries. Bacon was disgusted with ineffective *logical* speculations, and Socrates with ineffective *physical* researches.[1] He never suffered a general term to remain undetermined, but applied it at once to particulars, and by questions the purport of which was not comprehended. It was not by positive teaching, but by exciting scientific impulse in the minds of others, or stirring up the analytical faculties, which constitute his originality. "The Socratic dialectics, clearing away," says Grote,[2] "from the mind its mist of fancied knowledge, and, laying bare the real ignorance, produced an immediate effect like the touch of the torpedo; the newly created consciousness of ignorance was humiliating and painful, yet it was combined with a yearning after truth never before experienced. Such intellectual quickening, which could never commence until the mind had been disabused of its original illusion of false

1 Archer Butler, s. i. l. vii.

2 Grote, part ii. ch. 68; Maurice, *Ancient Philosophy*, p. 119.

knowledge, was considered by Socrates not merely as the index and precursor, but as the indisputable condition of future progress." It was the aim of Socrates to force the seekers after truth into the path of inductive generalization, whereby alone trustworthy conclusions could be formed. He thus improved the method of speculative minds, and struck out from other minds that fire which sets light to original thought and stimulates analytical inquiry. He was a religious and intellectual missionary preparing the way for the Platos and Aristotles of the succeeding age by his severe dialectics. This was his mission, and he declared it by talking. He did not lecture; he conversed. For more than thirty years he discoursed on the principles of morality, until he arrayed against himself enemies who caused him to be put to death, for his teachings had undermined the popular system which the Sophists accepted and practiced. He probably might have been acquitted if he had chosen it, but he did not wish to live after his powers of usefulness had passed away. He opened to science new matter and a new method, as a basis for future philosophical systems. He was a "colloquial dialectician," such as this world has never seen, and may never see again. He was a skeptic respecting physics, but as far as man and society are concerned, he thought that every man might and ought to know what justice, temperance, courage, piety, patriotism, etc., were, and unless he did know what they were he would not be just, temperate, etc. He denied that men can know that on which they have bestowed no pains, or practice what they do not know. "The method of Socrates survives still in some of the dialogues of Plato, and is a process of eternal value and universal application. There is no man whose notions have not been first got together by spontaneous, unartificial associations, resting upon forgotten particulars, blending together disparities or inconsistencies, and having in his mind old and familiar

The great aim of the Socratic method.

phrases and oracular propositions of which he has never rendered to himself an account; and there is no man who has not found it a necessary branch of self-education to break up, analyze, and reconstruct these ancient mental compounds."[1] The services which he rendered to philosophy, as enumerated by Tennemann,[2] "are twofold, — negative and positive: *Negative*, inasmuch as he avoided all vain discussions; combated mere speculative reasoning on substantial grounds, and had the wisdom to acknowledge ignorance when necessary, but without attempting to determine accurately what is capable, and what is not, of being accurately known. *Positive*, inasmuch as he examined with great ability the ground directly submitted to our understanding, and of which man is the centre."

Socrates cannot be said to have founded a school, like Xenophanes. He did not bequeath a system of doctrines; he rather attempted to awaken inquiry, for which his method was admirably adapted. He had his admirers, who followed in the path which he suggested. Among these were Aristippus, Antisthenes, Euclid of Megara, Phædo of Elis, and Plato, all of whom were disciples of Socrates, and founders of schools. Some only partially adopted his method, and all differed from each other. Nor can it be said that all of them advanced science. Aristippus, the founder of the Cyreniac School, was a sort of Epicurean, teaching that pleasure was the end of life. Antisthenes, the founder of the Cynics, was both virtuous and arrogant, placing the supreme good in virtue, but despising speculative science, and maintaining that no man can refute the opinions of another. He made it a virtue to

[1] Grote has written very ably, and at unusual length, respecting Socrates and his philosophy. Thirlwall has also reviewed Hegel and other German authors on Socrates' condemnation. Ritter has a full chapter of great value. See Donaldson's continuation of Müller. The original sources of knowledge respecting Socrates are found chiefly in Plato and Xenophon. Cicero may be consulted in his *Tusculan Questions.*

[2] Tennemann; Schliermacker, *Essay on the Worth of Socrates as a Philosopher*, translated by Bishop Thirlwall, and reprinted in Dr. Wigger's *Life of Socrates.*

be ragged, hungry, and cold, like the ancient monks; an austere, stern, bitter, reproachful man, who affected to despise all pleasures, like his own disciple Diogenes, who lived in a tub, and carried on a war between the mind and body — brutal, scornful, proud. To men who maintained that science was impossible, philosophy is not much indebted, although they were disciples of Socrates. Euclid merely gave a new edition of the Eleatic doctrines, and Phædo speculated on the oneness of the good.

It was not till Plato arose that a more complete system of philosophy was founded. He was born of noble Athenian parents B. C. 429, the year that Pericles died, and the second year of the Peloponnesian War, and the most active period of Grecian thought. He had a severe education, studying poetry, music, rhetoric, and blending these with philosophy. He was only twenty when he found out Socrates, with whom he remained ten years, and from whom he was separated only by death. He then went on his travels, visiting every thing worth seeing in his day, especially in Egypt. When he returned, he commenced to teach the doctrines of his master, which he did, like him, gratuitously, in a garden near Athens, planted with lofty plane-trees, and adorned with temples and statues. This was called the Academy, and gave a name to his system of philosophy. And it is this only with which we have to do. It is not the calm, serious, meditative, isolated man that I would present, but *his contribution* to the developments of philosophy on the principles of his master. And surely no man ever made a richer contribution. He may not have had the originality or breadth of Socrates, but he was more profound. He was preëminently a great thinker — a great logician — skilled in dialectics, and his "Dialogues" are such exercises of dialectical method that the ancients were divided whether he was a skeptic or a dogmatist. He adopted the Socratic method, and en-

Plato.

His education and travels.

He adopts the Socratic method.

larged it. "Socrates relied on inductive reasoning, and on definitions, as the two principles of investigation. Definitions form the basis of all philosophy. To know a thing, you must know what it is not. Plato added a more efficient process of analysis and synthesis, of generalization and classification."[1] "Analysis," continues the same author, "as insisted on by Plato, is the decomposition of the whole into its separate parts — is seeing the *one* in many. Definitions were to Plato, what general or abstract ideas were to later metaphysicians. The individual thing was transitory; the abstract idea was eternal. Only concerning the latter could philosophy occupy itself. Socrates, insisting on proper definitions, had no conception of the classification of those definitions which must constitute philosophy. Plato, by the introduction of this process, shifted philosophy from the ground of inquiries into man and society, which exclusively occupied Socrates, to that of dialectics." Plato was also distinguished for skill in composition. Dionysius of Halicarnassus classes him with Herodotus and Demosthenes in the perfection of his style, which is characterized by great harmony and rhythm, as well as the variety of elegant figures.[2]

His doctrines.

Plato made philosophy to consist in the discussion of general terms, or abstract ideas. General terms were synonymous with real existences, and these were the only objects of philosophy. These were called *Ideas;* and ideas are the basis of his system, or rather the subject matter of dialectics. He was a Realist, that is, he maintained that every general term, or abstract idea, has a real and independent existence. Here he probably was indebted to Pythagoras, for Plato was a master of the whole realm of philosophical speculation; but his conception of *ideas* is a great advance on the conception of *numbers*. He was taught by Socrates that beyond

1 Lewes, *Biog. Hist. of Philos.*

2 See Donaldson's quotations, *Hist. Lit. of Greece*, vol. ii. p. 257.

this world of sense, there was the world of eternal truth, and that there were certain principles concerning which there could be no dispute. The soul apprehends the idea of goodness, greatness, etc. It is in the celestial world that we are to find the realm of ideas. Now God is the supreme idea. To know God should be the great aim of life. We know him by the desire which like feels for like. The divinity within feels for the divinity revealed in beauty, or any other abstract idea. The longing of the soul for beauty is *Love.* Love then is the bond which unites the human to the divine. Beauty is not revealed by harmonious outlines which appeal to the senses, but is *Truth.* It is divinity. Beauty, truth, love, these are God, the supreme desire of the soul to comprehend, and by the contemplation of which the mortal soul sustains itself, and by perpetual meditation becomes participant in immortality. The communion with God presupposes immortality. The search for the knowledge of God is the great end of life. Wisdom is the consecration of the soul to the search; and this is effected by dialectics, for only out of dialectics can correct knowledge come. But man, immersed in the flux of sensualities, can never fully attain this high excellence — the knowledge of God, the object of all rational inquiry. Hence the imperfection of all human knowledge. The supreme good is attainable; it is not attained. God is the immutable good, and justice the rule of the universe. "The vital principle of his philosophy is to show that true science is the knowledge of the good; is the eternal contemplation of truth, or ideas; and though man may not be able to apprehend it in its unity, because he is subject to the restraints of the body, he is, nevertheless, permitted to recognize it, imperfectly, by calling to mind the eternal measure of existence, by which he is in his origin connected."[1] He was unable to find a transition from his world of ideas to that of sense,

The end of science is the contemplation of truth.

[1] Ritter, *Hist. of Phil.*, b. viii. p. 2, chap. i.

and his philosophy, vague and mystical, though severely logical, diverts the mind from the investigations of actual life — from that which is the object of experience.

The object of Plato's inquiries.

The writings of Plato have come down to us complete, and have been admired by all ages for their philosophical acuteness, as well as beauty of language. He was not the first to use the form of dialogue, but he handled it with greater mastery than any one who preceded him, or has come after him, and all with a view to bring his hearers to a consciousness of knowledge or ignorance. He regarded wisdom as the attribute of the godhead; that philosophy is the necessity of the intellectual man, and the greatest good to which he can attain. This wisdom presupposes, however, a communion with the divine. He regarded the soul as immortal and indestructible. He maintained that neither happiness nor virtue can consist in the attempt to satisfy our unbridled desires; that virtue is purely a matter of intelligence; that passions disturb the moral economy.

God the immutable good.

"When we review the doctrines of Plato, it is impossible to deny," says Ritter, "that they are pervaded with a grand view of life and the universe. This is the noble thought which inspired him to say, that God is the constant and immutable good; the world is good in a state of becoming, and the human soul that in and through which the good in the world is to be consummated. In his sublimer conception, he shows himself the worthy disciple of Socrates. His merit lies chiefly in having advanced certain distinct and precise rules for the Socratic method, and in insisting, with a perfect consciousness of its importance, upon the law of science, that to be able to descend from the higher to the lower ideas by a principle of the reason, and reciprocally from the multiplicity of the lower to the higher, is indispensable to the perfect possession of any knowledge. He thus imparted to this method a more liberal character. While he adopted many of the opinions of his predecessors, and gave due consideration to the results of the earlier philosophy, he did not allow himself to be disturbed by the mass of conflicting theories, but breathed into them the life-giving breath of unity. He may have erred in his attempts to determine the nature of good; still he pointed out to all who aspire to a knowledge of the divine nature, an excellent road by which they may arrive at it."

Plato is very much admired by the Germans, who look upon him as the incarnation of dialectical power; but it were to be hoped that, some day, these great metaphysicians may make a clearer exposition of his doctrines, and of his services to philosophy, than they have as yet done. To me, Ritter, Brandis, and all the great authorities, are obscure. But that Plato was one of the greatest lights of the ancient world, there can be no reasonable doubt. Nor is it probable that, as a dialectician, he has ever been surpassed; while his purity of life, and his lofty inquiries, and his belief in God and immortality, make him, in an ethical point of view, the most worthy of the disciples of Socrates. He was to the Greeks what Kant was to the Germans, and these two great thinkers resemble each other in the structure of their minds and their relations to society.

The ablest part of the lectures of Archer Butler of Dublin, is devoted to the Platonic philosophy. It is a criticism and an eulogium. No modern writer has written more enthusiastically of what he considers the crowning excellence of the Greek philosophy. The dialectics of Plato, his ideal theory, his physics, his psychology, and his ethics, are most ably discussed, and in the spirit of a loving and eloquent disciple. He represents the philosophy which he so much admires as a contemplation of, and the tendency to, the absolute and eternal good. The good is enthroned by Plato in majesty supreme at the summit of the whole universe, and the sensible world is regarded as a development of supreme perfection in an inferior and transitory form. Nor are ideas abstractions, as some suppose, but archetypal conceptions of the divine mind itself — the eternal laws and reasons of things. The sensible world is regarded as an imperfect image of ideal perfection, yet the uncertainty of physical researches is candidly admitted. The discovery of theological and moral truth, is the great object even of the "*Timæus.*" Hence the physics of Plato have a theological character — are mathematical rather than experimental. The psychology represents the body as the prison of the soul, somewhat after the spirit of oriental theogonists, and the aim of virtue is to preserve the distinctness of both, and realize liberty in bonds. The doctrine of preëxistence is maintained, as well as a future state. In the ethics, the perfection of the human soul — the perfection which it may attain — is distinctly unfolded, and also the unity of the great ideas of the beautiful, just, and good. The "*Phœdo*" enforces the supremacy of wisdom, and the "*Philebus*" the "*summum bonum.*" *Love* is the aspiration after a communion with perfection. The chief excellence of the philosophy which Plato taught, consists in the immutable basis assigned to the principles of moral truth; the defects are a want of distinct apprehension of the claims of divine justice in consequence of human sin, and an indirect discouragement of active virtue.

The great disciple of Plato was Aristotle, and he carried on the philosophical movement which Socrates had started to the highest limit that it ever reached in the ancient world. He was born at Stagira B. C. 384, of wealthy parents, and early evinced an insatiable thirst for knowledge. When Plato returned from Sicily he joined his disciples, and was his pupil for seventeen years, at Athens. On the death of Plato, he went on his travels, and became the tutor of Alexander the Great, and B. C. 335, returned to Athens, after an absence of twelve years, and set up a school, and taught in the Lyceum. He taught while walking up and down the shady walks which surrounded it, from which he obtained the name of Peripatetic, which has clung to his name and philosophy. His school had a great celebrity, and from it proceeded illustrious philosophers, statesmen, historians, and orators. He taught thirteen years, during whic he composed most of his greater works. He not only wrote on dialectics and logic, but also on physics in its various departments. His work on "The History of Animals" was deemed so important that his royal pupil presented him with eight hundred talents — an enormous sum — for the collection of materials. He also wrote on ethics and politics, history and rhetoric; letters, poems, and speeches, three fourths of which are lost. He was one of the most voluminous writers of antiquity, and probably the most learned man whose writings have come down to us. Nor has any one of the ancients exercised upon the thinking of succeeding ages so great an influence. He was an oracle until the revival of learning.

Genius of Aristotle.

"Aristotle," says Hegel, "penetrated into the whole mass, and into every department of the universe of things, and subjected to the comprehension its scattered wealth; and the greater number of the philo sophical sciences owe to him their separation and commencement."[1] He is also the father of the history of philosophy, since he gives an historical review of the way in which the subject has been hitherto treated by the earlier philosophers.

"Plato made the external world the region of the incomplete and bad, of the contradictory and the false, and recognized absolute truth only in the eternal immutable ideas. Aristotle laid down the proposition that the idea, which cannot of itself fashion itself into reality, is powerless, and has only a potential existence, and that it becomes a living reality, only by realizing itself in a creative manner by means of its own energy."[2]

[1] Hegel is said to have comprehended Aristotle better than any modern writer, and the best work on his philosophy is by him.

[2] Adolph Stahr, Oldenburg.

But there can be no doubt as to his marvelous power of systematization. Collecting together all the results of ancient speculation, he so elaborated them into a coördinate system, that for two thousand years he reigned supreme in the schools. In a literary point of view, Plato was doubtless his superior, but Plato was a poet making philosophy divine and musical; but Aristotle's investigations spread over a far wider range. He wrote also on politics, natural history, and ethics, in so comprehensive and able manner, as to prove his claim to be one of the greatest intellects of antiquity, the most subtle and the most patient. He differed from Plato chiefly in relation to the doctrine of ideas, without however resolving the difficulty which divided them. As he made matter to be the eternal ground of phenomena, he reduced the notion of it to a precision it never before enjoyed, and established thereby a necessary element in human science. But being bound to matter, he did not soar, as Plato did, into the higher regions of speculation; nor did he entertain as lofty views of God, or of immortality. Neither did he have as high an ideal of human life. His definition of the highest good was a perfect practical activity in a perfect life.

Vast attainments of Aristotle.

With Aristotle closed the great Socratic movement in the history of speculation. When Socrates appeared there was the general prevalence of skepticism, arising from the unsatisfactory speculations respecting nature. He removed this skepticism by inventing a new method, and by withdrawing the mind from the contemplation of nature, to the study of man himself. He bade men to look inward.

Plato accepted his method, but applied it more universally. Like Socrates, however, ethics were the great subject of his inquiries, to which physics were only subordinate. The problem he sought to solve was the way to live like the gods. He would contemplate truth as the great aim of life.

Ethics the great subject of inquiry with Plato.

With Aristotle, ethics formed only one branch of his attention. His main inquiries were in reference to physics and metaphysics. He thus, by bringing these into the region of inquiry, paved the way for a new epoch of skepticism.[1]

Main inquiries of Aristotle had reference to physics and metaphysics.

It is impossible, within the proper limits of this chapter, to enter upon an analysis of the philosophy of either the three great lights of the ancient world, or to enumerate and describe their other writings. I merely wish to show what are considered to be the vital principles on which their systems were based, and the general spirit of their speculations. The student must examine these in the elaborate treatises of modern philosophers, and in the original works of Plato and Aristotle.

Both Plato and Aristotle taught that reason alone could form science; but Aristotle differed from his master respecting the theory of ideas. He did not deny to ideas a *subjective* existence, but he did deny that they have an objective existence. And he maintained that the individual things alone *existed*, and if individuals only exist, they can only be known by *sensation*. Sensation thus becomes the basis of knowledge. Plato made reason the basis of knowledge, but Aristotle made *experience*. Plato directed man to the contemplation of ideas; Aristotle, to the observations of Nature. Instead of proceeding synthetically and dialectically like Plato, he pursues an analytic course. His method is hence inductive — the derivation of certain principles from a sum of given facts and phenomena. It would seem that positive science commenced with him, since he maintained that experience furnishes the principles of every science; but, while his conception was just, there was not sufficient experience then accumulated from which to generalize with effect. He did not sufficiently verify his premises. His reasoning

Their characteristic inquiries.

1 Lewes, Ritter, Hegel, Maurice, Diogenes Laertius. See fine article in *Encyclopedia Britannica*. Schwegler, translated by Seelyn.

was correct upon the data given, as in the famous syllogism, "All black birds are crows; this bird is black; therefore this bird is a crow." The defect of the syllogism is not in the reasoning, but in the truth of the major premise, since all black birds are not crows. It is only a most extensive and exhaustive examination of the accuracy of a proposition which will warrant reasoning upon it. Aristotle reasoned without sufficient examination of the major premise of his syllogisms.

Logic of Aristotle.

Aristotle was the father of logic, and Hegel and Kant think there has been no improvement upon it since his day. And this became to him the real organon of science. "He supposed it was not merely the instrument of thought, but the instrument of investigation." Hence it was futile for purposes of discovery, although important to aid the processes of thought. Induction and syllogism are the two great instruments of his logic. The one sets out from particulars already known to arrive at a conclusion; the other sets out from some general principle to arrive at particulars. The latter more particularly characterized his logic, which he presented in sixteen forms, showing great ingenuity, and useful as a dialectical exercise. This syllogistic process of reasoning would be incontrovertible, if the *general* were better known than the *particular*. But it is only by induction, which proceeds from the world of experience, that we reach the higher world of cognition. We arrive at no new knowledge by the syllogism, since the major premise is more evident than the conclusion, and anterior to it. Thus he made speculation subordinate to logical distinctions, and his system, when carried out by the schoolmen, led to a spirit of useless quibbling. Instead of interrogating Nature, as Bacon led the way, they interrogated their own minds, and no great discoveries were made. From a want of a proper knowledge of the conditions of scientific inquiry, the method of Aristotle became fruitless.[1]

[1] Maurice, *Anc. Phil.* See Whewell, *Hist. Ind. Science.*

Though Aristotle wrote in a methodical manner, yet there is great parsimony of language. There is no fascination in his style. It is without ornament, and very condensed. His merit consisted in great logical precision, and scrupulous exactness in the employment of terms.

Philosophy, as a great system of dialectics, as an analysis of the power and faculties of the mind, as a method to pursue inquiries, as an intellectual system merely, culminated in Aristotle. He completed the great fabric of which Thales laid the foundation. The subsequent schools of philosophy directed attention to ethical and practical questions, rather than to intellectual phenomena. The skeptics, like Pyrrho, had only negative doctrines, and had a disdain of those inquiries which sought to penetrate the mysteries of existence. They did not believe that absolute truth was attainable by man. And they attacked the prevailing systems with great plausibility. Thus Sextus attacked both induction and definitions. "If we do not know the thing we define," said he, "we do not comprehend it because of the definition, but we impose on it the definition because we know it; and if we are ignorant of the thing we would define, it is impossible to define it." Thus the skeptics pointed out the uncertainty of things and the folly of striving to comprehend them.

The Skeptics.

The Epicureans despised the investigations of philosophy, since, in their view, they did not contribute to happiness. The subject of their inquiries was happiness, not truth. What will promote this, was the subject of their speculation. Epicurus, born B. C. 342, contended that pleasure was happiness; that pleasure should not be sought for its own sake, but with a view of the happiness of life obtained by it. He taught that it was inseparable from virtue, and that its enjoyments should be limited. He was averse to costly pleasures, and regarded contentedness with a little to be a great good. He placed wealth not in great possessions, but few wants. He sought to widen the domain of pleasure, and narrow that of pain, and regarded a passionless state of life the highest. Nor did he dread death, which was deliverance from misery. Epicurus has been much misunderstood, and his doctrines were subsequently perverted, especially when the arts of life were brought into the service of luxury, and a gross materialism was the great feature of society. Epicurus had much of the practical spirit of a philosopher, although very little of the earnest cravings of a religious man. He himself led a virtuous life, because it was wiser and better to be virtuous, not because it was his duty. His writings were very voluminous, and in his tranquil garden he led a peaceful life of study and enjoyment. His followers, and they were numerous, were led into luxury and effeminacy, as was to be expected from a skeptical and irreligious philosophy, the great principle of which was that whatever is pleasant should be the object of existence.[1]

The Stoics were a large and celebrated sect of philosophers; but they added nothing to the domain of thought, — they created no system, they invented no new method, they were led into no new psychological inquiries. Their inquiries were chiefly ethical. And if ethics are a part of the great system of Grecian philosophy, they are well worthy of attention. Some of the greatest men of antiquity are numbered among them — like Seneca and Marcus Aurelius. The philosophy they taught was morality, and this was eminently practical and also elevated.

Zeno.

The founder of this sect, Zeno, born rich, but reduced to poverty by misfortune, was a very remarkable man, and a very good one, and profoundly revered by the Athenians, who intrusted him with the keys of their citadel. The date of his birth is unknown, but he lived in a degenerate age, when skepticism and sensuality were eating out the life and vigor of Grecian society,

1 The doctrines of the Epicureans are best set forth in Lucretius.

when Greek civilization was rapidly passing away, when ancient creeds had lost their majesty, and general levity and folly overspread the land. Deeply impressed with the prevailing laxity of morals and the absence of religion, he lifted up his voice, more as a reformer than as an inquirer after truth, and taught for more than fifty years in a place called the Porch, which had once been the resort of the poets. He was chiefly absorbed with ethical questions, although he studied profoundly the systems of the old philosophers. He combated Plato's doctrine that virtue consists in contemplation, and of Epicurus, that it consisted in pleasure. Man, in his eyes, was made for active duties. He also sought to oppose skepticism, which was casting the funereal veil of doubt and uncertainty over every thing pertaining to the soul, and God, and the future life. "The skeptics had attacked both perception and reason. They had shown that perception is, after all, based upon appearance, and appearance is not a certainty; and they showed that reason is unable to distinguish between appearance and certainty, since it had nothing but phenomena to build upon, and since there is no criterion to apply to reason itself." Then they proclaimed philosophy a failure, and without foundation. But he, taking a stand on common sense, fought for morality, as did Reid and Beattie, when they combated the skepticism of Hume.

Doctrines of the Stoics.

Philosophy, according to Zeno and other Stoics, was intimately connected with the duties of practical life. The contemplation, recommended by Plato and Aristotle, seemed only a covert recommendation of selfish enjoyment. The wisdom, which it should be the aim of life to attain, is virtue. And virtue is to live harmoniously with nature. To live harmoniously with nature is to exclude all personal ends. Hence pleasure is to be disregarded, and pain is to be despised. And as all moral action must be in harmony with nature, the law of destiny is supreme, and all things move according to immutable fate. With the predominant tendency to the universal which characterized their system, the Stoics taught that the sage ought to regard himself as a citizen of the world rather than of any particular city or state. They made four things to be indispensable to virtue: a knowledge of *good and evil*, which is the province of the reason; *temperance*, a knowledge of the due regulation of the sensual passions; *fortitude*, a conviction that it is good to suffer what is necessary; and *justice*, or acquaintance with what ought to be to every individual. They made *perfection* necessary to virtue, and saw nothing virtuous in the mere advance to it. Hence the severity of their system. The perfect sage, according to them, is raised above all influence of external events; he submits to the law of destiny; he is exempt from desire and fear, joy or sorrow; he is not governed even by what he is exposed to necessarily, like sorrow and pain; he is free from the restraints of passion; he is like a god in his mental placidity. Nor must the sage live only for himself, but for others; he is a member of the whole body of mankind; he ought to marry, and to take part in public affairs, but he will never give way to compassion or forgiveness, and is to attack error and vice with uncompromising sternness. But with this ideal, the Stoics were forced to admit that virtue, like true knowledge, although attainable, is beyond the reach of man. They were discontented with themselves, and with all around them, and looked upon all institutions as corrupt. They had a profound contempt of their age, and of human attainments; but it cannot be denied they practiced a lofty and stern virtue, and were the best people in their degenerate times. Their God was made subject to Fate, and he was a material god, synonymous with Nature. Thus their system was pantheistic. But they maintained the dignity of reason, and the ideal in nature, the actualization of which we should strive after, though without the hope of reaching it. "As a reaction

Influence of the Stoics.

against effeminacy, Stoicism may be applauded; as a doctrine, it is one-sided, and ends in apathy and egotism." [1]

With the Stoics ended all inquiry among the Greeks of a philosophical nature worthy of especial mention, until philosophy was revived in the Christian schools of Alexandria, where faith was united with reason. The Stoics endeavored to establish the certitude of human knowledge in order that they might establish the truth of moral principles, and the basis of their system was common sense, with which they attacked the godless skepticism of their times, and raised up a barrier, feeble though it was, to prevailing degeneracy. The struggles of so many great thinkers, from Thales to Aristotle, all ended in doubt and in despair. It was discovered that all of them were wrong, but that their error was without a remedy.

Bright period of Grecian philosophy.

The bright and glorious period of Grecian philosophy was from Socrates to Aristotle. Philosophical inquiries began about the origin of things, and ended with an elaborate systematization of the forms of thought, which was the most magnificent triumph that the unaided intellect of man ever achieved. Socrates founds a school, but does not elaborate a system. He reveals most precious truths, and stimulates the youth who listen to his instructions by the doctrine that it is the duty of man to pursue a knowledge of himself, which is to be sought in that divine reason which dwells within him and which also rules the world. He confides in science; he loves truth for its own sake; he loves virtue, which consists in the knowledge of the good.

Summary.

Plato seizes his weapons and is imbued with his spirit. He is full of hope for science and humanity. With soaring boldness he directs his inquiries to futurity, dissatisfied with the present, and cherishing a fond hope of a better existence. He speculates on God and the

[1] See Cicero, *De Fin.* and *Tusculan Questions;* Diogenes Laertius on Zeno. This historian is quite full on this subject, and seems to furnish the basis for Ritter.

soul. He is not much interested in physical phenomena. He does not, like Thales, strive to find out the beginning of all things, but the highest good, by which his immortal soul may be refreshed and prepared for the future life he cannot solve, yet in which he believes. The sensible is an impenetrable empire, but ideas are certitudes, and upon these he dwells with rapt and mystical enthusiasm, — a great poetical rhapsodist like Xenophanes, severe dialectician as he is, believing in truth and beauty and goodness.

Then Aristotle, following out the method of *his* teachers, attempts to exhaust experience, and directs his inquiries into the outward world of sense and observation, but all with the view of discovering from phenomena the unconditional truth, in which he, too, believes. But every thing in this world is fleeting and transitory, and, therefore, it is not easy to arrive at truth. A cold doubt creeps into the experimental mind of Aristotle with all his learning and all his logic.

The Epicureans arise. They place their hopes in sensual enjoyment. They despair of truth. But the world will not be abandoned to despair. The Stoics rebuke the impiety which is blended with sensualism, and place their hopes on virtue. But it is unattainable virtue, while their God is not a moral governor, but subject to necessity.

Thus did those old giants grope about, for they did not know the God who was revealed unto Abraham, and Moses, and David, and Isaiah. They solved nothing, since they did not *know*, even if they speculated on, the *Great First Cause.* And yet, with all their errors, they were the greatest benefactors of the ancient world. They gave dignity to intellectual inquiries, while they set, by their lives, examples of a pure morality — not the morality of the gospel, but the severest virtue practiced by the old guides of mankind.

Philosophy among the Romans.

The Romans added absolutely nothing to the philosophy of the Greeks. Nor were they much interested in any speculative inquiries. It was only the ethical views of the old sages which had attraction or force to them. They were too material to love pure subjective inquiries. They had conquered the land; they disdained the empire of the air.

Followers of the Greeks.

There were, doubtless, students of the Greek philosophy among the Romans, perhaps as early as Cato the Censor. But there were only two persons of note who wrote philosophy, till the time of Cicero, Aurafanius and Rubinus, and these were Epicureans.

Cicero.

Cicero was the first to systematize the philosophy which contributed so greatly to his intellectual culture. But even he added nothing. He was only a commentator and expositor. Nor did he seek to found a system or a school, but merely to influence and instruct men of his own rank. He regarded those subjects, which had the greatest attraction for the Grecian schools, to be beyond the power of human cognition, and, therefore, looked upon the practical as the proper domain of human inquiry. Yet he held logic in great esteem, as furnishing rules for methodical investigation. He adopted the doctrine of Socrates as to the pursuit of moral good. He regarded the duties which grow out of the relations of human society preferable to the obligations of pursuing scientific researches. Although a great admirer of Plato and Aristotle, he regarded patriotic calls of duty as paramount to any study of science or philosophy, which he thought was involved in doubt. He had a great contempt for knowledge which could neither lead to the clear apprehension of certitude, nor to practical applications. He thought it impossible to arrive at a knowledge of God, or the nature of the soul, or the origin of the world. And he thus was led to look upon the sensible and the present as of more importance than inconclusive inductions, or deductions from a truth not satisfactorily established.

Cicero was an Eclectic, seizing on what was true and clear in the ancient systems, and disregarding what was simply a matter of speculation. This is especially seen in his treatise "De Finibus Bonorum et Malorum," in which the opinions of all the Grecian schools concerning the supreme good are expounded and compared. Nor does he hesitate to declare that happiness consists in the cognition of nature and science, which is the true source of pleasure both to gods and men. Yet these are but hopes, in which it does not become us to indulge. It is the actual, the real, the practical, which preëminently claims attention; in other words, the knowledge which will but furnish man with a guide and rule of life.[1] Indeed, the sum of Philosophy, to the mind of Cicero, is that she is an instructress and a comforter. He takes an entirely practical view of the end of philosophy, which is to improve the mind, and make a man contented and happy. For philosophy as a science, — a series of inductions and deductions, — he had profound contempt. He also regards the doctrines of philosophy as involved in doubt, and even in the consideration of moral questions he is pursued by the conflict of opinions, although, in this department, he is most at home. The points he is most anxious to establish are the doctrines of God and the soul. These are most fully treated in his essay, "De Natura Deorum," in which he submits the doctrines of the Epicureans and the Stoics to the objections of the Academy.[2] He admits that man is unable to form true conceptions of God, but acknowledges the necessity of assuming one supreme God as the creator and ruler of all things, moving all things, remote from all mortal mixture, and endued with eternal motion in himself. He seems to believe in a divine providence ordering good to man; in the soul's immortality, in free-will, in the dignity of human nature, in the dominion of reason, in the restraint of the passions as necessary to virtue, in a life of public utility, in an immutable morality, in the imitation of the divine.

His eclecticism.

1 *De Fin.*, v. 6.

2 *De Nat. D.*, iii. 10.

The doctrines of Cicero on ethical subjects, are chiefly drawn from the Stoics and Peripatetics. They are opinions drawn sometimes from one system and sometimes from another. Thus he agrees with the disciples of Aristotle, that health, honors, friends, country, are worthy objects of desire. Then again, he coincides with the Stoics that passions and emotions of the soul are vices. But he recedes from their severe tone, which elevated the sage too high above his fellow-men.

His ethics.

Thus there is little of original thought in the moral theories of Cicero, and these are the result of observation rather than of any philosophical principle. We might enumerate his various opinions, and show what an enlightened mind he possessed; but this would not be the development of philosophy. His views, interesting as they are, and generally wise and lofty, yet do not indicate any progress of the science. He merely repeats earlier doctrines. These were not without their utility, since they had great influence on the Latin fathers. They were esteemed for their general enlightenment. He softened down the extreme views of the great thinkers before his day, and clearly unfolded what had become obscured. He is a critic of philosophy; an expositor whom we can scarcely spare.

Character of his philosophical writings.

If any body advanced philosophy among the Romans, it was Epictetus, and he even only in the realm of ethics. Quintius Sextius, in the time of Augustus, had revived the Pythagorean doctrines. Seneca had recommended the severe morality of the Stoics, but they added nothing that was not previously known. The Romans had no talent for philosophy, although they were acquainted with its various systems. Their greatest light was a Phrygian slave.

Epictetus taught in the time of Domitian, and though he did not leave any written treatises, his doctrines were preserved and handed down by his

Epictetus.

disciple Arrian, who had for him the reverence that Plato had for Socrates. The loftiness of his recorded views makes us feel that he must have been indebted to Christianity; for no one, before him, has revealed precepts so much in accordance with its spirit. He was a Stoic, but he held in the highest estimation Socrates and Plato. It is not for the solution of metaphysical questions that he was remarkable. He was not a dialectician, but a moralist, and, as such, takes the highest ground of all the old inquirers after truth. With him, philosophy, as it was to Cicero and Seneca, is a wisdom of life. He sets no value on logic, nor much on physics; but he reveals sentiments of great simplicity and grandeur. His great idea is the purification of the soul. He believes in the severest self-denial; he would guard against the syren spells of pleasure; he would make men feel that, in order to be good, they must first feel that they are evil; he condemns suicide, although it had been defended by the Stoics; he would complain of no one, not even of injustice; he would not injure his enemies; he would pardon all offenses; he would feel universal compassion, since men sin from ignorance; he would not easily blame, since we have none to condemn but ourselves; he would not strive after honor or office, since we put ourselves in subjection to that we seek or prize; he would constantly bear in mind that all things are transitory, and that they are not our own; he would bear evils with patience, even as he would practice self-denial of pleasure; he would, in short, be calm, free, keep in subjection his passions, avoid self-indulgence, and practice a broad charity and benevolence. He felt he owed all to God; that all was his gift, and that we should thus live in accordance with his will; that we should be grateful not only for our bodies, but for our souls, and reason, by which we attain to greatness. And if God has given us such a priceless gift, we should be contented, and not even seek to alter our external relations,

His lofty ethical system.

which are doubtless for the best. We should wish, indeed, for only what God wills and sends, and we should avoid pride and haughtiness, as well as discontent, and seek to fulfill our allotted part.[1]

Such were the moral precepts of Epictetus, in which we see the nearest approach to Christianity that had been made in the ancient world. And these sublime truths had a great influence, especially on the mind of the most lofty and pure of all the Roman emperors, Marcus Aurelius, who *lived* the principles he had learned from a slave, and whose "Maxims" are still held in admiration.

Marcus Aurelius.

Thus did the speculations about the beginning of things lead to elaborate systems of thought, and end in practical rules of life, until, in spirit, they had, with Epictetus, harmonized with many of the revealed truths which Christ and his Apostles laid down for the regeneration of the world. Who cannot see in the inquiries of the old philosopher, whether into nature, or the operations of mind, or the existence of God, or the immortality of the soul, or the way to happiness and virtue, a magnificent triumph of human genius, such as has been exhibited in no other department of human science? We regret that our limits preclude a more extended view of the various systems which the old sages propounded — systems full of errors, yet also marked by important truths, but whether false or true, showing a marvelous reach of the human understanding. Modern researches have discarded many opinions which were highly valued in their day, yet philosophy, in its methods of reasoning, is scarcely advanced since the time of Aristotle; while the subjects which agitated the Grecian schools, have been from time to time revived and rediscussed, and are still unsettled. If any science has gone round in perpetual circles, incapable, apparently, of progression or rest, it is that glorious

General observations.

1 A fine translation of Epictetus has been published by Little and Brown.

field of inquiry which has tasked more than any other the mightiest intellects of this world, and which, progressive or not, will never be relinquished without the loss of what is most valuable in human culture.

For original authorities in reference to the matter of this chapter, read Diogenes Laertius' Lives of the Philosophers; the Writings of Plato and Aristotle; Cicero, De Nat., De Or., De Offic., De Div., De Fin., Tusc. Quæst.; Xenophon, Memorabilia; Boethius, De Idea Hist. Phil.; Lucretius.

The great modern authorities are the Germans, and these are very numerous. Among the most famous writers on the history of philosophy, are Bruckner, Hegel, Brandis, I. G. Buhle, Tennemann, Ritter, Plessing, Schwegler, Hermann, Meiners, Stallbaum, and Speugel. The history of Ritter is well translated, and is always learned and suggestive. Tennemann, translated by Morell, is a good manual, brief, but clear. In connection with the writings of the Germans, the great work of Cousin should be consulted.

The English historians of ancient philosophy are not so numerous as the Germans. The work of Enfield is based on Bruckner, or is rather an abridgment. Archer Butler's Lectures are suggestive and able, but discursive and vague, as is the History of Ancient Philosophy by Maurice. Grote has written learnedly on Socrates and the other great lights. Lewes' Biographical History of Philosophy has the merit of clearness, and is very interesting, but rather superficial. Henry has written a good epitome. See also Stanley's History of Philosophy, and the articles in Smith's Dictionary, on the leading ancient philosophers. Donaldson's continuation of Müller's History of the Lit. of Greece, is learned, and should be consulted with Thompson's Notes on Archer Butler. There are also fine articles in the Encyclopedias Britannica and Metropolitana. Schleirmacher, on Socrates, translated by Bishop Thirlwall.

CHAPTER IX.

SCIENTIFIC KNOWLEDGE AMONG THE ROMANS.

It would be absurd to claim for the ancients any great attainments in science, such as they made in the field of letters or the realm of art. It is in science, especially when applied to practical life, that the moderns show their great superiority to the most enlightened nations of antiquity. In this great department, modern genius shines with the lustre of the sun. It is this which most strikingly attests the advance of society, which makes their advance a most incontestible fact. It is this which has distinguished and elevated the races of Europe more triumphantly than what has resulted from the combined energies of Greeks and Romans in all other departments combined. With the magnificent discoveries and inventions of the last three hundred years in almost every department of science,—especially in physics, in the explorations of distant seas and continents, in the analysis of chemical compounds, in the explanation of the phenomena of the heavens, in the wonders of steam and electricity, in mechanical appliance to abridge human labor or destroy human life, in astronomical researches, in the miracles which inventive genius has wrought,—seen in our ships, our manufactories, our wondrous instruments, our printing-presses, our observatories, our fortifications, our laboratories, our mills, our machines to cultivate the earth, to make our clothes, to build our houses, to multiply our means of offense and defense, to make weak children do the work of Titans, to measure our time with the accuracy

Wonders of modern science.

of the orbit of the planets, to use the sun itself in perpetuating our likenesses to distant generations, to cause a needle to guide the mariner with assurance on the darkest night, to propel a heavy ship against the wind and tide without oars or sails, to make carriages ascend mountains without horses at the rate of thirty miles an hour, to convey intelligence with the speed of lightning from continent to continent, under oceans that ancient navigators never dared to cross; these and other wonders attest an ingenuity and audacity of intellect which would have overwhelmed with amazement the most adventurous of Greeks and the most potent of Romans. The achievements of modern science settle forever the question as to the advance of society and the superiority of modern times over those of the most favored nations of antiquity. But the great discoveries and inventions to which we owe this marked superiority are either accidental or the result of generations of experiment, assisted by an immense array of ascertained facts from which safe inductions can be made. It is not, probably, the superiority of the Teutonic races over the Greeks and Romans to which we may ascribe the wonderful advance of modern society, but the particular direction which genius was made to take. Had the Greeks given the energy of their minds to mechanical forces as they did to artistic creations, they might have made wonderful inventions. But it was so ordered by Providence. Nor was the world in that stage of development when this particular direction of intellect would have been favored. There were some things which the Greeks and Romans exhausted, some fields of labor and thought in which they never have been, and, perhaps, never will be, surpassed; and some future age may direct its energies into channels which are as unknown to us as clocks and steam-engines were to the Greeks. This is the age of mechanism and of science, and mechanism and science sweep every thing before them, and will probably

Every great age distinguished for something never afterwards equaled.

be carried to their utmost capacity and development. Then the human mind may seek some new department, some new scope for energies, and a new age of wonders may arise, — perhaps after the present dominant races shall have become intoxicated with the greatness of their triumphs and have shared the fate of the old monarchies of the East. But I would not speculate on the destinies of the European nations, whether they are to make indefinite advances, until they occupy and rule the whole world, or are destined to be succeeded by nations as yet undeveloped, — savages, as their fathers were when Rome was in the fullness of material wealth and grandeur. We know nothing of the future. We only know that all nations are in the hands of God, who setteth up and pulleth down according to his infinite wisdom.

I have shown that in the field of artistic excellence, in literary composition, in the arts of government and legislation, and even in the realm of philosophical speculations, the ancients were our schoolmasters, and that among them were some men of most marvelous genius, who have had no superiors among us.

The ancients deficient in the application of science.

But we do not see the exhibition of genius in what we call science, at least in its application to practical life. It would be difficult to show any department of science which the ancients carried to any degree of perfection. Nevertheless, there were departments in which they made noble attempts, and in which they showed considerable genius, even if they were unsuccessful in great practical results.

Labors of the ancients in astronomy.

Astronomy was one of these. So far as mathematical genius is concerned, so far as astronomy taxed the reasoning powers, such men as Eratosthenes, Aristarchus, Hipparchus, and Ptolemy were great lights, of whom humanity may be proud; and, had they been assisted by our modern accidental inventions, they might have earned a fame scarcely eclipsed by that of Kepler and

Newton. The Ionic philosophers added but little to the realm of true philosophy, but they were pioneers of thought, and giants in their native powers. The old astronomers did as little as they to place science on a true foundation, but they showed great ingenuity, and discovered some great truths which no succeeding age has repudiated. They determined the circumference of the earth by a method identical with that which would be employed by modern astronomers. They ascertained the position of the stars by right ascension and declination. They knew the obliquity of the ecliptic, and determined the place of the sun's apogee as well as its mean motion. Their calculations on the eccentricity of the moon prove that they had a rectilinear trigonometry and tables of chords. They had an approximate knowledge of parallax.[1] They could calculate eclipses of the moon, and use them for the correction of their lunar tables. They understood spherical trigonometry, and determined the motions of the sun and moon, involving an accurate definition of the year, and a method of predicting eclipses. They ascertained that the earth was a sphere, and reduced the phenomena of the heavenly bodies to uniform movements of circular orbits.[2] We have settled, by physical geography, the exact form of the earth, but the ancients arrived at their knowledge by astronomical reasoning. "The reduction of the motions of the sun, moon, and five planets to circular orbits, as was done by Hipparchus, implies deep concentrated thought and scientific abstraction. The theory of eccentrics and epicycles accomplished the end of explaining all the known phenomena. The resolution of the apparent motions of the heavenly bodies into an assemblage of circular motions, was a great triumph of genius,[3] and was equivalent to the most recent and improved processes by which modern astronomers deal with such motions."

1 Delambre, *Hist. d'Astr. Anc.*, tom. 1, p. 184.
2 Lewis, *Hist. of Astron.*, p. 209.
3 Whewell, *Hist. Induc. Science*, v. i. p. 181.

But I will not here enumerate the few discoveries which were made by the Alexandrian school. I only wish to show that there are a few names among the ancients which are inscribed on the roll of great astronomers, limited as were the triumphs of the science itself. But, until the time of Aristarchus, most of the speculations were crude and useless. Nothing can be more puerile than the notions of the ancients respecting the nature and motions of the heavenly bodies.

Astronomy born in Chaldea.

Astronomy was probably born in Chaldea as early as the time of Abraham. The glories of the firmament were impressed upon the minds of the rude primitive races with an intensity which we do not feel with all the triumphs of modern science. The Chaldean shepherds, as they watched their flocks by night, noted the movements of the planets, and gave names to the more brilliant constellations. Before religious rituals were established, before great superstitions arose, before poetry was sung, before musical instruments were invented, before artists sculptured marble or melted bronze, before coins were stamped, before temples arose, before diseases were healed by the arts of medicine, before commerce was known, before heroes were born, those oriental shepherds counted the hours of anxiety by the position of certain constellations. Astronomy is, therefore, the oldest of the ancient sciences, although it remained imperfect for more than four thousand years. The old Assyrians, Egyptians, and Greeks made but few discoveries which are valued by modern astronomers, but they laid the foundation of the science, and ever regarded it as one of the noblest subjects which could stimulate the faculties of man. It was invested with all that was religious and poetical.

Discoveries made by oriental nations.

The spacious level and unclouded horizon of Chaldea afforded peculiar facilities of observation; and its pastoral and contemplative inhabitants, uncontaminated by the vices and superstitions of subsequent ages, active-minded and fresh, discovered, after a long observation of eclipses — some say extending over nineteen centuries — the cycle of two hundred and twenty-three lunations, which brings back the eclipses in the same order. Having once established their cycle, they laid the foundation for the most sublime of all the sciences. Callisthenes transmitted from Babylon to Aristotle a collection of observations of all the eclipses that preceded the conquests of Alexander, together with the definite knowledge which the Chaldeans had collected about the motions of the heavenly bodies. It was rude and simple, and amounted to little beyond the fact that there were spherical revolutions about an inclined axis, and that the poles pointed always to particular stars. The Egyptians also recorded their observations, from which it would appear that they observed eclipses at least one thousand six hundred years before the commencement of our era. Nor is this improbable, if the speculations of modern philosophers respecting the age of the world are entitled to respect. The Egyptians discovered, by the rising of Sirius, that the year consists of three hundred and sixty-five and one quarter days, and this was their sacred year, in distinction from the civil, which consisted of three hundred and sixty-five days. They also had observed the courses of the planets, and could explain the phenomena of the stations and retrogradations, and it is even asserted that they regarded Mercury and Venus as satellites of the sun. Some have maintained that the obelisks which they erected served the purpose of gnomons, for determining the obliquity of the ecliptic, the altitude of the pole, and the length of the tropical year. It is thought that even the Pyramids, by the position of their sides toward the cardinal points, attest their acquaintance with a meridional line. The Chinese boast of having noticed and recorded a series of eclipses extending over a period of three thousand eight hundred and fifty-eight years, and it is probable that they anticipated the Greeks two thousand years in the discovery of the Metonic cycle, or the cycle of nineteen years, at the end of which time the new moons fall on the same days of the year. They determined the obliquity of the ecliptic, one thousand one hundred years before our era, to be 23° 54′ 3–15″. The Indians, at a remote antiquity, represented celestial phenomena with considerable exactness, and constructed tables by which the longitude of the sun and moon are determined. Bailly thinks that astronomy was cultivated in Siam three thousand one hundred and two years before Christ, which hardly yields in accuracy to that which modern science has built on the theory of universal gravitation. The Greeks divided the heavens into constellations fourteen centuries before Christ. Thales, born 640 B. C., taught the rotundity of the earth, and that the moon shines with reflected light. He also predicted eclipses. Anaximander, born 610 B. C., invented the gnomon, and constructed geographical charts.

The early Greek investigators.

But the Greeks, after all, were the only people of antiquity who elevated astronomy to the dignity of a science. They however confessed that they derived their earliest knowledge from the Babylonian and Egyptian priests, while the priests of Thebes asserted that they were the originators of exact astronomical observations.[1] Diodorus asserts that the Chaldeans used the Temple of Belus, in the centre of Babylon, for their survey of the heavens.[2] But whether the Babylonians or the Egyptians were the earliest astronomers, it is of little consequence, although the pedants make it a grave matter of investigation. All we know is, that astronomy was cultivated by both Babylonians and Egyptians, and that they made but very limited attainments. The early Greek philosophers, who visited Egypt and the East in search of knowledge, found very little to reward their curiosity or industry; not much beyond preposterous claims to a high antiquity,

[1] Diod., i. 50.

[2] Diod., ii. 9.

and an esoteric wisdom which has not yet been revealed. They approximated to the truth in reference to the solar year, by observing the equinoxes and solstices, and the heliacal rising of particular stars. Plato and Eudoxus spent thirteen years in Heliopolis for the purpose of extracting the scientific knowledge of the priests, but they learned but little beyond the fact that the solar year was a trifle beyond three hundred and sixty-five days. No great names have come down to us from the priests of Babylon or Egypt. No one gained an individual reputation. The Chaldean and Egyptian priests may have furnished the raw material of observation to the Greeks, but the latter alone possessed the scientific genius by which indigested facts were converted into a symmetrical system. The East never gave valuable knowledge to the West. It gave only superstition. Instead of astronomy, it gave astrology ; instead of science, it gave magic and incantations and dreams — poison which perverted the intellect.[1] They connected their astronomy with divination from the stars, and made their antiquity reach back to two hundred and seventy thousand years. There were soothsayers in the time of Daniel, and magicians, exorcists, and interpreters of signs.[2] They were not men of scientific research, seeking truth. It was power they sought, by perverting the intellect of the people. The astrology of the East was founded on the principle that a star or constellation presided over the birth of an individual, and either portended his fate, or shed a good or bad influence upon his future life. The star which looked upon a child at the hour of his birth, was called the horoscopus, and the peculiar influence of each planet was determined by professors of the genethliac art. The superstitions of Egypt and Chaldea unfortunately spread both among the Greeks and Romans, and these were about all that the western nations learned from the boastful priests

[1] Sir G. G. Lewis, *Hist. of Anc. Astron.*, p. 293.

[2] Dan. i. 4, 17, 20.

of occult science. Whatever was known of real value among the ancients, is due to the earnest inquiries of the Greeks.

Researches of the Greeks.

And yet their researches were very unsatisfactory until the time of Hipparchus. The primitive knowledge, until Thales, was almost nothing. The Homeric poems regarded the earth as a circular plain, bounded by the heaven, which was a solid vault or hemisphere, with its concavity turned downwards. And this absurdity was believed until the time of Herodotus, five centuries after; nor was it exploded fully in the time of Aristotle. The sun, moon, and stars, were supposed to move upon, or with, the inner surface of the heavenly hemisphere, and the ocean was thought to gird the earth around as a great belt, into which the heavenly bodies sunk at their setting.[1] Homer believed that the sun arose out of the ocean, ascending the heaven, and again plunging into the ocean, passing under the earth, and producing darkness.[2] The Greeks even personified the sun as a divine charioteer driving his fiery steeds over the steep of heaven, until he bathed them at evening in the western waves. Apollo became the god of the sun, as Diana was the goddess of the moon. But the early Greek inquirers did not attempt to explain how the sun found his way from the west back again to the east. They merely took note of the diurnal course, the alternation of day and night, the number of the seasons, and their regular successions. They found the points of the compass by determining the recurrence of the equinoxes and solstices; but they had no conception of the ecliptic — of that great circle in the heaven, formed by the sun's annual course, and of its obliquity when compared with the equator. Like the Egyptians and Babylonians, they ascertained the length of the year to be three hundred and sixty-five days; but perfect accuracy was wanting for want of scientific

[1] *Il.*, vii. 422; *Od.*, iii. i. xix. 433.

[2] *Il.*, viii. 485.

instruments, and of recorded observations of the heavenly bodies. The Greeks had not even a common chronological era for the designation of years. Thus Herodotus informs us that the Trojan War preceded his time by eight hundred years:[1] he merely states the interval between the event in question and his own time; he had certain data for distant periods. Thus the Greeks reckoned dates from the Trojan War, and the Romans from the building of their city. And they divided the year into twelve months, and introduced the intercalary circle of eight years, although the Romans disused it afterwards until the calendar was reformed by Julius Cæsar. Thus there was no scientific astronomical knowledge worth mentioning among the primitive Greeks.

Immense research and learning have been expended by modern critics, to show the state of scientific astronomy among the Greeks. I am equally amazed at the amount of research, and its comparative worthlessness, for what addition to science can be made by an enumeration of the puerilities and errors of the Greeks, and how wasted and pedantic the learning which ransacks all antiquity to prove that the Greeks adopted this or that absurdity.[2]

1 *Il.*, ii. 53.

2 The style of modern historical criticism may thus be exemplified, like the discussions of the Germans, whether the Arx on the Capitoline Hill occupied the northeastern or southwestern corner, which take up nearly one half of the learned article in Smith's *Dictionary*, on the Capitoline. "Thales supposed the earth to float on the water, like a plank of wood": οἱ δ' εφ' ὕδατος κεῖσθαι τουτον γὰρ ἀρχαιότατον παρειλήφαμεν τον λόγον ὅν φασιν εἰπειν θαλή τὸν Μιλήσιον. Aristot., *De Cæl.*, ii. 13: "*Quæ sequitur Thaletis inepta sententia est. Ait enim terrarum orbem aquâ sustineri.*" Seneca, *Nat. Quæst.*, iii. 13. This notion is mentioned in *Schol. Iliad*, xiii. 125. This doctrine Thales brought from Egypt. See Plut., *Pac.*, iii. 10; Galen, c. 21. But this may be doubted. Callimach., *Frag.*, 94; Hygin, *Poet. Astr.*, ii. 2; Martin, *Timée de Platon.*, tom. ii. p. 109, thinks it questionable whether Thales saw Egypt. Diog. Laert., viii. 60. Compare, however, Sturz, *Thales*, p. 80; Proclus, *in Tim.*, i. p. 40; *Schol. Aristophanes*, *Nub.*, ii. 31; Varro, ii. vi. 10. See also, *Ideler Chron.*, vol. i. p. 300. But Brandis sheds light upon the point, though his suggestions conflict with Origen, *Phil.*, p. 11; also with Aristotle, *De Cæl.*, ii. 13.

This style of expending learning on nothing, meets with great favor with the pedants, who attach no value to history unless one half of the page is filled with

But to return. The earliest historic name associated with astronomy in Greece was Thales, the founder of the Ionic school of philosophers, born 639 B. C. He is reported to have predicted an eclipse of the sun, to have made a visit to Egypt, to have fixed the year at three hundred and sixty-five days, and to have determined the course of the sun from solstice to solstice. He attributed an eclipse of the moon to the interposition of the earth between the sun and moon; and an eclipse of the sun to the interposition of the moon between the sun and earth.[1] He also determined the ratio of the sun's diameter to its apparent orbit. As he first solved the problem of inscribing a right-angled triangle in a circle,[2] he is the founder of geometrical science in Greece. He left, however, nothing to writing, hence all accounts of him are confused. It is to be doubted whether in fact he made the discoveries attributed to him. His speculations, which science rejects, such as that water is the principle of all things, are irrelevant to a description of the progress of astronomy. That he was a great light, no one questions, considering the ignorance with which he was surrounded. Anaximander, who followed him in philosophy, held to puerile doctrines concerning the motions and nature of the stars, which it is useless to repeat. His addition to science, if he made any, was in treating the magnitudes and distances of the planets. He attempted to delineate the celestial sphere, and to measure time by a sun-dial. Anaximenes of Miletus taught, like his predecessors, crude notions of the sun and stars, and speculated on the nature of the moon, but did nothing to advance his science on true grounds, except the construction of sun-dials. The same may be said of Heraclitus, Xenophanes, Parmenides, Anaxagoras. They were great men,

Thales.

Anaximander and Anaximenes.

erudite foot-notes which few can verify, and which prove nothing, or nothing of any consequence.

[1] Sir G. G. Lewis, *Hist. of Astron.*, p. 81.

[2] Diog. Laert., i. 24.

but they gave to the world mere speculations, some of which are very puerile. They all held to the idea that the heavenly bodies revolved around the earth, and that the earth was a plain. But they explained eclipses, and supposed that the moon derived its light from the sun. Some of them knew the difference between the planets and the fixed stars. Anaxagoras scouted the notion that the sun was a god, and supposed it to be a mass of ignited stone, for which he was called an atheist.

Socrates. Socrates, who belonged to another school, avoided all barren speculations concerning the universe, and confined himself to human actions and interests. He looked even upon geometry in a very practical way, so far as it could be made serviceable to land measuring. As for the stars and planets, he supposed it was impossible to arrive at a true knowledge of them, and regarded speculations upon them as useless. The Greek astronomers, however barren were their general theories, still laid the foundation of science. Pythagoras, born 580 B. C., taught the obliquity of the ecliptic, probably learned in Egypt, and the identity of the morning and evening stars. It is supposed that he maintained that the sun was the centre of the universe, and that the earth revolved around it. But this he did not demonstrate, and his whole system was unscientific, assuming certain arbitrary principles, from which he reasoned deductively. "He assumed that fire is more worthy than earth; that the more worthy place must be given to the more worthy; that the extremity is more worthy than the intermediate parts; and hence, as the centre is an extremity, the place of fire is at the centre of the universe, and that therefore the earth and other heavenly bodies move round the fiery centre." But this was no heliocentric system, since the sun moved like the earth, in a circle around the central fire. This was merely the work of the imagination, utterly unscientific, though bold and original. Nor did this hypothesis gain credit, since it was the fixed opinion of philosophers, that the earth was the centre of the universe, around which the sun and moon and planets revolved. But the Pythagoreans were the first to teach that the motions of the sun, moon, and planets, are circular and equable. Their idea that they emitted a sound, and were combined into a harmonious symphony, was exceedingly crude, however beautiful. "The music of the spheres" belongs to poetry, as well as the speculations of Plato."

Eudoxus.

Eudoxus, who was born 406 B. C., may be considered the founder of scientific astronomical knowledge among the Greeks. He is reputed to have visited Egypt with Plato, and to have resided thirteen years in Heliopolis, in constant study of the stars, communing with the Egyptian priests. His contribution to the science was a descriptive map of the heavens, which was used as a manual of sidereal astronomy to the sixth century of our era. He distributed the stars into constellations, with recognized names, and gave a sort of geographical description of their position and limits, although the constellations had been named before his time. He stated the periodic times of the five planets visible to the naked eye, but only approximated to the true periods.

The error of only one hundred and ninety days in the periodic time of Saturn, shows that there had been, for a long time, close observations. Aristotle, whose comprehensive intellect, like that of Bacon, took in all forms of knowledge, condensed all that was known in his day in a treatise concerning the heavens.[1] He regarded astronomy as more intimately connected with mathematical science than any other branch of philosophy. But even he did not soar far beyond the philosophers of his day, since he held to the immobility of the earth — the grand error of the ancients. Some few speculators in science, like Heraclitus of Pontus and Hicetas, conceived a motion of the

[1] Delambre, *Hist. de l'Astron. Anc.*, tom. i. p. 301.

earth itself upon its axis, so as to account for the apparent motion of the sun, but they also thought it was in the centre of the universe.

The introduction of the gnomon and dial into Greece advanced astronomical knowledge, since they were used to determine the equinoxes and solstices, as well as parts of the day. Meton set up a sun-dial at Athens in the year 433 B. C., but the length of the hour varied with the time of the year, since the Greeks divided the day into twelve equal parts. Dials were common at Rome in the time of Plautus, 224 B. C.;[1] but there was a difficulty of using them, since they failed at night and in cloudy weather, and could not be relied on. Hence the introduction of water-clocks instead.

Meton.

Aristarchus is said to have combated (280 B. C.) the geocentric theory so generally received by philosophers, and to have promulgated the hypothesis "that the fixed stars and the sun are immovable; that the earth is carried round the sun in the circumference of a circle of which the sun is the centre; and that the sphere of the fixed stars having the same centre as the sun, is of such magnitude that the orbit of the earth is to the distance of the fixed stars, as the centre of the sphere of the fixed stars is to its surface."[2] This speculation, resting on the authority of Archimedes, was ridiculed by him; but if it were advanced, it shows a great advance in astronomical science, and considering the age, was one of the boldest speculations of antiquity. Aristarchus also, according to Plutarch,[3] explained the apparent annual motion of the sun in the ecliptic, by supposing the orbit of the earth to be inclined to its axis. There is no evidence that this great astronomer supported his heliocentric theory with any geometrical proof, although Plutarch maintains that he demonstrated it.[4] This theory gave great offense, especially to the Stoics, and Cleanthes, the head of the

Aristarchus.

1 Ap. Gell., *N. A.*, iii. 3.

2 Lewis, p. 190.

3 Plut., *Plac. Phil.*, ii. 24.

4 *Quæst. Plat.*, viii. 1.

school at that time, maintained that the author of such an impious doctrine should be punished. Aristarchus has left a treatise "On the Magnitudes and Distances of the Sun and Moon," and his methods to measure the apparent diameters of the sun and moon, are considered sound by modern astronomers,[1] but inexact owing to defective instruments. He estimated the diameter of the sun at the seven hundred and twentieth part of the circumference of the circle, which it describes in its diurnal revolution, which is not far from the truth; but in this treatise he does not allude to his heliocentric theory.

Archimedes.

Archimedes, born 287 B. C., is stated to have measured the distance of the sun, moon, and planets, and he constructed an orrery in which he exhibited their motions. But it was not in the Grecian colony of Syracuse, but of Alexandria, that the greatest light was shed on astronomical science. Here Aristarchus resided, and also Eratosthenes, who lived between the years 276 and 196 B. C. He was a native of Athens, but was invited by Ptolemy Euergetes to Alexandria, and placed at the head of the library. His great achievement was the determination of the circumference of the earth. This was done by measuring on the ground the distance between Syene, a city exactly under the tropic, and Alexandria situated on the same meridian. The distance was found to be five thousand stadia. The meridional distance of the sun from the zenith of Alexandria, he estimated to be 7° 12′, or a fiftieth part of the circumference of the meridian. Hence the circumference of the earth was fixed at two hundred and fifty thousand stadia, not far from the truth. The circumference being known, the diameter of the earth was easily determined. The moderns have added nothing to this method. He also calculated the diameter of the sun to be twenty-seven times greater than of the earth, and the distance of the sun from the earth to be eight hundred and

Eratosthenes.

[1] Lewis, p. 193.

four million stadia, and that of the moon seven hundred and eighty thousand stadia — a very close approximation to the truth.

Astronomical science received a great impulse from the school of Alexandria, and Eratosthenes had worthy successors in Aristarchus, Aristyllus, Apollonius. But the great light of this school was Hipparchus, whose lifetime extended from 190 to 120 years B. C. He laid the foundation of astronomy upon a scientific basis. "He determined," says Delambre, "the position of the stars by right ascensions and declinations; he was acquainted with the obliquity of the ecliptic. He determined the inequality of the sun, and the place of its apogee, as well as its mean motion; the mean motion of the moon, of its nodes and apogee; the equation of the moon's centre, and the inclination of its orbit; he likewise detected a second inequality, of which he could not, for want of proper observations, discover the period and the law. His commentary on Aratus shows that he had expounded, and given a geometrical demonstration of, the methods necessary to find out the right and oblique ascensions of the points of the ecliptic and of the stars, the east point and the culminating point of the ecliptic, and the angle of the east, which is now called the nonagesimal degree. He could calculate eclipses of the moon, and use them for the correction of his lunar tables, and he had an approximate knowledge of parallax."[1] His determination of the motions of the sun and moon, and method of predicting eclipses, evince great mathematical genius. But he combined, with this determination, a theory of epicycles and eccentrics, which modern astronomy discards. It was, however, a great thing to conceive of the earth as a solid sphere, and reduce the phenomena of the heavenly bodies to uniform motions in circular orbits. "That Hipparchus should have succeeded in the first great steps of the resolu-

Hipparchus.

Greatness of Hipparchus.

[1] Delambre, *Hist. de l'Astron. Anc.*, tom. i. p. 184.

tion of the heavenly bodies into circular motions is a circumstance," says Whewell, "which gives him one of the most distinguished places in the roll of great astronomers."[1] But he even did more than this. He discovered that apparent motion of the fixed stars round the axis of the ecliptic, which is called the Precession of the Equinoxes, one of the greatest discoveries in astronomy. He maintained that the precession was not greater than fifty-nine seconds, and not less than thirty-six seconds. Hipparchus framed a catalogue of the stars, and determined their places with reference to the ecliptic, by their latitudes and longitudes. Altogether, he seems to have been one of the greatest geniuses of antiquity, and his works imply a prodigious amount of calculation.

Posidonius.

Astronomy made no progress for three hundred years, although it was expounded by improved methods. Posidonius constructed an orrery, which exhibited the diurnal motions of the sun, moon, and five planets. Posidonius calculated the circumference of the earth to be two hundred and forty thousand stadia by a different method from Eratosthenes. The barrenness of discovery, from Hipparchus to Ptolemy, in spite of the patronage of the Ptolemies, was owing to the want of instruments for the accurate measure of time, like our clocks, to the imperfection of astronomical tables, and to the want of telescopes. Hence the great Greek astronomers were unable to realize their theories. Their theories were magnificent, and evinced great power of mathematical combination; but what could they do without that wondrous instrument by which the human eye indefinitely multiplies its power? — by which objects are distinctly seen, which, without it, would be invisible? Moreover, the ancients had no accurate almanacs, since the care of the calendar belonged to the priests rather than to the astronomers, who tampered with the computation of time for temporary and personal

[1] *Hist. Ind. Science*, vol. i. p. 181.

objects. The calendars of different communities differed. Hence Julius Cæsar rendered a great service to science by the reform of the Roman calendar, which was exclusively under the control of the college of pontiffs. The Roman year consisted of three hundred and fifty-five days, and, in the time of Cæsar, the calendar was in great confusion, being ninety days in advance, so that January was an autumn month. He inserted the regular intercalary month of twenty-three days, and two additional ones of sixty-seven days. These, together of ninety days, were added to three hundred and sixty-five days, making a year of transition of four hundred and forty-five days, by which January was brought back to the first month in the year after the winter solstice. And to prevent the repetition of the error, he directed that in future the year should consist of three hundred and sixty-five and one quarter days, which he effected by adding one day to the months of April, June, September, and November, and two days to the months of January, Sextilis, and December, making an addition of ten days to the old year of three hundred and fifty-five. And he provided for a uniform intercalation of one day in every fourth year, which accounted for the remaining quarter of a day.[1]

The Roman calendar.

> "Ille moras solis, quibus in sua signa rediret,
> Traditur exactis disposuisse notis.
> Is decies senos tercentum et quinqui diebus
> Junxit; et pleno tempora quarta die.
> Hic anni modus est. In lustrum accedere debet
> Quæ consummatur partibus, una dies." [2]

Cæsar was a student of astronomy, and always found time for its contemplation. He is said even to have written a treatise on the motion of the stars. He was assisted in his reform of the calendar by Sosigines, an Alexandrian astronomer. He took it out of the hands of the priests, and made it a matter of pure civil regulation. The year was defined by the sun, and not, as before, by the moon.

Cæsar's labors.

[1] Suet., *Cæsar*, 40; Plut., *Cæsar*, 59.

[2] Ovid, *Fast.*, iii.

Thus the Romans were the first to bring the scientific knowledge of the Greeks into practical use; but while they measured the year with a great approximation to accuracy, they still used sun-dials and water-clocks to measure diurnal time. And even these were not constructed as they should have been. The hours on the sun-dial were all made equal, instead of varying with the length of the day, so that the hour varied with the length of the day. The illuminated interval was divided into twelve equal parts, so that, if the sun rose at five A. M. and set at eight P. M., each hour was equal to eighty minutes. And this rude method of measurement of diurnal time remained in use till the sixth century. But clocks, with wheels and weights, were not invented till the twelfth century.

The earlier Greek astronomers did not attempt to fix the order of the planets; but when geometry was applied to celestial movements, the difference between the three superior planets and the two inferior was perceived, and the sun was placed in the midst between them, so that the seven movable heavenly bodies were made to succeed one another in the following order: 1. Saturn; 2. Jupiter; 3. Mars; 4. The Sun; 5. Venus; 6. Mercury; 7. The Moon. Archimedes adopted this order, which was followed by the leading philosophers.[1]

Ptolemy and his system.

The last great light among the ancients in astronomical science was Ptolemy, who lived from 100 to 170 A. D. in Alexandria. He was acquainted with the writings of all the previous astronomers, but accepted Hipparchus as his guide. He held that the heaven is spherical and revolves upon its axis; that the earth is a sphere, and is situated within the celestial sphere, and nearly at its centre; that it is a mere point in reference to the distance and magnitude of the fixed stars, and that it has no motion. He adopted the views of the ancient

[1] Lewis, p. 247.

astronomers, who placed Saturn, Jupiter, and Mars next under the sphere of the fixed stars, then the sun above Venus and Mercury, and lastly the moon next to the earth. But he differed from Aristotle, who conceived that the earth revolves in an orbit round the centre of the planetary system, and turns upon its axis — two ideas in common with the doctrines which Copernicus afterward unfolded. But even he did not conceive the heliocentric theory that the sun is the centre of the universe. Archimedes and Hipparchus both rejected this theory.

In regard to the practical value of the speculations of the ancient astronomers, it may be said that, had they possessed clocks and telescopes, their scientific methods would have sufficed for all practical purposes. The greatness of modern discoveries lies in the great stretch of the reasoning powers, and the magnificent field they afford for sublime contemplation. "But," as Sir G. Cornwall Lewis remarks, "modern astronomy is a science of pure curiosity, and is directed exclusively to the extension of knowledge in a field which human interests can never enter. The periodic time of Uranus, the nature of Saturn's ring, and the occultation of Jupiter's satellites, are as far removed from the concerns of mankind as the heliacal rising of Sirius, or the northern position of the Great Bear." This may seem to be a utilitarian view with which those philosophers, who have cultivated science for its own sake, finding in the same a sufficient reward, as in truth and virtue, can have no sympathy.

Result of ancient investigations.

The upshot of the scientific attainments of the ancients, in the magnificent realm of the heavenly bodies, would seem to be that they laid the foundation of all the definite knowledge which is useful to mankind; while in the field of abstract calculation they evinced reasoning and mathematical powers which have never been surpassed. Eratosthenes, Archimedes, and Hipparchus were geniuses worthy to be placed by the side of Kepler,

Newton, and La Place. And all ages will reverence their efforts and their memory. It is truly surprising that, with their imperfect instruments, and the absence of definite data, they reached a height so sublime and grand. They explained the doctrine of the sphere and the apparent motions of the planets, but they had no instruments capable of measuring angular distances. The ingenious epicycles of Ptolemy prepared the way for the elliptic orbits and laws of Kepler, which, in turn, conducted Newton to the discovery of the laws of gravitation — the grandest scientific discovery in the annals of our race.

Closely connected with astronomical science was geometry, which was first taught in Egypt, — the nurse and cradle of ancient wisdom. It arose from the necessity of adjusting the landmarks, disturbed by the inundations of the Nile. Thales introduced the science to the Greeks. He applied a circle to the measurement of angles. Anaximander invented the sphere, the gnomon, and geographical charts, which required considerable geometrical knowledge. Anaxagoras employed himself in prison in attempting to square the circle. Pythagoras discovered the important theorem that in a right-angled triangle the squares on the sides containing the right angle are together equal to the square on the opposite side of it. He also discovered that of all figures having the same boundary, the circle among plane figures and the sphere among solids, are the most capacious. The theory of the regular solids was taught in his school, and his disciple, Archytas, was the author of a solution of the problem of two mean proportionals. Democritus of Abdera treated of the contact of circles and spheres, and of irrational lines and solids. Hippocrates treated of the duplication of the cube, and wrote elements of geometry, and knew that the area of a circle was equal to a triangle whose base is equal to its circumference, and altitude equal to its radius. The disciples of Plato invented

Geometry.

Ancient Greek geometers.

conic sections, and discovered the geometrical loci. They also attempted to resolve the problems of the trisection of an angle and the duplication of a cube. To Leon is ascribed that part of the solution of a problem, called its *determination*, which treats of the cases in which the problem is possible, and of those in which it cannot be resolved. Euclid has almost given his name to the science of geometry. He was born B. C. 323, and belonged to the Platonic sect, which ever attached great importance to mathematics. His "Elements" are still in use, as nearly perfect as any human production can be. They consist of thirteen books, — the first four on plane geometry; the fifth is on the theory of proportion, and applies to magnitude in general; the seventh, eighth, and ninth are on arithmetic; the tenth on the arithmetical characteristics of the division of a straight line; the eleventh and twelfth on the elements of solid geometry; the thirteenth on the regular solids. These "Elements" soon became the universal study of geometers throughout the civilized world. They were translated into the Arabic, and through the Arabians were made known to mediæval Europe. There can be no doubt that this work is one of the highest triumphs of human genius, and has been valued more than any single monument of antiquity. It is still a text-book, in various English translations, in all our schools. Euclid also wrote various other works, showing great mathematical talent. But, perhaps, a greater even than Euclid was Archimedes, born 287 B. C., who wrote on the sphere and cylinder, which terminate in the discovery that the solidity and surface of a sphere are respectively two thirds of the solidity and surface of the circumscribing cylinder. He also wrote on conoids and spheroids. "The properties of the spiral, and the quadrature of the parabola were added to ancient geometry by Archimedes, the last being a great step in the progress of the science, since it was the first curvilineal space legitimately

Euclid.

Archimedes.

squared." Modern mathematicians may not have the patience to go through his investigations, since the conclusions he arrived at may now be reached by shorter methods, but the great conclusions of the old geometers were only reached by prodigious mathematical power. Archimedes is popularly better known as the inventor of engines of war, and various ingenious machines, than as a mathematician, great as were his attainments. His theory of the lever was the foundation of statics, till the discovery of the composition of forces in the time of Newton, and no essential addition was made to the principles of the equilibrium of fluids and floating bodies till the time of Stevin in 1608. He detected the mixture of silver in a crown of gold which his patron, Hiero of Syracuse, ordered to be made, and he invented a water-screw for pumping water out of the hold of a great ship he built. He used also a combination of pulleys, and he constructed an orrery to represent the movement of the heavenly bodies. He had an extraordinary inventive genius for discovering new provinces of inquiry, and new points of view for old and familiar objects. Like Newton, he had a habit of abstraction from outward things, and would forget to take his meals. He was killed by Roman soldiers when Syracuse was taken, and the Sicilians so soon forgot his greatness that in the time of Cicero they did not know where his tomb was.[1]

Eratosthenes.

Eratosthenes was another of the famous geometers of antiquity, and did much to improve geometrical analysis. He was also a philosopher and geographer. He gave a solution of the problem of the duplication of the cube, and applied his geometrical knowledge to the measurement of the magnitude of the earth — one of the first who brought mathematical methods to the aid of astronomy, which, in our day, is almost exclusively the province of the mathematician.

[1] See article in Smith's *Dictionary*, by Prof. Darkin, of Oxford.

Apollonius of Perga, probably about forty years younger than Archimedes, and his equal in mathematical genius, was the most fertile and profound writer among the ancients who treated of geometry. He was called the Great Geometer. His most important work is a treatise on conic sections, regarded with unbounded admiration by contemporaries, and, in some respects, unsurpassed by any thing produced by modern mathematicians. He, however, made use of the labors of his predecessors, so that it is difficult to tell how far he is original. But all men of science must necessarily be indebted to those who have preceded them. Even Homer, in the field of poetry, made use of the bards who had sung for a thousand years before him. In the realms of philosophy the great men of all ages have built up new systems on the foundations which others have established. If Plato or Aristotle had been contemporaries with Thales, would they have matured so wonderful a system of dialectics? and if Thales had been contemporaneous with Plato, he might have added to his sublime science even more than Aristotle. So of the great mathematicians of antiquity; they were all wonderful men, and worthy to be classed with the Newtons and Keplers of our times. Considering their means, and the state of science, they made as *great*, though not as *fortunate*, discoveries — discoveries which show patience, genius, and power of calculation. Apollonius was one of these — one of the master intellects of antiquity, like Euclid and Archimedes — one of the master intellects of all ages, like Newton himself. I might mention the subjects of his various works, but they would not be understood except by those familiar with mathematics.[1]

Apollonius of Perga.

Other famous geometers could also be mentioned, but such men as Euclid, Archimedes, and Apollonius are enough to show that geometry was cultivated to a great extent by the philosophers of antiquity.

Cultivation of geometry by the Greeks.

[1] See Bayle's *Dict.*; Bossuet, *Essai sur l'Hist. Gén. des Math.*; Simson's *Sectiones Conicæ.*

It progressively advanced, like philosophy itself, from the time of Thales, until it had reached the perfection of which it was capable, when it became merged into astronomical science. It was cultivated more particularly by the disciples of Plato, who placed over his school this inscription, "Let no one ignorant of geometry enter here." He believed that the laws by which the universe is governed are in accordance with the doctrines of mathematics. The same opinion was shared by Pythagoras, the great founder of the science, whose great formula was, that number is the essence or first principle of all things. No thinkers ever surpassed the Greeks in originality and profundity, and mathematics, being highly prized by them, were carried to the greatest perfection their method would allow. They did not understand algebra, by the application of which to geometry modern mathematicians have climbed to greater heights than the ancients. But then it is all the more remarkable that, without the aid of algebraic analysis, they were able to solve such difficult problems as occupied the minds of Archimedes and Apollonius. No positive science can boast of such rapid development as geometry for two or three hundred years before Christ, and never was the intellect of man more severely tasked than by the ancient mathematicians.

Empirical sciences.

No empirical science can be carried to perfection by any one nation or in any particular epoch. It can only expand with the progressive developments of the human race itself. Nevertheless, in that science which for three thousand years has been held in the greatest honor, and which is one of the three great liberal professions of our modern times, the ancients, especially the Greeks, made considerable advance. The science of medicine, having in view the amelioration of human misery, and the prolongation of life itself, was very early cultivated. It was, indeed, in old times, another word for *physics*, — the science of nature, — and the *physician* was the observer and expounder of physics. The physician was supposed to be acquainted with the secrets of nature — that is, the knowledge of drugs, of poisons, of antidotes to them, and the way to administer them. He was also supposed to know the process of preserving the body after death. Thus Joseph commanded his physician to embalm the body of his father seventeen hundred years before the birth of Christ, and the process of embalming was probably known to the Egyptians beyond the period when history begins. Helen, of Trojan fame, put into wine a drug that "frees man from grief and anger and causes oblivion of all ills."[1] Solomon was a great botanist, with which the science of medicine is indissolubly connected. The "Ayur Veda," written nine hundred years before Hippocrates was born, sums up the knowledge of previous periods relating to obstetric surgery, to general pathology, to the treatment of insanity, to infantile diseases, to toxicology, to personal hygiene, and to diseases of the generative functions.[2] The origin of Hindu medicine is lost in remote antiquity.

Hippocrates.

Thus Hippocrates, the father of European medicine, must have derived his knowledge, not merely from his own observations, but from the writings of men unknown to us, and systems practiced for an indefinite period. The real founders of Greek medicine are fabled characters, like Hercules and Æsculapius — that is, benefactors whose names have not descended to us. They are mythical personages, like Hermes and Chiron. One thousand two hundred years before Christ temples were erected to Æsculapius in Greece, the priests of which were really physicians, and the temples themselves were hospitals. In them were practiced rites apparently mysterious, but which modern science calls by the names of mesmerism, hydropathy, mineral springs, and other essential elements of empirical science. And these temples were also

1 *Odyssey*, b. iv.

2 Wise, *On the Hindu System of Medicine*, p. 12.

medical schools. That of Cos gave birth to Hippocrates, and it was there that his writings were commenced. Pythagoras — for those old Grecian philosophers were the fathers of all wisdom and knowledge, in mathematics and empirical sciences, as well as philosophy itself — studied medicine in the schools of Egypt, Phœnicia, Chaldea, and India, and came in conflict with sacerdotal power, which has ever been antagonistic to new ideas in science. He traveled from town to town as a teacher or lecturer, establishing communities in which *medicine* as well as *numbers* was taught.

The greatest name in medical science, in ancient or in modern times, — the man who did the most to advance it; the greatest medical genius of whom we have record, — is Hippocrates, born on the island of Cos B. C. 460, of the great Æsculapian family, and was instructed by his father. We know scarcely more of his life than we do of Homer himself, although he lived in the period of the highest splendor of Athens. And his writings, like those of Homer, are thought by some to be the work of different men. They were translated into Arabic, and were no slight means of giving an impulse to the Saracenic schools of the Middle Ages in that science in which the Saracens especially excelled. The Hippocratic collection consists of more than sixty works, which were held in the highest estimation by the ancient physicians. Hippocrates introduced a new era in medicine, which, before his time, had been monopolized by the priests. He carried out a system of severe induction from the observation of facts, and is as truly the creator of the inductive method as Bacon himself. He abhorred theories which could not be established by facts. He was always open to conviction, and candidly confessed his mistakes. He was conscientious in the practice of his profession, and valued the success of his art more than silver and gold. The Athenians revered him for his benevolence as well as genius. The great principle of his practice was trust in nature. Hence he was accused of allowing his patients to die ; but this principle has many advocates among scientific men in our day, and some suppose the whole philosophy of homeopathy rests on the primal principle which Hippocrates advanced. He had great skill in diagnosis, by which medical genius is most severely tested. His practice was cautious and timid in contrast with that of his contemporaries. He is the author of the celebrated maxim, "Life is short and art is long." He divides the causes of disease into two principal classes, — the one comprehending the influence of seasons, climates, and other external forces ; the other from the effects of food and exercise. To the influence of climate he attributes the conformation of the body and the disposition of the mind. He also attributes all sorts of disorders to a vicious system of diet. For more than twenty centuries his pathology was the foundation of all the medical sects. He was well acquainted with the medicinal properties of drugs, and was the first to assign three periods to the course of a malady. He knew, of course, but little of surgery, although he was in the habit of bleeding, and often employed his knife. He was also acquainted with cupping, and used violent purgatives. He was not aware of the importance of the pulse, and confounded the veins with the arteries. He wrote in the Ionic dialect, and some of his works have gone through three hundred editions, so highly have they been valued. His authority passed away, like that of Aristotle, on the revival of European science. Yet who have been greater ornaments and lights than these distinguished Greeks ?

Galen.

The school of Alexandria produced eminent physicians, as well as mathematicians, after the glory of Greece had departed. So highly was it esteemed that Galen went there to study five hundred years after its foundation. It was distinguished for inquiries into scientific anatomy and physiology, for which Aristotle had prepared the way. He was the Humboldt of his day, and gave great attention to physics. In eight books he developed the general principles of natural science known to the Greeks. On the basis of the Aristotelian researches, the Alexandrian physicians carried out extensive inquiries in physiology. Herophilus discovered the fundamental principles of neurology, and advanced the anatomy of the brain and spinal cord.

Although the Romans had but little sympathy for science or philosophy, being essentially political and warlike in their turn of mind, yet when they had conquered the world, and had turned their attention to arts, medicine received great attention. The first physicians were Greek slaves. Of these was Asclepiades, who enjoyed the friendship of Cicero. It is from him that the popular medical theories as to the "pores" have descended. He was the inventor of the shower-bath. Celsus wrote a work on medicine which takes almost equal rank with the Hippocratic writings. Medical science at Rome culminated in Galen, as it did at Athens in Hippocrates. He was patronized by Marcus Aurelius, and availed himself of all the knowledge of preceding naturalists and physicians. He was born at Pergamus about the year A. D. 165, where he learned, under able masters, anatomy, pathology, and therapeutics. He finished his studies at Alexandria, and came to Rome at the invitation of the emperor. Like his patron, he was one of the brightest ornaments of the heathen world, and one of the most learned and accomplished men of any age. "*Medicorum dissertissimus atque doctissimus.*"[1] He left five hundred treatises, most of them relating to some branch of medical science, which give him the merit of being one of the most voluminous of authors. His celebrity is founded chiefly on his anatomical and physiological works. He was familiar with practical anatomy, deriving his knowl-

Medical science among the Romans.

[1] St. Jerome, *Comment. in Aoms*, c. 5, vol. vi.

edge from dissection. His observations about health are practical and useful. He lays great stress on gymnastic exercises, and recommends the pleasures of the chase, the cold bath in hot weather, hot baths to old people, the use of wine, three meals a day, and pork as the best of animal food. The great principles of his practice were that disease is to be overcome by that which is contrary to the disease itself, and that nature is to be preserved by that which has relation with nature. As disease cannot be overcome so long as its cause exists, that, if possible, was first to be removed, and the strength of the patient is to be considered before the treatment is proceeded with. His "Commentaries on Hippocrates" served as a treasure of medical criticism, from which succeeding annotators borrowed. No one ever set before the medical profession a higher standard than Galen, and few have more nearly approached it. He did not attach himself to any particular school, but studied the doctrines of each — an eclectic in the fullest sense.[1] The works of Galen constituted the last production of ancient Roman medicine, and from his day the decline in medical science was rapid, until it was revived among the Arabs.

The physical sciences, it must be confessed, were not carried by the ancients to any such length as geometry and astronomy. In physical geography they were particularly deficient. Yet even this branch of knowledge can boast of some eminent names. When men sailed timidly on the coasts, and dared not explore distant seas, the true position of countries could not be ascertained with the definiteness that it is at present. But geography was not utterly neglected, nor was natural history.

Physical geography.

Herodotus gives us most valuable information respecting the manners and customs of oriental and barbarous nations, and Pliny has written a natural

[1] See Leclerc, *Hist. de la Medicine;* Hartt Shoengel, *Geschichte der Arzneykunde.* W. A. Greenhill, M. D., of Oxford, has a very learned article in Smith's *Dictionary.*

history, in thirty-seven books, which is compiled from upwards of two thousand volumes, and refers to twenty thousand matters of importance. He was born A. D. 23, and was fifty-three when the eruption of Vesuvius took place which caused his death. Pliny cannot be called a scientific genius, in the sense understood by modern savants; nor was he an original observer. His materials are drawn up second hand, like a modern encyclopedia. Nor did he evince great judgment in his selection. He had a great love of the marvelous, and is often unintelligible. But his work is a wonderful monument of human industry. It treats of every thing in the natural world — of the heavenly bodies, of the elements, of thunder and lightning, of the winds and seasons, of the changes and phenomena of the earth, of countries and nations, seas and rivers, of men, animals, birds, fishes, and plants, of minerals and medicines and precious stones, of commerce and the fine arts. He is full of errors; but his work is among the most valuable productions of antiquity. Buffon pronounced his natural history to contain an infinity of knowledge in every department of human occupation, conveyed in a dress ornate and brilliant. It is a literary rather than a scientific monument, and as such it is wonderful — a compilation from one hundred and sixty volumes of notes. In strict scientific value, it is inferior to the works of modern research; but there are few minds, even in these times, who have directed inquiries to such a variety of subjects.

Strabo.

Geographical knowledge was advanced by Strabo, who lived in the Augustan era; but researches were chiefly confined to the Roman empire. Strabo was, like Herodotus, a great traveler, and much of his geographical information is the result of his own observations. It is probable he is much indebted to Eratosthenes, who preceded him by three centuries, and who was the first systematic writer on geography. The authorities of Strabo are chiefly Greek, but his work is defective, from the imperfect notions which the ancients had of astronomy; so that the determination of the earth's figure by the measure of latitude and longitude, the essential foundations of geographical description, was unknown. The enormous strides, which all forms of physical science have made since the discovery of America, throw all ancient descriptions and investigations into the shade, and Strabo appears at as great disadvantage as Pliny or Ptolemy; yet the work of Strabo, considering his means, and the imperfect knowledge of the earth's surface, and astronomical science, was really a great achievement of industry. He treats of the form and magnitude of the earth, and devotes eight books to Europe, six to Asia, and one to Africa. His great authorities are Eratosthenes, Polybius, Aristotle, Antiochus of Syracuse, Posidonius, Theopompus, Artemidorus Ephorus, Herodotus, Anaximenes, Thucydides, and Aristo, chiefly historians and philosophers. Whatever may be said of the accuracy of the great geographer of antiquity, it cannot be denied that he was a man of immense research and learning. His work in seventeen books is one of the most valuable which have come down from antiquity, both from the discussions which run through it, and the curious facts which can be found nowhere else. It is scarcely fair to estimate the genius of Strabo by the correctness and extent of his geographical knowledge. All men are lost in science, and science is progressive. The great scientific lights of our day may be insignificant, compared with those who are to arise, if profundity and accuracy of knowledge is the test. It is the genius of the ancients, their grasp and power of mind, their original labors which we are to consider. Anaxagoras was one of the greatest philosophical geniuses of all ages; but, as philosophy is a science, and is progressive, his knowledge could not be compared with that of Aristotle. Again, who doubts the original genius and grasp of Aristotle, but what was he, in accuracy of knowledge and true method, in comparison with the savants of the nineteenth century; yet, it would be difficult to show that Aristotle was inferior to Bacon or Cuvier, or Stuart Mill. If, however, we would compare the geographical knowledge of the ancients with that of the moderns, we confess to the immeasurable inferiority of the ancients in this branch. When Eratosthenes began his labors, it was known that the surface of the earth was spherical. He established parallels of latitude and longitude, and attempted the difficult undertaking of measuring the circumference of the globe by the actual measurement of a segment of one of its great circles. Posidonius determined the arc of a meridian between Rhodes and Alexandria to be a forty-eighth part of the whole circumference — an enormous calculation, yet a remarkable one in the infancy of astronomical science. Hipparchus introduced into geography a great improvement, namely, the relative situation of places, by the same process that he determined the positions of the heavenly bodies. He also pointed out how longitude might be determined by observing the eclipses of the sun and moon. This led to the construction of maps; but none have reached us except those which were used to illustrate the geography of Ptolemy. Hipparchus was born B. C. 276, the first who raised geography to the rank of a science. He starved himself to death, being tired of life, like Eratosthenes, more properly an astronomer, and the most distinguished among the ancients, born about 160 B. C., although none of his writings have reached us. The improvements he pointed out were applied by Ptolemy himself, an astronomer who flourished about the year 160 at Alexandria. His work was a presentation of geographical knowledge known in his day, so far as geography is the science of determining the position of places on the earth's surface. The description of places belongs to Strabo. His work was accepted as the textbook of the science till the fifteenth century, for in his day

Construction of maps.

Ptolemy.

the Roman empire had been well surveyed. He maintained that the earth is *spherical*, and introduced the terms *longitude* and *latitude*, which Eratosthenes had established, and computed the earth to be one hundred and eighty thousand stadia in circumference, and a degree five hundred stadia in length, or sixty-two and a half Roman miles. His estimates of the length of a degree of latitude were nearly correct; but he made great errors in the degrees of longitude, making the length of the world from east to west too great, which led to the belief in the practicability of a western passage to India. He also assigned too great length to the Mediterranean, arising from the difficulty of finding the longitude with accuracy. But it was impossible, with the scientific knowledge of his day, to avoid errors, and we are surprised that he made so few.

REFERENCES. — An exceedingly learned work has recently been issued in London, by Parker and Son, on the Astronomy of the Ancients, by Sir George Cornwall Lewis, though rather ostentatious in his parade of authorities, and minute on points which are not of much consequence. Delambre's History of Ancient Astronomy has long been a classic, but richer in materials for a history than a history itself. There is a valuable essay in the Encyclopedia Britannica, which refers to a list of authors, among which are Riccoli, Weilder, Bailly, Playfair, La Lande. Lewis makes much reference to Macrobius, Vitruvius, Diogenes Laertius, Plutarch, and Suidas, among the ancients, and to Ideler, Unters. über die Art. Beob. der Alten.

Whewell's History of the Inductive Sciences may also be consulted with profit. Leclerc, Hist. de Med.; Spengel, Gesch. der Arzneykunde. Strabo's Geography is the most valuable of Antiquity. See also Polybius.

CHAPTER X.

INTERNAL CONDITION OF THE ROMAN EMPIRE.

WE have now surveyed all that was glorious in the most splendid empire of antiquity. We have seen a civilization which, in many respects, rivals all that modern nations have to show. In art, in literature, in philosophy, in laws, in the mechanism of government, in the cultivated face of nature, in military strength, in æsthetic culture, the Romans were our equals. And this high civilization was reached by the native and unaided strength of man; by the power of will, by courage, by perseverance, by genius, by fortunate circumstances; by great men, gifted with unusual talents. We are filled with admiration by all these trophies of genius, and cannot but feel that only a superior race could have accomplished such mighty triumphs.

But all this splendid external was deceptive. It was hollow at heart. And the deeper we penetrate the social condition of the people, their real and practical life, the more we feel disgust and pity supplanting all feelings of admiration and wonder. The Roman empire, in its shame and degradation, suggests melancholy feelings in reference to the destiny of man, so far as his happiness and welfare depend upon his own unaided strength. And we see profoundly the necessity of some foreign aid to rescue him from his miseries.

It is a sad picture of oppression, of injustice, of poverty, of vice, and of wretchedness, which I have now to present. Glory is succeeded by shame, and strength by weakness, and virtue by vice. The condition of the great mass is deplorable, and even the great and fortunate shine in a false and fictitious light. We see laws, theoretically good, practically perverted; monstrous inequalities of condition, selfishness, and egotism the mainsprings of life. We see energies misdirected, and art corrupted. All noble aspirations have fled, and the good and the wise retire from active life in despair and misanthropy. Poets flatter the tyrants who trample on human rights, and sensuality and Epicurean pleasures absorb the depraved thoughts of a perverse generation.

The imperial despotism.

The first thing which arrests our attention as we survey the grand empire which embraced the civilized countries of the world, is the imperial despotism. It may have been a necessity, an inevitable sequence to the anarchy of civil war, the strife of parties, great military successes, and the corruptions of society itself. It may be viewed as a providential event in order that general peace and security might usher in the triumphs of a new religion. It followed naturally the subversion of the constitution by military leaders, the breaking up of the power of the Senate, the encroachments of democracy and its leaders, the wars of Sulla and Marius, of Pompey and Julius. It succeeded massacres and factions and demagogues. It came when conspiracies and proscriptions and general insecurity rendered a stronger government desirable. The empire was too vast to be intrusted to the guidance of conflicting parties. There was needed a strong, central, irrepressible, irresistible power in the hands of a single man. Safety and peace seemed preferable to glory and genius. So the people acquiesced in the changes which were made; they had long anticipated them; they even hailed them with silent joy. Patriots, like Brutus, Cassius, and Cato, gave themselves up to despair; but most men were pleased with the revolution that seated Augustus on the throne of the world. For twenty years the empire had been desolated by destructive and exhaustive wars. The cry of the whole empire was for peace, and peace could be secured only by the ascendency of a single man, ruling with absolute and unresisted sway.

Historians generally have regarded the revolution, which changed the republic to a monarchy, as salutary in its influences for several generations. The empire was never so splendid as under the Cæsars. The energies of the people were directed into peaceful and industrial channels. A new public policy was inaugurated by Augustus — to preserve rather than extend the limits of the empire. The world enjoyed peace, and the rich consoled themselves with riches. Society was established upon a new basis, and was no longer rent by factions and parties. Demagogues no longer disturbed the public peace, nor were the provinces ransacked and devastated to provide for the means of carrying on war. So long as men did not oppose the government they were safe from molestation, and were left to pursue their business and pleasure in their own way. Wealth rapidly increased, and all mechanical arts, and all elegant pleasures. Temples became more magnificent, and the city was changed from brck to marble. Palaces arose upon the hills, and shops were erected in the valleys. There were fewer riots and mobs and public disturbances. Public amusements were systematized and enlarged, and the people indulged with sports, spectacles, and luxuries. Rome became a still greater centre of wealth and art as well as of political power. The city increased in population and beautiful structures. The emperors were great patrons of every thing calculated to dazzle the eyes of their subjects, whether amusements, or palaces, or baths, or aqueducts, or triumphal monuments. Artists and scholars flocked to the great emporium, as well as merchants and foreign princes. Nor was imperial cruelty often visited on the humble classes. It was the policy of the emperors to amuse and flatter the people, while they deprived them of political rights. But

Necessity of revolution.

Imperial rule.

social life was free. All were at liberty to seek their pleasures and gains. All were proud of their metropolis, with its gilded glories and its fascinating pleasures. The city was probably supplied with better water, and could rely with more certainty on the necessaries of life, than under the old regime. The people had better baths, and larger houses, and cheaper corn. The government, for a time, was splendidly administered, even by tyrants. Outrages, extortions, and disturbances were punished. Order reigned, and tranquillity, and outward and technical justice. All classes felt secure. They could sleep without fear of robbery or assassination. And all trades flourished. Art was patronized magnificently, and every opportunity was offered for making and for spending fortunes. In short, all the arguments which can be adduced in favor of despotism in contrast with civil war and violence, and the strife of factions and general insecurity of life and property, can be urged to show that the change, if inevitable, was beneficial in its immediate effects.

Despotism of the emperors.

Nevertheless, it was a most lamentable change from that condition of things which existed before the civil wars. Roman liberties were prostrated forever. Tyrants, armed with absolute and irresponsible power, ruled over the empire; nor could their tyranny end but with their lives. Noble sentiments and aspirations were rebuked. The times were unfavorable to the development of genius, except in those ways which subserved the interests of the government. Under the emperors we read of no more great orators like Cicero, battling for human rights, and defending the public weal. Eloquence was suppressed. Nor was there liberty of speech in the Senate. The usual jealousy of tyrants was awakened to every emancipating influence on the people. They were now amused with shows and spectacles, but could not make their voices heard regarding public injuries. The people were absolutely in the hands of iron masters. So was the Senate. So were all orders and conditions of men. One man reigned supreme. His will was law. Resistance to it was vain. It was treason to find fault with any public acts. From the Pillars of Hercules to the Caspian Sea one stern will ruled all classes and orders. No one could fly from the agents and ministers of the empire. He was the vicegerent of the Almighty, worshiped as a deity, undisputed master of the lives and liberties of one hundred and twenty millions of people. There was no restraint on his inclinations. He could do whatever he pleased, without rebuke and without fear. No general or senator or governor could screen himself from his vengeance. He controlled the army, the Senate, the judiciary, the internal administration of the empire, and the religious worship of the people. All offices and honors and emoluments emanated from him. All opposition ceased, and all conspired to elevate still higher that supreme arbiter of fortune whom no one could hope successfully to rival. Revolt was madness, and treason absurdity. And so perfect was the mechanism of the government that the emperor had time for his private pleasures. It was never administered with greater rigor than when Tiberius secluded himself in his guarded villa. And a timid, or weak, or irresolute emperor was as much to be feared as a monster, since he was surrounded with minions who might be unscrupulous. Nor was the imperial power exercised to check the gigantic social evils of the empire, — those which were gradually but surely undermining the virtues on which strength is based. They did not seek to prevent irreligion, luxury, slavery, and usury, the encroachments of the rich upon the poor, the tyranny of foolish fashions, demoralizing sports and pleasures, money-making, and all the follies which lax principles of morality allowed. They fed the rabble with corn and oil and wine, and thus encouraged idleness and dissipation. The world never saw a more rapid retrograde in human rights, or a greater prostration of liberties. Taxes

Tyranny of the emperors.

were imposed according to the pleasure or necessities of the government. Provincial governors became still more rapacious and cruel. Judges hesitated to decide against the government. A vile example was presented to the people in their rulers. The emperors squandered immense sums on their private pleasures, and set public opinion at defiance. Patriotism, in its most enlarged sense, became an impossibility. All lofty spirits were crushed. Corruption, in all forms of administration, fearfully increased, for there was no safeguard. Women became debased from the pernicious influences of a corrupt and unblushing court. Adultery, divorce, and infanticide became still more common. The emperors thought more of securing their own power and indulging their own passions than of the public good. The humiliating conviction was fastened upon all classes that liberty was extinguished, and that they were slaves to an irresponsible power. There are those who are found to applaud a despotism ; but despotism presupposes the absence of the power of self-government, and the necessity of severe and rigorous measures. It presupposes the tendency to crime and violence, that men are brutes and must be coerced like wild beasts. We are warranted in assuming a very low condition of society when despotism became a necessity. Theoretically, absolutism may be the best government, if rulers are wise and just; but, practically, as men are, despotisms are cruel and revengeful. There are great and glorious exceptions ; but it cannot be denied that society is mournful when tyrants bear rule. And it is seldom that society improves under them, without very powerful religious influences. It generally grows worse and worse. Despotism implies slavery, and slavery is the worst condition of mankind, — doubtless a wholesome discipline, under certain circumstances, yet still a great calamity.

The Roman world was fortunate in having such a man as Augustus for supreme ruler, after all liberties were subverted. He was one of the wisest and greatest of the emperors. He inaugurated the policy of his successors, from which the immediate ones did not far depart. He was careful, in the first place, to disguise his powers, and offend the moral sentiments of the people as little as possible. He met with but little opposition in his usurpation, for the most independent of the nobles had perished in the wars, and the rest consulted their interests. He selected the ablest and most popular men in the city to be his favorite ministers — Mæcenas and Agrippa. His policy was peace. He declined the coronary gold proffered by the Italian states. He was profuse in his generosity, without additional burdens on the state, for, as the heir of Cæsar, he came into possession of eight hundred and fifty millions of dollars, the amount which the Dictator had amassed from the spoils of war. He was but thirty-three years of age, in the prime of his strength and courage. He purged the Senate of unworthy members, and restored the appearance of its ancient dignity. He took a census of the Roman people. He increased the largesses of corn. He showed confidence in the people whom he himself deceived. He was modest in his demeanor, like Pericles at Athens. He visited the provinces and settled their difficulties. He appointed able men as governors, and perpetuated a standing army. He repaired the public edifices, and adorned the city.

Augustus.

But he gradually assumed all the great offices of the state. He clothed himself with the powers and the badges of the consuls, the prænomen of imperator, the functions of perpetual dictator. He exacted the military oath from the whole mass of the people. He became *princeps senatus*. He claimed the prerogatives of the tribunes, which gave to him inviolability, with the right of protection and pardon. He was also invested with the illustrious dignity of the supreme pontificate. As the Senate and the people continued to meet still for the purpose of legislation, he controlled the same by assuming the initiative, of proposing the laws. He took occasion to give to his edicts, in his consular or tribunitian capacity, a perpetual force; and his rescripts or replies which issued from his council chamber, were registered as laws. He was released from the laws, and claimed the name of Cæsar. The people were deprived of the election of magistrates. All officers of the government were his tools, and through them he controlled all public affairs. The prefect of the city became virtually his minister and lieutenant. Even the proconsuls received their appointment from him. Thus he became supreme arbiter of all fortunes, the fountain of all influence, the centre of all power, absolute over the lives and fortunes of all classes of men. Strange that the people should have submitted to such monstrous usurpations, although decently veiled under the names of the old offices of the republic. But they had become degenerate. They wished for peace and leisure. They felt the uselessness of any independent authority, and resigned themselves to a condition which the Romans two centuries earlier would have felt to be intolerable.

General character of the emperors.

Of the immediate successors of Augustus, none equaled him in moderation or talents. And with the exception of Titus and Vespasian, the emperors who comprised the Julian family, were stained with great vices. Some were monsters; others were madmen. But, as a whole, they were not deficient in natural ability. Some had great executive talents, like Tiberius — a man of vast experience. But he was a cruel and remorseless tyrant, full of jealousy and vindictive hatred. Still, amid disgraceful pleasures, he devoted himself to the cares of office, and exhibited the virtues of domestic economy. Nor did he take pleasure in the sports of the circus and the theatre, like most of his successors. But he destroyed all who stood in his way, as most tyrants do. Nor did he spare his own relatives. He was sensual and intemperate in his habits, and all looked to him with awe and trepidation. There was a perfect reign of terror at Rome during his latter days, and every body rejoiced when the tyrant died.

Caligula, who succeeded Tiberius, belonged to the race of madmen. He put to death some of the most eminent Romans, in order to seize on their estates. He repudiated his wife; he expressed the wish that Rome had but one neck, that it could be annihilated by a blow; he used to invite his favorite horse to supper, setting before him gilded corn and wine in golden goblets; he wasted immense sums in useless works; he took away the last shadow of power from the people; he impoverished Italy by senseless extravagance; he wantonly destroyed his soldiers by whole companies; he was doubtless as insane as he was cruel, luxurious, rapacious, and prodigal; he adorned the poops of galleys with precious stones, and constructed arduous works with no other purpose than caprice; he often dressed like a woman, and generally appeared with a golden beard; he devoted himself to fencing, driving, singing, and dancing, and was ruled by gladiators, charioteers, and actors. Such was the man to whom was intrusted the guardianship of an empire. No wonder he was removed by assassination.

Caligula.

His successor was Claudius, made emperor by the Prætorians. He took Augustus for his model, was well disposed, and contributed greatly to the embellishment of the capital. But he was gluttonous and intemperate, and subject to the influence of women and favorites. He was feeble in mind and body. He was married to one of the worst women in history, and Messalina has passed into a synonym for infamy. By this woman he was influenced, and her unblushing effrontery and disgraceful intrigues made the reign unfortunate. She trafficked in the great offices of the state, and sacrificed the best blood of the class to which she belonged. Claudius

Claudius.

was also governed by freedmen, who performed such offices as Louis XV. intrusted to his noble vassals. Claudius resembled this inglorious monarch in many respects, and his reign was as disastrous on the morals of the people. When the death of his wife was announced to him at the banquet, he called for wine, and listened to songs and music. But she was succeeded by a worse woman, Agrippina, and the marriage of the emperor with his niece, was a scandal as well as a misfortune. Pliny mentions having seen this empress in a sea-fight on the Fucine Lake, clothed in a soldier's cloak. Daughter of an emperator, sister of another, and consort of a third, she is best known as the mother of Nero, and the patroness of every thing that was shameful in the follies of the times. That an emperor should wed and be ruled by two such infamous women, indicates either weakness or depravity, and both qualities are equally fatal to the welfare of the state over which he was called to rule.

Nero.

The supreme power then fell into the hands of Nero. He gave the promise of virtue and ability, and Seneca condescended to the most flattering panegyrics; but the prospects of ruling beneficently were soon clouded by the most disgraceful enormities. He destroyed all who were offensive to those who ruled him, even Seneca who had been his tutor. Lost to all dignity and decency, he indulged in the most licentious riots, disguising himself like a slave, and committing midnight assaults. He killed his mother and his aunt, and divorced his wife. He sung songs on the public stage, and was more ambitious of being a good flute-player than a public benefactor. It is even said that he fiddled when Rome was devastated by a fearful conflagration. He built a palace, which covered entirely Mount Esquiline, the vestibule of which contained a colossal statue of himself, one hundred and twenty feet high. His gardens were the scenes of barbarities, and his banqueting halls of orgies which were a reproach to humanity. He wasted the empire by enormous contributions, and even plundered the temples of his own capital. His wife, Poppæa, died of a kick which she received from this monster, because she had petulantly reproved him. Longinus, an eminent lawyer, Lucan the poet, and Petronius the satirist, alike, were victims of his hatred. This last of the Cæsars, allied by blood to the imperial house of Julius, killed himself in his thirty-first year, to prevent assassination, to the universal joy of the Roman world, without having done a great deed, or evinced a single virtue. Flute-playing and chariot races were his main diversions, and every public interest was sacrificed to his pleasures, or his vengeance — a man delighting in evil for its own sake.

Nero was succeeded by Galba, who also was governed by favorites. He was a great glutton, exceedingly parsimonious, and very unpopular. In the early stages of his life, he appeared equal to the trust and dignity reposed in him; but when he gained the sovereignty, he proved deficient in those qualities requisite to wield it. Tacitus sums up his character in a sentence. "He appeared superior to his rank before he was emperor, and would have always been considered worthy of the supreme power, if he had not obtained it." He was assassinated after a brief reign.

Galba.

His successor, Otho, finding himself unequal to the position to which he was elevated, ended his life by suicide. Vitellius, who wore the purple next to him, is celebrated for cruelty and gluttony, and was removed by assassination. Titus and Vespasian were honorable exceptions to the tyrants and sensualists that had reigned since Augustus, but Domitian surpassed all his predecessors in unrelenting cruelty. He banished all philosophers from Rome and Italy, and violently persecuted the Christians, and was dissolute and lewd in his private habits. He also met a violent death from the assassin's

Otho.

dagger, the only way that infamous monsters could be hurled from power. Yet such was the fulsome flattery to which he and all the emperors were accustomed, that Martial addressed this monster, preëminent of all in wickedness and cruelty, —

> "To conquer ardent, and to triumph shy,
> Fair Victory named him from the polar sky.
> Fanes to the gods, to men he manners gave;
> Rest to the sword, and respite to the brave;
> So high could ne'er Herculean power aspire:
> The god should bend his looks to the Tarpeian fire." [1]

Of Nerva, Trajan, Hadrian, and the Antonines, I will not speak, since they were great exceptions to those who generally ruled at Rome. Their virtues and their talents are justly eulogized by all historians. Great in war, and greater in peace, they were ornaments of humanity. Under their sway, the empire was prosperous and happy. Their greatness almost atoned for the weakness and wickedness of their predecessors. If such men as they could have ruled at Rome, the imperial regime would have been the greatest blessing. But with them expired the prosperity of the empire, and they were succeeded by despots, whose vices equaled those of Nero and Vitellius. Commodus, Caracalla, Elagabalus, Maximin, Philip, Gallienus, are enrolled on the catalogue of those who have obtained an infamous immortality. At last no virtue or talent on the part of the few emperors who really labored for the good of the state, could arrest the increasing corruption. The empire was doomed when Constantine removed the seat of government to Constantinople. Forty-four sovereigns reigned at Rome from Julius to Constantine, in a period of little more than three hundred and fifty years, of whom twenty were removed by assassination. What a commentary on imperial despotism! In spite of the virtues of such men as Trajan and the Antonines, the history of the emperors is a

The latter emperors.

[1] Book ix. 101.

loathsome chapter of human depravity, and of its awful retribution. Never were greater powers exercised by single men, and never were they more signally abused. From the time of Augustus those virtues which give glory to society steadily declined. The reigns of the emperors were fatal to all moral elevation, and even to genius, as in the latter days of Louis XIV. The great lights which illuminated the Augustan age, disappeared, without any to take their place. Under the emperors there are fewer great names than for one hundred years before the death of Cicero. Eloquence, poetry, and philosophy were alike eclipsed. Noble aspirations were repressed by the all-powerful and irresistible despotism.

The tyranny of these emperors was rendered endurable by the general familiarity with cruelty. In every Roman palace, the slave was chained to the doorway; thongs hung upon the stairs, and the marks of violence on the faces of the domestics impressed the great that they were despots themselves. They were accustomed to the sight of blood in the sports of the amphitheatre. They ruled as tyrants in the provinces they governed.

But it must be allowed that the system of education was left untrammeled by the government, provided politics were not introduced; and it produced men of letters, if not practical statesmen. It sharpened the intellect and enlivened thought. The text-books of the schools were the most famous compositions of republican Greece, and the favorite subjects of declamation were the glories of the free men of antiquity. Nor was there any restriction placed upon writing or publication analogous to our modern censorship of the press, and many of the emperors, like Claudius and Hadrian, were patrons of literature. Even the stoical philosophers who tried to persuade the emperor that he was a slave, were endured, since they did not attempt to deprive him of sovereignty.

Nor could the imperial tyranny be resisted by minds

enervated by indulgence and estranged from all pure aspirations, by the pleasures of sense. They crouched like dogs under the uplifted arm of masters. They did not even seek to fly from the tyranny which ground them down.

Character of the emperors.

It cannot be denied that, on the whole, this long succession of emperors was more intellectual and able than oriental dynasties, and even many occidental ones in the Middle Ages, when the principle of legitimacy was undisputed. The Roman emperors, as men of talents, favorably compare with the successors of Mohammed, and the Carlovingian and Merovingian kings. But if these talents were employed in systematically crushing out all human rights, the despotism they established became the more deplorable.

Nor can it be questioned that many virtuous princes reigned at Rome, who would have ornamented any age or country. Titus, Hadrian, Marcus Aurelius, Antoninus Pius, Alexander Severus, Tacitus, Probus, Carus, Constantine, Theodosius, were all men of remarkable virtues as well as talents. They did what they could to promote public prosperity. Marcus Aurelius was one of the purest and noblest characters of antiquity. Theodosius for genius and virtue ranks with the most illustrious sovereigns that ever wore a crown — with Charlemagne, with Alfred, with William III., with Gustavus Adolphus.

Of these Roman emperors some stand out as world heroes — greatest among men — remarkable for executive ability. Julius is the most renowned name of antiquity. He ranks only with Napoleon Bonaparte in modern times. His genius was transcendent; and, like Napoleon, he had great traits which endear him to the world — generosity, magnanimity, and exceeding culture; orator, historian, and lawyer, as well as statesman and general. But he overturned the liberties of his country to gratify a mad ambition, and waded through a sea of blood to the mastership of the world. Augustus was a profound statesman, and a successful general; but he was stained with the arts of dissimulation and an intense ambition, and sacrificed public liberties and rights to cement his power. Even Diocletian, tyrant and persecutor as he was, was distinguished for masterly abilities, and was the greatest statesman whom the empire saw, with the exception of Augustus. Such a despot as Tiberius ruled with justice and ability. Constantine ranks with the greatest monarchs of antiquity. The vices and ambition of these men did not dim the lustre of their genius and abilities.

The imperial despotism.

Their cause was wrong. It matters not whether the emperors were good or bad, if the regime, to which they consecrated their energies, was exerted to crush the liberties of mankind. The imperial despotism, whether brilliant or disgraceful, was a mournful retrograde in the polity of Rome. It implied the extinction of patriotism, and the general degradation of the people, or else the fabric of despotism could not have been erected. It would have been impossible in the days of Cato, Scipio, or Metellus. It was simply a choice of evils. When nations emerge from utter barbarism into absolute monarchies, like the ancient Persians or the modern Russians, we forget the evils of a central power in the blessings which extend indirectly to the degraded people. But when a nation loses its liberties, and submits without a struggle to tyrants, it is a sad spectacle to humanity. The despotism of Louis XIV. was not disgraceful to the French people, for they never had enjoyed constitutional liberty. The despotism of Louis Napoleon is mournful, because the nation had waded through a bloody revolution to achieve the recognition of great rights and interests, and dreamed that they were guaranteed. It is a retrograde and not a progress; a reaction of liberty, which seats Napoleon on the throne of Louis Philippe; even as the reign of Charles II. is the

26

saddest chapter in English history. If liberty be a blessing, if it be possible for nations to secure it permanently, then the regime of the Roman emperors is detestable and mournful, whatever necessities may have called it into being, since it annulled all those glorious privileges in which ancient patriots gloried, and prevented that scope for energies which made Rome mistress of the world. It was impossible for the empire to grow stronger and grander. It must needs become weaker and more corrupt, since despotism did not kindle the ambition of the people, but suppressed their noblest sentiments, and confined their energies to inglorious pursuits. Men might acquire more gigantic fortunes under the emperors than in the times of the republic, and art might be more extensively cultivated, and luxury and refinement and material pleasures might increase; but public virtue fled, and those sentiments on which national glory rests vanished before the absorbing egotism which pervaded all orders and classes. The imperial despotism may have been needed, and the empire might have fallen, even if it had not existed; still it was a sad and mournful necessity, and gives a humiliating view of human greatness. No lover of liberty can contemplate it without disgust and abhorrence. No philosopher can view it without drawing melancholy lessons of human degeneracy — an impressive moral for all ages and nations.

If we turn to the class which, before the dictatorship of Julius, had the ascendency in the state, and, for several centuries, the supreme power, we shall find but little that is flattering to a nation or to humanity.

The Roman aristocracy.

The Roman aristocracy was the most powerful, most wealthy, and most august that this world has probably seen. It was under patrician leadership that the great conquests were made, and the greatness of the state reached. The glory of Rome was centred in those proud families which had conquered and robbed all the nations known to the Greeks. The immortal names of ancient Rome are identified with the aristocracy. It was not under kings, but under nobles, that military ambition became the vice of the most exalted characters. In the days of the republic, they exhibited a stern virtue, an inflexible policy, an indomitable will, and most ardent patriotism. The generals who led the armies to victory, the statesmen who deliberated in the Senate, the consuls, the prætors, the governors, originally belonged to this noble class. It monopolized all the great offices of the state, and it maintained its powers and privileges, in spite of conspiracies and rebellions. It may have yielded somewhat to popular encroachments, but when the people began to acquire the ascendency, the seeds of public corruption were sown. The real dignity and glory of Rome coexisted with patrician power.

Great families.

And powerful families existed in Rome until the fall of the empire. Some were descendants of ancient patrician houses, and numbered the illustrious generals of the republic among their ancestors. Others owed their rank and consequence to the accumulation of gigantic fortunes. Others, again, rose into importance from the patronage of emperors. All the great conquerors and generals of the republic were founders of celebrated families, which never lost consideration. Until the subversion of the constitution, they took great interest in politics, and were characterized for manly patriotism. Many of them were famous for culture of mind as well as public spirit. They frowned on the growing immoralities, and maintained the dignity of their elevated rank. The Senate was the most august assembly ever known on earth, controlling kings and potentates, and making laws for the most distant nations, and exercising a power which was irresistible.

Degeneracy of the nobles.

Under the emperors this noble class had degenerated in morals as well as influence. They still retained their enormous fortunes, originally acquired as governors of provinces, and continually increased by fortunate marriages and speculations. Indeed, nothing was more marked and melancholy at Rome than the disproportionate fortunes, the general consequences of a low or a corrupt civilization. In the better days of the republic, property was more equally divided. The citizens were not ambitious for more land than they could conveniently cultivate. But the lands, obtained by conquest, gradually fell into the possession of powerful families. The classes of society widened as great fortunes were accumulated. Pride of wealth kept pace with pride of ancestry. And when Plebeian families had obtained great estates, they were amalgamated with the old aristocracy. The Equestrian order, founded substantially on wealth, grew daily in importance. Knights ultimately rivaled senatorial families. Even freedmen, in an age of commercial speculation, became powerful for their riches. Ultimately the rich formed a body by themselves. Under the emperors, the pursuit of money became a passion ; and the rich assumed all the importance and consideration which had once been bestowed upon those who had rendered great public services. The laws of property were rigorous among the Romans, and wealth, when once obtained, was easily secured and transmitted.

Gigantic fortunes.

Such gigantic fortunes were ultimately made, since the Romans were masters of the world, that Rome became a city of palaces, and the spoils and riches of all nations flowed to the capital. Rome was a city of princes, and wealth gave the highest distinction. The fortunes were almost incredible. It has been estimated that the income of some of the richest of the senatorial families equaled a sum of five million dollars a year in our money. It took eighty thousand dollars a year to support the ordinary senatorial dignity. Some senators owned whole provinces. Trimalchio — a rich freedman whom Petronius ridiculed — could afford to lose thirty millions of sesterces in a single voyage without sensibly diminishing his fortune. Pallas, a freedman of the Emperor Claudius, possessed a fortune of three hundred millions of sesterces. Seneca, the philosopher, amassed an enormous fortune.

The Romans were a sensual, ostentatious, and luxurious people, and they accordingly wasted their fortunes by an extravagance in their living which has had no parallel. The pleasures of the table and the cares of the kitchen were the most serious avocation of the aristocracy in the days of the greatest corruption. They had around them a regular court of parasites and flatterers, and they employed even persons of high rank as their chamberlains and stewards. Carving was taught in celebrated schools, and the masters of this sublime art were held in higher estimation than philosophers or poets. Says Juvenal: —

Character of the nobles.

> "To such perfection now is carving brought,
> That different gestures, by our curious men
> Are used for different dishes, hare or hen."

Their entertainments were accompanied with every thing which could flatter vanity or excite the passions. Musicians, male and female dancers, players of farce and pantomime, jesters, buffoons, and gladiators, exhibited while the guests reclined at table. The tables were made of Thuja-root, with claws of ivory or Delian bronze, and cost immense sums. Even Cicero, in an economical age, paid six hundred and fifty pounds for his banqueting table. These tables were waited upon by an army of slaves, clad in costly dresses. In the intervals of courses they played with dice, or listened to music, or were amused with dances. They wore a great profusion of jewels — such as necklaces and rings and bracelets. They reclined at table after the fashion of the Orientals. They ate, as delicacies, water-rats and white worms. Gluttony was carried to such a point that the sea and earth scarcely

Excessive luxury.

sufficed to set off their tables. The women passed whole nights at the table, and were proud of their power to carry off an excess of wine. As Cleopatra says of her riotings with Antony, —

> "O times! —
> I laughed him out of patience; and that night
> I laughed him into patience: and next morn,
> Ere the ninth hour, I drank him to his bed."

The wines were often kept for two ages, and some qualities were so highly prized as to sell for about twenty dollars an ounce. Large hogs were roasted whole at a banquet. The ancient epicures expatiate on ram's-head pies, stuffed fowls, boiled calf, and pastry stuffed with raisins and nuts. Dishes were made of gold and silver, set with precious stones. Cicero and Pompey one day surprised Lucullus at one of his ordinary banquets, when he expected no guests, and even that cost fifty thousand drachmas — about four thousand dollars. His beds were of purple, and his vessels glittered with jewels. The halls of Heliogabalus were hung with cloth of gold, enriched with jewels. His beds were of massive silver, his table and plate of pure gold, and his mattresses, covered with carpets of cloth of gold, were stuffed with down found only under the wings of partridges. Crassus paid one hundred thousand sesterces for a golden cup. Banqueting rooms were strewed with lilies and roses. Apicius, in the time of Trajan, spent one hundred millions of sesterces in debauchery and gluttony. Having only ten millions left, he ended his life with poison, thinking he might die of hunger. The suppers of Heliogabalus never cost less than one hundred thousand sesterces. And things were valued for their cost and rarity, rather than their real value. Enormous prices were paid for carp, the favorite dish of the Romans. Drusillus, a freedman of Claudius, caused a dish to be made of five hundred pounds weight of silver. Vitellius had one made of such pro-

Luxury of the aristocracy.

digious size that they were obliged to build a furnace on purpose for it; and at a feast in honor of this dish which he gave, it was filled with the livers of the scarrus (fish), the brains of peacocks, the tongues of a bird of red plumage, called Phæsuicopterus, and the roes of lampreys caught in the Carpathian Sea. Falernian wine was never drunk until ten years old, and it was generally cooled with ices. The passion for play was universal. Nero ventured four hundred thousand sesterces on a single throw of the dice. Cleopatra, when she feasted Antony, gave each time to that general the gold vessels, enriched with jewels, the tapestry and purple carpets, embroidered with gold, which had been used in the repasts. Horace speaks of a debauchee who drank at a meal a goblet of vinegar, in which he dissolved a pearl worth a million of sesterces, which hung at the ear of his mistress. Precious stones were so common that a woman of the utmost simplicity dared not go without her diamonds. Even men wore jewels, especially elaborate rings, and upon all the fingers at last. The taste of the Roman aristocracy, with their immense fortunes, inclined them to pomp, to extravagance, to ostentatious modes of living, to luxurious banquets, to conventionalities and ceremonies, to an unbounded epicureanism. They lived for the present hour, and for sensual pleasures. There was no elevation of life. It was the body and not the soul, the present and not the future, which alone concerned them. They were grossly material in all their desires and habits. They squandered money on their banquets, their stables, and their dress. And it was to their crimes, says Juvenal, that they were indebted for their gardens, their palaces, their tables, and their fine old plate. The day was portioned out in the public places, in the bath, the banquet. Martial indignantly rebukes these extravagances, as unable to purchase happiness, in his Epigram to Quintus: "Because you purchase slaves at two hundred thousand sesterces; because you drink wines stored during the reign

Luxury of the nobles.

of Numa; because your furniture costs you a million; because a pound weight of wrought silver costs you five thousand; because a golden chariot becomes yours at the price of a whole farm; because your mule costs you more than the value of a house — do not imagine that such expenses are the proof of a great mind." [1]

Unbounded pride, insolence, inhumanity, selfishness, and scorn marked this noble class. Of course there were exceptions, but the historians and satirists give the saddest pictures of their cold-hearted depravity. The sole result of friendship with a great man was a meal, at which flattery and sycophancy were expected; but the best wine was drunk by the host, instead of by the guest. Provinces were ransacked for fish and fowl and game for the tables of the great, and sensualism was thought to be no reproach. They violated the laws of chastity and decorum. They scourged to death their slaves. They degraded their wives and sisters. They patronized the most demoralizing sports. They enriched themselves by usury, and enjoyed monopolies. They practiced no generosity, except at their banquets, when ostentation balanced their avarice. They measured every thing by the money-standard. They had no taste for literature, but they rewarded sculptors and painters, if they prostituted art to their vanity or passions. They had no reverence for religion, and ridiculed the gods. Their distinguishing vices were meanness and servility, the pursuit of money by every artifice, the absence of honor, and unblushing sensuality.

Gibbon's account of the nobles.

Gibbon has eloquently abridged the remarks of Ammianus Marcellinus, respecting these people: "They contend with each other in the empty vanity of titles and surnames. They affect to multiply their likenesses in statues of bronze or marble; nor are they satisfied unless these statues are covered with plates of gold. They boast of the rent-rolls of their estates. They meas-

[1] Book iii. p. 62.

ure their rank and consequence by the loftiness of their chariots, and the weighty magnificence of their dress. Their long robes of silk and purple float in the wind, and, as they are agitated by art or accident, they discover the under garments, the rich tunics embroidered with the figures of various animals. Followed by a train of fifty servants, and tearing up the pavement, they move along the streets as if they traveled with post-horses; and the example of the senators is boldly imitated by the matrons and ladies, whose covered carriages are continually driving round the immense space of the city and suburbs. Whenever they condescend to enter the public baths, they assume, on their entrance, a tone of loud and insolent command, and maintain a haughty demeanor, which, perhaps, might have been excused in the great Marcellus, after the conquest of Syracuse. Sometimes these heroes undertake more arduous achievements: they visit their estates in Italy, and procure themselves, by servile hands, the amusements of the chase. And if, at any time, especially on a hot day, they have the courage to sail in their gilded galleys from the Lucrine Lake to their elegant villas on the seacoast of Puteoli and Cargeta, they compare these expeditions to the marches of Cæsar and Alexander. Yet, should a fly presume to settle on the silken folds of their gilded umbrellas, should a sunbeam penetrate through some unguarded chink, they deplore their intolerable hardships, and lament, in affected language, that they were not born in the regions of eternal darkness. In the exercise of domestic jurisdiction they express an exquisite sensibility for any personal injury, and a contemptuous indifference for the rest of mankind. When they have called for warm water, should a slave be tardy in his obedience, he is chastised with an hundred lashes; should he commit a willful murder, his master will mildly observe that he is a worthless fellow, and should be punished if he repeat the offense. If a foreigner of no contemptible rank

Sarcasms of Ammianus Marcellinus.

be introduced to these senators, he is welcomed with such warm professions that he retires charmed with their affability; but when he repeats his visit, he is surprised and mortified to find that his name, his person, and his country are forgotten. The modest, the sober, and the learned are rarely invited to their sumptuous banquets; but the most worthless of mankind — parasites who applaud every look and gesture, who gaze with rapture on marble columns and variegated pavements, and strenuously praise the pomp and elegance which he is taught to consider as a part of his personal merit. At the Roman table, the birds, the squirrels, the fish which appear of uncommon size, are contemplated with curious attention, and notaries are summoned to attest, by authentic record, their real weight. Another method of introduction into the houses of the great is skill in games, which is a sure road to wealth and reputation. A master of this sublime art, if placed, at a supper, below a magistrate, displays in his countenance a surprise and indignation which Cato might be supposed to feel when refused the prætorship. The acquisition of knowledge seldom engages the attention of the nobles, who abhor the fatigue and disdain the advantages of study; and the only books they peruse are the 'Satires of Juvenal,' or the fabulous histories of Marius Maximus. The libraries they have inherited from their fathers are secluded, like dreary sepulchres, from the light of day; but the costly instruments of the theatre, flutes and hydraulic organs, are constructed for their use. In their palaces sound is preferred to sense, and the care of the body to that of the mind. The suspicion of a malady is of sufficient weight to excuse the visits of the most intimate friends. The prospect of gain will urge a rich and gouty senator as far as Spoleta; every sentiment of arrogance and dignity is suppressed in the hope of an inheritance or legacy, and a wealthy, childless citizen is the most powerful of the Romans. The distress which follows and chastises extravagant luxury often reduces the great to use the most humiliating expedients. When they wish to borrow, they employ the base and supplicating style of the slaves in the comedy; but when they are called upon to pay, they assume the royal and tragic declamations of the grandsons of Hercules. If the demand is repeated, they readily procure some trusty sycophant to maintain a charge of poison or magic against the insolent creditor, who is seldom released from prison until he has signed a discharge of the whole debt. And these vices are mixed with a puerile superstition which disgraces their understanding. They listen with confidence to the productions of haruspices, who pretend to read in the entrails of victims the signs of future greatness and prosperity; and this superstition is observed among those very skeptics who impiously deny or doubt the existence of a celestial power." [1]

Such, in the latter days of the empire, was the leading class at Rome, and probably in the cities which aped the fashions of the capital. There was a melancholy absence of elevation of sentiment, of patriotism, of manly courage, and of dignity of character. Frivolity and luxury loosened all the ties of society. The animating principle of their lives was a heartless Epicureanism. They lived for the present hour, and for their pleasures, indifferent to the great interests of the public, and to the miseries of the poor. They were bound up in themselves. They were grossly material in all their aims. They had lost all ideas of public virtue. They degraded women; they oppressed the people; they laughed at philanthropy; they could not be reached by elevated sentiments; they had no concern for the future. Scornful, egotistical, haughty, self-indulgent, affected, cynical, all their thoughts and conversation were directed to frivolities. Nothing made any impression upon them but passing vanities. They ignored both Heaven and Hell. They were like the courtiers of Louis XV. in the

1 Found in the sixth chapter of the fourteenth, and the fourth of the twenty-eighth, book of Ammianus Marcellinus.

most godless period of the monarchy. They were worse, for they superadded pagan infidelities. There were memorable exceptions, but not many, until Christianity had reached the throne. "One after another, the nobles sunk into a lethargy almost without a parallel. The proudest names of the old republic were finally associated with the idlest amusements and the most preposterous novelties. A Gabrius, a Callius, and a Crassus were immortalized by the elegance of their dancing. A Lucullus, a Hortensius, a Philippus estimated one another, not by their eloquence, their courage, or their virtue, but by the perfection of their fish-ponds, and the singularity of the breeds they nourished. They seemed to touch the sky with their finger if they had stocked their preserves with bearded mullets, and taught them to recognize their masters' voices, and come to be fed from their hands." [1]

As for the miserable class whom they oppressed, their condition became worse every day from the accession of the emperors. The Plebeians had ever disdained those arts which now occupy the middle classes. These were intrusted to slaves. Originally, they employed themselves upon the lands which had been obtained by conquest. But these lands were gradually absorbed or usurped by the large proprietors. The small farmers, oppressed with debt and usury, parted with their lands to their wealthy creditors. In the time of Cicero, it was computed that there were only about two thousand citizens possessed of independent property. These two thousand people owned the world. The rest were dependent; and they were powerless when deprived of political rights, for the great candidate for public honors and offices liberally paid for votes. But under the emperors the commons had subsided into a miserable populace, fed from the public stores. They would have perished but for largesses. Monthly distributions of corn were converted into daily allowance for

[1] Merivale, chap. ii.

bread. They were amused with games and festivals. From the stately baths they might be seen to issue without shoes and without a mantle. They loitered in the public streets, and dissipated in gaming their miserable pittance. They spent the hours of the night in the lowest resorts of crime and misery. As many as four hundred thousand sometimes assembled to witness the chariot races. The vast theatres were crowded to see male and female dancers. The amphitheatres were still more largely attended by the better populace. They expired in wretched apartments without attracting the attention of government. Pestilence and famine and squalid misery thinned their ranks, and they would have been annihilated but for constant succession to their ranks from the provinces. In the busy streets of Rome might be seen adventurers from all parts of the world, disgraced by all the various vices of their respective countries. They had no education, and but little of religious advantages. They were held in terror by both priests and nobles. The priest terrified them with Egyptian sorceries, the noble crushed them by iron weight. Like lazzaroni, they lived in the streets, or were crowded into filthy apartments. Several families tenanted the same house. A gladiatorial show delighted them, but the circus was their peculiar joy. Here they sought to drown the consciousness of their squalid degradation. They were sold into slavery for trifling debts. They had no home. The poor man had no ambition or hope. His wife was a slave; his children were precocious demons, whose prattle was the cry for bread, whose laughter was the howl of pandemonium, whose sports were the tricks of premature iniquity, whose beauty was the squalor of disease and filth. He fled from a wife in whom he had no trust, from children in whom he had no hope, from brothers for whom he felt no sympathy, from parents for whom he felt no reverence. The circus was *his* home, the wild beast *his* consolation. The future was a blank.

Condition of the people.

Death was the release from suffering. Historians and poets say but little of his degraded existence; but from the few hints we have, we infer depravity and brutal tastes. If degraded at all, they must have been very degraded, since the Romans had but little sentiment, and no ideality. They were sunk in vice, for they had no sense of responsibility. They never emerged from their wretched condition. The philosophers, poets, scholars, and lawyers of Rome, sprang uniformly from the aristocratic classes. In the provinces, the poor sometimes rose, but very seldom. The whole aspect of society was a fearful inequality — disproportionate fortunes, slavery, and beggary. There was no middle class, of any influence or consideration. It was for the interest of people without means to enroll themselves in the service of the rich. Hence the immense numbers employed in the palaces in menial work. They would have been enrolled in the armies, but for their inefficiency. The army was recruited from the provinces — the rural population — and even from the barbarians themselves. There were no hospitals for the sick and the old, except one on an island in the Tiber. The old and helpless were left to die, unpitied and unconsoled. Suicide was so common that it attracted no attention, but infanticide was not so marked, since there was so little feeling of compassion for the future fate of the miserable children. Superstition culminated at Rome, for there were seen the priests and devotees of all the countries which it governed — "the dark-skinned daughters of Isis, with drum and timbrel and wanton mien; devotees of the Persian Mithras, imported by the Pompeians from Cilicia; emasculated Asiatics, priests of Berecynthian Cybele, with their wild dances and discordant cries; worshipers of the great goddess Diana; barbarian captives with the rites of Teuton priests; Syrians, Jews, Chaldean astrologers, and Thessalian sorcerers." Oh, what scenes of sin and misery did that imperial capital witness in the third and fourth centuries — sensualism and superstition, fears and tribulations, pestilence and famine, even amid the pomps of senatorial families, and the grandeur of palaces and temples. "The crowds which flocked to Rome from the eastern shores of the Mediterranean, brought with them practices extremely demoralizing. The awful rites of initiation, the tricks of magicians, the pretended virtues of amulets and charms, the riddles of emblematical idolatry, with which the superstition of the East abounded, amused the languid voluptuaries who neither had the energy for a moral belief, nor the boldness requisite for logical skepticism." They were brutal, bloodthirsty, callous to the sight of suffering, and familiar with cruelties and crimes. They were superstitious, without religious faith, without hope, and without God in the world.

We cannot pass by, in this enumeration of the different classes of Roman society, the number and condition of slaves. A large part of the population belonged to this servile class. Originally introduced by foreign conquest, it was increased by those who could not pay their debts. The single campaign of Regulus introduced as many as a fifth part of the whole population. Four hundred were maintained in a single palace, at a comparatively early period. A freedman in the time of Augustus left behind him four thousand one hundred and sixteen. Horace regarded two hundred as the suitable establishment for a gentleman. Some senators owned twenty thousand. Gibbon estimates the number at about sixty millions, one half of the whole population. One hundred thousand captives were taken in the Jewish war, who were sold as slaves, and sold as cheap as horses.[1] Blair supposes that there were three slaves to one freeman, from the conquest of Greece to the reign of Alexander Severus. Slaves often cost two hundred thousand ses-

The slaves.

[1] Wm. Blair, *On Roman Slavery*, Edinburgh, 1833 ; Robertson, *On the State of the World at the Introduction of Christ.*

terces.[1] Every body was eager to possess a slave. At one time his life was at the absolute control of his master. He could be treated at all times with brutal severity. Fettered and branded he toiled to cultivate the lands of an imperious master, and at night he was shut up in subterranean cells. The laws did not recognize his claim to be considered scarcely as a moral agent. He was *secundum hominum genus*. He could acquire no rights, social or political. He was incapable of inheriting property, or making a will, or contracting a legal marriage. His value was estimated like that of a brute. He was a thing and not a person — "a piece of furniture possessed of life." He was his master's property, to be scourged, or tortured, or crucified. If a wealthy proprietor died, under circumstances which excited suspicion of foul play, his whole household was put to the torture. It is recorded, that, on the murder of a man of consular dignity by a slave, every slave in his possession was condemned to death. Slaves swelled the useless rabbles of the cities, and devoured the revenues of the state. All manual labor was done by slaves, in towns as well as the country. Even the mechanical arts were cultivated by the slaves. And more, slaves were schoolmasters, secretaries, actors, musicians, and physicians. In intelligence, they were on an equality with their masters. They came from Greece and Asia Minor and Syria, as well as from Gaul and the African deserts. They were white as well as black. All captives in war were made slaves, and unfortunate debtors. Sometimes they could regain their freedom ; but, generally, their condition became more and more deplorable. What a state of society when a refined and cultivated Greek could be made to obey the most offensive orders of a capricious and sensual Roman, without remuneration, without thanks, without favor, without redress.[2] What was to be

1 Martial, xii. 62.

2 Says Juvenal, *Sat.* vi., "Crucify that slave. What is the charge to call for

expected of a class who had no object to live for. They became the most degraded of mortals, ready for pillage, and justly to be feared in the hour of danger. Slavery undoubtedly proved the most destructive canker of the Roman state. It destroyed its vitality. It was this social evil, more than political misrule, which undermined the empire. Slavery proved at Rome a monstrous curse, destroying all manliness of character, creating contempt of honest labor, making men timorous yet cruel, idle, frivolous, weak, dependent, powerless. The empire might have lasted centuries longer but for this incubus, the standing disgrace of the pagan world. Paganism never recognized what is most noble and glorious in man; never recognized his equality, his common brotherhood, his natural rights. There was no compunction, no remorse in depriving human beings of their highest privileges. Its whole tendency was to degrade the soul, and cause forgetfulness of immortality. Slavery thrives best, when the generous instincts are suppressed, and egotism and sensuality and pride are the dominant springs of human action.

Slavery.

The same influences which tended to rob man of the rights which God has given him, and produce cruelty and heartlessness in the general intercourse of life, also tended to degrade the female sex. In the earlier age of the republic, when the people were poor, and life was simple and primitive, and heroism and patriotism were characteristic, woman was comparatively virtuous and respected. She asserted her natural equality, and led a life of domestic tranquillity, employed upon the training of her children, and inspiring her husband to noble deeds. But, under the emperors, these virtues had fled. Woman was miserably educated, being taught by a slave, or some Greek chambermaid, accustomed to ribald conversation,

such a punishment? What witness can you present? Who gave the information? Listen! Idiot! So a slave is a man then! Granted he has done nothing. I *will* it. I insist upon it, Let my will stand instead of reason." Read Martial, Juvenal, and Plautus.

27

and fed with idle tales and silly superstitions. She was regarded as more vicious in natural inclination than man, and was chiefly valued for household labors. She was reduced to dependence; she saw but little of her brothers or relatives; she was confined to her home as if it were a prison; she was guarded by eunuchs and female slaves; she was given in marriage without her consent; she could be easily divorced; she was valued only as a domestic servant, or as an animal to prevent the extinction of families; she was regarded as the inferior of her husband, to whom she was a victim, a toy, or a slave. Love after marriage was not frequent, since she did not shine in the virtues by which love is kept alive. She became timorous, or frivolous, without dignity or public esteem. Her happiness was in extravagant attire, in elaborate hair-dressings, in rings and bracelets, in a retinue of servants, in gilded apartments, in luxurious couches, in voluptuous dances, in exciting banquets, in demoralizing spectacles, in frivolous gossip, in inglorious idleness. If virtuous, it was not so much from principle as from fear. Hence she resorted to all sorts of arts to deceive her husband. Her genius was sharpened by perpetual devices, and cunning was her great resource. She cultivated no lofty friendships; she engaged in no philanthropic mission; she cherished no ennobling sentiments; she kindled no chivalrous admiration. Her amusements were frivolous, her taste vitiated, her education neglected, her rights violated, her sympathy despised, her aspirations scorned. And here I do not allude to great and infamous examples which history has handed down in the sober pages of Suetonius and Tacitus, or that unblushing depravity which stands out in the bitter satires of the times. I speak not of the adultery, the poisoning, the infanticide, the debauchery, the cruelty of which history accuses the Messalinas and Agrippinas of imperial Rome. I allude not to the orgies of the Palatine Hill, or the abominations which are inferred from the paint-

Degradation of woman.

ings of Pompeii. But there was a general frivolity and extravagance among women which rendered marriage inexpedient, unless large dowries were brought to the husband. Numerous were the efforts of emperors to promote honorable marriages, but the relation was shunned. Courtesans usurped the privilege of wives, and with unblushing effrontery. A man was derided who contemplated matrimony, for there was but little confidence in female virtue or capacity. And woman lost all her fascination when age had destroyed her beauty. Even her very virtues were distasteful to her self-indulgent husband. And whenever she gained the ascendency by her charms, she was tyrannical. Her relations incited her to despoil her husband. She lived amid incessant broils. She had no care for the future, and exceeded men in prodigality. "The government of her house is no more merciful," says Juvenal, "than the court of a Sicilian tyrant." In order to render herself attractive, she exhausted all the arts of cosmetics and elaborate hair-dressing. She delighted in magical incantations and love-potions. In the bitter satire of Juvenal, we get an impression most melancholy and loathsome : —

"'T were long to tell what philters they provide,
What drugs to set a son-in-law aside.
Women, in judgment weak, in feeling strong,
By every gust of passion borne along.
To a fond spouse a wife no mercy shows;
Though warmed with equal fires, she mocks his woes,
And triumphs in his spoils; her wayward will
Defeats his bliss and turns his good to ill.
Women support the *bar;* they love the law,
And raise litigious questions for a straw;
Nay, more, they fence! who has not marked their oil,
Their purple rigs, for this preposterous toil!
A woman stops at nothing, when she wears
Rich emeralds round her neck, and in her ears
Pearls of enormous size; these justify
Her faults, and make all lawful in her eye.
More shame to Rome! in every street are found
The essenced Lypanti, with roses crowned,
The gay Miletan, and the Tarentine,
Lewd, petulant, and reeling ripe with wine!"

In the sixth satire of Juvenal is found the most severe delineation of woman that ever mortal penned. Doubtless he is libellous and extravagant, for only infamous women can stoop to such arts and degradations, which would seem to be common in his time. But, with all his exaggeration, we are forced to feel that but few women, even in the highest class, except those converted to Christianity, showed the virtues of a Lucretia, a Volumnia, a Cornelia, or an Octavia. There was but a universal corruption. The great virtues of a Perpetua, a Felicitas, an Agnes, a Paula, a Blessilla, a Fabiola, would have adorned any civilization. But the great mass were, what they were in Greece, even in the days of Pericles, what they have ever been under the influence of Paganism, what they ever will be without Christianity to guide them, victims or slaves of man, revenging themselves by squandering his wealth, stealing his secrets, betraying his interests, and deserting his home.

Condition of woman.

Another essential but demoralizing feature of Roman society, were the games and festivals and gladiatorial shows, which accustomed the people to unnatural excitements, and familiarity with cruelty and suffering. They made all ordinary pleasures insipid. They ended in making homicide an institution. The butcheries of the amphitheatre exerted a fascination which diverted the mind from literature, art, and the enjoyments of domestic life. Very early it was the favorite sport of the Romans. Marcus and Decimus Brutus employed gladiators in celebrating the obsequies of their fathers, nearly three centuries before Christ. "The wealth and ingenuity of the aristocracy were taxed to the utmost, to content the populace and provide food for the indiscriminate slaughter of the circus, where brute fought with brute, and man again with man, or where the skill and weapons of the latter were matched against the strength and ferocity of the first." Pompey let loose six hundred lions in the arena

Games and festivals.

in one day. Augustus delighted the people with four hundred and twenty panthers. The games of Trajan lasted one hundred and twenty days, when ten thousand gladiators fought, and ten thousand beasts were slain. Titus slaughtered five thousand animals at a time. Twenty elephants contended, according to Pliny, against a band of six hundred captives. Probus reserved six hundred gladiators for one of his festivals, and massacred, on another, two hundred lions, twenty leopards, and three hundred bears. Gordian let loose three hundred African hyenas and ten Indian tigers in the arena. Every corner of the earth was ransacked for these wild animals, which were so highly valued that, in the time of Theodosius, it was forbidden by law to destroy a Getulian lion. No one can contemplate the statue of the Dying Gladiator which now ornaments the capitol at Rome, without emotions of pity and admiration. If a marble statue can thus move us, what was it to see the Christian gladiators contending with the fierce lions of Africa. The "Christians to the lions," was the watchword of the brutal populace. What a sight was the old amphitheatre of Titus, five hundred and sixty feet long, and four hundred and seventy feet wide, built on eighty arches, and rising one hundred and forty feet into the air, with its four successive orders of architecture, and inclosing its eighty thousand seated spectators, arranged according to rank, from the emperor to the lowest of the populace, all seated on marble benches, covered with cushions, and protected from the sun and rain by ample canopies! What an excitement when men strove not with wild beasts alone, but with one another, and when all that human skill and strength, increased by elaborate treatment, and taxed to the uttermost, were put forth in the needless homicide, and until the thirsty soil was wet and matted with human gore! Familiarity with such sights must have hardened the heart and rendered the mind insensible to refined pleasures. What theatres are to the French, what bull-fights are to the Spaniards, what horse-races are to the English, these gladiatorial shows were to the ancient Romans. The ruins of hundreds of amphitheatres attest the universality of the custom, not in Rome alone, but in the provinces.

The circus.

The sports of the circus took place from the earliest periods. The Circus Maximus was capable of containing two hundred and sixty thousand, as estimated by Pliny. It was appropriated for horse and chariot races. The enthusiasm of the Romans for races exceeded all bounds. Lists of the horses, with their names and colors, and those of drivers, were handed about, and heavy bets made on each faction. The games commenced with a grand procession, in which all persons of distinction, and those who were to exhibit, took part. The statues of the gods formed a conspicuous feature in the show, and were carried on the shoulders as saints are carried in modern processions. The chariots were often drawn by eight horses, and four generally started in the race.

The theatre was also a great place of resort. Scaurus built one capable of seating eighty thousand spectators. That of Pompey, near the Circus Maximus, could contain forty thousand. But the theatre had not the same attraction to the Romans that it had to the Greeks. They preferred scenes of pomp and splendor.

The circus and theatre.

No people probably abandoned themselves to pleasures more universally than the Romans, after war ceased to be the master passion. All classes alike pursued them with restless eagerness. Amusements were the fashion and the business of life. At the theatre, at the great gladiatorial shows, at the chariot races, senators and emperors and generals were always present in conspicuous and reserved seats of honor; behind them were the ordinary citizens, and in the rear of these, the people fed at the public expense. The Circus Maximus, the Theatre of Pompey, the Amphitheatre of Titus, would collectively accommodate over four hundred thousand spectators. We may presume that over five hundred thousand people were in the habit of constant attendance on these demoralizing sports. And the fashion spread throughout all the great cities of the empire, so that there was scarcely a city of twenty thousand people which had not its theatres, or amphitheatres, or circus. The enthusiasm of the Romans for the circus exceeded all bounds. And when we remember the heavy bets on favorite horses, and the universal passion for gambling in every shape, we can form some idea of the effect of these amusements on the common mind, destroying the taste for home pleasures, and for all that was intellectual and simple. What are we to think of a state of society, where all classes had leisure for these sports. Habits of industry were destroyed, and all respect for employments which required labor. The rich were supported by the contributions from the provinces, since they were the great proprietors of conquered lands. The poor had no solicitude for a living, for they were supported at the public expense. They, therefore, gave themselves up to pleasure. Even the baths, designed for sanatory purposes, became places of resort and idleness, and ultimately of improper intercourse. When the thermæ came fully into public use, not only did men bathe together in numbers, but even men and women promiscuously in the same baths. In the time of Julius Cæsar, we find no less a personage than the mother of Augustus making use of the public establishments; and in process of time the emperors themselves bathed in public with the meanest of their subjects. The baths in the time of Alexander Severus were not only kept open from sunrise to sunset, but even the whole night. The luxurious classes almost lived in the baths. Commodus took his meals in the bath. Gordian bathed seven times in the day, and Gallienus as often. They bathed before they took their meals, and after meals to provoke a new appetite. They did not content themselves with a single bath, but went through a

Baths.

course of baths in succession, in which the agency of air as well as water was applied. And the bathers were attended by an army of slaves given over to every sort of roguery and theft. "*O furum optume balmariorum,*" exclaims Catullus, in disgust and indignation. Nor was water alone used. The common people made use of scented oils to anoint their persons, and perfumed the water itself with the most precious perfumes. Bodily health and cleanliness were only secondary considerations; voluptuous pleasure was the main object. The ruins of the baths of Titus, Caracalla, and Diocletian, in Rome, show that they were decorated with prodigal magnificence, and with every thing that could excite the passions — pictures, statues, ornaments, and mirrors. Says Seneca, Epistle lxxxvi., "*Nisi parietis magnis et preciosis orbibus refulserunt.*" The baths were scenes of orgies consecrated to Bacchus, and the frescoes on the excavated baths of Pompeii still raise a blush on the face of every spectator who visits them. I speak not of the elaborate ornaments, the Numidian marbles, the precious stones, the exquisite sculptures, which formed part of the decorations of the Roman baths, but the demoralizing pleasures with which they were connected, and which they tended to promote. The baths became, according to the ancient writers, ultimately places of excessive and degrading debauchery.

"*Balnea, vina, Venas corrumpunt corpora nostra.*"

Dress and ornament.

The Romans, originally, were not only frugal, but they dressed with great simplicity. In process of time, they became extravagantly fond of elaborately ornamented attire, particularly the women. They wore a great variety of rings and necklaces; they dyed their hair, and resorted to expensive cosmetics; they wore silks of various colors, magnificently embroidered. Pearls and rubies, for which large estates had been exchanged, were suspended from their ears. Their hair glistened with a net-work of golden thread. Their stolæ were ornamented with purple bands, and fastened with diamond clasps, while their pallæ trailed along the ground. Jewels were embroidered upon their sandals, and golden bands, pins, combs, and pomades raised the hair in a storied edifice upon the forehead. They reclined on luxurious couches, and rode in silver chariots. Their time was spent in paying and receiving visits, at the bath, the spectacle, and the banquet. Tables, supported on ivory columns, displayed their costly plate; silver mirrors were hung against the walls, and curious chests contained their jewels and money. Bronze lamps lighted their chambers, and glass vases, imitating precious stones, stood upon their cupboards. Silken curtains were suspended over the doors and from the ceilings, and lecticæ, like palanquins, were borne through the streets by slaves, on which reclined the effeminated wives and daughters of the rich. Their gardens were rendered attractive by green-houses, flower-beds, and every sort of fruit and vine.

But it was at their banquets the Romans displayed the greatest luxury and extravagance. No people ever thought more of the pleasures of the table. And the prodigality was seen not only in the indulgence of the palate by the choicest dainties, but in articles which commanded, from their rarity, the highest prices. They not only sought to eat daintily, but to increase their capacity by unnatural means. The maxim, "*Il faut manger pour vivre, et non pas vivre pour manger*," was reversed. At the fourth hour they breakfasted on bread, grapes, olives, and cheese and eggs; at the sixth they lunched, still more heartily; and at the ninth hour they dined; and this meal, the *cœna*, was the principal one, which consisted of three parts: the first — the *gustus* — was made up of dishes to provoke an appetite, shell-fish and piquant sauces; the second — the *fercula* — composed of different courses; and the third — the dessert, a *mensœ secundœ* — composed of fruits and pastry. Fish were the chief object of the Roman epicures, of which the *mullus*, the *rhombus*, and the *asellus* were the most valued. It is recorded that a mullus (sea barbel), weighing but eight pounds, sold for eight thousand sesterces. Oysters, from the Lucrine Lake, were in great demand. Snails were fed in ponds for the purpose, while the villas of the rich had their piscinæ filled with fresh or salt-water fish. Peacocks and pheasants were the most highly esteemed among poultry, although the absurdity prevailed of eating singing-birds. Of quadrupeds, the greatest favorite was the wild boar, the chief dish of a grand *cœna*, and came whole upon the table, and the practiced gourmand pretended to distinguish by the taste from what part of Italy it came. Dishes, the very names of which excite disgust, were used at fashionable banquets, and held in high esteem. Martial devotes two entire books of his "Epigrams" to the various dishes and ornaments of a Roman banquet. He refers to almost every fruit and vegetable and meat that we now use — to cabbages, leeks, turnips, asparagus, beans, beets, peas, lettuces, radishes, mushrooms, truffles, pulse, lentils, among vegetables; to pheasants, ducks, doves, geese, capons, pigeons, partridges, peacocks, Numidian fowls, cranes, woodcocks, swans, among birds; to mullets, lampreys, turbots, oysters, prawns, chars, murices, gudgeons, pikes, sturgeons, among fish; to raisins, figs, quinces, citrons, dates, plums, olives, apricots, among fruit; to sauces and condiments; to wild game, and to twenty different kinds of wine; on all of which he expatiates like an epicure. He speaks of the presents made to guests at feasts, the tablets of ivory and parchment, the dice-boxes, style-cases, toothpicks, golden hair-pins, combs, pomatum, parasols, oil-flasks, tooth-powder, balms and perfumes, slippers, dinner-couches, citron-tables, antique vases, gold-chased cups, snow-strainers, jeweled and crystal vases, rings, spoons, scarlet cloaks, table-covers, Cilician socks, pillows, girdles, aprons, mattresses, lyres, bath-bells, statues, masks, books, musical instruments, and other articles of taste, luxury, or necessity. The pleasures of the table, however, are ever uppermost in his eye, and the luxuries of those whom he could not rival, but which he reprobates: —

> "Nor mullet delights thee, nice Betic, nor thrush;
> The hare with the scut, nor the boar with the tusk;
> No sweet cakes or tablets, thy taste so absurd,
> Nor Libya need send thee, nor Phasis, a bird.
> But capers and onions, besoaking in brine,
> And brawn of a gammon scarce doubtful are thine.
> Of garbage, or flitch of hoar tunny, thou 'rt vain;
> The rosin's thy joy, the Falernian thy bane." [1]

He thus describes a modest dinner, to which he, a poet, invites his friend Turanius: "If you are suffering from dread of a melancholy dinner at home, or would take a preparatory whet, come and feast with me. You will find no want of Cappadocian lettuces and strong leeks. The tunny will lurk under slices of egg; a cauliflower hot enough to burn your fingers, and which has just left the garden, will be served fresh on a black platter; white sausages will float on snow-white porridge, and the pale bean will accompany the red-streaked bacon. In the second course, raisins will be set before you, and pears which pass for Syrian, and roasted chestnuts. The wine you will prove in drinking it. After all this, excellent olives will come to your relief, with the hot vetch and the tepid lupine. The dinner is small, who can deny it? but you will not have to invent falsehoods, or hear them invented; you will recline at ease, and with your own natural look; the host will not read aloud a bulky volume of his own compositions, nor will licentious girls, from shameless Cadiz, be there to gratify you with wanton attitudes; but the small reed pipe will be heard, and the nice Claudia, whose society you value even more than mine." [2]

A poet's dinner.

How different this poet's dinner, a table spread without luxury, and enlivened by wit and friendship, from that

[1] Martial, b. iii. p. 77.

[2] *Ibid.* b. v. p. 78.

which Petronius describes of a rich freedman, which was more after the fashion of the vulgar and luxurious gourmands of his day.

Next to the pleasures of the table, the passion for expensive furniture seemed to be the prevailing folly. We read of couches gemmed with tortoise-shell, and tables of citron-wood from Africa. Silver and gold vases. Tables, also, of Mauritanian marble, supported on pedestals of Lybian ivory ; cups of crystal ; all sorts of silver plate, the masterpieces of Myro, and the handiwork of Praxiteles, and the engravings of Phidias. Gold services adorned the sideboard. Couches were covered with purple silks. Chairs were elaborately carved; costly mirrors hung against the walls, and bronze lamps were suspended from the painted ceilings. But it was not always the most beautiful articles which were most prized, but those which were procured with the greatest difficulty, or brought from the remotest provinces. That which cost most received uniformly the greatest admiration.

Expensive furniture.

If it were possible to allude to an evil more revolting than the sports of the amphitheatre, or the extravagant luxuries of the table, I would say that the universal abandonment to money-making, for the enjoyment of the factitious pleasures it purchased, was even still more melancholy, since it struck deeper into the foundations which supported society. The leading spring of life was money. Boys were bred from early youth to all the mysteries of unscrupulous gains. Usury was practiced to such an incredible extent that the interest on loans, in some instances equaled, in a few months, the whole capital. This was the more aristocratic mode of making money, which not even senators disdained. The pages of the poets show how profoundly money was prized, and how miserable were people without it. Rich old bachelors, without heirs, were held in the supremest honor. Money was the first object in all matrimonial alliances, and pro-

Money making.

vided that women were only wealthy, neither bridegroom nor parent was fastidious as to age, or deformity, or meanness of family, or vulgarity of person. The needy descendants of the old Patricians yoked themselves with fortunate Plebeians, and the blooming maidens of a comfortable obscurity sold themselves, without shame or reluctance, to the bloated sensualists who could give them what they supremely valued, chariots and diamonds. It was useless to appeal to elevated sentiments when happiness consisted in an outside, factitious life. The giddy women, in love with ornaments and dress, and the godless men, seeking what they should eat, could only be satisfied with what purchased their pleasures. The haughtiest aristocracy ever known on earth, tracing their lineage to the times of Cato, and boasting of their descent from the Scipios and the Pompeys, accustomed themselves at last to regard money as the only test of their own social position. There was no high social position disconnected with fortune. Even poets and philosophers were neglected, and gladiators and buffoons preferred before them. The great Augustine found himself utterly neglected at Rome, because he was dependent on his pupils, and his pupils were mean enough to run away without paying. Literature languished and died, since it brought neither honor nor emolument. No dignitary was respected for his office, only for his gains; nor was any office prized which did not bring rich emoluments. And corruption was so universal, that an official in an important post was sure of making a fortune in a short time. With such an idolatry of money, all trades and professions fell into disrepute which were not favorable to its accumulation, while those who administered to the pleasures of a rich man were held in honor. Cooks, buffoons, and dancers, received the consideration which artists and philosophers enjoyed at Athens in the days of Pericles. But artists and scholars were very few indeed in the more degenerate days of the empire. Nor would they have had influence. The wit of a Petronius, the ridicule of a Martial, the bitter sarcasm of a Juvenal, were lost on a people abandoned to frivolous gossip and demoralizing excesses. The haughty scorn with which a sensual beauty, living on the smiles and purse of a fortunate glutton, would pass, in her gilded chariot, some of the impoverished descendants of the great Camillus, might have provoked a smile, had any one been found, even a neglected poet, to have given them countenance and sympathy. But, alas! every body worshiped the shrine of Mammon. Every body was valued for what he *had*, rather than for what he *was;* and life was prized, not for those pleasures which are cheap and free as heaven, not for quiet tastes and rich affections and generous sympathies and intellectual genius, — the glorious certitudes of love, esteem, and friendship, which, "be they what they may, are yet the fountain-life of all our day," — but for the gratification of depraved and expensive tastes; those short-lived enjoyments which ended with the decay of appetite, and the *ennui* of realized expectation, — all of the earth, earthy; making a wreck of the divine image which was made for God and heaven, and preparing the way for a most fearful retribution, and producing, on contemplative minds, a sadness allied with despair, driving them to caves and solitudes, and making death the relief from sorrow. Cynicism, scorn, unbelief, and disgusting coarseness and vulgarity, made grand sentiments an idle dream. The fourteenth satire of Juvenal is direted mainly to the universal passion for gain, and the demoralizing vices it brings in its train, which made Rome a Pandemonium and a Vanity Fair. "Flatterers," says he, "consider misers as men of happy minds, since they admire wealth supremely, and think no instance can be found of a poor man that is also happy; and therefore they exhort their sons to apply themselves to the arts of money making. Come, boys; sack the Numidian hovels and the forts of Brigantes, that your sixtieth year may bestow on you the eagle which will make you rich. Or, if you shrink from the long-protracted labors of the camp, then bring something that you may profitably dispose of, and never let disgust of trade enter your head, nor think that any difference can be drawn between perfumes and leather. The smell of gain is good from any thing whatever. No one asks you *how* you get money, but *have* it you must." The poet Persius paints this passion for gold, displayed in the customs of the day, in a strain at once lofty and mournful, bitter and satirical:[1] —

> "O that I could my rich old uncle see
> In funeral pomp! O that some deity
> To pots of buried gold would guide my share!
> O that my ward, whom I succeed as heir,
> Were once at rest! Poor child! he lies in pain,
> And death to him must be accounted gain.
> By will thrice has Nerius swelled his store,
> And now is he a widower once more.
> O groveling souls, and void of things divine!
> Why bring our passions to the immortal's shrine?"

The old Greek philosophers gloried in their poverty; but poverty was the greatest reproach to a Roman. "In exact proportion to the sum of money a man keeps in his chest," says Juvenal,[2] "is the credit given to his oath. And the first question ever asked of a man is in reference to his income, rather than his character. How many slaves does he keep? How many acres does he own? What dishes are his table spread with? — these are the universal inquiries. Poverty, bitter though it be, has no sharper sting than this, — that it makes them ridiculous. Who was ever allowed at Rome to become a son-in-law if his estate was inferior, and not a match for the portion of the young lady? What poor man's name appears in any will? When is one summoned to a consultation even by an ædile?"

> "Long, long ago, in one despairing band,
> The poor, self-exiled, should have left the land."

And with this reproach of poverty there was no means

[1] *Satire* ii. [2] *Satire* iii.

to escape from it. Nor was there alleviation. A man was regarded as a fool who gave any thing except to the rich. Charity and benevolence were unknown virtues. The sick and the miserable were left to die unlamented and unknown. Prosperity and success, no matter by what means they were purchased, secured reverence and influence.

Indeed, the Romans were a worldly, selfish, Epicurean people, for whom we can feel but little admiration in any age of the republic. They never were finely moulded. They had no sentiment, unless in the earlier ages, it took the form of glory and patriotism. In their prosperity, they were proud and scornful. In adversity, they buried themselves in low excesses. They were not easily moved by softening influences. They had no lofty idealism, like the Greeks; nor were they even social, as they were. They were disgustingly *practical. Cui bono?* — "who shall show us any good?" — this was their by-word, this the sole principle of their existence. They were jealous of their dignity, and carried away by pomps and show. They were fond of etiquette and ceremony, and were conventional in all their habits. They had very little true intellectual independence, and were slaves of fashion as they were of ceremony and dress. They were inordinately greedy of social position and of social distinctions. They loved titles and surnames and inequalities of rank. They plumed themselves on taking a common-sense view of life, disdaining all lofty standards. They were dazzled by an outside life, and cared but little for the great certitudes on which real dignity and happiness rest. They had no conception of philanthropy. They lived for themselves. Nor had they veneration for ideal worth or beauty or abstract truth. They were reserved and reticent and haughty in social life. They were superstitious, and believed in dreams and omens and talismans. They were hospitable to their friends, but chiefly to display their wealth and pomp. They were coarse and indecent in banquets. They loved money supremely, but squandered it recklessly to gratify vanity. They had no high conceptions of art. They were copyists of the Greeks, and never produced any thing original but jurisprudence. They did not even add to the arts and sciences, which they applied to practical purposes. Their literature never produced a sentimentalist; their philosophy never soared into idealism; their art never ventured upon new creations. Their supreme ambition was to rule, and to rule despotically. They gloried in slavery, and degraded women and trod upon the defenseless. They had no pity, no gentleness, no delicacy of feeling. They could not comprehend a disinterested action. They lived to eat and drink, and wear robes of purple, and ride in chariots of silver, and receive greetings in the market-place, and be attended by an army of sycophants, flatterers, and slaves. What was elevated and what was pure were laughed at as unreal, as dreamy, as transcendental. All science was directed to *utilities*, and utilities were wines, rare fishes and birds, carpets, silks, cooking, palaces, chariots, horses, pomps. Their supreme idea was conquest, dominion over man, over beast, over seas, over nature — all with a view of becoming rich, comfortable, honorable. This was their Utopia. Epicurus was their god. Sensualism was the convertible term for their utilities, and pervaded their literature, their social life, and their public efforts; extinguishing poetry, friendship, affections, genius, self-sacrifice, lofty sentiments — the real utilities which make up our higher life, and fit man for an ever-expanding felicity. Practically, they were atheists — unbelievers of what is fixed and immutable in the soul, and glorious in the soul's aspirations. They had will and passion, sagacity and the power to rule, by which they became aggrandized; but they were wanting in those elements and virtues which endear their memory to mankind. They were both tyrants and sensualists; fitted to make conquests, unfitted to enjoy them. In an important sense, they were great civilizers, but their civilization pertained to material life. They worshiped the god of the sense, rather than the god of the reason; and, compared with the Greeks, bequeathed but little to our times which we value, except laws and maxims of government, and ideas of centralized power.

Such was imperial Rome, in all the internal relations of life, and amid all the trophies and praises which resulted from universal conquest. I cannot understand the enthusiasm of Gibbon for such a people, or for such an empire, — a grinding and resistless imperial despotism, a sensual and proud aristocracy, a debased and ignorant populace, disproportionate fortunes, slavery flourishing to a state unprecedented in the world's history, women the victims and the toys of men, lax sentiments of public morality, a whole people given over to demoralizing sports and spectacles, pleasure the master passion of the people, money the mainspring of society, all the vices which lead to violence and prepare the way for the total eclipse of the glory of man. What was a cultivated face of nature, or palaces, or pomps, or a splendid material civilization, or great armies, or a numerous population, or the triumph of energy and skill, when the moral health was completely undermined? The external grandeur was nothing amid so much vice and wickedness and wretchedness. A world, therefore, as fair and glorious as our own, must needs crumble away. There were no proper conservative forces. The poison had descended to the extremities of the social system. A corrupt body must die when vitality had fled. The soul was gone. Principle, patriotism, virtue, had all passed away. The barbarians were advancing to conquer and desolate. There was no power to resist them, but enervated and timid legions, with the accumulated vices of all the nations of the earth, which they had been learning for four hundred years. Society must needs resolve itself into its original elements when men would not make sacrifices, and so few belonged to their country. The machine was sure to break up at the first great shock. No state could stand with such an accumulation of wrongs, with such complicated and fatal diseases eating out the vitals of the empire. The house was built upon the sands. The army may have rallied under able generals, in view of the approaching catastrophe; philosophy may have gilded the days of a few indignant citizens; good emperors may have attempted to raise barriers against corruption; and even Christianity may have converted by thousands: still nothing, according to natural laws, could save the empire. It was doomed. Retributive justice must march on in its majestic course. The empire had accomplished its mission. The time came for it to die. The Sibylline oracle must needs be fulfilled: "O haughty Rome, the divine chastisement shall come upon thee; the fire shall consume thee; thy wealth shall perish; foxes and wolves shall dwell among thy ruins: and then what land that thou hast enslaved shall be thy ally, and which of thy gods shall save thee? for there shall be confusion over the face of the whole earth, and the fall of cities shall come."[1]

REFERENCES. — Mr. Merivale has written most fully of modern writers on the condition of the empire. Gibbon has occasional paragraphs which show the condition of Roman society. Lyman's Life of the Emperors should be read, and also DeQuincy's Lives of the Cæsars. See, also, Niebuhr, Arnold, and Mommsen, though these writers have chiefly confined themselves to republican Rome. But, if one would get the truest and most vivid description, he must read the Roman poets, especially Juvenal and Martial. The work of Petronius is too indecent to be read. Ammianus Marcellinus gives us some striking pictures of the latter Romans. Suetonius, in his Lives of the Cæsars, furnishes many facts. Becker's Gallus is a fine description of Roman habits and customs. Smith's Dictionary of Antiquities should be consulted, as it is a great thesaurus of important facts. Lucian does not describe Roman manners, but he aims his sarcasms on the hollowness of Roman life, as do the great satirists generally. Tillemont is the basis of Gibbon's history, so far as pertains to the emperors.

[1] If any one thinks this general description of Roman life and manners exaggerated, he can turn from such poets as Juvenal and Martial, and read what St. Paul says in the first chapter of the *Epistle to the Romans.*

CHAPTER XI.

THE FALL OF THE EMPIRE.

WE have contemplated the grandeur and the glory of the Roman empire ; and we have also seen, in connection with the magnificent triumphs of art, science, literature, and philosophy, a melancholy degradation of society, so fatal and universal, that all strength was undermined, and nothing was left but worn-out mechanisms and lifeless forms to resist the pressure of external enemies. So vast, so strong, so proud was this empire, that no one dreamed it could ever be subverted. With all the miseries of the people, with that hateful demoralization which pervaded all classes and orders and interests, there was still a splendid external, which called forth general panegyrics, and the idea of public danger was derided or discredited. If Rome, in the infancy of the republic, had resisted the invading Gauls, what was there to fear from the half-naked barbarians who lived beyond the boundaries of the empire ? The long-continued peace and prosperity had engendered not merely the vices of self-interest, those destructive cankers which ever insure a ruin, but a general feeling of security and self-exaggeration. The eternal city was still prosperous and proud, the centre of all that was grand in the civilization of the ancient world. Provincial cities vied with the capital in luxuries, in pomps, in sports, and in commercial wealth. The cultivated face of nature betokened universal prosperity. Nothing was wanting but energy, genius, and virtue among the people.

But all this prosperity was deceptive. All was rotten

and hollow at heart; and, had there not been universal delusion, it would have been apparent that the machine would break up at the first great shock. There was no spring in the splendid mechanism. It was broken, and society had really been retrograding from the time of Trajan — from the moment that it had completed its task of conquest. There was a strange torpor everywhere, so soon as external antagonism had ceased, and if the barbarians had not come the empire would have been disintegrated, and would scarcely have lasted two centuries longer.

Prosperity deceptive.

Moreover, the empire had fulfilled its mission. It had conquered the world that a great centralization of power might be created, under which peace and plenty might reign, and a new religion might spread.

The empire had fulfilled its mission.

Still, whatever the plans of Providence may have been in allowing that imperial despotism to grow and spread from the banks of the Tiber to the uttermost parts of the civilized world, we cannot but feel that a great retribution was deserved for the crimes which Rome had committed upon mankind. He that takes the sword shall perish with the sword. Rome had drank of the blood of millions, and was foul with all the abominations of the countries she had subdued, and her turn must come, and a new race must try new experiments for humanity.

The great instrument of God in punishing wicked nations and effecting important changes, is war. There are other forms of divine displeasure. Plague, pestilence, and famine are often sent upon degraded peoples. But these are either the necessary attendants on war itself, or they are limited and transient. They do not produce the great revolutions in which new ideas are born and new forms of social life arise.

War the instrument of punishment.

But war seems to be the ultimate scourge of God, when he dooms nations to destruction, or to great changes. It combines within itself all kinds of evil and calamity —

poverty, sickness, captivity, disgrace, and death. A conquered nation is most forlorn and dismal. The song of the conquered is — "By the rivers of Babylon we sat down and wept."

The passions which produce war are born in hell. They are pride, ambition, cruelty, avarice, and lust. These are the natural causes which array nation against nation, or people against people. But these are second causes. The primary cause is God, who useth the passions and interests of men, as his instruments of punishment.

Illustrated by the history of nations.

How impressive the history of the different civilized nations, which formed so large a part of the universal monarchy of the Romans. Assyria, Egypt, Persia, Asia Minor, Palestine, Greece, had successively been great empires and states — independent and conquering. They arose from the prevalence of martial virtues, of courage, temperance, fortitude, allied with ambition and poverty. Then monarchs craved greater power and possessions. Their passions were inexcusable; but they possessed men who were powerful and not enslaved to enervating vices. They made war on nations sunk in effeminacy and vile idolatries — men worse than they. The conquered nations needed chastisement and reconstruction; and, generally, by their blindness and arrogance, provoked the issue. Wealth and power had inflated them with false security, with egotistic aims; or else had enervated them and undermined their strength. They became subject to a stronger power. Their pride was buried in the dust. They became enslaved, miserable, ruined. They were punished in as signal, though not miraculous manner, as the Antediluvians, or the cities of Sodom and Gomorrah. The same hand, *however*, is seen in vengeance and in mercy. They regained in adversity the strength they had lost in prosperity, and civilization lost nothing by their sufferings.

The conquering powers, in their turn, became powerful,

wealthy, and corrupt. Effeminacy and weakness succeeded; war came upon them, and they became the prey of the stronger. Their conquerors, again, were enslaved by their vices, and their empire passed away in the same gloom and despair.

Wars overruled.

We see, however, in each successive conquest, the destruction, not of civilization, but of men. Countries are overrun, thrones are subverted, the rich are made slaves, the proud utter cries of despair; but the land survives, and arts and science take a new direction, and the new masters are more interested in great improvements than the old tyrants. The condition of Babylonia was probably better for the Persian conquest, while the whole oriental world gained by the wars of Alexander. Grecian culture succeeded Persian misrule. The Romans came and took away from Grecian dynasties, in Asia and Egypt, when they became enfeebled by prosperity and self-indulgence, the powers they had usurped, without destroying Grecian civilization. That remained, and will remain, in some form, forever, as an heirloom of priceless value to all future nations. The Greeks, when they conquered the Persians, had also spared the most precious monuments of their former industry and genius. The Romans, also, when they conquered Greece itself, guarded and prized her peculiar contributions to mankind. And they gave to all these conquered territories, something of their own. They gave laws, and a good government. The Grecian and Asiatic cities were humiliated by what they regarded as barbaric inroads; for the culture of Athens, Corinth, Antioch, and Ephesus, was higher than that of Rome, at that time; but who can doubt a beneficent change in the administration of public affairs? Society was doubtless improved everywhere by the Roman conquests. It is not probable that Athens, after she became tributary to Rome, was equal to the Athens of Pericles and Plato; but it is probable that society in Athens was better than what it was for a century before her fall. But what if particular cities suffered? These did not constitute the whole country. Can it be doubted that Syria, as a province, enjoyed more rational liberty and more scope for energy, under the Roman rule, than under that of the degenerate scions of the old Grecian kings? We see a retribution in the conquest, and also a blessing in disguise.

The Celtic nations.

But still more forcibly are these truths illustrated in the conquest of the Celtic nations of Europe. They were barbarians; they had neither science, nor literature, nor art; they were given over to perpetual quarrels, and to rude pleasures. Ignorance, superstition, and unrestrained passions were the main features of society. Other rude warriors wandered from place to place, with no other end than pillage. They had fine elements of character, but they needed civilization. They were conquered. The Romans taught them laws, and language, and literature, and arts. Cities arose among them, and these conquered barbarians became the friends of order and peace, and formed the most prosperous part of the whole empire. It was from these Celtic nations that the Roman armies were recruited. The great men of Rome, in the second and third centuries, came from these Celtic provinces. They infused a new blood into the decaying body. Who can doubt the benefit to mankind by the conquests of Britain, of Gaul, and of Spain? The Romans proved the greatest civilizers of the ancient world, with all their arrogance and want of appreciation of those things which gave a glory to the Greeks. They introduced among the barbaric nations their own arts, language, literature, and laws; and the civilization which they taught never passed away. It was obscured, indeed, during the revolutions which succeeded the fall of the empire, but it was gradually revived, and beamed with added lustre when its merits were at last perceived.

Thus wars are not an unmixed calamity, since the evils

are overruled in the ultimate good of nations. But they are a great calamity for the time, and they are sent when nations most need chastisement.

The Romans triumphed, by their great and unexampled energy and patience and heroism, over all the world, and erected their universal empire upon the ruins of all the states of antiquity. They were suffered to increase and prosper, that great ends might be accomplished, either by the punishment of the old nations, or the creation of a new civilization.

Conquest of the Celts.

But they, in their turn, became corrupted by prosperity, and enervated by peace. They had been guilty of the most heartless and cruel atrocities for eight hundred years. Their empire was built upon the miseries of mankind. They also must needs suffer retribution.

It was long delayed. It did not come till every conservative influence had failed. The condition of society was becoming worse and worse, until it reached a depravity and an apathy fatal to all genius, and more disgraceful than among those people whom they stigmatized as barbarians. Then must come revolution, or races would run out and civilization be lost.

God sent war — universal, cruel, destructive war, at the hands of unknown warriors; and they effected a total eclipse of the glory of man. The empire was resolved into its original elements. Its lands were overrun and pillaged; its cities were burned and robbed; and unmitigated violence overspread the earth, so that the cry of despair ascended to heaven, from the Pillars of Hercules to the Caspian Sea. Indeed, the end of the world was so generally believed to be at hand, on this universal upturning of society, that some of the best men fled to caves and deserts; and there were more monks that sought personal salvation by their austerities, than soldiers who braved their lives in battle.

Barbaric conquests.

It is this great revolution which I seek to present, this

great catastrophe to which the Romans were subjected, after having conquered one hundred and twenty millions of people. It was probably the most mournful, in all its aspects, ever seen on the face of this earth since the universal deluge. Never, surely, were such calamities produced by the hand of man. The Greeks and Romans, when they had conquered a rebellious or enervated nation, introduced their civilization, and promoted peace and general security. They brought laws, science, literature, and arts, in the train of their armies; they did not sweep away ancient institutions; they left the people as they found them, only with greater facilities of getting rich; they preserved the pictures, the statues, and the temples; they honored the literature and revered the sages who taught it; they may have brought captives to their capitals as slaves, but they did not root out every trace of cultivation, or regarded it with haughty scorn. But, when their turn of punishment came, the whole world was filled with mourning and desolation, and all the relations of society were reversed.

Infatuation of the Romans.

It was a sad hour in the old capital of the world, when its blinded inhabitants were aroused from the stupendous delusion that they were invincible; when the crushing fact stared every one in the face, that the legions had been conquered, that province after province had been overrun, that proud and populous cities had fallen, that the barbarians were advancing, treading beneath their feet all that had been deemed valuable, or rare, or sacred, that they were advancing to the very gates of Rome, — that her doom was sealed, that there was no shelter to which they could fly, that there was no way by which ruin could be averted, that they were doomed to hopeless poverty or servitude, that their wives and daughters would be subject to indignities which were worse than death, and that all the evils their ancestors had inflicted in their triumphant march, would be visited upon them with tenfold severity. The Romans, even then, when they cast their eyes upon external nature, saw rich corn-fields, smiling vineyards, luxurious gardens, yea, villas and temples and palaces without end; and how could these be destroyed which had lasted for centuries? How could the eternal city, which had not seen a foreign enemy near its gates since the invasion of the Gauls, which had escaped all dangers, so rich and gay, how could she now yield to naked barbarians from unknown forests? They still beheld the splendid mechanism of government, the glitter and the pomp of armies, triumphal processions, new monuments of victory, the proud eagles, and all the emblems of unlimited dominion. What had *they* to fear? "*Nihil est, Quirites, quod timere possitis.*"

Fatal security of the Romans.

Nor to the eye of contemporaries was the great change, which had gradually taken place since the reign of Trajan, apparent. Cowardice and weakness were veiled from the view of men. In proportion to the imbecility of the troops, were the richness of their uniform, and the insolence of their manners. It was the day of boasts and pomps. All forms and emblems had their ancient force. All men partook of the vices and follies which were praised. In their levity and delusion, they did not see the real emptiness and hollowness of their institutions. A blinded generation never can see the signs of the times. Only a few contemplative men hid themselves in retired places, but were denounced as croakers or evil minded. Every body was interested in keeping up the delusion. Panics seldom last long. The world is too fond of its ease to believe the truths which break up reposo and gains. All felt safe, because they had always been protected. Ruin might come ultimately, but not in their day. "*Apres moi le deluge.*" No one would make sacrifices, since no one feared immediate danger. Moreover, public spirit and patriotism had fled. If their cities were in danger, they said, better perish here with our wives and children than die on the frontiers after having suffered every privation and exposure. There must have been a universal indifference, or the barbarians could not have triumphed. The Romans had every inducement which any people ever had to a brave and desperate resistance. Not merely their own lives, but the security of their families was at stake. Their institutions, their interests, their rights, their homes, their altars, all were in jeopardy. And they were attacked by most merciless enemies, without pity or respect, and yet they would not fight, as nations should fight, and do sometimes fight, when their country is invaded. Why did they offer no more stubborn resistance? Why did the full-armed and well-trained legions yield to barbaric foes, without discipline and without the most effective weapons? Alas, dispirited and enervated people will never fight. They prefer slavery to death. Thus Persia succumbed before Alexander, and Asia Minor before the Saracen generals. Martial courage goes hand in hand with virtue. Without elevation of sentiment there will be no self-sacrifice. There is no hope when nations are abandoned to sensuality or egotism.

Weakness of the empire.

We must believe in a most extraordinary degeneracy of society, or Rome would not have fallen. With any common degree of courage, the empire should have resisted the Goths and Vandals. They were not more numerous than those hordes which Marius and Cæsar annihilated even in their own marshes and forests. It was not like the Macedonians, with their impenetrable phalanx, and their perfected armor, contending with semi-barbarians. It was not like the Spaniards, marching over Peru and Mexico. It was not like the English, with all the improved weapons of our modern times, firing upon a people armed with darts and arrows. But it was barbarians, without defensive armor, without discipline, without prestige, attacking legions which had been a thousand years learning the art of war. *Proh Pudor!* The soldiers of the empire must have lost their ancient spirit. They must have represented a most worthless people. We lose our pity in the strength of our indignation and disgust. A civilized nation that will yield to barbarians must deserve their fate. Nóble as were the elements of character among the Germanic tribes, they were yet barbarians in arts, in manners, in knowledge, in mechanisms. They had nothing but brute force. Science should have conquered brute force ; but it did not. We cannot but infer a most startling degeneracy. It is to be regretted that we have no more satisfactory data as to the precise state of society. I am inclined to the opinion that society was much more degraded than it is generally supposed. When for two centuries the whole empire scarcely produced a poet, or a philosopher, or an historian ; when even the writings of famous men in the time of Augustus were lost or unread ; when, from Trajan to Honorius, a period of three hundred and fifty years, scarcely a work of original genius appeared, it must be that society was utterly demoralized, and all life and vigor had fled.

Conquerors of Rome.

Then it was time for the empire to fall. And it is our work to sketch the ruin — and such a ruin. The bloody conquerors were Goths and Vandals, and other Teutonic tribes — Franks, Sueves, Alans, Heruli, Burgundians, Lombards, Saxons. They came originally from Central Asia, in the region of the Caspian Sea, and were kindred to the Medes and Persians. They drove before them older inhabitants, probably Celtic nations, and ultimately settled in the vast region between the Baltic and the Danube, the Rhine and the Vistula, embracing those countries which are now called Norway, Sweden, Denmark, and Germany.

All these tribes were probably similar in manners, habits, tastes, and natural elements of character. Tacitus has furnished us with the most authentic record of their customs and peculiarities.[1] Their eyes were stern and blue,

[1] Tacitus, *De Moribus Germanorum.*

their hair red, their bodies large, their strength great. They were ruled by kings, but not with unlimited power. The priests had also an extraordinary influence, which they shared with the women, who were present in battles, and who were characterized for great purity and courage. Even the power to predict the future was ascribed to women.

The Germanic nations. The Germans were superstitious, and were given to divinations by omens and lots, by the flight of birds and the neighing of horses. They transacted no business, public or private, without being armed. They were warlike in all their habits and tastes, and the field of battle was the field of glory. Their chief deity was an heroic prince. Odin, the type-man of the nation, was a wild captain, who taught that it was most honorable to die in battle. They hated repose and inactivity, and, when not engaged in war, they pursued with eagerness the pleasures of the chase; yet, during the intervals of war and hunting, they divided their time between sleeping and feasting. They loved the forests, and dangerous sports, and adventurous enterprises. They abhorred cities, which they regarded as prisons of despotism. A rude passion for personal independence was one of their chief characteristics, as powerful as veneration for the women and religious tendency of mind. They would brook no restraint on their wills or their passions. Their wills were stern and their passions impetuous. They only yielded to the voice of entreaty or of love. They were ordinarily temperate, except on rare occasions, when they indulged in drunken festivities. Chastity was a virtue which was rigorously practiced. There were few cases of adultery among them, and the unfaithful wife was severely punished. Men and women, without seductive spectacles or convivial banquets, were fenced around with chastity, and bound together by family ties. Polygamy was unknown, and the marriage obligation was sacred. The wife brought no dowry to her husband, but received one from him, not frivolous presents, but oxen, a caparisoned steed, a shield, spear, and sword, to indicate that she is to be a partner in toil and danger, to suffer and to dare in peace and war. Hospitality was another virtue, extended equally to strangers and acquaintances, but, at the festive board, quarrels often took place, and enmities once formed were rarely forgiven. Vindictive resentments were as marked as cordial and frank friendships. They drank beer or ale, instead of wine, at their feasts, although their ordinary drink was water. Their food was fruits, cheese, milk, and venison. They had an inordinate passion for gambling, and would even stake their very freedom on a throw. Slavery was common, but not so severe and ruthless as among the Romans. They had but little commerce, and were unacquainted with the arts of usury. Their agriculture was rude, and corn was the only product they raised. They had the ordinary domestic animals, but their horses were neither beautiful nor swift.

The native elements of character of the barbarians.

It is easy to see that, in their manners and traits, they had a great resemblance to the Celts, before they were subdued and civilized, but were not so passionate, nor impulsive, nor thoughtless, nor reckless as they. Nor were they so much addicted to gluttony and drunkenness. They were more persevering, more earnest, more truthful, and more chaste. Nor were they so much enslaved by the priesthood. The Druidical rule was confined to the Celts, yet, like the Celts, they worshiped God in the consecrated grove. Their religion was pantheistic: they saw God in the rocks, the rain, the thunder, the clouds, the rivers, the mountains, the stars. He was supposed to preside everywhere, and to be a supreme intelligence. Their view of God was quite similar to the early Ionic philosophers of Greece: "*Regnator omnium deus, cœtera subjecta atque parentia.*" They were never idol-worshipers; they worshiped nature, and called its wonders gods. But this worship of nature was modified by the worship of a hero. In Odin they beheld strength, courage, magnanimity, the attributes they adored. To be brave was an elemental principle of religion, and they attributed to the Deity every thing which could inspire horror as the terrible, — the angry god who marked out those destined to be slain. Hence their groves, where he was supposed to preside, were dark and mysterious. We adore the gloom of woods, the silence which reigns around. "*Lucos, atque in iis silentia, ipsa adoremus.*" While the priests of this awful being were not so despotic as the Druids, they still exercised a great ascendency: they conjured the storms of internal war; they pronounced the terrible anathema; they imparted to military commanders a sacred authority; and they carried at the head of their armies the consecrated banner of the Deity. In short, they wielded those spiritual weapons which afterward became thunderbolts in the hands of the clergy, and which prepared the way for the autocratic reign of the popes, in whom the Germanic nations ever recognized the vicegerent of their invisible Lord. They were most preëminently a religious people, governed by religious ideas — by which I mean they recognized a deity to whose will they were to be obedient, and whose favor could only be purchased by deeds of valor or virtue. Their morality sprung out of veneration for the Great Unseen, in whose hands were their destinies.

This trait is the most remarkable and prominent among the Germans, next to their fierce passion for war, their veneration for woman, and their love of personal independence, to which last Guizot attaches great importance. The feeling one's self a man in the most unrestricted sense, was the highest pleasure of the German barbarian. There was a personality of feeling and interest hostile to social forms and municipal regulations. They cared for nothing beyond the gratification of their inclinations. To be unrestrained, to be free in the wildest sense, to do what they pleased under the impulse of the moment, this was their leading characteristic. Who cannot see that such a trait was hostile to civilization, and would prevent obedience to law — would make the uncultivated warrior unsocial and solitary, and lead him, in after-times, when he got possession of the lands of the conquered Romans, to build his castle on inaccessible heights and rugged rocks? Hence isolated retreats, wild adventures, country life, the pleasures of the chase, characterized the new settlers. They avoided cities, and built castles.

National traits.

This passion for liberty, accompanied with the spirit of daring, adventure, and war, would have been fatal but for the rule of priests, and the great influence of woman. In this latter element of character, the barbarians from Scandinavia stand out in interesting contrast with the civilized nations whom they subverted. They evidently had a greater respect for woman than any of the nations of antiquity, not excepting the Jews. In her they beheld something sacred and divine. In her voice was inspiration, and in her presence there was safety. There was no true enthusiasm for woman in Greece even when Socrates bowed before the charms of Aspasia. There was none at Rome when Volumnia screened the city from the vengeance of her angry son. But the Germans worshiped the fair, and beheld in her the incarnation of all virtue and loveliness. And thus, among such a race, arose the glorious old institution of chivalry, which could not have existed among the Romans or the Greeks, even after Christianity had softened the character and enlarged the heart. In the baronial mansion of the Middle Ages this natural veneration was ripened into devotion and gallantry. Among the knights, zeal for God and the ladies was enjoined as a single duty; and "he who was faithful to his mistress," says Hallam, "was sure of salvation, in the theology of castles, if not of cloisters." This devotion was expressed in the rude poetry of barba-

Character of the Germanic nations.

rous ages, in the sports of the tournament and tilt, in the feasts of the castle, in the masculine pleasures of the chase, in the control of the household, in the education of children, in the laws which recognized equality, in the free companionship with man, in the trust reposed in female honor and virtue, in the delicacy of love, and in the refinements of friendship. This trait alone shows the superior nature of the Germanic races, especially when taught by Christianity, and makes us rejoice that the magnificent conquests of the Romans were given to them for their proud inheritance.

Such were the men who became the heirs of the Romans, — races never subdued by arms or vices, among whom Christianity took a peculiar hold, and gradually developed among them principles of progress such as were never seen among the older nations. Can we wonder that such men should prevail? — men who loved war as the Romans did under the republic; men who gloried in their very losses, and felt that death in the field would secure future salvation and everlasting honor; men full of hope, energy, enthusiasm, and zeal; men who had, what the old races had not, — a soul, life, uncorrupted forces.

Yet, when they invaded the Roman world, it must not be forgotten that they were rude, ignorant, wild, fierce, and unscrupulous. They were held in absolute detestation, as the North American Indians, whom they resembled in many important respects, were held in this country two hundred years ago. Their object was pillage. They roamed in search of more fruitful lands and a more congenial sky. They were bent on conquest, rapine, and violence. They were called the Northern Hordes — barbarians — and even their vices were exaggerated. They were, indeed, most formidable and terrific foes; and when conquered in battle would rally their forces, and press forward with renewed numbers.

The first of these Teutonic barbarians who made successful inroads were the Goths. I do not now allude to the Celtic nations who were completely subdued and incorporated with the empire before the accession of the emperors. Nor do I speak of the Teutons whom Marius defeated one hundred years before the Christian era, nor yet of the Germanic tribes who made unsuccessful inroads during the reigns of the earlier emperors. Augustus must have had melancholy premonitions of danger when his general, Varus, suffered a disgraceful defeat by the sword of Arminus in the dark recesses of the Teuto-burger Wald, even as Charlemagne covered his face with his iron hands when he saw the invasion of his territories by the Norman pirates. For three centuries there was a constant struggle between the Roman armies and the barbarians beyond the Rhine. In the reign of Marcus Antoninus they formed a general union for the invasion of the Roman world, but they were signally defeated, and the great pillar of Marcus Aurelius describes his victories on the Danube, who died combating the Vandals, A. D. 180. In the year 241 A. D., the great Aurelian is seen fighting the Franks near Mayence, who, nevertheless, pressed forward until they made their way into Spain.

The Goths.

The most formidable of the enemies of Rome were the Goths. When first spoken of in history they inhabited the shores of the Baltic. They were called by Tacitus, Gothones. In the time of Caracalla they had migrated to the coast of the Black Sea. Under the reign of Alexander Severus, 222–235, A. D., they threatened the peace of the province of Dacia. Under Philip, A. D. 244–249, they succeeded in conquering that province, and penetrated into Mœsia. In the year 251, they encountered a Roman army under Decius, which they annihilated, and the emperor himself was slain. Then they continued their ravages along the coasts of the Euxine until they made themselves masters of the Crimea. With a large fleet of flat-boats they sailed to all the north-

Invasion of the Goths.

ern parts of the Euxine, took Pityus and Trapezus, attacked the wealthy cities on the Thracian Bosphorus, conquered Chalcedon, Nicomedia, and Nice, and retreated laden with spoil. The next year, with five hundred boats — they cannot be called ships, — they pursued their destructive navigation, destroyed Cyzicus, crossed the Ægean Sea, and landed at Athens, which they plundered. Thebes, Argos, Corinth, and Sparta were unable to defend their dilapidated fortifications. They advanced to the coasts of Epirus and devastated the whole Illyrian peninsula. In this destructive expedition they destroyed the famous temple of Diana at Ephesus, with its one hundred and twenty-seven marble columns sixty feet in height, and its interior ornamented with the choicest sculptures of Praxiteles. But they at length got wearied of danger and toil, and returned through Mœsia to their own settlements. Though this incursion was a raid rather than a conquest, yet what are we to think of the military strength of the empire and the condition of society, when, in less than three hundred years after Augustus had shut the temple of Janus, fifteen thousand undisciplined barbarians, without even a leader of historic fame, were allowed to ravage the most populous and cultivated part of the empire, even the classic cities which had resisted the Persian hosts, and retire unmolested with their spoils? The Emperor Gallienus, one of the most frivolous of all the Cæsars, received the intelligence with epicurean indifference, and abandoned himself to inglorious pleasures; and as Nero is said to have fiddled while his capital was in ashes, so he, in this great emergency, consumed his time in gardening and the arts of cookery, and was commended by his idolatrous courtiers as a philosopher and a hero.

In fact, this invasion of the Goths was not contemplated with that alarm which it ought to have excited, but rather as an accidental evil, like a pestilence or a plague. Moreover, it was lost sight of in the general misery and misfortunes of the times. The Emperor Valerian had just been defeated and taken prisoner by Sapor. Pretenders had started up in nineteen different places for the imperial purple. Banditti had spread devastation in Sicily. Alexandria was disturbed by tumults. Famine and the plague raged for ten years in nearly all parts of the empire. Rome lost by the pestilence five thousand daily, while half the inhabitants of Alexandria were swept away. Soldiers, tyrants, barbarians, and the visitation of God threatened the ruin of the Roman world.

But the ruin was staved off one hundred years by the labors and genius of a series of great princes, who traced their origin to the martial province of Illyricum. And all that was in the power of the emperors to do was done to arrest destruction. No empire was ever ruled by a succession of better and greater men than the calamities of the times raised up on the death of Gallienus, A. D. 268. But what avail the energy and talents of rulers when a nation is doomed to destruction? We have the profoundest admiration for the imperial heroes who bore the burdens of a throne in those days of tribulation. They succeeded in restoring the ancient glories — but glories followed by a deeper shame. They attempted impossibilities when their subjects were sunk in sloth and degradation.

Success and defeat of the Goths.

Claudius, one of the generals of Gallienus, was invested with the purple at the age of fifty-four. He restored military discipline, revived law, repressed turbulence, and bent his thoughts to head off the barbaric invasions. The various nations of Germany and Sarmatia, united under the Gothic standard, and in six thousand vessels, prepared once more to ravage the world. Sailing from the banks of the Dniester, they crossed the Euxine, passed through the Bosphorus, anchored at the foot of Mount Athos, and assaulted Thessalonica, the wealthy capital of the Macedonian provinces. Claudius advanced to meet these three hundred and twenty thousand barbarians. At Naissus, in Dalmatia, was fought one of the most memorable and bloody battles of ancient times, but not one of the most decisive. Fifty thousand Goths were slain in that dreadful fight. Three Gothic women fell to the share of every imperial soldier. The discomfited warriors fled in consternation, but their retreat was cut off by the destruction of their fleet; and on the return of spring the mighty host had dwindled to a desperate band in the inaccessible parts of Mount Hemus.

Claudius survived his victory but two years, and was succeeded, A. D. 270, by a still greater man — his general Aurelian, whose father had been a peasant of Sirmium. Every day of his short reign was filled with wonders. He put an end to the Gothic war; he chastised the Germans who invaded Italy; he recovered Gaul, Spain, and Britain, from the hands of an usurper; he destroyed the proud monarchy which Zenobia had built up in the deserts of the East; he defeated the Alemanni who, with eighty thousand foot and forty thousand horse, had devastated the country from the Danube to the Po; and, not least, he took Zenobia herself a prisoner — one of the most celebrated women of antiquity, equaling Cleopatra in beauty, Elizabeth in learning, and Artemisia in valor — a woman who blended the popular manners of the Roman princes with the stately pomp of oriental kings.

Victories of Claudius.

Zenobia, queen of Palmyra, the widow of Odenatus, ruled a large portion of Asia Minor, Syria, and Egypt, and with a numerous army she advanced to meet the imperial legions. Conquered in two disastrous battles, she retired to the beautiful city which Solomon had built, shaded with palms, ornamented with palaces, and rich in oriental treasure. Then again, attacked by her persevering enemy, she mounted the fleetest of her dromedaries, but was overtaken on the banks of the Euphrates, and brought a captive to the tent of the martial emperor, while Palmyra, her capital, with all its riches, fell into the hands of the conqueror.

Aurelian, with the haughty queen who had presumed to rise up in arms against the empire, returned to Rome, and then was celebrated the most magnificent triumph which the world had seen since the days of Pompey and of Cæsar. And since the foundation of the city, no conqueror more richly deserved a triumph than this virtuous and rugged soldier of fortune. And as the august procession, with all the pomp and circumstance of war, moved along the Via Sacra, up the Capitoline Hill, and halted at the Temple of Jupiter, to receive the benediction of the priests, and to deposit within its sacred walls the treasures of the East, it would seem that Rome was destined to surmount the ordinary fate of nations, and reign as mistress of the world *per secula seculorum.*

Successes of Aurelian.

But this grand pageant was only one of the last glories of the setting sun of Roman greatness. Aurelian had no peace or repose. "The gods decree," said the impatient emperor, "that my life should be a perpetual warfare." He was obliged to take the field a few months after his triumph, and was slain, not in battle, but by the hands of assassins — the common fate of his predecessors and successors — "the regular portal" through which the Cæsars passed to their account with the eternal Judge. He had boasted that public danger had passed — "*Ego efficiam ne sit aliqua solicitudo Romana. Nos publicæ necessitates teneant; vos occupent voluptates.*" But scarcely had this warlike prince sung his requiem to the agitations of Rome before new dangers arose, and his sceptre descended to a man seventy-five years of age.

Tacitus, the new emperor, was however worthy of his throne. He was selected as the most fitting man that could be found. Scarcely was he inaugurated, before he was obliged to march against the Alans, who had spread their destructive ravages over Pontus, Cappadocia, Cilicia, and Galatia. He lost his life, though successful in battle, amid the hardships of a winter campaign, and Probus, one of his generals, who had once been an Illyrian peasant, was clothed with the imperial purple, A. D. 278.

The successes of Probus.

This vigorous monarch was then forty-five years of age, in the prime of his strength, popular with the army, and patriotic and enlarged in his views. He reigned six years, and won a fame equal to that of the ancient heroes. He restored peace and order in every province of the empire ; he broke the power of the Sarmatian tribes ; he secured the alliance of the Gothic nation ; he drove the Isaurians to their strongholds among the mountains ; he chastised the rebellious cities of Egypt ; he delivered Gaul from the Germanic barbarians, who again inundated the empire on the death of Aurelian ; he drove back the Franks into their morasses at the mouth of the Rhine ; he vanquished the Burgundians, who had wandered in quest of booty from the banks of the Oder ; he defeated the Lygii, a fierce tribe from the frontiers of Silesia, and took their chieftain Semno alive ; he passed the Rhine and pursued his victories to the Elbe, exacting a tribute of corn, cattle, and horses, from the defeated Germans ; he even erected a bulwark against their future encroachments — a stone wall of two hundred miles in length, across valleys and hills and rivers, from the Danube to the Rhine — a feeble defense indeed, but such as to excite the wonder of his age ; he, moreover, dispersed the captive barbarians throughout the provinces, who were afterward armed in defense of the empire, and whose brethren were persuaded to make settlements with them, so that, at length, " there was not left in all the provinces," says Gibbon, " a hostile barbarian, a tyrant, or even a robber."

After having destroyed four hundred thousand barbarians, the victor returned to Rome, and, like Aurelian, celebrated his successes in one of those gorgeous triumphs to which modern nations have no parallel. Then he again, like the conqueror of Zenobia, mounted the Pisgah of hope, and descried the Saturnian ages which, in his vision of Peace, he fancied were to follow his victories. "*Respublica orbis terrarum, ubique secura, non arma fabricabit. Boves habebuntur aratro; equus nasciter ad pacem. Nulla erunt bella; nulla captivitas. Æternos thesauros haberet Romana respublica.*" But scarcely had the pæans escaped him, before, in his turn, he was assassinated in a mutiny of his own troops — a man of virtue and abilities, although his austere temper insensibly, under military power, subsided into tyranny and cruelty.

Without the approbation of the Senate, the soldiers elected a new emperor, and he too was a hero. Carus had scarcely assumed the purple, A. D. 282, before he marched against the Persians, through Thrace and Asia Minor, in the midst of winter, and the ambassadors of the Persian king found the new emperor of the world seated on the grass, at a frugal dinner of bacon and pease, in that severe simplicity which afterward marked the early successors of Mohammed. But before he could carry his victorious arms across the Tigris, he suddenly died in his tent, struck, as some think, by lightning. His son Carinus was unworthy of the throne to which he succeeded, and his reign is chiefly memorable for the magnificence of his games and festivals. His reign, and that of his brother Numerian, was however short, and a still greater man than any who had mounted the throne of the Cæsars since Augustus, took the helm at the most critical period of Roman history, A. D. 285.

Diocletian.

This man was Diocletian, rendered infamous in ecclesiastical history, as the most bitter persecutor the Christians ever had; a man of obscure birth, yet of most distinguished abilities, and virtually the founder of a new empire. He found it impossible to sustain the public burdens in an age so disordered and disorganized, when every province was menaced by the barbarians, and he associated with himself three colleagues who had won fame in the wars of Aurelian and Carus, and all of whom had rendered substantial services — Galerius, Maximian, and Constantius. These four Cæsars, alive to the danger which menaced the empire, took up their residence in the distant provinces. They were all great generals; and they won great victories on the banks of the Rhine and the Danube, in Africa and Egypt, in Persia and Armenia. Their lives were spent in the camp; but care, vexation, and discontent pursued them. The barbarians were continually beaten, but they continually advanced. Their progress reminds one of the rising tide on a stormy and surging beach. Wave after wave breaks upon the shore, recedes, returns, and nothing can stop the gradual advance of the waters. So in the hundred years after Gallienus, wave after wave of barbaric invasion constantly appeared, receded, returned, with added strength. The heroic emperors were uniformly victors; but their victories were in vain. They were perpetually reconquering rebellious provinces, or putting down usurpers, or punishing the barbarians, who acquired strength after every defeat, and were more and more insatiable in their demands, and unrelenting in their wills. They were determined to conquer, and the greatest generals of the Roman empire during four hundred years could not subdue them, although they could beat them.

Constantine.

The empire is again united under Constantine, after bloody civil wars, A. D. 324, thirty-four years after Diocletian had divided his power and provinces with his associates. He renews the war against the Goths and Sarmatians, severely chastises them as well as other enemies of Rome, and dies leaving the empire to his son, unequal to the task imposed upon him. The inglorious reigns of Constantius and Gallus only enabled the barbarians to renew their strength. They are signally defeated by the Emperor Julian, A. D. 360, who alone survives of all the heirs of Constantius Chlorus. The studious Julian, who was supposed to be a mere philosopher, proves himself to be one of the most warlike of all the emperors. He repulses the Alemanni, defeats the Franks, delivers Gaul, and carries the Roman eagles triumphantly beyond the Rhine. His victories delay the ruin of the empire; they do not result in the conquest of Germany, and he dies, mortally wounded, not by a German spear, but by the javelin of a Persian horseman, beyond the Tigris, in an unsuccessful enterprise against Sapor, A. D. 363.

After his death the ravages of the barbarians became still more fearful. The Alemanni invade Gaul, A. D. 365, the Persians recover Armenia, the Burgundians appear upon the Rhine, the Saxons attack Britain, and spread themselves from the Wall of Antoninus to the shores of Kent, the Goths prepare for another invasion; in Africa there is a great revolt under Firmus. The empire is shaken to its centre.

New invasions of barbarians.

Valentinian, a soldier of fortune, and an able general, now wears the imperial purple. Like Diocletian, he finds himself unable to bear the burdens of his throne. He elects an associate, divides the empire, and gives to Valens the eastern provinces. All idea of reigning in peace, and giving the reins to pleasure, has vanished from the imperial mind. The office of emperor demands the severest virtues and the sternest qualities and the most incessant labors. "Uneasy sits the head that wears a crown," can now be said of all the later emperors. The day is past for enjoyment or for pomp. The emperor's presence is required here and there. Valentinian rules with vigor, and gains successes over the barbarians. He is one of the great men of the day. He reserves to himself the western provinces, and fixes his seat at Milan, but cannot preserve tranquillity, and dies in a storm of wrath, by the bursting of a blood-vessel, while reviling the ambassadors of the Quadi, A. D. 375, at the age of fifty-four.

His brother, Valens, Emperor of the East, had neither his talents nor energy; and it was his fate to see the first great successful inroads of the Goths. For thirty years the Romans had secured their frontiers, and the Goths had extended their dominions. Hermanric, the first historic name of note among them, ruled over the entire nation, and had won a series of brilliant victories over other tribes of barbarians after he was eighty years of age. His dominions extended from the Danube to the Baltic, including the greater part of Germany and Scythia. In the year 366 his subjects, tempted by the civil discords which Procopius occasioned, invaded Thrace, but were resisted by the generals of Valens. The aged Hermanric was exasperated by the misfortune, and made preparations for a general war, while the emperor himself invaded the Gothic territories. For three years the war continued, with various success, on the banks of the Danube. Hermanric intrusted the defense of his country to Athanaric, who was defeated in a bloody battle, and a hollow peace was made with Victor and Arintheus, the generals of Valens. The Goths remained in tranquillity for six years, until, driven by the Scythians, who emerged in vast numbers from the frozen regions of the north, they once more advanced to the Danube and implored the aid of Valens.[1] The prayers of the Goths were answered, and they were transported across the Danube — a suicidal act of the emperor, which imported two hundred thousand warriors, with their wives and children, into the Roman territories. The Goths retained their arms and their greed, and pretended to settle peaceably in the province of Mœsia. But they were restless and undisciplined barbarians, and it required the greatest adroitness to manage them in their new abodes. They were insolent and unreasonable in their demands and expectations, while the ministers of the emperor were oppressive and venal. Difficulties soon arose, and, too late, it was seen by the emperor that he had introduced most dangerous enemies into the heart of the empire.

Disasters of Valens

[1] See Ammianus Marcellinus, b. xxi., from which Gibbon has chiefly drawn his narratives.

The great leader of these Goths was Fritigern, who soon kindled the flames of war. He united under his standard all the various tribes of his nation, increased their animosities, and led them to the mouth of the Danube. There they were attacked by the lieutenants of Valens, and a battle was fought without other result than that of checking for a time the Gothic progress. But only for a time. The various tribes of barbarians, under the able generalship of Fritigern, whose cunning was equal to his bravery, advanced to the suburbs of Hadrianople. Under the walls of that city was fought the most disastrous battle, A. D. 378, to the imperial cause which is recorded in the annals of Roman history. The emperor himself was slain with two thirds of his whole army, while the remainder fled in consternation. Sixty thousand infantry and six thousand cavalry were stretched in death upon the bloody field — one third more than at the fatal battle of Cannæ. The most celebrated orator of the day, though a Pagan,[1] pronounced a funeral oration on the vanquished army, and attributed the catastrophe, not to the cowardice of the legions, but the anger of the gods. "The fury of the Goths," says St. Jerome, "extended to all creatures possessed of life: the beasts of the field, the fowls of the air, and the fishes of the sea." The victors, intoxicated with their first great success, invested Hadrianople, where were deposited enormous riches. But they were unequal to the task of taking so strong a city; and when the inhabitants aroused themselves in a paroxysm of despair, they raised the siege and departed to ravage the more unprotected West. Laden with spoils, they retired to the western boundaries of Thrace, and thence scattered their forces to the confines of Italy. From the shores of the Bosphorus to the Julian Alps nothing was to be seen but conflagration and murders and devastations. Churches were turned into stables, palaces were

Fritigern, leader of the Goths.

Death of the Emperor Valens.

[1] Libanius of Antioch.

burned, works of priceless value were destroyed, the relics of martyrs were desecrated, the most fruitful provinces were overrun, the population was decimated, the land was overgrown with forests, cultivation was suspended, and despair and fear seized the minds of all classes. So great was the misfortune of the Illyrian provinces that they never afterward recovered, and for ten centuries only supplied materials for roving robbers. The empire never had seen such a day of calamity.

Desperate condition of the Romans.

This melancholy state of affairs, so desperate and so general, demanded a deliverer and a hero; but where was a hero to be found? Nothing but transcendent ability could now arrest the overthrow. Who should succeed to the vacant throne of Valens?

Theodosius.

The Emperor Gratian, who wielded the sceptre of Valentinian in the West, in this alarming crisis, cast his eyes upon an exile, whose father had unjustly suffered death under his own sanction three years before. This man was Theodosius, then living in modest retirement on his farm in Spain, near Valladolid, as unambitious as David among his sheep, as contented as Cincinnatus at the plough. Great deliverers are frequently selected from the most humble positions; but no world hero, in ancient or modern times, is more illustrious than Theodosius for modesty and magnanimity united with great abilities. No man is dearer to the Church than he, both for his services and his virtues. The eloquent Fléchier has emblazoned his fame, as Bossuet has painted the Prince of Condé. Even Gibbon lays aside his sneers to praise this great Christian Emperor, although his character was not free from stains. He modestly but readily accepted the vacant sceptre and the conduct of the Gothic war. He was thirty-three years of age, in the pride of his strength, and well instructed in liberal pursuits. No better choice could have been made by Gratian. He was as prudent as Fabius, as magnanimous as Richard, as persevering as

His character and illustrious deeds.

Alfred, as comprehensive as Charlemagne, as beneficent as Henry IV., as full of resources as Frederic II. One of the greatest of all the emperors, and the last great man who swayed the sceptre of Trajan his ancestor, his reign cannot but be too highly commended, living in such an age, exposed to so many dangers, invested with so many difficulties. He was the last flickering light of the expiring monarchy, beloved and revered by all classes of his subjects. "The vulgar gazed with admiration on the manly beauty of his face and the graceful majesty of his person, which they were pleased to compare with the pictures and medals of the Emperor Trajan; while intelligent observers discovered, in the qualities of the heart and understanding, a more important resemblance to the best and greatest of the Roman emperors." [1]

Mr. Long, of Oxford, in a fine notice of Theodosius, thinks that the praises of Gibbon are extravagant, and that the emperor was probably a voluptuary and a persecutor. But Gibbon is not apt to praise the favorites of the Church. Tillemont presents him in the same light as Gibbon.[2] A man who could have submitted to such a penance as Ambrose imposed for the slaughter of Thessalonica, could not have been cast in a different mould from old David himself. For my part I admire his character and his deeds.

Soon as he was invested with the purple, he gave his undivided energies to the great task intrusted to him; but he never succeeded in fully revenging the battle of Hadrianople, which was one of the decisive battles of the world in its ultimate effects. He had the talents and the energy and the prudence, but he was beset with impossibilities. Still, he staved off ruin for a time. The death of Fritigern unchained the passions of the barbarians, and they would have been led to fresh revolts had they not submitted to the authority of Athanaric, whom the emperor invited to his capital and feasted at his table,

Defeat of the Goths.

1 Gibbon, chap. xxvi.

2 Tillemont, *Hist. des Emp.*, vol. v.

and astonished by his riches and glory. The Visigoths, won by the policy or courtesy of Theodosius, became subjects of the empire. The Ostrogoths, who had retired from the provinces of the Danube four years before, returned recruited with a body of Huns, and crossed the Danube to assail the Roman army, but were defeated by Theodosius; and a treaty was made with them, by which they were settled in Phrygia and Lydia. Forty thousand of them were kept in the service of the emperor; but they were doubtful allies, as subsequent events proved, even in the lifetime of the magnanimous emperor.[1]

Honorius and Arcadius.

Theodosius died at Milan in the arms of Ambrose, A. D. 395, and with his death the real drama of the fall of Rome begins. His empire was divided between his two sons, Honorius and Arcadius, who were unworthy or unequal to maintain their great inheritance. The barbarians, released from the restraint which the fear of Theodosius imposed, recommenced their combinations and their ravages, while the soldiers of the empire were dispirited and enervated. About this time they threw away their defensive armor, not able to bear the weight of the cuirass and the helmet; and even the heavy weapons of their ancestors, the short sword and the pilum, were supplanted by the bow, — a most remarkable retrograde in military art. Without defensive armor, not even the shield, they were exposed to the deadly missiles of their foes, and fled at the first serious attacks, especially of cavalry, in which the Goths and Huns excelled.

Alaric, king of the Visigoths.

History has taken but little notice of the leaders of the various tribes of barbarians until Alaric appeared, the leader of the Visigoths, the able successor of Fritigern. He belonged to the second noblest family of his nation, and first appears in history as a general of the Gothic auxiliaries in the war of Theodosius against Eugenius, A. D. 394. In 396, stimulated by anger or ambition,

[1] Zosimus, l. 4.

or the instigation of Rufinus,[1] he invaded Greece at the head of a powerful body, and devastated the country. He descended from the plains of Macedonia and Thessaly, and entered the classic land, which for a long time had escaped the ravages of war, through the pass of Thermopylæ. Degenerate soldiers, half armed, now defended the narrow passage where three hundred heroes had once arrested the march of the Persian hosts. But Greece was no longer Greece. The soldiers fled as Alaric advanced, and the fertile fields of Phocis and Bœotia were at once covered with hostile and cruel barbarians, who massacred the men and ravished the women in all the villages through which they passed. Athens purchased her preservation by an enormous ransom. Corinth, Argos, Sparta, yielded without a blow, but did not escape the fate of vanquished cities. Their palaces were burned, their works of art destroyed, their women subjected to indignities which were worse than death, and their families were enslaved.[2]

Only one hope remained to the feeble and intimidated Arcadius, and that was the skill and courage of Stilicho, by birth a Vandal, but who had risen in the imperial service until he was virtually intrusted by Theodosius with the guardianship of his sons and of the empire. He was the lieutenant of Honorius, who had espoused his daughter, but summoned by the dangers of Arcadius, he advanced to repulse the invaders of Greece, who had not met with any resistance from Thermopylæ to Corinth. A desperate campaign followed in the woody country where Pan and the Dryads were fabled to reside in the olden times. The Romans prevailed, and Alaric was in imminent peril of annihilation, but was saved by the too confident spirit of Stilicho, and his indulgence in the pleasures of the degenerate Greeks. He effected his release by piercing the lines of his besiegers and performing a rapid march to the Gulf of Corinth, where he embarked his soldiers, his captives,

Successes of the Goths.

1 Socrates, *Eccles. Hist.*, vii. 10.

2 Gibbon, chap. xxx.

and his spoil, and reached Epirus in safety, from which he effected a treaty with the ministers of Arcadius, which he never intended to keep, and was even made master-general of Eastern Illyricum. Successful war brings irresistible *éclat*, equally among barbarians and civilized nations. There is no fame like the glory of a warrior. Poets and philosophers drop their heads in the presence of great military chieftains; and those people who rest their claims to the gratitude or the admiration of the world on their intellectual and moral superiority, are among the first to yield precedence to conquering generals, whether they are ignorant, or unscrupulous, or haughty, or ambitious. The names of warriors descend from generation to generation, while the benefactors of mind are forgotten or depreciated. Who can wonder at military ambition when success in war has been uniformly attended with such magnificent rewards, from the times of Pompey and Cæsar to those of Marlborough and Napoleon?

The Gothic robber and murderer was rewarded by his nation with all the power and glory it could bestow. He was made a king, and was assured of unlimited support in all his future enterprises.

Danger of Italy.

He cast his eyes on Italy, for many generations undefiled by the presence of a foreign enemy, and enriched with the spoils of three hundred triumphs. He marched from Thessalonica, through Pannonia to the Julian Alps; passed through the defiles of those guarded mountains, and appeared before the walls of Aquileia, one of the most important cities of Northern Italy, enriched by the gold mines of the neighboring Alps, and a prosperous trade with the Illyrians and Pannonians. Here the great Julius had made his head-quarters when he made war upon Illyria, and here the younger Constantine was slain. It was the capital of Venetia, and had the privilege of a mint. It was the ninth city of the whole empire, inferior in Italy to Rome, Milan, and Capua alone. It was situated on a plain, and was strongly fortified with walls and towers. And it seems to have resisted the attacks of Alaric, who retired to the Danube for reinforcements for a new campaign.

The Emperor Honorius, weak, timid, and defenseless at Milan, was overwhelmed with fear, and implored the immediate assistance of his only reliable general. Stilicho responded to the appeal, and appreciated the danger. He summoned from every quarter the subjects or the allies of the emperor. The fortresses of the Rhine were abandoned; the legions were withdrawn from Britain; the Alani were enlisted as auxiliaries, and Stilicho advanced to the relief of his fugitive sovereign, who had fled from Milan to a town in Piedmont, just in time to rescue him from the grasp of Alaric, who, in his turn, became besieged by the troops which issued from all the passes of the Alps. The Goths were attacked in their intrenchments at Pollentia, and were obliged to retreat, leaving the spoils of Corinth and Argos, and even the wife of Alaric. The poet Claudian celebrated the victory as greater than even that achieved by Marius over the Cimbri and Teutones. The defeated Goth, however, rose superior to misfortune and danger. He escaped with the main body of his cavalry, broke through the passes of the Apennines, and spread devastation on the fruitful fields of Tuscany, and was resolved to risk another battle for the great prize which he coveted — the possession of Rome itself. He was, however, foiled by Stilicho, who *purchased* the retreat of the enemy for forty thousand pounds of gold. But the Goths respected no treaties. Scarcely had they crossed the Po, before their leader resolved to seize Verona, which commanded the passes of the Rhætian Alps. Here he was again attacked by Stilicho, and suffered losses equal to those incurred at Pollentia, and was obliged to retreat from Italy, A. D. 404.

Stilicho commands the Romans.

The conqueror was hailed with joy and gratitude; too

soon succeeded by envy and calumny, as is usual with benefactors in corrupt times. The retreat of Alaric was regarded as a complete deliverance; and the Roman people abandoned themselves to absurd rejoicings, gladiatorial shows, and triumphant processions. In the royal chariots, side by side with the emperor, Stilicho was seated, and the procession passed under a triumphal arch which commemorated the complete destruction of the Goths. For the last time, the amphitheatre of Rome was polluted with the blood of gladiators, for Honorius, exhorted by the poet Claudian, abolished forever the inhuman sacrifices.

Infatuation of the Romans.

Yet scarcely was Italy delivered from the Goths, before an irruption of Vandals, Suevi, and Burgundians, under Rodogast or Rhadagast, two hundred thousand in number of fighting men, beside an equal number of women and children, issued from the coast of the Baltic. One third of these crossed the Alps, the Po, and the Apennines, ravaged the cities of Northern Italy, and laid siege to Florence, which was reduced to its last necessity, when the victor of Pollentia appeared beneath its walls, with the *last* army which the empire could furnish, and introduced supplies. Moreover, he surrounded the enemy in turn with strong intrenchments, and the barbaric host was obliged to yield. The leader Rodogast was beheaded, and the captives were sold as slaves. Stilicho, a second time, had delivered Italy; but one hundred thousand barbarians still remained in arms between the Alps and the Apennines. Shut out of Italy, they invaded Gaul, and never afterward retreated beyond the Alps. Gaul was then one of the most cultivated of the Roman provinces; the banks of the Rhine were covered with farms and villas, and peace and plenty had long accustomed the people to luxury and ease. But all was suddenly changed, and changed for generations. The rich cornfields and fruitful vineyards became a desert.

New hordes of barbarians.

Devastation of Gaul.

Mentz was destroyed and burned. Worms fell after an obstinate siege, and experienced the same fate. Strasburg, Spires, Rheims, Tournay, Arras, Amiens, passed under the German yoke, and the flames of war spread over the seventeen provinces of Gaul. The country was completely devastated, and all classes experienced a remorseless rigor. Bishops, senators, and virgins were alike enslaved. No retreat was respected, and no sex or condition was spared. Gaul ceased to exist as a Roman province.

Assassination of Stilicho.

Italy, however, had been for a time delivered, and by the only man of ability who remained in the service of the emperor. He might possibly have checked the further progress of the Goths, had the weak emperor intrusted himself to his guidance. But imperial jealousy, and the voice of faction, removed forever this last hope of Rome. The frivolous Senate which he had saved, and the timid emperor whom he had guarded, were alike demented. The savior of Italy was an object of fear and hatred, and the assassin's dagger, which cut short his days, inflicted a fatal and suicidal blow upon Rome herself.

Alaric ravages Italy.

The Gothic king, in his distant camp on the confines of Italy, beheld with undissembled joy, the intrigues and factions which deprived the emperor of his best defender, and which placed over his last army incompetent generals. So, hastening his preparations, he again descends like an avalanche upon the plains of Italy. Aquileia, Altinum, Concordia, and Cremona, yielded to his arms, and increased his forces. He then ravaged the coasts of the Adriatic; and, following the Flaminian way, crossed the passes of the Apennines, ravaged the fertile plains of Umbria, and reached without obstruction the city which for six hundred years had not been violated by the presence of a foreign enemy. But Rome was not what she was when Hannibal led his Africans to her gates. She was surrounded with more extensive fortifications, indeed, and contained within her walls, which were twenty-one miles in circuit, a large population. But where were her one hundred and fifty thousand warriors? Where were even the three armies drawn out in battle array, that had confronted the Carthaginian leader? She could boast of senators who traced their lineage to the Scipios and the Gracchi; she could enumerate one thousand seven hundred and eighty palaces, the residence of wealthy and proud families, many of which were equal to a town, including within their precincts, markets, hippodromes, temples, fountains, baths, porticoes, groves, and aviaries; she could tell of senatorial incomes of four thousand pounds of gold, about eight hundred thousand dollars yearly, without computing the corn, oil, and wine, which were equal to three hundred thousand dollars more — men so rich that they could afford to spend five hundred thousand dollars in a popular festival, and this at a time when gold was worth at least eight times more than its present value; she could point with pride to her Christian saints, one of whom, the illustrious Paula, the friend of St. Jerome, was the sole proprietor of the city of Nicopolis, which Augustus had founded to commemorate his victory over Antony; she could count two millions of inhabitants, crowded in narrow streets, and four hundred thousand pleasure-seekers who sought daily the circus or the theatre, and three thousand public female dancers, and three thousand singers who sought to beguile the hours of the lazy rabble who were fed at the public expense, and who, for a small copper coin, could wash their dirty bodies in the marble baths of Diocletian and Caracalla; but where were her defenders — where were her legions?

Rome without defenders.

The day of retribution had come, and there was no escape. Alaric made no efforts to storm the city, but quietly sat down, and inclosed the wretched citizens with a cordon through which nothing could force its way. He cut off all communications with the country, intercepted the navigation of the Tiber, and commanded

Alaric besieges Rome.

the twelve gates. The city, unprovided for a siege, and never dreaming of such a calamity, soon felt all the evils of famine, to which those of pestilence were added. The most repugnant food was eagerly devoured, and even mothers are said to have tasted the flesh of their murdered children. Thousands perished daily in the houses, and the public sepulchres infected the air. Despair at last seized the haughty citizens, and they begged the clemency of the Gothic king. He derided the ambassadors who were sent to treat, and insulted them with rude jests. At last he condescended to spare the lives of the people, on condition that they gave up *all* their gold and silver, *all* their precious movables, and *all* their slaves of barbaric birth. More moderate terms were afterward granted; but the victor did not retreat until he had loaded his wagons with more wealth and more liberated captives than the Romans had brought from both Carthage and Antioch. He retired to the fertile fields of Tuscany to make negotiations with Honorius ; and it was only on condition that he were appointed master-general of the armies of the emperor, with an annual subsidy of corn and money, and the free possession of the provinces of Dalmatia, Noricum, and Venetia, for the seat of his kingdom, that he would grant peace to the emperor, who had entrenched himself at Ravenna. These terms were disregarded, and once more Alaric turned his face to Rome. He took possession of Ostia, one of the most stupendous works of Roman magnificence, and the port of Rome secured, the city was once again at his mercy. Again the Senate, fearful of famine and impelled by the populace, consented to the demands of the conqueror. He nominated Atticus, prefect of the city, emperor instead of the son of Theodosius, and received from him the commission of master-general of the armies of the West.

Disgraceful terms of peace.

The new emperor had a few days of prosperity, and the greater part of Italy submitted to his rule, backed by the Gothic forces. But he was after all a mere puppet in the hands of Alaric, who used him as a tool, and threw him aside when it suited his purposes. Atticus, after a brief reign, was degraded, and renewed negotiations took place between Alaric and Honorius. The emperor, having had a temporary relief, broke finally with the barbarians, who held Italy at their mercy, and Alaric, vindictive and

Alaric takes Rome.

indignant, once again set out for Rome, now resolved on plunder and revenge. In vain did the nobles organize a defense. Cowardice and treachery opened the Salarian gate. No Horatius kept the bridge. No Scipio arose in the last extremity. In the dead of night the Gothic trumpet rang unanswered in the streets. The Queen of the World, the Eternal City, was the prey of savage soldiers. For five days and nights she was exposed to every barbarity and license. Only the treasures collected in the churches of St. Peter and St. Paul were saved. Although the captor had promised to spare the lives of the people, a cruel slaughter was made, and the streets were filled with the dead. Forty thousand slaves were let loose by the bloody conquerors to gratify their long-stifled passions of lust and revenge. The matrons and virgins of Rome were exposed to every indignity, and

The miseries of the Romans.

suffered every insult. The city was abandoned to pillage, and the palaces were stripped even of their costly furniture. Sideboards of massive silver, and variegated wardrobes of silk and purple, were piled upon the wagons. The works of art were destroyed or injured. Beautiful vases were melted down for the plate. The daughters and wives of senatorial families became slaves — such as were unable to purchase their ransom. Italian fugitives thronged the shores of Africa and Syria, begging daily bread. They were scattered over various provinces, as far as Constantinople and Jerusalem. The whole empire was filled with consternation. The news made the tongue of old St. Jerome to cleave to the roof of his mouth in his cell at Bethlehem, which even was besieged with beggars. "For twenty years," cried he, "Roman blood has been flowing from Constantinople to the Julian Alps. Scythia, Thrace, Macedonia, Dacia, Epirus, Dalmatia, Achaia, the two Pannonias," yea, he might have added, Gaul, Britain, Spain, and Italy, "all belong to the barbarians. Sorrow, misery, desolation, despair, death, are everywhere. What is to be seen but one universal shipwreck of humanity, from which there is no escape save on the plank of penitence." The same bitter despair came from St. Augustine. The end of the world was supposed to be at hand, and the great churchmen of the age found consolation only in the doctrine that the second coming of our Lord was at hand to establish a new dispensation of peace and righteousness on the earth, or to appear as a stern and final judge amid the clouds of heaven.

The Goths in Italy.

After six days the Goths evacuated the city they had despoiled, and advanced along the Appian way into the southern provinces of Italy, destroying ruthlessly all who opposed their march, and loading themselves with still greater spoils. The corn, wine, and oil of the country were consumed within the barbarian camp, and the beautiful villas of the coast of Campania were destroyed or plundered. The rude inhabitants of Scythia and Germany stretched their limbs under the shade of the Italian palm-trees, and compelled the beautiful daughters of the proud senators of the fallen capital to attend on them like slaves, while they quaffed the old Falernian wines from goblets of gold and gems. Nothing arrested the career of the Goths. Their victorious leader now meditated the invasion of Africa, but died suddenly after a short illness, and the world was relieved, for a while, of a mighty fear.

Ravages in other provinces.

His successor Adolphus suspended the operations of war, and negotiated with the emperor a treaty of peace, and even enlisted under his standard to chastise his enemies in Gaul. But the oppressed provincials were cruelly ravaged by their pretended friends, who occupied the cities of Narbonne, Toulouse, and Bordeaux, and spread from the Mediterranean to the Ocean. Adolphus espoused Placidia, a sister of Honorius, to the intense humiliation of the ministers of Honorius. But the marriage proved fortunate for the empire, and the Goths settled down in the fertile provinces they had conquered, and established a Gothic kingdom. Among the treasures which the Goths carried to Narbonne, was a famous dish of solid gold, weighing five hundred pounds, ornamented with precious stones, and exquisitely engraved with the figures of men and animals. But this precious specimen of Roman luxury was not to be compared with the table formed from a single emerald, encircled with three rows of pearls, supported by three hundred and sixty-five feet of gems and massive gold, which was found in the Gothic treasury when plundered by the Arabs, and which also had been one of the ornaments of a senatorial palace.[1] The favor of the Franks was, in after times, purchased with this golden dish by a Spanish monarch, who stole it back, but compensated by a present of two hundred thousand pieces of gold, with which Dagobert founded the Abbey of St. Denys.[2]

New barbaric invasions.

The sack of Rome by the Goths was followed by the successful inroads of other barbaric tribes. The Suevi, the Alans, and the Vandals invaded Spain, which for four hundred years had been prosperous in all the arts of peace. The great cities of Corduba, Merida, Seville, Bracara, and Barcelona, testified to her wealth and luxury, while science and commerce both elevated and enfeebled the people. Yet no one of the Roman provinces suffered more severely. Gibbon thus quotes the language

[1] This emerald table was probably colored glass. It was valued at five hundred thousand pieces of gold.

[2] Gibbon, chap. xxx.

of a Spanish historian. "The barbarians exercised an indiscriminate cruelty on the fortunes of both Spaniards and Romans, and ravaged with equal fury the cities and the open country. Famine reduced the miserable inhabitants to feed on the flesh of their fellow-creatures, and pestilence swept away a large portion of those whom famine spared. Then the barbarians fixed their permanent seats in the country they had ravaged with fire and sword; Galicia was divided between the Suevi and the Vandals; the Alani were scattered over the provinces of Carthagenia and Lusitania, and Bœtica was allotted to the Vandals." But he adds, and this is a most impressive fact, "that the greater part of the Spaniards preferred the condition of poverty and barbarism to the severe oppressions of the Roman government."[1]

Permanent settlement of the Goths in Spain.

The successors of Alaric, A. D. 419, established themselves at Toulouse, forty-three years after they had crossed the Danube, which became the seat of the Gothic empire in Gaul. About the same time the Burgundians and the Franks obtained a permanent settlement in that distracted but wealthy province, and effected a ruin of all that had been deemed opulent or fortunate.

Meanwhile, Britain had been left, by the withdrawal of the legions, to the ravages of Saxon pirates, and the savages of Caledonia. The island was irrevocably lost to the empire, A. D. 409, although it was forty years before the Saxons obtained a permanent footing, and secured their conquest.

The Romans leave Britain.

But a more savage chastisement than Rome received from the Goths — the most powerful and generous of her foes — was inflicted by the Vandals, whose name is synonymous with all that is fierce and revolting.

These barbarians belonged to the great Teutonic race, although some maintain that they were of Slavonic origin. Their settlements were between

The Vandals.

[1] Gibbon, chap. xxx.

the Elbe and the Vistula; and, during the reign of Marcus Aurelius, they had, with other tribes, invaded the Roman world, but were defeated by the Roman emperor. One hundred years later they settled in Pannonia, where they had a bitter contest with the Goths. Defeated by them, they sought the protection of Rome, and enlisted in the imperial armies. In 406, they crossed the Rhine and invaded Gaul, and it was not in the power of the Franks to resist them. They advanced to the very foot of the Pyrenees, inflicting every atrocity upon the Celtic and Roman inhabitants. Neither age, nor sex, nor condition was spared, and the very churches were given to the flames. They then crossed into Spain, A. D. 409, and settled in Andalusia, and under its sunny skies resumed the agricultural life they had led in Pannonia.[1] The land now wore an aspect of prosperity; rich harvests covered the plains, while the hills were white with flocks. They seem to have lived in amity with the Romans, so that "there were found those who preferred freedom with poverty among the barbarians, to a life rendered wretched by taxation among their own countrymen."[2] This testimony is confirmed by Salvian, who declares, "they prefer to live as freemen under the guise of captivity, rather than as captives under the guise of freedom."[3] If this be true, it would seem that the rule of the barbarians was preferred to the taxation and oppression with which they were ground down by the Roman officials. And this conclusion is legitimate, when we remember the indifference and apathy that seized the old inhabitants when the empire was seriously threatened. It may have been that the irruptions of the barbarians were not regarded as so great a calamity after all, if they should break the bondage and alleviate the misery which filled the Roman world.

The Roman government, it would seem,[4] would not tol-

[1] Sheppard's *Fall of Rome*, p. 364.
[2] Orosius, vii. 41.
[3] *De Gub. Dei*, v.
[4] Sheppard, p. 364.

erate the Vandals in Spain, and intrigued with the Goths, their hereditary enemies, to make an attack upon them, perhaps with the view of weakening the strength of the Goths themselves, A. D. 416. Wallia, king of the Goths, was successful, and the Vandals were worried. The Romans also sent an army to reconquer Spain from their grasp, which drove the Vandals into Andalusia. But the Vandals turned upon their enemies and entirely discomfited them, and twenty thousand men were left dead upon the field. Spain was now entirely at the mercy of these infuriated barbarians, who might have peacefully settled had it not been for the jealousy of the imperial government, which, in those days, drew upon itself evils by its own mismanagement. For two years "Vandalism" reigned throughout the peninsula, which was pillaged and sacked.

Successes of the Vandals.

The king of these Vandals was Genseric, the worthy rival of Alaric and Attila, as a "scourge of God." If we may credit the writers who belonged to the people whom he humbled,[1] he was one of the most hideous monsters ever clothed with power. He was ambitious, subtle, deceitful, revengeful, cruel, and passionate. But he was temperate, of clear vision, and inflexible purpose.

Genseric.

He cast his eyes on Africa, the granary of Rome, and the only province which had thus far escaped the ravages of war. In the hour of triumph, and in the plenitude of power, he resolved on leaving Spain, which he held by uncertain tenure, since he was only an illegitimate son of the late monarch Gunderic, and founding a new kingdom in Africa. It was rich in farms and cities, whose capital, Carthage, had arisen from her ashes, and was once again the rival of Rome in majesty and splendor. She had even outgrown Alexandria, and her commerce was more flourishing than that of the capital of Egypt.

The Vandals threaten Africa.

[1] Procopius, *Bell. Vand.*, i. 3.

She was even famous for schools and chairs of philosophy; but more for those arts which material prosperity ever produces.

Dissensions of Roman generals.

There were, at that time, two distinguished generals in the service of the empire — Boniface and Ætius, the former of whom was governor of Africa. They were, unfortunately, rivals, and their dissensions and jealousies compromised the empire. United, they could have withstood, perhaps, the torrent which was about to sweep over Africa and Italy. Ætius persuaded the emperor to recall Boniface, while he advised the Count to disobey the summons, representing it as a sentence of death. Boniface put himself in the attitude of a rebel, and fearing the imperial forces, invited Genseric and his Vandals to Africa, with the proposal of an alliance and an advantageous settlement. Doubtless he was driven to this grand folly by the intrigues of Ætius.

Genseric gladly availed himself of an invitation which held out to him the richest prize in the empire. With fifty thousand warriors he landed on the coast of Africa, formed an alliance with the Moors, and became as dangerous an ally to Count Boniface, as Lord Clive was to the native princes of India. Africa was then disturbed by the schism of the Donatists, and these fanatical people were taken under the *protection* of the Vandals. The Moors always hated their Roman masters. With Vandals, Moors, and Donatists, leagued together, Africa was in serious danger.

The Vandals invade Africa.

The landing of the Vandals, who, of all barbarians, bore the most terrible name, was the signal of headlong flight. Consternation seized all classes of people. The gorges and the caverns of Mount Atlas were crowded with fugitives. The Vandals burned the villages through which they marched, and sacked the cities, and destroyed the harvests, and cut down the trees. The Moors swelled the ranks of the invaders, and indulged their common hatred of civilization and of Rome. Boniface, too late, perceived his mistake, and turned against the common foe; but was defeated in battle, and forced to cede away three important provinces as the price of peace, A. D. 432. But peace was not of long duration. The Vandals continually encroached upon more valuable territory. Moreover, they had been nominally converted to Christianity, and were bitter zealots of the Arian faith, and most relentlessly persecuted the Catholic Christians who adhered to the Nicene Creed.

Genseric at Carthage.

At last (439 A. D.), the storm burst out, and the world was thunderstruck with the intelligence that Genseric had seized and plundered Carthage. Suddenly, without warning, in a day looked not for, this magnificent city was plundered, and her inhabitants butchered by the most faithless and perfidious barbarians, who trampled out the dying glories of the empire. Her doom was like that pronounced upon Tyre and Sidon. The bitter cry which went up from the devastated city proclaimed the retribution of God for sins more hideous than those of Antioch or Babylon. Of all the cities of the world, Carthage was probably the wickedest — a seething caldron of impurities and abominations, the home of all the vices which disgraced humanity — so indecent and scandalous as to excite the disgust of the barbarians themselves. According to one of the authors of those times, as quoted by Sheppard,[1] "they were notorious for drunkenness, avarice, and perjury — the peculiar sins of degenerate commercial capitals. The Goths are perfidious but chaste, the Franks are liars but hospitable, the Saxons are cruel but continent; but the Africans are a blazing fire of impurity and lust; the rich are drunk with debauchery, the poor are ground down with relentless oppression, while other vices, too indecent to be named, pollute every class. Who can wonder at the fall of Roman

Fate of the city.

[1] Salvian, *De Gub. Dei*, vii. 251.

society? What hope can there be for Rome, when barbarians are more chaste and temperate than they?"

In the sack of Carthage, the voluminous writings of Augustine, then breathing his last in prayer to God that the fate of Sodom might be averted, were fortunately preserved, and have doubtless done more to instruct, and perhaps civilize, the western nations, than all the arts and sciences of the commercial metropolis. It is singular how little remains of the commercial cities of antiquity, which we value as trophies of civilization. A few sculptured ruins are all that attest ancient pride and glory. The poems of a blind schoolmaster at Chios, and the rhapsodies of a wandering philosopher on the hills of Greece, have proved greater legacies to the world than the combined treasures of Africa and Asia Minor. Where is the literature of Carthage, except as preserved in the writings of Augustine, the influence of which in developing the character of the barbarians cannot be estimated.

Renewed dangers of Rome.

The cry of agony which went from Carthage across the Mediterranean, announced to Rome that her turn would come. She looked in vain to every quarter for assistance. Every city and province had need of their own forces. Theodoric, king of the Visigoths, was contending with Ætius; in Spain the Sueves were extending their ravages; Attila menaced the eastern provinces; the Emperor Valentinian was forced to hide in the marshes of Ravenna, and see the second sack of the imperial capital, now a prostrate power — a corpse in a winding-sheet.

The Vandals in Italy.

The Vandals landed on the Italian coast. They advanced to the Tiber's banks. The Queen of Cities wrapped around her the faded folds of her imperial purple, rent by faction, pierced with barbaric daggers, and trampled in the dust. Yet not with the dignity of her great Julius did she die. She begged for mercy, not proud and stately amid her executioners, but like a withered hag, with the wine-cup of sorceries in her hand, pale, haggard, ghastly, staggering, helpless.

The last hope of Rome was her Christian bishop, and the great Leo, who was to Rome what Augustine had been to Carthage, in his pontifical robes, hastened to the barbarians' camp. But all he could secure was the promise that the unresisting should be spared, the buildings protected from fire, and the captives from torture. Even this promise was only partially fulfilled. The pillage lasted fourteen days and fourteen nights, and all that the Goths had spared was transported to the ships of Genseric. Among the spoils were the statues of the old pagan gods which adorned the capitol, the holy vessels of the Jewish temples which Titus had brought away from Jerusalem, and the shrines and altars of the Christian churches enriched by the liberality of popes and emperors. The gilding of the capitol had cost Domitian twelve million dollars, or twelve thousand talents, but the bronze on which it was gilt was carried away. The imperial ornaments of the palace, the magnificent furniture and wardrobe of senatorial mansions, and the sideboards of massive plate, gold, silver, brass, copper, whatever could be found, were transported to the ships. The Empress Eudoxia herself was stripped of her jewels, and carried away captive with her two daughters, the only survivors of the great Theodosius. Thousands of Romans were forced upon the fleet, while wives were separated from their husbands, and children from their parents, and sold into slavery.[1]

Sack and fall of Rome.

Such was the doom of Rome, A. D. 455, forty-five years after the Gothic invasion. The haughty city had met the fate she had inflicted upon her rivals. And she never would probably have arisen from her fall, but would have remained ruined and desolate, had not her great bishop, rising with the greatness of the crisis, and inspired with the old imperishable idea of national unity, which had for three hundred years sustained the crumbling empire, exclaimed to the rude spoliators, now con-

The doom of Rome.

[1] Gibbon, chap. xxxvi.

verted to *his* faith, while all around him were desolation and ruin, weeping widows, ashes, groans, lamentations, bitter sorrows — nothing left but recollections, nothing to be seen but the desolation spoken of by Jeremy the prophet, as well as the Cumean Sybil; all central power subverted, law and justice by-words, literature and art crushed, vice rampant multiplying itself, the contemplative hiding in cells, the rich made slaves, women shrieking in terror, bishops praying in despair, the heart of the world bleeding, barbarians everywhere triumphant — in this mournful crisis, did Leo, the intrepid Pontiff, alone and undismayed, and concentrating within himself all that survived of the ambition and haughty will of the ancient capital, exclaim to the superstitious victors, in the spirit if not in the words of Hildebrand, "Beware, I am the successor of St. Peter, to whom God has given the keys of the kingdom of heaven, and against whose church the gates of hell cannot prevail; I am the living representative of divine power upon the earth; I am Cæsar, a Christian Cæsar, ruling in love, to whom all Christians owe allegiance; I hold in my hands the curses of hell, and the benedictions of heaven; I absolve all subjects from allegiance to kings; I give and take away, by divine right, all thrones and principalities of Christendom — beware how you desecrate the patrimony given me by your invisible king, yea, bow down your necks to me, and pray that the anger of God may be averted." And the superstitious conquerors wept, and bowed their faces to the dust, in reverence and in awe, and Rome again arose from her desolation — the seat of a new despotism more terrible than the centralized power of the emperors, controlling the wills of kings, priests, and people, and growing more majestic with the progress of ages; a vital and mysterious power which even the Reformation could not break, and which even now gives no signs of decay, and boldly defies, in the plenitude of spiritual power, a greater prince than

The heroism of the Pope.

he who stood in the winter time three days and nights before the gates of the castle of Canossa, bareheaded and barefooted, in abject submission to Gregory VII.

While the Vandals were thus plundering Rome, a still fiercer race of barbarians were trampling beneath their feet the deserted sanctuaries of the empire. **Renewed invasion of barbarians.** The Huns, a Slavonic race, most hideous and revolting savages, Tartar hordes, with swarthy faces, sunken eyes, flat noses, square bodies, big heads, broad **The Huns.** shoulders, low stature, without pity, or fear, or mercy — equally the enemies of the Romans and the Germans — races thus far incapable of civilization, now spread themselves from the Volga to the Danube, from the shores of the Caspian to the Hadriatic. They were a nomadic people, with flocks and herds, planting no seed, reaping no harvest, wandering about in quest of a living, yet powerful with their horses and darts. For fifty years after they had invaded Southern Europe, their aid was sought and secured by the rash court of Constantinople, as a counterpoise to the power of the Goths and other Germanic tribes. They were obstinate pagans, and had an invincible hatred of civilization. They had various fortunes in their migrations and wars, and experienced some terrible defeats. But they had their eyes open to the spoil of the crumbling empire — "ripe fruit" for them to pluck, as well as for the Goths and Vandals.

The leader of the Huns at this period was Attila — a man of great astuteness and military genius, who **Attila.** succeeded in conquering, one after another, every existing tribe of barbarians beyond the Danube and the Rhine, and then turned his arms against the eastern empire. This was in the year 441. They ravaged Pannonia, routed two Roman armies, laid Thessaly in waste, and threatened Constantinople. The Emperor Theodosius, A. D. 446, purchased peace by an ignominious tribute, so great as to reduce many leading families to poverty. "The scourge of

God" then turned his steps to the more exhausted fields of the western provinces, and invaded Gaul. The Visigoths had there established a kingdom, hostile to the Vandal power. The Huns and the Vandals united, with all the savage legions which could be collected from Lapland to the Indus, against the Goths and imperial forces under the command of Ætius. "Never," says Thierry,[1] "since the days of Xerxes, was there such a gathering of nations as now followed the standard of Attila, some five hundred thousand warriors — Huns, Alans, Gepidæ, Neuvi, Geloni, Bastarnæ, Heruli, Lombards, Belloniti, Rugi, some German but chiefly Asiatic tribes, with their long quivers and ponderous lances, and cuirasses of plaited hair, and scythes, and round bucklers, and short swords." This heterogeneous host, from the Sarmatian plains, and the banks of the Vistula and Niemen, extended from Basle to the mouth of the Rhine. Attila directed it against Orleans, on the Loire, an important strategic position. Ætius went to meet him, bringing all the barbaric auxiliaries he could collect — Britons, Franks, Burgundians, Sueves, Saxons, Visigoths. It was not so much Roman against barbarian, as Europe against Asia, which was now arrayed upon the plains of Champagne, for Orleans had fallen into the hands of the Huns. There, at Châlons, was fought the most decisive and bloody battle of that dreadful age, by which Europe was delivered from Asia, even as at a later day the Saracens were shut out of France by Charles Martel. "*Bellum atrox, multiplex, immane, pertinax, cui simile nulla usquam narrat antiquitas.*"[2] Attila began the fight; on his left were the Ostrogoths under Vladimir, on his right were the Gepidæ, while in the centre were stationed the Huns, with their irresistible cavalry. Ætius stationed the Franks and Burgundians, whose loyalty he doubted, in the centre, while he strengthened his wings, and assumed the command of his own left.

The hosts of the barbarians.

Battle of Châlons.

1 *Histoire d'Attilla*, vol. i. p. 141.

2 Jornandes.

The Huns, as expected, made their impetuous charge; the Roman army was cut in two; but the wings of Ætius overlapped the cavalry of Attila, and drove back his wings. Attila was beaten, and Gaul was saved from the Slavonic invaders. It is computed that three hundred thousand barbarians, on both sides, were slain — the most fearful slaughter recorded in the whole annals of war. The discomfited king of the Huns led back his forces to the Rhine, ravaging the cities and villages through which he passed, and collected a new army. The following year he invaded Italy.

Defeat of the Huns.

Ætius alone remained to stem the barbaric hosts. He had won one of the greatest victories of ancient times, and sought for a reward. And considering the brilliancy of his victory, and the greatness of his services, the marriage of his son with the princess Eudoxia was not an unreasonable object of ambition. But his greatness made him unpopular with the debauched court at Ravenna, and he was left without a sufficient force to stem the invasion of the Huns. Aquileia, the most important and strongly fortified city of Northern Italy, for a time stood out against the attack of the barbarians, but ultimately yielded. Fugitives from the Venetian territory sought a refuge among the islands which skirt the northern coast of the Adriatic — the haunts of fishermen and sea-birds. There Venice was born, which should revive the glory of the West, and write her history upon the waves for a thousand years. Attila had spent the spring in his attack on Aquileia, and the summer heats were unfavorable for further operations, and his soldiers clamored for repose; but, undaunted by the ravages which sickness produced in his army, he resolved to cross the Apennines and give a last blow to Rome. Leo again sought the barbarians' camp, and met with more success than he did with the Vandals. Attila consented to leave Italy in consideration of an annual tribute, and the prom-

The Roman general Ætius.

Retreat of Attila.

ise of the hand of the princess Honoria, sister of the Emperor Valentinian, who, years before, in a fit of female spitefulness for having been banished to Constantinople, had sent her ring as a *gage d'amour* to the repulsive barbarian. He then retired to the Danube by the passes of the Alps, where he spent the winter in bacchanalian orgies and preparations for an invasion of the eastern provinces. But his career was suddenly cut off by the avenging poniard of Ildigo, a Bactrian or Burgundian princess, whom he had taken for one of his numerous wives, and whose relations he had slain.

Disasters of the Huns.

On his death, the German tribes refused longer to serve under the divided rule of his sons, and after a severe contest with the more barbarous Huns, the empire of Attila disappeared as one of the great powers of the world, and Italy was delivered forever from this plague of locusts. The battle of Netâd, in which they suffered a disastrous defeat, was perhaps as decisive as the battle of Châlons. They returned to Asia, or else were gradually worn out in unavailing struggles with the Goths.

The Avars.

The Avars, a tribe of the great Turanian race, and kindred to the Huns, a few years after their retreat, crossed the Danube, established themselves between that river and the Save, invaded the Greek empire, and ravaged the provinces almost to the walls of Constantinople. It would seem from Sheppard that the Avars had migrated from the very centre of Asia, two thousand miles from the Caspian Sea, fleeing from the Turks who had reduced them to their sway.[1] In their migration to the West, they overturned every thing in their way, and spread great alarm at Constantinople. Justinian, then an old man, A. D. 567, purchased their peace by an annual tribute and the grant of lands. In 582, the Avar empire was firmly established on the Danube, and in the valleys of the Balkan. But it was more hostile to the Slavic tribes, than

[1] Sheppard, Lect. iv.

to the Byzantine Greeks, who then occupied the centre and southeast of Europe, and who were reduced to miserable slavery. With the Franks, the Avars also came in conflict, and, after various fortunes, were subdued by Charlemagne. Their subsequent history cannot here be pursued, until they were swept away from the roll of the European nations. Moreover, it was not until *after* the fall of Rome, that they were formidable.

The real drama of the fall of Rome closes with the second sack of the city by the Vandals, since the imperial power was nearly prostrated in the West, and shut up within the walls of Ravenna. But Italy was the scene of great disasters for twenty years after, until the last of the emperors — Augustulus Romulus; what a name with which to close the series of Roman emperors!—was dethroned by Odoacer, chief of the Heruli, a Scythian tribe, and Rome was again stormed and sacked, A. D. 476. During these twenty years, the East and the West were finally severed, and Italy was ruled by barbaric chieftains, and their domination permanently secured. Valentinian, the last emperor of the race of Theodosius, was assassinated in the year 455 (at the instigation of the Senator Maximus, of the celebrated Anician family, whose wife he had violated), a man who had inherited all the weaknesses of his imperial house, without its virtues, and under whose detestable reign the people were so oppressed with taxes and bound down by inquisitions that they preferred the barbarians to the empire. The successive reigns of Maximus, Avitus, Majorian, Severus, Anthemius, Olybrius, Glycerius, Nepos, and Augustulus, nine emperors in twenty-one years, suggests nothing but disorder and revolution. The murderer of Valentinian reigned but three months, during which Rome was sacked by the Vandals. Avitus was raised to his vacant throne by the support of the Visigoths of Gaul, then ruled by Theodoric, a majestic barbarian, and the most enlightened

Final disasters of the empire.

Imbecile emperors.

and civilized of all the leaders of the Gothic hosts who had yet appeared. He fought and vanquished the Suevi, who had established themselves in Spain, in the name of the emperor whom he had placed upon the throne, but he really ruled on both sides of the Alps, and Avitus was merely his puppet, and distinguished only for his infamous pleasures, although, as a general, he had once saved the empire from the Huns.

Last days of Rome.

He was in turn deposed by Count Ricimer, a Sueve, and generalissimo of the Roman armies, and Majorian, whom Ricimer thought to make a tool, was placed in his stead. But he was an able and good man, and attempted to revive the traditions of the empire, and met the fate of all reformers in a hopeless age, doubtless under the influence of Ricimer, who substituted Severus, a Lucanian, who perished by poison after a reign of four years, so soon as he became distasteful to the military subordinate, who was all-powerful at Rome, and who ruled Italy for six years without an emperor with despotic authority. During these six years Italy was perpetually ravaged by the Vandals, who landed and pillaged the coast, and then retired with their booty. Ricimer, without ships, invoked the aid of the court of Constantinople, who imposed a Greek upon the throne of Italy. Though a man of great ability, Anthemius, the new emperor, was unpopular with the Italians and the barbarians, and he, *again*, was deposed by Ricimer, and Olybrius, a senator of the Anician house, reigned in his stead, A. D. 472. It was then that Rome for the third time was sacked by one of her own generals. Olybrius reigned but a few months, and Glycerius, captain of his guard, was selected as his successor — an appointment disagreeable to the Greek Emperor Leo, who opposed to him Julius Nepos — a distinguished general, who succeeded in ejecting Glycerius. The Visigoths, offended, made war upon Roman Gaul. Julius sent against them Orestes, a Pannonian, called the

Patrician, who turned a traitor, and, on the assassination of Julius, entered Ravenna in triumph. His son, christened Romulus, the soldiers elevated upon a shield and saluted Augustus; but as he was too small to wear the purple robe, they called him Augustulus — a bitter mockery, recalling the battle of Actium, and the foundation of Rome. He was the last of the Cæsars. It was easier to make an emperor than keep him in his place. The bands of Orestes clamored for lands equal to a third of Italy. Orestes hesitated, and refused the demand. The soldiers were united under Odoacer — chief of the Heruli, a general in the service of the Patrician — one of the boldest and most unscrupulous of those mercenaries who lent their arms in the service of the government of Ravenna. The standard of revolt was raised, and the barbarian army marched against their former master. Leaving his son in Ravenna, Orestes, himself an able general trained in the service of Attila, went forth to meet his enemy on the Lombard plains. Unable to make a stand, he shut himself up in Pavia, which was taken and sacked, and Orestes put to death. The barbarians then marched to Ravenna, which they took, with the boy who wore the purple, who was not slain as his father was, but pensioned with six thousand crowns, and sent to a Campanian villa, which once belonged to Sulla and Lucullus. The throne of the Cæsars was hopelessly subverted, and Odoacer was king of Italy, and portioned out its lands to his greedy followers, A. D. 476. He was not unworthy of his high position, but his kingdom was in a sad state of desolation, and after a reign of fourteen years he was in turn supplanted by the superior genius of Theodoric, king of the Ostrogoths, under whom a new era dawned upon Italy and the West, A. D. 490.

The Roman empire was now dismembered, and the various tribes of barbarians, after a contest of two hundred years were fairly settled in its provinces.

Dismemberment of the empire.

The settlement of the Ostrogoths in Italy.

In Italy we find the Ostrogoths as a dominant power, who, migrating from the mouth of the Danube, with all the barbarians they could enlist under the standard of Theodoric, prevailed over Odoacer, and settled in Italy. The Gothic kingdom was assailed afterward by Belisarius and Narses, the great generals of Justinian, also by the Lombards under Alboin, who maintained themselves in the north of Italy.

The settlement of the Franks in Gaul.

Gaul was divided among the Franks, the Burgundians, and the Visigoths, whose perpetual wars, and whose infant kingdom, it is not my object to present.

The settlement of the Saxons in Britain.

Britain was possessed by the Saxons, Spain by the Vandals, Suevi, and Visigoths, and Africa by the Vandals, while the whole eastern empire fell into the hands of the Saracens, except Constantinople, which preserved the treasures of Greek and Roman civilization, until the barbarians, elevated by the Christian religion, were prepared to ingraft it upon their own rude laws and customs.

It would be interesting to trace the various fortunes of these Teutonic tribes in the devastated provinces which they possessed by conquest. But this would lead us into a boundless field, foreign to our inquiry. It is the fall of Rome, not the reconstruction by the new races, which I seek to present. It would also be interesting to survey the old capital of the world in the hands of her various masters, pillaged and sacked by all in turn ; but her doom was sealed when Alaric entered the gates which had been closed for six hundred years to a foreign enemy, and the empire fell, virtually, when the haughty city, so long a queen among the nations, yielded up her palaces as spoil. The eastern empire had a longer life, but it was inglorious when Rome was no longer the superior city.

The story of the fall of the grandest empire ever erected on our earth is simple and impressive. Genius, energy, and patience led to vast possessions, which were retained by a uniform policy which nothing could turn aside. Prosperity and success led to boundless self-exaggeration and a depreciation of enemies, while the vices of self-interest undermined gradually all real strength. Society became utterly demoralized and weakened, and there were no conservative forces sufficiently strong to hold it together. Vitality was destroyed by disproportionate fortunes, by slavery, by the extinction of the middle classes, by the degradation of woman, by demoralizing excitements, by factitious life, by imperial misrule, by proconsular tyranny, by enervating vices, by the absence of elevated sentiments, by an all-engrossing abandonment to money-making and the pleasures it procured, so that no lofty appeal could be made to which the degenerate people would listen, or which they could understand. The empire was rotten to the core — was steeped in selfishness, sensuality, and frivolity, and the poison pervaded all classes and orders, and descended to the extremities of the social system. What could be done? There was no help from man. The empire was on the verge of dissolution when the barbarians came. They only gave a shock and hastened the fall. The empire was ripe fruit, to be plucked by the strongest hand.

Reflections on the fall of the empire.

Three centuries earlier a brave resistance would have been made, and the barbarians would have been overthrown and annihilated or sold as slaves. But they were now the stronger, even with their rude weapons, and without the arts of war which the Romans had been learning for a thousand years. Yet they suffered prodigious losses before they became ultimately victorious. But they persevered, driven by necessity as well as the love of adventure and rapine. Wave after wave was rolled back by desperate generals; but the tide returned, and swept all away.

Fortunately, they reconstructed after they had once

destroyed. They were converts of Christianity, and had sympathy with many elements of civilization. "Some solitary sparks fell from the beautiful world that was passed upon the night of their labors." These kindled a fire which has never been extinguished. They had, with all their barbarism, some great elements of character, and in all the solid qualities of the heart, were superior to the races they subdued. They brought their fresh blood into the body politic, and were alive to sentiments of religion, patriotism, and love. They were enthusiastic, hopeful, generous, and uncontaminated by those subtle vices which ever lead to ruin. They made innumerable mistakes, and committed inexcusable follies. But, after a long pilgrimage, and severely disciplined by misfortunes, they erected a new fabric, established by the beautiful union of German strength and Roman art, on the more solid foundations of Christian truth.

The authorities for this chapter are not numerous. They are the historians of the empire in its decline and miseries. Gibbon's history is doubtless the best in English. He may be compared with Tillemont's Hist. des Emperors. Sheppard has written an interesting and instructing book on this period, but it pertains especially to the rise of the new barbaric states. Tacitus' chapter on the Manners of the Germans should be read in connection with the wars. Gibbon quotes largely from Ammianus Marcellinus, who is the best Latin historian of the last days of Rome. Zosimus is an authority, but he is brief. Procopius wrote a history of the Vandal wars. Gregory of Tours describes the desolations in Gaul, as well as Journandes. The writings of Jerome, Augustine, and other fathers, allude somewhat to the miseries and wickedness of the times. But of all the writers on this dark and gloomy period, Gibbon is the most satisfactory and exhaustive; nor is it probable he will soon be supplanted in a field so dreary and sad.

CHAPTER XII.

THE REASONS WHY THE CONSERVATIVE INFLUENCES OF PAGAN CIVILIZATION DID NOT ARREST THE RUIN OF THE ROMAN WORLD.

It is a most interesting inquiry why art, literature, science, philosophy, and political organizations, and other trophies of the unaided reason of man, did not prevent so mournful an eclipse of human glory as took place upon the fall of the majestic empire of the Romans. There can be no question that civilization achieved most splendid triumphs, even under the influence of pagan institutions. But it was not paganism which achieved these victories; it was the will and the reason of a noble race, in spite of its withering effects. It was the proud reason of man which soared to such lofty heights, and attempted to secure happiness and prosperity. These great ends were measurably attained, and a self-sufficient philosopher might have pointed to these victories as both glorious and permanent. When the eyes of contemporaries rested on the beautiful and cultivated face of nature, on commerce and ships, on military successes and triumphs, on the glories of heroes and generals, on a subdued world, on a complicated mechanism of social life, on the blazing wonders of art, on the sculptures and pictures, the temples and monuments which ornamented every part of the empire, when they reflected on the bright theories which philosophy proposed, on the truths which were incorporated with the system of jurisprudence, on the wondrous constitution which the experience of ages had framed, on the genius of poets and historians, on the whole system of social life, adorned with polished manners and the graces of genial intercourse — when they saw that all these triumphs had been won over barbarism, and had been constantly progressing with succeeding generations, it seemed that the reign of peace and prosperity would be perpetual. It is nothing to the point whether the civilization of which all people boasted, and in which they trusted, was superior or inferior to that which has subsequently been achieved by the Gothic races. The question is, *Did* these arts and sciences produce an influence sufficiently strong to conserve society? That they polished and adorned individuals cannot be questioned. Did they infuse life into the decaying mass? Did they prolong political existence? Did they produce valor and moral force among the masses? Did they raise a bulwark capable of resisting human degeneracy or barbaric violence? Did they lead to self-restraint? Did they create a lofty public sentiment which scorned baseness and lies? Did they so raise the moral tone of society that people were induced to make sacrifices and noble efforts to preserve blessings which had already been secured.

Nothing conservative in a mere human creation.

I have to show that the grandest empire of antiquity perished from the same causes which destroyed Babylon and Carthage; that all the magnificent trophies of the intellect were in vain; that the sources of moral renovation were poisoned; that nothing worked out, practically and generally, the good which was intended, and which enthusiasts had hoped; that the very means of culture were perverted, and that the savor unto life became a savor unto death. In short, it will appear from the example of Rome, that man cannot save himself; that he cannot originate any means of conservation which will not be foiled and rendered nugatory by the force of human corruption; that man, left to himself, will defeat his own purposes, and that all his enterprises and projects will end in shame and humiliation, so far as they are intended to preserve society. The history of all the pagan races and countries show that only a limited height can ever be reached, and that society is destined to perpetual falls as well as triumphs, and would move on in circles forever, where no higher aid comes than from man himself. And this great truth is so forcibly borne out by facts, that those profound and learned historians who are skeptical of the power of Christianity, have generally embraced the theory that nations *must* rise and fall to the end of time; and society will show, like the changes of nature, only phases which have appeared before. Their gloomy theories remind us of the perpetual swinging of a pendulum, or the endless labors of Ixion — circles and cycles of motion, but no general and universal progress to a perfect state of happiness and prosperity. And if we were not supported by the hopes which Christianity furnishes, if we adopted the pagan principles of Gibbon or Buckle, history would only confirm the darkest theories. But the history of Greece and Rome and Egypt are only chapters in the great work which Providence unfolds. They are only acts in the great drama of universal life. The history of those old pagan empires is full of instruction. In one sense, it seems mournful, but it only shows that society must be a failure under the influences which man's genius originates. This world is not destined to be a failure, although the empires of antiquity were. I fall in with the most cheerless philosophy of the infidel historians, if there is no other hope for man, as illustrated by the rise and fall of empires, than what the pagan intellect devised. But this induction is not sufficiently broad. They have too few facts upon which to build a theory. Yet the theory they advance *is* supported by all the facts brought out by the history of pagan countries. And this is my reason for bringing out so much that is truly glorious, in an important sense, in Roman history, to show that these glories did not,

Civilization can only rise to a certain height by unaided reason.

and could not, save. And the moral lesson I would draw is, that *any* civilization, based on what man creates or originates, even in his most lofty efforts, will fail as signally as the Grecian and the Roman, so far as the conservation of society is concerned, in the hour of peril, when corruption and degeneracy have also accomplished their work. Paganism cannot give other than temporary triumphs. Its victories are not progressive. They do not tend to indefinite and ever-expanding progress. They simply show an intellectual brilliancy, which is soon dimmed by the vapors which arise out of the fermentations of corrupt society.

The virtues of the primitive races.

The question here may arise why the Greeks and Romans themselves arose from a state of barbarism to the degree of culture which has given them immortality? Why did they not remain barbarians, like the natives of Central Africa? But they belonged to a peculiar race — that great Caucasian race which, in all of its ramifications, showed superior excellences, and which, in the earliest times, seems to have cherished ideas and virtues which probably were learned from a primitive revelation. The Romans, in the early ages of the republic, were superior to their descendants in the time of the emperors in all those qualities which give true dignity to character. I doubt if there was ever any great improvement among the Romans in a moral point of view. They acquired arts as they declined in virtue. If strictly scrutinized I believe it would appear that the Roman character was nobler six hundred years before Christ than in the second century of our era. It was the magnificent material on which civilizing influences had to work that accounts for Roman greatness, in the same sense that there was a dignity in the patriarchal period of Jewish history not to be found under the reigns of the kings. The same may be said of the Greeks. The Homeric poems show a natural beauty and simplicity more attractive than the rationalistic character of the Athenians in the time of Socrates. There was a progress in arts which was not to be seen in common life. And this is true also of the Persians. They were really a greater people under Cyrus than when they reigned in Babylon. There are no records of the Indo-Germanic races which do not indicate a certain greatness of character in the earliest periods. The Germanic tribes were barbarians, but in piety, in friendship, in hospitality, in sagacity, in severe morality, in the high estimation in which women were held, in the very magnificence of superstitions, we see the traits of a noble national character. It would be difficult to show absolute degradation at any time among these people. How they came to have these grand traits in their primeval forests it is difficult to show. Certainly they were never such a people as the Africans or the Malay races, or even the Slavonic tribes. These natural elements of character extorted the admiration of Tacitus, even as the Orientals won the respect of Herodotus. It is more easy to conceive why such a people as the Greeks and Romans were, in their primitive simplicity, when they were brave, trusting, affectionate, enterprising, should make progress in arts and sciences, than why they should have degenerated after a high civilization had been reached. They made the arts and sciences. The arts and sciences did not make them. They were great before civilization, as technically understood, was born. Why they were so superior to other races we cannot tell. They were either made so, or else they must have received a revelation from above, or learned some of the great truths which by God were taught to the patriarchs. Possibly the wisdom they very early evinced had come down from father to son from the remotest antiquity. The divine savor may have leavened the whole race before history was written. With their uncorrupted and primitive habits, they had a moral force which enabled them to make great improvements. Without this force they never would have reached so high a culture. And when the moral force was spent, the civilization they created also passed away from them to other uncorrupted races. The Greeks learned from Egyptians, as Romans learned from Greeks. Civilization only reached a limited state among the Egyptians. It never advanced for three thousand years. Greek culture retrograded after the age of Pericles. There were but few works of genius produced at Rome after the Antonines. The age of Augustus saw a higher triumph of art than the age of Cato, yet the moral greatness of the Romans was more marked in the time of Cato than in that of Augustus. If moral elevation kept pace with art, why the memorable decline in morals when the genius of the Romans soared to its utmost height? The virtues of society were a soil on which art prospered, and art continued to be developed long after real vigor had fled, but only reached a certain limit, and declined when life was gone. In other words, the force of character, which the early Romans evinced, gave an immense impulse to civilization, whose fruits appeared after the glory of character was gone; but, having no soil, the tree of knowledge at last withered away. If the old civilization had a life of itself, it would have saved the race. But as it was purely man's creation, his work, it had no inherent vitality or power to save him. The people were great before the fruits of their culture appeared. They were great in consequence of living virtues, not legacies of genius. They ran the usual course of the ancient nations. The sterling virtues of primitive times produced prosperity and material greatness. Material greatness gave patronage to art and science. Art and science did not corrupt the people until they had also become corrupted. But prosperity produced idleness, pride, and sensuality, by which science, art, and literature became tainted. The corruption spread. Society was undermined, and the arts fell with the people, except such as ministered to a corrupt taste, like demoralizing pictures and inflammatory music. Why did

Decline of civilization in the ancient races.

not the arts maintain the severity of the Grecian models? Why did philosophy degenerate to Epicureanism? Why did poetry condescend to such trivial subjects as hunting and fishing? Why did the light of truth become dim? Why were the great principles of beauty lost sight of? Why the discrepancy between the laws and the execution of them? Why was every triumph of genius perverted? It was because men, in their wickedness, were indifferent to truth and virtue. Good men had made good laws; bad men perverted them. A corrupted civilization hastened rather than retarded the downward course, and civilization must needs become corrupt when men became so. We cannot see any progress in peoples without moral forces, and these do not originate in man. They may be retained a long time among a people; they are not natural to them. They are *given* to them; they are given originally by God. They are the fruit of his revelations. Neither in the wilderness nor in the crowded city are they naturally produced. A perfect state of nature, without light from Heaven, is extreme rudeness, poverty, ignorance, and superstition, where brutal passions are dominant and triumphant. The vices of savages are as fatal as the vices of cities. They equally destroy society. Place man anywhere on the earth, or under any circumstances, without religious life, and moral degradation follows. Whence comes religious life? Where did Abraham and Isaac and Jacob, those eastern herdsmen and shepherds, get their moral wisdom? Surely it was inherited from earlier patriarchs, taught them by their fathers, or given directly from God himself.

Virtues of primitive life.

The most that can be said of a primitive state of society is that it is favorable for the *retention* of religious and moral truth, more so than populous cities, since it has fewer temptations to excite the passions. But a savage in any country will remain a savage, unless he is elevated and taught through influences independent of himself. Hottentots make no progress. Greeks made progress, since they had moral wisdom communicated to them by their ancestors: the divine light struggled with human propensities. When outward circumstances were favorable the virtues were retained; they were not born, and these were the stimulus to all improvement; and when they were lost, all improvement that is real vanished away. Civilization is the fruit of man's genius, when man is virtuous. But it does not renovate races. It is only religion coming from God which can do this.

It would be an interesting inquiry how far the religion of the old Greeks and Romans was pure — how far it was uncontaminated by superstitions. I think it would be found on inquiry, if we had the means of definite knowledge, that all that was elevating to the character had descended from a remote antiquity, and that the superstitions with which it was blended were more recent inventions. The ancestors of the Greeks were probably more truly religious than the Greeks themselves. And as new revelations were not made by God, the primitive revelations were obscured by increasing darkness, until superstition formed the predominant element.

Hence the revelations of God can only be preserved in a written form, without change or comment. Christianity is perpetuated by the Bible. So long as the Bible exists Christianity will have converts, and will be able to struggle successfully with human degeneracy. The revelations originally made to the eastern nations became traditions. The standard was not preserved in a written form to which the people had access.

Christianity the only conservative power.

Moreover, the Greeks and Romans, when they were most virtuous, when they were in a state to produce a civilization, had great obstacles to surmount and difficulties to contend with. These ever develop genius and keep down destructive passions. Strength ever comes through weakness and dependence. This is the stern condition of our moral nature. It is a primeval and unalterable law that man must earn his living by the sweat of his brow, even as woman can only be happy and virtuous when her will is subject to that of her husband. A condition where labor is not necessary engenders idleness, sensuality, indifference to suffering, self-indulgence, and a conventional hardness that freezes the soul. Never, in this world, have more exalted virtues been brought to light than among the Puritans in their cold and dreary settlements in New England, even those which it is the fashion to attribute to congenial climates and sunny skies. The Puritan character was as full of passion as it was of sacrifice. We read of the existence and culture of friendship, love, and social happiness when the country was most sterile, and the difficulty of earning a living greatest. There was an outward starch and acerbity produced by toil and danger. But when people felt they could unbend, they were not icebergs but volcanoes, because the fires which burned unseen were those of the soul. The mirth of wine is maudlin and short-lived. It prompts to no labor, and kindles no sacrifices. It is satanic ; it blazes and dies, a horrid mockery, exultant and evanescent. But the joy of homes, the beaming face of forgiveness, the charity which covers a multitude of faults, the assistance rendered in hours of darkness and difficulty, enthusiasm for truth, the aspiration for a higher life, the glorious interchange of thoughts and sentiments, these are well-springs of life, of peace, and of power. Nothing is to be relied upon which does not stimulate the higher faculties of the mind and soul. Ease of living blunts the moral sensibilities, and even the beauty of nature is not appreciated, when " all save the spirit of man is divine." But when men are earnest and true, uncorrupted by the vices of self-interest, and unseduced by the pleasures of factitious life, then even nature, in all her wildness, is a teacher and an inspiration. The grand land-

Primitive life favors virtue.

scape, the rugged rocks, the mystic forests, and the lofty mountains, barren though they be, bring out higher sentiments than the smiling vineyard, or the rich orange-grove, or the fertile corn-field, where slaves do the labor, and lazy proprietors recline on luxurious couches to take their mid-day sleep, or toy with frivolous voluptuousness. Neither a great nor a rich country is anything, if only pride and folly are fostered; while isolation, poverty, and physical discomfort, if accompanied by piety and resignation, are frequently the highest boons which Providence bestows to keep men in mind of Him. Prosperity may have been the blessing of the Old Testament, but adversity is the blessing of the New — the mysterious benediction of Christ and Apostles and martyrs. A rich country does not make great men, except in craft or politics or business calculations; nor is there a more subtle falsehood than that which builds a nation's hope on the extent of its prairies, or the deep soil of its valleys, or the rich mines of its mountains, or the great streams which bear its wealth to the ocean. Mr. Buckle, fallaciously and sophistically, instances Egypt as peculiarly fortunate and happy, because it possessed the Nile; but all that was glorious in Egypt passed away before authentic history was written, while Greece, with her barren mountains, laid the foundation of all that was valuable in the ancient civilization. What survives of Carthage or Antioch or Tyre that society now cherishes? Yet much may be traced to Greece when the people were poor, and struggling with the waves and the forests. It is not nature that ennobles man; it is man that consecrates nature. The development of mind is greater than the development of material resources. True greatness is not in an easy life, but in the struggle against nature and the victory over adverse influences. Even in our own country, it will be seen that schools and colleges and religious institutions have more frequently flourished when the people were

Evils of prosperity.

The superiority of the early to the later Greeks in virtue.

poor and industrious than when they were rich and prodigal. Why has New England produced so many educators? Why is it that so few eminent men of genius and learning have arisen out of the turmoil and vanity of prosperous cities? Why is it that money cannot create a college, and is useless unless there is a vitality among its professors and students? The condition of national greatness is the same as that seen in the rise and fortunes of individuals. Industry, honesty, and patience are greater than banks and storehouses. Character, even in a wicked and busy city, is of more value than money.

These truths are most emphatically illustrated by the civilization of the Romans. We are attracted by the glitter and the glare of arts and sciences. Let us see what they did for Rome, when Rome became degenerate. Let us review the chapters that have been written in this book. We point with pride to the trophies of genius and strength. We do not disparage them. They were human creations. Let us see how far they had a force to save.

The first great development of genius among the Romans was military strength. We are dazzled by the glory of warlike deeds. We see a grand army, the power of the legions, the science of war. Why did not military organizations save the empire in the hour of trial?

The Roman armies in the republic.

The legions who went forth to battle in the days of Aurelian and Severus, were not such as marched under Marius and Cæsar. The soldiers of the republic went forth to battle expecting death, and ready to die. The sacrifice of life in battle was the great idea of a Roman hero, as it was of a Germanic barbarian. Without this idea deeply impressed upon a soldier's mind, there can be no true military enthusiasm. It has characterized all conquering races. Mere mechanism cannot do the work of life. Under the empire, the army was mere machinery. It had lost its ancient spirit; it was not inspired by patriotic glory; it maintained the defensive. The citizens were unwilling to enlist, and the ranks were gradually filled with the very barbarians against whom the Romans had formerly contended. The army was virtually composed of mercenaries from all nations, adventurers who had nothing to lose, who had but little to gain. They were turbulent and rebellious. Revolts among the soldiers were common. They brought new vices to the camps, and learned in addition all the vices of the Romans. They were greedy, unreliable, and cherished concealed enmities. They had no common interest or bond of union. They were always ready for revolt, and gave away the highest prizes to fortunate generals. They sold the imperial dignity, and became the masters rather than the servants of the emperors. Diocletian was obliged to disband the Prætorian band. The infantry, which had penetrated the Macedonian phalanx, threw away their defensive armor, and were changed to troops of timid horsemen, whose chief weapon was the bow. And they wasted their strength in civil contests more than against barbaric foes. They no longer swam rivers, or climbed mountains, or marched with a burden of eighty pounds. They scorned their ancient fare and their ancient pay. They sought pleasure and dissipation. The expense of maintaining the army kept pace with its inefficiency. Soldiers were a nuisance wherever they were located, and fanned disturbances and mobs. Their license and robbery made them as much to be dreaded by friends as by enemies. They assassinated the emperors when they failed to comply with their exorbitant demands. They often sympathized with the very enemies whom they ought to have fought. Enfeebled, treacherous, without public spirit, caring nothing for the empire, degenerate, they were thus unable to resist the shock of their savage enemies. Finally, they could not even maintain order in the provinces. "There was not," says Gibbon, "a single province in the empire in which a uniform gov-

Decline of military virtues.

Degeneracy of the legions.

ernment was maintained, or in which man could look for protection from his fellow man." What could be hoped of an empire when people were unwilling to enlist, and when troops had lost the prestige of victory? The details of the military history of the latter Romans are most sickening — revolts, rival generals, an enfeebled central power, turbulence, anarchy. Even military obedience was weakened. What would Cæsar have thought of the soldiers of Valentinian siding with the clergy of Milan, when Ambrose was threatened with imperial vengeance? What would Tiberius have thought of the seditions of Constantinople, when the most trusted soldiers demanded the head of a minister they detested? Where was the power of mechanism, without genius to direct it? What could besieged cities do, when treachery opened the gates? The empire fell because no one would belong to it. How impotent the army, without spirit or courage, when the hardy races of the North, adventurous and daring, were pouring down upon the provinces — men who feared not death; men who gloried in their very losses! The legions became utterly unequal to their task; they were recalled from the distant provinces in the greater danger of the capitals; and the boundaries of the empire were left without protectors. The empire was created by strength, enthusiasm, and courage; when these failed, it melted away. And even if the old discipline were maintained, how inadequate the army against the overwhelming tide of barbarians, fully armed, and bent on conquest. In all the victories of Valerian, Constantine, and Theodosius, we see only the flickering lights of departing glory. Military genius, united with patriotism, might have delayed the fall, but where was the glory of the legions in those last days? Military science belonged to the republic, not the empire. One reason why the army did not save the empire was, because there was no army capable of meeting the exigencies of the fourth and fifth centuries. It was corrupted, perverted, conquered.

The hopeless imbecility of the army under emperors.

Nor could *any* army, however strong, do more than prop up existing institutions. These themselves were rotten. Despotism cannot save a state. The reign of Louis XIV. was one of the most brilliant in modern annals. But no reign ever more signally undermined the state. It is the patriotism of soldiers that saves, not their physical force. Their force can be turned against the interests of a state as well as employed in its favor. Despotism sows the seeds of future ruin. No state was ever supported by military strength, except for a time, and then only when the soldiery were animated by noble sentiments. The imperial forces of Rome, while they preserved the throne of absolutisms, destroyed the self-reliance of the citizens, and supported wicked institutions. The difference in the aims of government under the Cæsars, and under the consuls, was heaven-wide. The military genius which created an empire, was misdirected when that empire sought to perpetuate wrong. How different is the spirit which animated the armies of the United States, when they sought to preserve the institutions of liberty and the integrity of the state, from that spirit which animates the armies of the Sultan of Turkey! The Roman empire under the later emperors was more like the Ottoman empire, than the republic in the days of Cato. It was sick, and must die. A great army devoted to the interests of despotism generates more evils than it cures. It eats out the vitals of strength, and poisons the sources of renovation. It suppresses every generous insurrection of human intelligence. It merely arms tyrants with the power to crush genius and patriotism. It prevents the healthful development of energies in useful channels. The most that can be said in favor of the armies of the empire is, that they preserved for a time the decaying body. They could not restore vitality; they warded off the blows of fate. They could only keep the empire from falling until the forces of enemies were organized. No generalship could have saved Rome. The great military emperors must have felt that they were powerless against the combination of barbaric forces. The soul of Theodosius must have sunk within him to see how fruitless were his victories, how barren *any* victories to such a diseased and crumbling empire. Diocletian retired, in the plenitude of his power, to die of a broken heart. The utmost the emperors could do, was to erect on the banks of the Bosphorus a new capital, and virtually make a new combination of those provinces most removed from danger. The old capital was abandoned to its fate.

Despair of the military emperors.

The elaborate and complicated constitution of the Romans, on which so much genius and experience were employed, *was* subverted when Cæsar passed the Rubicon. Only forms remained, a bitter mockery, and a thin disguise. These were nothing. Neither consuls, nor prætors, nor pontiffs, nor censors, nor tribunes existed, except in name. Every office of the republic was absorbed in the imperial despotism. The glorious constitution, which gave authority to Cato and dignity to Cicero, was a dead-letter. Flatterers, and sycophants, and courtiers, took the place of senators. The imperial despotism crushed out every element of popular power, every protest of patriots, every gush of enthusiasm. The constitution could not save when it was itself lost. Never was there a more wanton and determined disregard of those great rights for which the nations had bled, than under the emperors. Every conservative influence that came from the people was hopelessly suppressed. The reign of beneficent emperors, like the Antonines, and of monsters like Nero and Caracalla, was alike fatal. The seal of political ruin was set when Augustus was most potent and most feared. Government simply meant an organized mechanism of oppression. There is nothing conservative in government which does not have in view the interests of the governed. When it is merely used to augment gigantic fortunes, or

The Roman constitution.

create inequalities, or encourage frivolities, and allows great evils to go unredressed, then its very mechanism becomes a refinement of despotic cruelty. When sycophants, jesters, flatterers, and panderers to passions become the recipients of court favor, and control the hand that feeds them, then there is no responsible authority. The very worst government is that of favorites, and that was the government of Rome, when only courtiers could gain the ear of the sovereign, and when it was for their interest to cover up crimes. What must have been the government when even Seneca accumulated one of the largest fortunes of antiquity as minister? What must have been the court when such women as Messalina and Agrippina controlled its councils? The ascendency of women and sycophants is infinitely worse than the arbitrary rule of stern but experienced generals. The whole empire was ransacked for the private pleasure of the emperors, and those who surrounded them. "*L'état, c'est moi*," was the motto of every emperor from Augustus to Theodosius. With such a spirit, so monopolizing and so proud, the rights of subjects were lost in an all-controlling despotism, which crushed out both grand sentiments and noble deeds. None could rise but those who administered to the pleasures of the emperor. All were sure to fall who opposed his will. From this there was no escape. Resistance was ruin. There was a perfect system of espionage established in every part of the empire, and it was impossible to fly from the agents of imperial vengeance. And the despotism of the emperors was particularly hateful, since it veiled its powers under the forms of the ancient republic, until in the very wantonness of its vast prerogatives it threw away its vain disguises, and openly and insultingly reveled on the forced contributions of the world. There were good and wise emperors who sought the welfare of the state, but these were exceptions to the general rule. Octavius,

Infamy of the imperial regime.

Abortive efforts of good emperors.

that Ulysses of state craft, checked open immoralities by legal enactments, discouraged celibacy, expelled unworthy members from the Senate, appointed able ministers and governors, and sought to prevent corruption, which was then so shameful. Vespasian introduced a severe military discipline among the legions, permitted citizens to have free access to his person, and promoted many great objects of public utility.

Hadrian attempted to give dignity to the Senate, and visited in person nearly all the provinces of his empire, impartially administered justice, magnificently patronized art, and encouraged the loftiest form of Greek philosophy. Antoninus Pius and Marcus Aurelius set, in their own lives, examples of the sternest virtue, although they were deceived in the character of those to whom they delegated their powers, and were even ruled by unworthy favorites. Marcus Aurelius was, after all, the finest character of antiquity who was intrusted with absolute power. Contrasted with Solomon, or Augustus, or even Theodosius, he was a model prince, for he had every facility of indulging his passions, but his passions he restrained, and lived a life of the severest temperance and virtue to the end, sustained by the severest doctrines of the Stoical school. All that his rigid severity and moral elevation could do to save a decaying empire was done. He sought to base the stability of the throne on a rigid morality, on self-denial and self-sacrifice. When only twelve, he adopted the garb and the austerities of a philosopher, believing in virtue for its own sake.

Hadrian.

Marcus Aurelius.

From his earliest youth he associated with his instructors in the greatest freedom, and it was the happiness of his life to reward philosophers and scholars. He promoted men of learning to the highest dignities of the empire, and even showed the greatest reverence for the cultivation of the mind. Philosophy was the great object of his zeal, but he also gave his attention to all branches of science, to law, to music, and to poetry. His disposition was kind and amiable, and he succeeded in acquiring that self-command and composure which it was the professed object of the Stoics to secure. He was firm without being obstinate, gentle without being weak. He was modest, retiring, and studious. He believed that it was necessary for good government that rulers should be under the dominion of philosophy. He was so universally beloved and esteemed, that everybody who could afford it had his statue in his house. No man on a throne was ever held in such profound veneration. If ever there was, in a heathen country, an example of sublime virtue, it shone in the life of Marcus Aurelius; if ever there was an expression of supernal beauty, it was in his features beaming with love and gentleness and humility. He never neglected the duties of his office. He was noble in all the relations of a family. He was the model of an emperor. He only complained of want of time to prosecute his literary labors. He was probably the most learned man in his dominions. The Romans called him brother and father, and the Senate felt that its ancient dignity was restored. He had great causes of unhappiness. The barbarians invaded his territories; a long peace had destroyed martial energies; the Roman world was sinking into languor and decay; his adoptive brother Verus lived in luxury and dissoluteness; his wife Faustina was a second Messalina, abandoned to promiscuous profligacy; a pestilence ravaged Asia Minor, Greece, Italy, and Gaul, still this great man preserved his serenity, his virtues, and his fame. He was unseduced by any kind of mortal temptation, and left an unstained character, and an unrivaled veneration for his memory. And when we consider that he was the absolute master of one hundred and twenty millions, having at his disposal the riches of the world, and all its pleasures, — above public opinion, with no law to check him — a law only to himself, we find more to admire than in Solomon before his fall. *His meditations* have lately been translated and published — a work full of moral wisdom, rivaling Epictetus in morality, and the sages of the Middle Ages in contemplative piety. Niebuhr says it is more delightful to speak of him than of any man in history. The historical critic can see but one defect — his persecution of the Christians. He was doubtless a bigoted Stoic, as Paul was, at one time, a bigoted Pharisee; and the great delusion of his life was to rear a basis of national prosperity on the sublime morality of the philosophers whom he copied. He sought to save the state by the Stoical philosophy. Never were nobler efforts put forth on the part of a philosophic prince; but neither his patronage of philosophers, nor his own bright example, nor the doctrines of the Porch, conservative as they are, were of any avail. The Roman world could not be saved by the philosophy of Aurelius any more easily than the imperial despotism could be averted by the patriotism of Cicero. He was succeeded, after a glorious reign of twenty years, by his son Commodus, as incapable of managing an empire as Rehoboam was the kingdom of his father Solomon. Thus are the schemes and enterprises of the best men baffled by a mysterious power above us, who holds in his own hands the destinies of nations — the Divine Providence who giveth and who withholdeth strength.

Marcus Aurelius did all that human virtue could do to arrest the ruin which he saw, with the saddest grief, was impending over the empire, in spite of all the external prosperity which called forth such universal panegyric. And the empire was also favored by a succession of military emperors, who tried the force of arms, as Aurelius had philosophy.

Never did abler men reign on an absolute throne. All that genius and experience and skill could do to arrest the waves of the barbarians was done. A succession of most brilliant victories marked these later days of Rome. Amid unparalleled disasters, there were also most memorable triumphs. The glory of the Roman name was revived in Claudius, Aurelian, Probus, Carus, Diocletian, Constantius, Galerius, Constantine, Julian, all of whom rendered important services. These great emperors were uniformly victors, yet were doomed to hurl back perpetually advancing forces of Teutonic warriors, who were resolved on conquest. Diocletian was a second Augustus, and Constantine another Julius. But their conquests and reconstructions were all in vain. The barbarians advanced. They were getting more and more powerful with defeat; the Romans weaker and weaker after victory. In the middle of the fourth century the Goths were firmly settled in Dacia, the Persians had recovered the provinces between the Euphrates and the Tigris, Gaul was invaded by Germans, the Saxons had ravaged Britain, the Scots and Picts had spread themselves from the wall of Antoninus to the shores of Kent, Africa had revolted, Sapor had broken his treaties, the Goths had crossed the Danube, the Emperor Valens had been slain, with sixty thousand infantry and six thousand cavalry. From the shores of the Bosphorus to the Julian Alps, nothing was to be seen but rapes, murders, and conflagrations. Palaces were destroyed, churches were turned into stables, the relics of martyrs were desecrated, women were ravished, bishops were praying in despair, cities had fallen, the country was laid waste; the desolation extended to fishes and birds. Fruitful fields became pastures, or were overgrown with forests. The day of ruin was at hand. There was needed a hero to arise, a deliverer, a second Moses. And a great man appeared in the person of Theodosius — the most able and valiant of all the emperors after Julius Cæsar.

Theodosius.

The career of Theodosius is exceedingly interesting, since it shows that every thing which imperial genius could do to arrest ruin, was done by him.

Theodosius was thirty-three years of age when summoned from retirement to govern the world. He had learned the art of war from his father in Britain, and had, in his lifetime, defeated the Sarmatians. The Romans, disheartened by the tremendous defeat they had sustained under the walls of Adrianople, and the death of Valens the emperor, had no longer the courage to brave the Goths in the open field, and Theodosius was too prudent to lead them against a triumphant enemy. He retired to Thessalonica to watch the barbarians. In four years he had revived the courage of his troops, even as Alfred subsequently rekindled the martial ardor of the Saxons after their defeat by the Danes. On the death of Fritigern, the first great historic name among the Visigoths, his soldiers were demoralized, and divided by jealousies, and were won over by the arts and statesmanship of Theodosius, and a treaty was made with them by which they obtained a settlement within the limits of the empire, and became the allies of the emperor. The Ostrogoths were soon after defeated in a decisive battle on the Danube, and all fears were removed, at least for the present, of these hostile barbarians.

Theodosius was equally fortunate in his conflicts with Maximus, who had usurped the provinces of Gaul, Spain, and Britain, and who meditated the conquest of Italy. At Aquileia the usurper was seized, after a succession of defeats, stripped of his imperial ornaments, and delivered to the executioner, and Theodosius reigned without a rival in the renovated empire, practicing the virtues of domestic life, rewarding eminent merit, and protecting the interests of the church. He restored the authority of the laws, and corrected the abuses of the preceding reigns. Whatever rival or enemy, in those distracted times, raised himself up against the imperial authority, was easily subdued. Eugenius met the fate of Maximus, and Arbogastes turned his sword against his own breast. Theodosius reigned in peace and wisdom, the idol of the church, and the object of fear to the barbaric world. He had his defects and vices, and committed errors and crimes, but his reign was beneficent, and the Christian world hoped that the evils which threatened the empire were removed. Alas, the empire was doomed. The death of Theodosius was the signal for renewed hostilities. His sons, the feeble Arcadius and Honorius, were unequal to the task of governing the empire, and it fell into the hands of the barbarians, who ruthlessly marched over the crumblings ruins, regardless of the treasures of the classic soil and of the guardians which Christianity presented in the presence of protesting bishops. The empire could not be saved by able emperors, however great their military genius. Absolutism, whether wielded by tyrants, or philosophers, or generals, was alike a failure. What hope for the empire when the Senate inculcated maxims of passive obedience to tyrants; when such lawyers as Papinias and Paulus declared that emperors were freed from all restraints? What could Alexander Severus do when the most illustrious man in the empire — the learned and immortal Ulpian — was murdered before his eyes by the guards, of which he was the prefect, and when such was the license of the soldiers, that the emperor could neither revenge his murdered friend, nor his insulted dignity; when his own life was sacrificed to the discontents of an army which had become the master of the emperors themselves? After the murder of this brave and enlightened prince, no emperor was safe upon his throne, or could do more than oppose a feeble barrier to the barbarians upon the frontiers. External dangers may have raised up able commanders, like Decius, Aurelian, and Probus; but they could not prevent the inroads of the Goths, or heal the miseries of society. Of the nineteen tyrants who arose during the reign of Gallienus, not one died a natural death. And when, after a disgraceful period of calamities, Diocletian ascended the throne, the ablest perhaps of all the emperors after Augustus, no talents could

Successors of Theodosius.

Diocletian.

sustain the weight of public administration, and even this emperor attempted to extinguish the only influence that had power to save. Absolutism had sowed seeds of ruin, which were destined to bear most wretched fruit.

Roman jurisprudence.

Jurisprudence was the science of which the Romans have the most to boast; and this was not perfected until the time of the emperors. It was closely connected with the constitution, but was superior to it, since it was based upon the principles of natural justice or equity. This has lasted when all material greatness has vanished, and still forms the basis of the laws of European nations. This was a great element of civilization itself; it was part of the mechanism of social order; it pervaded all parts of the empire; it made the reign of tyrants endurable.

There is no doubt that the excellence of the laws formed one of the most powerful conservative influences of pagan antiquity. We glory in those laws as one of the proudest achievements of the human mind. But laws are rather an exponent of the state of society than a controlling force which modifies it. If a murderer is to be hung, or a thief imprisoned, the rigid law shows simply no mercy to murderers and thieves; it does not create a sentiment which prevents, though it may punish, iniquity. The wise division of property among heirs may operate against injurious accumulations, but does not prevent disproportionate fortunes. The more complicated the jurisprudence, the more need it seems that society has of restraints and balances. The law cannot go higher than the fountain. The more perfect the state of society, the less need there is of laws. The cautious guards against fraud simply show that frauds are common and easy. The minute regulations in reference to the protection of property and contracts, show that the prevailing customs and habits of dealers were corrupt, and needed the strong arm of a protecting government. As a general thing, it will be found that the laws are best, and most rigidly enforced, when iniquity prevails. A man is safe in Paris when he is not in Boston, but we do not infer from this fact that society is higher, but that there is a sterner necessity on the part of government to restrain crime. The laws of the Romans give the impression of the necessity of a constant watchfulness and supervision to prevent the strong preying upon the weak. Other influences are more necessary than laws to keep men virtuous and orderly. Laws are necessary, indeed; but they are not the first conditions of social existence.

Perversion of the laws.

But what are we to think of laws when they are either evaded or perverted, when there is not wisdom to feel their justice, or virtue to execute them? What are laws if judges are corrupt? The venality of the judges of Rome was proverbial. Even in the comparatively virtuous age of Cicero, a friend wrote to him not to recall a certain great functionary, since he himself was implicated in his robberies, and the request was granted. The empire was regarded as spoil, and the provinces were robbed of their most valuable treasures. Witness the extortions of Verres in Sicily, when a residence of two years was enough to make the fortune of a provincial governor. Nor was Roman law ever independent of political power. The prætors were politicians having ambitious aims beyond the exercise of judicial authority. Influential men could ever buy verdicts, and the government winked at the infamy. There *was* justice in the *abstract*, but not in the *reality*. And when jurisprudence became complicated, judgments were made on technical points rather than on principles of equity. It was as ruinous to go to law at Rome as in London. Lawyers absorbed the money at issue by their tricks and delays. They made the practice of their noble profession obscure and uncertain. Clients danced attendance on eminent jurists, and received promises, smiles, and oyster-shells. It was, too, often better to submit to an injury than seek to redress it. Cases were decided *against* justice, if some technical form or ancient usage favored the more powerful party. Lawyers formed a large and powerful class, and they had fortunes to make. Instead of protecting the innocent, they shielded the guilty. Those who paid the highest fees were most certain of favorable verdicts. The laws practically operated to make the rich richer and the poor poorer. Between the venality of the court and the learned jugglery of advocates, there was little hope for the obscure and indigent. Says Merivale: "The occupation of the bench of justice was the great instrument by which powerful men protected their monopolies; for, by keeping this in their own hands, they could quash every attempt at revealing, by legal practice, the enormities of their administration. And the means of seduction allowed by law, such as the covert bribery of shows and festivals, were used openly and boldly." What, then, could be hoped from the laws when they were made the channel of extortion and oppression? Law, the glory of Rome in the abstract, became the most dismal mockery of the rights of man. Salt is good, but if the salt has lost its savor it is good for nothing, not even for the dunghill. When the laws practically add to the evils they were intended to cure, what hope is there in their conservative influence? The practice of the law ever remained an honorable profession, and the sons of the great were trained to it; but we find such men as Cyprian, Chrysostom, and Augustine, who originally embarked in it, turning from it with disgust, as full of tricks and pedantries, in which success was only earned by a prostitution of the moral powers. Laws perverted were worse than no laws at all, since they could be turned by cunning and sharp lawyers against truth and innocence. It would be harsh and narrow to say that lawyers were not necessary; but they did very little to avert evils. A wicked generation pressed over the feeble barriers which the laws presented against iniquity. They were only cobwebs to catch the insignificant. Unless good laws are enforced by virtue and intelligence, they prove a snare. It is the enforcement of laws, on the principles of justice, not the creation of them, that saves a state.

If a complicated system of laws and government, on which the reason and experience of ages were expended, did not prevent the empire from falling into the hands of barbarians, much less was to be expected of art, for which the Romans were also distinguished in common with the Greeks. Much is said of the ennobling influence of those great creations which gave so great lustre to ancient civilization. Founded on imperishable ideas, we naturally attribute to them a great element of national preservation, as they were of glory and pride.

Art among the later Romans.

It cannot be denied that art, when in harmony with the exalted ideals of beauty and grace, which it seeks to perpetuate on canvas or in marble, does much to improve the taste, to promote refinement and æsthetic culture. And when art is pursued with a lofty end, seeking, like virtue, its own reward, there is much that is ennobling in it. Even that literature is most prized and most enduring which is artistic, like the odes of Horace, the epics of Virgil, the condensed narrative of Tacitus; like the "Elegy in a Country Churchyard," or the "Deserted Village," or "Corinne," or "Waverley." Varro was the most learned writer whom Rome produced, and the most voluminous. Yet scarcely any thing remains of his productions. They were deficient in art, like German histories — very useful in their day, but only survive in the writings of those who made use of their materials. Hence science is not so enduring as poetry, when poetry is exalted, since it is superseded by new discoveries. Hence style in writing, when of great excellence, gives immortality to works which could not have lived without it, even had they been ever so profound. Voltaire's "Charles XII." is still a classic, like the numbers of the "Specta-

Its inherent beauty.

tor," although superficial, and, perhaps, unreliable. A great painting is like the history of Thucydides — it lives because it is a creation. Hence art, when severe and lofty, cannot be too highly praised or cherished. A man cannot write for bread as he writes for fame; and he cannot write for fame as he writes to satisfy his own ideal. The immortal poets are those who sing themselves away to the regions of bliss, in a divine ecstacy, from love of art, or to give expression to the feelings which fill the soul. Sir Walter Scott could write his "Ivanhoe" when inspired by the sentiments which warmed the chivalrous ages; he became a mere literary hack when he wrote to pay his debts.

The true artist is one of the favorites of Heaven, in a great measure exalted above mortal commiseration, even if his days are clouded with cares and sorrows. He lives in a different and purer atmosphere than ordinary men. He may not banquet on the pleasures of sense, but he revels in the joys of the soul. A Dante may be sad and sorrowful, as when, in his gloomy wanderings and isolations, he asked of Fra Ilario the rest and peace of his sacred monastery; but he was sad as a greater than he wept over Jerusalem, in the profound seriousness of superior knowledge, in the sublime solitariness of an inhabitant of another and grander sphere. Genius ever partakes of this sadness, and it is as shallow to mistake it for misery as it would be to pity the saint passing through the tribulations of our worldly pilgrimage, in full view of the unending glories which are in store for him in the celestial city. The higher joys of the soul are foreign to frivolity, tumult, and the mirth of wine, — those pleasures most prized by the weak or sensual. There is nothing more sublime in this world than the example of a lofty nature seeking the imperishable, the true, the beautiful, the good, amid discomfort, or reproach, or neglect.

The true artist.

Such are truly great artists. Sometimes they are munificently rewarded by their generation with praises and material goods, as was Apelles among the Greeks, and Raphael among the Italians. Sometimes their excellence was unappreciated, except by a few. But whether appreciated or not, the great artists of antiquity belong to the constellation of men of genius which shall shine forever. They lived in their own glorious realm of thought and feeling, which the world can neither understand nor share. They did not live for utilities. They lived to realize their own exalted ideas of excellence.

But this was not the case in imperial Rome. All writers speak of a most signal decline in the arts from Augustus to Diocletian. Even architecture became corrupted. It was without taste, or a mere copy, like the arch of Constantine, from the older models. There were no original edifices erected, and such as were built were in defiance of all the principles that were established by the Greek architects. Least of all did art encourage grand sentiments. It did not paint ethereal beauty. It did not chisel the marble to elevate or instruct. Statues were made to please the degraded taste of rich but vulgar families, to give pomp to luxury, to pander wicked passions. Painting was absolutely disgraceful; and we veil our eyes and hide our blushes as we survey the decorations of Pompeii. How degrading the pictures which are found amid the ruins of ancient baths! Art was sensualized, perverted, corrupting. Paintings appealed either to perverted tastes, or fostered a senseless pride, or stimulated unholy passions, or flattered the vanity of the rich — brought angels down to earth, not raised mortals to heaven. They commemorated the regime of tyrants, or amused the wealthy classes, whose wealth had bought alike the muse of the poets and the visions of the sculptor. Art was venal. She sold her glories, which ought to be as unbought as the graces of life and the smiles of beauty; and she became a painted Hætera, drunk with the wine-cups of Babylon, and fantastic with the sorceries of Egypt.

Decline of art.

Prostitution of art.

How could she, thus prostituted, elevate the people, or arrest degeneracy, or consecrate the ancient superstitions? She facilitated rather than retarded the ruin. It is marvelous how soon art degenerated with the progress of luxury, reproducing evil more rapidly than good, and obscuring even truth itself. Pleasures that appeal to the intellect will ever be in accordance with prevailing tastes, and the more exquisite the art the more fatally will it lead astray by the insidious entrance of a form as an angel of light. We cannot extinguish art without destroying one of the noblest developments of civilization ; but we cannot have civilization without multiplying the dangers and temptations of human society. And even granting that the arts of the pagan world had a refining influence on the few, what is this unless accompanied with the virtues which grow out of self-sacrifice? I am not speaking of those glories which art ought to represent, but of those attractions which it presents when degraded. What conservative influence can result from the Venus of Titian? Why did not art reform morals, as morals elevated art? And why did art degenerate? Why did it not keep its own? The truth is, that art is esoteric, and not popular. The imagination of the vulgar is not sufficiently cultivated to see, in the emblems which art typifies, those passions or sentiments which have moved generations with enthusiasm. A Gothic cathedral is infinitely more interesting to a man of sentiment or learning than to an unlettered boor. The ignorant cannot appreciate the historical fidelity and marvelous study of races which appear in such a statue as the African Sybil. We must comprehend the character of Moses before we can kindle with admiration at the dignity and majesty which Michael Angelo impersonated in his statue. When Phidias, Praxiteles, and Lysippus moulded their clay models, they had a Pericles, a Plato, or a Demosthenes for their critics and admirers. It was for them they worked, and by them

The later Romans incapable of appreciating art.

they were stimulated — not the rabble crowd of slaves and sycophants. But when, at Rome, there was no Cicero, no Octavius, no Mecænas, no Horace, the artists toiled to please imperial gluttons, pretentious freedmen, ignorant generals, drunken senators, and venal judges. Their sublime art became the handmaid of effeminacy, of vanity, of sensuality. It could not rise above the level of those who dedicated themselves to its service. It did not make men better. Was Leo X. a wiser Pope because he delighted in pictures? Did art make the Medici at Florence more susceptible to religious impressions? Does art sanctify Dresden or Florence? Does it make modern capitals stronger, or more self-sacrificing, better fitted to contend with violence, or guard against the follies which undermine a state? What are the true conservative forces of our world? On what did Luther and Cranmer build the hopes of regeneration? The cant of dilettanti would be laughed at by the old apostles and martyrs. Art amuses, and may refine when it is itself pure. It does not brace up the soul to conflict. It does not teach how to resist temptation. It presents temptations rather. It gilds the fascinations of earth. It does not point to duties, or the life to come. That which is conservative is what saves, not what adorns. We want ideas, invisible agencies, that which exalts the mind above the material. So far as art can do this it is well. It is a great element of civilization. So far as gardens and flowers and villas and groves can do this, let us have them. Let us make a paradise out of a desert. Man was put into Eden to dress and to keep it. The material, rightly directed and used, is part of our just inheritance. Man is physical as well as intellectual. It is monkish and erratic to spurn the outward blessings of Providence. An inheritance in Middlesex is worth more than one in Utopia. Give us beauty and grace — they are invaluable. But let us remember, also, that it is chiefly from moral truth that the soul expands —

The degradation of art.

the recognition of responsibilities and duties. No matter how splendid we make the triumphs of art in its æsthetic influence, the question returns, Did these, in their best estate, in Greece and Rome, lead to patriotism, to sacrifice, to an elevated social home? And if these did not arrest corruption, how could art, when perverted, save a falling empire? All profound inquiries as to the progress of the race centre in moral truths, — those which have reference to the spiritual rather than the material, the future rather than the present. Art failed because it did not propound grand ideas which pertain to spiritual and future interests. It especially failed when it pandered to perverted tastes, when it was the mere pastime of the rich, and diverted the mind from what is greatest and holiest. St. Paul, when he wandered through the Grecian cities, said very little of the sculptures and the temples which met his eye at every turn. He was not insensible to beauty and grandeur. But he felt that all renovating forces came from the ideas which he was sent to preach. He did not condemn art; he probably admired it; but this he saw was a poor foundation of national happiness and strength. If the severe morality of the Stoics was a feeble barrier against corruption, how much more feeble were temples to Minerva, and statues to Jupiter, and pictures of Venus? Great was Diana of the Ephesians, but not as an influence to stem degeneracy. Exalt art as highly as we can, it is not a renovating power, and it is this of which we speak.

Utter failure of art as a conservative power.

Literature attempted something higher than art; nor need we expatiate on its transcendent excellence in the classical ages. This itself was art, art in the highest and most enduring form, and will live when marbles moulder away. Virgil, Cicero, Horace, Tacitus, Livy, Ovid, were great artists, and civilization will perpetuate their fame. They cannot die. What more immortal than the artistic delineations of man and of nature which

Attempts of literature.

the poets and historians wrought out with so much labor and genius? When did men, uninspired by Christianity, utter sentiments more tender, or thoughts more profound, or aspirations more lofty? They are our perpetual study and marvel — prodigies of genius, such as appear only at great intervals. All that is most valuable in the ancient civilization is perpetuated in its literature, and survives empires and changes. The men who were amused and instructed by these great masterpieces *have* passed away, as well as their empire, but these will interest remotest generations. These live by their own vitality. If the unaided intellect of man could soar so high under the withering influence of paganism and political slavery and social degradation, we cannot but feel that Christianity has higher missions to accomplish than to stimulate the intellectual faculties of man; and, while we remember that, in our own times, some of the highest creations of genius have been made by those who have repudiated the spirit of Christianity, we cannot but feel that conservative influences do not come from literature, in its best estate, unless its ideas are inspired by the Gospel. The great writers of the Augustan age did not arrest degeneracy, any more than Goethe and Bulwer and Byron and Hugo have in our own day. They amused, they cultivated, they adorned; they did not save. Nor is it probable that the great masterpieces of antiquity were favorite subjects of study, except with a cultivated few, any more than Milton, Bacon, and Pascal are read in our times by the people. They enriched libraries; they were venerated and preserved in costly bindings; but they were not familiar guides. The people read nothing. The great writers of antiquity complain of the frivolity of the public taste. Moreover, the troubles of the empire and the corruptions of society were unfavorable to lofty creations of genius. Men were absorbed in passing events; and literary men generally pandered to the vile taste of the people, or stooped to adulate the monsters whom they feared. Hunting and hawking furnished subjects for the muse of the poets. History was reduced to dull and dry abridgments, and still drier commentaries. The people sought scandalous anecdotes, or demoralizing sketches, or frothy poetry. **Degradation of literature.** The decline in letters, like the decline in art, kept pace with the public misfortunes. When lofty and contemplative characters were saddened and discouraged, in view of public and private corruption, and saw ruin approaching, they had no spirit to make great exertions — and exertions which would not be appreciated. They sought retreats. There was no life, no enthusiasm in literature. It was conventional — to suit fashionable coteries, with whom strength was unpalatable and dignity a rebuke. Sound was preferred to sense. Rhetoric supplanted thought. A sentimental flow of words passed current for poetry. Literary men united into mutual admiration societies, and exalted their own frivolous productions. As the penny-a-liners of our day enumerate in their catalogue of great men chiefly those who have written romances and poetry for magazines, and pass unnoticed the stern thinkers of the age, so the literary gossips of Rome made the city ring, like grasshoppers, with their importunate chink. Unfortunately they were the only inhabitants of the field, for "no great cattle" kept silence under the shadow of the protecting oak. Nero suppressed the writings of Lucan, because he painted, in his "Pharsalia," the follies of the time. Lucian gave vent to his bitter sarcasms, and raised the veil of hypocrisy in which his generation had wrapped itself; but his mockery, like that of Voltaire, demolished, without seeking to substitute any thing better instead. Petronius laughed at the vices he did not wish to remove, and in which he himself shared. Juvenal and Martial both flattered the tyrants they detested. The nobles may have laughed at their bitter sarcasms, but they pursued their pleasures. Literature, under Augustus, did but little to elevate the Roman mind. What could be expected when it was coarse, feeble, and frivolous? If intellectual strength will not keep men from vices, what can be expected when intellect panders to passions and interests? There is no more absurd cant than that the culture of the mind favors the culture of the heart. What do operas and theatres for the elevation of society? Does a sentimental novel prompt to duty? Education seldom keeps people from follies when the will is not influenced by virtues. If Socrates sought the society of Aspasia, if Seneca amassed a gigantic fortune in the discharge of great public trusts, if Cicero languished in his exile because deprived of his accustomed pleasures, if Marcus Aurelius was blind to the rights and virtues of Christians, what could be hoped of the literary sensualists of the fourth century? If knowledge did not restrain the passions of philosophers, how could passions be restrained when every influence tended to excite them? Athens fell when her arts and schools were in the zenith of their glory, how could Rome stand when arts and schools undermined the moral health? Neither poets, nor historians, nor critics had in view the regeneration of society. They wrote, as poets and novelists write now, for bread, for fame, for social position. If such a man as Racine, so lofty and severe, was killed by a frown from Louis XIV., how could such an elaborate voluptuary as Petronius live out of the smiles of Nero and the flatteries of the court? If literature is feeble to arrest degeneracy when it is lofty, inasmuch as it reaches only the cultivated few, how inadequate it is when it is itself corrupted! The taste of our times, with all our glorious Christian literature, and our public libraries, our lecturers, our preachers, our professors, and our standard classical authorities, is scarcely kept from being perverted by the flimsy literature which has inundated us, and the newspaper platitudes which we devour with our breakfast. With every effort of true and Christian philanthropists, it is questionable whether there is any moral progress among us. There is a material growth ; but does the moral correspond, with all our immense machinery for the elevation of society? What, then, could be expected at Rome, where there were no public libraries, no newspapers, no lyceums, no pulpits, no printing-presses, and where books were the solace of a few aristocrats, and where these aristocrats could only be amused by scandalous anecdotes and frivolous poetry. Literature did not even hold its own. It steadily declined from the Augustan age. It declined in proportion as the people had leisure to read it. Instead of elevating society, society corrupted literature. The same may be said of literature as was said of art. It did not fulfill its mission, if it was intended to save. It could reach only a small part of the population, and those whom it did reach were simply amused.

It would be too sweeping to affirm that the better forms of Roman literature did not refine and elevate, but unfortunately they reached only a few minds, and not always those who had political and social power. Literature was not powerful enough, was not sufficiently circulated, and the greater part of it was demoralizing, thus proving a savor of death rather than a savor of life. When a civilization reproduces evil more rapidly than good, there is not much hope for society, except from some signal interposition of Almighty power. Society is infinitely gloomy to a contemplative man, when there are no antidotes to the poison which is rapidly consuming the vitality of states. We contemplate approaching death, and death amid the array of physical glories. It is like a rich man laid on the bed from which he will never rise, surrounded with every comfort and every pleasure that men seek. Literature was a feeble medicine to the dying patient. Had all classes banqueted on the rich treasure of the mind, and been content, then there might have been some hope. But this was not the fact. Only a few

Failure of literature.

reveled in the glories of thought. And these scorned the people.

But philosophy attempted something higher and nobler —even to reform morals, especially at Rome. The Romans had but little taste for abstract speculations. And hence they did not extend the boundaries of thought and reason beyond the limits which the Greeks arrived at. But they adopted what was most practical in the Grecian philosophy, and applied it to common life.

Ancient philosophy.

If there is any thing lofty in paganism, it is philosophy. It proposed to seek the beautiful, the true, the good; to divert men from degrading pursuits; to set a low estimate on money, and material gains, and empty pleasures. It was calm, fearless, and inquiring. All sects of philosophers despised the pursuits of the vulgar, and affected wisdom. Minerva, not Venus, not Diana, was the goddess of their idolatry. It deified reason, and sought to control the passions. It longed for the realms of truth and love. It believed in the divine, and detested the gross. Hence the philosophers were not eager for outward rewards, and kept aloof from the demoralizing pleasures of the people. They attired themselves in a different garb, lived retired, and studied the welfare of the soul. Mind was adored, and matter depreciated. They were esoteric men who abhorred vice, and sought the higher good. Morally, they were in general superior to other men, as they were in intellectual gifts and attainments. And they opposed the popular current of opinions, and stemmed popular vices. They were the reformers of the ancient world, the sages — earnest men, advocating the great certitudes of love and friendship and patriotism — the lofty spirits of their time, preoccupied and rapt in their noble inquiries into nature and God. Look at Socrates, so careless of dress, walking barefooted, giving what he had away, courting mortification, and disdaining popular favor, if he could only persuade his pupils of the greatness of the infinite and imperishable. Look at Pythagoras, refusing political office, and consecrating himself to teaching. Look to Xenophanes, wandering over Sicily in the holy enthusiasm of a rhapsodist of truth. Look at Parmenides, forsaking patrimonial wealth, that he might teach the distinction between ideas obtained through the reason, and ideas obtained through the senses. Look at Heraclitus, refusing the splendid offers of Darius, and retiring to solitudes, that he might explore the depths of his own nature. See Anaxagoras, allowing his fortune to melt away, that he might discover the many faces of nature. See Empedocles, giving away his fortune to poor girls, that he might attack the Anthropomorphism of his day; or Democritus declining the sovereignty of Abdera, that he might have leisure to speculate on the distinction between reflection and sensation; or Diogenes living in a tub; or Plato in his garden; or Aristotle in the shady side of the Lyceum; or Zeno guarding the keys of the citadel. See the good Aurelius, in later and more corrupt ages, forsaking the pleasures of an imperial throne, that he might meditate on his soul's welfare, or the slave Epictetus, unfolding the richest lessons of moral wisdom to a corrupt and listless generation.

The Romans fail to appreciate philosophy.

The loftier forms of the ancient philosophy were never popular, even at Athens. The popular teachers were sophists and rhetoricians, who, as men of fashion and ambition, despised the sublime speculations of Socrates and Plato. The Platonic philosophy had a hold only of a few, and these were men of powerful minds, but stood aloof from the prevailing tastes and pleasures. It had still less influence on the Roman mind, which was practical and worldly. Platonism opposed the sensualism and materialism of the times, believed in eternal ideas, sought the knowledge of God as the great end of life — a sublime realism which was hardly more appreciated than Christianity itself. Platonism was doubtless the highest effort of uninspired men, under the influence of pagan ideas and institutions, to attain a knowledge of God and the soul. It gloried in immortality, and claimed for man a nature akin to the deity, and destined to a higher development after death. It endeavored to understand our complex nature, and trace a connection between earth and heaven. It sought to distinguish between forms and essence, the spiritual and the sensual. It spiritualized the popular mythology, and insisted on the unity on which it fundamentally rests. It did not sneer at religious earnestness, and looked upon the beatitudes of the soul as the highest good of earth.

But such knowledge was too wonderful for the Romans. It was high, and they could not attain unto it. Its ends were too spiritual and elevated. There was scarcely an eminent Roman who adopted the system. Cicero came the nearest to understand its spiritual import, but it was too lofty even for him. He composed a republic and a treatise of laws, in which reason and the rule of right should be made the guide of states and empires. In this way Platonism, as a sublime hypothesis, entered into jurisprudence. It affected the thinking of master minds, even as it entered into Christianity at a later period, and formed an alliance with it. But, practically, it did not have much effect on life and manners. It was regarded as a system of mysticism, cherished by a very small esoteric body of believers, who were spurned as dreamers. They were looked upon very much as the transcendentalists of our own day are regarded, with whom the great body of even thinkers had but little sympathy. There was no more respect for Plato at Rome than there is for Kant among the merchants of London. His name may have been pronounced with an oracular admiration, but there was no profound appreciation of him, no general knowledge of his writings, no sympathy for his doctrines. They were to the Romans foolishness, somewhat after the sense that

Platonism.

Christianity was to the Greeks. They transcended their experience, went beyond the limits of their thoughts, and sought spiritual certitudes which they disdained.

The philosophy of Aristotle was nearly as distasteful to the Romans as that of Plato, and it was less lofty. It had a skeptical tendency, and excluded scientific light from the sphere of activity, and inculcated a proud and self-reliant spirit. The academics denied the possibility of arriving at truth with certainty; and, therefore, held it uncertain whether the gods existed or not, whether the soul is mortal or survives the body, whether virtue is preferable to vice, or the contrary. They sneered at religious earnestness, and tacitly encouraged influences greatly to be dreaded. They held in supreme contempt the popular religion, and made a mockery of religious ceremonies. They undermined superstition, but weakened religion also by substituting nothing instead of the absurdities they brushed away. Lucian was a type of these philosophers, and his bitter sarcasms were more powerful than the logic of Cicero to destroy what could not be proved. The academics may be said to have been the rationalists of antiquity. The old religions could not maintain their ground before the inquiring skepticism and sarcastic wit of these irreligious philosophers, who contented themselves with a lifeless deism — a system which did not, indeed, deny the existence and providence of God, but which attributed to the Deity an indifference respecting the affairs of men. Dr. Neander, in the first volume of the "History of the Church," has shown the effects of the unbelief of the academics on the state of society at Rome, especially on the men of rank and fashion. Infidelity, in any form, can have no conservative influence. It is designed to pull down, and not to build up. Superstition, with all its puerilities, is better than a scornful and proud philosophy which takes no cognizance of popular wants and aspirations.

The Aristotelian philosophy.

Its failure.

The Stoical philosophy.

If any form of ancient philosophy could have renovated society, it was the Stoical school, which Zeno had founded. It commended itself, in a corrupt age, to many noble and powerful minds, because it raised them above the corruption around them, and proclaimed an ideal standard of morality. The Romans cared very little for mere speculations on God or the universe; but they did revere that which proposed a practical aim. The Stoics despised prevailing baseness, and set examples of a severe morality. Marcus Aurelius, one of the loftiest followers of this school, was a model of every virtue, and he looked upon his philosophy as a means of salvation to a crumbling empire. But the Stoics, with all their morality, were the Pharisees of pagan antiquity. They held themselves superior to all other classes of men. They gloried in their proud isolation. And with all the loftiness of Stoicism, it did not teach of a God who governed the world in mercy and love, but according to the iron decrees of necessity. It attacked error with a stern severity, but had no toleration for human weakness. It confounded the idea of God with that of the universe, and therefore destroyed his personality, making the Deity himself an influence, or a development. The Stoic despised the age, and despised every influence to elevate it which did not come from himself. He treated the most wholesome truths so partially as to be led into the greatest absurdities of doctrine and inconsistencies with their general principle. Epictetus, indeed, infused a new life into the Stoical philosophy. He taught the doctrine of passive endurance so forcibly that the Christians claimed him for their own. But there was nothing which appealed to the people in Stoicism. It was too stern and cold. It had no humanity. Hence they stood aloof, as they did from all the systems of Grecian philosophy. It was not for them, but for the learned and the cultivated. It was a system of thought; it was not a religion — a speculation and not a life. Like Platonism, the Stoical philosophy was esoteric, and only appealed to a few elevated minds, who had affected indifference to the evils of life, and had learned to conquer natural affections. The Stoical doctrines of Epictetus had a more practical end in view than those of Zeno, since they were applied to Roman thought and life. We cannot deny the purity and beauty of his aphorisms, but he was like Noah preaching before the flood. He had his disciples and admirers, but they made a feeble barrier against corruptions. It was the protest of a man before a mob of excited and angry persecutors resolved on his death. It was no more heard than the dying speech of Stephen. It was lost utterly on a people abandoned to inglorious pleasure.

The Epicurean philosophy.

The only form of philosophy which was popular with the Romans, and which was appreciated, was the Epicurean. The disciples of this school were, of course, the luxurious, the fashionable, the worldly, and it exercised upon them but a feeble restraining influence. It denied the providence of God; it maintained that the world was governed by chance; it denied the existence of moral goodness; it affirmed that the soul was mortal, and that pleasure was the only good. If the more contemplative and the least passionate rebuked gross vices, they still advocated a tranquil indifference to outward events that showed neither loftiness nor fear of judgment. Their system was openly based upon atheism. Self-love was the foundation of all action, and self-indulgence was the ultimate good. The Epicureans were the patrons of the circus, and the theatre, and the banquet, and, indeed, of all those vanities and follies which disgraced the latter days of Rome. Their influence tended to enervate and corrupt. Their philosophy, instead of preserving old forms of life, old customs, old institutions, old traditions and associations, made a mockery of them all, and was as efficient in producing decay as was the philosophy of the eighteenth century in France in paving the way for the revolution.

The purest type of Epicureanism may have refined a few of the better sort, but the prevailing influence, doubtless, undermined society. The god of the reason was allied with the god of the sense, and the maniac soul of the lying prophet entered the schools. Education, as directed by them, served only to make youth worldly and frivolous. Teachers sought to amuse and not to instruct, to make royal roads to knowledge, to exalt the omnipotence of money, to set a high value on what passes away. They limited man to himself, and acknowledged no other object of human exertion than is to be found within the compass of the fleeting phenomena of the present life. They had no wish beyond the present hour, and only aimed to console man in the corruption and misery which he saw around him. They had no high aims; nor did they seek to produce profound impressions. They adapted themselves to what was, rather than what ought to be. They were easy and gracious, but utterly without earnestness. The Peripatetic inquired, sneeringly, "What *is* truth?" The Epicurean languidly said, "What is truth to *me*. There is no truth nor virtue, nor is there a God, nor a place of rewards and punishments. This world is my theatre. Let me eat and drink, for to-morrow I die. I will abstain from inordinate self-indulgence, for it will shorten my life, or produce satiety, ennui, disgust — not because it is wrong. I will make the most of earth and of my faculties for pleasure. Wealth is the greatest blessing, poverty the greatest calamity. Friends are of no account, unless they amuse me or help me. The sentiment of friendship is impossible, and would be unsatisfactory." The true Epicurean quarreled with no person and with no opinions. Nothing was of consequence but ease, prosperity, self-forgetfulness. The soul of man could aspire to nothing beyond this life; and when death came, it was a release, a thing neither to be regretted nor rejoiced in, but an irresistible fate. What could be expected from such a system?

What renovation in such a cold, barren, negative faith, without hope, without God in the world? The most prevalent of all the systems of philosophy, so far from doing good, did evil. How could it save when its ends were destructive of all those sentiments on which true greatness rests? What could be expected of a philosophy which only served to amuse the great, to throw contempt on the people, to undermine religious aspirations, to vitiate the moral sense, to ignore God and duty and a life to come?

Thus every influence at Rome, whether proceeding from art, or literature, or philosophy, or government, instead of saving, tended to destroy. All these things came from man, and could not elevate him beyond himself. Even religion was a compound of superstitions, ritual observances, and puerilities. It did not come from God. It was neither lofty nor pure. What good there was soon became perverted, and the evil was reproduced more rapidly than good. Only error seemed to have vitality. The false lights which sin had kindled shed only a delusive gleam. The soul occasionally asserted the dignity which God had given it, and great men swept and garnished houses, but devils reëntered, and the normal condition of humanity was what the Bible declares it to be since Adam was expelled from Paradise. Genius, energy, ambition, were allowed to win their victories, and they shed a glorious light, and for a time exalted the reason of man, but alas, were soon followed by shame and degradation.

All forms of civilization fail to be conservative.

And what is the logical inference — the deduction which we are compelled to draw from this mournful history of the failure of all those grand trophies of the civilization which man has made? Can it be other than this: that man cannot save himself; that nothing which comes from him, whether of genius or will, proves to be a conservative force from generation to generation; that it will be perverted, however true, or beautiful, or glorious, because "men love darkness rather than light." All that is truly conservative, all that grows brighter and brighter with the progress of ages, all that is indestructible and of permanent beauty, must come from a power higher than that of man, whether supernatural or not — must be a revelation to man from Heaven, assisted by divine grace. It must be divine truth in conjunction with divine love. It must be a light from Him who made us, and which alone baffles the power of evil.

He did send Christianity, when every thing else had signally failed, as it will forever fail. And this is the seed of the woman which shall bruise the serpent's head.

We have now to show why this great renovating and life-giving influence did not prevent the destruction of the empire; and we may be convinced that if this great end could not be accomplished in accordance with the plans of Providence, and in accordance with the laws by which He rules the world, Christianity was in no sense a failure, as man's devices were; but, through the mouths and writings of great bishops, saints, and doctors, projected its saving truths far into the shadows of barbaric Europe, and laid the foundation for a new and more glorious civilization — a civilization not destined to perish, so far as it is in harmony with divine revelation.

CHAPTER XIII.

WHY CHRISTIANITY DID NOT ARREST THE RUIN OF THE ROMAN EMPIRE.

ONE of the most interesting inquiries which is suggested by history is, Why Christianity did not prevent the glory of the old civilization from being succeeded by shame? This is not only a grand inquiry, but it is mysterious. We are naturally surprised that literature, art, science, laws, and the perfect mechanism of government should have proved such feeble barriers against degeneracy, for these are among the highest triumphs of the human mind, and such as the world will not willingly let die. But a still more potent and majestic influence than any thing which proceeds from man still remained to the haughty masters of the ancient world. A new religion had been proclaimed with the establishment of the empire, which gradually broke down the old superstitions, conquered the hatred and prejudices of both Greeks and Romans, supplanted the old systems of Paganism, and went on from conquering to conquer, until it seated itself on the imperial throne, and proved itself to be the wisdom and the power of God.

But we see that as this wonderful religion gained ground, whether in changing the lives of individuals, or in allying itself with dominant institutions, the Roman Empire declined. When Christianity was first proclaimed, the Roman eagles surmounted the principal cities of antiquity, and the central despotism on the banks of the Tiber was the law of the world. When it was a feeble light on the mountains of Galilee, the glory of Rome was the object of universal panegyric, and the city of the seven hills rejoiced in a magnificence which promised to be eternal. But when Paganism yielded to Christianity, and when the latter had spread to every city and village in the empire, with its grand hierarchy of bishops and doctors, the proud empire was in ruins. It would even seem that its decline and fall kept pace with the triumphs of a religion it had spurned and persecuted.

Society retrograded as Christianity spread.

What is the explanation of this grand mystery? Why should society have declined as Christianity spread, if, as we believe, Christianity is the great conservative force of the world, and is destined to regenerate all government, science, and social life? If the stability of the empire rested on virtues, and was undermined by vices, virtue must have declined and vice increased. But how can we reconcile such a fact with the progress of a religion which is the mainspring of all virtue, and the destruction of all vice? We do know that Christianity did not prevent the empire from falling, but also we have the testimony of poets and historians to the exceeding wickedness of society when Christianity was fairly established.

A mysterious fact.

In presenting the strange phenomenon of a falling empire with an all-conquering religion, it is necessary to grapple with the gloomy problem. We have unbounded faith in the power of Christianity to save the world, and yet we see a mighty empire crumbling to pieces from vices which Christianity did not subdue. What a deduction might be drawn from this strange fact, that Christianity *can*, but *but did not, save*. How mournful the future of modern Christian nations if the same fact should be repeated — if civilization should decline as Christianity achieves its triumphs! Is it possible that civilization, the triumph of human genius and will, may fade away as Christianity, which gives vitality to society, advances? Has civilization nothing to do with Christianity?

But there can be nothing mournful in the developments of a divine religion — nothing discouraging in the conquests which seemed incomplete. Nor did it really, in any important task, prove a failure; but amid the ashes of the old world, as it disappeared, we see the new creation, and listen to melodious birth-songs. Indeed, the fall of the empire, when we profoundly survey it, instead of detracting from Christianity, only prepared the way for higher triumphs, and for a loftier development of civilization itself. Future ages have probably lost nothing by the ruin of Rome, while the world has gained by the establishment of Christianity, even by the seeds of truth planted by the early church.

Christianity not however a failure.

Still, it cannot be questioned that, in the Roman empire, vices and corruptions spread with terrific and mournful rapidity even after Christianity was revealed — so rapidly, indeed, that Christianity opposed but a feeble barrier.

The history of Christianity among the Romans suggests these three inquiries: —

First, why it proved so feeble in arresting degeneracy; secondly, how far it conserved old institutions; and thirdly, how far it created a new and higher civilization.

The first inquiry, on a superficial view, is discouraging. We see a sublime realism making quietly its converts by thousands, without seemingly checking ordinary vices. We are reminded of Socrates creating Platos, yet failing to reform Athens. We behold witnesses of the truth in every land, which gradually sinks deeper and deeper in infamy as the witnesses increase. And, when the land is about to be overrun by barbarians, when despair seizes the public mind, and desolation overspreads the earth, and good men hide in rocks, and dens, and caves, we see the church resplendent with wealth and glory, her bishops enthroned as dignitaries, princes doing homage to saints, and even the barbarians themselves bowing down in reverence and awe. How barren these ecclesiastical vic-

Christianity fails to check degeneracy.

tories seem to a superficial or infidel eye! If Christianity is what its converts claim, why did it accomplish so little?

But, in another aspect, the victories do not seem so barren; and they even appear more and more majestic the more they are contemplated. There is something grand in the spread of new ideas which are unpalatable to the mighty and the wise. Considering the humble characters of the early Apostles and their disciples, their triumphs were really magnificent. It is astonishing that the teachings of fishermen should have supplanted the teachings of Jewish rabbis and Grecian philosophers, amid so great and general opposition. It is remarkable that their doctrines should have so completely changed the lives of those who embraced them. It is wonderful that emperors who persecuted and sages who spurned the religion of Jesus, should have been won over by a moral force superior to all the venerated influences of the old religion of which they were guardians and expounders. It is surprising that such relentless and bloody persecutions as took place for three hundred years should have been so futile. When we remember the extension of Christianity into all the countries known to the ancients, and the marvelous fruits it bore among its converts, making them brothers, heroes, martyrs, saints, doctors — a benediction and a blessing wherever they went; and when we see these little esoteric bands, in upper chambers or in catacombs, persecuted, tormented, despised, yet gaining daily new adherents, without the aid of wealth, or learning, or social position, or political power, until generals, senators, and kings came willingly into their fraternity, and bound themselves by their rules, and changed the whole habits of their lives, looking to the future rather than the present — the infinite rather than the finite; blameless in morals, lofty in faith, heavenly in love; sheep among wolves, yet not devoured — we feel that Christianity cannot be too highly exalted as a conquering power.

Yet still a conquering religion.

But the point is, not that Christianity failed to conquer, but that it failed to save the Roman world. The conquests of the church are universally admitted and universally admired. They were the most wonderful moral victories ever achieved. But, while Christianity conquered Rome, why did she fail to arrest its ruin? Vice gained on virtue, rather than virtue gained on vice, even when the cross was planted on the battlements of the imperial palaces.

The victories of Christianity came not too late for the human race, but for the stability of the Roman empire. Had Christianity completely triumphed when Julius Cæsar overturned the republic, the empire might have lasted. But when Constantine was converted, the empire was shaken to its foundations, and the barbarians were advancing. No medicine could have prevented the diseased old body from dying. The time had come. When the wretched inebriate embraces a spiritual religion with one foot in the grave, with a constitution completely undermined, and the seeds of death planted, then no repentance or lofty aspiration can prevent physical death. It was so in Rome. Society was completely undermined long before the emperors became Christians. The fruits of iniquity were being reaped when Chrysostom and Augustine lifted up their voices. The body was diseased, so that no spiritual influence could work upon it. Had every man in the empire been a Christian, yet, when the army had lost its discipline and efficiency, when patriotism had fled, when centuries of vices had enfeebled the physical forces, when puny races had lost all martial ardor, and could present nothing but weakness and cowardice — all from physical causes, how could they have successfully contended with the new and powerful barbaric armies? Christianity saves the soul; it does not restore exhausted physical functions. The vices which had undermined were learned before Christianity protested, and

Christianity too late to save.

were dominant when Christianity was feeble. The effects of those vices were universal before a remedy could be applied.

Moreover, when Christianity itself was a vital and conquering force, the number of its converts formed but a small proportion of the inhabitants of the empire. Witnesses of the truth were sent into every important city in the world, but they simply protested in a dark corner. Their warning voice was unheeded except by a few, and these were unimportant people in a social or political or intellectual point of view. Even when Constantine was converted, the number of Christians in the empire, according to Gibbon, whose statement has not been refuted, was only one fifth of the whole population. And this accounts for the insignificant social changes that Christianity wrought. A vast majority was opposed to them even in the fourth century. There were doubtless large numbers of Christians at Rome, Antioch, Alexandria, Corinth, Ephesus, and other populous cities, in the third century, and also there were powerful churches in the great centres of trade, where people of all nations congregated; but they were exposed to bitter persecutions, and they durst not be ostentatious, not even in those edifices where they congregated for the worship of Jehovah. For two centuries they worshiped God in secret and lonely places, exposed to persecution and scorn. Not only were the Christians few in number, when compared with the whole population, but they were chiefly confined to the humble classes. In the first century not many wise or noble were called. No great names have been handed down to us. Now and then a centurion was converted, or some dependent on a great man's household, or some servant in the imperial family; but no philosophers, or statesmen, or nobles, or generals, or governors, or judges, or magistrates. In the first century the Christians were not of sufficient importance to be generally persecuted by the

Limited number of the converts.

government. They had not even arrested public attention. Nobody wrote against them, not even Greek philosophers. We do not read of protests or apologies from the Christians themselves. No contemporary historian or poet alludes to them. They had no great men in their ranks, either for learning, or talents, or wealth, or social position. In the cities they were chiefly artisans, slaves, servants, or mechanics, and in the country they were peasants. They were unlettered, plebeian, unimportant. If there were distinguished converts, we do not know their names. Ecclesiastical history is silent as to distinguished persons except as persecutors, or as great contemporaries. We read of the calamities of the Jews, of Herod Agrippa, of Philo, of Nero's persecution, of the emperors, but not of Christians. Eusebius does not narrate a single interesting or important fact which took place in the first century through the agency of a great man. We know scarcely more than what is contained in the New Testament. We read that Clement was bishop of Rome, but know nothing of his administration. We do not know whether or not he was a man of any worldly consideration. Nothing in history is more barren than the annals of the church in the first century, so far as great names are concerned. Yet in this century converts were multiplied in every city, and traditions point to the martyrdoms of those who were prominent, including nearly all of the Apostles.

Early Christians unimportant.

In the second century there are no greater names than Polycarp, Irenæus, Ignatius, Justin Martyr, Clement Melito, and Apollonius — quiet bishops or intrepid martyrs — bishops who addressed their flocks in upper chambers, and who held no worldly rank — famous only for their sanctity or simplicity of character, and only mentioned for their sufferings and faith. We read of martyrs, some of whom wrote valuable treatises and apologies; but among them we find no people of

Obscurity of the early Christians.

rank, not even ladies like Paula and Marcella and Fabiola, in the time of Jerome, unless Symphorosa is an exception. It was a disgrace to be a Christian in the eye of fashion or power. Even the great Marcus Aurelius, so distinguished as a man and a philosopher, had supreme contempt of the new apostles of truth, and was one of their most unrelenting persecutors. The early Christian literature is chiefly apologetic, and the doctrinal character of the fathers of this century is simple and practical, showing no great acquaintance with the system of heathen thought. There were controversies in the church — an intense religious life — great activities, great virtues, but no outward conflicts, no secular history, nothing to arrest public notice. But the converts to Christianity, plebeian as they were, were yet of sufficient consequence to be persecuted. They had attracted the notice of government. They were looked upon as fanatics who sought to destroy a reverence for existing institutions. But they had not as yet assailed the government, or the great social institutions of the empire. In this century the polity of the church was quietly organized. There was an organized fellowship among the members: bishops had become influential, not in society, but among the Christians; dioceses and parishes were established; there was a distinction between city and rural bishops; delegates of churches assembled to discuss points of faith, or suppress nascent heresies; the diocesan system was developed, and ecclesiastical centralization commenced; deacons began to be reckoned among the higher clergy; the weapons of excommunication were forged; missionary efforts were carried on; the festivals of the church were created; Gnosticism — a kind of philosophical religion — was embraced by many leading minds; catechetical schools taught the faith systematically; the formulas of baptism and the other sacraments became of great importance; marriage with unbelievers was discouraged; and monachism became pop-

Their intense religious life.

ular. The internal history of the church becomes interesting, but still the Christians had no great influence outside their own body; it was esoteric, quiet, unobtrusive; and it was a very small body of pure and blameless men, who did not aspire to control society.

While the church was thus laying the foundation of its future polity and power, but nothing more, and failed to attract the great, or men of ambitious views — those who led society — the empire was approaching a most fearful crisis. Hadrian had built a wall from the Rhine to the Danube to arrest the incursions of barbarians; the Roman garrisons beyond the Danube were withdrawn; the Goths had advanced from the Vistula and the Oder to the shores of the Black Sea; the Jews were dispersed; a chaos of deities was in the Roman Pantheon; Grecian philosophy had degenerated; the taste of the people had become utterly corrupt; games and festivals were the business and the amusement of the people; the despotism of the emperors had utterly annulled all rights; a succession of feeble and wicked princes ruled supreme; the empire was falling into a state of luxury and inglorious peace; the middle classes had become extinct; and disproportionate fortunes had vastly increased slavery. The work of disintegration had commenced.

The empire in a hopeless state.

The third century saw the church more powerful as an institution. Regular synods had assembled in the great cities of the empire; the metropolitan system was matured; the canons of the church were definitely enumerated; great schools of theology attracted inquiring minds; the doctrines of faith were systematized; Christianity had spread so extensively that it must needs be persecuted or legalized; great bishops ruled the growing church; great doctors speculated on the questions which had agitated the Grecian schools; church edifices were enlarged, and banquets instituted in honor of the martyrs. The church was rapidly advancing to a posi-

The church of the third century.

tion which extorted the attention of mankind. But even so late as the close of the third century, there were but few Christians eminent for riches or rank. There were some great bishops like Cyprian, Hippolytus, Victor, Demetrius; some great theologians like Origen, Tertullian, and Clement; some great heretics like Hermogones, Sabellius, and Novatian — all marked men, immortal men; but of no great influence outside their ranks.

What could they do in a time of so much public misery and misfortune as marked the empire when it was ruled by monsters; when the barbarians had obtained a foothold in the provinces; when the capital was deserted by the emperors for the camp; and when signs of decay and ruin were apparent to all thoughtful minds?

The church of the fourth century.

It was not till the fourth century—when imperial persecution had stopped; when Constantine was converted; when the church was allied with the state; when the early faith was itself corrupted; when superstition and vain philosophy had entered the ranks of the faithful; when bishops became courtiers; when churches became both rich and splendid; when synods were brought under political influence; when monachists had established a false principle of virtue; when politics and dogmatics went hand in hand, and emperors enforced the decrees of councils — that men of rank entered the church, and the church had a visible influence on the state. It was not till the fourth century that such great names as Arius, Athanasius, Hosius, Eusebius, Cyril of Alexandria, Hilary of Poictiers, Martin of Tours, Diodorus of Tarsus, Ambrose of Milan, Basil of Cæsarea, Cyril of Jerusalem, Gregory Nazianzen, Theophilus of Alexandria, Chrysostom of Constantinople, arose and made their voices heard in the council chambers of the great.

But when the church had become a mighty and recognized power, when it had assailed social institutions, when it drew men of rank into its folds, when it was no longer an obloquy to be a Christian — then the seat of empire had been removed to the banks of the Bosphorus; then the Goths and Vandals had become most formidable enemies, and Theodosius, the last great emperor, was making a brave but futile attempt to revive the glories of Trajan and the Antonines. The empire was crumbling to pieces — was dying — and even Christianity could not save it politically.

The empire dismembered before the political triumphs of Christianity.

Thus, when Christianity was pure, and a truly renovating religion, it had no social influence on the leaders of rank and fashion. How could people of no political or social position, who were objects of ridicule and contempt, have effected great social or political changes? Until their conversion, they had not modified a law, and still less enacted one. How could they reach the ear of those who disdained, repelled, and persecuted them? They had no influence on the makers or the executors of laws. They could not call in the vast power of fashion, for they had no social prestige. They could not create a public opinion, for they were obliged to hide to save their lives. They had no learning to attract philosophers. They were not allowed to preach in public, and could not reach the people. They had no schools, nor books, nor colleges. They could not assail public institutions, for despotism was established and was irresistible. There was no liberty of speech by which they might have made converts above their rank. They could not subvert slavery without influencing those who controlled it. They could not destroy disproportionate fortunes, since the wealthy were protected by government. They could not interfere with games and demoralizing spectacles, for these were controlled by the emperor and his ministers, whose ear they could not reach, and upon whom all lofty arguments would have been wasted. The court, the army, the aristocracy, rushed with headlong eagerness into excesses and pleasures, which could not have been arrested by the wise and good of their own rank; much less by a class who were obnoxious and forgotten. The Christians could not even utter indignant protests without personal danger, to which they were not called. There was no possible way of presenting a barrier against corruption, outside their own ranks. Obscure men in these times can write books, but not under the empire; now they can lecture and preach, but not then. They were obliged to conceal their sentiments when there was danger of being suspected of being Christians. Those who have observed the resistless tyranny of fashion in our times — how even Christians are drawn into its eddies, not merely in such matters as dress, and houses, and education, but even in pleasures which are questionable, and in opinions which are false — what are we to think of the overwhelming influence of fashion at Rome, when society was still more artificial, when its leaders were kings and tyrants, and when all the propensities of human nature were in accordance with the customs handed down for centuries, and endorsed by all who were powerful in ordinary life. If Christians are so feeble in Paris, London, and New York, in suppressing acknowledged evils which come from the world, how could the early Christians prevent the ascendency of evils among those over whom they had no influence — perhaps those who did not feel them to be evils at all. If Christians who affect great social position in our cities cannot break up theatres and other demoralizing pleasures, how could the early Christians bring the games of the amphitheatre into disrepute? If social evils increase among us in spite of churches and schools and a free press and lectures, how could we expect them to decrease when no power was exerted to bring them into disrepute, and when the general tone of society was infinitely lower than in the worst capitals of modern times? What would wealthy senators, with their armies of clients and slaves, or the frivolous courtiers of godless emperors, or the sensual

The Christians form an imperfect barrier against corruption.

equestrians who composed a moneyed class, care for opposition to their pleasures from those whom they despised, and with whom they never associated, and who had no influence on public opinion? The Christians could not, and dared not, make their voices heard, to any extent, outside their own esoteric circle. They had an influence, or their circle could not have increased, but it was private and concealed. Artisans talked with artisans, servants with servants, soldiers with soldiers. They converted, quietly and unobtrusively, by private talk and blameless lives, those with whom alone they freely mingled. Thus their numbers multiplied, but their prestige did not increase, until these mechanics and laborers and slaves exercised some fortunate influence, by occasional entreaties, on their haughty masters. A favorite slave could sometimes gain the ear of the lady whose hair she dressed; or some veteran and trusted servant might persuade an indulgent master to listen to the new truths which were such a life to him. Thus the circle of the Christians gradually embraced some of the more candid and intellectual and fearless of the great. But it should be borne in mind that as the circle was enlarged, especially so as to embrace people whose lives had been egotistical and self-indulgent, the standard of morality was lowered. Also we should remember, as the circle increased, even of devout believers, that vice and degeneracy increased also outside the circle, and also as rapidly. The overwhelming current of corruption swept every thing away before it. What if the small minority were virtuous, when the vast majority were vicious. They were only witnesses of truth; they were not triumphant conquerors of error. If the state could have lasted a thousand years longer in peace and prosperity, then the leaven of the Gospel might have leavened the whole lump. But the barbarians could not wait for society to be renovated. They came when society

The Christians an esoteric band of worshipers.

Christians powerless outside their ranks.

was most enervated. When the Christians had gained sufficient influence to stop the games of the circus and the amphitheatre; when they had induced emperors to modify slavery; when they uttered protests against demoralizing amusements, the barbarians had advanced, and were becoming the new masters of the empire. The prayers of Augustine, the letters of Jerome, the sermons of Chrysostom, the ascetic example of Basil, could no more arrest the march of the avengers of centuries of misrule than the intercession of Abraham could stop the thunderbolts of God on the guilty inhabitants of Sodom. The Roman world, so long abandoned to every folly and sin, must reap the bitter fruit. It was no reproach to Christianity that it did not avert the consequences of sin, any more than it was a reproach to Jonah that he could not save Nineveh. If Christianity effects so little with us, when there are no opposing religions, and all institutions are professedly in harmony with it; when it controls the press and the schools and the literature of the country; when its churches are gilded with the emblem of our redemption in every village; when its ministers go forth unopposed, and have every facility of delivering their message, even to the wise and mighty; when philanthropy comes in with its mighty arm and knocks off the fetters of the slave, and sends the Gospel to every land — how could it affect society when every influence was against it. If religion wanes before the dazzling forces of a brilliant material civilization, and scarcely holds her own, when all profess to be governed by Christian truth, so that in a moral and spiritual view, society rather retrogrades than advances, I am amazed that it made so considerable a progress in the Roman empire, and increased from generation to generation until it shook the throne of emperors. And the example of the early church would seem to indicate that religion can only spread in a healthy manner by constantly guarding and purifying those who profess it. It would seem that the true mission of the church is to elevate her own members rather than to mingle in scenes which have a corrupting influence. It is not easy to make the theatre a means of moral improvement, for it will be deserted when it rises above popular tastes, and the more it panders to these tastes the more it flourishes. The theatre may have been elevated at Athens, when the citizens who thronged to hear the plays of Sophocles were themselves cultivated. Racine may have been relished at Versailles, but only because the court of a great king composed the audience. The theatre never rises *above* the taste of those who patronize it. Christian teachings would have been spurned at Rome even had there been no persecution. The church flourished because it instructed its own members, and quietly gained an extension of its influence, not because it appealed to those who opposed it. The church, in those days, was not a philanthropical institution, or an educational enterprise, or a network of agencies and "instrumentalities" to bring to bear on society at large certain ameliorating influences or benignant reforms. These were beyond its reach. But it was a secret body of believers, a kind of freemasonry which aimed to control and reform those who belonged to it. Its rules were for members, not the outside world. Hence the history of the early church refers chiefly to its discipline, to its officers, to the management of dioceses, to councils, holydays, festivals, liturgies, creeds, bearing only on its own internal organization. The members of this secret society lived apart from the world, absorbed in their own spiritual interests, or seeking to save the souls of those with whom they came in contact. The true triumphs of Christianity were seen in making good men of those who professed her doctrines, rather than changing outwardly popular institutions, or government, or laws, or even elevating the great mass of unbelievers. And it is more comforting to feel that the church was small and

The church powerless outside its circle.

pure than that it was large and corrupt. And for three centuries there is reason to believe that the Christians, if feeble in influence and few in numbers when compared with the whole population, were remarkable for their graces and virtues — for their noble resistance to those temptations which enthrall so great a number of our modern believers. Insignificant in every public sense, they may not have lifted up their voices against the system of slavery which did so much to undermine the state; they may not have lectured against the despotic power of the imperator; they may have taken but little interest in politics, rendering unto Cæsar whatever was due, whether taxes or obedience; they may not have formed schools or colleges or lyceums; they may not have meddled with any thing outside their ranks, except to preach temperance, justice, and a judgment to come, and a Saviour who was crucified, and a heaven to be obtained; but they did practice among themselves all the duties enjoined by Christ and his Apostles; they refused to sacrifice to the gods of pagan antiquity; they visited no shows; they attended no pageants; they gave no sumptuous banquets; they did not witness the games of the theatre and the circus; they did not play at dice, or take usury, or dye their hair, or wear absurd ornaments, or indulge in unseemly festivities; they detested astrologers and soothsayers, shrines, images, and idolatry; they kept the Sabbath, educated their children in the faith, settled their disputes without going to law, were patient under injuries, were charitable and unobtrusive, were full of faith and love, practicing the severest virtues, devout and spiritual when all were worldly and frivolous around them, ready for the martyr's pile, and looking to the martyr's crown. That Christianity should have rescued so many from the pollution of paganism in such general degeneracy, is very wonderful. That it should have extended its circle of sincere believers amid increasing degeneracy, is still more so, and is a most encouraging fact to the friends of religious progress. If it could not reach the fashionable and the worldly wise before society was undermined, and the provinces had become the prey of barbarians, it still could boast of a glorious army of martyrs, witnesses of the truth, whom all ages will hold in veneration, precious seed for future and better times. If Christianity, when it was a life, — a great transforming and renovating power, reforming what was bad, conserving what was good, — had but little influence beyond the circle of believers, still less could it save the empire when it was itself corrupted, when it was a mere nominal religion, however extensively it had spread. When it became the religion of the court and of the fashionable classes, it was used to support the very evils against which it originally protested, and which it was designed to remove.

Christianity itself corrupted.

It first adopted many of the errors of the oriental philosophy. Gnosticism was embraced by many of the leading intellects of the church. It was the reaction of that old aristocratic spirit which had ruled the pagan world. It was an eclecticism of knowledge and culture which had originally despised the doctrines of the Cross. It united the oriental theosophy with the Platonic philosophy, both of which were proud, exclusive, disdainful. "It drew a distinction between the man of intellect, whose vocation it was to know, and the man who could not rise above blind and implicit faith." The early Christians were characterized for the simplicity of their faith. But with the triumphs of faith arose the cravings for knowledge among the more cultivated part of the converts.

It adopts oriental errors.

Paul had seemingly discouraged all vain speculations, and the Grecian spirit of philosophy, believing that they would not avail to the explanation of the Christian mysteries, but rather prove a stumbling-block and a folly, since the realm of faith was essentially different from the realm of reason — not necessarily antagonistic, but distinct. This fundamental principle has ever been maintained by the more orthodox leaders of the church — by Athanasius, Augustine, Bernard, Pascal, Calvin — even as the fundamental principle of sound philosophy which Bacon advocated, that the world of experience and observation could not be explained by metaphysical deductions, has been the cause of all great modern progress in the sciences. The Gnostics, the men who aimed at superior knowledge, disdained the humbling doctrine of Paul, which made faith supreme over all forms of philosophy, and were the first to seek solutions of difficult points of theology by abstruse inquiries — honorable to the intellect, but subversive of that docile spirit which Christianity enjoined. This tendency to speculation was unfortunate, but natural to those active minds who sought to discover a connection between the truths taught by revelation, and those which we arrive at by consciousness. Grecian philosophy, when most lofty, as expressed by Plato, was based on these mental possessions — these internal convictions reached by logic and reflection. What more harmless, and even praiseworthy, to all appearance, than was this earnest attempt to reconcile reason with faith? The finest minds and characters of the church entered into the discussion with singular intensity and ardor. They would explain the Man-God, the Trinity, the Word made flesh, and all the other points which grew out of grace and free will. A dialectical spirit arose, which combated or explained what had formerly been received with unquestioning submission. In the first century there was scarcely any need of creeds, for the faith of the Christians was united on a few simple doctrines, such as are expressed in the Apostles' Creed. In the second and third centuries agitations and speculations began, and with the Gnostics, that class who invoked the aid of Oriental and Grecian philosophies in the propagation of the new religion. It was to be made dependent on human speculation — a most

Attempts to reconcile reason with faith.

dangerous error, since it reintroduced the very *wisdom* which knew not God, and which the Apostles ignored. It ushered in the reign of rationalism, which still refuses to abdicate her throne, and which is absolutely rampant and exulting in the great universities of the most learned and inquiring of European nations.

Gnosticism.

But Gnosticism partook more of the haughty and exclusive spirit of the eastern sages, than of the patient and inquiring nature of the Grecian schools. It soared into regions whither even Platonism did not presume to venture. It sought to subject even the Grecian mind to its wild and lofty flights. The doctrines which Zoroaster taught pertaining to the two antagonistic principles of good and evil — the oriental dualism — Parsism had great fascination, especially to those who were inclined to monastic seclusion. The spirit of Evil, which seemed to be dominant on earth, and which was associated with material things, chained the soul to sense. The soul, longing for truth and holiness — for God and heaven — panted to be free of the corrupting influences of matter, which imprisoned the noblest part of man. The oriental Christian, not fully emancipated from the spirit which Buddhism communicated to all the countries of the East — that is, the longing of the soul for the release from matter, its reunion with the primal power from which all life has flowed, and the estrangement from human passions and worldly interests — sought repose and retirement where the mind would be free to dwell on the great questions which pertained to God and immortality. The dualistic principle, one of the chief elements of Gnosticism, harmonized with the prevailing temper of that age, even as the pantheistic principle rules the schools of philosophy in our own. All Christians were alive to consciousness of the power of evil. Gnosticism recognized it. Christianity triumphs over it by the power of the Cross which procures redemption. Gnosticism would work out salvation by abstractions, by ascetic severities, by a renunciation of the pleasures of the world. Hence it is the real father of monasticism — that spirit of seclusion and self-abnegation which became so prevalent in the third and fourth centuries, and which remained in the church through the mediæval period. Gnosticism busied itself with the solution of insoluble questions respecting the origin of evil, which Christianity justly relinquished to the domain of useless inquiries — "the wisdom of the world." Gnosticism would acknowledge no limits to human speculation; Christianity accepts mysteries hidden from the wise and prudent, and yet revealed unto babes. Hence all sorts of crudities of belief crept into the church, such as the idea of the demiurge, and the different ways of contemplating the person of Christ. Moreover, the Gnostics subjected the New Testament to the boldest criticism, affirming it to be impossible to arrive at the true doctrines of Christ; and hence they sought to go beyond Christ, explaining difficult subjects by rationalistic interpretations. Cerinthus placed a boundless chasm between God and the world, and filled it up with different orders of spirits as intermediate beings. Basilides supposed an angel was set over the entire earthly course of the world. Valentine announced the distinction between a psychical and pneumatical Christianity. Ptolemæus maintained that the creation of the world did not proceed from the supreme God. Bardesanes sought to trace the vestiges of truth among people of every nation. Carpocrates maintained that all existence flowed from one supreme original being, to whom it strives to return. Prodicus asserted that as men were sons of the supreme God, a royal race, they were bound by no law. Saturnine advanced a fanciful system on the creation. Tatian advocated the mortality of the soul. Marcion attempted to sunder the God of Nature and the God of the Old Testament from the God of the Gospel. It is difficult to enumerate all the fanciful theories propounded by the Gnostics, and which arose from the attempt to engraft Orientalism upon Christianity.

Manicheism.

A still greater attempt to blend Christianity with the religions of ancient Asia was made by Mani, a Persian, who especially attempted to fuse Zoroastrian with Christian doctrines. He aimed to produce the utmost estrangement from all mundane influences, since the evil principle held in bondage the elements springing out of the kingdom of light. Deliverance from this bondage he regarded as the great end and aim of life. His spirit was pantheistic, probably derived from Buddhism, which he had learned during his extensive journeys into India and China. He adopted the dualism of Zoroaster, and supposed two principles antagonistic to each other, on the one side God, the primal light, from whom all light radiates, on the other side Evil, whose essence is self-conflicting uproar, matter, darkness. Most nearly connected with the supreme God were Æons, — the channels for the diffusion of light, — innumerable in number and of surpassing greatness. The Æon-mother of life generated the primitive man to oppose the powers of darkness. Hence man's nature is full of dignity, although he was worsted in the conflict with Evil. But the spirit raises him once more to the kingdom of light, and purifies his soul which sprung from the primitive man. The pure soul is Christ, enthroned in the sun, superior to all contact with matter, and incapable of suffering.

These were some of the features of that mystical philosophy which made Christ the spirit of the sun, giving light and life to the soul imprisoned in the kingdom of darkness. Man thus becomes a copy of the world of light and darkness, struggling against matter, elevated by the source of life — a soul living in the kingdom of light, and a body derived from the kingdom of darkness, and enticed by all the pleasures of sense, and thus drawn down to the world which is matter and evil, counteracted by the angel of light. This is the dualism which formed the essential element of the Manichean speculations, so congenial to the mystic theogonies of the East, and which was embraced by a portion of the eastern church, especially by those who were fascinated by the refinements and pretensions of a philosophy which aimed to solve the highest problems of existence — the nature of God, and the creation of man.

Mysticism. These daring speculations, which led astray so many inquiring minds, were, however, too mystical and indefinite to reach the popular mind, and they pertained to questions which did not shock Christian instincts, like those which attacked the person or the offices of Christ. Gnosticism was viewed as a sort of Judaism, inasmuch as it did not rest its exclusiveness on the title of birth, but on especial knowledge communicated to the enlightened few. It was a philosophy whose esoteric doctrines soared above the comprehension of the vulgar; but it affected more than the surface of society; it poisoned the minds of those who aspired to lead the intelligence of the age. Its spirit was antagonistic to the simplicity of the faith, and so, as it prevailed, was an influence much to be dreaded, and called forth the greatest energies of the Alexandrian school, in order to defeat it and nullify it. But its dangerous seeds remained to germinate a rationalistic theology, especially when united with the Neo-Platonic philosophy.

Adoption of oriental ceremonies and pomps. But the church was not only impregnated with the errors of pagan philosophy, but it adopted many of the ceremonials of oriental worship, which were both minute and magnificent. If any thing marked the primitive church it was the simplicity of worship, and the absence of ceremonies and festivals and gorgeous rites. The churches became, in the fourth century, as imposing as the old temples of idolatry. The festivals became authoritative; at first they were few in number, and purely voluntary. It was supposed that when Christianity superseded Judaism, the obligations to observe the ceremonies of the Mosaic law were abrogated. Neither the apostles nor evangelists imposed the yoke of servitude, but left Easter and every other feast to be honored by the gratitude of the recipients of grace. The change in opinion, in the fourth century, called out the severe animadversion of the historian Socrates, but it was useless to stem the current of the age. Festivals became frequent and imposing. The people clung to them because they obtained a cessation from labor, and obtained excitement. The ancient rubrics mention only those of the Passion, of Easter, of Whitsunday, Christmas, and the descent of the Holy Spirit. But there followed the celebration of the death of Stephen, the memorial of John, the commemoration of the slaughter of the Innocents, the feast of Epiphany, the feast of Purification, and others, until the Catholic Church had some celebration for some saint and martyr for every day in the year. They contributed to create a craving for an outward religion, which appealed to the senses and the sensibilities rather than the heart. They led to innumerable quarrels and controversies about unimportant points, especially in relation to the celebration of Easter. They produced a delusive persuasion respecting pilgrimages, the sign of the cross, and the sanctifying effects of the sacraments. Veneration for martyrs ripened into the introduction of images — a future source of popular idolatry. Christianity was emblazoned in pompous ceremonies. The veneration for saints approximated to their deification, and superstition exalted the mother of our Lord into an object of absolute worship. Communion-tables became imposing altars typical of Jewish sacrifices, and the relics of martyrs were preserved as sacred amulets.

Monastic life.

Monastic life ripened also into a grand system of penance, and expiatory rites, such as characterized oriental asceticism. Armies of monks retired to gloomy and isolated places, and abandoned themselves to rhapsodies and fastings and self-expiations, in opposition to the grand doctrine of Christ's expiation. They despaired of society, and abandoned the world to its fate — a dismal and fanatical set of men, overlooking the practical aims of life. They lived more like beasts and savages than enlightened Christians — wild, fierce, solitary, superstitious, ignorant, fanatical, filthy, clothed in rags, eating the coarsest food, practicing gloomy austerities, introducing a false standard of virtue, regardless of the comforts of civilization, and careless of those great interests which were intrusted them to guard. They were often men of extraordinary virtue and influence, and their lives were not assailed by great temptations. They abstained from marriage, and celibacy came to be regarded as the angelic virtue — a proof of the highest and purest Christian life. Vast numbers of men left the sanctities and beatitudes of home for a cheerless life in the desert, and their gloomy and repulsive austerities were magnified into extraordinary virtues. The monks and hermits sought to save themselves by climbing to Heaven by the same ladder that had been sought by the soofis and the fakirs, — which delusion had an immense influence in undermining the doctrines of grace. Christianity was fast merging itself into an oriental theosophy.

Ambition and wealth of the clergy.

Again the clergy became ambitious and worldly, and sought rank and distinction. They even thronged the courts of princes, and aspired to temporal honors. They were no longer supported by the voluntary contributions of the faithful, but by revenues supplied by government, or property inherited from the old temples. Great legacies were made to the church by the rich, and these the clergy controlled. These bequests became sources of inexhaustible wealth. As wealth increased, and was intrusted to the clergy, they became indifferent to the wants of the people, no longer supported by them. They became lazy, arrogant, and independent. The people were shut out of the government of the church. The bishop became a grand personage, who controlled and appointed his clergy. The church was allied with the state, and religious dogmas were enforced by the sword of the magistrate. An imposing hierarchy was established, of various grades, which culminated in the bishop of Rome. The emperor decided points of faith, and the clergy were exempted from the burdens of the state. There was a great flocking to the priestly offices when the clergy wielded so much power, and became so rich; and men were elevated to great sees, not because of their piety or talents, but influence with the great. What a falling off from the teachings of the original clergy, when bishops were the companions of princes rather than preachers to the poor, and when the clergy could live without the offerings of the people, and were appointed from favor and not from merit. The spiritual mission of the church was lost sight of in a degrading alliance with the state and the world. "Make me bishop of Rome," said a pagan general, "and I too would become a Christian."

The church conforms to the world.

When Christianity itself was in such need of reform, when Christians could scarcely be distinguished from pagans in love of display, and in egotistical ends, how could it reform the world? When it was a pageant, a ritualism, an arm of the state, a vain philosophy, a superstition, a formula, how could it save, if ever so dominant? The corruptions of the church in the fourth century are as well authenticated as the purity and moral elevation of Christians in the second century. Isaac Taylor has presented a most mournful view of the state of Christian society when the religion of the cross had become the religion of the state. And the corruptions kept pace with the outward triumphs of the faith, especially when the pagans had yielded to the supremacy of the cross. The same fact is noticeable in the history of Mohammedanism. When it was first declared by the extraordinary man who claimed to be the greatest of the prophets of God, when it was a sublime theism, immeasurably superior to the prevailing religions of Arabia, and especially when it was promulgated by moral means, its converts were few, but these were lofty. When it was extended by an appeal to the sword, and to the bad passions of men, when it gave a promise of demoralizing joys, and was embraced by powerful classes and chieftains, it had rapidly extended over Asia and Africa, and even invaded Europe. Mohammedanism doubtless prevailed in consequence of its very errors, by adapting itself to the corrupt inclinations of mankind. If it prospered by means of its truths, why was its progress so slow when it was comparatively pure and elevated? The outward triumphs of a religion are no indications of its purity, since the more corrupt it is the more popular it will be, and the purer it is the less likely it is to be embraced, except by a few, whom God designs to be witnesses of his power and truth. Buddhism and Brahminism have more adherents than Mohammedanism, and Mohammedanism more than Christianity, and Roman Catholic Christianity has more than Protestantism, and Protestantism, when it is a life, is narrowed down to a very small body of believers. Christianity which is popular and fashionable, is not necessarily elevated and ennobling, and when it is fashionable or popular is very apt to assume the forms of an imposing ritualism, or to be blended with philosophical speculations, or to sink to the degradation of superstitious rites and ceremonies. When Christianity falls to the level of prevailing fashions and customs and opinions, it has not a very powerful renovating influence on human life. The Jesuits made great conquests in Japan and China, but how barren they have proved. The Puritans planted the barren hills of New England with stern and rugged believers in a spiritual and personal God, and they have extended their principles throughout the country. What renovating influence has the nominal

Christianity of South America, or Spain, or Italy? The religion embraced by the wise and great is apt to become a rationalism, and that professed by the degraded populace to become a superstition. The reception of Christianity in the heart implies sacrifices and self-denial, and will not be cordially embraced except by a few thus far, in any age. The Lollards in England, in the time of Henry VII., were a feeble body, but they did more to infuse a religious life than the whole machinery and influence of the Roman Catholic Church. And as soon as the Church of England gained over the state, and became established, it began to degenerate, and had need of successive reforms. How feeble every form of dissent as a truly renovating power when it has become triumphant! What have the fashionable court religions of Europe done towards the real regeneration of society? Protestantism in Germany, when it was protesting, had a mighty life. When universities and courts accepted it, it became a poisonous rationalism, or a dead formula. Puritanism, established in New England just previous to the Revolution, was a very different thing from what it was when its adherents were exiles and wanderers. It spread and was honored, but retained chiefly its forms, its traditions, its animosities. How rapidly the Huguenots degenerated after the battle of Ivry! Even Jesuitism could not stand before its own triumphs. Its real life was in the times of Xavier and Aquaviva, not of Escobar and La Chaise. Any dominant faith will find its supporters among those whose practical lives are false to the original principles. Its powers of renovation depend upon its exalted doctrines, not upon the numbers who profess it, because, when dominant, men are drawn to it by ambition or interest. They degrade it more than it elevates them. Hence it would almost seem that Christianity, in this dispensation, is designed to call out witnesses of its truths, in every land, the elect of God, rather than to be a universally renovative power on hu-

Christianity produces witnesses, but is not all conquering.

man institutions. But if it is destined to be all-conquering, bringing government and science and social life in harmony with its spirit, as most people believe, and perhaps with the greatest evidence on their side, still its *real* conquests must be slow, without supernatural aid. It will spread, from its inherent life and power; it will become corrupted, and fail to exert as great a spiritual influence as was hoped; it will be reformed, after great debasements, when it is scarcely more than a nominal faith, except among the few witnesses; and the reforming party or sect will gain ascendency, and in its turn become degenerate and powerless as a renovating force. So history seems to indicate, from the times of Theodosius to our own, specially illustrated by the establishment of the different monastic orders, the great awakenings under Luther and Calvin and Knox, the successes of Jesuits and Jansenists, the triumphs of the Puritans, the Quakers, and the Methodists, the rise of Puseyism, or the Church of England. That Christianity remains vital in the world, and makes true advances from generation to generation, can scarcely be questioned. But these advances are slow and delusive. Spiritual power will pass away as the conquering party gains adherents from the world of fashion and of rank. It will not become extinct, but the difference between its true influence, when it is persecuted and when it is triumphant, is less than generally supposed. The spiritual cannot be measured by the material. Who can tell wherein true and permanent influence abides? Who can estimate the power of spiritual agencies? It is common to speak of enlarged spheres of usefulness; but a clergyman in a humble parish may set in motion ideas which will have more effect on the age in which he lives, and on succeeding times, than by any splendid position in a large and populous city. God seeth not as man seeth. To fill the sphere which Providence appoints is the true wisdom; to discharge trusts faithfully and live exalted ideas, that is the mission of good men.

Christianity, then, in the fourth century was not more of a renovating power in consequence of its rapid extension and vast external influence. It was never more sublime than when it made martyrs and heroes of the few who dared to embrace its doctrines. There was more hope of its regenerating the world when it was a continually expanding circle of devout believers, uncompromising and aggressive, than when it numbered the wise and noble and mighty, with their old vices and follies. Its external triumphs rather diminished its spiritual power.

Reasons why Christianity did not save the empire.

If Christianity failed as a gorgeous ritualism, armed with the weapons of the state, and allied with pagan philosophy, attractive as it was made to different classes, where is the hope of the renovation of this world from the effects of climate, soil, material wealth, and the other boasts of physical improvements and culture? What a poor basis for the hopes of man to rest upon is furnished by such guides as the Comtes, the Buckles, and the Mills? If a fashionable and popular religion could not save, how can a cold materialism which chains the thoughts to sense, and confines aspirations to worldly success.

Christianity, as it would seem, did not avert the ruin of the empire, because, when pure, it had but little influence outside its circle of esoteric believers, while society was rotten to the core, and was rapidly approaching a natural dissolution. When it was dominant it failed, because it was itself corrupted, and the ruin had begun. The barbarians were advancing to desolate and destroy, were routing armies and sacking cities and enslaving citizens, when the great fathers of the church were laying the foundation of a Christian state. The ruin of the empire was threatening when Christianity was a proscribed and persecuted faith; it was inevitable when it was grasping the sceptre of princes.

Moreover, we take a low and material view of Christianity when we wonder why it did not save the empire.

It was sent to save the world, not the institutions of an egotistical people. Why should we grieve that it failed to perpetuate such an organization of government as that wielded by the emperors? What was a central and proud despotism, with vast military machinery, and accompanying aristocracies and inequalities, and the accumulated treasure of all ages and nations on the banks of the Tiber, compared with a state more favorable for the development of a new civilization? What does humanity care for the perpetuation of Roman pride? Providence attaches but little value to human sorrows and sacrifices, to the melting away of delusions, pomps, vanities, and follies, compared with the spread of those indestructible ideas on which are based the real happiness of man. If the empire had withstood the shock of barbarians, a state would have existed unfavorable to the higher and future triumphs of the cross. Where was hope, when imperial despotism, and disproportionate fortunes, and slavery, and the reign of conventional forms and traditions, and the tyranny of foolish fashions were likely to be perpetuated? How could Christianity have subverted these monstrous evils without producing revolutions more blasting than even barbaric violence? There seem to be some evils so subtle, poisonous, and deeply-rooted that nothing but violence can remove them. How long before slavery would have been destroyed in the United States by any moral means? How could slavery be destroyed when the most eloquent of Christian teachers were its defenders, and all its kindred institutions were upheld by the church? So of slavery in the Roman Empire. There were sixty millions of slaves, not of the posterity of Ham, but of Shem and Japhet. Every prosperous person was eager to possess a slave, nor had Christianity openly and signally rebuked such a gigantic institution. Where was the hope of the abolition of such an evil when Christianity adapted itself to prevailing fashions and opinions, and only thought of

True mission of the church.

alleviating some of its worst forms? Would slaves decrease when worldly men became the overseers of the church, and emperors presided at councils? Where were the hopes of its abolition when the whole world was its theatre, and every rich man its defender; where, instead of four millions, there were sixty millions, and where the general level of morality and intelligence was lower than it is at present? So of disproportionate fortunes. They were a hopeless evil. If aristocratic institutions keep their ground in the best country of Europe, what must have been the grasp of nobles in the Roman world? Abandonment to money-making was another social evil. If we in America cannot weaken its power, even in the most Christian communities; if we cannot prevent the tyranny of money in our very churches, where we are reminded every Sunday that it is the root of all evil, yea, when we have Bibles in our hands, — what could a corrupted Christianity do with it when material pleasures were more prized than they are with us, and when philanthropic institutions were unborn? If the whole power of the Gallican Church was exerted to prop up the feudal privileges of the French noblesse, and there was needed a dreadful and bloody revolution to destroy them, much more was a revolution needed at Rome to destroy the inherited powers of a still prouder and more powerful aristocracy. If the rights of women are so slowly recognized among the descendants of chivalrous nations, with all the moral forces of the Gospel, how hopeless the elevation of women among peoples where woman for thousands of years was regarded as a victim, a toy, or a slave? When we remember the inherited opinions of Orientals, Greeks, and Romans as to the condition and duties and relations of the female sex, it seems as if no ordinary instruction could have broken the fetters of woman for an indefinite period. The institutions of the pagan world were too firmly rooted to afford hope to Christian teachers, if ever so enlightened. The great cardinal principle of the common brotherhood of man could only be applied under more favorable circumstances. The unity of the empire *did* facilitate the outward triumphs and spread of Christianity, and perhaps that was the great mission which the Roman empire was designed by God to promote. But the social and political institutions of the Romans were exceedingly adverse to a healthy development of Christian virtue. The teachers of the new religion originally aimed entirely at the salvation of the soul. It was to save men from the wrath to come, and publish tidings of great joy to the miserable populace of the ancient world, that apostles labored. They did not attack political or great organized systems of corruption openly and directly. It was enough to promise Heaven, not to change the structure of society. For four centuries neither the condition of woman nor of the slave was radically improved. Christianity could not, without miraculous power, bear its best fruit on a Roman soil. It could not do its best work on degenerate and worn-out races. How many centuries would it take for Christianity, even if embraced by all the people of Japan or China, to make as noble Christians as in Scotland or New England? There must be a material to work upon. There was not this material in the Roman empire. A dreadful revolution was necessary, in which new and uncorrupted races should obtain ascendency, and on whom Christianity could work with renewed power. In such a catastrophe, the good must suffer with the evil, the just with the unjust. A Gothic soldier would not spare a cloister any sooner than a palace, or a palace sooner than a hut, a philosopher more readily than a peasant. Christians as well as pagans must drink the bitter cup, for natural law has no tears to shed and no indulgence to give. The iniquities of the fathers were visited upon the children, even to the third and fourth generation. And what if there was suffering on the earth? Tribulation is generally a blessing in disguise. Men are

The fall of the empire a necessity.

not born for undisturbed happiness on earth, but for a preparation for heaven. Whatever calls the thoughts from a lower to a higher good is the greatest boon which Providence gives. The monstrous calamities of the fourth and fifth centuries had a marked influence in opening the portals of the church, even for the barbarians themselves — for they were not converted until they became conquerors. A new life, in spite of calamities, was infused into the empire, tottering and falling. It was among the new races that the new creation began, and it is among their descendants that the loftiest triumphs of civilization have been achieved. So it was ultimately a good thing for the world that the empire and all its bad institutions were swept away. Creation followed destruction, and the death-song was succeeded by a melodious birth-song. All suffering and sorrow were overruled. Future ages were the better for such sad calamities. Temples were destroyed, but the sublime ideas of beauty and grace by which they were erected still survive. Armies were annihilated, but military science was not lost. Libraries were burned, but models of ancient style survived to incite to new creation. Anarchy prevailed, but new states arose on the ruins of the old provinces. Men passed away, but not the fruits of the earth, nor the relics of genius. The new races gave a new impulse, when fairly established, to agriculture, to commerce, and to art. The fall of the empire was the destruction of fortunes and of farms, the change of masters, the dissolution of the central power of emperors, the breaking up of proconsular authority, the dissipation of conventionalities and fashions; but these were not the ruin of human hopes or the bondage of human energies. Genius, poetry, faith, sentiment, and piety, remained. Nor was the earth depopulated; it was decimated. All the substantial elements of greatness were moulded into new forms. A fresh and beautiful life arose among the simple and earnest people who had descended

The creation which succeeds destruction.

from the Oder and the Vistula. Entirely new institutions were formed. The old fabric was shattered to pieces, but of the ruins a new edifice was constructed more calculated to shelter the distressed and miserable. The barbarians seized the old traditions of the church and invested them with poetical beauty. The Teutonic civilization, more Christian than the Roman, surpassed it in all popular forms, and became more adapted to the wants of man. Probably nothing really great in civilization has ever perished, or ever will perish. I don't believe in "lost arts." They are only buried for a time, like the glorious sculptures of Praxiteles or Lysippus, amid the debris of useless fabrics, to be dug up when wanted and valued, as models of new creations. I doubt if any thing really valuable in even the Egyptian, or Assyrian, or Indian civilization has hopelessly passed away, which can be made of real service to mankind. It is, indeed, a puzzle how the capstones of the Pyramids were elevated — such huge blocks raised five hundred feet into the air; but I believe the mechanical forces are really known, or will be known, at the proper time, and will be again employed, if the labor is worth the cost. We could build a tower of Babel in New York, or a temple of Carnac, or a Colosseum, and would build it, if such a structure were needed or we could afford the waste of time, material, and labor. There is nothing in all antiquity so grand as a modern railroad, or the *Great Eastern* steamship, or the Erie Canal. Nebuchadnezzar's palace would not compare with St. Peter's Church or Versailles, nor his hanging gardens with the Croton reservoirs. Gibraltar or Ehrenbreitstein is more impregnable than the walls of Babylon, which Cyrus despaired to scale or batter down. Every succeeding generation inherits the riches and learning of the past, even if Rome and Carthage are sacked, and the library of Alexandria is burned. The barbarians destroyed the monuments of former greatness— temples, palaces, statues, pictures, libra-

What is truly valuable never perishes.

ries, schools, languages, and laws. These *they* did not restore, but they were restored by their descendants, as there was need, and new creations added. The Parthenon reappears in the Madeleine; the Golden House of Nero in the Tuileries and the Louvre; Jupiter of Phidias in the Moses of Michael Angelo; the Helen of Zeuxis in the Venus of Titian; the library of Alexandria in the Bibliothèque Imperiale; the Academy of Plato in the University of Oxford; the orations of Cicero in the eloquence of Burke; the Institutes of Justinian in the Code Napoleon. In addition, we have cathedrals whose architectural effect Vitruvius could not have conceived; pictures that Polygnotus could not have painted; books which Aristotle could not have imagined; universities before which Zeno would have stood awestruck; courts of law that would have called out the admiration of Paul and Papinian; houses which Scaurus would have envied; carriages that Nero would have given the lives of ten thousand Christians to possess; carpets that Babylon could not have woven; dyes surpassing the Tyrian purple; silks, velvets, glass mirrors, sideboards, fabrics of linen and cotton and wool, ships, railroads, watches, telescopes, compasses, charts, printing-presses, gunpowder, fire-arms, photographs, engravings, bank-notes, telegraphic wires, chemical compounds, domestic utensils, mills, steam-engines, balloons, and a thousand other wonders of a civilization which no ancient race attained. *We* have lost nothing of the old trophies of genius, and have gained new ones for future civilization. The Romans, if left in possession of the provinces they had conquered for two thousand years longer, would never, probably, have made our modern discoveries and inventions. They would have been more like the modern inhabitants of China. A new race was required to try new experiments and achieve new triumphs. The Greeks and Romans did their share, fulfilled a great mission for humanity, but they could not monopolize forever the human race itself.

Reconstruction.

Every great nation and age has its work to do in the field of undeveloped energies; but the field is inexhaustible in resources, for the intellect of man is boundless in its reserved powers. No limit can be assigned to the future triumphs of genius and strength. We are as ignorant of some future wonders as the last century was of steam and telegraphic wires. Nor can we tell what will next arise. The wonders of the Greeks and Romans would have astonished Egyptians and Assyrians. The Oriental civilization gave place to the Hellenic and the Roman; and the Hellenic and Roman gave place to the Teutonic. So the races and the ages move on. They have their missions, become corrupt, and pass away. But the breaking up of their institutions, even by violence, when no longer a blessing to the world, and the surrender of their lands and riches to another race, not worn out, but new, fresh, enthusiastic, and strong, have resulted in permanent good to mankind, even if we feel that the human mind never soared to loftier flights, or put forth greater and more astonishing individual energies than in that old and ruined world.

Every age has a peculiar mission.

How far Christianity conserved the treasures of the past we cannot tell. No one can doubt the influence of Christianity in reviving letters, in giving a stimulus to thought, in creating a noble ambition for the good of society, and producing that moral tone which fits the soul to appreciate what is truly great. It was the church which preserved the manuscripts of classical ages; which perpetuated the Latin language in chants and litanies and theological essays; which gave a new impulse to agriculture and many useful arts; which preserved the traditions of the Roman empire; which made use of the old canons of law; which gave a new glory to architecture in the Gothic vaults of mediæval cathedrals; which encouraged the rising universities; which gave wisdom to rulers and laws to social life. The monasteries and con-

How far Christianity conserved.

vents, in their best ages, were receptacles of arts, bee-hives of industry, schools of learning, asylums for the miserable, retreats for sages, hospitals for the poor, and bulwarks of civilization which rude warriors dared not assail. What did not the Christian clergy guard and perpetuate?

That the Teutonic nations would have arisen to as lofty a platform as the ancient Greeks or Romans, without Christianity, is probable enough. There is no limit to the intellect of a noble race until corrupted. Without Christianity, society might still have possessed our modern discoveries, since the Gothic races have shown a distinguishing genius in mechanical inventions. I apprehend that Christianity has not much to do with many of the wonders of our present day; and I find some classes of men who have made great attainments in certain channels in antagonism to Christianity. I question whether a spiritual religion has given an impulse to steam navigation, or rifled cannons, or electrical machines, or astronomical calculations, or geological deductions. It has not created scientific schools, or painters' studios, or Lowell mills, or Birmingham wares, or London docks. Material glories we share with the ancients; we have simply improved upon them. In some things they are our superiors. We do not see the superiority of modern over ancient civilization in material wonders, so much as in immaterial ideas. What is really greatest and noblest in our civilization comes from Christian truths. Certainly, what is most characteristic is the fruit of spiritual ideas, such as paganism never taught — never could have conceived; such, for instance, as pertains to social changes, to popular education, to philanthropic enterprise, to enlightened legislation, to the elevation of the poor and miserable, to the breaking off the fetters of the slave, and to the true appreciation of the mission of woman. Nor was the Roman empire swept away until the seeds of all these great modern improvements, which raise society, were planted by the sainted fathers and doctors of the church. They worked for us, for all future ages, for all possible civilizations, as well as for their own times. They are, therefore, immortal benefactors of the human race, since they were the first to declare great renovating ideas. The early church is the real architect of European civilization. She laid the foundation of the noble edifice under which the nations still shelter themselves against the storms of life. Christianity not only rescued a part of the population of the Roman empire from degradation and ruin; it not only had glorious witnesses of its transcendent power and beauty in every land, thus triumphing over human infirmity and misery as no other religion ever did; but it has also proved itself to be a progressively conquering power by the great and beneficent ideas which were planted in the minds of barbarians, as well as oriental Christians, and which from time to time are bearing fruit in every land, so as to make it evident to any but a perverted intellect, that Christianity is the source of what we most prize in civilization itself, and that without it the nations can only reach a certain level, and will then, from the law of depravity, decline and fall like Greece, Asia Minor, and Rome. If we had no Christianity, we should be compelled, so far as history teaches us lessons, to adopt the theory of Buckle and his school, of the necessary progress and decline of nations — the moving round, like systems of philosophy, in perpetual circles. But, with the indestructible ideas which the fathers planted, there must be a perpetual renovation and an unending progress, until the world becomes an Eden.

The real triumphs of Christianity.

REFERENCES. — The reader is directed only to the ordinary histories of the church. The great facts are stated by all the historians, and few new ones have been brought to light. Historians differ merely in the mode of presenting their subject. The ecclesiastical histories are generally deficient in art, and hence are uninteresting. The ablest and the most learned of modern historians is doubtless

Neander. He is also the fullest and most satisfactory; but even he is unattractive. Mosheim is dry and dull, but learned in facts. Dr. Schaff has most ably presented primitive Christianity, and his recent work is both popular and valuable. Milman is the best English writer on the church, and he is the most readable of modern historians. Tillemont and Dupin are very full and very learned. But a truly immortal history of the church, exhaustive yet artistic, brilliant as well as learned, is yet to be written. The ancient historians, like Eusebius and Socrates and Zosimus, are very meagre. The genius and spirit of the early church can only be drawn from the lives and writings of the fathers.

CHAPTER XIV.

THE LEGACY OF THE EARLY CHURCH TO FUTURE GENERATIONS.

It is my object in this chapter to show the great Christian ideas which the fathers promulgated, and which have proved of so great influence on the Middle Ages and our own civilization. These were declared before the Roman empire fell; and if they did not arrest ruin, still alleviated the miseries of society, and laid the foundation of all that is most ennobling among modern nations. The early church should be the most glorious chapter in the history of humanity. While the work of destruction was going on in every part of the world, both by vice and violence, there was still the new work of creation proceeding with it, a precious savor of life to future ages. If there is any thing sublime, it is the power of renovating ideas amid universal degeneracy. They are seeds of truth, which grow and ripen into grand institutions. These did not become of sufficient importance to arrest the attention of historians until they were cultivated by the Germanic nations in the Middle Ages.

It could be shown that almost everything which gives glory to Christian civilization had its origin in the early church. Few are aware what giants and heroes were those fathers and saints whom this age has been taught to despise. We are really reaping the results of those conflicts — conflicts with bigoted Jewish sects, conflicts with the high priests of paganism, with Greek philosophers, with Gnostic Manichæan illuminati; with the symbolists, soothsayers, astrologers, magicians, which mystic superstition conjured up among degenerate people. And not merely their conflicts with the prince of the power of the air alone, but with themselves, with their own fiery passions, and with tangible outward foes. They were illustrious champions and martyrs in the midst of a great Vanity Fair, in a Nebuchadnezzar fire of persecutions, an all-pervading atmosphere of lies, impurities, and abominations which cried to heaven for vengeance. They solved for us and for all future generations the thousand of new questions which audacious paganism proposed in its last struggles; they exposed the bubbles which charmed that giddy generation of egotists; they eliminated the falsehoods which vain-glorious philosophers had inwrought with revelation; and they attested, with dying agonies, to the truth of those mysteries which gave them consolation and hope amid the terrors of a dissolving world. They absorbed even into the sphere of Christianity all that was really valuable in the system they exploded, whether of philosophy or social life, and transmitted the same to future ages. And they set examples, of which the world will never lose sight, of patience, fortitude, courage, generosity, which will animate all martyrs to the end of time. And if, in view of their great perplexities, of circumstances which they could not control, utter degeneracy and approaching barbarism, they lent their aid to some institutions which we cannot endorse, certainly when corrupted, like Manichæism and ecclesiastical domination, let us remember that these were adapted to their times, or were called out by pressing exigencies. And further, let us bear in mind that, in giving their endorsement, they could not predict the abuse of principles abstractly good and wise, like poverty, and obedience, and chastity, and devout meditation, and solitary communion with God. In all their conduct and opinions, we see, nevertheless, a large-hearted humanity, a toleration and charity for human infirmities, and a beautiful spirit of brotherly love. If they advocated definite creeds with great vehemence and earnestness, they yet soared beyond them, and gloried in the general name they bore, until the fundamental doctrines of their religion were assailed.

For two centuries, however, they have no history out of the records of martyrdom. We know their sufferings better than any peculiar ideas which they advocated. We have testimony to their blameless lives, to their irreproachable morals, to their good citizenship, and to their Christian graces, rather than to any doctrines which stand out as especial marks for discussion or conflict, like those which agitated the councils of Nice or Ephesus. But if we were asked what was the first principle which was brought out by the history of the early church, we should say it was that of martyrdom. Certainly the first recorded act in the history of Christianity was that memorable scene on Calvary, when the founder of our religion announced the fulfillment of the covenant made with Adam in the Garden of Eden. And as the deliverance of mankind was effected by that great sacrifice for sin, so the earliest development of Christian life was the spirit of martyrdom. The moral grandeur with which the martyrs met reproach, isolation, persecution, suffering, and death, not merely robbed the grave of its victory, but implanted a principle of inestimable power among all future heroes. Martyrdom kindled an heroic spirit, not for the conquest of nations, but for the conquest of the soul, and the resignation of all that earth can give in attestation of grand and saving truths. We have a few examples of martyrs in pagan antiquity, like Socrates and Seneca, who met death with fortitude, — but not with faith, not with indestructible joy that this mortal was about to put on immortality. The Christian martyrdoms were a new development of humanity. They taught the necessity of present sacrifice for future glory, and more, for the great interests of truth and virtue, with which good men had been identified. They brought life and immortality to the view of the people, who had not dared to speculate on their future condition. Their martyrs inspired a spirit into society that nothing could withstand; a practical belief that the life was more than meat; that the future was greater than the present: and this surely is one of the grand fundamental principles of Christianity. They incited to a spirit of fortitude and courage under all the evils of life, and gave dignity to men who would otherwise have been insignificant. The example of men who rejoiced to part with their lives for the sake of their religion, became to the world the most impressive voice which it yet heard of the insignificance of this life when compared with the life to come. "What will it profit a man to gain the whole world and lose his own soul?" became thus one of the most stupendous inquiries which could be impressed on future generations, and affected all the relations of society. Martyrdom was one solution of this mighty question which introduced a new power upon the earth, for we cannot conceive of Christianity as an all-conquering influence, except as it unfolds a new and superior existence, in contrast with which the present is worthless. The principle of martyrdom, setting at defiance the present, led to unbounded charity and the renunciation of worldly possessions. What are they really worth? Every martyr had the comparative worthlessness of wealth and honor and comfort profoundly impressed upon his mind, in view of the greatness of the Infinite and the importance of the future.

The early martyrdoms thus brought out with immeasurable force the principle of faith, without which life can have no object, — faith in future destinies, faith in the promises of God, faith in the power of the Cross to subdue finally all forms of evil. The sacrifice of Christ introduced into the world sentiments of unbounded love and gratitude, that He, the most perfect type of humanity, and the Son of God himself, should come into this world to bear its sins upon the cross, and thus give a heaven which could not be bought by expiatory gifts. It was love which prompted the crucifixion of Jesus; and love produced love, and stimulated thousands to bear with patience the evils under which they would have sunk. The martyrdoms of the early Christians did not indeed kindle sentiments of gratitude; but they inspired courage, and led to immeasurable forms of heroism. The timid and the shrinking woman, the down-trodden slave, and the despised pauper, all at once became serene, lofty, unconquerable, since they knew that though their earthly tabernacle would be destroyed, they had a dwelling in the heavens free from all future toil and sorrow and reproach. Martyrdoms made this world nothing and heaven everything. They proved a powerful faith in the ultimate prevalence of truth, and created an invincible moral heroism, which excited universal admiration; and they furnished models and examples to future generations, when Christians were subjected to bitter trials.

We cannot but feel that martyrdom is one of the most impressive of all human examples, since it is the mark of a practical belief in God and heaven. And while we recognize it as among the most interesting among spiritual triumphs, we are persuaded that the absence of its spirit, or its decline, is usually followed by a low state of society. Epicureanism is its antagonistic principle, and is as destructive as the other is conservative. The moment men are unwilling to sacrifice themselves to a great cause, they virtually say that temporal and worldly interests are to be preferred to the spiritual and the future. The language of the Epicurean is intensely egotistic. It is: "Soul, take thine ease; eat, drink, and be merry;" to which God says, "Thou fool." Christianity was sent to destroy this egotism, which undermined the strength of the ancient world; and it created a practical belief in the future, and a faith in truth. Without this faith, society has ever retrograded; with it there have been continual reforms. It is an important element of progress, and a mark of dignity and moral greatness.

Shall we seek a connection between their martyrdoms and civilization? They bore witness to a religion which is the source of all true progress upon earth; they attested to its divine truth amid protracted agonies; they were illustrious examples for all ages to contemplate.

Perhaps the most powerful effect of their voluntary sacrifice was to secure credence to the mysteries of Christianity. Socrates died for his own opinions; but who was ever willing to die for the opinions of Socrates? But innumerable martyrs exulted in the privilege of dying for the doctrines of Him whose sacrifice saved the world. Nor to these had death its customary terrors, since they were assured of a glorious immortality. They impressed the pagan world with a profound lesson that the future is greater than the present; that there is to be a day of rewards and punishments. Amid all the miseries and desolations of society, it was a great thing to bear witness to the reality of future happiness and misery. The hope of immortality must have been an unspeakable consolation to the miserable sufferers of the Roman Empire. It gave to them courage and patience and fortitude. It inspired them with hope and peace. Amid the ravages of disease, and the incursions of barbarians, and the dissolution of society, and the approaching eclipse of the glory of man, it was a great and holy mystery that the soul should survive these evils, and that eternal bliss should be the reward of the faithful. Nothing else could have reconciled the inhabitants of the decaying empire to slavery, war, and pillage. There was needed some powerful support to the mind under the complicated calamities of the times. This support the death and exultation of the martyrs afforded. It was written on the souls of the suffering millions that there was a higher life, a glorious future, an exceeding great reward. It was impossible to see thousands ready to die, exulting in the privilege of martyrdom, anticipating with confidence their "crown," and not feel that immortality was a certitude brought to light by the Gospel. And the example of the martyrs kindled all the best emotions of the soul into a hallowed glow. Their death, so serene and beautiful, filled the spectators with love and admiration. Their sufferings brought to light the greatest virtues, and diffused their spirit into the heart of all who saw their indestructible joy. Is it nothing, in such an age, to have given an impulse to the most exalted sentiments that men can cherish? The welfare of nations is based on the indestructible certitudes of love, friendship, faith, fortitude, self-sacrifice. It was not Marathon so much as Thermopylæ which imparted vitality to Grecian heroism, and made that memorable self-sacrifice one of the eternal pillars which mark national advancement. So the sufferings of the martyrs, for the sake of Christ, warmed the dissolving empire with a belief in Heaven, and prepared it to encounter the most unparalleled wretchedness which our world has seen. They gave a finishing blow to Epicureanism and skeptical cynicism; so that in the calamities which soon after happened, men were buoyed with hope and trust. They may have hidden themselves in caves and deserts, they may have sought monastic retreats, they may have lost faith in man and all mundane glories, they may have consumed their lives in meditation and solitude, they may have anticipated the dissolution of all things, but they awaited in faith the coming of their Lord. Prepared for any issue or any calamity, a class of heroes arose to show the moral greatness of the passive virtues, and the triumphs of faith amid the wrecks of material grandeur. Were not such needed at the close of the fourth century? Especially were not such bright examples needed for the ages which were to come? Polycarp and Cyprian were the precursors of the martyrs of the Middle Ages, and were of the Reformation. Early persecutions developed the spirit of martyrdom, which is the seed of the church, impressed it upon the mind of the world, and prepared the way for the moral triumphs of the Beckets and Savonarolas of remote generations. Martyrdoms were the first impressive facts in the history of the church, and the idea of dying for a faith one of the most signal evidences of superiority over the ancient religions. It was a new idea, which had utterly escaped the old guides of mankind.

Another great idea which was promulgated by the church long before the empire fell, was that of benevolence. Charities were not one of the fruits of paganism. Men may have sold their goods and given to the poor, but we have no record of such deeds. Hospitals and eleemosynary institutions were nearly unknown. When a man was unfortunate, there was nothing left to him but to suffer and die. There was no help from others. All were engrossed in their schemes of pleasure or ambition, and compassion was rare. The sick and diseased died without alleviation. "The spectator who gazed upon the magnificent buildings which covered the seven hills, temples, arches, porticoes, theatres, baths and palaces, could discover no hospitals and asylums, unless perchance the temple of Æsculapius, on an island in the Tiber, where the maimed and sick were left in solitude to struggle with the pangs of death." But the church fed the hungry, and clothed the naked, and visited the prisoner, and lodged the stranger. Charity was one of the fundamental injunctions of Christ and of the Apostles. The New Testament breathes unbounded love, benevolence so extensive and universal that self was ignored. Self-denial, in doing good to others, was one of the virtues expected of every Christian. Hence the first followers of our Lord had all things in common. Property was supposed to belong to the whole church, rather than to individuals. "Go and sell all that thou hast" was literally interpreted. It devolved on the whole church to see that strangers were entertained, that the sick were nursed, that the poor were fed, that orphans were protected, that those who were in prison were visited. For these purposes contributions were taken up in all assemblies convened for public worship. Individuals also emulated the whole church, and gave away their possessions to the poor. Matrons, especially, devoted themselves to these works of charity, feeding the poor, and visiting the sick. They visited the meanest hovels and the most dismal prisons. But "what heathen," says Tertullian, "will suffer his wife to go about from one street to another to the houses of strangers? What heathen would allow her to steal away into the dungeon to kiss the chain of the martyr?" And these works of benevolence were not bestowed upon friends alone, but upon strangers; and it was this, particularly, which struck the pagans with wonder and admiration — that men of different countries, ranks, and relations of life, were bound together by an invisible cord of love. A stranger, with letters to the "brethren," was sure of a generous and hearty welcome. There were no strangers among the Christians; they were all brothers; they called each other brother and sister; they gave to each other the fraternal kiss; they knew of no distinctions; they all had an equal claim to the heritage of the church. And this generosity and benevolence extended itself to the wants of Christians in distant lands; the churches redeemed captives taken in war, and even sold the consecrated vessels for that purpose on rare occasions, as Ambrose did at Milan. A single bishop, in the third century, supported two thousand poor people. Cyprian raised at one time a sum equal to four thousand dollars in his church at Carthage, to be sent to the Manichæan bishops for the purposes of charity. Especially in times of public calamity was this spirit of benevolence manifested, and in striking contrast with the pagans.[1] When Alexandria was visited with the plague during the reign of Gallienus, the pagans deserted their friends upon the first symptoms of disease; they left them to die in the streets, without even taking the trouble to bury them when dead; they only thought of escaping from the contagion themselves. The Christians, on the contrary, took the bodies of their brethren in their arms, waited upon them without thinking of themselves, ministered to their wants, and buried them with all possible care, even while the best people of the community, presbyters and deacons, lost their own lives by their self-sacrificing generosity.[2] And when Carthage was ravaged by a similar pestilence in the reign of Gallus, the pagans deserted the sick and the dying, and the streets were filled with dead bodies, which greatly increased the infection. No one came near them except for purposes of plunder; but Cyprian, calling his people together in the church, said: "If we do good only to our own, what do we more than publicans and heathens." Animated by his words, the members of the church divided the work between them, the rich giving money, and the poor labor, so that in a short time the bodies which filled the streets were buried.

And this principle of benevolence has never been relinquished by the church. It was one of the foundation-pillars of monastic life in the Middle Ages, when monasteries and convents were blessed retreats for the miserable and unfortunate, where all strangers found a shelter and a home; where they diffused charities upon all who sought their aid. The monastery itself was built upon charities, upon the gifts and legacies of the pious. In pagan Rome men willed away their fortunes to favorites; they were rarely bestowed upon the poor. But Christianity inculcated everywhere the necessity of charities, not merely as a test of Christian hope and faith, but as one of

1 Neander, vol. i. § 3.

2 Eusebius, l. vii. chap. 22.

the conditions of salvation itself. One of the most glorious features of our modern civilization is the wide-spread system of public benevolence extended to missions, to destitute churches, to hospitals, to colleges, to alms-houses, to the support of the poor, who are not left to die unheeded as in the ancient world. Every form of Christianity, every sect and party, has its peculiar charities; but charities for some good object are a primal principle of the common creed. What immeasurable blessings have been bestowed upon mankind in consequence of this law of kindness and love! What a beautiful feature it is in the whole progress of civilization!

The early church had set a good example of patience under persecution, and practical benevolence extended into every form of social life which has been instituted in every succeeding age, and to which the healthy condition of society may in a measure be traced.

The next mission of the church was to give dignity and importance to the public preaching of the Gospel, which has never since been lost sight of, and has been no inconsiderable element of our civilization. This was entirely new in the history of society. The pagan priest did not exhort the people to morality, or point out their religious duties, or remind them of their future destinies, or expound the great principles of religious faith. He offered up sacrifices to the Deity, and appeared in imposing ceremonials. He wore rich and gorgeous dresses to dazzle the senses of the people, or excite their imaginations. It was his duty to appeal to the gods, and not to men; to propitiate them with costly rites, to surround himself with mystery, to inspire awe, and excite superstitious feelings. The Christian minister had a loftier sphere. While he appealed to God in prayer, and approached his altar with becoming solemnity, it was also his duty to preach to the people, as Paul and the Apostles did throughout the heathen world, in order to convert them to Christianity, and change the whole character of their lives and habits. The presbyter, while he baptized believers and administered the symbolic bread and wine, also taught the people, explained to them the mysteries, enforced upon them the obligations, appealed to their intellects, their consciences, and their hearts. He plunged fearlessly into every subject bearing upon religious life, and boldly presented it for contemplation.

What a grand theatre for the development of mind, for healthy instruction and commanding influence, was opened by the Christian pulpit. There was no sphere equal to it in moral dignity and force. It threw into the shade the theatre and the forum. And in times when printing was unknown, it was almost the only way by which the people could be taught. It vastly added to the power of the clergy, and gave them an influence that the old priests of paganism could never exercise. It created an entirely new power in the world, a moral power, indeed, but one to which history presents no equal. The philosophers taught in their schools, they taught a few admiring pupils; but the sphere of their teachings was limited, and also the number whom they could address. The pulpit became an institution. All the Christians were required to assemble regularly for public instruction as well as worship. On every seventh day the people laid aside their secular duties and devoted themselves to religious improvement. The pulpit gave power to the Sabbath; and what an institution is the Christian Sabbath. To the Sabbath and to public preaching Christendom owes more than to all other sources of moral elevation combined. It is true that the Jewish synagogue furnished a model to the church; but the Levitical race claimed no peculiar sanctity, and discharged no friendly office beyond the precincts of the temple. In the synagogue the people assembled to pray, or to hear the Scriptures read and expounded, not to receive religious instruction. The Jewish religion was as full of ceremonials as the pagan, and the intellectual part of it was confined to the lawyers, to the rabbinical hierarchy. But the preaching of the great doctrines of Christianity was made a peculiarly sacred office, and given to a class of men who avoided all secular pursuits. The Christian priest was the recognized head of the society which he taught and controlled. In process of time, he became a great dignitary, controlling various interests; but his first mission was to preach, and his first theme was a crucified Saviour. He ascended the pulpit every week as an authorized as well as a sacred teacher, and, in the illustration of his subjects, he was allowed great latitude in which to roam. It is not easy to appreciate what a difference there was between pagan and Christian communities from the rise of this new power, and we might also say institution, since the pulpit and the Sabbath are interlinked and associated together. Whatever the world has gained by the Sabbath, that gain is intensified and increased vastly by public teaching. It placed the Christian as far beyond the Jew, as the Jew was before beyond the pagan. It also created a sacerdotal caste. The people may have had the privilege of pouring out their hearts before the brethren, and of speaking for their edification, but all the members were not fitted for the secular office of teachers. Christianity claims the faculties of knowledge, as well as those of feeling. Teaching was early felt to be a great gift, implying not only superior knowledge, but superior wisdom and grace. Only a few possessed the precious charisma to address profitably the assembled people, *χάρισμα διδασκαλίας*, and those few became the appointed guides of the Christian flocks, *διδασκαλοί*. Other officers of the new communities shared with them the administration, but the teacher was the highest officer, and he became gradually the presbyter, whose peculiar function it was to discourse to the people on the great themes which it was their duty to learn. And even after the presbyter became a bishop, it was his chief office to teach publicly, even as late as the fourth and fifth centuries.

Leo and Gregory, the great bishops of Rome, were eloquent preachers.

Thus the church gradually claimed the great prerogative of eloquence. Eloquence was not born in the church, but it was sanctified, and set apart, and appropriated to a thousand new purposes, and especially identified with the public teaching of the people. The great mysteries, the profound doctrines, the suggestive truths, the touching histories, the practical duties of Christianity were seized and enforced by the public teacher; and eloquence appeared in the sermon. In pagan ages, eloquence was confined to the forum or the senate chamber, and was directed entirely into secular channels. It was always highly esteemed as the birthright of genius — an inspiration, like poetry, rather than an art to be acquired. But it was not always the handmaid of poetry and music; it was brought down to earth for practical purposes, and employed chiefly in defending criminals, or procuring the passage of laws, or stimulating the leaders of society to important acts. The gift of tongue was reserved for rhetoricians, lawyers, politicians, philosophers; not for priests, who were intercessors with the Divine. Now Christianity adopted all the arts of eloquence, and enriched them, and applied them to a variety of new subjects. She carried away in triumph the brightest ornament of the pagan schools, and placed it in the hands of her chosen ministers. The pulpit soon began to rival the forum in the displays of a heaven-born art, which was now consecrated to far loftier purposes than those to which it had been applied. As public instruction became more and more learned, it also became more and more eloquent, for the preacher had opportunity, subject, audience, motive, all of which are required for great perfection in public speaking. He assembled a living congregation at stated intervals; he had the range of all those lofty inquiries which entrance the soul; and he had souls to save — the greatest conceivable motive to a good man who realizes the truths of the Gospel. All human enterprises and schemes become ultimately insipid to a man who has no lofty view of benefiting mankind, or his family, or his friend. We were made to do good. Take away this stimulus, and energy itself languishes and droops. There is no object in life to a seeker of pleasure or gain, when once the passion is gratified. What object of pity so melancholy as a man worn out with egotistical excitements, and incapable of being amused. But he who labors for the good of others is never ennuied. The benevolent physician, the patriotic statesman, the conscientious lawyer, the enthusiastic teacher, the dreaming author, all work and toil in weary labors, with the hope of being useful to the bodies, or the intellects, or the minds of the people. This is the great condition of happiness. There is an excitement in gambling as in pleasure, in money-making as in money-spending; but it wears out, or exhausts the noble faculties, and ends in ennui or self-reproach and bitter disappointment. It is not the condition of our nature, which was made to be useful, to seek the good of others. They are the happiest and most esteemed who have this good constantly at heart. There can be no unhappiness to a man absorbed in doing good. He may be poor and persecuted like Socrates; he may walk barefooted, and have domestic griefs, and be deprived of his comforts — but he is serene, for the soul triumphs over the body. Now, what motive so grand as to save the immortal part of man. This desire filled the ancient Christian orator with a preternatural enthusiasm, as well as gave to him an unlimited power, and an imposing dignity. He was the most happy of mortals when led to the blazing fire of his persecutors, and he was the most august. The feeling that he was kindling a fire which should never be quenched, even that which was to burn up all the wicked idols of an idolatrous generation, unloosed his tongue and animated his features. The most striking examples of seraphic joy, of a sort of divine beauty playing upon the features, are among orators. In animated conversation, a person ordinarily homely, like Madame de Staël, becomes beautiful and impressive. But in the pulpit, when the sacred orator is moving a congregation with the fears and hopes of another world, there is a majesty in his beauty which is nowhere else so fully seen. There is no eloquence like that of the pulpit, when the preacher is gifted and in earnest. Greece had her Pericles and Demosthenes, and Rome her Hortensius and Cicero. Many other great orators we could mention. But when Greece and Rome had an intellectual existence such as that to which our modern times furnish no parallel, in our absorbing pursuit of pleasure and gain, and amid the wealth of mechanical inventions, there were, even in those classic lands, but few orators whose names have descended to our times; while, in the church, in a degenerated period, when literature and science were nearly extinct, there were a greater number of Christian orators than what classic antiquity furnished. Yea, in those dark and miserable ages which succeeded the fall of the Roman empire, there were in every land remarkable pulpit orators, like those who fanned the Crusades. There was no eloquence in the Middle Ages outside the church. Bernard exercised a far greater moral power than Cicero in the fullness of his fame. And in our modern times, what orators have arisen like those whom the Reformation produced, both in the Roman Catholic church, and among the numerous sects which protested against her? What orator has Germany given birth to equal in fame to Luther? What orator in France has reached the celebrity of Bossuet, or Bourdaloue, or Massillon? Even amid all the excitements attending the change of government, who have had power on the people like a Lacordaire or Monod? In England, the great orators have been preachers, with a very few exceptions; and these men would have been still greater in the arts of public speaking had they been trained in the church. In our day, we have seen great orators in secular life, but they yield in fascination either to those who are accustomed to speak from the sacred desk, or to those whose training has been clerical, like many of our popular lecturers. Nothing ever opened such an arena of eloquence as the preaching of the Gospel, either in the ancient, the mediæval, or the modern world, not merely from the grandeur and importance of the themes discussed, but also from the number of the speakers. In a legislative assembly, where all are supposed to be able to address an audience, and some are expected to be eloquent, only two or three can be heard in a day. Only some twenty or thirty able speeches are delivered in Congress or Parliament in a whole session; but in England, or the United States, some thirty thousand preachers are speaking at the same time, many of whom are far more gifted, learned, and brilliant than any found in the great councils of the nation. Nor is this eloquence confined to the Protestant church; it exists also in the Roman Catholic in every land. There are no more earnest and inspiring orators than in Italy or France. Even in rude and unlettered and remote districts, we often hear specimens of eloquence which would be wonderful in capitals. What chance has the bar, in a large city, compared with the pulpit, for the display of eloquence? Probably there are more eloquent addresses delivered every Sunday from the various pulpits of Christendom than were pronounced by all the orators of Greece during the whole period of her political existence. Doubtless there are more touching and effective appeals made to the popular heart every Sunday in every Christian land, than are made during the whole year beside on subjects essentially secular. Then what an impulse has pulpit oratory given to objects of a strictly philanthropic character! The church has been the nurse and mother of all schemes of benevolence since it was organized. It is itself a great philanthropic institution, binding up the wounds of the prisoner, relieving the distressed, and stimulating great enterprises. For all of this the pulpit has been called upon, and has lent its aid; so that the world has been more indebted to the eloquence of divines than to any other source. Who can calculate the moral force of one hundred and fifty thousand to two hundred thousand Christian preachers in a world like ours, most of whom are arrayed on the side of morality and learning. It may be said that these benefits may more properly be considered to flow from Christianity as revealed in the Bible; that the Bible is the cause of all this great impulse to civilization. We do not object to such an interpretation; nevertheless, in specifying the influence of the church, even before the empire fell, the creation of pulpit eloquence should be mentioned, since this has contributed so much to the moral elevation of Christendom. Christianity would be shorn of half her triumphs were it not for the public preaching of her truths. Paganism had no public teachers who regularly taught the people and stimulated their noblest energies. It was a new institution, these Sabbath-day exercises, and has had an inconceivable influence on the progress and condition of the race. The power of the Gospel was indeed the main and primary cause; but the church must have the credit of appropriating what was most prized in the intellectual centres of antiquity, and giving to it a new direction. Christian oratory is also an interesting subject to present in merely its artistical relations. Its vast influence no one can question.

Again, who can estimate the debt which civilization, in its largest and most comprehensive sense, owes to the fathers of the early church, in the elaboration of Christian doctrine. They found the heathen world enslaved by a certain class of most degrading notions of God, of deity, of goodness, of the future, of rewards and punishments. Indeed, its opinions were wrong and demoralizing in almost every point pertaining to the spiritual relations of man. They met the wants of their times by seizing on the great radical principles of Christianity, which most directly opposed these demoralizing ideas, and by giving them the prominence which was needed. Moreover, in the church itself, opinions were from time to time broached, so intimately allied with pagan philosophies and oriental theogonies, that the faith of Christians was in danger of being subverted. The Scriptures were indeed recognized to contain all that is essential in Christian truth to know; but they still allowed great latitude of belief, and contradictory creeds were drawn from the same great authority. If the Bible was to be the salvation of man, or the great thesaurus of religious truth, it was necessary to systematize and generalize its great doctrines, both to oppose dangerous heathen customs and heretical opinions in the church itself. And more even than this, to set forth a standard of faith for all the ages which were to come; not an arbitrary system of dogmas, but those which the Scriptures most directly and emphatically recognized. Christian life had been set forth by the martyrs in the various forms of teaching, in the worship of God, in the exercise of those virtues and graces which Christ had enjoined, in benevolence, in charity, in faith, in prayer, in patience, in the different relations of social life, in the sacraments, in the fasts and festivals, in the occupations which might be profitably and honorably carried on. But Christianity influenced thought and knowledge as well as external relations. It did not declare a rigid system of doctrines when first promulgated. This was to be developed when the necessity required it. For two centuries there were but few creeds, and these very simple and comprehensive. Speculation had not then entered the ranks, nor the pagan spirit of philosophy. There was great unity of belief, and this centered around Christ as the Redeemer and Saviour of the world. But, in process of time, Christianity was forced to contend with Judaism, with Orientalism, and with Greek speculation, as these entered into the church itself, and were more or less embraced by its members. With downright Paganism there was a constant battle; but in this battle all ranks of Christians were united together. They were not distracted by any controversies whether idolatry should be or should not be tolerated. But when Gnostic principles were embraced by good men, those which, for instance, entered into monastic or ascetic life, it was necessary that some great genius should arise and expose their oriental origin, and lay down the Christian law definitely on that point. So when Manichæism, and Arianism, and other heretical opinions, were defended and embraced by the Christians themselves, the fathers who took the side of orthodoxy in the great controversies which arose, rendered important services to all subsequent generations, since never, probably, were those subtle questions pertaining to the Trinity, and the human nature of Christ, and predestination, and other kindred topics, discussed with so much acumen and breadth. They occupied the thoughts of the whole age, and emperors entered into the debates on theological questions with an interest exceeding that of the worldly matters which claimed their peculiar attention. It is not easy for Christians of this age, when all the great doctrines of faith are settled, to appreciate the prodigious excitement which their discussion called forth in the times of Athanasius and Augustine. The whole intellect of the age was devoted to theological inquiries. Everybody talked about them, and they were the common theme on all public occasions. If discussions of subjects which once had such universal fascination can never return again, if they are passed like Olympic games, or the discussions of Athenian schools of philosophy, or the sports of the Colosseum, or the oracles of Dodona, or the bulls of mediæval popes, or the contests of the tournament, or the "field of the cloth of gold," they still have a historical charm, and point to the great stepping-stones of human progress. If they are really grand and important ideas, which they claimed to be, they will continue to move the most distant generations. If they are merely dialectical deductions, they are among the profoundest efforts of reason in the Christian schools of philosophy.

We cannot, of course, enter into the controversies through which the church elaborated the system of doctrines now generally received, nor describe those great men who gave such dignity to theological inquiries. Clement was raised up to combat the Gnostics, Athanasius to head off the alarming spread of Arianism, and Augustine to proclaim the efficacy of divine grace against the Pelagians. The treatises of these men and of other great lights on the Trinity, on the incarnation, and on original sin, had as great an influence on the thinking of the age and of succeeding ages, as the speculations of Plato, or the syllogisms of Thomas Aquinas, or the theories of Kepler, or the expositions of Bacon, or the deductions of Newton, or the dissertations of Burke, or the severe irony of Pascal. They did not create revolutions, since they did not labor to overturn, but they stimulated the human faculties, and conserved the most valued knowledge. Their definite opinions became the standard of faith among the eastern Christians, and were handed down to the Germanic barbarians. They were adopted by the Catholic church, and preserved unity of belief in ages of turbulence and superstition. One of the great recognized causes of modern civilization was the establishment of universities. In these the great questions which the fathers started and elaborated were discussed with renewed acumen. Had there been no Origen, or Tertullian, or Augustine, there would have been no Anselm, or Abelard, or Erigena. The speculations and inquiries of the Alexandrian divines controlled the thinking of Europe for one thousand years, and gave that intensely theological character to the literature of the Middle Ages, directing the genius of Dante as well as that of Bernard. Their influence on Calvin was as marked as on Bossuet. Pagan philosophy had no charm like the great verities of the Christian faith. Augustine and Athanasius threw Plato and Aristotle into the shade. Nothing more preëminently marked the great divines whom the Reformation produced, than the discussion of the questions which the fathers had systematized and taught. Nor was the interest confined to divines. Louis XIV. discussed free will and predestination with Racine and Fenelon, even as the courtiers of Louis XV. discussed probabilities and mental reservations. And in New England, at Puritan firesides, the passing stranger in the olden times, when religion was a life, entered into theological discussions with as much zest as he now would describe the fluctuations of stocks or passing vanities of crinoline and hair dyes. Nor is it one of the best signs of this material age that the interest in the great questions which tasked the intellects of our fathers is passing away. But there is a mighty permanence in great ideas, and the time, we trust, will come again when indestructible certitudes will receive more attention than either politics or fashions.

The influence of the fathers is equally seen in the music and poetry which have come down from their times. The church succeeded to an inheritance of religious lyrics unrivaled in the history of literature. The *Magnificat* and the *Nunc dimittis* were sung from the earliest Christian ages. The streets of the eastern cities echoed to the seductive strains of Arius and Chrysostom. Flavian and Diodorus introduced at Antioch the antiphonal chant, which, improved by Ambrose, and still more by Gregory, became the joy of blessed saints in those turbulent ages, when singing in the choir was the amusement as well as the duty of a large portion of religious people. So numerous were the hymns of Ambrose, Hilary, Augustine, and others, that they became the popular literature of centuries, and still form the most beautiful part of the service of the Catholic church. Who can estimate the influence of hymns which have been sung for fifty successive generations? What a charm is still attached to the mediæval chants! The poetry of the early church is preserved in those sacred anthems. They inspired the barbarians with enthusiasm, even as they had kindled the rapture of earlier Christians in the church of Milan. The lyrical poets are immortal, and exert a wide-spread influence. The fervent stanzas of Watts, of Steele, of Wesley, of Heber, are sung from generation to generation. The hymns of Luther are among the most valued of his various works. "From Greenland's icy mountains" — that sacred lyric — shall live as long as the "Elegy in a Country Church-yard," or the "Cotter's Saturday Night," yea, shall survive the "Night Thoughts," and the "Course of Time." There is nothing in Grecian or Roman poetry that fills the place of the psalmody of the early church. The songs of Ambrose were his richest legacy to triumphant barbarians, consoling the monk in his dreary cell and the peasant on his vine-clad hills, speaking the sentiment of a universal creed, and consecrating the most tender recollections. So that Christian literature, in its varied aspects, its exegesis, its sermons, its creeds, and its psalmody, if not equal in artistic merit to the classical productions of antiquity, have had an immeasurable influence on human thought and life, not in the Roman world merely, but in all subsequent ages.

But the great truths which the fathers proclaimed in reference to the moral and social relations of society are still more remarkable in their subsequent influence.

The great idea of Christian equality struck at the root of that great system of slavery which was one of the main causes of the ruin of the empire. Christianity did not break up slavery ; it might never have annihilated it under a Roman rule, but it protested against it so soon as it was clothed with secular power. As in the sight of heaven there is no distinction of persons, so the idea of social equality gained ground as the relations of Christianity to practical life were understood. The abolition of slavery, and the general amelioration of the other social evils of life, are all a logical sequence from the doctrine of Christian equality, — that God made of one blood all the nations of the earth, that they are equally precious in his sight, and have equal claims to the happiness of heaven. All theories of human rights radiate from, and centre around, this consoling doctrine. That we are born free and equal may not, practically, be strictly true ; but that the relations of society ought to be viewed as they are regarded in the Scriptures, which reveal the dignity of the soul and its glorious destinies, cannot be questioned ; so that oppression of man by man, and injustice, and unequal laws militate with one of the great fundamental revelations of God. Impress Christian equality on the mind of man, and social equality follows as a matter of course. The slave was recognized to be a man, a person, and not a thing. Whenever he sat down, as he did once a week, beside his master, in the adoration of a common Lord, the ignominy of his hard condition was removed, even if his obligations to obedience were not abrogated. As a future citizen of heaven, his importance on the earth was more and more recognized, until his fetters were gradually removed.

From the day when Christian equality was declared, the foundations of slavery were assailed, and the progress of freedom has kept pace with Christian civilization, although the Apostles did not directly denounce the bondage that disgraced the ancient world. It was something to declare the principles which, logically carried out, would ultimately subvert the evil, for no evil can stand forever which is in opposition to logical deductions from the truths of Christianity. Moral philosophy is as much a series of logical deductions from the doctrine of loving our neighbor as ourself as that great network of theological systems which Augustine and Calvin elaborated from the majesty and sovereignty of God. Those distinctions which Christ removed by his Gospel of universal brotherhood can never return or coexist with the progress of the truth. A vast social revolution began when the eternal destinies of the slave were announced. It will not end with the mere annihilation of slavery as an institution; it will affect the relations of the poor and the rich, the unlucky and the prosperous, in every Christian country until justice and love become dominant principles. What a stride from Roman slavery to mediæval serfdom! How benignant the attitude of the church, in all ages, to the poor man! The son of a peasant becomes a priest, and rises, in the Christian hierarchy, to become a ruler of the world. There was no way for a poor peasant boy to rise in the Middle Ages, except in the church. He attracts the notice of some beneficent monk; he is educated in the cloister; he becomes a venerated brother, an abbot, perhaps a bishop or a pope. Had he remained in service to a feudal lord, he never could have risen above his original rank. The church raises him from slavery, and puts upon his brow her seal and in his hands the thunderbolts of spiritual power, thus giving him dignity and consideration and independence. Rising, as the clergy did in the Middle Ages, in all ages, from the lower and middle classes, they became as much opposed to slavery as they were to war. It was thus in the bosom of the church that liberty was sheltered and nourished. Nor has the church ever forgotten her mission to the poor, or sympathized, as a whole, with the usurpations of kings. She may have aimed at dominion, like Hildebrand and Innocent III., but it was spiritual domination, control of the mind of the world. But she ever sympathized with oppressed classes, like Becket, even as he defied the temporal weapons of Henry II. The Jesuits, even, respected the dignity of the poor. Their errors were trust in machinery and unbounded ambition, but they labored in their best ages for the good of the people. And in our times, the most consistent and uncompromising foes of despotism and slavery are in the ranks of the church. The clergy have been made, it is true, occasionally, the tools of despotism, and have been absurdly conservative of their own privileges, but on the whole, have ever lifted up their voices in defense of those who are ground down.

The elevation of woman, too, has been caused by the doctrine of the equality of the sexes which Christianity revealed; not "woman's rights" as interpreted by infidels; not the ignoring of woman's destiny of subservience to man, as declared in the Garden of Eden and by St. Paul, but her glorious nature which fits her for the companionship of man. Heathendom reduces her to slavery, dependence, and vanity. Christianity elevates her by developing her social and moral excellences, her more delicate nature, her elevation of soul, her sympathy with sorrow, her tender and gracious aid. The elevation of woman did not come from the natural traits of Germanic barbarians, but from Christianity. Chivalry owes its bewitching graces to the influence of Christian ideas. Clemency and magnanimity, gentleness and sympathy, did not spring from German forests, but the teachings of the clergy. Veneration for woman was the work of the church, not of pagan civilization or Teutonic simplicity. The equality of the sexes was acknowledged by Jerome when he devoted himself to the education of Roman matrons, and received from the hand of Paula the means of support while he labored in his cell at Bethlehem. How much more influential was Fabiola or Marcella than Aspàsia or Phryne! It was woman who converted barbaric kings, and reigned, not by personal charms, like Bastern beauties, but by the solid virtues of the heart. Woman never occupied so proud a position in an ancient palace as in a feudal castle. When Paula visited the East, she was welcomed by Christian bishops, and the proconsul of Palestine surrendered his own palace for her reception, not because she was high in rank, but because her virtues had gone forth to all the world; and when she died, a great number of the most noted people followed her body to the grave with sighs and sobs. The sufferings of the female martyrs are the most pathetic exhibitions of moral greatness in the history of the early church. And in the Middle Ages, whatever is most truly glorious or beautiful can be traced to the agency of woman. Is a town to be spared for a revolt, or a grievous tax remitted, it is a Godiva who intercedes and prevails. Is an imperious priest to be opposed, it is an Ethelgiva who alone dares to confront him even in the king's palace. It is Ethelburga, not Ina, who reigns among the Saxons — not because the king is weak, but his wife is wiser than he. A mere peasant-girl, inspired with the sentiment of patriotism, delivers a whole nation, dejected and disheartened, for such was Joan of Arc. Bertha, the slighted wife of Henry, crosses the Alps in the dead of winter, with her excommunicated lord, to remove the curse which deprived him of the allegiance of his subjects. Anne, Countess of Warwick, dresses herself like a cook-maid to elude the visits of a royal duke, and Ebba, abbess of Coldingham, cuts off her nose, to render herself unattractive to the soldiers who ravage her lands. Philippa, the wife of the great Edward, intercedes for the inhabitants of Calais, and the town is spared.

The feudal woman gained respect and veneration because she had the moral qualities which Christianity developed. If she entered with eagerness into the pleasures of the chase or the honor of the banquet, if she listened with enthusiasm to the minstrel's lay and the crusader's tale, her real glory was her purity of character and unsullied fame. In ancient Rome men were driven to the circus and the theatre for amusement and for solace, but among the Teutonic races, when converted to Christianity, rough warriors associated with woman without seductive pleasures to disarm her. It was not riches, nor elegance of manners, nor luxurious habits, nor exemption from stern and laborious duties which gave fascination to the Christian woman of the Middle Ages. It was her sympathy, her fidelity, her courage, her simplicity, her virtues, her noble self-respect, which made her a helpmeet and a guide. She was always found to intercede for the unfortunate, and willing to endure suffering. She bound up the wounds of prisoners, and never turned the hungry from her door. And then how lofty and beautiful her religious life. History points with pride to the religious transports and spiritual elevation of Catharine of Sienna, of Margaret of Anjou, of Gertrude of Saxony, of Theresa of Spain, of Elizabeth of Hungary, of Isabel of France, of Edith of England. How consecrated were the labors of woman amid feudal strife and violence. Whence could have arisen such a general worship of the Virgin Mary had not her beatific loveliness been reflected in the lives of the women whom Christianity had elevated? In the French language she was worshiped under the feudal title of Notre Dame, and chivalrous devotion to the female sex culminated in the reverence which belongs to the Queen of Heaven. And hence the qualities ascribed to her, of Virgo Fidelis, Mater Castissima, Consolatrix Afflictorum, were those to which all lofty women were exhorted to aspire. The elevation of woman kept pace with the extension of Christianity. Veneration for her did not arise until she showed the virtues of a Monica and a Nonna, but these virtues were the fruit of Christian ideas alone.

We might mention other ideas which have entered into our modern institutions, such as pertain to education, philanthropy, and missionary zeal. The idea of the church itself, of an esoteric band of Christians amid the temptations of the world, bound together by rules of discipline as well as communion of soul, is full of grandeur and beauty. And the unity of this church is a sublime conception, on which the whole spiritual power of the popes rested when they attempted to rule in peace and on the principles of eternal love. However perverted the idea of the unity of the church became in the Middle Ages, still who can deny that it was the mission of the church to create a spiritual power based on the hopes and fears of a future life? The idea of a theocracy forms a prominent part of the polity of Calvin, as of Hildebrand himself. It is the basis of his legislation. He maintained it was long concealed in the bosom of the primitive church, and was gradually unfolded, though in a corrupt form, by the popes, the worthiest of whom kept the idea of a divine government continually in view, and pursued it with a clear knowledge of its consequences. And those familiar with the lofty schemes of Leo and Gregory, will appreciate their efforts in raising up a power which should be supreme in barbarous ages, and preserve what was most to be valued of the old civilization. The autocrat of Geneva clung to the necessity of a spiritual religion, and aimed to realize that which the Middle Ages sought, and sought in vain, that the church must always remain the mother of spiritual principles, while the state should be the arm by which those principles should be enforced. Like Hildebrand, he would, if possible, have hurled the terrible weapon of excommunication. In cutting men off from the fold, he would also have cut them off from the higher privileges of society. He may have carried his views too far, but they were founded on the idea of a church against which the gates of hell could not prevail. Who can estimate the immeasurable influence of such an idea, which, however perverted, will ever be recognized as one of the great agencies of the world? A church without a spiritual power, is inconceivable; nor can it pass away, even before the material tendencies of a proud and rationalistic civilization. It will assert its dignity when thrones and principalities shall crumble in the dust.

Such are among the chief ideas which the fathers taught, and which have entered even into the modern institutions of society, and form the peculiar glory of our civilization. When we remember this, we feel that the church has performed no mean mission, even if it did not save the Roman empire. The glory of warriors, of statesmen, of artists, of philosophers, of legislators, and of men of science and literature in the ancient world, still shines, and no one would dim it, or hide it from the admiration of mankind. But the purer effulgence of the great lights of the church eclipses it all, and will shine brighter and brighter, until the seed of the woman shall bruise the serpent's head. This is the true sun which shall dissipate the shadows of superstition and ignorance that cover so great a portion of the earth, and this shall bring society into a healthful glow of unity and love.

In another volume I shall present, more in detail, the labors of the Christian Fathers in founding the new civilization which still reigns among the nations. And in the creation which succeeded destruction we shall be additionally impressed with the wisdom and beneficence of the Great First Cause, through whose providences our fallen race is led to the new Eden, where truth and justice and love reign in perpetual beauty and glory.

THE END.

www.ingramcontent.com/pod-product-compliance
Lightning Source LLC
LaVergne TN
LVHW021218110826
845150LV00002B/195